ALSO BY
KENNETH M. POLLACK

—

THINGS FALL APART:
Containing the Spillover from an Iraqi Civil War

THE PERSIAN PUZZLE:
The Conflict Between Iran and America

THE THREATENING STORM:
The Case for Invading Iraq

ARABS AT WAR:
Military Effectiveness, 1948–1991

A PATH OUT *of the* DESERT

A PATH OUT
of the DESERT

—

A GRAND STRATEGY FOR AMERICA
IN THE MIDDLE EAST

—

KENNETH M. POLLACK

RANDOM HOUSE | NEW YORK

Published in the United States by Random House,
an imprint of The Random House Publishing Group,
a division of Random House, Inc., New York.

RANDOM HOUSE and colophon are registered
trademarks of Random House, Inc.

LIBRARY OF CONGRESS CATALOGING-IN-
PUBLICATION DATA
Pollack, Kenneth M. (Kenneth Michael).
A path out of the desert : a grand strategy for America
in the Middle East / Kenneth M. Pollack.
p. cm.
1. Middle East—Foreign relations—United States.
2. United States—Foreign relations—Middle East.
3. United States—Politics and government—2001–
4. United States—Foreign relations—2001–   I. Title.
DS63.2.U5P67   2008
327.73056—dc22   2008004328

ISBN 978-1-4000-6548-6

Printed in the United States of America
on acid-free paper

www.atrandom.com

2 4 6 8 9 7 5 3 1

FIRST EDITION

Book design by Barbara M. Bachman

For Martin Sokolow,
who inspired me

Strobe Talbott

It IS ONE OF THE GREAT IRONIES OF BOTH HISTORY AND current events that the Middle East should be the source of so much trouble for those who live there, for the United States, and for the world as a whole. After all, consider to what degree that region has enriched, ennobled, and shaped humanity over the millennia: it is the birthplace of the three great monotheistic religions and, in a very real sense, of civilization itself. Anthony Pagden, a professor of intellectual history at the University of California, Los Angeles, could have substituted the phrase "Middle Eastern" for "Asian" in the following passage from his masterly 2008 book, *Worlds at War: The 2,500-Year Struggle Between East and West*: "An abducted Asian woman gave Europe her name; a vagrant Asian exile gave Europe its political and finally its cultural identity; and an Asian prophet gave Europe its religion." The lady in question—Europa—was a Phoenician, from today's Lebanon; Aeneas was from today's Turkey; and Jesus Christ was born in a town on the West Bank of the Jordan River that today is occupied by Israel.

Yet in the sixty-plus years since World War II, the very words "Middle East" have been virtually synonymous with bad news. Whatever their vast differences, the residents have suffering in common. They have waged at least a dozen wars of their own. About half of those conflicts have pitted Arabs against Israel, but the rest have been among Arabs or between Arabs and Kurds, Persians, Africans, Americans, Europeans, and a host of others. Indeed, the longest and bloodiest conventional war of the postwar era was the eight years of carnage between Iraqis and Iranians, who are descended, respectively, from subjects of Hammurabi and Cyrus the Great.

What President George W. Bush calls "the global war on terror" began on September 11, 2001, with a plot hatched and carried out primarily by rogue Saudis. "Democratizing" the Middle East was, briefly, the administration's proclaimed strategic priority for its foreign policy as a whole.

For all ten of Mr. Bush's predecessors in the Oval Office—five Republicans and five Democrats—the Middle East has been a major challenge and in almost all cases a perennial cause of frustration as well as a source of geopolitical danger, not to mention an exceedingly difficult and sensitive matter to be managed on the home front of U.S. domestic politics.

Harry Truman had to wrestle with his own State Department over U.S. support for the creation of an independent Israel—and then cope with the first Arab-Israeli war that immediately erupted. Dwight Eisenhower roiled transatlantic relations when he put the kibosh on the ill-conceived British-French-Israeli military action against Egypt during the Suez Crisis of 1956. Richard Nixon rushed to help Israel and went to DEFCON 3 against the Soviet Union when the Kremlin armed the Arabs during the Yom Kippur War of 1973. Jimmy Carter, George H. W. Bush, and Bill Clinton all became diplomats in chief in their efforts to advance the Middle East peace process. The current President Bush, who has bet his place in history on his conduct of an ongoing war in the region, is devoting at least some of his energy in his last year in office to burnishing his credentials as peacemaker between the Arabs and Israelis.

For decades, ever since 1908, when oil was discovered at Masjed Solayman, in southwestern Iran, the region has been important as the world's gas station—a distinction that brings with it sticker shock as the price of oil hovers around $100 per barrel.

In more recent years, the Middle East has taken on another global significance of a much more ominous kind: it is the part of the world most susceptible to nuclear proliferation and most likely to produce a nuclear war if that proliferation occurs. Israel is widely assumed to have nukes already. Pakistan has the world's first "Islamic bomb." Iran has made no secret—or at least a badly kept one—that it wants the option of being the second. Saddam Husayn's aspiration to have a full range of weapons of mass destruction was the pretext for the Bush invasion and occupation of Iraq.

If, as is all too imaginable, the global nonproliferation regime, already fraying at the edges, were to collapse in the years ahead, other states in the region—Egypt, Turkey, Saudi Arabia, the United Arab Emirates (no doubt an incomplete list)—might make the most chronically troubled and troublesome region on Earth also the most heavily nuclearized.

For all these reasons, there are not just shelves but whole libraries filled with books on the Middle East. They keep coming for two reasons: first, the sheer importance of the subject; second, its fluidity; the story keeps unfolding and requires updating.

My colleague Ken Pollack's book, now in your hands, is much more than just "another" book on the region. It is an audacious and successful attempt—highly successful, in my view—to do something that has rarely ever been attempted before and certainly not recently—which is to say, in the post-9/11 world. Ken's multiple achievement is to weave together three strands in this book. First, he lays out, in accessible narrative form, the historical backdrop of the multiple, mutually exacerbating crises that rage today from Algeria to Iran. Second, he explains, in a way that is both balanced and authoritative, the consequences (many of them unwanted) of recent American policy in the region (and not just those of the current administration). And third, he advocates specific policy recommendations and a grand strategy for Mr. Bush's successor, for whom the Middle East will almost certainly be—to use a word Ken invokes frequently—"headache" number one.

This is the right book at the right time by the right author. Ken has spent twenty years studying the region as an intelligence analyst, White House policy maker, scholar, and commentator. He has traveled to the region dozens of times over the years, including three visits during the year he spent writing this book.

Ken has earned a reputation as an expert who goes to where the action is (including when it is dangerous to do so), sees with his own eyes what is happening there, then calls it straight, never mind peer pressure or conventional wisdom. When he and another Brookings colleague, Mike O'Hanlon, returned from a visit to Iraq in July 2007, they wrote a *New York Times* op-ed arguing that the "surge" in U.S. forces showed signs of success in tamping down the insurgency, while noting that progress on the security front had not yet been translated into political reconciliation in Baghdad. They took flak from those who had written off Iraq as an unmitigated and irretrievable disaster. Within about three months, the essence of Ken and Mike's judgment had itself gone a long way toward becoming conventional wisdom itself, including among Democratic candidates for the presidency and all but the most die-hard and blinkered critics of the administration.

For me, one of the most important services that Ken has performed is to establish the connection between terrorism—the export commodity from the Middle East that now preoccupies the world as much as oil—and social, political, economic, and cultural factors. Like President Bush, Ken believes that political reform is needed in the Middle East, not least because its own people want and deserve that eventual outcome. But unlike President Bush, Ken understands the complexity of the challenge, the extent to which it will have to be defined and met in the region rather than imposed from Washington, and how long it will take.

Another contribution Ken has made is to bring some sanity to the issue of Islam itself. One reason the phrase "Islamic bomb" sends a shiver up spines around the world is that the first word has, absurdly, become to many ears almost as terrifying as the second. Ken is especially forceful in dealing with the shibboleths and prejudices that haunt the debate over "political Islam." Thanks in part to the scope of his book and the depth of his background as a student of culture and religion, he treats Islam, along with the other two great faiths to which it is related historically and theologically, as a force that, when politicized, need not explode, either in the vest of a suicide bomber or in a mushroom cloud; rather, political Islam can be managed, both by its own adherents and practitioners and by the world as a whole, in a way that benefits communities, both national and international.

Finally, I admire the way Ken has, in the pages that follow, found the right angle of attack to come at the subjects at hand—and thereby the right voice to address his readers. Without oversimplifying or patronizing, he conveys the sense of engaging nonexperts in a civil discussion that has too often been monopolized either by connoisseurs of the esoteric or by people who have long stopped listening to one another. Ken gives a highly accessible overview of why the Middle East matters so much and, in language free of jargon and cant, offers guidelines on how Americans—and their principal partners around the world and in the Middle East itself—should think about the best way to advance U.S. and Western interests there. He takes account, respectfully but often critically, of the various orthodoxies, from those of the neocons to those of the liberal internationalists and those of the various regional actors as well. He also surveys what other experts have to say, thereby providing yet another service: readers of this book will not only have a far better understanding of the subject at hand, but they will have taken a crash course in the relevant literature on the subject. This book will, I'm confident, instantly establish a proud and enduring place on those shelves—and your own.

I F YOU BOTHERED TO PICK UP THIS BOOK, WHETHER TO READ it, flip through it, or throw it across the room, it is probably because you are frustrated with the Middle East. Join the club. We're all frustrated with the Middle East. It is a very frustrating place.

It is frustrating for Americans because most Americans understand (at least intuitively) that our country has important interests in the region that are threatened by the problems there, but it is often hard to understand those interests, and the problems all seem to defy solution. It is frustrating for Europeans, Asians, and others because they too have critical interests in the region (in some ways more immediate than America's), but not only are they equally perplexed about how to secure those interests in the face of the Middle East's labyrinthine problems, but they typically lack the power of the United States even to attempt to solve those problems and protect their interests. It is frustrating for Israelis because most Israelis want to live in peace and security, but since the early twentieth century, the vast majority of the other people of the region have refused to grant them either. It is also frustrating for the Arabs, Iranians, Berbers, Circassians, Kurds, Chaldeans, Azeris, Armenians, and other peoples of the region. In some ways, they are the most frustrated of all. And one of the themes of this book is that their frustration is the most important problem and lies at the heart of most of what frustrates everyone else about the Middle East.

This book is about recognizing both the nature of America's vital interests in the Middle East and how those vital interests are threatened by the anger and frustration of the people of the region, caused by an interlocking set of crippling societal problems. It is also about how the United States must stop trying to run away from the problems of the region and adopt a balanced, long-term approach to its problems if it is to secure its interests. Only when we have done that will it be safe for us to diminish our engagement with this troublesome part of the world.

Personally, I would love to be able to tell other Americans that we can just forget about the Middle East; that it's really not that important, that we really don't face meaningful threats from the region, and that those we do face threaten us only because we have tried to do too much there. Such an argument would be especially popular after our tragic experiences in Iraq and Afghanistan, which seem to have reinforced many Americans' desires to just forget about the Middle East altogether.

But the problem is that turning our backs on the Middle East now is neither possible nor wise. And one of the main reasons why America's problems in the region seem to get worse and worse is that our inclination has always been to try to have as little to do with this confused and confusing part of the world as we could. As a result, we have consistently tried to do things on the cheap. Even when we have taken on herculean tasks, like invading, occupying, and rebuilding Iraq, Washington's inclination has been to try to do it with too few troops, too few resources, too few allies, and too little time. As in Iraq, the result of this shortsighted approach has always been to prolong our involvement and make it more costly than it needed to be, even if it were always going to be more costly than we wanted to admit.

Consequently, the principal theme of this book is that to secure America's interests in the Middle East over the long term, the United States must embrace a long-term commitment to encourage and enable the countries of the Middle East to pursue a gradual process of political, economic, and social reform—one that grows from within, rather than being imposed from without; one that reflects the values, traditions, history, and aspirations of the people of the region themselves, not a Western guess at them; one that recognizes that reform and stability are not mutually exclusive but mutually reinforcing—and ultimately mutually essential. As I readily acknowledge and discuss at some length, this is a difficult undertaking, but I believe it is ultimately the only good path we can follow.

The Middle East

In this book, I am going to talk about the Middle East as encompassing all of the countries from Morocco in the west to Iran in the east. For the purposes of this book, the northernmost borders of the Middle East are the northern borders of Syria, Iraq, and Iran, and it reaches as far south as Sudan and Yemen. For those looking for a more precise list, it includes the countries of Morocco, Algeria, Tunisia, Libya, Egypt, Sudan, Israel, the Palestinian territories, Lebanon, Syria, Jordan, Iraq, Iran, Saudi Arabia, Kuwait, Bahrain, Qatar, the United Arab Emirates (UAE), Oman, and Yemen. Excluding Israel from this list leaves the countries that I refer to frequently as "the Muslim Middle East" because their populations are predominantly, although not exclusively, Muslim.

There are important differences among the countries of the Muslim Middle East. Some are fairly large, like Egypt and Iran, and others are tiny, like Bahrain and the Palestinian territories. Some are fabulously wealthy, like Kuwait and the UAE, and others are destitute, like Sudan and Yemen. Some are fairly homogeneous, like Saudi Arabia, while others, like Lebanon, are very diverse in their composition. Some are dictatorships, like Tunisia and Syria, and others are monarchies, like Jordan and Morocco.

Nevertheless, it is one of the themes of this book that there is also a great deal that they have in common—something that the people of the region readily assert. In most of these countries, Arabs are the predominant ethnic group, although there are plenty of Berbers, Africans, Kurds, Circassians, and others mixed in—not to mention the Persians who constitute a narrow majority in Iran. All speak dialects of Arabic as their principal language, except in Iran, where they speak Persian (Farsi), although this has much in common with Arabic, including a similar alphabet. There are strong similarities in culture and social structures, derived from their common heritage as descendants of the Islamic empire that encompassed all of this region for five centuries or more. As a result, their economic, political, educational, and social systems tend to resemble one another more than they resemble other countries. Egypt and Saudi Arabia have a lot of obvious differences, but they are much more like each other than Saudi Arabia is like other oil producers such as Venezuela and Nigeria, or than Egypt is like other midsize developing nations such as Argentina or the Philippines. Different as they are, their societies remain very similar.

Indeed, one of the things that is striking is how similar the societal problems facing all of these states are, despite their apparent differences. The persistence of autocracy—and not just of autocracy, but of a certain form of autocracy. The dominance of traditional Middle Eastern patronage systems, the bloated bureaucracies, and the stifling of dissent. The same inadequacies of education derived largely from the failure to modernize the same traditional teaching methods. Although unemployment is the greater problem in the poor states of the region, and underemployment the greater problem in the rich states of the region, both stem from the same problems of poor worker productivity, inappropriate skills, low foreign investment (except in the narrow oil sector), little trade (especially nonoil exports), and rapid demographic growth. And the reasons for the manifestation of these problems are also remarkably similar across this group of countries.

Moreover, the people see the commonalities with each other in what they fear, what they dislike, what they desire, what they like, and how they seek to achieve their desires. When the people of the Muslim Middle East look around them, it is these countries that they recognize as being like them and part of their world. Iran is not an Arab country, but it shares many of the problems of the Arab states, and its strategic focus has been westward—toward the Arab heartlands—since Cyrus the Great first conquered Mesopotamia in the sixth century B.C. Israel is considered an alien entity by a great many of the people of the Muslim Middle East, but its problems are intimately intertwined with those of the Muslim Middle East because of its location. Sudan is arguably as much a sub-Saharan African country as a Middle Eastern state. Indeed, its misery is particularly acute because it seems to suffer from all of the problems of the Muslim Middle East *and* all of the problems of sub-Saharan Africa. But Sudan is ruled over by the Arab element of its population, whose aspirations lie northward. And because it does evince so many of the problems of the Arab world, it is useful to include Sudan as well.

Throughout this book I have tried to note the many differences among the countries of the region wherever appropriate, even as I focus more often on their commonalities. Indeed, in places I provide a few more examples or a bit more data than I otherwise might feel the need for in part to demonstrate the universality of different phenomena across the region. Still, it is worth keeping in mind as you read this book that as similar as these countries are in many respects, there are differences, even in those areas where they seem most alike.

THERE ARE SOME obvious other countries I might have included but chose not to. There are states like Mauritania, Somalia, and Eritrea that are all members of the Arab League. But they tend to look more like other sub-Saharan African nations than like the countries of the Muslim Middle East, and their problems are mostly those of sub-Saharan Africa.

Then there is Turkey. Turkey truly spans two worlds, Europe and the Middle East. Like Iran, it is not Arab, but it is predominantly Islamic. Turkey also shares at least some of the problems of other states of the Muslim Middle East, from some of its economic challenges, to the rise of political Islam, to a Kurdish population eager for its own state. I have chosen not to include Turkey because the Middle Eastern aspects of Turkey seem increasingly outweighed by its European and simply unique features. The Turks themselves insist that they are Europeans, not Middle Easterners, and they have doggedly sought membership in the European Union (EU). Moreover, those problems that they do share with the Middle East appear in much milder form in Turkey, and the Turks have been able to rely on solutions to those problems not available to their neighbors to the south. This is why Turkey seems increasingly to be moving in a different direction from the Middle East, even if it has not yet fully left the region's ambit.

Pakistan is a country that falls into a similar category. There are certainly similarities between Pakistan and a number of the Middle Eastern states—Islam, a government caught between autocracy and democracy, a similar set of economic problems, and a culture that feels under threat from the forces of secular globalization. Indeed, several of the people I asked to comment on the book while it was in manuscript form observed that many of the problems I discuss in the Arab world sound similar to those of Pakistan—and many of the solutions I propose would be equally applicable to Pakistan. Be that as it may, I have chosen not to include Pakistan in this book. Despite its similarities, Pakistan belongs to South Asia, not the Middle East. It has many important differences from the Muslim Middle East, including a wholly different language and a legacy as part of the subcontinent and then under the British Raj that was very different from the experience of the Middle East. This, in turn, left Pakistan with different political, economic, military, educational, and legal institutions. Muslim Middle Easterners look on the Pakistanis as more distant cousins than close kin. Similarly, Pakistan's strategic problems are not the same as those of the states of the Middle East, nor is there a Middle Eastern analogy for its relationship with India, which dominates its foreign policy. Thus, while the reader may see many parallels to Pakistan, I would caution that it is not a perfect fit, and so I have chosen not to include it in this work.

What I Hope You Will Get from This Book

I wrote this book with a number of different audiences in mind. I hope that all will find something of value and interest in it.

For those struggling to make sense of the Middle East, I have tried to provide a structured way of thinking about the region and understanding what America's interests are (and are not) there, what the problems facing the region consist of, how the problems are creating threats to our interests (particularly terrorism and the potential for instability to cause sudden, massive economic crises because of the world's dependence on Middle Eastern oil), and how we as a nation should attempt to fashion a new approach to address those problems, eliminate the threats, and so secure our interests over the long term. In particular, I have attempted to spell out a number of important connections that are often misunderstood in the media and public debate, leading to a lot of confusion about what is actually going on in the Middle East and what the United States should or should not be trying to achieve.

In fact, you may find that this book contains a number of arguments that seem counterintuitive. If that is the case, it is largely because a pernicious "common wisdom" currently pervades our country's discussion of the Middle East that is, to a great extent, flat-out wrong. It reflects a tendency on the part of the media and large swathes of the punditocracy to draw erroneous conclusions from partial information. In a number of places, I've gone out of my way to try to correct some of the worst misunderstandings about the contemporary Middle East.

My hope is that policy makers, both once and future, will find this book useful and thought-provoking by providing in one place a fully developed version of an argument that has been swirling around piecemeal in policy circles for over a decade: the idea that the United States and its allies in Europe and Asia should support a gradual process of economic, political, and social transformation in the Muslim Middle East—albeit one different from the way we have done so in the past, particularly under the George W. Bush administration.

Many in the policy community, of which I am part, are now trying to make the case that the United States cannot let the many missteps of the Bush 43 administration cause us to abandon this goal because it actually is the right thing for us to do despite the fact that President Bush said it was. It is a hard argument to make because of this painful, recent history, but it is also an important argument to make. This book is an effort to lay out the evidence and analysis in support of such a policy, in the hope that putting it all in one place will help us get over the problem of our recent past and the bad taste it has left in the mouths of so many Americans.

In addition, I have tried to show how the different strands of America's Middle East policies—our Iraq policy, our Iran policy, our efforts in the Middle East peace process—are all interrelated and why we need to devise policies toward each that are properly harmonized toward all. Again, this is a concept that is generally understood by many in the Middle East policy community, but the case is typically made in bits (like why we can't forget about the Arab-Israeli conflict as we try to contain Iran), and I think it far more compelling and understandable when seen from the perspective of U.S. policy toward the region as a whole.

The Middle East expert is going to find a lot of things that he or she already knows about the region in these pages—but that is inevitably true of any book written on the Middle East. Instead, what I hope the expert will find is two things. First, some new ways of thinking about critical issues that Middle East experts have been debating for decades. For example, in part III, which deals with the threats to American interests, I argue that the problems of both terrorism and instability in the region are best understood through the prism of revolutions (and thus through the extensive scholarship on revolutions). Seeing both problems as manifestations of a general prerevolutionary state gripping the Middle East helps explain many important features of both phenomena that experts have long struggled to connect (like why so many terrorists are middle class and the linkages among terrorism, instability, and economic problems).

Second, like the policy community, the expert community has been wrestling with the question of whether the West should support a process of economic, political, and social reform in the Middle East for a long time. This book weighs in strongly on the side of those who believe that we should, albeit not necessarily in the same way that we have been. Many other Middle East experts are largely in agreement with this argument, and for them, I hope this book will provide an explication of that argument presented in a way that explains how the United States should advance that agenda both across the region and over the long term and puts it all in one place. For those who don't agree with this perspective, I hope this book will challenge you to reexamine your position.

As a final point, it should be clear that I wrote this book principally for other Americans, at least in the sense that it's written very much with American interests in mind. I hope that people from elsewhere around the world will find it thought-provoking and perhaps even convincing, even as they excuse the America-centric perspective: I am an American, and I am writing this book primarily for my countrymen. Of course, every nation around the world has its own interests in the Middle East, few are identical to one another, and almost none has the exact same interests as the United States, if only because none of the others has the same power and the same place in the contemporary international system as the United States does. As I note at various points, the current international system benefits a great many countries around the world, but none in the same way (and few to the same extent) as it benefits the United States. And it is the role of the Middle East, and particularly its oil exports, in that international system that makes it so important to America and the world. Although I could not list all of the Middle Eastern interests of all of the other countries in the world and how they subtly differ from one another, if nothing else, I hope that this book helps other people to understand America's interests and policies in this part of the world and how their own country might interact with the United States as we pursue what are inevitably common interests in the stability, prosperity, and peace of this vital region.

Cards on the Table

I am a liberal internationalist (what sometimes gets called a liberal interventionist). What that means is that I believe strongly in the importance of U.S. involvement in the world and that that involvement should be conditioned by American values. I believe this for both moral and strategic reasons. I believe that the United States can be a force for good in the world and that we have been on many occasions, from World War II to Bosnia. I also believe that America's efforts to promote progress, to help other nations, to oppose those who would use violence to bring about change have been vital to our own security and prosperity. For most of our history, the United States was admired, not feared, despite our great strength. That is something very unusual in world history. Other states did not band together to oppose us, as is often the case when one state becomes very powerful. Instead, most sided with us and helped us to achieve our goals because we were willing to help them achieve theirs as well. This, in turn, has been a tremendous source of strength and security to the United States: we have not had to fear attack by most of the countries of the world and have typically been able to count on their friendship and assistance instead.

I am certainly not blind to the fact that the United States has not always acted in so benevolent a fashion—that we have, especially in the past four or five decades, ignored human rights abuses, turned a deaf ear to the pleas of the downtrodden, aided tyrants, trampled over the rights of others, and even perpetrated some horrific deeds of our own. In fact, it is another of the principal themes of this book that such conduct in the Middle East was a tragic miscalculation that helped produce the greatest threats to our security today. As Talleyrand might have judged, such conduct on our part was worse than a crime, it was a mistake.

Like the vast majority of Americans, I believe that our nation's foreign policy should hew to the highest values of our national credo. Nevertheless, I also believe that national self-interest is not a sin; that we must protect what we hold most dear, and that such considerations must also be a primary source of our foreign policy goals. For me, this is where "realism" comes into the mix. The goals of American foreign policy must be determined by both our interests and our ideals, but our pursuit of them must be firmly grounded in realistic strategies and equally realistic assessments of the likelihood and difficulty of those courses of action.

One reason that I tend toward liberal internationalism is that I believe history has strongly and repeatedly demonstrated that America's strategic interests have been best served by ensuring that our actions are consistent with our values. The hard part is to distinguish between short-term interests and long-term interests. In the short term, we can often benefit from taking the easy way out, minding our own business, or doing what is expedient—in short, by ignoring our values. In the long run, such policies have usually left us much worse off. For instance, by the mid–twentieth century, the United States was paying dearly for a century or so of amoral, "realist" policies regarding Latin America. We backed dictators, condoned their abuses, toppled popular governments that did not agree with us, and sucked every dollar we could out of the region's economies with little regard for the long-term welfare of the people. The result was widespread hatred of the United States and a major impetus to instability, revolutions, civil wars, and a Soviet presence in what we considered "our" hemisphere. These underlying problems manifested themselves in a seemingly endless series of Latin American calamities, from Argentina's dirty war, to the Cuban revolution and Missile Crisis, to the Latin American debt crisis, to Colombia's drug wars, to name only a handful.

My belief that American foreign policy ought to be guided by both our values and our strategic interests (and that, over the long term, our strategic interests are themselves best served by adhering to our values) led me to support America's interventions in Somalia, Haiti, Bosnia, and Kosovo, although I was not always thrilled with how we went about intervening. For similar reasons, I always hoped that we would find a way to intervene in Rwanda to end its genocide and I still hope that the United States will find a way to do something for the people of Congo, who are trapped in a horrible civil war. The realist in me recognizes that doing so will be difficult, but the liberal internationalist in me believes we should try, for both moral and strategic reasons.

I have spent most of my professional career working on Iraq, although never exclusively so. Among other positions, I was a Persian Gulf military analyst at the CIA and twice served on President Clinton's National Security Council staff, working on Persian Gulf issues. By the time of September 11, 2001, those experiences and my liberal internationalist perspective had increasingly focused me on the desirability of removing Saddam Husayn's regime altogether. Thus, when the George W. Bush administration turned its attention to Iraq in 2002, like many other members of the Clinton administration, I was sympathetic to that goal. The containment of Iraq was crumbling, a truth reinforced by postwar revelations, and I believed my old colleagues in the intelligence community when they asserted that Saddam was reconstituting his weapons of mass destruction programs, including his nuclear program. Saddam was also one of the worst tyrants since his idol, Josef Stalin, and I felt that the Iraqi people deserved to be freed from his cruelty. In 2002, I wrote a book titled *The Threatening Storm: The Case for Invading Iraq,* which laid out this perspective. In that book, I argued that certainly for strategic but also for moral reasons, a war to remove Saddam Husayn's regime would be necessary—although not at the time or in the way that the Bush 43 administration actually mounted it. (For instance, I placed tremendous emphasis on a range of factors that the administration ignored, like the importance of eliminating al-Qa'ida before turning on Iraq, making a major effort to revive the Arab-Israeli peace process, and committing ourselves to a long and difficult effort to build a viable Iraqi state after we had toppled Saddam. I also made clear that, despite the Bush administration's claims to the contrary, there was no evidence of meaningful Iraqi ties to al-Qa'ida.) Since the revelation that Saddam had actually eliminated virtually all of his WMD programs in the late 1990s, I have written several pieces for *The Atlantic Monthly, The New Republic, Slate, The New York Times,* and other publications in which I tried to look back at my own thinking before the war to determine the mistakes that I (and others) made before it.

Given the fiasco of our intervention in Iraq, you might wonder why anyone would recommend greater American involvement in the Muslim Middle East. There is a natural inclination after such a foreign policy disaster to simply turn away from the region entirely—to look inward, concentrate on our problems at home and forget that we ever tried something that proved so unpleasant. The distaste of Iraq is already engendering such a reaction among many Americans. While it is understandable, it is also unwise. The United States has vital interests in the Middle East, and the Middle East is a region with many deep-seated problems that are unlikely to solve themselves. Indeed, many of these problems contributed to the maelstrom of Iraq. We ignore these problems at our peril. Thus, one hope for this book is that it will help Americans to look past Iraq and recognize the importance of remaining engaged with this frustrating part of the world. Only this time we must do so with humility and a willingness to see the region as it is, not as we would like it to be.

CONTENTS

—

Why a Grand Strategy for the Middle East?

IT HASN'T SEEMED THAT WAY IN RECENT YEARS, BUT THE United States largely tried to avoid playing a major role in the Middle East for most of its history. The United States has certainly played an active, even decisive, role from time to time, but America never really wanted to be the dominant power in the region, at least not in the military or political sense. It was trade (and missionary work) that brought the first Americans to the region, and trade was the nation's abiding interest there for decades thereafter. The erroneous but ubiquitous Middle Eastern conspiracy theories that conjure an America hell-bent on colonizing the region notwithstanding, the United States was mostly dragged into its leading role there, digging in its heels nearly every step of the way.

In the latter half of the nineteenth century and the first half of the twentieth, Great Britain, not the United States, was the dominant power in the Middle East. Britain safeguarded the petty emirates of the Persian Gulf, held dominion over Egypt and Sudan, and controlled the key choke points from Suez to the Bab al-Mandeb to the Strait of Hormuz. Britain propped up the Ottoman Empire during much of this time, until the First World War, when it saw to the Sick Man of Europe's swift euthanasia. Afterward, London was the principal beneficiary of Istanbul's eclipse, picking up the lands of Palestine, Transjordan, and Iraq; helping 'Abd al-Aziz Ibn Sa'ud create the Kingdom of Saudi Arabia; and acquiring the region's most important newly discovered oil fields in northern Iraq and south-western Persia. Indeed, as oil emerged as a critical commodity, it was the United Kingdom, not the United States, that was both the principal consumer and "protector" of the region's oil production.

A funny thing happened to the British along the way: they came to be despised by the people of the region, most of whom had welcomed the Union Jack when it first arrived on the scene. Back then, in the eighteenth and early nineteenth centuries, the British had come almost solely as traders, often bringing fabulous wares to be sold at astonishingly low prices. They cared little or nothing about how the peoples of the region governed themselves, whom they worshiped, whom they fought, or who ruled which state. But as British trade with the Middle East grew, so too did the region's importance in the Crown's calculations—helped also by its proximity to India and its position astride the quickest route from Bombay to Portsmouth. Some of the potentates of the Middle East avidly courted London, hoping to involve it more in the region. They saw the English principally as a benign counterweight to their more traditional (and immediate) foes. So the Kuwaitis used the British to secure their independence from the Ottomans, just as the Trucial States (which would become the UAE), Bahrain, Qatar, and the Sultanate of Muscat (which would become Oman) all used the British to prevent the Saudis from gobbling them up as Ibn Sa'ud's armies overran the rest of the Arabian Peninsula in the 1920s.

Of course, British involvement in the region was hardly benign. A great many British entrepreneurs and businesses sought to rob the people of the region blind, just as the Arabs, Persians, Jews, Kurds, and other peoples of the Middle East sought to swindle the British. Yet the British typically stole far more than was stolen from them. For instance, the forerunner of British Petroleum managed to cheat the Persians of all but a pittance of their oil revenues, and Britain (along with Russia) effectively governed Persia by the turn of the twentieth century. All of this only made the Middle East more profitable to British industry and therefore more important to the British economy. And the more important the Middle East became to the British economy (and the cohesiveness of the British Empire), the more London realized that it needed to care about how Middle Easterners governed their own affairs because a sudden political change in the region could have a dramatic impact on British fortunes.

So the British increasingly began to involve themselves in the affairs of the region to ensure that nothing happened—no sudden regime change, no catastrophic war, no undisciplined revolution—that could threaten their economic stake in the region, their oil supplies, or their passage to India. They went from trading to owning to governing. And in so doing, they became deeply hated.

Before there was anti-Americanism, there was bitter anti-Anglicism, traces of which linger on in myriad corners of the Middle East. During the early 1950s, when the United States attempted to mediate the dangerous confrontation over British control of Iran's oil, Iran's popular prime minister, Muhammad Mossadiq, stunned Averell Harriman by his consuming fear of and hatred for the British. He told the former American ambassador to London, "You do not know how crafty they are. You do not know how evil they are. You do not know how they sully everything they touch."[1]

It wasn't just that the British ruled only to protect their own interests (though they largely did) and that they typically picked pliant incompetents to serve as the new kings of their Middle Eastern possessions; it was to a great extent simply the fact that they were seen as being "in charge" everywhere. And so every problem, whether it was their fault or not (and many *were* their fault, at least in part), was blamed on them. Every policy that London pursued that Middle Easterners did not like was magnified to become a grave affront, because it provided a tangible focus for the otherwise inchoate frustration of the people of the region. Indeed, the legacy of this exists to this day, with British troops in Iraq being blamed for every misfortune, including—believe it or not—a sudden increase in attacks by badgers on cattle. Even today, journalists typically find that, for Iranians of all walks of life, "The idea that Britain is behind much of what goes wrong in Iran is not just another conspiracy theory, but rather a prism through which many domestic events are often viewed. Indeed, America—the Great Satan itself—is often portrayed as merely a hapless, muscle-bound child manipulated by smarter, craftier, more deceitful forces in London."[2]

By the time of the Second World War, the Middle East was largely a British protectorate, a fact only reinforced during the war when the British invaded Vichy-controlled Syria and Lebanon, put down a pro-Nazi uprising in Iraq, and carved up Iran (the country formerly known as Persia) with the Russians to open a second route to provide supplies to the Red Army. Although the British had nowhere attempted to impose their own democratic system of government on the region (largely because they condescendingly believed the people of the region unsuited for the rigors of democracy), they were still hated. In Palestine, they were hated by the Arabs for allowing *any* Jews to emigrate there and for promising the Jewish community it could become a self-governing homeland. They were hated by the Jews for preventing *most* Jews from emigrating there, even those fleeing the Nazis, and preventing the Zionists from establishing that promised homeland. In Iran, they were hated for stealing the country's oil revenues, usurping the regulation of the Iranian economy, and a host of other real and imagined grievances.

Among the Arabs, the reasons for hating Great Britain were too many to list easily. To a great extent, the Arabs were simply miserable. They were poor; they were weak; they were oppressed; they were plagued by disease, war, and starvation; and they felt themselves powerless before the vicissitudes of fortune and the whims of their overlords. And since they believed that the British controlled the Middle East (which they certainly did, to a much greater extent than the United States does today), they blamed most, if not all, of its problems, rightly or wrongly, on London. The British were so hated in Iraq that the only one of Iraq's three British-imposed kings that the Iraqis really warmed to was their short-ruling second king, Ghazi, and only because he used to give radio addresses denouncing his British masters. (For which London may have had him assassinated.) Most of the most popular leaders of the early years of Middle Eastern independence, from Gamal 'Abd al-Nasser of Egypt to 'Abd al-Karim al-Qassim of Iraq to David Ben-Gurion of Israel to Muhammad Mossadiq of Iran, all rose to prominence or solidified their hold on power by publicly opposing and vilifying the British.

THIS MAY SEEM vaguely familiar. It should. It is remarkably similar to the trajectory that the United States seems to have followed in the region. Americans first stumbled on the Middle East in the early nineteenth century and by the latter half had begun to develop modest trade relations that grew slowly prior to the Second World War. The war itself provided the circumstances for America's first real involvement with the region. American strategists quickly recognized the importance of Middle Eastern oil production to Britain, and potentially to Germany, if the Nazis could get their hands on it. America was pumping nearly a quarter of the world's oil in those days, so we did not care about the region for our own needs.[3] American naval forces began to patrol the Red Sea and Persian Gulf, and American ground forces would participate in the routing of Axis forces from North Africa (where Erwin Rommel's Afrika Korps threatened the safety of the Middle East and its oil fields). The United States also dispatched 30,000 troops to Iran, to help the British and Russians funnel mostly American supplies from the Persian Gulf to the USSR.

In those days, the United States was generally welcomed in the Middle East and even encouraged to play a greater role in the region—with some Iranians going so far as to suggest that Franklin D. Roosevelt evict the British and Russians from their land and have the Americans rule it alone.[4] America was widely admired for its values of equality, democracy, and national self-determination—all of which made us the principal anti-imperialist power in the world. Throughout the war, American officials warned our allies that after it was over, we expected their colonial empires to be emancipated. What's more, as the British had been before us, we were then unknown in the Middle East, and, more important still, we were not the oppressor the local populations knew. As a result, Middle Easterners projected a great many of their hopes onto the United States without knowing very much about America or Americans.

Early on, Washington took a number of actions that seemed to vindicate the outsized expectations of the people of the region that America would be their savior from the old imperialist powers. In

1946, the Truman administration demanded that Russia and Britain end their occupation of Iran, going so far as to threaten war with Moscow.[5] In 1948, Harry Truman recognized the newly independent state of Israel, igniting the hopes of Jews everywhere, although this did little for the sympathies of the Arabs. In 1950–1952, Secretary of State Dean Acheson labored to convince the British government and its avaricious oil giant, the Anglo-Iranian Oil Company, to accept a revised oil concession that would grant Iranians a fairer share of their own petroleum exports. (And he and President Truman forbade the British from mounting an invasion of Iran to topple Mossadiq, as London wanted to do.) Most famously, in 1956, the Eisenhower administration intervened to force the British and French to end their unprovoked invasion of Suez, which was intended to overthrow Gamal 'Abd al-Nasser, Egypt's highly popular, nationalistic leader.

At that time, it was easy for the United States to seem benignly disinterested in the Middle East because we were largely uninterested in it.[6] Our economic interests in the region were growing but still small, largely because we continued to produce so much more oil than our economy consumed. We continued to leave the military and political stability of the region largely to the British. Though Truman had recognized the state of Israel, he then promptly abandoned it, refusing to provide meaningful military or economic assistance, and instead imposing an arms embargo on all of the "confrontation states," which in turn prompted many of the Arab states to develop an arms relationship with the Soviet Union and forced the Israelis to turn to France. Naturally, there were exceptions along the way, like the infamous CIA coup d'état that overthrew Mossadiq in 1953, based on the British-fabricated claim that he was pro-Communist, and an American intervention in Lebanon in 1958 (which was paired with a simultaneous British intervention in Jordan), also to stave off illusory Communist threats. But by and large the United States showed remarkably little interest in the Middle East.

All of this began to change in the late 1960s and early 1970s for a host of converging reasons. First, America switched from being a net exporter of oil to being a net importer.[7] Second, in 1968, the British announced that, for financial reasons, they would be forced to end their military commitments "east of Suez" by 1971, opening up the prospect that there would be no great power minding the stability of the Persian Gulf and its oil. Moreover, the Kennedy, Johnson, and Nixon administrations all concluded that America's neglect of the region had allowed the Soviet Union to make considerable inroads with important client states in Egypt, Syria, Libya, South Yemen, and (to a much lesser extent) Iraq. The Six-Day War of 1967 also fed into that equation. It convinced the Johnson administration that Israel could be a very effective regional ally to counter Moscow's proxies in the Middle East or even to help thwart a Russian offensive into the region.[8] Consequently, beginning in 1967–1970, the United States began to take on the role of Israel's principal backer, which it has played ever since.

Even then, the United States proved to be a reluctant replacement as the region's dominant power. There was no massive buildup of American forces to supplant the British. The Johnson administration looked to Israel to help balance the Soviet Union and its proxies in the region. The Nixon administration went further still, devising the policy of "Twin Pillars" by which the United States would rely on the shah of Iran (and, to a much lesser degree, the Saudis) as our "policeman" in the region, to keep the peace and mind our interests so that we did not have to. Nixon and Kissinger also chose to try to wean Moscow's most important ally in the region, Egypt, away from the Soviet camp so as to diminish both the threat to regional peace and Soviet domination without requiring any increase in America's presence in the region. The Camp David Peace Accords between Egypt and Israel (along with the massive aid packages that followed them, eventually furnishing over $3 billion to Israel and over $2 billion for Egypt every year) were a seminal event, important to the United States because they seemed once again to promise that we could find ways to stabilize and pacify the region (and so ensure our interests, particularly the free flow of oil), without playing the same kind of dominating role Britain had assumed in the first half of the twentieth century.

Quickly, however, events proved these fixes to be inadequate. The Iranian Revolution of 1978–1979 toppled America's great ally in the Gulf region. The Soviet invasion of Afghanistan in 1979 then drove home the unfortunate reality that because the United States had not established a network of bases in the region, it was incapable of defending the Persian Gulf oil fields if the Soviets decided to try the same sort of offensive into Iran. Next, Israel's horribly misguided invasion of Lebanon in 1982, which inflamed the Lebanese Civil War it was meant to end, demonstrated that, whatever value the Israel Defense Forces might provide in a war with the Soviet Union, the Jewish state had little ability to use its military might to help bring greater stability to the region. Saddam Husayn's equally foolish invasion of Iran—leading eventually to Iraq's use of chemical warfare, missile attacks against the civilian populations of both countries, and large-scale military strikes against each other's oil exports (and later against those of Saudi Arabia and Kuwait)—struck another blow to America's efforts to remain disengaged from the Middle East. It illustrated that trying to maintain a balance of power between Iran and Iraq, which Washington had adopted when the Iranian Revolution killed the Twin Pillars approach, was not an effective way to keep the peace and ensure the free flow of Persian Gulf oil. Consequently, in 1987, the United States grudgingly agreed to provide Kuwaiti oil tankers with American naval escorts. This in turn led to a series of naval and air clashes with the Iranians. For all its jingoism, however, the Reagan administration tried mightily to avoid that commitment and then took extraordinary steps to prevent each instance of U.S.-Iranian combat from escalating. Saddam's even more misguided invasion of Kuwait in 1990 was yet another nail in the coffin of America's aloofness from the Middle East. It repudiated the idea that the United States could take a purely "offshore balancing" approach to the region, because an Iraq that was strong enough to balance Iran was plenty strong enough to overrun Kuwait and Saudi Arabia. And so, after the Persian Gulf War, for the first time in its history, the United States agreed to maintain a long-term commitment of military forces not just afloat on the region's waters but with combat troops on the ground.

Worse still, like the British before us, we began to realize that intrastate issues in the Middle East could be just as problematic for our interests as could interstate conflicts. The first inkling of this came with the Iranian Revolution, which created a serious threat to U.S. interests in the region during much of the 1980s. It was the first lesson that problems internal to the countries of the region couldn't just be ignored.

A second lesson came in the 1990s, when the Clinton administration saw its painstaking efforts to forge a comprehensive peace between Israel and the Arab states dashed on the internal politics of the Arab world. As Ambassador Martin Indyk has explained, the United States assumed that the best thing it could do was to set aside the internal unhappiness of the Muslim populace of the Middle East (at least for some time) under the assumption that the autocrats of the region could keep them under control and would be willing to work with the United States to help us achieve our interests— including making peace with Israel and containing Iranian and Iraqi efforts to overturn the status quo through violence and subversion. Ultimately, of course, the Arab regimes were not able to do either. Their fear of their own public unrest made them unwilling to go along with key elements of U.S. policy.[9] Neither Hafiz al-Asad nor Yasser Arafat could bring himself to accept peace deals with Israel brokered by the Clinton team. Meanwhile, throughout the decade, the United States saw its freedom of maneuver in the Middle East increasingly circumscribed by its closest Arab allies—including Egypt, Jordan, Saudi Arabia, and Morocco—all of which concluded that their angry populations would not tolerate greater cooperation with the United States. So much for that Faustian bargain.

EVEN THE GEORGE W. BUSH administration was far less interested in playing an active role in the Middle East than is commonly imagined. It is certainly true that some of the more ardent neoconservatives in the administration had from the outset been clamoring for an attack on Iraq (in some way, shape, or form) to topple Saddam Husayn in the mystical (and badly mistaken) belief that doing so would eliminate virtually all of America's problems in the region. But prior to 9/11 and the Afghan war, their views had not prevailed in the groupthink that dominated the Bush administration's decision making. None of the administration's seniormost members—the president, Vice President Dick Cheney, Secretary of State Colin Powell, National Security Advisor Condoleezza Rice, or Secretary of

Defense Donald Rumsfeld—really cared about the Middle East at all. They decided to try "smart sanctions" on Iraq as a last-ditch effort to maintain a coalition in the U.N. Security Council to keep the pressure on Saddam to comply with his various obligations to the United Nations. In practice, this amounted to allowing the U.N. sanctions to continue to wither away. They had no policy of any kind toward Iran, except to try to ignore it. Al-Qa'ida and the terrorist threat were famously low on their list of priorities. And they all agreed to avoid mounting a new effort to broker peace between Israelis and Palestinians like the plague.[10] In short, before the twin towers fell, the Bush 43 administration wanted little to do with the Middle East.

September 11 changed that, but not as much as is often assumed. The United States invaded both Afghanistan and Iraq, but what was so important—and so tragic—about both invasions was the absolute determination of the Bush administration not to involve itself seriously in postwar reconstruction. Infamously in the case of Iraq, the Bush administration refused to accept the need for a major effort to secure the country and rebuild its mangled institutions. Instead, it insisted that the United States would need to do little more than hand the country over to the neocons' favorite Iraqi expatriate, Ahmed Chalabi, before we could walk away from it.[11] Nor did its new involvement in the Middle East change its members' minds about the importance of brokering a peace between Israelis and Palestinians. The president's "road map" for Israeli-Palestinian peace, which involved a series of steps to be taken by both sides that was to produce a Palestinian state and a peace treaty between it and Israel, was effectively a farce, and it generally required a looming catastrophe or (most remarkable of all) the demands of Israeli Prime Minister Ariel Sharon, for the administration to make even brief forays into the peace process. The administration backed the Cedar Revolution in Lebanon as a way of ousting the Syrians but then did nothing to help build a Lebanese state capable of filling the vacuum that Syria's departure left—until the Israeli-Hizballah war of 2006 demonstrated how shortsighted that had been. Even their much-ballyhooed and maligned effort to push for democratization in the region was conducted briefly and halfheartedly. It never had first call on the best personnel, resources, or the attention of senior policy makers and was quickly shunted aside when it became inconvenient.[12]

Perhaps the only area of the Middle East where the administration really stepped up its level of engagement, and did so in a reasonably competent (although hardly flawless) manner, was on Iran, where it adopted a diplomatic approach relying on carrots and sticks and forged an impressive (if fragile) international coalition to pressure Tehran to give up its nuclear enrichment efforts. Unfortunately, even then, the administration's hawks were unwilling to pony up the most meaningful carrots—like showing a willingness to lift unilateral U.S. sanctions in return for Iran's giving up its nuclear enrichment program and support for terrorism—which would have given the policy a much better shot at success. In the end, they were simply unwilling to offer meaningful concessions to get what the United States needed in the Middle East.

Overall, and in marked contrast to the common (mis)perceptions of the Muslim world, the United States has been a reluctant hegemon in the Middle East. Indeed, the worst of the many mistakes we have made in the Middle East over the years has been that we have never really reconciled ourselves to the fact that we need to remain deeply engaged with it for some time to come and therefore must develop a plan of action for the long term. Our involvement with the region has too frequently been episodic, tried on the cheap, and shortsighted. Too often, we have adopted policies toward the Middle East in the ridiculous expectation that a brief exertion would solve the immediate crisis, whatever it was, and then we could go back to whatever it was we had been doing and forget about this frustrating part of the world. More often than not, months, years, or even decades later, we found ourselves still trying to address the same deep-seated problem with the same quick-fix strategy we started out with, hoping that just a little bit more would do the job and let us leave again.

It is time to put away such foolishness and confront the Middle East in a mature and rational manner. One of the many painful paradoxes of the Middle East today is that only by committing to a major, sustained effort to address the problems of the region do we have any chance of eliminating it as a constant source of crises and threats to our vital interests. This deeply troubled part of the world cannot stabilize itself and if left to its own devices will wreak havoc on the interests of the United States and the rest of the world. We have tried to pretend that the problems there will just go away, and the result has been to make those problems worse and worse. Now it is time to try the opposite, as we should have all along. As Winston Churchill once remarked, "you can always count on the Americans to do the right thing, but only after they have exhausted every other possibility." Having exhausted all of the other possibilities, it is time for us to do the right thing in the Middle East.

The Necessity of a Grand Strategy for the Middle East

The principal theme of this book is that the United States needs to devise an integrated grand strategy to secure and manage its interests in the Middle East over the long term. I begin with the recognition that the Muslim states of the Middle East are plagued by crippling economic, political, social, and cultural problems that are giving rise to the twin threats of instability (and raising the risk of all forms of internal unrest from insurgencies to civil wars to revolutions) and terrorism. The latter is the most immediate and direct threat to American interests, but the former may be the more dangerous. Thus, rather than attempting to deal episodically with problems as they arise or to treat the symptoms of the disease, as has been our wont—and the reason our involvement with the Middle East has been so unhappy and unsuccessful over the years—we must make a concerted effort to help the states of the region deal with their societal problems.

A grand strategy is simply a strategy that employs all of the capabilities of a nation, whether they are military, political, economic, or anything else. Thus, a grand strategy for the Middle East would be an overarching conception of what it is that we seek to achieve, how we intend to do it, and how to employ the full panoply of foreign policy tools—military, diplomatic, economic, social, technological, and even cultural—in support of it. It means thinking through what it is that we are trying to accomplish in the Middle East and how best to do so. It also means rationalizing the welter of our current

Middle East policies (our policy toward Iraq, our policy toward Iran, our policy toward Israel and the Palestinians, and so on) so that they work in harmony with one another and with the broader objectives of the grand strategy.

For most of the postwar era, American policy toward the Middle East was itself seen largely as an outgrowth of the principal American grand strategy, containment of the Soviet Union. Since the fall of the Soviet Union, we have had no overarching foreign policy principle to take the place of containment. Moreover, especially since September 11, 2001, we have realized that the gravest threats we now face are from the Muslim Middle East. This troubled part of the world is riven by conflict, mired in backwardness, and seething with anger at America and other countries it holds responsible (rightly and wrongly) for its problems. What's more, global economic dependence on oil has risen to the point where the United States and its trading partners simply cannot tolerate the kind of instability for which the Middle East has become famous. A major calamity there could bring down the entire international economic order. In other words, we have every reason to make the development of a coherent Middle East policy one of our preeminent concerns.

Both the Clinton and Bush 43 administrations recognized this shift in the locus of America's foreign policy threats and attempted to craft grand strategies toward the Middle East. Clinton sought to conclude a comprehensive Arab-Israeli peace in the belief that doing so would make it easier to solve all of the region's other problems. While certainly a noble goal in itself and a well-implemented policy despite its ultimate failure, the policy did not fully take into account that those other problems had, to a great extent, eclipsed the Arab-Israeli conflict as the principal threat to American interests in the region. On the other hand, the Bush 43 administration did recognize (eventually) the nature of the problems gripping the region but tried to deal with those problems in a breathtakingly arrogant, ignorant, and reckless manner that brought the United States to a previously unimaginable nadir in the Middle East.

The failings of both the Clinton and Bush 43 approaches toward the Middle East should be cautionary tales but not reasons to abjure the effort. The Middle East will not cease to generate threats to our interests just because we would like to ignore it. But we must take care to properly diagnose the source of those threats and devise appropriate and realistic courses of action that can address both the threats and their underlying causes. A new grand strategy toward the Middle East is still desperately needed, but it has to have the right goals and be implemented soberly and realistically.

To that end, and as with containment, we need to be ready to commit to such a grand strategy for the long term. Helping the Middle East address its many problems is not going to be easy, and it is not going to happen quickly. Indeed, one of the many problems with the Bush administration's efforts to promote democracy and free-market economics in the region was its determination to press ahead quickly, demanding changes in real time. The results were disastrous. As the old expression has it, "If you want it bad, you'll get it bad." For instance, by demanding elections in Iraq and the Palestinian territories long before either of those societies had anything like the kind of institutions, leaders, and political parties that might have produced a reasonable outcome, the elections succeeded in empowering the worst elements in both societies. The civil wars raging in both countries are a direct outgrowth of this rush to elections.

Instead, we must think in terms of decades. Perhaps many decades. It took forty to fifty years for the United States to help Western Europe transform itself and end the endemic warfare, ethnic strife, internal conflict, revolutions, and oppression that had made it one of the most violent regions of the world for millennia. The nations of East Asia are undergoing a similar transformation, but their evolution has been slower still. In the case of the Middle East, we should not expect that a grand strategy designed to help the region transform itself can be accomplished in less than twenty to thirty years, and it may well take longer. In fact, we would probably not want the process to move any faster than that. The problem with fundamental change is that if it happens too quickly it can be tremendously destabilizing, and since our ultimate goal should be to produce a more stable, more peaceful region, we should always bear in mind that speed kills.

Last, we must recognize that all of the various country- or issue-specific policies that we pursue in the region can affect one another and, of greater importance still, can help or hamstring the pursuit of a larger grand strategy. For this reason, a grand strategy must also include broad guidelines to rationalize specific policies so that all are working in unity, rather than undermining one another, and all are at least not hindering our efforts to advance the overarching goal of the grand strategy. There were any number of problems with the Bush administration's policies toward various aspects of the Middle East. However, what even its critics have so far failed to recognize is that the greatest problem with its approach was its failure to conceive and promote a grand strategy toward the region and craft constituent policies toward specific issues that would support the pursuit of such a grand strategy. As a result, many of America's current policies are mutually contradictory: they hinder one another and actually make it harder for our nation to achieve what should be our principal goals in the region.

THE GRAND STRATEGY I propose that the United States adopt is one of gradual, indigenously driven, but internationally assisted transformation throughout the Muslim Middle East. By transformation, I mean helping the region to reform its stagnant economies; improve its educational systems; devise workable legal systems that establish the rule of law; restructure its political systems in accord with democratic principles; and allow its culture to come to grips with all these changes and the impact of globalization. I have called this a strategy of "enabling reform" because the role of the United States and other external powers is not to reform the region ourselves but simply to make it possible for those Middle Easterners trying to do so to be able to. It is a very tall order, but there are no other good alternatives. Quite frankly, we have been trying not to adopt such an approach, and that has only made our problems with the Middle East worse.

This effort must be gradual, because something so ambitious cannot possibly be done quickly, and, as I have already noted, to try to do so would only be to doom it to failure. It must be indigenously driven because outsiders cannot possibly know how to change the society of another people. In particular, the success of our efforts to do the same in Western Europe, East Asia, and now Eastern Europe and Latin America, have been directly related to the ability of the people of these parts of the world themselves to adapt various ideas and models to their specific circumstances.

Democracy is a perfect example of this. Democracy is based on malleable concepts: representative government, accountability, transparency, rule of law, minority protection, political and legal equality, and so on. Thus, different societies can mold their institutions in very different ways and yet still fulfill the conditions of democracy. It is for this reason that democracy in Japan looks fundamentally different from democracy in Germany, let alone the democratic system of the United States. All of these countries have democratic systems, but they are very different, because they were the results of Japanese, Germans, and Americans adapting the abstract principles of democracy to fit their own unique cultures, histories, traditions, demographies, geographies, and other specific circumstances. As I will show, contrary to popular belief, most Muslim Middle Easterners want democratic systems of government; but they want democratic systems that suit their own history, culture, traditions, and other specific circumstances. Though the United States and other nations can certainly help them devise a democratic system that could work for them, we absolutely should not try to impose one on them or even devise one for them. Only they can figure out what will work for them, and therefore transformation is something that must grow out of the region itself. It cannot be made in America.

Last, the process can and should be internationally assisted, and that is where the United States comes back in. While the peoples of the Muslim Middle East are going to have to do a great deal of the work themselves, we should not assume that they can do it all on their own. The international community, led by the United States, can be of great assistance. We can provide advice, know-how, and experience. We can prod, encourage, demonstrate, and even threaten to move the process of reform forward. We can provide much-needed resources to make change possible. We can work to remove external security threats (real, exaggerated, and imagined) that might otherwise consume resources or sidetrack reform efforts. We can dampen or even prevent wars that might do even worse.

Moreover, it must be an international effort because the United States, even working in harmony with the states of the region (which will often not be the case), cannot do it alone. We are going to need lots of partners to help. Even the vast resources of the United States are ultimately limited, if only by what the American people will be willing to put up for such an effort. It will be extremely important to have other nations willing to contribute to this effort as well. Many nations and international organizations have skills and knowledge that the United States lacks but that will be critical to assisting the peoples of the Muslim Middle East. In addition, while there are some things that only the United States can or will be trusted to do, so too are there things where it would be much better if the United States were not in the lead or even not involved at all. For that reason too, we will need help from other nations and other organizations. The one bit of good news I can provide at the outset is that there are a great many countries and a great many such organizations that are ready to help. Indeed, many of them came to understand the need for such a grand strategy years ago, and they have been waiting patiently for us to "exhaust all the other options," as Churchill might have put it.

Today, the United States is lost in the sands of the Middle East. We will extricate ourselves from this morass only if we commit to making the same kind of effort on behalf of the Middle East that we have for Europe and East Asia over the decades. If we do, there is every reason to believe that we can succeed there eventually. It is going to be a long, hard road, but there is a path out of the desert.

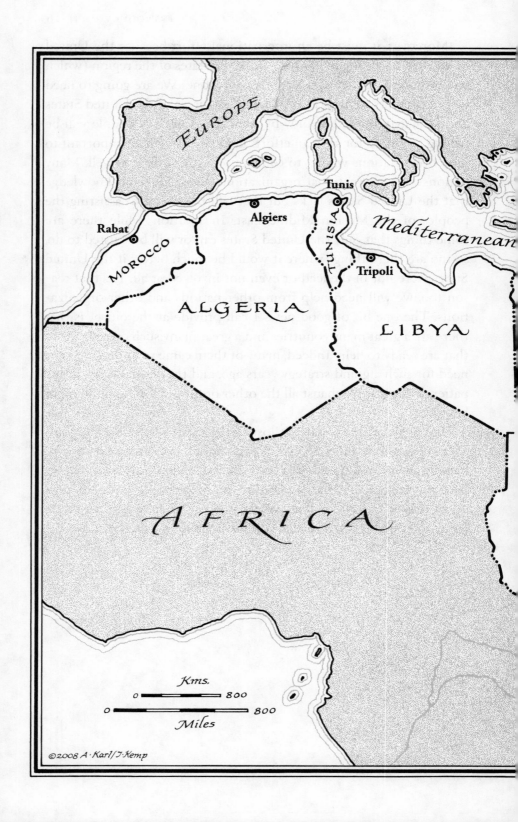

EUROPE

Mediterranean

Tunis

Algiers

Rabat

TUNISIA

Tripoli

MOROCCO

ALGERIA

LIBYA

A F R I C A

Kms.
0   800
0   800
Miles

©2008 A·Karl/J·Kemp

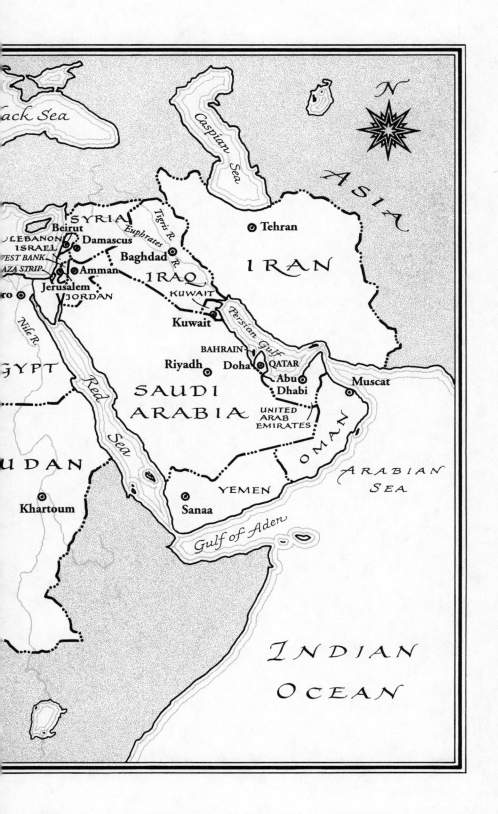

PART ONE

AMERICA'S INTERESTS

IN THE MIDDLE EAST

MANY AMERICANS HAVE ONLY A VAGUE SENSE OF THEIR country's interests in the Middle East. Some on all parts of the political spectrum believe our engagement in the region brings only trouble and that we should disengage as much as possible. Many who do support American engagement in the region do so without ever having thought through why. Still others overstate American interests, assuming that nothing that happens in the Middle East is unrelated to the well-being of the United States. In arguing for a new, activist grand strategy toward the Middle East (albeit one not quite so activist as the second Bush administration's), it is incumbent upon me to demonstrate why it is important that we should do so, and that means explaining specifically why and in what ways the region matters to the United States.

Along the same lines, it is impossible to devise a clear strategy without an equally clear understanding of that strategy's purpose. As the old expression has it, "If you don't know where you're going, any road will get you there." Its converse is also true: picking the right road requires you to know where you *are* going. Indeed, in the past, America's approach toward the Middle East and other countries or parts of the world has gone astray precisely because we did not have a clear sense of our own interests. In every instance where that was the case, the result was a bad one—ranging from mere missed opportunities to outright disasters. Thus it is important to articulate America's interests in the Middle East to have a clear sense of what we should be hoping to achieve, what we should care about, and what we should fear; but it is equally important to understand those interests to discern what it is that we should not fear, what should not concern us, and what is unnecessary for us to achieve.

This last point matters because one of the traps Washington has fallen into in the past is "goal displacement," in which our true interests become superseded by something else that seems to be consistent with them but really is not. For instance, many American interests in the Middle East are best served by the preservation of stability in the region, but that does *not* mean that stability itself is our interest. Change is often necessary, especially when the status quo becomes untenable, as is the case in the Middle East today. Unfortunately, for much of the last thirty years American administrations have failed to make that distinction and have often favored stability and opposed change at all costs. The result has been a series of American policies designed to preserve the status quo that have ended in disaster, from the Iranian Revolution to 9/11. Mistakenly substituting stability for our true interests in the Middle East is a dangerous example of goal displacement that we should avoid whenever possible. The best way to avoid it is to have a very clear sense of what our true interests entail.[1] Consequently, Part I examines America's most important interests in the region, starting with oil but also including some interests that apply all over the world but should not be lost amid our specific interests in the Middle East.

CHAPTER 1

—

OIL

LET'S NOT KID OURSELVES: AMERICA'S FIRST AND MOST important interest in the Middle East is the region's oil exports. However, this interest has *nothing* to do with how much oil we import from the Middle East. Instead, oil is our number one interest in the Middle East because our economic well-being relies generally on plentiful oil. That is true both because of the direct importance of oil to our own economy and, indirectly, because of its importance to the economies of the rest of the world—whose trade is vital to our economy. The Middle East plays a critical role in global oil production and therefore in the well-being of the *global* economy, of which our own economy is an irreducible part.

The American economy, as well as that of every other developed nation and ever-greater numbers of developing nations, is addicted to oil. In the words of one recent study, "Oil is the lifeblood of modern civilization. It fuels the vast majority of the world's mechanized transportation equipment: automobiles, trucks, airplanes, trains, ships, farm equipment, the military, etc. Indeed, according to the Department of Transportation, oil accounts for a whopping 97 percent of the energy used for transportation in the United States. Oil is also the primary feedstock for many of the chemicals that are essential to modern life."[1] Petroleum products are a critical input into the American economy not merely for transportation (which accounts for about two thirds of all American petroleum consumption) but also for industrial production (including plastics) and even some power generation. Petroleum accounts for 40 percent of all of the energy used in the United States, far more than either of the next two biggest sources of American energy, natural gas and coal, which account for only 23 and 22 percent, respectively.[2] In all, the United States consumes roughly 20 million barrels of oil per day, accounting for almost a quarter of global oil consumption by itself.[3]

What this means is that oil is a critical input into the United States' economy, and any major, sudden increase in the price of oil can have a calamitous effect on our way of life. As former Federal Reserve Chairman Alan Greenspan testified to the Congressional Joint Economic Committee in April 2002, "all economic downturns in the United States since 1973, when oil became a prominent cost factor in business, have been preceded by sharp increases in the price of oil."[4] In fact, nine of the last ten U.S. recessions were preceded by an increase in crude oil prices, and statistical tests have demonstrated that this was not coincidental.[5] Many economists already believe that the tripling of oil prices in the last four to five years is creating the conditions for another such recession.[6]

It is the price of oil, not its source, that is critical to our economy and those of our major trading partners. Oil is fungible, meaning that a barrel of oil can be burned anywhere in the world and have the same effect. That also means that a tanker full of oil can be sold anywhere in the world, to anyone—and always to the highest bidder. So the fact that we import most of our oil from Canada, Mexico, Venezuela, and Saudi Arabia does not mean that we are immune to problems with Russian oil exports; exactly the opposite. If there is a problem with Russian oil exports, the countries that normally buy from Russia will simply go looking for their oil somewhere else and will likely be willing to pay a higher price to get it. If they are, then our normal Canadian and Mexican suppliers will sell to them instead of to us, unless we meet the new price. Thus, the price of oil is determined by the classic patterns of supply and demand. Whenever the demand increases faster than the supply or the supply unexpectedly drops, the price of oil rises—and it rises for every country, including the United States, no matter where we get our oil from.[7]

Although the source of our imported oil is irrelevant, the amount of oil we import does have some relevance. The fact that the United States imports significant quantities of oil (about 65 percent of the oil we consume)[8] means that we cannot insulate ourselves from the direct impact of oil disruptions caused by sudden imbalances between the global oil supply and global consumption. If domestic American production accounted for all, or nearly all, of American consumption needs, then in time of crisis the government could suspend the impact of market forces by imposing price controls. In other words, if we imported only a very small amount of oil, we could divorce ourselves from the global price of oil at a rather low cost. But given how much we import, it is not economically feasible to do so. As long as we rely on oil for our energy needs while importing a significant amount of oil, our economy will be tied to the international oil market.[9]

It is also important to recognize that the *amount* of oil we import is not terribly meaningful, at least in terms of our interest in Middle Eastern oil production. Once we cross some immeasurable threshold of importation, after which it is no longer possible for us to cut off all imports without doing tremendous harm to our economy, the exact amount we import becomes irrelevant. Importing 75 percent of our oil is no more harmful than importing 25 percent: since the price of all of our oil will still be set by the international market in either case, we are no more vulnerable importing at the higher rate than at the lower. So merely trying to reduce the amount of oil we import is effectively useless, unless we can somehow get down to a fraction of current import levels.[10]

Even then, virtually eliminating oil imports, if it were somehow possible, would reduce the *direct* impact we would face from a major oil disruption but would hardly solve the problem because of the *indirect* impact of higher oil prices on the U.S. economy through their effects on our trade partners. In the globalized world of the twenty-first century, foreign trade is a large, and growing, input into the U.S. economy. The ratio of trade to gross domestic product (GDP) for the United States amounted to 17 percent in 1985, 23.6 percent in 1995, and 26.2 percent in 2005.[11] So even if we could somehow insulate our economy from the direct impact of a sudden spike in oil prices, we would still feel its impact due to a downturn in our trade relations. Higher oil prices would make foreigners less able to buy our goods and services, while driving up the prices we pay for theirs.

In particular, as a great deal of the annual U.S. deficit is funded by selling bonds to foreigners (meaning that a great deal of the U.S. national debt is held by foreigners), a worldwide recession could seriously affect U.S. finances by constricting global capital markets to the point where it becomes difficult for Washington to finance the deficit or service the national debt. These indirect forms of damage could cripple our economy even if the direct damage did not.[12]

Of course, it is highly unlikely that the United States will be able to greatly reduce, let alone eliminate, its oil dependency in the next decade or two, no matter how desirable that would be (and it *would* be highly desirable, obviously, for environmental and economic reasons).[13] It was a hopeful sign that even President George W. Bush recognized that America is addicted to oil and that this is potentially very dangerous for the country.[14] They say that admitting you have a problem is the first step to solving it, but we have a long, long way to go before we can solve this one.[15] Given the difficulty of either slashing domestic oil consumption or boosting domestic oil production to the level necessary to eliminate the direct impact of a major shortfall of oil in the next ten to twenty years, the reality we are stuck with is that major, sudden oil disruptions will hammer the U.S. economy *both* directly by jacking up the price we pay for oil *and* indirectly by suffocating trade and capital flows. Our economy would contract suddenly both from the increase in oil prices, which would boost inflation across the board, and from the sudden loss of trade as the economies of our business partners contracted as well. In the words of the oil expert Matthew Simmons, "Only energy has the potential to shut down the entire world."[16]

The Economic Impact of Major Oil Shocks

What the above discussion means for the average American is that when the international price of oil increases, either because the demand for oil is growing or because its supply has diminished, prices increase and the amount of disposable income we have drops. As the economist Keith Sill has put it, "Oil prices affect the economy through a multitude of channels. . . . The key is that oil-price changes affect both supply and demand. Changes in oil prices affect supply because they make it more costly for firms to produce goods; they affect demand because they influence wealth and can induce uncertainty about the future."[17]

First, rising oil prices mean that transportation costs more. That is most obviously true with car travel, because the price of gasoline at the pump increases. But oil prices also increase the cost of air, bus, truck, ship, and rail transportation—which are the ways we move goods from the factories, farms, and ports to the stores where we buy them and then to our homes. These transport costs are factored into the price of everything we buy. So if oil boosts the price of transportation, it ends up boosting the price of nearly everything else. Another reason that increased oil prices boost all other prices is that petrochemicals play a very large role in modern production, plastics being the best example. So anything made with plastic becomes more expensive, and in our modern world, a lot of things are made in part or in whole from plastics of one kind or another. Airline travel, train travel, and bus travel also increase in cost, which hurts everything from sales to tourism. When prices go up across the board (especially when it happens suddenly, because of an unexpected political problem affecting oil supplies), the average consumer has less disposable income and tends to spend less on major purchases—cars, appliances, even houses—all of which can depress major industries. An increase in the price of oil can also increase the nation's trade deficit because we pay more for all of the oil we import.[18] Thus prices typically go up (inflation), as do interest rates; manufacturing is hurt; unemployment increases and wages often decline in real terms; people have less money to spend because they are spending more on basics like food, heating oil, and transportation; which in turn hurts business, particularly in the sectors most closely tied to transportation.[19]

While even gradual oil price increases can be harmful to the U.S. economy, sudden shocks, in which oil prices skyrocket quickly (in a matter of months or even weeks) and unexpectedly, are of far greater consequence.[20] Over time, market forces allow the economy to accommodate itself to new oil prices. Higher prices will likely produce inflation, worsen the trade balance, possibly weaken the dollar, and overall cause some diminution of economic activity, but they are unlikely to be catastrophic. Gradual increases also allow people and businesses to switch over to other sources of energy, especially if the higher price of oil makes alternative sources more attractive. Moreover, businesses can plan for the changes and adjust their operations accordingly. Thus even the steep increase in the price of oil from $18 per barrel in 2001 to $70 per barrel in 2005 to $110 per barrel in 2008 has hurt the U.S. economy, but because it has transpired over years, not weeks, it has not been crippling.[21]

The problem with sudden, unforeseen shocks is that people cannot suddenly switch their cars or boilers from oil to another source overnight, nor can businesses plan to adjust their spending, revenues, and prices quickly enough. In many cases, people and businesses are simply prevented from doing things that are part of their daily lives (like driving to work) without any opportunity to adapt. It is why a major oil shock can almost literally bring the economy to a halt.

In economic terms, sudden disruptions in the oil supply serve as shocks to the U.S. economy that cause "stagflation," a very painful type of recession featuring both high inflation and high unemployment.[22] It is something of an economic "perfect storm" and can be very damaging. Relatively mild oil price shocks in 1973 and 1979 (both of which were caused by Middle East crises) were responsible for the worst recessions in the last forty years of U.S. history.[23] The problem is that it is possible to envision plausible scenarios in which future crises in the Middle East could cause much worse price shocks than those of 1973 and 1979, causing much worse recessions.

STRATEGIC RESERVES

One other piece of the complicated puzzle of American interest in Middle Eastern oil is the question of strategic oil reserves. After the 1973 oil shock and recession, the governments of the United States and several other industrialized countries decided to begin building strategic petroleum reserves to mitigate the impact of future disruptions.[24] Today, the United States has nearly 700 million barrels in its strategic reserve, and there are another 700 million barrels or so in the combined reserves of Germany, Japan, and several other countries. Since global oil consumption averaged 85 million barrels per day (bpd) in 2006, these reserves could theoretically cover *all* oil demand for sixteen to seventeen days. However, that is a ridiculous standard because it is impossible to imagine a scenario where *all* oil production was disrupted. The more relevant question when trying to ascertain the impact of an oil shock is "How much production is taken off the market and for how long—and how quickly can Washington and other governments release oil from their strategic reserves onto the market to make up for the amount of oil lost?" If past crises are any guide, the answer to the question of how quickly strategic reserves can be released onto the market is about 2.5 million barrels per day, which could be supported, in theory, for about 560 days.[25] This could eliminate the impact of a mild oil shock but would do no more than take the edge off a major disruption, and unfortunately, instability in the Middle East creates the potential for just such major disruptions.

The Importance of Middle Eastern (and Particularly Saudi) Oil Production

Of the 85 million barrels of oil per day (bpd) consumed globally in 2005, nearly 23 million bpd (27 percent) was produced by Middle Eastern countries, including roughly 19 million bpd (23 percent) by the Persian Gulf states—and roughly half of that (about 11 to 13 percent of total production) by Saudi Arabia alone. To make matters worse, virtually all of the world's excess production capacity, amounting to about 1 million to 2 million bpd, is located in the Persian Gulf region—and nearly all of that is in Saudi Arabia too.[26] This excess production capacity is important because it is the only way (other than the strategic oil reserves, which governments are loath to release) to compensate for lost production in the short and medium terms. In other words, if something were to happen to the Saudi oil network, not only would the world lose a huge chunk of current production, we would also lose any capacity we have to replace it quickly by bringing unused production capacity online.[27] For these reasons, Saudi oil production is irreplaceable at this time, and its loss would be devastating.

It is extremely difficult to predict what the sudden loss of a significant percentage of Middle East oil production would do to the U.S. economy, but all of the estimates are alarming. The 1973 Arab oil embargo resulted from a reduction of just 2.75 percent of global oil production. The 1979 Iranian Revolution pulled 5.68 percent of global production off the market.[28] Since 2000, Saudi Arabia has typically accounted for 11 to 13 percent of annual oil production alone. Clearly, the loss of its oil production would have a much greater impact than these previous two disruptions. What's more, in the 1970s there was considerable excess production capacity that helped to limit the damage of some of the earlier oil shocks, especially over time. Today, the tight oil market and concentration of available spare capacity in Saudi Arabia mean that the country's loss as an oil producer could be far worse than simply a straight-line extrapolation from the two historical cases.[29]

Another way to try to get at the same question is to consider that global expenditures on oil as a share of total world GDP have typically ranged from 1 to 3 percent. Whenever they have exceeded 4 percent, there has been a global recession. Above 7 percent has caused a severe global recession, such as occurred in 1979–1982, the worst global recession since the Great Depression. One recent study projected that a loss of 4 percent of oil production (hardly the 11 to 13 percent potentially represented by Saudi Arabia) resulting from a political crisis in the Middle East would cause an increase in global expenditures on oil as a share of total world GDP to 8 percent, causing a tripling of inflation in the United States and macroeconomic consequences that are simply incalculable.[30]

Other studies have shown that a 10 percent increase in the price of oil would lead to a 1.4 percent drop in real U.S. GDP growth. This is bad enough, given expectations that a major loss of Middle Eastern oil could produce price increases in the range of 200 to 500 percent in a few weeks, but it could be much worse, because the models economists use to determine such an impact are designed to deal with only modest price shocks (in which the price rises by only 10 to 30 percent over a period of months) and are not really able to extrapolate to such astronomical levels.

In 2001, my colleague at the Brookings Institution, the economist George Perry, examined several scenarios for a serious oil disruption as a result of political instability in the Middle East. In his worst-case scenario, Perry assumed that a crisis in the Middle East resulted in the loss of 13 percent of global oil production—roughly equivalent to the amount of oil produced by Saudi Arabia alone today. Even with a release of 2.5 million bpd from strategic reserves, Perry calculated that such an oil shock would cause oil prices to quintuple (from the 2001 price of $30 per barrel to the then-astronomical figure of $161 per barrel), adding 15 percent to inflation in the first year and causing a recession that would be "the steepest and deepest of the postwar period."[31] Perry estimated that GDP would suffer negative growth of 5 percent during the first year after the shock.[32] Just for comparison, during the first two years of the Great Depression the United States suffered negative growth rates of 9.8 percent in 1929 and 7.6 percent in 1930. Thus, by Perry's calculus, the recession caused by the loss of Saudi oil production might not cause another Great Depression, but it would be close.

Other economists and oil experts fear that a sudden loss of Saudi oil production could actually spark a global recession of the same magnitude as the Great Depression. They argue that the interconnectedness of the global economy and its greater reliance on oil as a basic input since the oil shocks of the 1970s mean that such a major shortfall could have geometrically greater ripple effects than a simple straight-line projection from the earlier crises would predict, bad as that would be. The truth is that, as former Clinton administration National Economic Adviser Gene Sperling warned in 2005, none of our current economic models can adequately predict the consequences of a sudden disruption that would cause the price of oil to triple, quadruple, or worse in a very brief period of time.[33] Even pondering the question typically leads oil experts and economists to say that such a development would range from "very bad" to "disastrous," "catastrophic," or even "unimaginable."[34]

Moreover, this situation is expected to get worse before it gets better—if it improves at all. By 2025, the U.S. Department of Energy's Energy Information Administration estimates, global demand for oil will grow from the current 85 million bpd to nearly 120 million bpd, with U.S. consumption rising from 20 million to 28 million bpd. By far, the largest increases are expected to come as China and India continue to modernize. Because the Persian Gulf has the greatest capacity to bring additional increments of oil at cheap prices online, the amount of oil produced by Middle Eastern OPEC countries is projected to rise from 23 million bpd (27 percent of all consumption) to 38 million bpd (31 percent of all consumption) in 2025.[35] The EIA estimates that Middle Eastern countries will supply 35 percent of global oil production by 2030.[36] In other words, the world will become more dependent on Middle Eastern oil, not less.

The Perils of Petroleum

Though the likelihood of a major loss of Middle Eastern oil in the next ten to twenty years is probably not high, unfortunately it is not "unimaginable"—even if the consequences of such a development might be. The history of the Middle East over the past sixty years has been chock-full of interstate wars, revolutions, civil wars, terrorist attacks, and the seizure of power by irrational zealots. A number of these events have caused oil shocks in the past, some very harmful to the U.S. and global economies, although none has come close to what the loss of Saudi oil production today would likely entail. Any of these occurrences in the future could produce just such a major oil disruption, and there is little reason to believe that the Middle East will be less prone to these events in the future than it has been in the past. Indeed, it is the frequency of these events in the Middle East, and their potential to cause major, sudden oil disruptions, that makes the region vital to America's national security and to the stability of the entire global economy.

The Persian Gulf War of 1990–1991 furnishes two good examples of how interstate war can lead to large-scale losses of oil exports. In 1990, Saddam Husayn invaded Kuwait. The world reacted by embargoing Iraqi oil as well as Kuwaiti oil, so that Saddam's regime could not make a penny off either. The result was the loss of about 3.9 million bpd at a time when global production amounted to 69.5 million bpd.[37] The impact of this shortfall was greatly mitigated by excess production capacity, particularly in Saudi Arabia, that was quickly brought on line to compensate—excess production capacity that would not be available if the same happened *to* Saudi Arabia. Then, in March 1991, as Iraqi troops fled pell-mell from Kuwait in the face of the onslaught of Operation Desert Storm, they ignited or destroyed 80 percent of Kuwait's oil wells. Although repairs went much better than expected, they were not completed until November 1991.[38] (Again, compensation by other producers with spare capacity—particularly Saudi Arabia—this time coupled with a release of oil from U.S. and other national petroleum reserves, helped diminish the impact of the loss of Kuwaiti oil.)

The Iranian Revolution demonstrated both how internal instability can cause sudden, massive oil production losses and the willingness of ideological zealots to choose not to pump oil. The Iranian Revolution played out for over a year in 1978 and 1979, during which time Iran's oil production dropped disastrously because of strikes, the loss of foreign workers (both highly skilled and unskilled), disruptions, the distraction of the people and government officials, and even skirmishes at oil facilities. In addition, the Ayatollah Ruhollah Khomeini and many of those around him were deeply ambivalent about Iran's oil exports, reasoning that it was the oil that had brought on so many of Iran's problems under the shah, from the cultural corruption of Iranian society to Western intervention in Iranian politics. Consequently, the imam did not make restoring Iranian oil production a priority, and Iranian oil production dropped from 5.9 million bpd in 1978 to just 1.3 million bpd before the start of the Iran-Iraq War.[39] It was an important lesson that zealotry, especially in the Middle East, can override economic need, with calamitous results for all. Khomeini's decision crippled the Iranian economy and caused the worst recession in post–World War II U.S. history. A future "Saudi Khomeini" who adopted the same approach could do far worse damage.

Insurgencies can also cause damage to oil production and export infrastructure. Insurgent and terrorist attacks in Nigeria have reduced that country's oil exports from 2.5 million bpd to less than 2 million bpd at various times.[40] Between June 2003 and March 2007, insurgents in Iraq conducted at least 402 attacks on Iraq's pipelines, oil fields, refineries, and export terminals, depressing its oil production by as much as 40 percent below its nominal capacity during some periods and preventing Iraq from rebuilding its devastated oil infrastructure, which is theoretically capable of exporting at nearly twice the current levels.[41]

There is also the ever-present danger of terrorist attack on Middle Eastern oil production and export facilities. Unfortunately, al-Qa'ida, its offshoots, and other terrorists know that oil is the Achilles' heel of the Western world.[42] As the former head of the CIA's al-Qa'ida unit, Michael Scheuer, has explained, "The steady and affordable supply of oil being crucial to the well-being of the economies of the United States and its allies, [oil] has naturally become a focus for al-Qa'ida, as well as a valued target in its overall plan to force the United States out of the Middle East by damaging its economy severely."[43] In December 2004, Usama bin Ladin explicitly called for attacks on oil facilities in the Persian Gulf and Caspian Sea—including on civilians working at these facilities.[44] In February 2006, bin Ladin's principal deputy, Ayman az-Zawahiri, added his voice to these calls. "I call on the mujahideen to concentrate their attacks on Muslims' stolen oil," he demanded, "most of the revenues of which go to the enemies of Islam, while most of what they leave is seized by the thieves who rule our countries."[45]

Moreover, these words have been translated into actions. For instance, in October 2002, al-Qa'ida extremists tried to attack the French oil tanker *Limbourg* with a suicide boat packed with explosives off the coast of Yemen. That same year, U.S. and Saudi intelligence discovered that al-Qa'ida sympathizers had infiltrated Saudi ARAMCO and were planning to destroy key Saudi oil facilities.[46] In 2004, al-Qa'ida operatives attacked the Saudi oil terminal at Yanbu, killing five Westerners working there.[47] More recently, in February 2006, terrorists were physically prevented by security personnel from crashing two car bombs into the Abqaiq oil-processing center in Saudi Arabia. Although few had heard of this facility before the attack, there is no more sensitive economic target on Earth—more than the City of London, Wall Street, the Fed, or Japan's Keihin Industrial Region, Abqaiq is the beating heart of the global economy. Roughly 75 percent of Saudi oil flows through the main mixing manifold at Abqaiq before being piped out to refineries and then export terminals. If there is any one facility on Earth whose loss could cause massive, widespread economic damage, Abqaiq is it—and the February 2006 attack signaled that the terrorists had figured this out and were going after it precisely because of its importance. Then, in

April 2007, Saudi officials revealed that they had arrested 172 "Islamic extremists" linked to al-Qa'ida who were planning to crash airplanes into Saudi oil targets.[48] Like striking at Abqaiq, using airplanes as weapons could give terrorists the ability to cause much greater damage than would normally be the case and might even allow them to do the kind of damage to Middle Eastern oil facilities that only wars (civil or interstate), revolutions, or misguided leaders might otherwise accomplish. A third approach would be to employ the lessons of Iraq and Nigeria to mount a sustained insurgent/terrorist campaign of attacks on a nation's oil infrastructure. Although each attack might have only a minor impact, over time the aggregate result could be devastating.[49]

So far, there has not yet been a case of any event like those mentioned above triggering a truly catastrophic oil disruption. Nevertheless, the worst oil disruptions since the Second World War were caused by the Suez-Sinai War of 1956, the October War of 1973, the Iranian Revolution of 1978, the Iran-Iraq War of 1980–1988, the Persian Gulf War of 1990–1991, and now the U.S. invasion of Iraq and the Iraqi civil war that has followed (although their impacts diverged significantly because of a range of factors).[50] As noted above, these Middle Eastern events in turn caused many of the worst recessions of the postwar era. Because all of these disruptions fell on the "low" to "modest" end of the spectrum of potential disruptions, the results were nasty recessions, but little else. If a similar event were to cause a major disruption, such as would happen if all Saudi oil (along with the country's spare production capacity) were removed from the market the way Iraq's was in 1990 or nearly all of Iran's was as a result of the Iranian Revolution in 1979–1980, the result could be disastrous. That is the most important reason that the steady flow of Middle Eastern oil is America's most important interest in the Middle East.

Too Much Oil in the Wrong Hands

Unfortunately, the global addiction to oil has created another American interest in the Middle East: the danger that a malevolent regime will gain control over a large chunk of Middle Eastern oil and use it to deliberately harm the United States and its allies.

One of the reasons that Washington has had a soft spot in its heart for the royal family of Saudi Arabia, the Al Sa'ud, is that they are interested principally in making money. Moreover, they have been wise enough to plan and act to maximize their ability to make money over the long term, rather than just make as much as they can in the short term. They understand that their oil wealth can keep their subjects happy and themselves living like princes (pardon the pun) for many decades as long as they ensure that oil is relatively cheap and relatively plentiful and that its price does not rise (or fall) too quickly.

This has made them the ideal custodians of the world's largest oil reserves and (at most times) the largest percentage of global oil exports. Because the Saudis really just want to make money, it means that they have generally allowed market forces to prevail and at times have even used their excess production capacity to maintain an orderly market by acting as a "swing producer"—increasing or decreasing production to prevent oil prices from fluctuating too erratically. The only occasions when they diverged from that policy—during the 1973 October War, in which they joined the oil "embargo" of the West and cut oil production, and to an even lesser extent after the Iranian Revolution—backfired on them by encouraging Westerners to adopt conservation practices and promote alternative sources of energy.[51] This threatened to get the West to kick its oil addiction, which in turn threatened Riyadh's long-term revenues. The Saudi response was to decide that they would never do something so foolish again, a position they have kept to ever since.[52]

The problem is that states and their leaders are not always motivated by economics alone or even by a long-term view of their economic interests. Others have seen oil wealth as a means to increase their military power or as a weapon itself. The last shah of Iran, our erstwhile ally, longed for his country to be the greatest military power in the Persian Gulf region and may even have hoped to make Iran the equal of America and the Soviet Union someday. Consequently, he was the worst of the oil "price hawks," constantly pressing the other OPEC members to agree to push up the price of oil in order to maximize his revenues in the short term, so that he would have more money to build up Iran's armies. Of course, the shah was our ally, so we did not oppose his push for power. However, his zeal to boost oil prices as fast as possible was the driving force behind the 1973 oil embargo, which threw the U.S. economy into recession (and helped his friends in the Republican Party lose the 1976 presidential election). Moreover, the shah's efforts proved to be his undoing, as Iran's runaway oil revenues—and his people's outrage that these riches were not trickling down to them—helped provoke the Iranian Revolution, which ousted him from his throne.[53] It would be something of an understatement to say that neither the sudden increase in the price of oil during the 1970s, which provoked the recession in the United States, nor the fall of the shah and his replacement by Ayatollah Khomeini were good for the United States.

Saddam Husayn, too, saw his country's oil wealth as a tool to increase his military and political power. His decision to invade Kuwait in 1990 was motivated by this, as well as a desire to alleviate Iraq's massive debt from the Iran-Iraq War. Saddam believed that by adding Kuwait's oil wealth to Iraq's, he would make himself the greatest economic and military power in the Middle East. At the time, the combination of Iraqi and Kuwaiti oil production amounted to roughly 9 percent of global production, just slightly less than Saudi Arabia's.[54] While we don't know for certain what Saddam would have done had he been allowed to digest his Kuwaiti conquest, his later behavior is not a source of comfort. Specifically, Saddam refused to export any Iraqi oil from 1991 to 1996 because the U.N. Security Council would allow him to use oil revenues only to buy food and medicine for his people. After 1996 he relented, largely because he realized that he had crippled Iraq's economy so badly that his country was teetering on the brink of financial collapse.[55] Even after he agreed to sell oil, Saddam frequently halted Iraqi oil production to try to blackmail the U.N. Security Council. He sold oil at cut-rate prices to advance his political agenda, regardless of the cost to his economy or people. Moreover, unlike the Saudis, Saddam believed that the Arab oil embargo of 1973 had been a great victory.[56] In a particularly gratuitous move, in April 2002, Saddam shut off all legal Iraqi oil exports to protest Israel's Operation Defensive Shield, which was aimed at Palestinian militants and had nothing to do with Iraq. Saddam simply hoped to use the maneuver to increase his popularity on the Arab street, regardless of the impact the lost oil revenue would have on the Iraqi people or economy.[57] All of this suggests that had Saddam ever gained control of the Gulf's oil resources, he would have been willing to restrict or even halt oil exports altogether whenever it suited him to make money or force concessions from his fellow Arabs, Europe, the United States, or anyone else.

Finally, there is the example of Ayatollah Khomeini, related earlier, whose antipathy toward Iran's "oil curse" caused him to disregard the reconstruction of Iran's own oil industry until the Iraqi invasion of September 1980 forced him to do so. This history, in particular, should illustrate the mistaken assumption that many make when they insist that the United States should not be concerned about political problems in the Middle East because "they can't drink the oil." They don't need to "drink the oil": they might not be able to pump or sell the oil; they might choose to leave it in the ground; or they might decide to sell only as much as they want to, not as much as we need. All of these alternatives would be bad, and potentially catastrophic, for the United States.

Indeed, what all of these examples make clear is that a war, revolution, or terrorist attack suddenly taking large amounts of oil off the market is not the only way that the United States could face a major threat because of our addiction to oil. Unscrupulous leaders might choose to manipulate the international oil market for their own political or strategic aims. Even if they do decide to pump as much as they could (like the shah in the 1970s and Saddam in the 1980s), they might decide to do so to make as much money as possible to build as big an arsenal as they could to launch wars of conquest, blackmail their neighbors, or mount other destabilizing adventures.

It should come as no surprise that Usama bin Ladin has already thought of all of this. What might be surprising is that he has said that when he has restored the Islamic caliphate, he does not believe that it should cut off all oil exports despite the fact that he seems to agree with Khomeini that oil has been a major source of political and cultural corruption in the 'Umma (the Islamic community). "Instead," according to Scheuer, "he has focused on finding ways to drive up the price of oil." He has stated that he believes that the United States and the West are "stealing our oil. The U.S. buys cheap oil from us and then sells us its own tanks and aircraft with [that is, on the basis of] the threat from Israel. This is how the U.S. takes its own money back from us."[58] He has promised that, once in power, the Islamists would boost the price of oil to the level they consider fair.[59] There is little reason to think that what bin Ladin considers fair would not prove disastrous for the global economy.

Of course, bin Ladin is not the only radical Islamic fundamentalist seeking to gain control over Saudi Arabia or another major oil-producing region of the Middle East. Others might see things Khomeini's way and decide not to sell oil at all. Still others might decide to cut oil production drastically (which would dramatically boost oil prices, at least in the short run, and therefore might actually cause their revenues to increase) to blackmail the international community or specific actors to give them what they want on any number of issues. It's not hard to imagine that if an Islamic fundamentalist regime were to take power in Saudi Arabia, it might demand that the United States withdraw its military forces from the region, then build up its own armies and attempt to re-create the Islamic conquests of the seventh century, while threatening to bring down the global economy by shutting off all oil sales if the United States or other outside powers attempted to stop it. It seems highly unlikely that any American administration would back down from such a challenge, but this is exactly the kind of situation that we ought to be trying to avoid.

What Does and Does Not Matter About Middle Eastern Oil

Although the United States has some very powerful interests in Middle Eastern oil, they are also fairly discrete, and it is important to be clear in our own minds where those interests lie. For as long as we and our trade partners remain addicted to cheap, plentiful oil, we need to ensure that there are no major, sudden losses of Middle Eastern oil exports. That means we have an interest in preventing wars (civil and interstate), revolutions, and terrorist attacks that could cause such a disruption. At least in the case of Saudi Arabia— but possibly in smaller but still important exporters like Iraq, Iran, Kuwait, and the UAE as well—we also have an interest in seeing that whoever governs there is committed to exporting as much oil as is economically feasible and not in halting or manipulating oil exports for ideological or diabolical purposes. In addition, we have an interest in preventing an unscrupulous regime from gaining control over a significant percentage of global production and using that position to undermine the global economy—or merely blackmail the United States and its allies with the threat of doing so. It would also be preferable to prevent such a regime from gaining control over major oil resources for fear of how it might use the revenues.

These are compelling interests, but they are also worst-case scenarios. Given the history of the Middle East and the potentially catastrophic impact of one of these threats becoming manifest, the United States and its allies ought to go to considerable lengths to prevent them—or at least mitigate the likelihood of their occurring. However, there is no reason to believe that any of these scenarios is likely, at least in the near term. I would not bet my salary that none of these things could happen over the next ten years, but neither would I bet that any of these things will happen tomorrow. That balance of potential cost and likelihood needs to be kept in mind as we consider the goals of an American grand strategy for the Middle East.

Perhaps of greater importance is what this examination of America's interests in Middle Eastern oil leaves out. While I do believe that preventing the sudden loss of a significant portion of the region's oil production (for instance, in the event of revolution or civil war in Saudi Arabia) is a vital American security interest, I do not believe that keeping the price of oil low falls into the same category. As an American, I feel that keeping the price of oil low would be desirable from an economic perspective but not necessary from a security perspective. The distinction I am drawing here is between the kind of oil disruption that could cause an economic collapse, perhaps approaching the scale of the Great Depression (or conceivably even worse), and other fluctuations that might cause milder (albeit still painful) recessions. I consider the former a security *threat* and the latter an economic *problem*. Security threats justify the expenditure of enormous resources, even the use of force, to prevent them. Economic problems don't.

What this suggests is that American involvement in the Middle East should be intended and designed principally to prevent catastrophic oil disruptions and the acquisition of massive oil resources by particularly nefarious characters. I raise this point because since 1973, American presidents have been tempted to use America's military and diplomatic position in the Persian Gulf region to try to influence the price of oil to stave off recessions. Though I don't think that the United States should necessarily sit idly by if OPEC decides to jack up prices, especially if it does so for political reasons, as it does from time to time, I also don't think that this is the sort of problem that should be the focus (let alone the justification) of an Amerian grand strategy toward the Middle East.

There is a constant tug-of-war between market forces and politics when it comes to American (and global) interests in Middle Eastern oil. The bad news is that our dependence on imported oil means that we are at the mercy of the market. The good news is that market forces can typically compensate for all but the severest problems. These compensations can sometimes be unpleasant, but as long as the problems remain modest they are also bearable. The problems arise when major political disruptions nullify the ability of market forces to compensate. To the extent that problems in the Middle East affect oil production, we can (and should) safely allow market forces to deal with most of them. The key concern for American security interests in the region is to prevent the kinds of worst-case political-military developments—like a revolution or civil war in Saudi Arabia or a massive terrorist attack on a key oil node—that market forces alone cannot handle.

CHAPTER 2

ISRAEL

Typically, Americans describe our interests in the Middle East as being "oil and Israel." Though that list is incomplete, it is true that these have been our highest priorities for decades. America's interest in Israel is typically thought of as being a sentimental one, and our support is certainly rooted in our core foreign policy values: the determination to help the suffering, the belief that people everywhere should be allowed to govern themselves and not be oppressed by others, and the conviction that the United States must stand in solidarity with democracies both because it is right and because the world is a better and more peaceful place for our doing so. These are the values that have shaped and inspired American foreign policy since the beginnings of the republic and that for many, many decades made the United States admired throughout the world.

However, the United States also has compelling strategic interests in its relationship with Israel, although those interests have changed since the end of the Cold War. Increasingly, Americans have recognized that the preservation and even spread of democracy around the world are not just a moral good but also a strategic one because of the considerable security benefits they bring to the United States. Moreover, since the 1970s, American support for Israel has often acted as an important source of peace and stability in the Middle East (thereby buttressing our primary interest in the region's oil exports). It is also the case that the arguments of those critical of the U.S. commitment to Israel's security are unpersuasive and mistaken, reflecting a misunderstanding of Middle Eastern history, the U.S.-Israeli relationship, and current regional dynamics.

Though I believe support for Israel does constitute a vital interest of the United States for *both* moral and strategic reasons, some people disagree, and it is worth being explicit in addressing their skepticism.[1] Moreover, it is important to understand the basis of the U.S. commitment to Israel to understand what it does and does not imply for American strategy and policies toward the Middle East. Finally, the rationales for America's interest in Israel's strength and security have varied over time, and if the United States is going to refashion its approach to the Middle East to address the problems of a new era, Israel's place in that approach at this time and for the foreseeable future also needs to be spelled out.

The Moral Debt

Over time, some American interests in Israel have come and gone while others have remained constant. One that overshadowed all others sixty years ago was a sense of moral obligation to the Jewish people in the aftermath of World War II and the Holocaust. Samuel W. Lewis, a former U.S. ambassador to Israel under Carter and Reagan, explains that "In the beginning was guilt . . . guilt about the Nazi Holocaust that nearly exterminated European Jewry while America turned a blind eye for too long."[2] Former Secretary of State George Shultz put it this way: "The United States supported the creation of the state of Israel almost four decades ago because of moral convictions deeply rooted in the American character. We knew of the centuries of persecution suffered by the Jews and we had witnessed the horror of the Nazi Holocaust. No decent American could fail to see the justice and necessity of a Jewish state where Jews could live without fear."[3] Even two scholars critical of America's support for Israel acknowledged that "[the] conviction that America had a moral obligation to Israel rested on several grounds. In part it derived from a sense of guilt that the Christian West in general and the United States in particular had done nothing to prevent the Nazi destruction of European Jewry and little even to mitigate its effects by accepting large numbers of Jewish refugees or by making the survival of European Jews a major priority of the military strategy of the war against Germany."[4]

Clark Clifford, the de facto national security advisor to President Truman at a time before that position had been formally created, explained that this sense of moral obligation was probably the most important of a range of motives that convinced Truman to recognize the new state of Israel when it proclaimed its independence pursuant to the United Nations' decision to partition Palestine in May 1947. (And, it is worth noting for the conspiracy theorists, who insist that all American support for Israel rests on the machinations of a "Jewish lobby" or similar ideas about domestic politics, Clifford did not believe that domestic political considerations had anything to do with Truman's decision.)[5]

Does the United States still owe Israel that same moral debt? Different Americans will answer that question differently, but a considerable number would likely answer in the affirmative, at least to some extent. That is my feeling about the matter: I believe that America's willingness to turn a blind eye to the horrors of the Holocaust, our failure to take military action to hinder it, our refusal to take in large numbers of refugees fleeing the Nazis (and, in some famous instances, actually turning away boatloads of Jews fleeing Europe so that they were forced to return and be killed there), and our unwillingness to press the British to allow greater Jewish emigration to Palestine remain a stain on our nation's conscience. However, while I would wholeheartedly agree with President Truman's decision and his rationale for doing so, I believe that that moral debt is no longer the principal consideration in America's interest in Israeli security.

National Self-Determination

Another element in Truman's thinking was that the United States stood for the right of groups of peoples—"nations"—to have their own states.[6] Support for national self-determination as a core principle of American foreign policy dates back at least to the goals that Woodrow Wilson espoused in his famous Fourteen Points for resolving the First World War. This concept also played a major role in American policies in redrawing the maps of Europe and Asia after World War II and lay at the heart of America's long opposition to imperialism and support for postwar decolonization.

National self-determination has remained an important principle guiding American foreign policy ever since, and our championing of that principle has served us well. National self-determination formed part of America's rationale for opposing the Soviet domination of Eastern Europe during the Cold War and has been one of our salient arguments in supporting the emergence of post-Soviet states against Moscow's neoimperialistic impulses. During the Balkan wars of the 1990s, national self-determination was the key intellectual principle guiding American support for Slovenian, Macedonian, Croatian, Bosnian, and eventually Kosovar independence. Indeed, on a number of occasions, the United States has been willing to go to war to up-hold this principle. Unfortunately, as the examples of Kosovo and the Kurds illustrate, American support for national self-determination has never been pristinely consistent. However, we have honored the ideal more in the observance than in the breach, and when we have backed away from it, we have done so only reluctantly (and typically only temporarily), in the face of difficult practical problems—like the need to hold Iraq together in the face of the massive centrifugal forces we unleashed after toppling Saddam and failing to be ready to deal with the consequences.

National self-determination deserves to remain an important principle in American foreign policy because, in addition to its moral desirability, it commands a compelling strategic logic. A great many nations have been grateful to the United States for our support of their bids for independence. Moreover, as Wilson recognized during World War I, advancing the cause of national self-determination was crucial to the causes of international peace and security: through-out human history, numerous wars, civil and interstate, could have been avoided had various nations been allowed to rule themselves rather than being subject to others. Multiethnic (or "multinational") states are a lovely idea in theory but have often proven difficult in practice—with the (successful) United States and India being notable exceptions and the (unsuccessful) Soviet Union, Austria-Hungary, Ottoman Empire, Yugoslavia, Czechoslovakia, and Ethiopia serving as more common examples. This is not to argue that the United States should oppose multiethnic states or even that we should support the right of every group to form its own country. However, when a people clearly constitute a nation, when they have made clear that they wish to rule themselves, and especially when they have already constituted themselves as a state, the United States ought to support them both because it is "right" and because in such circumstances a peaceful separation is generally much better for all involved than the civil strife that is the usual alternative.

ISRAEL AND NATIONAL SELF-DETERMINATION

The Jews were unquestionably a "nation" before the creation of the state of Israel, even though many had been scattered around the globe beginning with their forced diaspora from ancient Judaea by the Romans in the first century A.D. Beginning in the nineteenth century, spurred largely by the horrific pogroms they suffered in Russia, as well as the pervasive anti-Semitism they faced in Europe and, to a lesser extent, the Islamic world, many Jews began to advocate a return to their ancestral homes in the Levant and the establishment of a Jewish state built around the core of Jews who had never left. This aspiration fit the definition of national self-determination perfectly, and the savagery of the Nazi Holocaust only made that case more compelling.

Today, no objective observer would deny that the Jews of Israel constitute a nation deserving of their own state. While this is not the place to rehearse all of the claims and counterclaims of the Jews and Arabs to the land of Israel/Palestine, suffice it to say that for centuries there was a Jewish state in that parcel of land, and there has been a continuous Jewish presence there for millennia (although its population has varied widely over time). Moreover, beginning with the Muslim conquest in the seventh century, the Jews there were never treated better than second-class noncitizens. While Islam never inflicted anything like the terrors of European anti-Semitism on the Jews, neither was life particularly pleasant for them under Muslim rule. And on too many occasions, Muslims also engaged in more extreme forms of persecution and violence against Jews. As Jews from abroad began to buy land in the Levant starting in the 1880s to enable them to emigrate, the Arabs resisted violently—provoking both self-defense and retaliation by the Jews—all of which made it apparent that any effort to impose a multinational state on the entire territory of Palestine would be more likely to end in civil war than in harmony. [7]

Both the legitimate aspiration to self-determination by the Jewish community and the inability of Jews and Arabs to live in a successful multinational state were recognized at various points by the British, who ruled the area from 1919 till 1947. This recognition, in part, motivated Lord Balfour's famous declaration in 1917 that Britain would look favorably on the creation of a Jewish state there. Twenty years later, the Peel Commission came to the same conclusions and recommended that the mandatory territory of Palestine be partitioned to create a Jewish state (Israel) and an Arab state (Palestine) west of the Jordan River.[8] In 1947, the United Nations reached the same verdict as the Peel Commission, dividing the land west of the Jordan River between Arabs and Jews, apportioning specific areas to each based on which group predominated on the ground and decreeing that both peoples should be allowed to form their own states.

Of course, if the Jews clearly constitute a nation deserving of a state—and of the support of the United States in achieving and now preserving that goal—so too do the Palestinians. America's commitment to national self-determination for reasons both idealistic and strategic (in terms of reducing a major cause of conflict in the world) argues for American support for Israelis to have a Jewish homeland; but it also argues for American support for a separate Palestinian state. It should be self-evident that peace between Israelis and Palestinians requires the creation of a separate, independent Palestinian state. I believe strongly that the United States should continue to support national self-determination (including the eventual establishment of a Kurdish state), and specifically this means continued staunch support for Israel's right to exist as a Jewish state alongside a Palestinian state, sharing the territory of former mandatory Palestine west of the Jordan River.[9]

Democracy

For President Truman, democracy was another important reason to support the new Jewish state, albeit secondary to moral considerations. Today, I would argue that this order should be reversed. Israel is an imperfect democracy, but it is a true democracy—the only one in the Middle East. For the United States, that is a huge reason and, at this point, of far greater significance than guilt for our disgraceful behavior during the Holocaust. As with national self-determination, there are both moral and strategic imperatives for American foreign policy to support democracies, and these rationales form another important element in our interest in Israel's security.

It was Clark Clifford who first articulated the strategic component of the democracy argument when he fought for recognizing the new state of Israel in the debates during the Truman administration. In responding to his colleagues who opposed recognizing Israel, Clifford argued, "I fully understand and agree that vital national interests are involved. In an area as unstable as the Middle East, where there is not now and never has been any tradition of democratic government, it is important for the long-range security of our country— and indeed, the world—that a nation committed to the democratic system be established there, one on which we can rely. The new Jewish state can be such a place. We should strengthen it in its infancy by prompt recognition."[10]

America has supported democracies around the world since our own nation's inception. Our proudest moments have been when we have stood up, and even fought, for the cause of democracy, and our most shameful moments have typically been those when we sided with dictators (including against their own people) rather than other democracies. It is worth remembering that we took up arms in both of the world wars on the side of the democracies, and not by accident. In World War I, President Wilson announced that we were going to war to "Make the world safe for democracy" and that "A steadfast concert for peace can never be maintained except by a partnership of democratic nations."[11] Indeed, in the First World War there was not the same moral divide as in the Second to justify our opposition to Germany: the kaiser was hardly Adolf Hitler—Anglo-French propaganda aside—and therefore our decision to ally with the British and French was driven principally by our determination to support democracies against autocracies. For this reason, the U.S. government largely found Russia's exit from the war in 1917 after the Communist revolution a relief, because it made even clearer that American support for the Western Allies was based on democratic solidarity. At Versailles, we argued for national self-determination and democracy as the guiding principles for postwar reconstruction, not just because we thought it was morally right but because we believed (correctly, given the postwar history) that this was the best way to prevent another terrible conflict.[12] After the Second World War, the United States pushed to establish democracies in all of the states of Europe that fell within our sphere of influence, including West Germany. Our success in doing so proved critical both to our commitment to Western Europe and to the ultimate happiness of Europeans themselves. We likewise established a democracy in Japan and regularly demanded (if only rhetorically) that the Soviet Union allow true democracy in its zone of control in Eastern Europe. It is worth noting that this support for democracy is the foundation of the tranquillity and prosperity of Europe and Japan today and to our "victory" in the Cold War.

Of course, the Cold War also saw the United States support a range of outrageous autocrats, including at times even against democratic forces within their own societies, as in Iran in 1953 and Chile twenty years later. But today, most Americans see such support as having been largely misguided, and since the end of the Cold War, support for democracies around the world has been at the forefront of American policy, even if Washington still makes more than a few exceptions.

AMERICAN SUPPORT FOR DEMOCRACY has stemmed from a variety of sources. First has been the American conviction that it is simply right for people to control their own political systems and that it is America's obligation to help make the world a better place. Of course, one need not believe that it is America's God-given mission to bring democracy to the world to believe that with great power comes great responsibility. As the most powerful nation on Earth, the United States bears the greatest responsibility to advance the cause of all mankind, and until someone comes up with a better form of government, democracy is not just the best way for men and women to pursue prosperity and happiness, it is also, by far, the most popular form of government around the planet[13]—including in the Arab world, a point I will return to at some length later in this book.

As previously noted, American support for democracy can and should also be justified in much more hard-nosed, strategic terms. America's relationships with democracies have proven to be far more beneficial, predictable, and enduring than its ties to countries with other systems of government. Over the past hundred years, our greatest allies have been democracies and our greatest adversaries have been autocracies. The countries with which we have most often found common cause have been democracies; those whose behavior we have found most threatening have generally been autocracies of one kind or another. Mature democracies tend to be less prone to radical changes in government (like revolutions) and radical changes in policy, making it easier to predict their behavior and to expect them to honor the commitments they have made. Consequently, since the days when Pericles walked the streets of Athens, democracies have tended to be "natural" allies.

Likewise, scholars have noted that democracies seem much less inclined to fight one another, with some going so far as to claim that there have been no instances of democracies fighting in nearly two hundred years.[14] Whether this last claim is true or not, and even if it is true whether it will hold true in the future, are not critical to the recognition that America has clearly had much closer relations with democracies than with other kinds of states. Indeed, this is the principal reason that both the George H. W. Bush and Bill Clinton administrations made democracy promotion critical components of their foreign policy after the collapse of the Soviet Union, not only in Eastern Europe but around the world. As President Clinton put it, "Ultimately, the best strategy to ensure our security and to build a durable peace is to support the advance of democracy elsewhere. Democracies don't attack each other."[15]

Israel is a democracy (actually, one of the world's older democracies at this point), and the United States should support Israel as a democracy just as it supports democracies everywhere else in the world. We should not let its location in the Middle East and its conflict with the Arab world disqualify it for our support. If anything, the fact that Israel is a democracy surrounded by (mostly hostile) autocracies ought to make us *more* supportive of it, not less.

THERE IS LITTLE QUESTION that Israel is not a utopian democracy. Even within the confines of Israel and its democratic system, there is still considerable discrimination against Israel's Arab population.[16] However, a few points are in order here. While Israel's discriminatory practices should not be excused or condoned, neither should they disqualify it for American support as a democracy. In 2007, Freedom House put Israel in its highest category of "Free," for its overall adherence to democracy. On a scale of 1 to 7 (with 1 being the best) it ranked Israel as 1 for political rights and 2 for civil liberties. (It is worth noting that the next closest Middle East country was Kuwait, which scored a 4 in both categories. Even our NATO ally Turkey scored only 3s in both categories and is described as only "Partly Free").[17] Indeed, the reason we know so much about Israel's problems is that its own domestic civil liberties groups publicize them, its politicians debate them, and its courts punish them. Moreover, we should not forget our own shameful history of discrimination against African Americans and American Indians, much of which makes Israel's treatment of its Arab population pale by comparison. Nor are we alone: the Irish faced long years of oppression at the hands of the British, and even today much of Western Europe is guilty of racist and discriminatory treatment of its own Arab and Muslim minorities—discrimination that has begun to provoke violent backlashes like the riots in France and Belgium in the summer of 2006. There are few perfect democracies in this world, and although Israel's abuses should be condemned and we should press the Israelis to end their discriminatory practices, this should not disqualify Israel as a democracy any more than France's treatment of its Algerians or Germany's treatment of its Kurds and Turks should disqualify them.

Even Israel's repressive occupation of the West Bank should not be grounds to cut America's ties to it. First, because Israel remains so desirous of preserving its links to the United States, Washington has been able to prevail on Jerusalem at times (typically, whenever a U.S. administration felt it important, which has not often been the case under the George W. Bush administration) to modify or even halt Israeli activities in the Palestinian territories. Second, any number of American allies have waged similar campaigns without their actions calling into question American support, and Israel should not be treated any differently just because it is Jewish and/or located in the Middle East. Great Britain's handling of Ireland—complete with civil wars, massacres, bloody crackdowns, suppression of human rights, and military occupation—never disqualified it for U.S. support, and, especially when one factors in all of the aid we provided during the two world wars, our economic, political, and military assistance to Britain has dwarfed our support for Israel.

Washington should press Israel on its discrimination against Israeli Arabs and its occupation of the West Bank. Both countries have accepted UNSC Resolution 242, which established the formula of "land for peace," and we need to hold Israel to that as a general principle, just as we should criticize it when it falls short in meeting its own democratic values (and perhaps expect it to do the same when we fall short on ours, as in our handling of the prisoners at Guantánamo Bay). But none of this should obscure the commitment the United States should maintain to Israel as a flourishing democracy, just as we do for every other democracy from Great Britain to South Africa and from Taiwan to Mexico.[18] If there is any principle that can be said to be the core of America's foreign policy for both strategic and moral reasons, it is our commitment to support and defend democracies. Israel should be no exception.

The Arab-Israeli Conflict

As explained in chapter 1, war, revolution, or terrorist attacks could cause a major shortfall in the export of oil from the region. Consequently, our first and most important interest in the region is to avert wars (civil and foreign) and revolutions (or other radical changes of regime) for fear that they could directly or indirectly cause such an oil disruption. Over the past sixty years, even when wars, terrorism, and revolutions have not directly affected important oil-producing states, they have typically had ripple effects in those states—either by inspiring copycats who try to achieve the same (as many Islamists have been inspired to rebel against the Arab regimes by the example of the Iranian Revolution against the shah), by creating spillover effects like refugees, or by encouraging the oil-producing states to get involved in a fight that might not concern them directly, as happened in 1973 with the oil embargo.

The Arab-Israeli conflict has been a major source of such instability in the region, sparking at least six interstate wars since 1948, as well as numerous smaller clashes, military operations, raids, and the like, right up through the Israeli-Hizballah conflict of 2006.[19] These wars have had far-reaching ramifications, including for Arab states that did not participate in them in any significant way. Arab governments have been overthrown in response (in part or whole) to the Arab-Israeli wars: Egypt in 1952 (and almost again in 1970), Libya in 1969, Syria in 1949 (and almost in 1967 as well), and Iraq in 1958 and 1968. In 1970, the Jordanian monarchy was almost overthrown by the Palestine Liberation Organization (PLO), which was born of the Palestinian refugees from the Arab-Israeli wars and whose principal grievance with King Hussein was that he tried to limit its attacks on Israel. Both Jordan and Saudi Arabia have faced internal threats at different points stemming from their lukewarm support for the Arab cause in these wars. The Arab-Israeli wars have also helped give rise to terrorist organizations like the PLO, Hamas, Islamic Jihad, and Hizballah, and they led directly to disruptions in the flow of oil in 1956 and 1973.

America's unequivocal backing of Israel's security and existence, although not necessarily its policies, has actually helped dampen conflict throughout the region. Prior to 1967, American sentiment toward Israel was "cool and distant" at best.[20] The United States provided very little aid and even less military assistance. The results were the 1956 and 1967 Arab-Israeli wars, in which Israel launched preemptive or preventive offensives against Egypt and Syria (and in 1967 was simultaneously attacked by Jordan), as well as the Israeli decision to pursue a nuclear weapons capability to guarantee the continued survival of the Jewish state.[21] By comparison, after the United States committed itself to Israel's defense in the wake of the 1967 Six-Day War, the U.S. government has been able to exercise considerable pressure on Israel to restrain its military actions.[22] In 1969, according to newly declassified U.S. government documents, the United States prevailed on Israel not to test a nuclear device, which Washington feared would trigger a regional arms race.[23] In 1973, Israeli Prime Minister Golda Meir famously refused to launch a preemptive attack on Egypt and Syria because she knew that the United States would not condone it and American support was more important to her than getting in the first punch. In 1982, Israel sought America's permission before launching its disastrous invasion of Lebanon (which we foolishly granted) and then halted its military forces on the outskirts of Beirut at Washington's request—allowing the PLO leadership and many of its fighters to escape under the protection of a U.S.-led multinational force.[24] Likewise, during the 1991 Persian Gulf War, Saddam Husayn gratuitously launched thirty-nine Scud missiles at Israel in the hope of turning his conflict with the thirty-nation coalition into an Arab-Israeli war. The Israeli government, under the ultrahawk Yitzhak Shamir, grudgingly agreed not to retaliate because of tremendous pressure from the Bush 41 administration.[25] Finally, Israel's decisions to "take risks for peace" over the years would have been unimaginable without unstinting U.S. support for its existence and its security. Its peace treaties with Egypt and Jordan—and the near misses with Syria and the Palestinians in the 1990s—were possible only because Washington had made clear that it would come to Israel's rescue if the situation somehow fell apart and imperiled the Jewish state.[26] An insightful study by Jonathan Rynhold has suggested that the more Israelis believe that they can rely on the United States, the more willing they have been to trade land for peace.[27]

The American commitment to Israel was critical to peacemaking in the Middle East for another reason as well: it helped convince the

Arabs that they did not have a military option against Israel. To some extent, this was nothing but a facade—it was simply more palatable for Arab leaders to say that they could not win a war against Israel because of American support. In fact, the Israelis had defeated the Arabs just as handily without American support as they had with it, and American support for Israel during the 1973 October War has been vastly exaggerated. Ambassador Dennis Ross, who led the Clinton administration's effort to forge a comprehensive Arab-Israeli peace in the 1990s, has written, "Would the Arab world even believe it had to accommodate itself to Israel's existence if it had reason to question the staying power of the U.S. commitment to Israel? I also doubted that. When Anwar Sadat of Egypt made peace with Israel he explained that he could have fought Israel, but he could not fight the United States. Peacemaking required that the Arabs understand that no wedge could be driven between the United States and Israel and that Israel was not going to disappear."[28]

America's support for Israel over the years has even been a critical element in winning and securing Arab allies. A great many of the Arab states saw in American support for Israel the very aid that they sought themselves. This was another element in Sadat's decision to make peace with Israel—the fact that doing so would secure an alliance with the United States, which in turn would unlock America's vast economic and military assistance for Egypt. Sadat was proven right on all counts. During the 1973 October War, one aspect of the Nixon administration's decision to start an unprecedented airlift of war matériel to Israel was Washington's desire to convince the Arab states that allying with the United States brought far greater benefits than allying with the Soviet Union, a message that was not lost on the Arabs. At the time, the Saudi minister of the interior, the future King Fahd, summoned his senior aides and showed them clips of American weaponry being delivered to Israel. "This is why we need to maintain a close relationship with the U.S.," he told them. "They are the only ones capable of saving us in this manner should we ever be at risk."[29] It was a role fulfilled by Washington when the Saudis suddenly found themselves at risk after Saddam Husayn's invasion of Kuwait in the summer of 1990.

Other Strategic Considerations

The political scientist Steven David has pointed out that Israel is the one Middle Eastern country for which it would be inconceivable ever to turn against the United States: "The interests of Israel and the United States are not identical, and disputes will arise between the two countries. But it is unthinkable that Israel would ever engage in anti-American terrorism, support countries that threaten the United States, or confront American forces directly, as have so many of America's Arab allies."[30] As David also noted, Americans fear an Islamist takeover in virtually all of the states of the Middle East except Israel. Israel is not subject to coups or rebellions because it is a stable, mature democracy—another point about the importance of supporting democracies. "Second, Israel's pro-American orientation is rooted in the democratic values of its society. In no other Middle Eastern state are the roots of pro-American support so deep, widespread, and immutable."[31] Even our closest Arab allies have, at times, sided against us—the Saudis mounting the oil embargo that caused the first great oil shock (and triggered a particularly painful recession in the United States) in 1973, the Jordanians standing with Saddam Husayn in the 1990–1991 Persian Gulf War. Not Israel.

The Israelis have also helped the United States in a number of ways over the years. While this aid is not so important that it would constitute a compelling rationale of its own, neither has it been unimportant. For instance, in 1970, during the nadir of Jordanian fortunes during the Black September civil war with the PLO, Washington asked Jerusalem to move its forces to threaten Syria (which had invaded Jordan in support of the PLO) and prepare to intervene on behalf of Jordan if the Syrians did not withdraw. The Israelis did so, and although their role in the successful outcome of this crisis is still debated, their willingness to play such a part when the United States could not was gratefully acknowledged in Washington.[32] Since the United States began making major arms sales to Israel in 1970, the U.S. military has benefited from the experience the Israelis have gained with those weapons in battle. From conformal fuel tanks for fighter aircraft to the use of drones, from the 30 mm cannon on the

A-10 attack aircraft to identification markings on tanks, the U.S. military is stronger for sharing the expertise of the Israel Defense Forces. Similarly, Israeli intelligence has provided assistance to American intelligence agencies over the years, most notably in 1956, when Mossad was the only Western intelligence service to acquire a copy of Nikita Khrushchev's secret speech denouncing Stalin.

Israel is also a significant American trade partner, another factor that has been important in establishing American security relationships in the past. In 2003, out of 251 nations tracked by the Department of Commerce's International Trade Administration, Israel ranked as the United States' twenty-first most important trading partner, a position it has basically maintained since then.[33] In 2006, Israeli trade with the United States amounted to $22 billion, and the United States was both Israel's largest source of imports and its largest export market.[34]

Finally, there is the potential demonstration effect if the United States were to reverse course and end its alliance with (or merely distance itself from) Israel. While I am not very fond of arguments about reputation and commitment, there is something to this. In 1987, the U.S. Congress designated Australia, Egypt, Israel, Japan, and the Republic of Korea as "major non-NATO allies." If the United States were to cool its relations with Israel, one can only wonder how the Taiwanese, South Koreans, Turks, Japanese, and other countries might respond. At the very least, the United States would likely seem to them to be less reliable as an ally than they had formerly believed. Many of these states, particularly Taiwan and South Korea, might find themselves pondering whether the same could happen to them, given that American interests in their security are effectively identical to (and arguably weaker than) American interests in Israel. They might choose to take unilateral actions to guard against the possibility that the United States might abandon them too—actions like developing nuclear arsenals that might be highly provocative to China, North Korea, and other regional rivals.

While at some level the Jordanians, Saudis, Egyptians, and other Arabs might be glad to see the United States cut its ties to Israel, at another level they might find it deeply disturbing—both because of the loss of America as a restraint on Israeli behavior and because of what it might imply for their own security if the United States ever decided that they too had become inconvenient allies. As with South Korea and Taiwan, we should want our Arab allies to feel that they can rely on the United States so that they can focus on their internal problems and so that they do not take provocative unilateral actions that could spark a new war or other crisis. Divorcing ourselves from our longtime friends in Israel, the only country in the region with which the United States shares political, moral, and cultural ties, will not reassure our Arab allies and can only make the Middle East a less stable and more violent place.

The Counterargument

Had the state of Israel been founded on a deserted island, the moral arguments coupled with the strategic value of supporting national self-determination and solidarity with a fellow democracy would likely have been more than adequate to ensure American support for the Jewish state for as long as one could imagine since there would be no downside to doing so. Of course, Israel was not founded on a deserted island, and the most persistent reason why some have called American support for Israel into question is that the Israelis are, by and large, hated by the Arabs and our support for Israel has created problems in our relations with the Arab states. Consequently, since 1947, some have argued that the United States should not support Israel because we should support the Arabs instead. Although remarkably persistent, this argument is simplistic, weak, and wrongheaded.

In 1948, the consensus of the American foreign policy establishment was that the United States should oppose the creation of the state of Israel in order to curry favor with the Arabs so as to maintain access to their oil. Secretary of State George C. Marshall led this opposition, summed up and backed by a State Department analysis drafted by George Kennan, which argued that U.S. recognition of Israel would allow the Soviets to make inroads into the Middle East, threaten American basing rights in the region, and undermine profitable oil concessions.[35] Secretary of Defense James Forrestal bluntly scolded Clark Clifford, "You just don't understand. There are four hundred thousand Jews and forty million Arabs. Forty million Arabs are going to push four hundred thousand Jews into the sea. And that's all there is to it. Oil—that is the side we ought to be on."[36]

Though these arguments undoubtedly seemed cogent at the time, history has proven them otherwise. Even without American military assistance, the Israelis more than held their own against the "forty million" (now over 200 million) Arabs. They were not pushed into the sea. Instead they won stunning victories in 1948, 1956, 1967, and 1973. The United States did lose a few bases in the region as retaliation for our recognition of the state of Israel (notably Wheelus Air Base in Libya after Muammar Qadhafi took power in 1969), but this had no impact on America's strategic posture vis-à-vis the Russians because the advent of ballistic missiles with intercontinental ranges made those bases unnecessary. The Soviets did make inroads into the region starting in 1955, but this had nothing to do with American support for Israel; indeed, American support for Israel was negligible during the period when the Soviets made their greatest gains, and the sudden increase in American support to Israel after 1967 was actually a *response* to the major gains the Russians had made with Egypt, Syria, and other Arab states. Indeed, the strength of America's position in the Middle East improved only after the United States began to support Israel. Similarly, the United States did "lose" its oil concessions, but not because of Israel. The states of the region all decided to nationalize their oil industries so that they could enjoy greater control over and revenues from their oil reserves. And since then, American oil firms have continued to be the most desired business partners for most of the Arab national oil companies despite massive American support to Israel beginning after the Six-Day War.

This is the fundamental point missed by partisans of the argument that the United States should not support Israel because our interests really lie with the Arabs: it is not a zero-sum game. Much as the Arabs (and the Israelis) would like us just to pick one side and stick with it, the reality is that we have been able to maintain strong relations with both for decades. Might the United States have had even closer relations with some of the Arab states had it shunned Israel? Almost certainly yes, but to what end? What is it that we want from the Arabs that we are not getting now and that cutting our ties to Israel could somehow produce? The answer is, not much.

THE HEART OF THE anti-Israel argument is that Arab populations hate Israel and transfer that animosity to the United States for being Israel's principal patron in the region. There is no question that the Arab populace detests Israel and is largely anti-Semitic (in the colloquial sense of being "anti-Jewish") in general. Opinion polls regularly demonstrate Arab hostility to Israel,[37] as does open racism in media and educational materials. Anyone who has spent even an hour in the region has probably encountered Arab hostility toward the Jewish state, if not the Jewish people. (It is also worth noting that many Israelis hold equally racist views of their Arab neighbors.) To some extent, albeit typically less than their people, the governments of the region share this animosity toward Israel, and this does play a role in the fashioning of their policies. In addition, because the governments know that their people hate Israel (and, in most cases, use it to distract from other problems), they often tailor their policies so as not to be seen as overly kind to Israel or, to a lesser but still important extent, as overly kind to Israel's backer, the United States, for fear of being seen as out of step with public opinion. There is no question that all of this is true and that it does play a role in America's relationship with the Muslim Middle East, but what is important for America's interests is that the actual impact of these sentiments on America's economic and strategic interests in the region is actually quite marginal.

The biggest consideration is, obviously, oil. However, as noted in the last chapter, oil is fungible, producing an international market, and it is that market that determines 99 percent of what happens with oil. The Arab oil producers cannot use their oil exports to hurt the United States selectively for its support of Israel. As we have seen, the only thing they could do would be to curb production, which would diminish the flow of oil to the entire international market, hurting the United States and all other countries but also hurting themselves by encouraging their customers to cut back on oil consumption. Although the Arab states have realized that monkeying around with global oil supplies doesn't really make sense for them, they could still cut out American oil companies from doing business with them (as Kennan and company argued back in 1947). This has happened in a few instances, but rarely. Exxon, Amerada Hess, Chevron, Conoco, and their colleagues generally do extremely well throughout the Middle East because the Arab states want their skills and technology—which are second to none—and so "overlook" American support for Israel. Here as well, dollars speak louder than politics. In those cases where American oil corporations have been shut out, as in Iran, Syria, Sudan, and Iraq under Saddam Husayn, the cause has been American sanctions, not Muslim animosity toward Israel.[38] American oil companies are hugely profitable and create considerable wealth and jobs for the American economy—could they have gotten even more if the United States had not supported Israel? Perhaps a bit, but it isn't as if our economy has done poorly since 1947 or that whatever additional revenue the U.S. oil companies might have extracted from Libya would have made a significant difference to the American economy. Moreover, though I am not opposed to American policy being helpful to American oil companies when things work out that way, neither do I believe that the United States should devise its policy toward the Middle East or anywhere else based on what is best for the profit margins of Exxon and Conoco.

If not oil, what about allies? Did America's support for Israel prevent the United States from acquiring the most powerful allies in the region? Nope. As Charles Lipson of the University of Chicago has pointed out, "Close American ties to Israel have not prevented Saudi Arabia and Kuwait from relying heavily upon the United States for defense of state, crown, and oil."[39] America's closest allies in the Arab world are the most powerful and important states in the Arab world: Egypt, Saudi Arabia, Jordan, Morocco, Kuwait, the United Arab Emirates, Qatar, Bahrain, and Oman. We're also on good terms with Lebanon, Algeria, Tunisia, and Yemen. Even Libya is courting the United States aggressively these days. Some of those states chose to ally with us in part (and we should not push this too far) *because* of our relationship with Israel, as noted above. The only Arab states we count as our adversaries today are Syria and Sudan—where our support for Israel has definitely cost us, but not much. It would be nice to be on good terms with both the Syrians and the Sudanese, but these days the estrangement is a function mostly of our animosity toward their regimes and their policies (toward Lebanon and Darfur, for instance), not of their dislike of us because of our support for Israel.

Iran is not an Arab state, but it is an important member of the Muslim Middle East, and it is the one key state in that region that is our enemy. However, our enmity with Iran has little to do with our support for Israel. The Iranian people are actually quite well disposed toward the United States and mostly ambivalent about Israel. On the other hand, many members of the Iranian regime hate the United States, but their hatred is almost entirely based on our past support for the shah and our meddling (both real and perceived) in Iranian affairs. Even for the most ardent revolutionary ideologues, American support for Israel is largely an afterthought.[40]

Another possible way that American support for Israel might hurt America's interests would be if it diminished the positive assistance the United States receives from the Arabs. Here the idea is that the Arab states could be helping the United States more if it weren't Israel's great patron. But there are two problems with this claim: our Arab allies are actually pretty helpful to us, and it is not clear how much more helpful they could be. The Saudis have always offered financial assistance to other moderate Arab states—like Jordan and Morocco, largely because it is in their own interest. However, after the Iraqi invasion of Kuwait in 1990 and the subsequent American-led military operations to defend the kingdom and oust Saddam's army, both the Saudis and the Kuwaitis demonstrated their appreciation for Washington's aid by donating to a wide range of American causes, some of which had little intrinsic benefit to them (like supporting the Bosnians and Kosovars). Other countries like Egypt and Jordan, which lacked the financial resources of the Gulf states, ponied up military forces for peacekeeping operations in places like Angola, Liberia, Somalia, Cambodia, Haiti, and the former Yugoslavia at Washington's request.[41] Egypt has gone even further, committing its military to support U.S. foreign policy initiatives in Zaire in 1977 and Morocco in 1979, to block Libyan attacks on Sudan in 1983, and to Saudi Arabia in 1990, as well as to Somalia and Bosnia. In fact, the Egyptians not only participated in the U.S.-organized U.N. intervention in Somalia in 1992–1993, they opened their ports and air bases to the operation. U.S. Central Command essentially ran the entire logistical operation for the Somalia mission from Egypt. American military officers uniformly asserted that the intervention would not have been possible without Egypt's total cooperation.[42] Our relationship with Israel did not preclude any of this.

It is not clear what more the United States might want from friendly Arab states. Unfortunately, most of the Arab states have little military capacity and virtually no ability to project power beyond their borders. Problems with military professionalism have also made many Arab militaries undesirable even for peacekeeping missions, with the exceptions noted above.[43] Despite the caricatures of wealthy Arab oil shaykhs, most of the Arab states are very poor, with little trade, aid, investment, or technology to offer. Even in the richest states, dysfunctions in their governmental, legal, and educational systems make them poor models for other third-world countries. This is why, to a very considerable extent, it is money from the wealthy Gulf states that has been most helpful to American strategic and diplomatic efforts around the world. In this regard the Arab states are often quite generous, and it is not always clear how much more generous they could realistically be, especially given their own problems at home.

Thus there is no reason to believe that America's strategic position in the Middle East would be significantly better if we were to cut our ties to Israel, and, as noted earlier, doing so would likely hurt us more than it helped because of the strategic benefits we accrue from that relationship.

I do not want to suggest that American support for Israel is not a complicating factor in U.S. relations with the Arab world, only to demonstrate that it is not nearly as problematic as its critics claim. Military basing is an issue that illustrates the distinctions nicely. Though the United States was not shut out of the region, as Secretaries Marshall and Forrestal feared back in 1948, America has not always enjoyed unfettered access to the region either, and our relationship with Israel has been a part of that. In particular, in the late 1990s the Saudis increasingly limited U.S. military operations from bases in their country. First, they effectively quarantined virtually all American personnel at Prince Sultan Air Base (PSAB), out in the middle of the desert, far from any city, so that the vast majority of Saudis would never see an American. Then they began placing limits on what American planes based at PSAB could do. Eventually, they forbade us from mounting strike operations from the kingdom altogether. The problem they had was that their people were growing unhappy with the Anglo-American air missions over the no-fly zones in Iraq. Beginning in 1998, Saddam Husayn ordered his air defense forces to regularly attack American and British planes enforcing the no-fly zones, which prompted responses from these aircraft—which Saddam's regime invariably claimed were killing civilians, which in turn riled up the Saudi populace against the United States.

The Saudi population's general unhappiness with American support for Israel did play a role in all of this, but it was only one of a much larger set of issues. It should be noted that these problems emerged at a time when the Clinton administration's peace process was moving well, when there was a sense in the region that peace was right around the corner, and when there was less of a sense that America was unabashedly siding with Israel. Rather, the Saudi people were most bothered by their perception that the United States (acting through the United Nations) was purposely crippling Iraq (for standing up to us *and the Israelis* during the Gulf War) and starving many Iraqis to death. In addition, there was rising discontent within the kingdom because of growing economic, political, and social problems, which were blamed on the regime—and on the United States, which was seen as the regime's principal backer. Finally, a section of Saudi society (stirred up by bin Ladin and other Islamist extremists) did not like Americans on their soil because virtually all of the American soldiers were non-Muslims (and some were Jews, whom they considered even worse than Christians). Ultimately, the United States withdrew its forces from Saudi Arabia altogether in 2003, after the invasion of Iraq, to remove the American presence as an irritant in Saudi internal politics and to regain freedom of action for American military forces by redeploying them to Kuwait, Bahrain, and Qatar, where they were welcomed. America's support for Israel played a part in this complex series of events, but not a key one.

Another example of the problem came in 2000, when the Camp David meeting failed to produce an agreement between the Israelis and Palestinians and Yasser Arafat unleashed the al-Aqsa intifadah against Israel instead, leading to a wave of violence and terrorist attacks against Israelis.[44] The Israelis reacted with force—disproportionate in some cases—and this enraged feelings throughout the Arab world. There were riots and demonstrations across the Arab world that frightened many of the Arab governments. The people were angry at the Israelis, but also angry at the United States for being Israel's patron and at their own regimes for being allied to Israel's patron. In the end, little came of these demonstrations, but they were a caution to the Arab rulers: a reminder not to be seen as too close to the United States (or Israel) because of the potential for popular backlash. Yet even these unexpected events did not actually change America's strategic posture in the region. We did not lose any bases, and today, even omitting our temporarily massive presence in Iraq, we have pretty much everything we need.

Finally, there is the issue of terrorism. Again, there is no question that Arab rage at Israel does get partially transferred to the United States, and some of the inspiration for some terrorist attacks against Americans does come from Arab venom for Israel. I will discuss the causes of Middle Eastern terrorism at great length later in this book, so for now I will simply make this point. Anger at Israel is only one of a complex set of reasons that is inspiring the current wave of Arab-Muslim terrorism. In particular, the Palestinian cause may be an important element of al-Qa'ida's inspiration, but their pattern of attacks—which have not included Israel—suggest that it is not their principal motivation. Instead, for most of these groups and for their wider network of supporters and sympathizers, anger at their own governments, and at the United States for being the principal patron of those governments, appears to be their foremost source of anger, as indicated by whom and what they actually attack. Even the legacy groups from earlier waves of terrorism that have attacked the United

States in the past see U.S. support for Israel as only part of a panoply of hatreds for the United States. For instance, Hizballah's attacks on the United States in Lebanon in the 1980s were driven by American support for Israel; but they were also driven, probably in equal measure, by American support for the Maronite-dominated Lebanese government and by Iranian hatred of the United States (which, as noted earlier, has little to do with Israel). So there *is* displacement of anger onto the United States going on in the Muslim Middle East, but Israel is only one aspect of it and probably not the most important one. Again, this is not to dismiss American support for Israel as an inspiration to various terrorist groups, only to place it in its proper context and priority.

Overall, American support for Israel has been something more than an irritant in U.S. relations with the Arab world but something considerably less than a strategic dilemma. It has not precluded strong relationships with key Arab states. It has not prevented the United States from becoming the dominant power in the region. It has zero impact on America's oil imports. It has had a very modest impact on the profits of American oil companies. It has created a number of complications for issues like basing, but it is only one of several complicating factors there and the problems have typically been tactical, not strategic, in their nature and impact. The price that the United States pays in diplomatic frustration and even the occasional lost opportunity, though sometimes considerable to the individuals who have to endure it, is negligible from the perspective of our nation's economic and strategic interests.

Elsewhere in this book I note a number of other ways that U.S. support for Israel complicates American policy making in the Middle East. As with basing, these need to be kept in their proper perspective. None are insignificant. However, none are so meaningful, either individually or taken together, that they would justify the attenuation of U.S. support for Israel. Overall, they are greatly outweighed by the benefits we accrue from that relationship and our overarching national interests.

The only serious problem that we face for this support is the potentially catastrophic threat of Muslim zealots taking over the government of Saudi Arabia or another major oil producer and cutting its oil production. Even in these circumstances, American support for Israel is likely to be fairly far down on their list of grievances against the United States and dwarfed by our support (real and perceived) for their own autocratic governments, as well as our "infidel" presence in the Muslim Middle East. Of greater importance still, there is absolutely no reason to believe that ending American support for Israel would somehow eliminate (or even ameliorate) the risks of this scenario.

What America's Interest in Israel Means and Does Not Mean

The United States continues to have a range of powerful incentives to care about Israel's existence and security—incentives rooted in our core values as a nation and proven over the course of our history to be critical to our own security and prosperity. Moreover, the costs we pay for tending to that interest are more than tolerable; they are rather marginal. But that does not mean that America's interests are identical to Israel's or that staunch American support for Israel's security should translate into unqualified support for Israeli policies. In fact, some of the lowest points in our relationship have been when an American administration uncritically backed a misguided Israeli policy, such as the Reagan administration's decision to back the 1982 Israeli invasion of Lebanon, which led to disaster for both nations.

Moreover, though the U.S.-Israel alliance has brought benefits to the United States in its position in the Middle East that should not be minimized, we should not exaggerate them either. In truth, Israel cannot help the United States stabilize shaky Arab nations or intervene in intra-Arab affairs. As part of that, Israel borders only Lebanon, Syria, Jordan, and Egypt, none of which have significant oil reserves. To return to the Lebanese example, the one time that Israel did act to try to "stabilize" an Arab country that had descended into civil war, the Israelis made the situation worse for all concerned, including the United States. Thus, though the security of Israel should remain a key American interest in the region, it cannot be the cornerstone of American foreign policy toward the wider Middle East.

CHAPTER 3

—

AMERICA'S ARAB ALLIES

I T IS WORTH STARTING TO MAKE THE CASE FOR THE IMPORTANCE of our relationships in the Arab world with the simple proposition that many of the Arab states have generally proven to be our friends over the years, especially recent ones. Several of the Arab states have demonstrated that they share many of America's interests in the Middle East and the world. A great many more have come to share our interests over time. They have mostly helped us to achieve those goals, even if they did so because it was in their own interests as well as ours. Most have found ways to pay us back for the help that we offered them on many occasions, like the Saudis and Kuwaitis helping to fund American causes around the world and the Egyptians routinely providing access to their airspace or to Suez in spite of disagreement with us on specific policies. Indeed, the Gulf states (particularly Kuwait and Saudi Arabia), the Jordanians, the Moroccans, and the Egyptians have gone out of their way to help the United States with money and military operations from Zaire to the Gulf to Somalia to the Balkans over the past thirty years.

Friends should never be taken for granted—not for individuals and not by nations. The United States cannot have too many friends in this world, and we should not lightly write off those we do have. A number of the Arab states have proven to be our friends, and for as long as that remains the case, we should honor that friendship as a valuable asset of the American people.

Nevertheless, as Lord Palmerston once noted, nations have no permanent friends or enemies, only permanent interests. Thus, though we should not neglect the importance of our friendships with the Arab states, we must also look past them to our nation's strategic interests. In that light, the principal strategic rationale for our alignment with the Arab states is really an extension of our strategic interest in Middle Eastern oil.

Of course, as Rachel Bronson astutely noted in her book *Thicker Than Oil,* oil is a necessary but not sufficient cause for the closeness of the United States' relationship with Saudi Arabia.[1] The United States has had much rockier relationships with other major oil producers, like Iran, Iraq, Libya, and Algeria. What made the U.S.-Saudi relationship such a close one has been not only the kingdom's oil wealth but the perspective of the Al Sa'ud, the royal family of Saudi Arabia. The Al Sa'ud have opposed violent change in the region. They opposed the Soviet Union as godless atheists and a source of instability. They have opposed revolutionary ideology of every kind, from Nasserism to Khomeinism. They have supported the status quo throughout the region and, to a great extent, throughout the world in the belief that their lives were as good as they could get and change could only threaten their paradisical existence. Especially after the 1973 debacle, they opposed the use of Arab oil exports as a source of political leverage over the West and became prudent custodians of the global oil market. They have insisted on denominating oil in dollars, which has saved Americans a huge amount, especially when the dollar was weak, as at present. Had the Al Sa'ud not ruled in this manner, their oil wealth alone would not have made them such desirable allies for the United States.[2]

Even our interest in other Arab states can be traced, to a greater or lesser extent, back to oil, although the path is sometimes convoluted. Egypt is the most populous of the Arab states, one of its strongest military powers, and a center of culture and learning for the Arab world, and so, in diplomatic matters, many other Arab states will follow Cairo's lead. Building coalitions of Arab states is much easier with Egypt on board and much harder without it. In addition, Egypt rules some important real estate, including the Suez Canal, the gateway between the Mediterranean Sea and the Indian Ocean. Moreover, because of Egypt's symbolic importance, if a revolutionary ideology were somehow to take hold there, it could easily inspire others throughout the region—conjuring up the nightmare of revolution in the Gulf oil states. Thus, to the extent that it is in America's interests to see peace prevail and revolution dampened throughout the region (so as not to threaten the flow of oil), our strong relationship with Egypt is extremely important.

Jordan is another Middle Eastern state with which the United States has a close relationship, but largely because of Jordan's situation and how it relates to larger American interests, particularly oil. Why do we care about Jordan? To some extent, it is because the Hashemite dynasty that has ruled Jordan for the past eighty-five years has been highly pro-Western, and as a rule the United States looks favorably on governments that like us. Within the Arab world, Jordan is among the most committed to moving down the path of economic reform and democratization, something else the United States likes to see. But if Jordan were a reforming, pro-Western government located in sub-Saharan Africa, it seems highly unlikely that it would be considered of such importance to the United States. Instead, Jordan borders Syria, Iraq, Saudi Arabia, and Israel—and the security of the last two is of direct interest to the United States, while that of the first two is indirectly related to that of the latter two. Problems in Jordan can affect any of those countries. In the past, Jordan's stability has been particularly problematic for Israel because so many of the Palestinians who fled from Palestine/Israel in 1948 and from the West Bank in 1967 resettled in refugee camps in Jordan. Thus, Jordan matters because problems there could affect U.S. interests in Israel, Iraq, and (potentially of much greater significance) Saudi Arabia.

Helping Hands

Oil is also a major element of another interest in the Arab states of the region: their ability to contribute to American causes in the Middle East and beyond. Because of their oil revenues, some of the Arab states have massive financial resources that they have been willing to direct to areas beneficial to the United States. In many cases, but not always, they have funded causes that they saw as important to their interests as well. Over time, the Saudis and, to a lesser extent, the Kuwaitis, Emiratis, Qataris, and others have given billions of dollars in financial aid to poor nations in the Middle East, Europe, South Asia, Southeast Asia, and Africa.[3] The Saudis in particular have also been willing to fund American proxy wars and covert operations in places like Angola, Ethiopia (by funding Sudan and Somalia), Yemen, and even Nicaragua.[4] Whether you agree with the American involvement in these conflicts or not, it was certainly helpful to the U.S. government to have the Saudis bankrolling our side. Saudi financial assistance to the Afghan mujahidin following the 1979 Soviet invasion may have exceeded American contributions.[5]

In addition, we should not forget that the Arab states do recycle a significant amount of their "petrodollars" back into the U.S. economy in the form of imports from the United States and investment in the United States (including in U.S. government bonds). If the Arab states did not have oil, they would not have the money to make these purchases and investments, but given that they do, it is very important to the U.S. economy that so much of it comes back to us rather than going elsewhere. The Arab states have been among the largest consumers of major American industrial products—airliners, weapons, cars, refrigerators—over the years. For instance, the Congressional Research Service once calculated that between 1950 and 1997 Saudi Arabia alone had bought upward of $58 billion worth of American weaponry.[6] (And unlike Jordan and Egypt, the Saudis and other Gulf states can actually pay for these purchases themselves without U.S. financial assistance.) Indeed, overall, U.S. trade with Saudi Arabia amounted to nearly $44 billion in 2006.[7] While the vast majority (over 75 percent) of this consisted of Saudi oil sales to the United States, it is not an insignificant number.

To some extent, this trade relationship is driven by pure economics. As the world's largest and most advanced economy, the United States is a good investment for Arab capital and a great place to purchase goods. However, perhaps of equal importance, the Gulf states have purposely funneled their money and their contracts to the United States to ensure that Washington always has an interest in their safety and security. If the Arab states did not see us as their great protector, they would likely find other investment opportunities and places to buy weapons and airplanes. But that kind of money pumped back into the U.S. economy buys them a lot of goodwill and influence. Indeed, the Israel lobby in Washington often has its hands full battling the countervailing forces of Arab petrodollars.

Beyond their financial resources, our allies in the Arab world have been a source of help to the United States because of their Muslim credentials. In a number of instances over the past sixty years, having Muslim (or merely Arab) allies has been of great importance. For example, during the Persian Gulf War of 1990–1991 it was critical to Washington and Riyadh that the effort to evict Saddam Husayn's forces from Kuwait be seen as an international effort backed by the Muslim world, not a scheme of the Al Sa'ud and their American supporters. Consequently, securing the participation of two Egyptian divisions, a Syrian division, and smaller formations from Morocco, Kuwait, Qatar, Oman, Bahrain, and the UAE was crucial to building support for Operation Desert Storm throughout the Middle East. In the Balkans, too, it has been important to have Muslim troops as part of Western peacekeeping missions designed to secure the Muslim Bosnians and Kosovar Albanians. Egypt, Jordan, and Tunisia all provided troops for the U.N. Protection Force (UNPROFOR) in Bosnia from 1992 to 1995. Likewise, Egypt and Morocco provided troops for the Stabilization Force (SFOR) that secured Bosnia from 1996 to 2004, and Moroccan and Emirati troops have participated in the Kosovo Force (KFOR).

Moreover, America's relationships with various Arab states have helped dampen conflict in the Middle East. As Henry Kissinger once observed, "The Arabs cannot make war against Israel without Egypt," and by establishing strong relations with Egypt, the United States has made it unthinkable for Cairo to make war on Israel again. In another example, in July 1977, Anwar Sadat got fed up with Muammar Qadhafi, the unstable Libyan leader, who had begun supporting an insurgency against Egypt in response to Sadat's peace negotiations with Israel. He deployed two mechanized divisions to the border with Libya, mounted air strikes, and ordered his forces to push across the border in a move that Egyptian officials told foreign diplomats in Cairo was meant to be the start of an invasion to oust

Qadhafi altogether. But Sadat abruptly stopped the offensive as soon as it had begun because the United States pressed him to call it off, reportedly because Washington feared that Egyptian forces were not up to the challenge and that, if they failed, it would threaten Sadat's grip on power.[8] Likewise, during the 1990s, the United States could typically prevail upon the Syrians (often using the Saudis as intermediaries) to rein in Hizballah attacks on Israel and so prevent an escalation in violence.[9] During that same period, the Clinton administration was able to use its close ties to Egypt, Jordan, Morocco, and Saudi Arabia to push the Palestinian leadership to make compromises for peace and avoid steps likely to provoke violent Israeli responses, just as it used its ties to Israel to do the same. Ultimately, one of the worst gaffes of the Clinton team was its failure to sufficiently bring the Egyptians, Jordanians, and Saudis on board in the negotiations at Camp David to secure their support in moving Arafat to match Israeli Prime Minister Ehud Barak's proposed concessions.[10]

Furthermore, a number of the Arab states, including Egypt and Saudi Arabia, are heavily dependent on American military assistance. Specifically, their armed forces cannot logistically support military operations of any real size without U.S. assistance, effectively giving Washington the ability to prevent them from mounting a major attack should it choose to do so. As one example, in 1995, Cairo wanted to conduct airstrikes against Khartoum to retaliate for the assassination attack on Husni Mubarak in Addis Ababa earlier that year, which the Egyptians believed the Sudanese (and Iranians) had been behind. However, the Egyptians were forced to abort these plans because they could not mount combat operations against Sudan with even a squadron of F-16s from their bases in Upper Egypt without American logistical support, which the United States declined to provide for fear of setting off a wider war and having our Egyptian allies become bogged down in a useless conflict in Sudan.[11] This virtual "veto" has proven critical in reassuring Israel and keeping Jerusalem from taking provocative actions that might have touched off another war in response to Egypt's constant procurement of modern military equipment from the United States. Given the degree of their dependence on U.S. logistical support, it is hard to imagine that the Egyptian armed forces could mount another offensive like the one that opened the 1973 October War against Israel without America's active participation.

Geography

Strategists continue to make the argument that the Middle East is pivotal because of its geography, but in the present circumstances this is actually only of modest importance. The Middle East lost its status as a critical trade route from Asia to Europe back in the eighteenth century, when the maritime revolution made it cheaper to move goods by sea than by land and the camel caravans of the silk and spice roads were replaced by European sailing ships. Today, very little trade passes over the territory of the Middle East, with the major exceptions of oil and the ships that pass through the Suez Canal. In the case of the oil trade, obviously the issue is principally the region's oil exports, not its geographic position per se. The Suez Canal has strategic value, but not nearly as much as one might think. A considerable amount of trade still flows through the canal. However, free access to the canal is largely a matter of cost and convenience, not a matter of strategic necessity for either the United States or any of its allies. If the Suez Canal were closed or blocked (as it was from 1967 to 1975), ships would be rerouted around the Cape of Good Hope, which would mean longer voyages, which in turn would cost more money. But, as was the case in 1967–1975, the increased costs would hardly be crippling.

The same is largely true in the military realm. Today, and for the foreseeable future, there is only one blue-water navy—the U.S. Navy. Every other navy, including those of Britain, France, Russia, and China, is essentially a coastal defense force, able to project power across the oceans only on occasion and only if the U.S. Navy has no reason to prevent them from doing so. This means that control of strategic maritime chokepoints is not vital to our national security because there is no major foe against which we are seeking every advantage. The U.S. Navy does use the Suez Canal very frequently, but because it is convenient, not because it is necessary. Passage through the canal for American warships is another benefit of our alliance with Egypt, but its loss would not threaten the safety of the nation and would only marginally complicate the Navy's deployments.

In actuality, of greater significance to the U.S. military is Egyptian airspace. A lot of American military air traffic passes over Egypt. Since ships are always expected to take days or weeks to reach a destination, the added distance that would be required if the Suez Canal were off limits to us (thereby forcing maritime traffic around the Cape of Good Hope) would alter the schedule of naval movements within tolerable bounds. But air traffic is supposed to be much faster, and military cargo that moves by plane typically needs to reach its destination very quickly—if it didn't, it would go by ship, which is much cheaper. Of course, in a pinch, military air traffic could overfly Israel, Jordan, and Saudi Arabia rather than Egypt, if the Egyptians suddenly decided to close down their airspace to us. More important still is the fact that the vast majority of the American military air traffic crossing Egypt is bound for the Persian Gulf, and it is headed to the Persian Gulf to perform missions that are all ultimately intended, directly or indirectly, to safeguard the region's oil exports. Thus, even in this case, America's interest is really about the oil and not about geography per se.

The Limits of American Interest in the Arab States

It is important always to keep in mind two things about America's relationships with the Arab states: they are very important, and they are very important mostly because of oil. If we could find a way to eliminate our dependence on oil, our interests with the Arab states would diminish precipitously. The reason that we have common interests and we have aided each other over the years has been, to a considerable extent, our interest in their oil exports—which in turn has produced a number of other subinterests that matched some of theirs. I say this as an American who is very well disposed toward the Arab states and who believes staunchly in improving our relations with them. But the simple fact is that we have few *strategic* interests in the Arab world beyond oil. None of the Arab states except Lebanon is a democracy, although some are slowly creeping in that direction—and the more they move down that path, the greater a strategic interest it will create in the Arab world beyond oil. Modern transportation and information technology have greatly reduced the Middle East's geographic importance. The Arab world is not an economic or technological powerhouse. With oil removed from the picture, our trade relationships with the Arab states would shrivel to insignificance. There would be almost no Western investment in the Arab world and no Arab capital to invest in the West. Overall, in 2006, U.S. imports from the Arab states amounted to $74 billion, of which $61 billion, or 82 percent, consisted of petroleum products.[12] Even with the oil, this put the Arab world ahead of only the countries of the former USSR and sub-Saharan Africa, and if you were to remove oil from the equation, the $12 billion in American imports from the Arab world would exceed only the $3 billion in nonoil imports from sub-Saharan Africa.[13] Without oil and the financial resources it has brought them, the Arab states would also have little to contribute to the rest of the world in terms of peace and stability.

Although this might sound like a wonderful world to many Americans tired of the troubles of the Middle East and fed up with Arab anti-Americanism, for now it is nothing but fantasy. The reality is that the world is addicted to oil, and that makes the Arab states very important. Even the most draconian policies designed to wean the world off the oil habit will take a generation or more to have a real impact.[14] Yet even while recognizing the importance of the Arab states because of their oil wealth, we should also recognize that they are dependent on us for their peace and security, and they have learned that trying to use their oil production as leverage over us on specific issues has proven disastrous to their long-term interests. In addition, over time they have learned to use their oil wealth to harmonize many of their policies with those of the United States (and convinced us to tailor some of ours to better fit their interests) to ensure that we are working in tandem. That is not insignificant and is worth trying to expand to our mutual benefit.

CHAPTER 4

NONPROLIFERATION AND NONINTERESTS

THERE ARE A LOT OF OTHER, LESSER AMERICAN INTERESTS in the Middle East that one could also mention in compiling a complete list simply for the sake of being comprehensive. Some of these are global, in the sense that they apply to America's interests everywhere in the world—for instance, America's interest in maintaining freedom of navigation on all of the world's oceans, an interest that led to armed confrontations (and lopsided American victories) over Libyan naval and air forces during the 1980s. But few of these merit discussion because they generally do not have serious implications for American policy and strategy toward the region, and those that do generally do because they are really subsets of one of the major issues already discussed.

Nevertheless, there is at least one global interest of the United States that has important resonance in the Middle East, and that is preventing the further spread of nuclear weapons—in the region and in the rest of the world. From a regional perspective, nonproliferation makes sense because it buttresses our other main interests in oil, Israel, and our Arab allies. From a global perspective, preventing further proliferation in the Middle East is important because failure to do so could be the straw that breaks the camel's back of an increasingly fragile international nonproliferation regime.

In addition, there are a number of other notions that others have suggested as key American interests that are not interests per se (in most cases, they are actually threats to our interests) that are worth noting, if only for the sake of clarity.

Nonproliferation

Since the Second World War, the United States has tried to limit the number of countries with nuclear arsenals, although it has been famously inconsistent in applying that principle. A case can be made that an Israel with nuclear weapons is in the best interest of the United States (because it reassures the Israelis, thereby dampening their tendency to attack preemptively, and relieves us of the need to come to their defense in extremis). However, the fact is that the United States tried to dissuade Israel from going down this path.[1] And there is no question that the United States does not want to see any other country in the region acquire nuclear weapons.

Of course, in the Middle East, our interest in preventing the spread of nuclear weapons is only partly freestanding in the sense of springing from our general commitment to nonproliferation (peripatetic as that may be). The United States fears that the spread of nuclear weapons to Middle Eastern states, particularly those that have shown a determination to undermine or overturn the status quo, including by force, like Saddam Husayn's Iraq and the Islamic Republic of Iran, could result in a nuclear threat to the region's oil exports.[2] Similarly, the proliferation of nuclear weapons within the region could spark crises such as those between the United States and the USSR during the Cold War (the Cuban Missile Crisis, the Berlin crises, and the 1973 October War crisis), between Russia and China in 1969, and between India and Pakistan in 2000. In the Middle East, similar crises could threaten not just the oil but also our allies in Israel, Jordan, Egypt, Saudi Arabia, and other countries.

America's interest in nonproliferation in the Middle East also has a component that transcends our interests within the region. This is the more generalized threat to global security from the proliferation of weapons of mass destruction, and it rests upon two different fears. The first of these is that the more states that have WMD, the greater the likelihood that it will fall into the hands of terrorists or other truly dangerous individuals. This is purely statistical: the more countries with a nuclear arsenal, the greater the probability that one or more will fail to safeguard them properly (allowing weapons to be sold or stolen), the greater the probability that one or more will choose to sell a weapon or give one to terrorists, and the greater the probability that political instability (and even governmental collapse) will lead to "the worst weapons" falling into the hands of "the worst people," as President Bush has repeatedly warned us. Now that North Korea and Pakistan have nuclear weapons and Iran is making considerable progress in the same direction, these are not idle fears.

The other relates to the bad habit of nuclear proliferation to cause more nuclear proliferation. In a number of cases around the world, one country's possession of nuclear weapons has convinced another to follow suit. America's acquisition of the first nuclear weapons caused the Soviets to develop their own. To deter both superpowers, China decided to acquire its own nuclear arsenal. Fearing the Chinese, the Indians concluded that they too had to have a nuclear weapon, which in turn propelled the Pakistanis down the same path. The more Middle Eastern states acquire nuclear weapons, the more likely that others, inside the region and out, may feel the need to do the same to deter their Middle Eastern rivals. Thus, many people fear that if Iran were to acquire a nuclear weapons capability, Saudi Arabia, Egypt, and Turkey might all decide that they had to do so as well. While there is room for skepticism about each of these countries doing so, the best answer of all would be never to have to find out.

In addition, the more countries that are able to acquire nuclear weapons (or other WMD) without paying a heavy price for doing so, the more it convinces other countries that it would be worth it for them to do so as well. Since 1945, a number of countries have started down the path toward acquiring nuclear weapons but ultimately chose not to do so. Egypt, Sweden, Switzerland, Australia, Italy, Japan, South Korea, Taiwan, Brazil, and Argentina all discontinued nuclear programs before they had acquired a weapon, and in every case an important element in their decision to do so was the potential price they believed they would pay in terms of international opprobrium, if not formal sanctions, for doing so.[3] The more countries that are able to cross the nuclear weapons threshold without paying a high price—like Israel, India, and Pakistan[4]—the greater the sense among still more countries that there really isn't much of a price to be paid for proliferating. This is one reason why it is so important for the international community to punish Iran for its refusal to comply with the demands of the IAEA and the U.N. Security Council that it discontinue its uranium enrichment and plutonium separation programs. Moreover, the more states that have successfully proliferated in the face of international pressure not to do so, the less international pressure can be expected to be applied against the next state to try, causing the entire nonproliferation regime to lose its potency. Thus, America's interest in preventing the proliferation of nuclear weapons, and WMD more generally, throughout the world creates an interest in the Middle East that includes, but also transcends, our specific interests in the region's oil and our allies there.

Dogs That Aren't Barking

I have yet to deal in any sustained way with what may seem like some of America's most important interests in the Middle East—things like fighting terrorism and stabilizing Iraq. But though fighting terrorism and dealing with Iraq are very important problems for the United States and issues for a new American grand strategy to confront, they are not *interests*. In actuality, they are *threats* to our interests and are dealt with later in this book.

Terrorism, for example, is not what brought us to the Middle East or what keeps us involved there but is instead a by-product of our involvement in the region. The reason that we are being targeted by terrorists is that they do not like our involvement in the region. As neoisolationists argue, if the United States were not involved in the Middle East, the terrorists would likely leave us alone. Ridiculous rhetoric from the Bush administration aside, the Islamist extremists do not hate us for who we are or what we stand for or for our freedom; they hate us for what we are doing in the Middle East or, just as often, for what they imagine we are doing in the region.

Thus, terrorism is not an interest of the United States; rather, it is a threat to our interests and a by-product of those interests. We are involved in the region mostly for its oil, and it is that overriding interest that requires us to fight the terrorists who are trying to drive us out of the region. Though it is also true that many of the terrorists hate us for our support of Israel, there are far fewer examples of recent terrorist attacks against Americans specifically designed to end U.S. support for Israel than attacks against Americans meant to persuade us to end our support for the Arab regimes, particularly the Arab oil producers.

A Final Word About America's Interests in the Middle East

The United States does not have many interests in the Middle East, but those we have are of great importance—enough so that we will have to make the area a high priority for our foreign policy for some time to come. How long? Well, for at least as long as our own economy and those of our major trading partners remain addicted to oil and the Middle East continues to be a key supplier of petroleum products. If nothing else does, this should put front and center the importance of weaning the global economy from its dependence on oil, so that we no longer have to be so fearful of developments in such a fragile and troubled part of the world. If we could somehow kick the oil "habit," we would still have interests in the region, but they would be mere interests—not nightmarish fears of possible catastrophe. That might not solve the problems of the Middle East, but it would mean that regional problems need not take on global dimensions. And that would make both America and the world more secure and more tranquil.

The problem, of course, is that it is unrealistic to expect the United States, let alone the whole world, to seriously reduce its dependence on oil for several decades. That's no reason to stop trying, but it means that this cannot be our near-term answer to the problems of the Middle East. And the threats to American interests in the Middle East—war, revolution, instability, and terrorism—are growing worse, not better. That being the case, we have no choice but to devise a coherent, integrated approach that will allow us to manage, if not reduce or even eliminate, the problems of the Middle East. Because the problems are so deep-seated and the threats so complex, such an approach is likely to take decades to pay real dividends, but we don't have any alternatives.

PART TWO

—

THE PROBLEMS OF THE

MODERN MIDDLE EAST

It IS EASY TO UNDERSTAND WHY THE BUSH ADMINISTRATION decided to call its campaign in response to 9/11 a "War on Terror," but it is unfortunate that it did so. Though the phrase had considerable rhetorical appeal, especially in the wake of the destruction of the twin towers, for mobilizing the American people and announcing to the world that America's cause was righteous, it has created a great deal of confusion. In fact, this has not been a campaign against "terrorism"; the United States has done little or nothing against most of the world's terrorist groups. Our efforts have principally focused on al-Qa'ida, the group that actually attacked us, and rightly so. But by proclaiming a "war" on a widespread tactic, it opened us to charges of hypocrisy, perplexed many would-be allies, and created an opening for many regimes to crush their own troublesome domestic oppositions behind the excuse of fighting terrorism.

Perhaps of greater importance, the proclamation of a "War on Terrorism" created the mistaken impression that America's principal problem in the Middle East, if not the world, is terrorism. Although there is no question that terrorism is a threat to the United States and our allies and that we do need to make a much greater effort to combat it than we had for the twenty years prior to 9/11, the United States has other concerns in the world of equal, and potentially greater, importance, like peacefully managing the rise of China and helping to prevent Russia from receding into authoritarianism and xenophobia.

Moreover, terrorism isn't even the greatest problem facing the Middle East or even facing the United States in the region. Terrorism is an outgrowth of the problem, not the problem itself. Although we devote a disproportionate level of resources to fighting terrorism, we neglect the true problems that are giving rise to the terrorist threat as well as other threats we face in the region.

The principal problem of the Middle East—the underlying malady, one of the symptoms of which is the proliferation of terrorist groups from Hizballah to Hamas to al-Qa'ida—is the failure of the contemporary state system of the Muslim Middle East. To be blunt, the countries of the Muslim Middle East are broken. Their political, economic, and even social systems are stagnant. The people of the region feel that their culture is under assault by the forces of modernity, which, as it has around the globe, has made them fearful and caused them to retreat behind the familiar and comforting wall of their religion. They feel powerless, angry, frustrated, and frightened, and their leaders feed them a steady diet of lies, exaggeration, and blame shifting. It should be no wonder that this is a deeply troubled part of the world. Moreover, it is these powerful forces that have fed the rise of Islamist opposition groups and, at the extreme, vicious terrorist groups lashing out at a remarkable range of perceived enemies. The failures of the states and the sense of cultural assault have created a populace that is deeply disillusioned, receptive to calls for rebellion, and willing to turn a blind eye to actions they mostly consider immoral. Thus, if the United States is to address the range of threats to its vital interests in the Middle East, from terrorism to instability, it must first come to grips with the underlying problems that are spawning these threats.

CHAPTER 5

—

A SEA OF SOCIOECONOMIC PROBLEMS

Different people might begin to explain the problems of the modern Muslim Middle East in different ways. For me, the right place to start is with economics. Not because economics is necessarily the most important link in the skein of Middle Eastern troubles—although many would argue that it is—but because it is the problem that Arabs and Persians, Circassians and Kurds, Assyrians and Azeris feel most. Political oppression, a culture under attack, an inadequate legal system, even a misguided educational system generally require some event to touch the lives of the average person. It requires an act of political repression or (merely) disdain, an encounter with another culture that seems particularly alien, an incident with the legal system, or an epiphany about the nature of what you are being taught to be reminded of these other problems. But being unemployed and a burden on your family, living in a shantytown, being unable to marry or simply live the life you want because you cannot get an adequate job (or any job) is something that far too many people in the Muslim Middle East live with every moment of every day.

Moreover, a great many of the other problems of the Muslim Middle East relate to the underlying economic problems of the region. For instance, many of the worst failings of the Arab educational systems are manifested in how poorly they prepare both the average person and the members of the elite to compete in the globalized economy. One of the most tangible maladies of the legal system is the impact that it has on business. And one of the things that most Muslim Middle Easterners find most enraging about their governments is how badly they mismanage their economies—and how little they seem to care about the harm that this does to their citizens. To dismiss the socioeconomic problems of the region as being unrelated to the threats that the United States faces from it is to completely misunderstand the nature of the region, our interests, and how best to protect them.

Demographics

The population of the Muslim states of the Middle East has been growing by leaps and bounds in recent decades. Especially between 1980 and 2000, when the oil boom that began in the 1970s began to provide better medical care and nutrition in the Arab states and Iran, mortality rates began to fall and life expectancy began to rise very quickly. Infant mortality rates were cut in half. In typical fashion, fertility rates (the number of children the average woman bears in her lifetime) did not decline as quickly as the birthrate rose (and the death rate fell), and the result was a rapid increase in overall population.[1] In 1950, the region's total population stood at 78.6 million, and by 1980 it had reached nearly 180 million people. But by 2000, the regional population exceeded 307 million, and it is projected to reach 375 million in 2010.[2] To put it into some perspective, the Arab states had a higher rate of population growth during this period than all but a few sub-Saharan African countries.[3] At present, the region's overall population growth is 2.7 percent per year, the fastest rate of growth in the world—exceeding even that of sub-Saharan Africa. And this is actually a marked decline from the torrid 3.2 percent per year population growth of the 1980s and early 1990s.[4]

These high growth rates alone have been an important culprit in the region's economic woes. A major new study of the region by the economists Marcus Noland and Howard Pack begins by observing that "In part due to relatively high population growth rates, living standards in the Arab countries as a whole stagnated during the 1980s and 1990s, with per capita income in 2000 at roughly the same level as 20 years earlier."[5] Indeed, the traditional rule of thumb is that annual growth in GDP per capita needs to exceed annual population growth by 2 percentage points for a nation to "develop" at all—i.e., do more than keep pace with the growing needs of a burgeoning population.[6] As Table 5.1 demonstrates, few Arab states have been able to meet this benchmark during the past thirty years. For instance, not only did the growth of Egypt and Syria slow down over the years, but at no time since 1975 did their growth in GDP per capita exceed population growth by 2 percentage points or more. Jordan's GDP per capita growth never cleared the 2-point threshold above population growth during this time frame. Indeed, the great economist of the Middle East Alan Richards summed up the situation in 2004 as "per capita incomes in the Arab states today are little different from what they were in 1980; some analysts would argue that per capita growth has actually been negative. . . . Real wages and labor productivity today are about the same as in 1970. This performance is the worst of any other major region of the world except for the countries of the former Soviet Union. Even sub-Saharan Africa has done better."[7]

Rapid population growth can be a blessing or a curse. In societies with the right educational, legal, political, and economic trends, more and more people mean more and more consumers and workers, boosting economic activity and propelling development and growth. However, because of the problems in the Arab world in all of these other areas, rapid population growth has instead meant that the fragile economies of the region simply cannot cope with the ever-greater numbers of people being introduced into society and the workforce. It has created problems of overpopulation, driving up unemployment, driving down real wages, burdening housing markets and social welfare networks, and stimulating considerable disaffection among the populations of the Arab world and Iran.[8] As a World Bank study noted in 2007, the Middle East and North Africa (MENA) region is "facing an unprecedented challenge in labor markets. MENA's demographic bulge, the result of high population growth in the 1970s and 1980s, is now coming of age. Nearly 40 million additional people are expected to join MENA's labor force between 2000 and 2010—an astounding 40 percent increase."[9]

One of the biggest problems with this kind of rapid growth in population, and one that is already affecting the Muslim Middle

Table 5.1. GDP Per Capita Growth Compared to Annual Population Growth for Selected Arab Countries

COUNTRY	1975		1985		1995		2003	
	Population Growth	GDP Per Capita Growth	Population Growth	GDP Per Capita Growth	Population Growth	GDP Per Capita Growth	Population Growth	GDP Per Capita Growth
Algeria	3.1	1.8	3.1	0.6	1.9	1.8	1.5	5.1
Bahrain	4.8	N.A.	3.4	−7.9	3.2	0.6	1.4	5.7
Egypt	2.1	6.6	2.5	4.0	1.8	2.7	1.9	1.1
Iraq	3.3	N.A.	2.7	N.A.	3.1	N.A.	N.A.	N.A.
Jordan	3.5	N.A.	3.6	−0.2	3.3	2.8	2.6	1.4
Kuwait	6.2	−13.5	3.4	−7.4	N.A.	N.A.	2.6	6.9
Libya	4.3	3.0	3.8	−12.2	2.0	N.A.	2.0	7.0
Morocco	2.5	4.9	2.1	4.1	1.1	−7.6	1.1	4.3
Oman	4.7	18.8	4.5	8.9	3.0	1.9	0.7	0.6
Palestinian territories	N.A.	N.A.	N.A.	N.A.	3.9	−6.2	4.1	−5.6
Qatar	6.9	N.A.	7.8	N.A.	2.0	N.A.	6.6	N.A.
Saudi Arabia	5.1	0.1	5.6	−9.6	2.5	−2.2	2.7	4.7
Sudan	3.1	12.2	2.8	−8.8	2.4	3.5	1.9	4.0
Syria	3.4	15.5	3.7	2.3	2.7	2.4	2.5	−1.4
Tunisia	2.1	4.9	3.0	2.5	1.6	0.1	0.6	5.0
UAE	17.9	11.1	8.4	−14.1	8.4	−0.7	7.4	3.4
Yemen	2.4	N.A.	3.9	N.A.	4.1	7.1	3.1	−0.1

N.A.: *Not available.*
Source: *The World Bank,* World Development Indicators, 2006 (CD-ROM) *(Washington, D.C.: IBRD, World Bank, 2006).*

East, is a "youth bulge." This means that the population is producing very large numbers of young people at rates disproportionate to previous rates. It means that there are lots and lots of young people in the Arab countries and Iran and that the median age is very low. In the three most populous countries of the Arab world—Egypt, Algeria, and Morocco, in order—the median ages are 20, 20, and 21, respectively. Of all the Arab countries, only the UAE has a median age of 30 or more.[10] According to the International Labour Organization

(ILO), between 1995 and 2005, the youth labor force increased by 32.2 percent in the Middle East and North Africa region—again, the highest increase of any region in the world.[11]

Another demographic problem closely associated with rapid population growth (and modernization and industrialization) is urbanization, and here as well the Muslim Middle East has been no exception. Over time, and particularly in the last thirty years, larger and larger numbers of Arabs, Iranians, and other Muslim Middle Easterners have left the countryside for the cities, seeking better lives. Unfortunately, few have found what they sought. Fifty years ago, Riyadh, the capital of Saudi Arabia, was a tiny village of mud-brick homes clustered around a small fort. By 2000, it was a massive metropolis of over 4 million and its population was growing at the blistering pace of 8 percent annually because so many young people were leaving their villages in search of jobs.[12] Of course, urban planning and public spending on housing have been inadequate across the Muslim Middle East, and the result has been the sprawl of shantytowns and slums that now ring every major Arab and Iranian city. By 1995, 35 percent of Cairo's population and 16 percent of Egypt's entire population were living in horrible slums (including many who have been reduced to living in its cemeteries for lack of any other space).[13] Social services, jobs, sanitation, medical services, and the like have similarly failed to keep up with the growth in Middle Eastern cities, leading to the rise of disease, unemployment, and disaffection.[14]

As Table 5.2 shows, between 1990 and 2003, every one of these fifteen Arab states experienced an increase in its urban population. With the exception of Egypt and Iraq, the percentage of the population living in urban areas increased, and typically by a great deal—well over 5 percent—during this thirteen-year time span. Perhaps an even better way to get a sense of the extent of urbanization is to recognize that in just thirteen years, Egypt's cities grew by 6 million people—equal to 11 percent of the country's *total* population in 1990. Jordan's cities absorbed nearly 2 million people, 59 percent of the size of its total population at the start of this time span. Saudi Arabia's cities added a number of people equal to 46 percent of its total population in 1990, while the UAE's cities exploded, adding more people in thirteen years than even lived in the country in 1990.[15]

Table 5.2. Urbanization in the Arab World, 1990–2003

Country	Urban Population in 1990 (millions)	Urban Population in 2003 (millions)	Increase or Decrease (millions)	Increase in Urban Population as % of 1990 Total Population	% of Population Urban in 1990	% of Population Urban in 2003	Increase or Decrease
Algeria	12.9	18.7	+6.2	+25	51	59	+8
Egypt	22.9	28.9	+6.0	+11	44	43	−1
Iraq	12.6	16.7	+4.1	+23	70	68	−2
Jordan	2.3	4.2	+1.9	+59	72	79	+7
Kuwait	2.0	2.3	+0.3	+14	95	96	+1
Lebanon	3.1	4.1	+1.0	+32	84	91	+7
Libya	3.5	4.9	+1.4	+34	82	88	+6
Morocco	11.6	17.3	+5.7	+23	48	57	+9
Oman	1.0	2.0	+1.0	+56	62	78	+14
Saudi Arabia	12.4	19.7	+7.3	+46	78	88	+10
Sudan	6.6	13.0	+6.4	+24	27	39	+12
Syria	5.9	9.1	+3.2	+26	49	53	+4
Tunisia	4.7	6.7	+2.0	+24	58	67	+9
UAE	1.4	3.6	+2.2	+116	80	88	+8
Yemen	2.7	4.9	+2.2	+18	23	26	+3

Source: *The World Bank,* World Development Indicators, 2005, *pp. 166–168.*

Unemployment

As the discussion of demographic factors has already suggested, unemployment is a key manifestation of Middle Eastern economic problems. In 2005, the ILO reported that average annual growth in the Middle East workforce in 2000–2005 amounted to 3.7 percent, the highest of any region in the world.[16] This trend has held constant since at least 1980.[17] The economies of the Arab states and Iran simply cannot create jobs fast enough. For instance, in 2000, the Saudi economy was generating only 30,000 new jobs per year, although roughly 100,000 people were entering the workforce each year.[18] Similarly, in 2003, the Egyptian economy needed to produce about

750,000 new jobs every year but was creating only about 350,000 per year.[19]

As a result, in 2007, the Middle East had the highest unemployment rate in the world. The average unemployment rate across the entire region is 12.2 percent (compared to the global average of 6.3 percent), and the employment-to-population ratio (also the worst in the world) was only 47.3 percent (compared to the global average of 62.5 percent). It also had the lowest labor force participation rate (53.9 percent in 2006), meaning that relatively few Middle Easterners even wanted or tried to work compared to other regions of the world.[20] Believe it or not, these numbers are actually too optimistic because they rely on official government figures, which in many cases are believed to be considerably exaggerated.[21] For instance, in 2004, the real unemployment rate in Egypt was believed to be almost twice as high as the official government figure (25 versus 12.9 percent).[22] Similarly, while the Saudi government claimed that Saudi Arabia's unemployment rate was only 13 percent in 2003–2004, most experts believed that it was closer to 25 to 30 percent.[23] The Arab League Economic Unity Council estimated in 2006 that the members of the Arab League had an average unemployment rate of 20 percent, not the 12.2 percent cited by the World Bank.[24]

Naturally, unemployment was considerably worse for young people than for older generations. By 2002, unemployment rates across the region were eight to ten times higher for fifteen-to-twenty-four-year-olds than for twenty-five-to-thirty-four-year-olds, whereas in OECD countries, this difference generally does not exceed two to one.[25] The MENA region has the highest youth unemployment rate in the world, at 25.6 percent—compared to the global average of 7.4 percent. Similarly, it has the lowest rates of youth labor force participation in the world at 40 percent and the lowest youth employment to population ratio of 29.7 percent (compared to the global average of 47.3).[26]

In addition, urban unemployment was considerably worse than rural. Alan Richards and John Waterbury estimate that, across the Muslim states of the region, unemployment was generally two to four times higher in the cities than in the rural areas.[27] As one example of that, unemployment in Egypt rose from 5.4 percent to 7.9 percent (according to official figures) from 1988 to 1998. However, unemployment among urban males aged 15 to 19 increased from 14.6 percent to 21.8 during the same time frame.[28]

Nor is this trend expected to abate anytime soon. The Arab League projects that the labor force will grow at a rate of about 3 percent per year until 2032 and that unemployment could rise from 15 million people to 50 million during that same twenty-five-year period, more than tripling the current number at a time when the population is expected only to double.[29] In 2007, the World Bank predicted that the MENA labor force would expand from 120 million people in 2005 to 174 million in 2020. Just to maintain the current high rates of unemployment, this means that the region will need to create 54 million jobs in fifteen years. However, if the MENA countries were to actually try to *improve* their current economic circumstances, they would really need to create 68 million jobs to bring down the unemployment rate, or 4.5 million jobs per year—a very "daunting challenge," in their words.[30]

Unemployment captures only part of the region's job woes, as *under*employment is just as big a challenge. Although specific figures are hard to come by, equal or greater numbers of Muslim Middle Easterners are forced to accept part-time work, jobs that cannot fulfill their basic needs, or jobs requiring far less than their educational achievements would seem to qualify them for.[31] Economists of the Middle East believe that underemployment in the Muslim Middle East is quite high but extremely difficult to measure. However, they point to the region's strikingly low labor productivity as evidence of widespread underemployment.[32]

Failure to Compete

One of the reasons that Arab economies began to experience troubles beginning in the late 1970s and early 1980s is that globalization highlighted their dysfunctions and inefficiencies. The states of the Muslim Middle East have had tremendous difficulty competing on the broad playing field of the global economy. This has left them economically disadvantaged and psychologically humiliated as other states, not just in Europe and North America but in Asia and

Latin America, have surpassed them. Globalization has meant that the Arab states and Iran have to be ready to play in the big leagues, and so far they have not shown the ability to do so. Moreover, the entrance of gigantic competitors like China and India has made the global market even more competitive and has raised the bar for other countries to successfully integrate—as well as the costs for those that cannot.[33] As Noland and Pack summed up the problem:

> To date, the region's performance on numerous indicators of economic opening to the rest of the world has been unimpressive, and looking forward there is cause for concern as to the region's ability to successfully globalize and generate the necessary growth in employment. . . . Until the recent oil-fueled expansion of FDI [foreign direct investment], the region attracted less FDI than some small Scandinavian economies. The Middle East risks being left behind, precisely when it needs to accelerate growth to create jobs for its growing labor force.[34]

THE MOST OBVIOUS indicator of this is trade, where the Muslim Middle East underperforms badly. Nonoil exports from the MENA region grew very slowly during the twenty years between 1980 and 2000, with the result that the region's share of global nonoil exports plummeted, declining by more than 50 percent by 2000.[35] In 1980, the manufacturing export level of the Arab world was comparable to that of Eastern Europe, Latin America, South Asia, and sub-Saharan Africa and not much below that of East Asia. By 2003, the Arab states had fallen behind all of them, including even sub-Saharan Africa.[36] Egypt has a population greater than South Korea and Taiwan combined, but these two East Asian countries export more goods in two days than Egypt does in an entire year.[37] Likewise, the total manufactured exports of the 325 million people of the Arab world were exceeded by those of the Philippines (with less than one third the population), Turkey (with less than a quarter of the population), and even (worst of all) tiny Israel, with only 6 million citizens.[38] Overall, that year, the Arab world accounted for 5 percent of global population but no more than 3 percent of global trade, and the majority of that was in oil and gas.[39]

There are a great many reasons why trade, and particularly nonoil exports, from the region are so low. For instance, the Muslim Middle East states maintain unusually high tariffs, quantitative restrictions, and significant nontariff barriers to imports. To some extent, this is designed to protect domestic manufacturing, which has shown little ability to compete in the international market but is an important source of jobs. Arab bureaucracies also create interminable delays with customs regulations, inspections, and other red tape that add excessive (and sometimes prohibitive) delays to the importation of goods.[40] The Arab states and Iran also frequently dispense monopoly control over segments of the economy to favorite supporters, who use that privileged position to exclude competitors (including foreign businesses) and distort the market (thereby making it less desirable for foreign firms to do business there).[41]

Another important reason why trade is unusually austere among and with the Muslim Middle Eastern states is that all of them suffer from problems with low worker productivity.[42] Paralleling the Middle East's low standing in terms of trade, the World Bank reported that in 1995 and again in 2005, the whole MENA region accounted for only 3 percent of global productivity, despite comprising roughly 7.7 percent of the global population.[43] The 2003 *Arab Human Development Report* warned that "rates of productivity (the average production of one worker) in Arab countries were negative to a large and increasing extent in oil-producing countries during the 1980s and '90s. The gross national product per worker in all Arab countries is less than half of that in two advanced developing countries: South Korea in Asia and Argentina in Latin America."[44] In fact, GDP per worker was negative during the 1990s for both oil-producing and non-oil-producing Arab states.[45] The bottom line is that worker productivity in the Middle East is the lowest in the world.[46]

In a similar vein, the International Labour Organization found in 2007 that worker productivity in the Middle East and North Africa had grown between 1996 and 2006, but by only 9 percent—very low compared to the global average of 26 percent. Only Latin America showed lower growth.[47] A year earlier, the ILO had warned of "stagnant productivity" in the region because while GDP had grown by 5.5 percent annually between 1993 and 2003, productivity had increased by only 0.1 percent annually. Through this rate was better than that of sub-Saharan Africa, it was only one tenth of the global average during that same time frame.[48] To the extent that any of the countries in the region showed real increases in worker productivity, this tended to occur in the Gulf countries and largely because of their reliance on large numbers of foreign workers. As one expert on Saudi Arabia noted, "Saudis simply do not—as a rule—prove as productive as their foreign counterparts. Those who operate private-sector establishments consistently note this lack of productivity. The government, while aware of the difficulty of getting solid performance out of Saudi nationals, nevertheless indulges this attitude in that it too, like other governments in the region, uses employment as a means of easing any political tensions arising from unemployment."[49]

The region's ability to attract foreign direct investment (FDI) is as poor as its trade statistics.[50] Virtually all FDI coming into the Muslim Middle East goes to oil exploration, production, and export, where it has little impact on the wider society. Across the region, FDI "has accounted for less than 1 percent of GDP and a very small percentage of fixed capital formation."[51] One IMF study estimated that, on average, MENA countries attracted only one third of the FDI of developing nations of comparable size, and if investment in oil were excluded the figures would be (not surprisingly) much worse.[52] The reasons for this are fairly straightforward: What prudent investor would choose to sink huge amounts of his or her capital into a region dominated by low worker productivity, poor management practices, sclerotic bureaucracies, vague legal systems, a poor work ethic, arbitrary regimes against which there is effectively no legal recourse, threats of terrorism and civil unrest, and poor educational systems that cannot furnish large numbers of highly capable employees? Except in the oil and gas sectors, where the returns on investment are enormous and the ventures themselves are discretely (and purposely) separated from the rest of society, it just isn't worth it.

Not only can't the region attract foreign investors, it has great difficulty keeping local money in its own economies. The super-wealthy of the Gulf oil states typically keep huge portions of their assets "offshore" in foreign bank accounts and investments overseas. They understand better than foreigners the problems with the economies and labor forces of their own countries, and, much as some of them may want to help for reasons of pride and nationalism, when it comes to investing their own money, they typically follow their heads rather than their hearts. As a result, there is considerable "capital flight" from the region to go with the low levels of FDI coming in.[53]

The Oil Curse

The region's massive hydrocarbon wealth affects nearly every aspect of the economies of the Muslim states of the Middle East. Even those countries without oil themselves have frequently been able to count on aid from the oil-exporting states, remittances from expatriates working in the oil-producing states, and the provision of services to the citizens of the oil-producing states.[54] For instance, in 1975 remittances and economic assistance from the Gulf countries amounted to 27 percent of Egypt's GNP. In Morocco, economic assistance from other Arab states accounted for 12 percent of its GNP in 1981, 5 percent of Tunisia's in 1989, and a whopping 55 percent of Jordan's at its peak in 1986.[55] Consequently, all of the regional economies are tied, to some degree, to the price of oil (and increasingly natural gas) and the revenues it generates.[56]

Though higher oil prices since the oil shocks of the 1970s have brought tremendous wealth into the region and even produced something of a "trickle-down effect" in countries like Egypt and Jordan that produce little oil, it has hardly been an unmitigated good. In fact, the nearly effortless wealth generated by hydrocarbon production has badly distorted regional economies and political systems and helped create many of the region's current problems.[57]

In the economic realm, oil wealth has, in many cases, eliminated the impact of market forces in a vast range of economic sectors. Rather than shut down unprofitable businesses, governments simply subsidize them. With enough cash, traditional business practices that may no longer be suitable for a globalized economy can be sustained. Cultural tendencies that impede efficiency can be indulged. The costs of nepotism and cronyism can be papered over. Because there is so much cash sloshing around, corruption becomes extremely difficult to monitor, let alone curb, and with so many people using money to compensate for bad economic practices, bribes, "commissions," kickbacks, creative bookkeeping, and all other manner of graft can become routine.[58]

In the arena of politics, oil wealth can be equally damaging.[59] Massive oil revenues can eliminate the need for a government to impose taxes to pay for public goods (like security, education, justice, etc.), which eliminates an important incentive for the government to be responsive to its people. As many others have noted, without taxation, there is generally no representation. The regimes typically use the oil largesse to reward their cronies and other supporters, distorting the distribution of wealth and further insulating them from public pressure. As part of this effort, they can sustain a massive and, throughout the Muslim Middle East, massively inefficient, public sector as a way of taking the edge off unemployment and rewarding the regime's friends and supporters.

Oil wealth also creates perverse incentives for individuals. Because there is so much money available to the governments, it is almost always more remunerative for people to try to manipulate the political system to get a share of government revenues (legally or illegally) than to produce things with economic value.[60] As a result, many of the best and brightest in the Arab world spend their time angling for government largesse, rather than trying to figure out how to build a better mousetrap. Similarly, oil has allowed the development of a crippling work culture, especially in the oil-rich Gulf states. Many people in the Gulf region simply do not work at all, expecting the state, their family, and *bakshish* (fees and gifts of money) to provide for them. Others choose not to accept jobs they consider beneath them, causing societies where unemployment is already high to have to import workers from South and Southeast Asia to perform work that the Gulf Arabs will not. As the World Bank has noted, this has led to the bizarre situation in which two thirds of the workers in the Gulf region are expatriates while much of the population is either unemployed or does not participate in the workforce at all (and is increasingly unhappy about it).[61] "A generation has grown up within a dependency culture," bemoans Ismail Serageldin of the Bibliotheca Alexandrina, "that is ill-suited to cope with the expected increasing exposure to market pressures. That generation lacks 'achievement motivation, vision of opportunities, sense of discipline, work ethic commitment, and self esteem' that one generation passes on to another in a motivation and progressive society."[62]

As important as the "oil curse" may be in hindering Arab economic prospects, the claim can be pushed only so far. The simple fact is that even by the standards of other major oil producers, the Arab oil producers are underperforming badly. For instance, in 2000, oil represented 30 percent of Saudi Arabia's GDP, 33 percent of the UAE's GDP, 29 percent of Kuwait's GDP, and 25 percent of Algeria's GDP. By contrast, it made up only 7 percent of Venezuela's GDP in 2000 and only 7 percent of Indonesia's in 1999.[63]

Is the Oil Boom Good for the Region?

Since 2005, the steep increase in global oil prices has brought the Middle East a reprieve from some of its economic problems and even caused a boom in some sectors. However, though higher oil prices are helpful to Middle Eastern states in some ways, they can also be very dangerous. On the one hand, they allow the oil-exporting states to pay off their debts and fund their burdensome welfare systems. On the other hand, they raise popular expectations that the "rising tide" of oil revenues is going to lift all boats—and lift them *a lot*.

Because of the tremendous corruption of many of the regimes, the funneling of all oil revenues into the treasuries of the regime or the bank accounts of the royal family, and the ability of well-connected individuals to manipulate the political system to secure disproportionate shares of this government-controlled largesse, oil wealth has created very significant income gaps in all of the oil-producing states. As a result, real poverty persists in the region and in places is actually growing.[64] For example, most Americans think of Saudi Arabia as an enormously wealthy country, which it is in some ways. But in 2004, the economist Robert Looney estimated that 20 to 30 percent of Saudis were living below the poverty line.[65] He has quoted the journalist Kim Murphy as warning in 2003 that

> The dozen years since the Persian Gulf War have seen slums grow up on the outskirts of Jeddah and Riyadh, the capital. Beggars hawk bottles of water at intersections. Penniless women huddle in strips of shade outside their crumbling mud-brick houses, begging for money. Many families in the capital are so poor they can't afford electricity. Raw sewage runs through parts of Jeddah. . . . The increasingly perilous economic situation that all in Saudi Arabia but the royalty face today may be a big factor in recruiting young Saudis to terrorist groups such as Al Qaeda. Chronic joblessness, diminished incomes and difficulty in collecting enough money to marry and start families are all issues that can evoke anger.[66]

Moreover, over the years the consistent pattern has been that, for these same reasons, the more oil revenue pours into the country, the wider these gaps in income become. Although there is some "trickling down" of oil wealth, it tends to be merely a trickle. So in times of great oil profitability, the regime and its cronies tend to become immensely rich and the rest of the population is left behind—much to its anger and frustration. Many Middle Eastern oil exporters are smart enough to recognize this trend and make efforts to redistribute some of their oil wealth through various social welfare programs, construction projects, and other public efforts. However, it is rare that the benefits from such expenditures actually live up to public expectations, let alone compensate every citizen equally.

To their credit, this time around the governments of the region are trying to direct far more of the new revenues back into the region than they have in the past. However, a great deal of money is still flowing out of the region—in the form of investments, savings, and massive foreign purchases, particularly of weapons. The money that is being reinvested in the region is creating a considerable alleviation of immediate economic burdens, but so far, the improvements have been largely superficial. There are few signs that the reinvestment is actually affecting the deeper, structural problems. New industries are being built in the Arab world, but most of the jobs continue to go to newly imported South and Southeast Asians. To the extent that unemployment numbers are improving, they are doing so because of new public works, some increase in agricultural hires (where productivity is in decline), and the government practice of classifying informal work at home and cottage industries as "employment." For the most part, local employment has not been growing in industries with the potential for increased dynamism, technological development, or greater integration with the global economy. In contrast, the biggest returns from new local investment have been coming in areas that offer few prospects for dealing with the region's employment problems—the oil and petrochemical sectors, which need relatively few workers, can increasingly rely on automation and continue to prefer hiring foreigners.[67] Moreover, corruption and mismanagement remain the rule, and this can mean that all of the investment in infrastructure, industry, and education goes to waste, exacerbating the underlying economic problems rather than alleviating them. So far, the increase in oil prices is having little impact on what matters most to the citizenry: unemployment, real wages, inflation, and other determinants of the basic quality of life.

This can be very dangerous. It is the ultimate image of shattered dreams and unfulfilled expectations: large numbers of people who know that their government is making money by the basketful, and who are expecting that this windfall will just as quickly alleviate all of the onerous economic problems they face, only to find that vast sums are being siphoned off into graft; redirected back out of the country to private accounts; spent on luxury items, military hardware, or "white elephant" projects; or simply wasted. Moreover, the oil boom is creating the perception of real progress but may simply be papering over the problems, which means that when the oil boom passes—as it inevitably will—those problems will reemerge, probably worse than before.

It is worth noting that the shah's Iran experienced the same sort of oil boom just before the Iranian Revolution. The shah too attempted to use that oil wealth to build new industries and transform the Iranian workforce, but his efforts were so badly mismanaged and so riddled with corruption that they had little impact on the actual plight of the Iranian people, who became enraged when the flood of oil money flowing into Iran failed to raise their living standard while so many of the shah's cronies became fabulously wealthy overnight. Instead of solving Iran's economic difficulties, the oil boom triggered the Iranian Revolution.[68]

Education

To a certain degree, nearly all of the difficulties that the Arab world is experiencing with integration into the globalized economy derive from a common root problem: the low level of human development throughout its societies. This is not to suggest that there are not some very bright, very innovative, and very entrepreneurial Arabs who are willing and able to perform at high levels in the new information economy. It is to say instead that Arab society, in particular, is not producing nearly enough such people to enable it to compete in this environment. Though political, cultural, sociological, and even other economic aspects contribute to this dearth, the central problem lies in the educational systems of the Arab world. In the information age, knowledge is the most important commodity. Unfortunately, current Arab educational systems are not producing large numbers of people able to create and employ knowledge to enable the Arab states to compete in the global marketplace.

In some parts of the Arab world, the problem is still a matter of resources. Most of the Muslim states of the Middle East have made education one of their highest priorities in the last thirty years and have devoted admirable proportions of their national resources toward improving education. However, this is yet another area in which the torrid growth of their populations has diminished (although hardly eliminated) the gains being realized from such efforts. In many of the Arab states in particular, the resources allocated to education still cannot hire enough teachers, build enough schools, and buy enough textbooks to fully compensate for the numbers of new children who need educating. As a result, class sizes are still somewhat large, the ratio of students to teachers is at times too great, and the entire educational experience has not yet caught up to the standards set out for it.[69] For instance, World Bank figures demonstrate that student-teacher ratios in the Arab world remained higher than those of comparable developing nations elsewhere around the world from 1985 till 2000.[70] Moreover, though literacy rates in the Arab world have improved markedly over the past thirty years, they still remain low. The OECD countries and the countries of the former Soviet Union have literacy rates of 98 and 97 percent on average, respectively, whereas in the Muslim Middle East, the average literacy rate is under 60 percent—still better than in South Asia and sub-Saharan Africa but far from where the Arab states aspire to be.[71]

Nevertheless, it would be a mistake to make too much of these quantitative factors. In fact, the Arab governments have made a major investment in education over the past thirty to forty years, and most of the statistical evidence demonstrates a remarkable improvement in basic educational indicators in an absolute sense, even if they have not shown many relative gains compared to other parts of the world.[72] Literacy is way up on average, as is the average number of years of schooling—from 1.3 in 1970 to 4.5 in 2000.[73] Enrollment rates have increased markedly, especially for high school students.[74] Per capita spending on education across the region is very low by the standards of OECD nations but considerably higher than the average for the developing world.[75] The pupil-teacher ratio has declined very respectably.[76] Especially given the comparisons with other developing countries, it is hard to make the case that inadequate resources are the crux of the problem with Arab education when so many other developing nations are performing so much better than the Arab states in the educational field despite devoting fewer resources to it than the Arabs.

Moreover, spending on education in the Gulf states was nothing short of massive beginning in the 1970s. There was no shortage of schools, teachers, tutors, administrators, books, special programs, buses, pencils, or anything else.[77] Yet the Gulf states did not fare particularly better than the rest of the Muslim Middle East when it came to educational achievement. In 1995, Kuwait was the only Arab country to participate in the Third International Mathematics and Science Study, along with forty other countries from around the world. Kuwait was exceptional because of its small size and wealth: "It spends generously on education and has made outstanding progress in its quantitative expansion." But Kuwaiti students came in at the bottom of the list and ranked thirty-ninth out of forty-one overall in achievement in math and science. Kuwait's scores were far below the world average, let alone those of the leading countries. "The example points to an important conclusion," the 2003 *Arab Human Development Report* (AHDR) stated; "ultimately, the quality of education does not depend on the availability of resources or on quantitative factors but rather on other organizations of the educational process and the means of delivery and evaluation."[78]

Moreover, in subsequent international mathematics and science studies, more Arab states participated, and the results were noteworthy in two ways: (1) all of the Middle East states did poorly, with only one country in one of the tests (Jordan in science in 2003) exceeding the global average and most falling at the very bottom of the list; and (2) the Gulf states did just as poorly as other Muslim Middle Eastern countries. For example, in 1999, three Arab states (Jordan, Tunisia, and Morocco) took part along with thirty-five other countries. In math, Tunisia ranked twenty-ninth, Jordan thirty-second, and Morocco thirty-seventh out of the field of thirty-eight. In science, they did even worse, with Jordan placing thirtieth, Tunisia thirty-fourth, and Morocco again thirty-seventh. Four years later, in a field of forty-six countries, in math, Lebanon came in thirty-first, Jordan thirty-second, Tunisia thirty-fifth, Bahrain thirty-seventh, Morocco fortieth, and Saudi Arabia forty-third. In science, Jordan ranked twenty-fifth—just above the global average, the only Arab country to do so—but Bahrain came in thirty-third, the Palestinians thirty-fourth, Egypt thirty-fifth, Tunisia thirty-eighth, Saudi Arabia thirty-ninth, Morocco fortieth, and Lebanon forty-first.[79]

Clearly, access to resources is not the principal problem with education in the Arab world anymore. Indeed, it is unquestionably the case that Arab educational deficits are a function of poor *quality*, rather than inadequate *quantity*. It is what Arab students are being taught and how they are being taught that is the problem.[80] As various *Arab Human Development Reports* have repeatedly stressed, "the most important challenge facing Arab education is its declining quality."[81] Or as the international management expert Delwin A. Roy put it when discussing Saudi educational problems, "Although the government can point to dramatic increases in the numbers who have passed through the various educational levels, there is considerable doubt as to the degree to which it might be said that students have actually been 'educated.' "[82]

MIXING POLITICS AND EDUCATION

Some, though by no means all, of the problems with the quality of education in the Muslim Middle East can be traced to the impact of authoritarian politics on schooling. Except among the oil emirates of the Persian Gulf, where education is largely private, the state is the overwhelming provider of education in the Arab world. Even including the Gulf states, public funding still accounts for 89 percent of all spending on education among the Arab states.[83] This dependency on the government makes Arab education highly vulnerable to the vicissitudes of politics.

On the positive side, all of the Arab governments have acknowledged the importance of education and made considerable efforts to improve it, with the results described above. However, there is also a significant negative side. Specifically, the regimes of the region are notoriously deaf to the pleas of their people. They follow their own internal logic, driven by outdated notions of central planning and staffed by people who often do not know the first thing about educational practices around the world, let alone education theory. Ahmed Galal, a superb Egyptian political economist, has written of his home country, in a passage that is largely applicable throughout the Muslim Middle East, that bureaucrats have limited incentives

to efficiently monitor, regulate, and improve the education process. . . . Like teachers, their salaries are low, their performance is difficult to assess, and their career is not linked to measurable achievements. While tending to be process rather than outcome oriented, excessive centralization gives them enormous power over the expansion and oversight of schools. Centralization creates a distance between those responsible for delivering the education and those who benefit from education the most. Both the teachers and managers of schools only have incentives to respond to superiors at the Center instead of to parents and students."[84]

One result of this dependence is that schooling in the Arab world tends to be closely directed by strict guidelines handed down by education ministries. It is the ministry that chooses textbooks, sets curricula, formulates guidelines for advancement, and sets standards for teacher training.[85] In his study of Moroccan schooling, education researcher Gerald Miller found that, to revise the math curriculum of Moroccan public schools, the Ministry of Education sent out detailed lesson plans to the teachers with instructions to the teachers to carry them out exactly. If a lesson plan was delayed in reaching a teacher, the teacher normally would not improvise and instead would simply reteach the previous week's lesson plan verbatim—without even changing the examples or problems used.[86] The famed education expert Joseph Szyliowicz observed that in every Arab state, the Ministry of Education "permitted no deviations of any sort from its detailed regulations, thus effectively stifling any possible initiative or flexibility within particular schools."[87]

A CRIPPLING EDUCATIONAL METHOD

Ultimately, the most important problem undermining the quality of education throughout the Arab world is its reliance on a traditional teaching method that runs counter to the demands of modern economic life.[88] All societies have particular methods of imparting knowledge, values, and patterns of behavior to successive generations. This is the core of a people's culture. But cultures can have very different methods of education—methods that made sense for the community's needs in certain circumstances at some point in the not-too-distant past. A crucial problem for Arab society is that the cultural method of education that it devised is not preparing its young men and women for modern economic life in a globalized marketplace. This should not be terribly surprising—the patterns and values of Arab culture were derived in decades, even centuries, past to meet the needs of the community at that time and could not anticipate the radically different needs of the modern global economy. Like all cultures, Arab culture is constantly evolving and will no doubt change to accommodate the impact of globalization on the Middle East, but it is the nature of cultures to change slowly, and, especially when it comes to adapting traditional teaching methods, Arab culture is not changing quickly enough to provide young Arab men and women with the skills they most need right now.[89]

Education begins at home. Long before they ever set foot in a school, children begin to be taught knowledge, values, behavior, and ways of thinking and understanding the world by their parents and families. Not surprisingly, the methods of Arab informal education, the education that takes place in the home and social settings, are effectively identical to the formal methods employed in Arab schools from kindergarten through graduate schools. Moreover, because education often has the greatest impact at the earliest ages, many sociologists, psychologists, anthropologists, and educators believe that the informal education received in the home is the most important of all in creating patterns for future behavior and learning later in life.[90]

Most Middle East sociologists note that the cornerstone of educating a child in Arab families is teaching him or her complete obedience to authority.[91] "Studies indicate that the most widespread style of child rearing in Arab families is the authoritarian mode accompanied by the overprotective," according to the 2003 *Arab Human Development Report*. "This reduces children's independence, self-confidence and social efficiency, and fosters passive attitudes and hesitant decision-making skills. Most of all, it affects how the child thinks by suppressing questioning, exploration, and initiative."[92] The Lebanese psychologist 'Ali Zayour, in his monumental study *Psychoanalysis of the Arab Ego*, says that the Arab family is "relentless in its repression. . . . The young are brought up to be obedient, well-mannered and subservient to those above them."[93]

This relentless effort to force children to defer decision making and judgment to authority figures works to depress creativity and initiative among Arab youth. In essence, within the family structure, children are taught to obey rather than to think for themselves. Hamed Ammar, the great Arab education expert, concluded that Egyptian child rearing worked "to produce submissive, obedient children who lack the spirit of enterprise and initiative. Adults continuously wean their offspring from flights of imagination and spontaneity of action till they almost completely achieve their end by the time their offspring reach adolescence."[94] The scholar Raymond Cohen concurs with Ammar's findings that "the personal initiative and autonomy characteristic of child-rearing and education in the Western world is neglected by Egyptian culture, as it is indeed throughout the Arab world."[95] Cohen goes on to say that "denied freedom of choice, [Arab] children learn to do only what they are told. Self-reliance and personal initiative are not encouraged because they do not contribute to group needs."[96] Hisham Sharabi, a highly influential Arab intellectual historian, argues that, "Arab children [are] discouraged by their upbringing from exercising independent judgment. They are taught to accept unquestioningly the view of others."[97] Similarly, the sociologist Halim Barakat observes that Arab children "avoid taking risks and trying new ways of doing things, for independence of mind, critical dissent, and adventure beyond the recognized limits are constantly and systematically discouraged by parents and other older members of the family."[98]

Arab families often teach that group affiliation is paramount, and acceptance by the group is achieved by conforming to the accepted behavioral norms of the society. Thus teaching children to suppress their own judgment and needs to that of the larger group also contributes to a suppression of creativity and initiative. According to the renowned experts Saad Eddin Ibrahim and Nicholas S. Hopkins, "[Arab] children learned not only to expect emotional and material support from an expanded kinship group, but also that any of them was nothing by himself outside that group. The child's personality was not only shaped by, but also submerged in the kinship group. His loyalty to it was therefore very intense. He hardly questioned or entertained independent judgment. He developed a reflexive deference to authority."[99]

The primary method of teaching children in most Arab families has been rote memorization enforced by arbitrary punishment. Halim Barakat and Hisham Sharabi concur that "The typical urban,

Muslim, middle- and lower-middle class family—i.e. feudal, bourgeois family—uses the principal techniques of shaming, physical punishment and rote-learning (*Talqín*) in socializing its children."[100] Elsewhere, Sharabi and Muktar Ani have written that "the learning process in the Arab family (and beyond it) may be characterized by two aspects: it de-emphasizes persuasion (and reward), and it emphasizes physical punishment and rote-learning (*Talqín*)."[101] Both of these methods dampen analytical skills, degrade the ability of children to see beyond specifics, and discourage independent thought and action. Children are forced to memorize information without necessarily being taught to use it as a basis for analogical reasoning or as a beginning point for extrapolations to other situations. Information is often considered useful only for the specific purpose and context for which it is taught. Similarly, since punishment is arbitrary and frequently no explanation is given for the action that prompted it—or what other action would entail a reward—children become wary of all independent action and instead are conditioned to take action only when specifically sanctioned by an authority figure. The sociologist Sana al-Khayyat's work on Iraqi society led her to conclude that the constant disciplining of Iraqi children without explanation and punishing them for asking questions left them incapable of acting independently. In her words, "parents commonly give children commands rather than explaining. Thus children do not grow up to make their own decisions and develop as independent people."[102]

These patterns of education continue seamlessly in the formal educational processes of the Arab world—elementary and high school, college, and even graduate programs. The educational system of all the Arab states in the postwar era derives largely from the Qur'anic schools—the *kuttab* and the *madrasa*—that were essentially the only formal education in the Arab states until the nineteenth century, or even the twentieth century in some parts of the region.[103] Richards and Waterbury observe that when it comes to the problems of education in the Arab world, "More important than class size are pedagogical methods, teacher quality, and morale. Far too often, education in the region mimics traditional madrasas (Islamic schools, where boys memorize parts of the Koran), with their emphasis on rote learning, rather than stressing problem solving, writing skills, or creativity."[104] Since the 1980s, there has been some movement toward reforming the educational method in some parts of the Arab world. However, such efforts have been modest and are more often the exception than the rule.[105]

Drawing on their heritage in the kuttabs and madrasas, Arab education is generally organized around the central concept that knowledge is revealed, not created.[106] Teaching is conducted in Arab schools in mostly authoritarian fashion, and students are too often taught to remain passive and simply absorb what the teacher presents to them. In the classrooms of most Arab schools, the teacher generally presents the information to be learned without explanation, and students are taught to memorize this information and be able to repeat it on demand.[107] Critics and experts frequently note that the incentive structure of Arab schools encourages the student to memorize lessons without internalizing them and often leaves them little room to explore their imaginations or sharpen their analytic faculties.[108] The authors of the 2003 *Arab Human Development Report* bluntly stated, "In Arab countries, lectures seem to dominate. Students can do little but memorize, recite, and perfect rote learning. . . . Communication in education is didactic, supported by set books containing indisputable texts in which knowledge is objectified so as to hold incontestable facts, and by an examination process that only tests memorization and factual recall."[109]

In particular, advancement from one grade level to the next depends upon annual standardized tests that measure only the ability of the students to memorize their standardized textbooks.[110] As the political economist Mohamed Rabie put it, "Students are given thousands of facts to memorize instead of the research skills that will enable them to find the facts when needed. Memorization, together with the authoritarian method of instruction, serves to inhibit rather than encourage students' ability to think and take the initiative. Material memorized will be regurgitated on paper during examinations. A hypothesis may go long untested and be accepted as fact. The students' ability to develop realistic and imaginative solutions to whatever problems they may have to deal with is very much limited."[111] This is true even at the university level, with Bassam Tibi of Cornell University despairing that "All Arab Islamic . . . universities I know of have courses of study based solely on the capacity for rote learning in order to pass successfully."[112]

In his 1994 survey of the contemporary Middle East, Milton Viorst relates the following anecdote regarding the state of education in the Arab world:

> An Arab professor at a West Bank university, a Muslim who taught for many years in the United States, told me that his Palestinian students, though more highly motivated and more conscientious than American students, were far more timid about exploring the bounds of knowledge. "They cannot free themselves from the habit of learning by rote," he said. "They are more sensitive to community opinion. They are more dependent on the teacher. Most striking to me, their training in the Koran teaches them that all knowledge is in the book. One can memorize the book; one can even interpret it. But a book is not a point of departure; one cannot add to it. The Islamic tradition holds that learning is fixed. My students resist going beyond the book, any book."[113]

It is not hard to understand why an educational system that teaches in this fashion is failing its students. It is this obsolete method, more than any other problem, that accounts for the vast disparities in the quality and impact of education between the Arab world and other regions. A system that favors rote memorization of facts, that discourages innovation and initiative, that insists that subjects remain discrete (rather than promoting interdisciplinary thinking), that emphasizes conformity over independence, and that promotes hierarchic thinking is not an educational method well suited to the demands of the twenty-first century and the globalized economy. With all this in mind, it should not be surprising that between 1980 and 2000 tiny Israel, with a population less than onetenth that of Egypt's, registered nearly one hundred times as many patents.[114]

THE IMPACT: EDUCATED UNEMPLOYMENT

One of the most important results of the poor quality of education being provided to Arab children can be found in the dangerously high levels of educated unemployment found throughout the region. The educational system is failing its students; it is failing to provide them with the skills that they need to get jobs and compete effectively in a globalized economy. It is natural that the higher an individual has made it on the educational ladder, the higher his or her expectations for a job. The most educated expect the best jobs and are often unwilling to accept jobs that they consider unworthy of their achievements. But since more schooling in the Arab world is no guarantee of greater ability or skills, it is all too often the case that the best-educated Arabs do not get the best jobs—in fact, they don't get any jobs at all. Few multinational firms are interested in establishing major manufacturing, research, or even administrative facilities in the Muslim Middle East, in large part because they see the poor quality of the human capital produced by the regional educational system.[115]

Likewise, there is little foreign investment in the region outside the oil and gas sector—and much of the money from oil revenues is pumped out by shrewd Gulf investors who see little rationale in investing locally, given the low productivity of the workforce and the other economic problems of the Muslim Middle East. So comparatively few large, integrated firms are established by local entrepreneurs. As a result, there are few white-collar jobs available in the private sector, and many of the multinational corporations that do establish facilities in the region prefer to bring in foreign managers, researchers, salesmen, and other senior personnel, rather than try to find locals able to perform these tasks. In the past, the refuge for well-educated (but not properly educated) Middle Easterners was the public sector—both the bureaucracy and its network of state-owned enterprises (SOEs).[116] But in recent years, these have become so bloated that they have had to cut back on their hiring (and even do some downsizing) at the exact moment when the demographic trends are producing ever-greater numbers of supplicants for these jobs.[117]

The result of all this has been widespread unemployment (and

Table 5.3. Unemployment by Educational Level in Selected Muslim Middle East Countries in 2006 (Using Official Figures)

Country	Total, Official Unemployment Rate	Without Secondary Education	With Secondary and Intermediate Education	With Higher Education
Algeria	15.7	15.7	19.3	19.3
Egypt	10.3	1.4	13.5	13.7
Iran	15.0	5.7	16.4	17.1
Jordan	15.4	14.2	12.1	17.7
Morocco	7.7	5.2	20.5	26.8

Source: CIA, World Factbook, 2006; The World Bank, Middle East and North Africa Region Economic Developments and Prospects, 2007: Job Creation in an Era of High Growth (Washington, D.C.: World Bank, 2007), p. 64.

arguably even worse underemployment) among the educated elements of Arab and Iranian societies. Perversely, as Table 5.3 illustrates, in most of the states of the region, unemployment rates *increase* with education—so that the more educated you are, the *less* likely it is that you will be employed. Indeed, repeated studies of unemployment and education in the region have verified this dangerous phenomenon.[118] As Alan Richards and John Waterbury put it, "These young people have received enough education to have altered their expectations and aspirations, but not enough to compete effectively for the (very scarce) good jobs in the formal sector."[119]

A Culture Under Siege

As the education issue has already suggested, the last socioeconomic issue affecting the contemporary Muslim Middle East is the cultural conflict between its traditional values and patterns of life and those of the globalizing world. Over the past twenty to thirty years, the Muslim Middle East has also been confronted with the homogenized mass culture that first arose in the West with the development of postindustrial, information age economies, the growth of global trade and economic activity, and the explosion of real-time communications during the late twentieth century—what is typically called simply "modernity."

Every traditional society that modernity has touched in recent decades (including the more traditional communities of North America and Western Europe) has experienced a profound shock. Modernity brings with it a raft of new values, behavior patterns, and modes of thinking and acting that are either most compatible with or enabled by its own economic, communication, and social components. For example, the rise of mass media and instantaneous mass communication has made speed a cardinal virtue of modernity: both the speed of operations and the rate of change in the world have increased many times over. This has typically proven to be a shock to most traditional cultures where the pace of activity has been determined by much slower cadences—agricultural seasons or even early-industrial production, transportation, and communication. In the preindustrial age, the pace of activity was often measured in weeks or days; in the industrial age, it was measured in hours or perhaps minutes; but in the information age it is measured in nanoseconds. Making that adjustment is very difficult, especially if the society in question was still getting used to the demands of the industrial age. Likewise, modernity has empowered the individual, reducing the importance of collective activities and increasing the importance of individual beliefs and desires. Again, most traditional cultures emphasize collective thinking as being most beneficial to the society as a whole, and this change in focus can be equally wrenching. Moreover, because modernity is a transnational phenomenon, it has tended to promote secularism, multiculturalism, and a "lowest-common-denominator" approach to human values to create a common set of values and modes of behavior acceptable to all peoples. This has clashed with the unique values, national pride, and religiosity of most traditional societies.

Across the Muslim Middle East, the forces of modernity have sparked quintessentially negative reactions.[120] While many Middle Easterners love their new cell phones and satellite-dish TVs, they hate many of the lascivious Western music videos and movies from America and Europe that penetrate their world through these devices. They hate the emphasis on materialism they see. They fear what they see as "Christian" values infecting the Dar al-Islam (the house of Islam), although in truth it is modern secularism, not

Christianity, that modernity purveys. Of course, this is just as bad for many devout Muslims. Many Muslim Middle Easterners are alarmed by the new emphasis on the individual at the expense of traditional values built around family and community. They are bewildered by the demands of modernity for speed, innovation, competitiveness, and endless demands for bigger, better, and faster. As the authors of the *Arab Human Development Report* warned:

> Arabic culture, however, like other cultures, finds itself facing the challenges of an emerging global cultural homogeneity and related questions about cultural multiplicity, cultural personalities, the issue of the "self" and the "other," and its own cultural character. These and similar questions raise apprehensions, fears, and risks in the minds of its people. Concerns about the extinction of the language and culture and the diminution and dissipation of identity have become omnipresent in Arab thought and culture.[121]

In response, a great many people have rejected modernity or attempted to separate the material benefits of modernity from its cultural underpinnings, claiming that their society should embrace the former while shunning the latter. A great many have simply retreated to the safety of traditional religion.

Although certainly some manifestations of this pattern of behavior are unique to the Muslim Middle East, for the most part, there is nothing unique about this general reaction. Pretty much every traditional society confronted with modernity has reacted in a broadly similar fashion.[122] Even here in the United States, stop and think about how conservatives have decried the same materialism, licentiousness, secularism, and homogenization of culture. Protecting "family values" is the battle cry of American conservatives just as much as it is for Islamic conservatives. The impact of modernity has spurred greater religiosity here too as people frightened by or unhappy with modernity go looking for an alternative conception of how a person should conduct him- or herself and how a society should organize itself. Indeed, religion, as one of the most important vessels of a culture, is always a refuge when people are confronted with alien values and find them taking root in their society. Most world religions have tremendous resonance with their adherents and offer a fairly complete "plan" for living that feels far more comfortable, if only because it is long-standing, to those who feel themselves under assault. It is a fortress in which people can seek shelter when they feel that their culture has been invaded by another.

The Creeping Isolation of the Muslim Middle East

One particularly disturbing manifestation of this phenomenon in the Middle East has been the tendency of a number of elites and average people to respond to their confrontation with modernity by running from it—figuratively, not literally. Again, the confrontation between a traditional society and modernity has not been pleasant anywhere, including in the United States and Europe. However, the Middle East is the only region in which there is a broad current of opinion supporting the idea that its society should isolate itself from the rest of the world as a way of dealing with the problem. Again, there are certainly voices arguing that the people of the Muslim Middle East should find a way to take from the global community what is most useful (principally technology) while excluding its culture—another very typical reaction to modernity. But in the Arab world and Iran, these voices are not predominant. Moreover, the emirates of the Persian Gulf have largely embraced globalization, integrating into the global economy at "breakneck speed," in the words of Robert Looney.[123] However, far more are moving in the direction of attempting to keep out the forces of modernity by trying, consciously or unconsciously, to wall off their society—an effort that is doomed to failure but will cause considerable damage.[124] Anthony Cordesman has commented, on this phenomenon, "The fact that so many in the region have turned back to more traditional social structures and religion is scarcely surprising, but it is unclear that this offers any meaningful solution to the problems involved."[125]

Some of the signs of this pattern of isolation of Muslim Middle Eastern society include a lack of curiosity about the outside world, animosity to foreigners, and limited desire to learn about or even make contact with the rest of the world prevalent in some parts and strata of the Arab world. The authors of the *Arab Human Development*

Report have repeatedly bemoaned the limited interaction the Arab world has with the rest of the global community. They have pointed out that in the Arab states, the average number of newspapers per thousand people is just 53, compared with an average of 285 in the developed world. The number of telephone lines in the Arab world is one fifth that of developed countries. There are just 18 computers per 1,000 people in the Arab world, compared to a global average of 78.3 per 1,000 people. Only 1.6 percent of the population of the Arab states has Internet access.[126] They similarly note that between 1980 and 1985, on average, 4.4 books were translated into Arabic per million people. In Hungary, the same number at the same time was 519 books per million and in Spain 920 books per million.[127] Ultimately, about 330 books are translated into Arabic each year, which is one-fifth the number translated into Greek. Since the year 819, during the reign of the Caliph al-Mamun (who began translating works from Greek into Arabic), the Arab world has translated a grand total of about 10,000 books—fewer than what Spain translates in a single year.[128]

Some additonal passages from the 2003 *AHDR,* which focused on the particularly acute problem of knowledge creation, are worth quoting here as more evidence on the peculiar isolation of Arab society at a time when the rest of the world is moving toward greater integration. "It is relevant to observe here that facility with the English language is waning across the Arab world. With the exception of a few university professors and educated individuals, real proficiency in English has ebbed, preventing many Arab researchers from publishing their research in international scientific journals."[129] Arab elites, particularly university professors and researchers, increasingly speak only Arabic—as a result of "strained relations between some Western countries and Arab countries. . . . A new kind of monolingual professor and researcher has started to gradually replace the kind of bilingual academic who in the past dominated most Arab universities and research centres. It has also affected Arab participation at international scientific meetings and, consequently, the Arab presence in international scientific groups and networks."[130] "A form of Arab self-containment hobbles co-operation with international partners in the humanities and social sciences. The emphasis on 'specificity' of Arab societies, a common preoccupation in Arab countries, has played a negative role in this respect, leading to a neglect of anything that is not 'related to our reality' and a narrow focus in research on local or purely Arab subjects. . . . There is no accumulated tradition of Arab scholarship on the 'Other.' Institutions concerned with the study of other societies are almost non-existent."[131] "Meanwhile, this form of insularity also affects Arab students pursuing research abroad, the majority of whom concentrate on research topics about their own countries or region. Few Arab Ph.D. theses earned outside the region deal with the society in which the researcher temporarily resides."[132]

A noteworthy exception to this pattern is Iran, although it is hardly moving in a 180-degree opposite direction. There are a great many Iranians, particularly in the urban middle classes, who desire a better relationship with the West and embrace modernity rather than rejecting it. The society as a whole has been far more receptive to Western culture in recent years, in part because it is seen as being antithetical to the precepts of the clerical regime, which is widely unpopular. On the other hand, President Mahmoud Ahmedinejad and other Iranian hard-line conservatives have taken the idea of isolating Iranian society from the larger global community to ridiculous extremes. They have embraced it as a deliberate policy and want to apply it to all aspects of their economy in the pursuit of a chimerical autarky, in addition to what they perceive as globalization's corrupting cultural influences.

The many socioeconomic ills of the Middle East are not someone else's problems. They are our problems too, because they serve as the angry, unstable bedrock upon which the other dysfunctions of the region stand. You cannot understand the security problems of the region without understanding their roots in these deeper socioeconomic issues, nor can you hope to eradicate the threats to American interests in the region without addressing these foundational problems. Nevertheless, as bad as these socioeconomic failings are, they would not be nearly as dangerous as they are if they were not exacerbating and being exacerbated by pernicious political problems, to which we must turn next.

CHAPTER 6

THE CRISIS OF MIDDLE EASTERN POLITICS

LYING BEHIND VIRTUALLY EVERY ONE OF THE PROBLEMS of the Muslim Middle East, causing some and aggravating others, are the dysfunctional politics of the region.[1] This includes all of the socioeconomic problems described in the last chapter. The perverse politics of virtually all of the states of the region subvert weak economic systems, turn serious problems into existential threats, and create dangerous vicious cycles in which politics, economics, and culture mix to become far more lethal than any of them would be on its own. The fragility and irrationality of Middle Eastern political systems makes it hard, if not impossible, to address the structural problems of Arab economies and educational systems or to present acceptable pathways to deal with social and cultural change. The political systems introduce a range of problems of their own as well, some of which have little to do with the socioeconomic issues, but all add to the unhappiness of the Muslim Middle East and, in so doing, to the threats faced by the United States and our allies in the region.

The Persistence of Autocracy

To a very great extent, the Middle East is the last bastion of authoritarianism left on Earth.[2] In Freedom House's annual standings, the Arab world continues to rank last in the world when compared to other regions. In the 2007 edition of its *Freedom in the World* report, 61 percent of Middle East and North African countries ranked as "Not Free," and another 33 percent as "Partly Free." Only one country in the entire region qualified as free—and that was Israel. Even sub-Saharan Africa fared better, with only 31 percent of its countries falling into the "Not Free" category and another 46 percent assessed as "Partly Free." The MENA region managed to account for nearly one quarter of all of the countries ranked as "Not Free" in the world.[3] In a similar ranking, called the Polity IV Project ratings, which grades countries on a range from +10 (least authoritarian) to −10 (most authoritarian), all of the Arab states received negative scores. Jordan and Yemen scored "best" at −2, with Qatar and Saudi Arabia ranking worst with flat-out −10s. Overall, the regional average for the Muslim Middle East was a stunning −6. Every other region in the world had a positive average, except South Asia, which was still better than −1.[4]

The governments of the Muslim Middle East are composed of either dynastic monarchies or military (or merely militaristic) dictators. The one exception is the bizarre theocratic oligarchy ruling Iran, which is highly authoritarian but ruled over by a collective leadership and does include some pluralistic elements. None of these governments can claim a high degree of legitimacy. Although the monarchies tend to be much better accepted by their people than the dictatorships and do not have to employ anything like the same levels of repression to maintain their authority, none can claim the kind of legitimacy that can come only from a mandate from the masses. A number of the monarchies are of rather recent origin—the Al Sa'ud established Saudi Arabia only in 1932, and the Hashimites were not put on the throne of Jordan by the British until 1921— which means that they cannot even call on venerable tradition to justify their rule. Consequently, these governments must constantly fend off political changes; crush, divert, or buy off domestic unrest; and work assiduously to discredit rivals who might be able to challenge their legitimacy.

As a consequence, paranoia is a guiding principle of all of the Muslim Middle Eastern regimes, to a greater or lesser extent. For the first three decades after World War II, coups and rebellions occurred regularly. Those in power today, however, survived that Darwinian struggle precisely by evolving into what James Quinlivan of RAND has described as largely "coup-proof" regimes that maintain extensive internal security and internal intelligence capabilities to monitor the citizenry for any signs of dissension. The regimes tend to forbid organized opposition, and even where it is technically legal, they wage a relentless campaign to undermine it—locking up opposition leaders on trumped-up charges, preventing them from recruiting or holding meetings, hamstringing their participation in political activities, and preventing them from raising funds. The worst of the Middle Eastern regimes do not even bother with these niceties; they simply kill, banish, or imprison anyone they believe to oppose them politically, even if this opposition is modest and well within their draconian laws. The most extreme version of this system was Saddam Husayn's totalitarian state, which created a "Republic of Fear," in Kanan Makiya's famous phrase, that traumatized Iraqi society and created many of the pathologies that American mistakes unleashed after U.S. military forces toppled Saddam's regime in 2003. While none of the other states of the region matches the horrors of Saddam's Iraq, the nature of the psychological damage that he inflicted on his people is an extreme version of what others in Syria, Libya, Iran, Tunisia, and even Egypt, Yemen, and Saudi Arabia feel thanks to the (somewhat milder) paranoia of their regimes.[5]

Although virtually all of the regimes of the region have adopted modest liberal reforms of one kind or another (to be discussed at greater length later), all remain inherently autocratic. There is little participation by the general populace in matters of policy, let alone actual governance. Especially in the dictatorships (known euphemistically as "republics" and headed equally euphemistically by "presidents"), the chief executive retains all of the prerogatives of ultimate power without any checks on his authority. In the monarchies there tends to be more of a consultative process either with other members of the royal family or, rarer still, with a small circle of trusted technocratic advisers. A number of the monarchies, like Kuwait and Jordan, have also shown themselves to be relatively enlightened in considering what might be best for their people as well as what their people might want.

However, even in the most progressive of the Middle Eastern despotisms, the rulers sit atop huge, sclerotic bureaucracies that often reduce the citizenry to powerlessness in a more direct way than any arbitrary action by the king, amir, or president.[6] In part because of the dysfunctional legal system, which allows the average bureaucrat tremendous license for graft and arbitrariness while confounding the efforts of honest civil servants, and in part because of a governmental social system that seems to promote petty acts of abuse simply as a way of demonstrating authority, many of the region's civil servants compound the injustices inflicted on the people they are meant to serve.

The size of these bureaucracies also contributes to both their unwieldiness and their callousness to the plight of their people. To a considerable extent, the fantastic growth of Middle Eastern government bureaucracies stems from the illegitimacy and paranoia of the regimes, as well as traditional hierarchic relations in the Arab world. As the people of the region began to obtain independence from either the Turks or the Europeans in the first half of the twentieth century, their new regimes began to employ the government bureaucracy as a traditional Middle Eastern patronage network.

The linkage between politics and economics in the Muslim Middle East is one of the defining features of its traditional society, and its most important manifestation is that whoever controls political power invariably uses it to enrich himself and his community—his power base—or any other communities whose loyalty he requires. Providing government jobs to members of one's tribe, family, clan, religious sect, geographic community, or other grouping is both expected and ubiquitous. Eventually, to secure the support of larger segments of the population and virtually the entire "elite" of their country, nearly all of the Middle Eastern states began to guarantee government jobs to anyone with a university degree, so that any good son of the middle class could expect to be rewarded with a reasonably well-paying and prestigious government job upon completion of college.[7]

This practice has had profound consequences for the region. First, in just a few decades Middle Eastern governments ballooned into overstaffed monstrosities that did little but serve their own needs and were uninterested in properly supporting the wider populace and unable to do so.[8] For instance, when the French left Algeria in 1962, there were barely 30,000 Algerian civil servants; by the second half of the 1980s, the Algerian government employed 800,000 people, and ten years later the figure was up to 1.2 million (with another million working at equally unproductive state-owned enterprises). In the forty years after the overthrow of King Farouk in 1952, Egypt's civil service grew from 350,000 to over 4 million and by 2007 had grown to roughly 7 million.[9] The Saudis had only 37,000 government employees in 1962, but by 1999 this force had grown to 900,000 people, representing over 20 percent of the Saudi labor force (i.e., excluding foreigners).[10] In the non-oil-producing states of the region, public sector employment accounts for about 20 percent of total employment on average and exceeded 28 percent in Egypt, 25 percent in Algeria, and 34 percent in Jordan in 1996–2000.[11] More stunning still, the Kuwaiti government employed over 90 percent of its national workforce, while Qatar, Bahrain, Oman, and the UAE all had public sectors that employed 40 to 70 percent of their national labor forces.[12]

Providing jobs in government as a form of payment for political support—let alone guaranteeing a job to all college graduates regardless of their skills, the quality of their education, or what they may have studied—is a recipe for bureaucratic incompetence. A great many government jobs in the Muslim Middle East long ago became sinecures. Many of the people holding them, especially those with the best political connections, just don't show up for work at all. In other cases, they show up late, leave early, and take leave often. There is also a lot of make-work in Middle Eastern bureaucracies to justify creating new positions for new people. This creates the worst of both worlds: many people with important jobs who don't take their responsibilities seriously and so don't do their work, and many others with unimportant jobs (or, worse still, *unnecessary* jobs that simply add to the layers of red tape) who take their jobs very seriously so as to justify their lives and self-respect. Both hinder efficiency. Graft is rampant, especially because government salaries have been declining in real terms in most of the region as demographics outstrip economic performance. In fact, one reason that government jobs are still considered so desirable in the Middle East is that they leave a lot of free time for people to moonlight. Honest, well-meaning, well-qualified, and intelligent people who join the system typically are beaten down by the weight of this monolith and eventually make a Faustian peace with it. The best often do not rise to the top, and fewer still are able to actually change the system in any way.[13]

A third problem with the Middle Eastern patronage approach to government bureaucracy is that it encourages (or at least excuses) the poor educational practices described in the previous chapter. During the decades when Middle Eastern governments guaranteed a civil service job to any university graduate—and civil service jobs were then both remunerative and prestigious—there was no incentive to reform the educational system. It did not matter what you were taught or what you learned. A degree in Arabic or Islamic studies was rewarded exactly the same as a degree in molecular biology or engineering. Nor was one expected to utilize any of the skills learned in the new government job. Indeed, a great many government offices in the Arab world and Iran are occupied by people with the title of "engineer" whom you would not want building a bridge for you. Consequently, there was no incentive to reform education and adapt new teaching methods that could provide the kinds of skills needed in the modern globalized economy.[14] Along similar lines, there was also little incentive for graduates of Arab universities to seek employment (or the skills needed to gain such employment) in the private sector. As a result, between 1976 and 1986, 90 percent of all new jobs created for Egyptians came from either the government or emigration abroad—not a recipe for success.[15]

Many of the Middle Eastern governments put an excessive amount of effort into controlling their economies. In part this is a vestige of earlier, disproven ideologies that argued that central planning promoted economic efficiency, which many of the larger Arab states unfortunately continue to adhere to. Another motive, however, is the paranoia of the regimes—their desire to prevent the emergence of threatening power bases beyond their control (and economic resources can create such rival sources of power) and ensure that those loyal to the regime are well rewarded economically. Some regimes also try to ensure that the segments of the population they consider disloyal are punished by being impoverished. All of this combines with the massive size of government and the nature of the bureaucracies as patronage networks to create a fourth problem, namely, the massive consumption and diversion of national resources by the regimes.[16] In virtually every Muslim Middle Eastern country, the public sector accounts for an absurd percentage of economic activity and wealth. For instance, in 1980, total public expenditures represented 60 percent of Egypt's GDP.[17] Even in Saudi Arabia, where the oil sector contributes so much to the economy, public sector output still accounted for 18 percent of its GDP in 2003.[18]

A final problem created by the size of Middle Eastern bureaucracies and the excessive (and oppressive) role that they play is that they have simply gotten too big and are being forced to cut back. Although for many years the regimes resisted economic pressures to curb the growth of their bureaucracies because of their importance as sources of patronage and in absorbing the large numbers of educated young people entering the job force, eventually they became saturated and simply could not handle any more. Across the region, in the late 1990s and the early twenty-first century, the government bureaucracies became so bloated and such a drain on their societies that the political leadership realized that they had to call a halt.[19] They ended the guarantee of providing a government job for all university graduates, slowed their hiring in general, and in a few cases even allowed natural attrition to reduce the size of the bureaucracies.[20] They began to privatize some of the state-owned enterprises. They began to cap or even cut back on government spending. They allowed government salaries to lag behind inflation, meaning a decline in wages in real terms. Though this is all to the good from a long-term macroeconomic perspective (assuming they stick to it), the immediate impact has been to greatly exacerbate the problems of unemployment, poverty, and frustration among the population—especially among the sons (and daughters) of the middle class who had thought they could count on a government job once they graduated from college. For the first time, Arab university graduates were forced to look for "real" jobs, and many suddenly realized that the traditional educational practices by which they had been taught left them poorly equipped to get jobs—especially the kind of high-paying, high-prestige jobs to which they believed their social status and educational accomplishments entitled them.

As this point suggests, the unusual role of the public sector in the Muslim Middle East has also meant the creation of an unusual middle class, again to the detriment of the people of the region. Both because Arab society considered government jobs prestigious and because for many years the regimes themselves made them easily accessible and financially rewarding to those with education, the Arab societies developed a middle class that consisted largely of civil servants of one kind or another. This was further abetted by the stifling of entrepreneurship and other economic dysfunctions of the Arab states, which made the traditional path of the bourgeoisie much less attractive in the Arab world. The result has been a middle class closely aligned with the prospects of the regime. The middle classes that emerged in Europe, America, Asia, and even Latin America had economic interests that led them to oppose government taxation, regulations, and graft and so led them to demand the curbing of government prerogatives and the devolution of power to the populace. In contrast, much of the Arab middle class sees itself as benefiting from its governments' approach to taxation, regulations, and graft and so has been less willing to demand political change—and less able to do so because it lacks the economic resources and independence of a more traditional middle class.[21]

Another important impact of the paranoia of Middle Eastern regimes on their own economies concerns trade. The importance of authoritarian patronage networks and the regimes' fears of the growth of alternative power centers based on economic power incline them to rely on central planning, government control of manufacturing, and regulation of private industry, both to ensure that money flows to regime loyalists and to ensure that it does not flow to those considered disloyal. For the same reasons, the regimes tend to be inherently skeptical about trade, particularly any kind of international integration, because "Opening up would imply a loss of control and the concomitant ability to rig the local market to the benefit of regime supporters."[22] Real economic integration could be very dangerous because it would introduce powerful market forces into their states that might overpower their carefully constructed political, legal, and economic controls. The idea of creating an "Arab Common Market" fell apart in 1964 because the states of the region simply were not willing to allow greater openness and competition to undermine their patronage networks, political controls, byzantine regulations, and allocation based on political expediency rather than economic rationality—even if it was with their brother Arabs.[23] The net result is that "Lack of competition reduces productivity and therefore demand for knowledge in economic activity. Instead, competitive advantage and the ability to maximize profits derive from favouritism in power structures, manifested in money and politics."[24]

The Ripple Effect of Bad Governance

It is often difficult for Westerners living in a democracy to understand the myriad ways in which Muslim Middle Eastern autocracies have hampered the development of their societies. For instance, state ownership of banks has been a serious inhibiting factor on investment and entrepreneurship because it impedes efficiency and undermines risk analysis. Banks often give loans based on political directives, cronyism, and graft rather than economic viability because their state ownership means that they have no profit motive. Hence, often the *worst* investments are funded.[25] Another example is that many regional states impose high taxes on private enterprise, especially foreign-owned firms—as well as requirements for foreign firms to employ a certain percentage of local nationals—as yet another reward for cronies and a way of limiting unemployment. Unfortunately, all of this acts only as yet another disincentive for foreign firms to do business in the Arab world, especially given the low level of skills endowed by Arab educational systems and the poor work ethic of many of the citiizens of the oil-rich states.[26] The 2003 *Arab Human Development Report* warned:

> Healthy competition still eludes Arab economies where entrenched monopolies dominate several sectors. Uncompetitive firms do not seek out knowledge but instead concentrate on maintaining their traditional commercial footholds. In addition, a lack of transparency and accountability has created a certain overlap between political and business elites. This further reduces the competitive pressure to enhance the use of

knowledge in economic activities in Arab countries, since profits are mostly derived from access to power rather than through economic efficiency and performance.[27]

MANIPULATING INFORMATION

The Arab states and Iran are not exactly known for having a healthy relationship with information. The obsession with security and snuffing out any possible potential opposition plagues every aspect of information diffusion throughout their societies. The most obvious manifestation of this fear is the regime's efforts to control the press, which up until very recently were virtually absolute and even today remain daunting, although important cracks are allowing sunlight to penetrate the darkness.

Muslim Middle Eastern regimes routinely censor newspapers, magazines, TV and radio broadcasts, and even the Internet. However, the regimes go well beyond mere censorship. In fact, much of the media in the Arab world is simply controlled outright by the government, which exercises ultimate authority over whom to hire and fire, who will be promoted or demoted, and who will be allowed to write editorials, broadcast commentary, or even just report. On important issues, the regime lets it be known to their minions in the press how it wants a topic covered—or whether it wants it covered at all—and the press dutifully reports the news just the way that the regimes want it reported. So subservient is most of the Arab press that it rarely requires violence on the part of the regime to intimidate it into doing something; the regimes' control over their livelihoods, coupled with the knowledge that the regime could imprison, beat, or kill them, is more than adequate to ensure that they do as they are told.[28]

There are three important partial exceptions to this rule. The first is Iran, which has a semi-independent media, although this appears to be fading. There is a wide range of newspapers, magazines, Internet sites, and other forms of media in Iran, most of which are privately owned, and this allows for an infinitely more open and vibrant political debate than anywhere else in the Muslim Middle East. Nevertheless, TV and radio remain under the state's control (and are generally no better than their Arab counterparts), many

Iranian media outlets are closely connected to key regime figures and spout their particular viewpoints (although in Iran, regime figures frequently disagree with one another in fundamental ways), and the regime (and hard-line elements within the regime) frequently use violence—beatings, threats, imprisonment, and assassination—to silence journalists whose views they don't like. The second exception is Iraq, which has the freest press in the Arab world. However, as of this writing, Iraq remains trapped in civil strife with a weak government incapable of implementing its decisions without American assistance. Moreover, journalists in Iraq are routinely targeted by warring groups that don't like their coverage, injecting an element of self-censorship. Thus, Iraq's exceptional status is both compromised on the one hand and threatened on the other.

The last exception is the satellite television stations, such as Al Arabiya, MBC (Middle East Broadcasting Centre), Abu Dhabi TV, and the infamous Al Jazeera. For a variety of reasons, particularly the willingness of the government of Qatar to allow Al Jazeera to say what it likes as long as it says nothing bad about the government of Qatar, these channels have been given far greater latitude in covering the news and presenting opinions and information than any other form of Arab media. While there is no question that they still have a long way to go—and Al Jazeera, in particular, still leaves a great deal to be desired as an objective Arab fourth estate—these channels, and again Al Jazeera in particular, keep breaking important new ground in the Arab world. In many ways, they are transforming Arab media. They are willing to criticize other Arab governments, albeit cautiously, and typically do so by measuring the regimes against democratic yardsticks. Indeed, as Hugh Miles, the author of a book on Al Jazeera, has noted, that whipping boy of the Bush 43 administration has probably done more to educate Arabs about democracy than anything else—and certainly more than any program of the U.S. government.[29]

VIRTUALLY NO CORNER of Middle Eastern society is too remote or innocuous for the regimes to ignore when it comes to trying to control information. Indeed, their obsessions with security and patronage dominate the personnel policies, funding, and even research agendas of regional universities, think tanks, research institutes, and the like. The result is often cronies with no competence in under-funded positions doing government-directed research to support the regime's political objectives.[30] "Most laws governing higher education and university scientific research institutes include statutes and regulations that curb the independence of these institutions," in the words of the 2003 *Arab Human Development Report,* "and place them under the direct control of the ruling regimes. . . . Such laws effectively kill the spirit of enquiry and creativity in researchers."[31]

In some ways, pure censorship is not the worst of the ways that the Middle Eastern regimes manipulate information and attempt to prevent its free flow. The regimes of the region know full well that their people are very unhappy for all of the many reasons enumerated above. They also understand that their own policies have played a considerable role in that state of affairs. Unfortunately, one of their responses has been to try to deflect blame from themselves onto others, and typically onto outside powers. Israel has been their favorite, if only because it is so easy. The Arab populaces and, to a lesser extent, the Iranians as well and assume that the Israelis are trying to inflict harm on them in any way imaginable. A distressing number of people in the Muslim Middle East are predisposed to ridiculous conspiracy theories, especially when it comes to the Israelis, and the regime has typically fed their appetite by blaming Israel for its own mistakes and misdeeds.[32] Indeed, the scholar of militant Islam Joyce Davis observes that in mosques throughout the Arab world it is typical to hear clerics daily "lambasting the U.S. and Israel, whom they [blame] for the despotism of Middle Eastern governments, for the lack of jobs, and for the overall misery so prevalent in the Arab world."[33] It is a constant theme of the Arab world, that all of the injustices and miseries of their lives are somehow the fault of Israel.

The need to guard against Israeli (and American) plots and the need to mobilize resources to fight Israel have justified both the draconian security measures that the regimes have employed to suppress internal opposition and maintain their control over the economy and diversion of resources away from the common weal (and to the benefit of the regime and its cronies). Even in the era of Arab-Israeli peacemaking, the regimes have repeatedly deflected calls for political change, from both within and without, by arguing that the need to focus on solving the Arab-Israeli dispute, or prepare for its possible failure, makes it inappropriate to adopt any meaningful changes. The authors of the 2003 *Arab Human Development Report* courageously called attention to this problem, stating, "The threat of Israeli domination also creates a pretext for deferring political and economic reforms in the name of national solidarity against a formidably-armed external aggressor."[34]

Over the past ten to fifteen years, as the conditions in their countries have worsened, the Arab regimes have also increasingly condoned—and at times even sanctioned—diverting popular anger away from themselves and onto the United States, although this has been tricky for them, given their own ties to the United States. What is interesting is that in these conspiracy theories America is always connected to Israel, although sometimes the theory has the United States using Israel as its cat's-paw in the region and other times (occasionally even the same theory) it has Israel using the United States as its puppet. Along similar lines, the Arab regimes have implicitly or explicitly backed a range of terrorist groups against Israel, regional enemies, or even the United States as a way of deflecting popular anger away from themselves.[35]

Over the past sixty years, the regimes of the region have used the threat from Israel, or the wider "civilizational" threat from the West led by the United States, to excuse a wide range of failures and enable them to avoid taking the hard steps necessary to correct them. The specific "threats" they have used to justify their inaction have included colonialism, the Arab-Israeli conflict, the Egyptian–Saudi Arabian war in Yemen in the 1960s, pan-Arabism (considered threatening by the conservative states of the region, like Saudi Arabia), the conflict in Western Sahara between Algeria and Morocco, the Iraq-Iran War of the 1980s, Libya's war with Chad, and the Iraqi invasion of Kuwait, and eventually the U.S.-led invasion of Iraq. The economists Marcus Noland and Howard Pack note, however, that there is nothing obvious or common about this practice despite its prevalence in the Muslim Middle East. Historically, a considerable number of non–Middle Eastern states have done exactly the opposite. In fact, they argue, the most successful governments have typically employed such external challenges to mobilize their populations around wide-ranging reforms to strengthen their economic, educational, legal, and political systems in the interest of acquiring the power to defeat the external threat, whatever its nature. In the Muslim Middle East, the governments have almost invariably done the opposite, using such adversaries or adversity to justify *not* taking action to rationalize the economy, straighten out the legal system, reform the educational process, and overhaul politics—all of which could only undermine the privileged position of the regimes and their supporters.[36]

Stultifying Legal Systems

Rather than providing a set of fair and impartial guidelines for economic and social behavior, the legal codes of the Muslim Middle East are principally a source of further frustration and inertia. The laws and regulations of a great many of these states are vague, at times contradictory, and inaccessible, rendering the overall system highly opaque.[37] This makes it hard for the average person, whether a citizen or a foreigner, to know what is legal and allowed and what is illegal or otherwise forbidden. Moreover, many of the countries of the region operate under a "state of emergency"—a state of martial law, the provisions of which generally invalidate even the most basic civil rights, such as freedom of expression, freedom of association, protection from illegal search and seizure, habeas corpus, and a long list of other basic freedoms.[38]

The legal systems of the Arab states and Iran tend to be badly underfunded and understaffed, especially given the amount of adjudication that is expected of them. Positions within the legal system, particularly the state-run judiciary, are frequently doled out based on connections to the leader of the regime or important figures within it—or even "sold" to the highest bidder. This creates a legal system that is easily and regularly subverted by political intervention, manipulated by more powerful members of the government (as often for personal or financial as for political reasons), and rife with bribery and other forms of corruption.[39] As the 2003 *Arab Human Development*

Report starkly noted, Arab society generally "implements laws only when forced to."[40] The opacity of the system greatly contributes to this tendency: since it is hard to know what the law is and it is frequently suborned by officialdom, it is easy for members of the system to demand payment for a favorable verdict or interpretation of the law. Indeed, the complexity and opacity of regulations and laws make corruption ubiquitous—and even necessary, as the average person generally needs a fixer or a protector to interpret the law and guide the supplicant through the system, including knowing whom to bribe and how much to pay. And, of course, the fixers themselves want to be paid for doing so.[41] Worse still, individuals often need to pay bribes to get a favorable result even if the law is on their side and just as frequently do so to get a favorable result in the event the law is against them. And since it is often hard to know whether a given judgment was correct, it is hard to make the case that corruption was involved based on the outcome.

It is not surprising that most Muslim Middle Easterners have little confidence in their legal systems.[42] In the 2007 Transparency International ranking of corruption around the world, which ranks countries on a scale from 10 (least corrupt) to 1 (most corrupt), the average score for the Muslim Middle East states was a dismal 3.85.[43] (The full results are presented in Table 6.1.) Similarly, in global surveys of issues like the rule of law, judicial independence, the efficiency of the legal system, and the effectiveness of property rights, the states of the Muslim Middle East tend to score very poorly across the board—although some, like Jordan and Kuwait, tend to score better than others.[44] The corruption, arbitrariness, and opacity of their legal systems is an important element in the overall sense of frustration and powerlessness felt by so many Middle Easterners.

Of course, a defective legal system is also very bad for business. A recent study of Middle East businessmen concluded that, in their view, the greatest single obstacle to doing business in the region was the problematic and arbitrary enforcement of laws and regulations.[45] Both the World Bank and Ibrahim Akoum, a senior economist at the Arab Monetary Fund, have noted that as a result of inefficiency, poor regulatory practices, and corruption, the cost of starting a business in the Muslim Middle East is much higher than anywhere else

Table 6.1. Transparency International Corruption
Scores for the Muslim Middle East
(10 Is Least Corrupt, 1 Is Most Corrupt)

COUNTRY	TRANSPARENCY INTERNATIONAL CPI SCORE
Algeria	3.1
Bahrain	5.7
Egypt	3.3
Iran	2.7
Iraq	1.9
Jordan	5.3
Kuwait	4.8
Lebanon	3.6
Libya	2.7
Morocco	3.2
Oman	5.4
Qatar	6.0
Saudi Arabia	3.3
Sudan	2.0
Syria	2.9
Tunisia	4.6
UAE	6.2
Yemen	2.6

Source: Transparency International, "Corruption Perceptions Index, 2006," available at www.transparency.org/policy_research/surveys_indices/cpi/2006, downloaded May 30, 2007.

in the world.[46] The cost expressed as a percentage of GDP per capita ranges from 276 percent in the West Bank and 240 percent in Yemen to 110 percent in Lebanon and 105 percent in Egypt—with only the small Gulf states escaping this trend. By contrast, in Belgium the same average cost is 11 percent, in Brazil 10 percent, in Thailand 6 percent, in Taiwan 6 percent, in Finland 1.2 percent, in

Singapore 1.1 percent, and in Canada just 1 percent. Similarly, in another relevant measure of the impact of the legal system on the economy, the average time it takes to enforce a contract—which is about sixty to seventy-five days in Japan, Singapore, and South Korea and up to about 210 days in Taiwan and Hong Kong—is more than 400 days in virtually all of the Arab states. In extreme cases it can be even worse, averaging as many as 672 days in Syria, 721 days in Lebanon, and 915 days in Sudan.[47] On average, MENA countries ranked behind all other regions except South Asia with regard to business and regulatory reform during the 2003–2006 time frame.[48]

The legal dysfunctions are of course caused, in part, by the region's equally dysfunctional political systems, and these can combine in other ways to hinder economic activity. Because government regulations make it hard to create new businesses and operate them, the meager funds available that are not going into regional oil production tend to go to a relatively small number of politically connected enterprises, not to smaller or midsized businesses or start-ups.[49] Moreover, they make it hard to pull the plug on a failed business. Legal regulations in the Muslim Middle East make declaring bankruptcy extremely difficult, and this too frightens off would-be entrepreneurs and investors: if they have little expectation that they can save most of their assets if a business fails, they become much less willing to take the initial risk.[50]

A Whole That Is Worse Than the Sum of Its Parts

Believe it or not, this chapter and its predecessor provide merely a cursory overview of the many ills that beset the states of the Muslim Middle East. There is a range of other problems that I have not mentioned, and even those I have described have components, effects, and nuances beyond what I have depicted. Of greatest importance, there are critical and complex interactions among these problems that make the sum total far more dangerous and debilitating than a simple listing can convey.

Here is one simple way to understand some of the interactions among some of the most important of these variables. The rapid population growth depresses living standards, creating poverty in some areas and unemployment and underemployment throughout society. The children of the middle class graduate from colleges believing themselves entitled to lives at least as respectable and comfortable as their parents'. But they quickly find that there are no jobs for them—the government is no longer hiring, and there is too little private industry to provide the numbers of white-collar jobs that they want. There are few multinational corporations around—they have mostly been convinced to build their facilities elsewhere by the low worker productivity, poor work habits, labyrinthine government regulations, arbitrariness of government decisions, and corruption and nepotism that plague Middle Eastern economies. The few multinationals around may have brought in foreigners for many or all of their managerial positions, recognizing that the poor-quality education of Arab schools leaves most of the locals unequipped to perform at the level expected in the West or East Asia. So that too is not an option. These young men and women have the choice of taking a low-paying job that does not befit their education, their class, or their aspirations; or they can go back and live off their families and wait (and hope) that a "proper" job comes their way. Regardless of their choice, they are frequently deeply angry and frustrated by this situation, but their leaders do not seem to care. The regime pretends that the problems don't exist or that if they do, they are the fault of the Israelis, the Americans, or someone else, which goes only so far. Certainly there is no path for political redress. These people, their parents, their friends and family have no expectation that they can empower new leadership that would change the country's economic direction. If they try to complain to the bureaucracy, they find that their pleas fall on deaf ears, with the exception of the Mukhabarat, the secret police, who may take note of them as potential troublemakers. Nor is there any expectation that if they are patient, the regime will change its ways and the economy will turn around and provide them with the opportunities they so desperately desire.

In many ways, it is even worse in a material sense for the lower classes, although they may not feel the same sense of frustration and betrayal as the children of the middle class. The lower classes must contend with real poverty. The rapid pace of population growth has produced large numbers of young men and women who cannot be supported on local, rural economies. So they move to the cities to seek work. Most of these young men and women (but mostly men) are not too proud to take any job, but there are not enough jobs of any kind, and those that exist pay very little. Moreover, the rapid pace of urbanization has outstripped the housing market, with the result that finding a decent home or apartment is well beyond the means of the lower classes, even those who are employed. So instead they crowd in squalid shantytowns, some built on graveyards or in other appalling conditions. They too have no sense that their situation is going to improve, because they too feel that their leaders have forgotten them. On the occasions when they have anything to do with the government—whether it is with a policeman, a clerk, or a bank teller (most Middle Eastern banks are state-owned)—they find the civil servants callous and uninterested in their plight. With no legitimate economic or political path out of their situation, many turn to despair, to religion, or, in increasing numbers, to crime. Even in a country where the brutal punishments of Shari'a law are a huge deterrent, crime among young, jobless Saudis rose by 320 percent between 1990 and 1996 and was expected to go up by another 136 percent by 2005, although final statistics have not yet been released.[51]

The result of all of this is, inevitably, widespread disaffection, disillusionment, anger, resentment, frustration, humiliation, and a range of other powerful emotions that infect the population as a collective. It is not hard to understand why the people of the Muslim Middle East are a very angry lot.

PART THREE

—

THE THREATS WE FACE

FROM THE MIDDLE EAST

THE UNITED STATES CANNOT SOLVE ALL OF THE WORLD'S problems. There are a great many people who are unhappy and angry at their lot in life. There are many people living in poverty and many living in worse privation than even the poor of the Muslim Middle East. There are unemployment and underemployment in many countries. There are poor education systems and worse legal systems in other parts of the world. Although the region has an unusual and unhealthy attachment to authoritarianism, it is not the only place where there are still oppressive regimes, and some of the region's autocracies (particularly monarchies like Bahrain, Jordan, Kuwait, Morocco, Qatar, and the UAE) are quite enlightened, as far as autocracies go. Nor is it the only part of the world where people are frightened and mistrustful of modernity and globalization.

Though our better angels should prod us to help the nations of the Middle East deal with their economic, social, and political problems under any set of circumstances, they alone do not justify the kind of strategic focus required for a comprehensive new grand strategy for the region, one that would make America's Middle East policy a centerpiece of our foreign policy for the next several decades.

To make that case requires demonstrating the connection between these underlying problems and serious threats to America's vital national interests. It is because these underlying problems are giving rise to both our greatest immediate threat—terrorist attacks against the United States and American citizens—and potentially our greatest long-term threat—instability in the form of revolutions, civil wars, insurgencies, or coups d'état that could paralyze the global oil market upon which our economy rests—that the United States must finally bite the bullet and adopt a grand strategy that can ameliorate, if not eliminate, these problems over time.

CHAPTER 7

POLITICAL ISLAM

D URING THE TWENTIETH CENTURY, ANY NUMBER OF MUSLIM intellectuals alienated by the many economic, political, and social problems creeping into the Middle East even before World War II began looking for alternative ways to organize their societies and live their lives. Although at different times they espoused a wide variety of ideologies to fill this role, including pan-Arabism, Marxism, and even Fascism, in the end Islamism rose to the top. At its most basic level, Islamism, or political Islam, asserts that all of the answers to the problems of Middle Eastern society can be found in strict adherence to Islamic precepts. Many Islamists explicitly or implicitly argue that the misery of the people of the Muslim Middle East came about because they turned away from the strict preachings of the Qur'an and the Hadiths (the sayings of the Prophet Muhammad), and that salvation can come only from a return to the true path. Indeed, many Middle Easterners would argue that Islamism is not a new idea at all but a return to the way that Muslims have thought about politics for centuries, interrupted only during the twentieth century by the (temporary) ascendancy of secular philosophies that have now been discarded. Islamists also argue that Islam provides a complete set of guidance, not just for how individuals should behave but also for collectives, like nation-states, as well. Thus, political Islam argues that the religion of Islam can and should guide politics, economics, and social structure, not just personal behavior.

Political Islam is not necessarily a threat to the United States, but neither is it unrelated to the threats we face from the Muslim Middle East. For the most part, it is a product, a symptom, of the many problems of the region described in part II. Unfortunately, Islamism has become both a refuge and a motivation for many of the most extreme elements of Middle Eastern society, and so aspects or segments of it have become the vehicles for the phenomena that do threaten the United States and our interests in the Middle East. The first step in understanding these threats is to look at the rise of Islamism across the Middle East.

The Rise of Political Islam

No one has benefited more from the widespread disaffection of the people of the Muslim Middle East created by the toxic combination of stagnant economic, political, legal, and educational systems than have the Islamists.[1] As Fawaz Gerges, a well-known scholar of political Islam, has described it, "Since the 1970s religious fervor in the Arab world has fed into rage over economic, social, and political impotence. More and more Muslims turned to religion for spiritual sustenance and as a refuge from and a response to the seemingly unstoppable Westernization of their societies and oppressive political authoritarianism."[2]

In a superb article in early 2008 describing how the mix of economic, political, and social frustrations of the Muslim Middle East were driving young men to embrace political Islam (and some to go one step beyond, to terrorism), Michael Slackman of *The New York Times* identified the nexus of these problems precisely. "Here in Egypt and across the Middle East," Slackman wrote,

> many young people are being forced to put off marriage, the gateway to independence, sexual activity and societal respect. Stymied by the government's failure to provide adequate schooling and thwarted by an economy without jobs to match their abilities or aspirations, they are stuck in limbo between youth and adulthood. "I can't get a job, I have no money, I can't get married, what can I say?" Mr. Sayyid said one day after becoming so overwhelmed that he refused to go to work, or to go home, and spent the day hiding at a friend's apart-

ment. In their frustration, the young are turning to religion for solace and purpose, pulling their parents and their governments along with them.

As a result, Slackman notes, in 1986 there was one mosque for every 6,031 Egyptians, but by 2005 this had grown to one for every 745 people, despite the fact that the population of the country had doubled during that same time span.[3]

The Islamists' success can be further broken down into five factors. First, they have benefited from the discrediting of a range of other ideologies that previously were far more popular. Islamism is not the first "ism" to sweep the Middle East. For most of the twentieth century, it was pan-Arabism, Arab socialism, and variations on Arab nationalism that dominated Middle Eastern coffee-shop discussions and political platforms. Islamism already existed in those earlier periods—the Ikhwan al-Muslimun, the Muslim Brotherhood, the granddaddy of Islamist movements, was founded in Egypt by Hassan al-Banna in 1928—but it did not dominate the opposition movements then as it does today. There were certainly those who supported the tenets of the Islamists and, in the late 1940s, the Ikhwan may have boasted as many as a million members in Egypt. Yet this still paled beside the force of pan-Arabism, especially with the rise of the charismatic Gamal 'abd al-Nasser as its chief spokesman. Islamism was not a major force in Arab politics until the 1980s and '90s.[4] Today, pan-Arabism, Arab socialism, Arab nationalism, and a host of other ideologies are widely seen as having been refuted by the passage of history. All of them failed to produce the better world they promised, and so, like other failed ideologies, they have faded away. This has allowed Islamism not just to move to the fore but to effectively capture the field simply because it faces so little competition.[5] Indeed, a number of important Islamist leaders were once members of now-discredited secular nationalist movements.[6]

The second reason for the rise of the Islamist groups has been the successful efforts of their great adversaries, the autocratic regimes of the region, to snuff out all other viable opposition movements. In their paranoia, the authoritarian regimes of the region have done a masterful job of quashing every single manifestation of secular opposition: killing or imprisoning leaders, preventing fund-raising and recruiting, breaking up meetings and other attempts to mobilize support or coordinate activities, and attacking these groups in every other way conceivable. Although they certainly employed all of these tactics against the Islamists as well, at times many of the regimes of the region also demonstrated a certain degree of restraint that was often not present when they attacked the secular oppositionists.[7] The regimes often felt it necessary to leave the Islamist groups intact, whereas they were willing to completely exterminate secular opposition movements.

The principal reason for these manifestations of restraint is that in a society as religious as the Muslim Middle East, many of the dictators, amirs, and kings have been wary of taking actions that could be seen (and would inevitably be portrayed by the Islamists) as antireligious. Many of the regimes also rely on the support or even the sanction of their clergy: the Al Sa'uds' claim to legitimacy derives from the continuing seal of approval of their clergy (*ulamah* in Arabic) that they remain true to the principles of their Wahhabi sect of Islam. Similarly, even Husni Mubarak of Egypt, whose autocratic rule in Egypt is so complete that he is often jokingly referred to as "pharaoh," feels it important to have the ulamah of al-Azhar University, the great Sunni theological faculty, supportive of his rule and his actions. Consequently, attacking the Islamists has often entailed greater political risks for the autocrats than suppressing other, secular opposition groups. Many regimes have been loath to take on the Islamists and were willing to tolerate them in ways that they were not willing to tolerate Communists, socialists, anarchists, liberals, and opposing military factions. Again, this is not to say that the regimes did not arrest and harass these groups at times, but the level of oppression was often less than that meted out to their rivals.[8] That said, because of the popular connection between the Islamists and religion, whenever the regimes made the decision that the Islamists needed to be dealt with, they typically went after them root and branch, as Hafiz al-Asad did in crushing the Syrian Ikhwan in 1982.

As disaffection grew across the Arab world in the 1980s and '90s, people became increasingly frustrated by the many problems enumerated in the last chapter and resentful of their governments' inability or unwillingness to remedy them. Seeking an outlet for their grievances, they found only the Islamists—the only opposition movement left standing at just the moment when vast numbers of Arabs began feeling themselves increasingly at odds with the status quo, desirous of change, and looking for an opposition movement that would allow them to channel those sentiments into a political program of some kind.[9]

THERE ARE THREE OTHER elements important to the rise of the Islamist movements as the principal and, to some extent, only viable opposition to the authoritarian Arab regimes today. The first of these is the simple fact that in a society where most people are fairly religious and tend to see their religion as inherently "good," progressive, and a help in their lives, any political movement relying on the language of religion, claiming to be a political outgrowth of that religion, and promising to lead the society to a better, purer, and more righteous time is likely to be very popular.[10] Ted Robert Gurr of the University of Maryland has written that "When traditional norms and social patterns become irrelevant, people are ripe for conversion to new ideologies based on religion or nostalgia for a glorious, mythic past. Ideologies derived from Islamic principles are powerful because, for traditional people in Arab societies, religion covers all aspects of life and gives meaning, counsel, and justifications for actions."[11] This is why Islamism still commanded a fair degree of popularity even during the periods when other ideologies held sway.

Islamism is not Islam and should never be confused with it. There are plenty of devout Muslims who do not believe in even the most modest aspirations of the Islamist movements. However, the Islamists have derived much of their political agenda from their interpretation of Islamic theology and have cloaked their entire political platform in the language of Islam. This makes it appealing to a great many Muslims, especially those who have been praying for an alternative to their current situation for so long.[12]

Over time, the stagnation of the Arab economies has created considerable poverty across the region.[13] The dysfunctionality of the regimes, and particularly the decreasing willingness or ability of their bureaucracies to adapt or improve the lives of the people, have led to breakdowns in the provision of basic services to much of the populace. Ever-larger numbers of people (ever larger because of both population growth and impoverishment) have needed help finding food, shelter, medical services, child care, loans, and a range of other basic needs. The Islamist groups recognized these needs and, led by the example of the Muslim Brotherhood in Egypt and, later, Hizballah in Lebanon, have established large, efficient, and wide-ranging social services of their own. In so doing, they have demonstrated that they are more capable than the regimes, more concerned with the plight of the people, and better able to make concrete improvements in the lives of the people.[14]

Finally, the importance of Islamism's Islamic guise has been boosted further by the reaction to modernity discussed earlier.[15] As noted, part of the fear and frustration that so many Arabs feel comes from the cultural clash between the forces of modernity and their own traditional, and more comfortable and understandable (to them), culture and values. Historically, this clash has often prompted people to retreat into religiosity. So the current problems of the Middle East are not just causing general disaffection with the regimes, thereby causing people to search for any opposition; they are actually helping to channel them toward religious-based opposition. The Islamists benefit not just from the fact that their reliance on the language and ideas of religion make them inherently appealing to a fairly religious population but that some of the factors generating a movement in the direction of opposition movements is causing people to seek out greater religion in their lives. In late 2006 and early 2007, the National Democratic Institute conducted a series of focus groups in Morocco, Lebanon, and Jordan and found that the greatest source of Islamist political appeal in all three countries was the sense that Islamist parties would protect their society from the encroachment of modernity and other cultural threats to their way of life.[16]

The rise of political Islam is not necessarily bad for the region or for the United States. There are a great many varieties in the form, nature, and severity of the philosophies of political Islam practiced by different Islamist parties and movements in the Arab world. Some are entirely reasonable and would be fully consistent with the interests of the United States and, possibly, the best interests of the people of the region.[17]

However, the rise of political Islam has been associated with two important problems, both for the region and for the interests of the United States. The first is that many of the worst extremists in the region, whose pathological hatred of the status quo has led them to embrace mass slaughter as a political program, have chosen to take the same path. They have both attempted to justify their acts of murder through the medium of religion and expressed their vision of the "better world" that they mean their terrorist acts to generate in religious terms. Moreover, because of similarities in aspects of their thinking—in both what they oppose and what they hope to achieve—there is something of a continuum of Islamist movements from the truly moderate to the truly psychotic, with people and groups shifting across it and differences becoming difficult to discern at times. Because of these similarities, many of those on the more moderate end are sympathetic to the zealots and not infrequently have made common cause on specific issues. Thus, the rise of political Islam has generally also helped boost Islamic extremists and has created a larger population whose thinking and views are inherently sympathetic toward certain aspects of the extremists' goals (although typically not their methods).

The second problem with the rise of political Islam is that many elements within the much wider movement do advocate radical regime change and even theological authoritarianism (as in Iran), both of which could easily be inimical to American interests (especially when combined with the strong anti-Americanism prevalent in these movements). At some level, all of the Islamist movements seek fairly fundamental changes to the status quo. Graham Fuller, one of the most thoughtful scholars of the Islamic world, has written:

> Islamists by their very existence pose a challenge to the state, just as any opposition party does. Islamists seek to change the nature of political discourse in the country, to weaken the state monopoly over policy, to influence state decisions, to gain a voice in the conduct of state affairs, to work toward re-

moving or changing powerful elements within the state who oppose them, and ultimately to have a dominant voice or even control over the exercise of state power itself. . . . Overall these developments represent a profound threat to the authoritarian state.[18]

Those Islamist movements that seek a sudden and/or radical transformation of their state, or of the entire Islamic 'Umma, come in many forms. Some have always held these positions, while others were pushed into them by the unwillingness of the current regimes to allow them any meaningful participation in the political process—convincing some that started out willing to work with the regime to conclude that only its overthrow would do. As argued in part I, we don't have to like the governments of the Middle East to secure our interests. However, violent revolutions and sudden regime changes have the potential to create civil wars, interstate wars, and insurgencies, all of which could threaten the flow of Middle Eastern oil. They also harbor the potential to bring to power extremist leaders uninterested in exporting oil or desirous of exporting it for aggressive political and military reasons.

Thus, political Islam is not necessarily a threat to American interests, but neither is it unequivocally benign. That is one of the complexities of the region. There *are* moderate Islamists whose stated agendas seem largely compatible with American interests in the Middle East. They say that they are committed to democracy and are willing to work within a democratic system. They say that though they may not like American policies—or even America itself—they have no desire to go to war with us or gratuitously harm our interests. They say that they respect international law and international agreements and are looking to live in peace with their neighbors. But we cannot be certain how they will behave on any of those scores if they ever achieve supreme power, and some of their rhetoric leaves open the possibility that they will not prove true to their word. Moreover, they are often associated with other, much less moderate Islamist groups, many of whom espouse radical restructurings of their countries' domestic and foreign policies and too many of whom have close ties to terrorist groups.

CHAPTER 8

THE THREAT FROM
INSTABILITY AND INTERNAL STRIFE

UNDERSTANDING HOW THE UNDERLYING PROBLEMS OF THE Middle East have given rise to a wide range of Islamist opposition groups is barely half the matter, however. It is not just that people dislike their circumstances and the regimes they believe perpetuate them. It is also that the underlying problems create powerful emotions, not only driving people into the arms of opposition movements but firing those groups with a determination to seek far-reaching change and empowering individuals who are willing to go to extreme lengths to bring it about. The same emotions that are driving so many people across the Arab world into the arms of various Islamist opposition groups are also creating a more pervasive set of forces that feed a fundamental instability throughout the region. It is this instability that creates the greatest threats to American interests over the long term.

A History of Violence

Anger. Frustration. Disappointment. Disillusionment. Disaffection. Despair. Rage. To a tragic extent, these are the dominant emotions of the people of the Muslim states of the Middle East. They are everywhere in the region. Any traveler can tell you how easy it is to ignite such sentiments even in casual conversation with the mildest housewife, coffee-shop denizen, or businessman. Among the *shabab*, the "youth" of the Arab world, they are ubiquitous. The many economic, educational, legal, social, cultural, and political problems that beset the region have a profound impact on the lives of a great many of its inhabitants, breeding these powerful emotions.[1] Gerges expresses the thought that "It is a terrible time to be a young Muslim. Most feel profoundly depressed, incapable of realizing even their simplest aspirations. They are politically oppressed and socially repressed in their countries of birth, unable to find jobs so they can afford to rent apartments or even get married."[2] In particular, as noted, because the regimes are (not unreasonably) held responsible for so many of the problems that afflict their people and because the same regimes are typically so unwilling and unable to address these problems, much of the frustration, anger, and despair become focused on the regimes themselves.[3] This produces all manner of civil unrest, from riots to terrorist attacks to insurgencies to civil wars to revolutions, with various Islamist groups bound up with and effectively leading every one of them.[4]

Every state in the Muslim Middle East has suffered some form of civil unrest over the past fifteen to twenty years, and many have suffered radical regime changes (like Algeria, Iraq, Sudan, and Palestine) or pervasive domestic violence of one sort or another. For instance:

- From 1991 to 1999 Algeria was consumed by a devastating civil war in which 100,000 to 150,000 people died. The war began when Islamists threatened to take power in fair elections and the government and military canceled the elections and banned the Islamist parties.

- Bahrain has experienced constant problems between its Shi'ah majority and Sunni regime, including riots in 1996 and regular demonstrations since 2004.

- In the 1990s, Islamist and Salafi extremist* groups waged a terrorist insurgency against the government of Egypt that left

---

* The term "Salafi" or "Salafist" refers to Sunni Muslims who believe that the only proper way to live one's life is by strict adherence to the laws laid down in the Qur'an and Hadiths (the sayings of the Prophet Muhammad) as they were practiced by the early community of Muslims during the

over 2,500 people dead.[5] For long stretches of time, major swaths of upper Egypt were effectively beyond government control and under the demesne of the Islamist groups.

- Since the Iranian Revolution, the regime in Tehran has experienced regular ethnic tensions (including riots and terrorist attacks), periodic rioting in major cities to protest government economic and social policies, and a civil conflict with the country's Baluchi minority (among whom unemployment runs at 35 to 40 percent) that has claimed the lives of 3,000 to 4,000 members of the Iranian security services since 1979.[6]

- Even before the current American-made mess, Iraqi society was racked by repeated internal conflicts—including civil wars with the Kurds in every decade since the 1960s, the revolt of the Shi'ah majority after the Gulf War in 1991, and a subsequent protracted insurgency by various Shi'i groups. Although the total numbers of casualties from Iraq's civil wars are unknown, those with the Kurds in the 1980s and 1990s (alone) probably resulted in 100,000 to 250,000 people slaughtered, while the regime's campaign to crush the Shi'ah in 1991 killed another 30,000 to 60,000.[7]

---

time of the Prophet and the first four of his successors (*caliphs* in Arabic) during the seventh century A.D. For this reason, the term is often translated into English as "fundamentalists." The version of Islam propounded by the eighteenth-century Arabian cleric Muhammad ibn 'Abd al-Wahhab, which became the form of Islam practiced throughout the Kingdom of Saudi Arabia, is one common version of Salafism. This version is often referred to as "Wahhabism," a term that Saudis consider derogatory, preferring "Salafism" instead. Usama bin Ladin's al-Qa'ida and its affiliated and component groups are all Salafists of one kind or another. They are often referred to as "Salafi Jihadists," the name that they themselves prefer because it ennobles their actions. The term "jihad" does not mean "holy war," as many Westerners mistakenly believe; in fact, it means simply "to struggle (in the way of God)," referring to the struggle of all Muslims to be good people and to live by God's laws. In the past, we have typically allowed terrorist groups to name themselves—the Israelis certainly do not think of the Palestinian terrorists as being a "Palestine Liberation Organization," nor did the British think of Irish terrorists as constituting an "Irish Republican Army." In every case, the people being attacked by the terrorists considered them bandits, criminals, murderers, and other more descriptive terms, but the convention has always been to employ the term used by the terrorist group itself. Nevertheless, many Muslim friends have implored me not to perpetuate the myth that what bin Ladin and his ilk are doing is somehow condoned by Islam by referring to them as they would like to be known—using the salutary term "jihad" to excuse their acts of murder. Consequently, throughout this book I have chosen to call them "Salafi extremists" or "Salafi terrorists," which is a more accurate descriptor in any event.

- Jordan has had to deal with periodic demonstrations and riots, especially in 1989, 1998, and again in 2002, inspired at times by militant Islamist groups but growing out of popular unhappiness with its economy and political stagnation.[8] Now Amman must also deal with a growing threat from Salafi terrorists, highlighted by the thwarted "Millennium" terrorist plot set for 2000 and the tragic November 2005 hotel bombings.

- Lebanon suffered through a terrible civil war among various Christian, Sunni, and Shi'i sects from 1975 to 1990, resulting in the deaths of roughly 150,000 out of a population of 2.8 million.[9] Violence never fully ceased in Lebanon, although it tapered off dramatically. Today, the country teeters on the brink of renewed civil war.

- Aside from Muammar Qadhafi's many quixotic and humiliating foreign military adventures throughout the 1970s and '80s, beginning in the 1990s, the Libyan regime has had to deal with numerous tribal revolts, as well as a nascent insurgency/terrorist campaign by various Islamist and Salafi extremist groups.

- Morocco too has a local al-Qa'ida terrorism problem, with the best-known incidents the series of attacks in May 2003 and April 2007 on Western and Jewish targets in Casablanca.

- Even setting aside the constant violence between the Israelis and Palestinians, the Palestinians have had a stormy existence. In particular, since the death of Yasser Arafat in 2004, there have been numerous intra-Palestinian confrontations, many leading to violence. The worst so far has been the 2007 fighting, in which Arafat's party, Fatah, was savaged by the Islamist group Hamas and stripped of its rule in the Gaza Strip.

- Saudi Arabia itself has experienced periodic unrest and even violence both from, and directed against, its Shi'ah community since the Iranian Revolution. Salafi extremists have also been a problem for the kingdom since 1979, when one group took over the Grand Mosque in Mecca until its members were killed in a bloody shoot-out with Saudi security forces. In 1994, Salafi extremist clergy attempted to spark a revolt in the heartland town of Buraydah and its environs, which succeeded in creating a series of unprecedented antigovernment riots. And, of couse, al-Qa'ida has mounted numerous terrorist attacks against Saudi and Western targets in the kingdom over the years.

• Sudan has had very few years since becoming independent in 1956 when it has not been in a state of civil war. The Arab Islamic north (which controls the government) waged a civil war against the black Christian–animist south from 1956 to 1972 that resumed again in 1983 and did not burn out till 2005. At that point it was superseded by the conflict between government-backed forces and the Darfur tribes, which has resulted in 200,000 to 400,000 people slaughtered in a genocidal campaign.

• From 1976 to 1982, Syria was racked by civil war, with elements of its majority Sunni community, led by the Islamist Muslim Brotherhood, rebelling against the minority Alawi regime—and effectively seizing control of several northwestern Syrian cities until the government retook them forcibly in 1982 in a brutal campaign that resulted in the deaths of 20,000 to 40,000 people.

• The United Arab Emirates (UAE), long one of the Gulf region's islands of tranquillity, has recently begun to experience labor unrest problems with its large community of South and Southeast Asian expatriate workers imported to perform the menial jobs that Emiratis will not do themselves.[10]

• Yemen experienced a civil war between its north and south in 1994 in which roughly 10,000 people died. In addition, the Yemeni regime has had to battle numerous tribal revolts and insurgencies and, since the early 1990s, a growing Salafi extremist presence, highlighted by the attack on the U.S.S. *Cole* in August 2000.

Altogether, since 1980, the eighteen countries that make up the Muslim Middle East have experienced six major civil wars (Algeria, Iraq, Lebanon, Sudan, Syria, Yemen) and four smaller ones (Egypt, Iran, Libya, and the Palestinians). This is a remarkably violent and bloody record, demonstrating that internal conflict has become commonplace in much of the Muslim Middle East. Although the scale and duration of the violence have varied considerably from country to country, the number of states that have experienced major, protracted civil strife is striking and speaks to the impact of the pervasive sense of anger and grievance that characterizes modern Muslim Middle Eastern societies. There are a lot of people eager to see fundamental change in their societies and willing to employ (or condone) violence to get it. With that kind of kindling lying around, it does not take much for someone or something to strike the match that sets it all ablaze.

Of course, not all of that anger and frustration is unleashed on the regimes. A sizable slice is reserved for the United States and Israel. Still another portion is focused on minorities. For instance, as circumstances in Egypt have deteriorated, Egyptian Muslims have increasingly blamed the Christian Copts for their misery, indulging in persecution and even violence. One journalist reported in 2006 that "Increasingly radicalized Muslims, facing growing unemployment, have found it easier to take out their anger on the small Christian minority than confront the government of President Hosni Mubarak."[11] Egyptians are angry because of their economic circumstances; they blame the government, but they know that the regime does not care and will crush them brutally if they protest, so they take out their anger on someone else—a minority group unable to defend itself effectively. It is an unfortunate pattern of behavior but one with a long historical pedigree. It is worth adding that the incidents in Egypt in 2006 were really not about religion. In the eyes of a range of Egyptian political experts, "Those who have been clashing with Copts are in general people who don't pray except Fridays (the

Muslim day of prayer). Some have never set a foot in the mosque. Their motives arise from a deformed popular culture. They are the marginalized in society because of unemployment and economic hardships."[12]

The Roots of Instability

None of this should be surprising. There is a long historical record of the same kind of economic, social, and political problems that currently afflict the Middle East producing all sorts of instability, including civil wars and revolutions. The scholar Jack Goldstone concluded in his landmark work on revolutions in history that stagnant economic conditions coupled with high population growth are one of the most common causes of rebellion and revolution.[13] A recent study of the "Troubles" in Northern Ireland found that "Economic disparity between Catholics and Protestants was a principal aggravating factor in touching off and sustaining violence in Northern Ireland." It also concluded that "chronic and pervasive unemployment" was an important cause of the militancy of the Catholic community and that increased prosperity was a key feature in bringing the conflict to an end.[14] Similarly, an economic study of civil wars concluded, among other things, that "Male secondary education enrollment, per capita income and the growth rate" were key determinants of the likelihood of large-scale internal violence.[15]

Consequently, it is not surprising to find that the poor state of the Arab (and Iranian) economies, especially when combined with the effects of the other underlying problems, is producing this kind of violence. Looking back on the rise of political Islam and Salafi terrorism, the great French Arabist Gilles Kepel has written that "the region suffered from a disastrous combination of overpopulation, low employment and low pay, and deficient access to education and modern communications. This situation created fertile conditions for conflict, particularly over control of the dominant ideological system that maintained the region's political and social balance: Islam."[16] In a similar vein, Alan Richards warns that "Economic stagnation undermines regime legitimacy and even, in some cases, the capacity to govern. The problem is particularly serious because stagnant economies cannot provide adequate jobs for the rising tide of young job seekers. The mixture of regime incapacity, rising unemployment and poverty, and very young populations is politically highly volatile."[17]

Indeed, unemployment and underemployment are often the most dangerous forces in this mix. Widespread unemployment creates widespread disaffection, anger, and frustration. This in turn creates a large pool of people who are looking for change in the society and are often vulnerable to being recruited by those seeking to overturn the extant order by force. Unemployment typically afflicts the working class the most, while underemployment often has the greatest impact on the middle classes—whose education and sense of socioeconomic entitlement creates frustration when they cannot secure the kinds of jobs they believe they deserve.[18] Academic studies have consistently found that employment may be the most important determinant of overall happiness, as it allows an individual to support himself/herself, furnishes a sense of self-respect, and includes the individual in an important network of supportive social contacts.[19]

As one example of the impact of this phenomenon in the Muslim Middle East, frequent complaints of those who voted for Hamas in the January 2006 Palestinian elections—a most unwelcome "regime change" for the United States and its allies and one that has produced civil strife among the Palestinians—were unemployment and the need to bribe Fatah officials to get a government job.[20] Similarly, the crippling unemployment epidemic in Iraq after the fall of Saddam's regime (estimated at 50 to 80 percent depending on the community and other conditions) was one of the most important factors in the rise of vicious Sunni groups like al-Qa'ida in Iraq and their Shi'i counterparts, like Jaysh al-Mahdi, in the years after the invasion. Both groups, and their many clones and rivals, are overwhelmingly made up of dispossessed, angry, and unemployed young men who join up with the insurgents and militias for the money, the camaraderie, the sense of adventure, and the desire to lash out at those they believe have caused their unhappiness.[21]

Though the economic conditions of the Muslim Middle East are important in producing widespread anger and frustration and the violence that typically goes along with those sentiments, the problem is considerably magnified by the interrelated political problems of the region. It is not just that so many Arabs and Iranians are unhappy or disappointed with their economic circumstances, it is also that they have a strong sense (largely correct) that their governments are complicit in their misery. And this fuels the raw emotions dominating contemporary Middle Eastern society.[22] "Many Arabs believe they could do no worse than current leaders such as Mubarak," according to Joyce Davis, a journalist and author on Islamic radicalism, "who have kept their world in a state of perpetual decline, stifling dissent, rigging elections when they take place, lining the pockets of their cronies, and maintaining a system that provides few opportunities for smart, ambitious, and increasingly better-educated youths."[23] Former Jordanian Prime Minister Taher Masri has warned that the desire for more-democratic governments on the part of so many Arabs—because they want governments that are more responsive to the needs of the people—and the regimes' unwillingness to give it to them are paradoxically driving a great many into the arms of opposition groups, whose commitment to revolutionary change often exceeds their commitment to democracy.[24]

In many ways, the key intersection between the economic and political grievances of so many Arabs (and Iranians) lies in the wide gap between their expectations and their realities. Going back to Crane Brinton's pathbreaking work on revolutions, the greatest civil unrest typically occurs when large numbers of people feel that they are owed or have been promised a better life but are then deprived of it—either because the expectation was never realistic or because of changed circumstances. Revolutions and other internal revolts are typically the products of hope denied.[25]

As explained in chapters 5 and 6, this is precisely the circumstance of the Muslim Middle East today. The vast expansion of education in the Arab world has ignited the hopes of a prosperous middle-class existence in far more young people than the economies of the region can support. For the poor, the situation is inevitably worse: though their expectations are generally lower, their more precarious starting circumstances often mean that their frustration comes from being unable to find a job at all, which means they cannot support a family or even find decent housing.[26] The Israeli scholar Emmanuel Sivan addressed this same phenomenon in 1998 with the conclusion that "The 'retreating state' of the 1990s thus creates disgruntled citizens by the legion: university graduates no longer assured of a government job; workers barely able to eke out a living, let alone save for a dowry and establish a family; or masses of recent rural migrants who lack such basics as shelter. All these groups provide a pool of possible recruits for Islamic associations."[27] It is this sense of unfulfilled expectations and what the social scientist Caroline Ziemke calls "relative deprivation" that has fueled much of the Islamist anger at the government and the instability that this in turn has caused.[28]

The gap between expectations and reality in the Muslim Middle East also applies in a regional, strategic, or "macro" sense. A great many Arabs and Iranians understand their relative economic, diplomatic, and military weight in the world and are angry and humiliated that they are so weak. These tend to be proud people, virtually all of whom can look back on their history to earlier eras in which their nation (whichever one it happens to be) was among the strongest and richest on Earth.[29] They don't just wonder why their economies lag so far behind those of so many other (infidel) nations, they resent it. They likewise smolder when they see so many other countries in East Asia, Eastern Europe, South America, and even Africa achieve economic prosperity so much more quickly than they have. Decades earlier, many of the countries of those regions were poorer and less developed than the Middle Eastern states, but now they are more prosperous, and their citizens seem to live better than a great many Arabs and Iranians do. Moreover, this macrolevel sense of inequality and unfulfilled expectations is taken as another symptom of the incompetence and corruption of their governments—and another manifestation of the machinations of the United States (and Israel). Thus, anger at their own personal disappointment is exacerbated by a larger sense that their nation and their wider community are falling behind so many others because of the actions of their own corrupt and callous leaders and the plots of their external enemies.[30]

A Darker Future?

As bad as things are today for the countries of the Muslim Middle East, trends suggest that the situation is unlikely to improve anytime soon and could deteriorate still further. As population growth and its attendant "youth bulge" spur urbanization, the likely increases in unemployment and underemployment that will ensue and the decline in living standards (both relative and absolute) discussed in chapter 5 have the potential to create a lethal mixture for the states of the Muslim Middle East. All of these developments have historically produced internal violence, often including extreme forms such as civil war and revolution. They unquestionably have been doing so in the Middle East over the past several decades, and they doubtless will continue to do so for some time to come.

For example, in societies ill equipped to handle rapid population growth, like the Muslim Middle East, "the predominance of young adults constitutes a social challenge and a political hazard. This is particularly the case when employment opportunities are scarce and large numbers of young men feel frustrated in their search for status and livelihood. The evidence that a large proportion of young people is associated with the outbreak of political violence and warfare is among the best-documented literature on population and conflict."[31] This was one of the central conclusions of a seminal study of 182 countries between 1970 and 2000 tracing the relationship between civil unrest (and civil war) and demographic factors conducted by Robert P. Cincotta, Robert Engelman, and Daniele Anastasion. They found that countries with high proportions of young people have a high likelihood of becoming involved in civil conflict.[32] As the authors explained, "Why are youth bulges so volatile? The short answer is: too many young men with not enough to do."[33] This should not be surprising: young men are both deductively and statistically more prone to violence than are women or older men.[34] In fact, "A wealth of historical studies indicates that cycles of rebellion and military campaigns in the early-modern and modern world tended to coincide with periods when young adults comprised an unusually large proportion of the population."[35]

Specifically, the Cincotta, Engelman, and Anastasion study found that "Countries in which young adults [those aged 15 to 29] comprised more than 40 percent of the adult population were more than twice as likely as countries with lower proportions to experience an outbreak of civil conflict."[36] Overall, they found that between 1990 and 2000, 33 percent of states with a youth population of 40 percent or higher experienced civil conflict, compared to just 18 percent of those with a youth population of 30 to 39 percent and 11 percent of those with a youth population of less than 11 percent.[37] As Table 8.1 illustrates, in 2002, only the UAE and Qatar had youth populations that made up less than 30 percent of the population, and most of the Muslim Middle Eastern countries, including all of the biggest, most populous, and most important states, were over the 40 percent "danger" threshold. Although population growth rates are finally beginning to decline in the Middle East, they remain extremely high and the impact of even this diminution will not be felt for decades.[38] By 2025, the ILO estimates, 45 percent of the regional population as a whole will still be under twenty-five years old.[39] Indeed, 40 percent of the current population is under fifteen years of age, and these make up the next wave of the ongoing youth bulge, meaning that this dangerous set of pressures is likely to persist for years to come.[40]

Like rapid population growth in general and youth bulges specifically, rapid urbanization such as that taking place in the Muslim Middle East has been tied to problems of internal unrest. Rapidly growing cities breed violence and rebellion. Again, the mental leap from squalid, overcrowded living conditions without adequate sanitation, clean water, medical care, and even food—let alone satisfying jobs—to the kind of anger and frustration that contribute to riots, revolts, acts of terrorism, and even civil wars is not hard to make.[41] Alan Richards notes that these problems have already manifested themselves in the Middle Eastern states: "As rural poverty is 'exported' to the cities, not only do the number of potential militants rise, but also the difficulties of regimes in dealing with urban problems mount. Rapidly growing numbers of poor urban dwellers multiply the demands on urban administration. In an age of increasingly scarce governmental resources, meeting these demands becomes in-

Table 8.1. Percentage of the Population of Muslim Middle East States 15–29 Years Old in 2002

COUNTRY	% OF POPULATION 15–29 YEARS OLD
Algeria	45.1
Bahrain	35.0
Egypt	44.2
Iran	49.1
Iraq	47.5
Kuwait	31.6
Lebanon	38.0
Libya	46.4
Morocco	42.5
Oman	44.0
Palestinian territories	48.8
Qatar	26.7
Saudi Arabia	43.6
Sudan	45.3
Syria	50.5
Tunisia	40.8
UAE	29.9
Yemen	53.2

Source: Robert P. Cincotta, Robert Engelman, and Daniele Anastasion, The Security Demographic: Population and Civil Conflict After the Cold War (Washington, D.C.: Population Action International, 2003), pp. 96–101.

creasingly difficult. Such government failure further delegitimizes the governments in the eyes of both the poor urbanites themselves plus the intellectuals and students."[42] Indeed, rapid urbanization under similar conditions was an important (but hardly the only) element in the outbreak of the Iranian Revolution in 1978.[43]

Cincotta, Engelman, and Anastasion again found high correlations between rapid urbanization and civil strife, just as they did with youth bulges. In their words, "States with urban population growth rates above 4 percent were about twice as likely to sustain the outbreak of a civil conflict as countries with lower rates."[44] Of the fifteen Middle Eastern countries depicted in Table 8.1, eleven have urban population growth rates of 4 percent or higher. As a result, the Cincotta, Engelman, and Anastasion study rated Iran and every Arab state other than the UAE as suffering from either "high" or "extreme" demographic stress in 2002.[45]

The Prerevolutionary Middle East

The nature and extent of the many economic, social, cultural, and political problems in the Muslim Middle East has created a dangerous state of affairs: nearly every one of the Arab countries and Iran is in a "prerevolutionary" state to a greater or lesser extent. This means that in virtually every one of these countries the sense of grievance among the population is such that it is giving rise to revolutionary political groups that seek to overturn the current political order, that these groups receive enough support from the population (much of it merely passive support) that their numbers are growing and their activities create real problems for the regime, and that with the right admixture of other factors—a charismatic leader, a rallying event, a significant loss in the regime's power or willingness to employ that power—the situation could produce a true revolution.[46] This is arguably the most important threat to American interests in the Middle East, and it is a problem largely, if not entirely, derived from the underlying economic, social, and political problems of the region.

Having made such a bold statement, let me add some important caveats. First, some of the Arab states are in a far less precarious position than others. Second, a lot of countries over the course of history have existed in a prerevolutionary state for very long periods of time. Very few actually fell victim to successful revolutions. As the sociologist Theda Skocpol has pointed out, successful revolutions are heavily dependent on the regime losing either the willingness or the ability to employ repression, which is actually a rarity in history and therefore accounts for the small number of successful social revolutions despite the wide prevalence of prerevolutionary conditions.[47] And few of the Arab states appear to have lost either the will or the ability to employ large-scale repression.

However, just because few countries that slipped into prerevolutionary states suffered successful revolutions does not mean that they ended well. Many of these regimes were nevertheless subverted or overthrown as a direct or indirect result of the pressure from revolutionaries and other discontented domestic groups. During the 1950s, the Iraqi and Egyptian monarchies were both toppled in coups that were enabled by widespread internal unrest similar to the current conditions. In fact, both of these coups were actually hailed as "revolutions" because they came in the context of prerevolutionary states in which the majority of their populaces were eager to see the *anciens régimes* removed one way or another. Other regimes facing prerevolutionary states have been crippled by urban rioting, insurgencies, and civil wars, which in many cases produced the fall of the regime. The Chinese Communists came to power not through a classic revolution, as occurred in France, Russia, and Iran, but through a protracted insurgency against the Guomindang regime, which—thanks also to the regime's corruption and its weakness after World War II—produced its collapse. Indeed, far more regimes have fallen when a revolutionary movement could not mount a successful revolution but instead sparked a civil war or an insurgency (which in turn caused the fall of the regime) than have fallen to the archetypal social revolution along the lines of the French and Russian models. Other regimes have been transformed over time by constant internal strife, like the English government in the nineteenth century. Still others, such as South Vietnam and East Pakistan (now Bangladesh), were so weakened by internal problems that they were conquered by predatory neighbors. In other words, being in a prerevolutionary state does not mean that the sky is falling, but neither is it something to be cavalierly dismissed. Nations in a prerevolutionary state have very serious internal problems that, even if they do not provoke a successful revolution, can nevertheless convulse the country for many decades and/or cause the fall of the regime in myriad ways.

THE GROWTH OF REVOLUTIONARY PARTIES
IN THE MUSLIM MIDDLE EAST

Though we typically think of both Islamist political parties and the various Salafi extremist groups as being opposition parties and terrorists, it is important to recognize them first and foremost as revolutionary groups. Many of the Islamist groups and all of the Salafi extremists are not your garden-variety political party. They are not analogous to the Green Party or European social democrats waiting their turn to take power in a democratic system. Many of the Islamists and all of the Salafi extremists seek a radical reconstitution of the political system from its current form, and a number (including all of the Salafi extremists) have indicated a willingness to do so through violence. Keeping these basic points in mind puts the constant strife of the Muslim Middle East into a wholly different perspective.

Sheri Berman, one of the most insightful political scientists of her generation, was among the first to draw attention to this critical point.[48] Writing specifically about the situation in Egypt, she explained that

> What the case demonstrates is that the necessary precondition for the rise of Islamism has been the declining efficacy and legitimacy of the Egyptian state—just as many leading theories on revolutions would predict. This development alone, however, has not been sufficient to turn a potentially revolutionary situation into a successful revolution. Instead, what has occurred in Egypt and other parts of the Arab world is a peculiar kind of stalemate in which the existing regime retains political power while ceding substantial control over the societal and cultural spheres to the revolutionary challenger.[49]

Professor Halid Duran has made virtually the same point in observing that "Islamism is not a reaction of people feeling a loss of religious meaning, but a reaction to a sense of loss in the political sphere. It is a thrust for power, an attempt to conquer the state, not to regain independence for religion, and, least of all, independence for indvidual fate."[50] Both Gilles Kepel and Peter Bergen, one of the foremost authorities on bin Ladin and al-Qa'ida, have similarly argued that the constant bloodshed in Egypt in the 1980s and 1990s was an effort by various Islamist and Salafi extremist groups to inspire an Islamic revolution. Bin Ladin and his followers were effectively taking a page from the Marxist revolutionary Carlos Marighella's famous "handbook," *The Minimanual of the Urban Guerrilla,* and employing insurgent warfare, civil disobedience, riots, and terrorism to force the regime to crack down in such a way that it would (they hoped) cause the people to rise up against the government and overthrow it.[51] The fact that they have failed to do so (so far) should not obscure their ultimate goals.

Other scholars have echoed Berman in pointing out that the range of economic, social, and political problems of the region has collectively created widespread grassroots support for significant change in the status quo, which in turn has empowered a variety of political parties and militant groups, all of them advocating such changes— and often very radical versions of such changes.[52] Again, this is a pattern typical of previous revolutions and revolutionary movements. The groups fostered by the underlying political grievances often advocate a more radical agenda than do the bulk of their followers. In 1916, if you had polled Russians as to what they wanted in terms of political change, very few would have demanded communism. If you had polled Iranians regarding what kind of political system they would have liked to see established in 1977, few would have suggested the theological state that Khomeini imposed after 1979. Few Frenchmen would have demanded Robespierre's "Terror," nor did many American colonists want a complete break from England in the early 1770s. It is most often the case that the people in a prerevolutionary state simply want change, often of a fairly modest variety (at least in their eyes); however, this desire leads them to support leaders who promise it but who often harbor more radical aspirations.

The terrorism expert Martha Crenshaw and the Middle East scholar Michael Doran have both noted that the Islamists are waging civil wars in their own countries and that it is "spillover" from these civil wars that has led to terrorist attacks against the United States and Europeans.[53] This too buttresses the view of the Islamists as revolutionaries, because many civil wars are failed or ongoing bids at revolution. Those who start the civil war are rarely seeking the war itself; most often they seek some radical change in the political status quo (a new government, a new ruler, seceding from the existing state), and the civil war ensues when they are blocked by other groups and/or the government, which oppose the changes they seek. This is effectively the story of the Chinese civil war and its Communist "revolution." Mao and the Chinese Communist Party (CCP) sought to overthrow the Guomindang regime but were not able to imitate the Leninist model and so turned to a protracted guerrilla war against the regime instead. Eventually, after several decades of civil war (and World War II), the CCP prevailed and was able to radically transform China, as it had always wanted.

Indeed, the intellectual godfather of the Islamists and Salafi extremists was an Egyptian philosopher named Sayyid Qutb, whose work plays effectively the same role for them as the writings of Marx and Engels played for any number of leftist groups in the nineteenth and twentieth centuries. Sayyid Qutb explicitly called for the creation of a Leninist-style vanguard party of Islamists that would lead the way in a violent struggle to overthrow the governments of the region, all of which he branded *jahili*—"unbelievers" in Arabic, effectively declaring them to be pagans or apostates.[54] In the same vein, he argued that Egypt and the entire Arab world were living in the Dar al-Harb, the House of War, in which governments must be overthrown because they are un-Islamic and societies must be rebuilt completely in line with the teachings of Islam.[55] Qutb's most famous work, *Milestones,* was essentially just "a blueprint for destroying Nasser's regime—and by implication any regime deemed un-Islamic."[56] Not surprisingly, the political psychologist Jerrold Post and the terrorism expert Ehud Sprinzak have reported that in interviewing Middle Eastern terrorists, they found that many of them said that their heroes were revolutionaries like Che Guevara or Fidel Castro, whom they sought to emulate.[57]

There is no question that Usama bin Ladin, Ayman az-Zawahiri, and the other leaders of al-Qa'ida see themselves as constituting a Leninist vanguard party determined to overthrow the jahili governments of the Arab world, if not the entire Muslim 'Umma. Bin Ladin has applied Qutb's logic for overthrowing Nasser's regime in Egypt to his own homeland of Saudi Arabia, repeatedly calling for and attempting to spark a revolution there to oust the Al Sa'ud.[58] Of course, so far he has failed to do so, just as his Egyptian compatriots failed to topple Mubarak. In fact, it was this failure that prompted a number of bin Ladin's lieutenants to flee Egypt and join him in Afghanistan in the late 1990s. The most important of bin Ladin's Egyptian compatriots, Ayman az-Zawahiri, said himself, in his book *Knights Under the Prophet's Banner*, that al-Qa'ida's rationale for attacking the United States was that it had failed to spark a revolution by directly attacking the Arab governments. So instead, it had decided to try to attack the power it saw as standing behind the regional regimes in the hope that if it could weaken American power in the region, this would undermine the strength of the Arab regimes and leave them vulnerable to a new revolution.[59] After bin Ladin declared war on the United States in 1996, he told interviewers that "if the U.S. is beheaded, the Arab kingdoms will wither away," and as a result the Al Sa'ud would "suffer the same fate as the Shah of Persia."[60] In short, al-Qa'ida's decision to attack the "far enemy" (the United States) was intended to be an indirect method of accomplishing the Islamic revolution against the "near enemy" (the Arab regimes and, most important, Saudi Arabia), which is its paramount goal.

Nor is al-Qa'ida the only Sunni Islamist group to openly embrace revolutionary goals. In Libya, for example, Muammar Qadhafi is increasingly challenged by a broad range of Islamist and Salafi extremist factions, led by the Libyan Islamist Fighting Group (LIFG), the Muslim Brotherhood, and the Islamic Liberation Party (ILP). Though the LIFG has largely stuck to terrorism to try to bring down Qadhafi's regime, the ILP and the Ikhwan have followed the models of Hizballah and the Egyptian Muslim Brotherhood by creating efficient social welfare programs, demonstrating competence and integrity in responding to the needs of the people (which places them in stark contrast with the incompetence and corruption of the regime), and demanding change—via political reform or other means. Indeed, the rapid growth of these threats to Qadhafi's reign was an important element in his decision, after 2002, to give up his support for terrorism and pursuit of weapons of mass destruction so that the United Nations would lift its sanctions and allow Libya back into the good graces of the international community.[61]

Although it is composed of Shi'i Islamists (unlike the Sunnis of al-Qa'ida and other Salafi groups), Hizballah is another good example of an Islamist group whose objectives are ultimately revolutionary. Hizballah was founded by a number of Shi'i theologians who had been students and colleagues of Ayatollah Khomeini during his long exile in the *hawza* (seminary) of Najaf. When Khomeini seized control of the Iranian revolution from the eclectic group of secularists, leftists, and moderate Islamists who had triggered it and converted it into an Islamic revolution that went on to overthrow the shah, he electrified his old Lebanese followers. With the assistance of a couple thousand of Khomeini's new Revolutionary Guards, they set about forging the most radical Shi'i militias in Lebanon into a new organization, eventually called Hizballah, whose principal aim was to bring Khomeini's Islamic revolution to Lebanon. Even twenty-five years later, and despite the fact that Hizballah has become a major player in secular Lebanese politics, Hizballah's leadership continues to acknowledge Khomeini's successor as Iran's supreme leader, 'Ali Khamene'i, as their own ultimate overlord. For the hard core of Hizballah's leadership, dominating Lebanon—even destroying Israel—would not satisfy their aspirations; they still seek, perhaps only distantly, to bring about the "liberation" of the entire 'Umma that Khomeini preached.[62]

Hizballah is not the only Islamist group to be inspired by the Iranian Revolution. Though the many Sunni Islamist and Salafi extremist groups did not care for Iran's Shi'ism—let alone Khomeini's novel interpretation of it—they were enormously admiring of what the imam had accomplished.[63] He had done what they had only dreamt of. What's more, he had done it to the most feared autocrat in the Middle East: the shah of Iran, America's closest Muslim ally, the second leading oil producer, and the monarch who had commanded a terrifying secret police and the second most powerful military in the region. In fact, even before Lebanon's Shi'ah created Hizballah, a group of Sunni extremists was the first to try to emulate Khomeini by seizing the Grand Mosque of Mecca on November 20, 1979, in the midst of the *hajj,* the sacred Muslim pilgrimage to

Mecca. The rebels demanded the end of favorable terms for foreign oil companies, the withdrawal of all foreign military advisers from the country, the elimination of government corruption, and a return to the canons of what they considered "genuine" Islam.[64] Since then, Islamists of every stripe and a wide range of Salafi extremists have expressed admiration for and drawn inspiration from Khomeini's feat. The Iranian Revolution "was an inspiration to all Muslims who wished for radical change and for whom American influence in the Middle East was a Satanic force."[65]

HISTORICAL PARALLELS

The Iranian Revolution is a particularly appropriate source of inspiration for the region's other would-be revolutionaries because of the similarities between the underlying conditions in their countries and those that gave rise to revolution in Iran. The ultimate causes of the Iranian Revolution are complex, and I can present only a brief overview here.[66] Iran's economic situation, like that of most of the Arab states today, appeared good at a superficial level but was disastrous when examined closely. The nation was making phenomenal amounts of money from oil, generating apparently high GDP per capita and foreign exchange and trade balances. In addition, the government was spending prodigiously on education, infrastructure development, and industrialization. What all of that missed was that the government was horribly corrupt and largely incompetent. Its efforts to reform Iran's agricultural sector effectively destroyed Iran's peasantry, which, along with the country's high population growth rate, caused rural poverty; this in turn triggered large-scale urbanization as more and more young men fled the countryside to seek jobs in Iran's new urban industries. But the industries were misplanned and mismanaged, heavily reliant on foreign labor, and unable to support themselves, and so were unable to provide enough jobs. And even those who did get jobs found themselves barely able to eke out a living on their meager wages in the face of quickly rising prices, forcing them to crowd together in squalid slums around Tehran and several other Iranian cities. Meanwhile, the high inflation rate also destroyed the earning power and savings of the middle class, which meant that neither they nor the lower classes were available as customers for Iran's traditional merchants, the bazaaris. This situation produced ever-widening gaps between the rich and the poor and drove the middle class increasingly downward. Rather than being enriched by Iran's new oil wealth, far too many people were impoverished.

The political system only made these problems worse. As noted, the shah's regime was horribly corrupt and horribly incompetent, so that a great many wrongheaded (but very expensive) projects were undertaken by the government, as well as many other reasonable projects that were inadequately planned and improperly implemented, with the result that little that was promised to the people was actually delivered. The one aspect of the shah's regime that was extremely efficient was his secret police, SAVAK, which ensured that seemingly anyone who voiced even the slightest disappointment with the regime was dealt with swiftly and harshly. The regime restricted political activities, forbidding opposition parties and eventually even insisting that the entire population join a single political party (the Rastakhiz party). Inevitably, the people went looking for sources of psychological comfort, and they found it in religion. At the same time, many of the regime's policies had also enraged Iran's clergy. The shah's blatant secularism, as well as his efforts to reduce the power of the clergy and deprive them of their traditional sources of income, pushed many of them into bitter opposition just as his foolish economic and political policies were driving the bulk of the lower and middle classes into their arms as the Iranian people searched for guidance and meaning in their unhappy lives.

In 1978, Iran was a very rich country and seemed to be doing very well, but most of Iranian society was frustrated, enraged, and ripe for revolution. Unfortunately, Iran's frustration and anger at that time echo the same sentiments heard all across the Arab world today. Though it is hard to say that any Arab country currently possesses the exact same mix of problems as Iran or to the same degree, the similarities exceed the differences, and Arab countries are prey to other problems that the Iranians were not. Again, this is not to suggest that the entire Arab world is about to fall to Islamic revolutions as Iran did. They most likely won't, in large part because, as I noted earlier, a key variable in producing a successful revolution like Iran's is the unwillingness or inability of the regime to employ maximal violence to repress the population. However, it *is* to say that the rest of the Muslim Middle East suffers from many of the same problems, and often of similar orders of magnitude, as Iran did. Consequently, we should not assume that revolutions are impossible, and we *should* assume that other forms of civil unrest, which could be equally problematic for American interests, are likely to persist or even worsen.

How Long Can They Tread Water?

So far, the regimes have done a reasonably good job of snuffing out potential revolutions, mostly through repression, but it is not clear that they can continue to do so indefinitely. "Muddling through," as the Arab states largely have, is a common government policy and is often successful for some period of time, but when the stakes are so high, it is an ill-advised strategy. As Alan Richards warns:

> The durability of this seeming stability is doubtful. In particular, the mounting pressures . . . may well have a cumulative effect. Economic policies have changed—but the changes have not raised living standards much. One may be also highly skeptical concerning the sustainability of such limited growth as has occurred. Evidence from such sources as the World Bank strongly suggests that problems of environmental degradation in the region are sufficiently severe that recent increases in per capita income—desultory as they are—may be entirely illusory. When ecological constraints (especially those of water supplies) are included, the challenges facing the region during the medium term appear more daunting still. Just because regional elites have maintained their power so far does not mean that they will be able to continue to do so in the medium run.[67]

There are historical examples of regimes that successfully employed repression to snuff out terrorism for more than just the short term. However, doing so required an outrageous degree of repression—like that employed by Nazi Germany, Stalinist Russia, Saddam

Husayn's Iraq, and North Korea.[68] As successful as the Egyptians and Saudis have been in suppressing their dissident movements, terrorists, and would-be revolutionaries in the short term, we should not assume that their recent successes will last for very long absent meaningful changes in the perception of grievances among their population. Cairo and Riyadh have employed a fair degree of repression, but not as much as the historical record suggests would be needed to make it last for the long term—and it is not clear that they would be able or willing to employ the kind of totalitarian levels of repression needed to do so.

Moreover, the United States of America should always think long and hard before endorsing widespread repression on the part of friendly regimes to stave off internal demands for change, especially when those demands derive from legitimate economic, social, and political grievances. Not only is this path morally repugnant, but our frequent willingness to do so in the twentieth century produced numerous instances (like Iran, Cuba, Nicaragua, the Philippines, and South Vietnam) that backfired against us. Indeed, such a backlash against America's tolerance for repression is already a major component of the boiling anti-Americanism throughout the Muslim world.

History demonstrates that backing repression is like playing Russian roulette with your foreign policy: it can work for some time and then fail suddenly and catastrophically. The historical record shows that countries in prerevolutionary states can fend off outright revolution for considerable periods of time by employing repression, typically spiced with partial reforms designed to take the edge off popular anger (although their usual impact is actually the opposite: they just whet the popular appetite for more). However, as Skocpol warns, if at some point the regime is fundamentally weakened by some other factor—like a foreign war, a major economic problem, or the death of an important leader—this could quickly create the circumstances for a successful revolution. Berman worries that the repeated military defeats of the Arab states and their inability to cope with modernity, rapid population growth, and other problems may be weakening the Arab regimes in precisely this fashion, albeit doing so over a longer period of time than is typically the case.[69] Given the frequency of wars in the Middle East, the construction of these regimes around paramount leaders, and the fragility of their economies, such rapid changes in fortune are not unusual in the region and could be all that is required to turn a prerevolutionary state into a true revolution. Backing repression, like Russian roulette, is not a smart game to play.

Russia in the late nineteenth and early twentieth centuries furnishes a useful example of the phenomenon. By the 1870s, Russia had entered a prerevolutionary state. The country's economy was failing its people; the gap between rich and poor was vast and appeared to be worsening; Russians saw the development of western Europe and wondered why they were so backward; yet they bristled at many of the ideas emanating from western Europe as outgrowths of the Enlightenment and industrial age. Meanwhile, the tsar's government was corrupt, incapable of addressing its economic problems, and largely uninterested in the fate of its people. Inevitably, this situation spawned a number of revolutionary movements, beginning with the Nechaev group, which attempted to incite a peasant revolt against the tsar but could not mobilize the masses—at least not before the tsar's secret police stopped it.[70] Successor groups, particularly Narodnaya Volya ("People's Will"), learned the lesson from Nechaev's failure and opted for terrorism and insurgent warfare instead. Their goal remained absolutely the same: to spark a revolution in Russia that would topple the tsarist regime—but their tactics changed in light of the failure of their predecessors to mount a direct revolution.[71] Their terrorist campaign enjoyed significant success both tactically (they assassinated Tsar Alexander II) and strategically, as their pressure was an important element in Alexander II's decision to enact various political reforms before his death.[72]

In interesting further parallels with the contemporary Middle East, virtually all of the Russian revolutionaries/terrorists were well-educated, city-dwelling products of the middle class, even though their typical grievance was the oppression and misery of the Russian people and their goal was the "liberation" of the peasantry.[73] In fact, a great many of their terrorist attacks were actually suicide bombings. Dynamite was their weapon of choice, because its blast radius and ability to be thrown offered the best prospects for killing the intended target. However, both to maximize the odds of success and because the death of the attacker allowed them to distinguish their actions from those of common criminals, the Russian terrorists typically chose to throw their dynamite from distances so close that they were invariably killed along with their target.[74] Moreover, as the historian of terrorism David Rapoport has observed, after the wave of terrorist attacks began in Russia in the 1880s, it quickly spread to western Europe and even Asia.[75]

Subsequent tsars, Alexander III and Nicholas II, abandoned Alexander II's program of reform and instead opted for pure repression, beginning in about 1883. They were successful with this approach for a number of years—largely quashing the terrorist threat and fending off other efforts to trigger rebellions. But then problems emerged when Russia started losing wars, wars that it had not sought. In January 1905, after Russia's humiliating defeat in the Russo-Japanese War, a variety of mostly Marxist groups was able to start a nationwide revolt against the tsar. Although the regime did eventually prevail through savage repression, it was forced to make numerous concessions, including the establishment of a parliament. Of course, this was not enough to avert disaster, and in 1917, as Russia reeled from economic and military collapse during the First World War, the tsarist regime was finally overthrown altogether by a range of revolutionary groups, all of them composed overwhelmingly of well-educated, urban, middle-class young men. The group that eventually succeeded in taking power, the Bolshevik branch of the Russian Communist Party, was led by the man known to history as Vladimir Lenin. Lenin's brother just happened to be one of the terrorists of Narodnaya Volya, which had tried to bring about the same result decades earlier.

In short, even the most repressive regime can fall prey to revolution, although it may take decades rather than years or months. And just because repression has worked for many years, that is no guarantee that it will work forever.

Nor should we expect that the states of the region can use their oil wealth to simply "buy off" the opposition. In a study of this question, the Middle East scholar Gwenn Okruhlik found that oil wealth generally does not prevent internal unrest, and it can actually provoke conflict and revolts when it is distributed inequitably across class, ethnic, religious, or geographic lines. In the Middle East, inequitable division of oil revenues is the norm, not the exception. And Iraq furnishes an obvious example of how competition for oil revenues can fuel internal conflict.[76]

EVEN FAILED REVOLUTIONS ARE TROUBLE

Although we should not dismiss the threat of successful revolutions in the Muslim Middle East, we should recognize that they tend to be rare events and therefore should not exaggerate this particular threat either. The problem is that even failed revolutions, protorevolutions, or just revolutionary "wannabes" can still create real problems that can jeopardize American interests in the Middle East. Most revolutionary groups that are unable to pull off the same kind of feat as Lenin or Khomeini and actually topple an autocratic regime don't simply fade away. Especially if the underlying grievances among the wider populace that gave rise to the revolutionary movement persist, as is likely to be the case in the Middle East for some time to come, the revolutionaries will stay on the scene and will just change their methods. Like Mao Zedong, Ho Chi Minh, and Che Guevara, they may choose to mount an insurgency. Like Narodnaya Volya and al-Qa'ida, they might opt for a terrorist campaign. Or they might mount a coup d'état or a bid at revolution that devolves into civil war when it fails, as happened with the Spanish and Nigerian civil wars.

Indeed, civil wars, insurgencies, and terrorist campaigns are often (although not always) the product of failed revolutions. As noted above, bin Ladin and az-Zawahiri acknowledge turning to terrorism (including against the United States) when it became clear that they could not spark revolutions in Saudi Arabia and Egypt. As Martha Crenshaw has explained, terrorists usually have a revolutionary goal: "Their dissatisfaction with the policies of the government is extreme, and their demands usually involve the displacement of existing political elites."[77] In laying out the four "waves" of terrorism in modern history, David Rapoport makes virtually the same point: " 'Revolution' is the overriding aim in every wave, but revolution is understood in different ways."[78]

An example of the broader phenomenon that even "failed" revolutions can create real problems is the Algerian civil war of the

1990s. In the 1970s and '80s, various Islamist groups rose to prominence in Algeria just as they had throughout the region. Despite Algeria's oil wealth, the economy was floundering and the government was corrupt and callous toward the aspirations of the people.[79] Since the regime effectively shut down all other avenues of dissent and because Algerians were predisposed to approve of a political movement cloaked in the language and symbolism of Islam, the Islamists became the great beneficiary of their unhappiness. In 1988, several of the Islamist groups combined to form the Front Islamique du Salut (FIS, Islamic Salvation Front).[80] The goals of the FIS were unabashedly revolutionary: they sought to create a new Algerian state based upon the principles of Shari'a and a return to what they considered more traditional Islamic values, behavior, organization, and government. However, the FIS was divided between a moderate Islamist wing, which occasionally suggested that Islamism was compatible with democracy, and a hard-line Salafist wing, which demanded radical changes in Algerian political and social life, condemned democracy, and espoused a rather virulent anti-Americanism as well. Whereas the moderates argued for a process of working through the existing political system, the radicals demanded that they circumvent, if not topple, it. Although it was the radical wing that was most popular among young, less educated, urban lower classes, eventually the moderate wing prevailed in its internal debates and the FIS decided to participate in Algerian elections to try to gain power peacefully.[81]

Despite the regime's efforts to warp the results, the FIS won 188 of 231 seats in the first round of parliamentary elections in December 1991. The regime and the military feared that once the FIS had won a parliamentary majority, it would use its legitimate victory to dismantle the pluralist system and establish a theocratic autocracy. Though the regime was not certain that the FIS would do so, there was also no guarantee that it would not, especially given that one of its main election slogans was "No laws. No constitution. Only the laws of God and the Qur'an."[82] So in January 1992, the army canceled the second round of voting and installed a new president, and in March it dissolved the FIS. After that, a wide variety of Islamist groups took up arms against the government, including eventually the FIS itself. Among those waging the civil war were numerous Salafi extremists and other radicals, led by the highly violent terrorist/insurgent movement Groupe Islamique Armé (GIA, Armed Islamic Group), which saw itself as a Leninist "vanguard" party that would fulfill the revolution that had been derailed in 1992.[83] According to Antar Zouabri, one of its leaders, the GIA was waging an "all-out war" to "found a true Islamic state."[84]

Seven years and 100,000 to 150,000 deaths later, Algeria was finally able to start picking up the pieces.[85] Nevertheless, the GIA lived on for several more years, killing when it could. It has since been succeeded by another Salafi terrorist group more closely affiliated with al-Qa'ida, the Groupe Salafiste pour la Prédication et le Combat (GSPC, Salafist Group for Preaching and Combat), which in 2005 helpfully renamed itself al-Qa'ida of the Islamic Maghreb. This group continues to mount terrorist attacks in Algeria and possibly Tunisia as well. Thus the Algerian Civil War arose when an Islamist movement seeking revolutionary changes in the status quo had its bid for power blocked by conservative elements and so resorted to civil war and terrorism to achieve what it could not peacefully.

Moreover, the Algerian case illustrates a widespread phenomenon across the region: though most Islamist groups at one time hoped to mount a traditional revolution, when they found that they were unable to do so, they changed tactics, with many choosing to build grassroots support throughout society either so that they might be able to take power nonviolently in their own form of "velvet revolution" or else to better position themselves to mobilize the masses when an opportunity presented itself. As Berman remarks of the FIS's Egyptian counterparts, "The Islamists, finding themselves unable to achieve their revolutionary goals directly by conquering the state, turned to gradually remaking Egyptian society and culture."[86] Without overstating the problem, Berman cautions that Islamist control of civil society could allow the Islamists to subvert the governments and take power peacefully, as the Fascists in Italy and Germany did during the interwar years and as the Algerian military feared—rightly or wrongly—that the FIS would.[87] The historian Ira Lapidus has similarly argued that "The revival movements have two

strategies to reach these ends. One is education and community organizing to build an Islamic society from the bottom up which, as it
grows in power and mass appeal, will simply take over the state. The
other strategy calls for political violence to overthrow corrupt and/or
foreign-dominated governments by the direct seizure of the state. . . .
The two approaches are not mutually exclusive and indeed may be
pursued at once or substituted for each other as tactical situations
require."[88]

Having a radical Islamist in the mode of either bin Ladin or
Khomeini overthrow the regime and take power in Saudi Arabia or
Egypt would obviously be disastrous for American interests. However, what the Algerian example illustrates is that even their failure
to take power could produce various forms of civil war (including insurgencies and terrorist campaigns) that could be equally dangerous
to American interests. For example, Algeria's oil-exporting regions
were largely unaffected by the civil war, and, setting aside whether
the Army was right to step in and block the FIS from taking power,
its actions did ensure that Algeria's oil infrastructure remained in the
hands of a government determined to maximize oil production and
exports. The specter of Iraq, in contrast, demonstrates that civil war
and insurgency *can* greatly diminish a country's oil exports. And it's
not hard to imagine worse civil wars that might shut down a country's oil production altogether.

As a final point, all of these different problems (revolutions, civil
wars, insurgencies, terrorist campaigns) have a very bad habit of em-
broiling neighboring states, not just the country being targeted by
the revolutionary group in question. From France to Russia to China
to Iran to Ethiopia and a number of others, successful revolutions
seem invariably to provoke interstate wars—launched either by the
revolutionary state to spread the revolution or, more typically, by
neighboring states seeking to throttle it or to pick up quick gains
from its perceived weakness.[89] Civil wars also have a bad habit of
overflowing their borders. In the worst cases, like the Congolese civil
war and the civil war between Palestinian Jews and Palestinian Arabs
(which grew into the Arab-Israeli conflict), they have provoked regional wars or caused civil wars in other, neighboring states. Civil
war in Lebanon caused civil war in Syria, and civil war in Rwanda

triggered civil war in Congo. Indeed, even if spillover from such civil wars does not result in similarly catastrophic consequences, the impact can still be devastating. For instance, many of Pakistan's crippling problems are a direct outgrowth of various forms of spillover from the Afghan Civil War.[90] Insurgencies too have a bad habit of spreading into adjoining countries, as in Indochina in the 1960s and '70s, in Africa during the same era, and in Central America in the 1980s. Finally, as we have seen all across the Middle East and in South Asia as well, terrorism can spread from one country to another. Once one group sees it as a useful method of political opposition and/or a path to overthrow a hated government, others will doubtless be inspired to do the same. The spread of Salafi terrorist groups linked to al-Qa'ida from North Africa to Southeast Asia to sub-Saharan Africa and Europe is an obvious example of this phenomenon.

Internal strife is the usual precursor to another modern phenomenon that has plagued the Middle East and created major headaches for the United States: failed states. Somalia, Afghanistan, Lebanon, Iraq, Sudan, Algeria, and Yemen have, at times, all been described as failed states—countries where the mechanisms of governance simply broke down, leaving anarchy, if not chaos, in their wake. In every case, internal conflict both produced the state failure in these countries and was further intensified by it. Failed states create a range of problems for their neighbors, including refugees, terrorism (which typically flourishes in ungoverned spaces), and a power vacuum that can spur military intervention by neighboring states (and that rarely turns out well for the intervening countries). Thus the tendency of prerevolutionary states and failed bids at revolution to spawn internal strife also creates the potential for more failed states in a region that does not need them.

THE COUP THREAT

Prerevolutionary situations also frequently produce military coups d'état. Especially in countries with weak civil-military relations, military leaders constantly gauge the performance of the political leadership, and in states with politicized militaries and/or weak governmental legitimacy, the sense that the government is not performing as well as it should can trigger a military coup. Widespread economic problems (or merely the perception of such problems), an unhappy populace, a nation that is clearly lagging behind others (especially when it is believed to be capable of much more) can all prompt elements in the military to topple the government. Anytime a politicized military believes that the political leadership has left the country "weak" or otherwise failed the nation, there is risk of a coup d'état. Of course, there are plenty of other factors that can trigger a coup, and in many cases it is simply the ambitions of one or more officers to wield political power that is the primary force behind a coup. However, even then, widespread public disaffection with the government—as in the Iraqi and Egyptian cases—can provide cover and a permissive environment for would-be dictators.

By definition, a coup d'état is a sudden change in government that inevitably brings to power someone with little experience of governance and potentially very dangerous ideas about the world. Though there have been perfectly reasonable, even enlightened, dictators, most are at least internally repressive, which can create the conditions for another coup or a revolution, civil war, or insurgency, empowering more radical leadership down the road. In other cases, the new military dictator himself may be a radical determined to take his country in a direction that would threaten American interests.

Libya is a perfect example of this phenomenon. In the late 1960s there was considerable unhappiness with the lethargic government of King Idris. Libyans were poor despite their growing oil wealth, there was little development, and the king was seen as being too close to the West (particularly the British). All around them, the Libyans saw other Arab states having long since overthrown their own monarchies, embraced pan-Arabism and Arab socialism, and seemingly become modern nations at the cutting edge of international politics. The Libyan military, which yearned to be as strong as its Egyptian, Syrian, and Iraqi counterparts seemed to be, blamed the king and his British allies for preventing Libya from joining the front ranks of the Arab states. As a result, there were quite a few cabals in Tripoli and Benghazi scheming against the king in the 1960s. The man who seized the brass ring, however, was a major named

Muammar Qadhafi. Qadhafi led a band of officers who overthrew the monarchy in 1969 and, inevitably, proclaimed his actions a revolution, although they were little more than a military coup. Nevertheless, as in Iraq and Egypt, the fall of the monarchy was generally treated as a positive development by the populace, who believed that now their country would be able to make progress, just like its Arab brethren.

Of course, Qadhafi's coup created a lot more problems for the United States than merely the loss of King Idris as an ally and the loss of Wheelus Air Base as a staging facility from which to attack the USSR. We should leave it to the psychologists to determine whether Qadhafi is clinically insane—there is certainly a lot of evidence for that supposition. At the very least, he proved to be egomaniacal, reckless, aggressive, determined to overthrow the status quo in the region, and bitterly opposed to the United States. He used Libya's oil wealth to fund terrorism, acquire weapons of mass destruction (including a nuclear program), mount aggressive wars (mostly against Chad), and support other rulers determined to oppose the United States and its allies.

Qadhafi's actions were not disastrous for the United States, but they were unquestionably harmful. Before the 9/11 attacks, the destruction by Libya of Pan Am flight 103 over Lockerbie, Scotland, in 1988 was the single worst terrorist attack on Americans. His military adventures ended badly for him and for Libya, but he nearly provoked a war with Egypt that the United States had to step in and halt for fear that it would undermine Sadat's government.

Even if coups d'état in the Middle East did nothing but produce one or more new Qadhafis, this certainly would not be helpful to American interests. However, we cannot be certain that such coups would affect only weak peripheral states like Libya or that the reckless, aggressive, anti–status quo dictators brought to power would prove as incompetent as Qadhafi. Saddam Husayn created far greater problems for the United States and its interests both because he ruled Iraq and because he was better at harnessing its resources than Qadhafi. A coup d'état that brought to power a leader like Qadhafi or Saddam in Egypt or Saudi Arabia would potentially be a dire threat. Even if they were willing to pump and sell as much oil as possible, as both Qadhafi and Saddam (mostly) were, if they were using it to fund terrorism, weapons of mass destruction, and aggressive wars against their neighbors, the consequences would be very severe for U.S. interests—and possibly disastrous.

A Foolish Game

Thus, the underlying problems of the Muslim Middle East have created a daunting set of threats for the United States in the region. They have given rise to prerevolutionary states in most of the countries of the Middle East. This raises the possibility of a successful revolution, which would almost certainly be engineered by a radical Islamist, someone like Khomeini or bin Ladin. Though it is possible that the new revolutionary leader would prove to be more moderate than either of them, we should not assume that such would be the case. It is the nature of successful revolutions to be led by radicals, not moderates. Typically, the radicals kill off the moderates.

While the threat of revolution may have the lowest probability, it potentially raises the greatest risk: imagine the consequences of an Iranian-style revolution in Saudi Arabia. Not only might such a radical new leader decide to curb or cut off oil exports to suit his religious convictions and/or strategic plans, but he might decide to launch wars of aggression. Historically, revolutions have a very bad habit of doing so. The French Revolution launched multiple wars to try to spread the blessings of *liberté, égalité,* and *fraternité.* The Russian Revolution mounted a drive to the West to liberate Europe for communism, only to be stopped by Józef Piłsudski and the Polish Army at the gates of Warsaw. The Iranians turned Saddam Husayn's foolish attack into a crusade to liberate Basra and Baghdad on the road to Jerusalem and Mecca. Consequently, though a revolution in Saudi Arabia would be most threatening of all, a revolution in a nearby state would be equally problematic because of the potential for the new revolutionary government to attack a U.S. ally or major oil producer—and Saudi Arabia, in particular, to "liberate" Mecca and Medina. Alternatively, such a revolutionary state might make a renewed effort to attack Israel. The current crop of regimes has learned that they are no match for the Israel Defense Forces, but a zealous new regime, no doubt believing its revolutionary triumph to be a sign of divine favor, might not be so deterred. Moreover, as we have seen with Iran, Islamist-dominated states may feel more of a need to acquire nuclear weapons, if only to defend themselves against the United States and other forces that, in their conspiratorial worldview, they believe are determined to destroy them.

Even if these worst-case scenarios are never realized, there is a range of other potential threats that stem from this same underlying set of problems. Even failed revolutions could lead to civil wars, insurgencies, and terrorist campaigns, all of which could result in oil disruptions as described in chapter 1. Alternatively, they might simply create the circumstances for a successful revolution or other form of regime change later on. The same conditions might encourage and enable military officers to stage a coup d'état, with the potential not just to remove governments that have been helpful to the United States in the past but also to install new ones that could be very harmful to U.S. interests.

Finally, even revolutions, coups d'état, civil wars, insurgencies, and terrorist campaigns that start in countries in the region that are not themselves intrinsically important to American interests (and particularly to our interest in Middle Eastern oil) could still have that impact eventually because of the spillover effects of all of these problems. The fact that civil wars are already raging in Iraq, Sudan, and the Palestinian territories, with a latent conflict smoldering in Lebanon, ought to give us real concern that they may threaten other countries that are even more important to American interests. We are already seeing manifestations of a wide range of spillover effects from the Iraqi Civil War on all of Iraq's neighbors, including Saudi Arabia. Though they have been tolerable so far, if the Iraqi Civil War intensifies, so too may its spillover. Given this already precarious state of affairs, America's interests demand a focus on quelling the ongoing civil conflicts and preventing new ones. The time for ignoring the underlying problems of the Muslim Middle East is long past.

CHAPTER 9

THE THREAT OF TERRORISM

THE LAST CHAPTER EXPLAINED THAT ONE THREAT TO AMERI-can interests produced by the economic, political, and social problems of the Muslim Middle East is widespread instability in the form of civil unrest, coups, insurgencies, civil wars, and possibly even revolutions, all of which are meant to topple the governments of the region. Though this may be the most dangerous threat we face in the region, at this moment it is somewhat farther down the road. Instability in the region has not caused a sudden, massive loss of regional oil exports, has only marginally contributed to Israel's security problems, and has not provoked sudden regime change in any of our regional allies since the fall of the shah. It *has* reduced oil exports, invariably affecting the price of oil and causing recessions in the United States, and it has also contributed meaningfully to the threat of proliferation, insofar as the Iranian Revolution was born of similar, underlying factors and the regime installed by that revolution is now seeking a nuclear enrichment capability that would allow it to build nuclear weapons. However, the Iranians do not yet possess a weapon, so that too is still only a potential threat that is at least several years in the future.[1]

In contrast, the other threat that the underlying problems help create is a much more immediate and direct one, although it might not be of as much consequence for American interests as a revolution or civil war in Saudi Arabia. This is the threat of Middle Eastern terrorist attacks against the United States and American citizens. In the aftermath of 9/11 it should not require any additional proof that this is a real threat that needs to be dealt with promptly and, one hopes, permanently.

Terrorism and Terrorism

There are a great many terrorist groups in the world, and the Middle East has more than its fair share. Indeed, the Middle East is lousy with terrorist groups. But not all terrorism is the same. In particular, for our purposes, not all terrorist groups present the same threat to the United States. Many terrorist groups present no real threat to the United States at all, either because they are not interested in attacking Americans (or our allies) and/or they have little real capacity to do so even if they were. This is an important distinction and an important starting point when thinking about the terrorist threat the United States faces from the Middle East.

Jerrold Post, a respected political psychologist, draws a useful distinction between social revolutionary terrorists and ethnic-nationalist terrorists.[2] Social revolutionary terrorists are those looking to radically transform their nation, their region, or even the whole world by tearing down the old order and replacing it with a utopian new order. Many Marxist terrorists fell into this category, but in the Middle East, it applies in particular to the Salafi extremists, like al-Qa'ida, that are looking to overthrow the existing regimes and replace them with utopian, Islamist states. In contrast, ethnic-nationalist terrorists are those looking to achieve more concrete results (freedom, territory, greater rights) for their people, who are typically being oppressed—in reality or merely in the minds of the terrorists—by some other group. Most national liberation movements fall into this category. In the Middle East, all of the Palestinian terrorist groups, along with the Kurdistan Workers' Party (the PKK) and the Polisario Front, are examples of this form of terrorism. Naturally, there are groups that are hybrids of the two, and here the most important examples are Hamas and Hizballah. Both are ethnic-nationalist in the sense that they are using violence to reclaim land they believe belongs to them; however, both are also social revolutionary since they subscribe to Islamist ideologies that seek to transform the entire Muslim world. (In practice, both have behaved more like ethnic-nationalist groups than like social revolutionaries.)

While the ethnic-nationalist terrorist groups present only a minor threat to American interests, the social revolutionary groups present serious direct and indirect threats.

Few of the ethnic-nationalist terrorist groups of the Middle East have ever attacked Americans or U.S. interests directly. Hizballah has, but not since the 1980s. Once the Lebanese Civil War ended in 1990, Hizballah became careful not to fall afoul of the United States. The only exceptions to this have been that a member of Lebanese Hizballah participated in the Iranian-directed bombing of the Khobar Towers American military housing facility in Saudi Arabia in 1996 and some members of Lebanese Hizballah appear to have assisted Shi'i militants attacking U.S. forces in Iraq. Both cases seem to be instances of the Iranian Revolutionary Guard using members of Lebanese Hizballah as "hired guns" to help it with its covert action projects—not necessarily causes of Lebanese Hizballah itself. The PFLP-GC, Hamas, and Palestinian Islamic Jihad (PIJ) have never deliberately attacked American targets. The PLO did in the 1970s, but the last attacks that can be tied to elements of the PLO coalition are the 1985 *Achille Lauro* hijacking by the Palestine Liberation Front and the 1986 hijacking of an American airliner by the Abu Nidal Organization. Since then, the Palestinian militant groups have all concentrated on Israel and one another. Moreover, none has shown any inclination to mount attacks on the United States despite the tremendous levels of anti-Americanism in the region, the popularity that al-Qa'ida has garnered for its attacks on the United States, and the lopsided pro-Israel policies of the George W. Bush administration.

Consequently, it is difficult to suggest that Palestinian terrorist groups are a direct threat to the United States. This does *not* mean that the United States should condone or overlook them. It is simply meant to demonstrate that, odious as their actions may be, they do not constitute the same kind of threat to American interests as al-Qa'ida and therefore do not merit the same response. Moreover, it should be borne in mind that the Palestinian terrorist groups are an *indirect* problem for the United States because they attack our Israeli ally, prevent the conclusion of a peace between Israel and the Arabs (which means that the Arab-Israeli conflict continues to boil, creating problems for U.S. regional interests), have helped create chaos in Lebanon, and have tried to do the same in other countries, like Jordan, in the past. But they are not a direct threat to the United States, and the extent of the indirect threat they pose is open to wide variations in interpretation.

Beyond Hizballah and the Palestinian militants, none of the region's other ethnic-nationalist groups has ever posed a threat to the United States. The PKK, the Polisario, and Baluchi terrorist groups, not to mention Jewish terrorist groups like Kach and Kahane Chai, have never attacked the United States and seem to have little interest in doing so. At most, they too create indirect problems, for instance by attacking American allies (like the PKK's attacks on Turkey), or by hindering progress toward an Arab-Israeli peace settlement (as has been the case with the Jewish terrorists).

In contrast, al-Qa'ida and other Salafi extremist groups attack America directly and therefore are a direct threat to our interests— as well as being an indirect threat because of their attacks and efforts to overthrow the governments of America's Arab allies. Consequently, when we talk about the threat that the United States faces from Middle Eastern terrorists, we are really talking about al-Qa'ida and other Salafi terrorist groups.

The Revolutionary Angle

By now, the first link between the underlying problems of the Muslim Middle East and the threat of terrorism the United States faces should be obvious. The underlying economic, social, and political problems of the region have pushed nearly all of the countries of the region into prerevolutionary states. As typically follows, these circumstances have produced numerous revolutionary groups seeking to overthrow the regimes by any means possible, and most of these groups are associated with political Islam in one way or another because of the specific history and conditions of the region. This was the essential origin of many of al-Qa'ida's component and affiliated groups, as well as most other Salafi extremist groups.

It is also the first reason why solving the problem of terrorism requires addressing the underlying problems of the region. If you simply kill or arrest all of the current crop of terrorists without changing the prerevolutionary conditions that produced them, more revolutionary movements will arise and, assuming they do not succeed in mounting successful revolutions (which could be even worse for U.S. interests), some of them will turn to terrorism as well. The destruction of Narodnaya Volya by the tsarist secret police did not prevent the emergence of new terrorist groups later on, nor did it prevent other revolts or the eventual success of the 1917 Russian Revolution, for that matter.

Just as the answer to the question "What could the tsar have done to eliminate terrorism and head off the Russian Revolution?" is "He should have mounted a comprehensive program of reform to address Russia's economic, social, and political backwardness," so too it is the first answer to the question "How can we help end the scourge of anti-American terrorism from the Middle East and head off the potential for future revolutions, civil wars, and insurgencies in this part of the world?" In the end, the Salafi terrorists are not nihilists looking to kill lots of people for no reason; they have an agenda and a cause, and eliminating the Salafi terrorist groups will require eliminating their cause and the perceived need for their agenda. Indeed, throughout history, that has been a key component of eliminating every social revolutionary terrorist group—from the Bolsheviks to the Baader-Meinhof Gang.

Nevertheless, the causes of terrorism are exceptionally complicated and/or exceptionally poorly understood. As important as the connection to revolutionary aspirations is—and it is extremely important—it is not the only thing going on. Thus, in trying to understand the link between the underlying problems of the region and the terrorist threat, there are other considerations worth exploring because they too can help flesh out how best to meet this threat and, *inshallah,* eradicate it.

The Roots of Terrorism

Experts have been studying terrorists and terrorist groups for a long time. Though the results of their many studies are certainly interesting, no one has yet been able to develop a sophisticated psychological profile of the average terrorist.[3] Nor is there a consensus about the common traits of terrorists' psychological makeup.[4] At some level, there has always been a belief that since what terrorists do is not "normal" by any stretch of the imagination, there must be something about the terrorists too that is "abnormal."[5] However, what these studies have repeatedly found is that most, perhaps a large majority, of the terrorists whom experts have been able to interview *were* surprisingly "normal." Very few were pathological or otherwise insane. They were not all Charles Mansons and David Berkowitzes, just looking for an opportunity to slaughter as many people as they could because their dog told them to.[6]

Of course, although most are not abnormal, they are typically "different."[7] For instance, some studies of terrorist leaders have found that they are typically highly alienated from society, narcissistic to the point of feeling no empathy or pity for those they kill, and highly egotistical.[8] Consequently, many psychologists continue to maintain that it is likely that at some point we will discover that there is something about terrorists that does predispose them to violence and that many do join terrorist groups because at some deep, subconscious level, they are seeking violence. But so far, we simply do not have the evidence to make that case.[9]

Some caveats are in order here. Although there has been a lot of work done on terrorists' motivation, this work has to be taken with more than a few grains of salt. The number of terrorists whom the experts have been able to observe, let alone study, is comparatively small. Terrorism may dominate the world's newspaper headlines, but it is actually a pretty rare phenomenon, and from a global perspective, there are comparatively few people actually engaged in terrorism. Moreover, terrorists tend to operate in secrecy and many would prefer to die than be captured, which makes it difficult to capture and study them. This is especially true of suicide bombers, few of whom are apprehended before they launch their attacks (and fewer still afterward). A number of intrepid experts have interviewed terrorists while they were still operating, but in those conditions it is much harder to get at the information needed for these kinds of evaluations. In prison a terrorist might choose to tell you whether his mommy loved him, but if he is out and waging his war he is unlikely to do so—and might even kill you for asking. You never know.

Consequently, the pool of information on terrorists is weak. Moreover, it tends to be heavily skewed toward a few groups, particularly the Palestinian militants, largely because the Israelis have captured and imprisoned so many of them over the years and the Israelis have been eager to try to get a better grip on what motivates them. However, as already noted, Palestinian terrorists may not be good surrogates for the Salafi extremist groups posing the greatest threat to the United States because of the very different motives of the groups (ethnic-nationalist versus social revolutionary). Similarly, quite a few Palestinians belong to the various Palestinian militant groups, especially when compared to the tiny size of the Palestinian population of 3.5 million. On the other hand, al-Qa'ida and its affiliates are relatively small, certainly smaller than the Palestinian groups, but are drawing from a far larger pool—the entire Islamic world of 1.2 billion people. In other words, the people who join al-Qa'ida represent a much smaller fraction of the pool of people from whom it is recruiting than do the Palestinian militant groups. What this suggests is that at a societywide level, joining a group like Hamas is much more common—and therefore considered more "normal"—among the Palestinian population than is joining a group like al-Qa'ida for the much larger Muslim population.

Another related factor is the difference in methods between the Palestinian terrorist groups and al-Qa'ida. The Palestinian militants are building a mass movement and therefore tend to be much more inclusive and welcoming of anyone willing to fight Israel in some way. In contrast, al-Qa'ida thinks of itself (at least for now) as a Leninist-style vanguard revolutionary party, which is necessarily highly selective in whom it recruits and accepts for membership. This allows al-Qa'ida to choose only those who match its specific needs and in particular allows it to select only those recruits with higher education, technical skills, and other unusual backgrounds that are useful to its terrorist operations. For all of these reasons, there may be considerable differences in the motivations of the individuals joining these groups. At the very least, those joining al-Qa'ida may prove to be far more different from the norm for their population (although not necessarily to the extent of being considered insane) than are Palestinian militants for the Palestinian population.

Nevertheless, even this discussion of the limits of our knowledge regarding who joins various terrorist organizations continues to suggest that most who join are not crazy. At some level, they may be "abnormal" in the strictest sense of not representing something close to the norm, but this can be judged only for each group. For the Palestinians, it may actually be perfectly "normal" for a young man to join a terrorist group, given that a relatively large percentage of young Palestinian men do so. But although it is certainly not "normal" for a Muslim to join al-Qa'ida, nothing from the evidence gathered on that group or other Salafi terrorists indicates that the people who join it are crazy. In fact, given the difficulties involved in planning and pulling off the kind of spectacular terrorist operations that al-Qa'ida favors, it often requires people who are intelligent, good under pressure, charismatic, and clear-eyed—at least for the leaders of any operation. This too suggests that many al-Qa'ida members are not average. Many are above average (which is also in keeping with their self-image as a vanguard party), but they are not crazy.[10]

The fact that most terrorists are not psychotic, sociopathic, or otherwise psychologically damaged suggests the importance of environmental factors in their decision to join a terrorist organization. It takes *something,* or a number of somethings, to convince an otherwise psychologically healthy person to commit acts of indiscriminate slaughter. Part of that is the psychological "molding" (we might say "brainwashing") that goes on once a person joins a terrorist group. This pattern has been well documented over the years. When a recruit joins a terrorist group, the group puts him (or her) through an established process that shapes his thinking to ensure that he is willing and psychologically able to conduct acts of mayhem—or whatever else it is the group has in mind for him."¹¹ This process is an interesting one for counterterrorism experts but not terribly important for our purposes because the only way to interrupt that process of psychological molding is to physically interrupt it by getting to the recruit. Since that is rarely an option for the United States, adopting policies meant to interrupt this process is not really an option either, let alone a necessary component of a grand strategy toward the Middle East.

However, what is of real importance is the second set of environmental factors, those at work on the larger society that can cause some of its members to make the decision to join terrorist groups in the first place. Since it is not the case that the terrorist groups seek out the psychologically damaged members of society (although there is evidence that they do just that when it comes to suicide bombers) but instead mostly recruit people who seem to fall within the "normal" spectrum of values and behavior for the society, there must be forces at work in the society itself that in turn cause some of its members (since it is never the case that all members of a society react the same way to the same set of influences) to join terrorist groups. It also opens up another line of attack for the United States to fight the problem of terrorism: it allows us to treat the forces afflicting the wider society in the expectation that doing so will remove the incentives leading some of its members to conduct terrorist attacks.

Of course, this is a less precise method than identifying the terrorists and killing them or identifying potential terrorist recruits and heading them off before they join up. However, because we cannot identify any distinguishing traits that would readily expose a "latent" terrorist, that's not really an option. Indeed, throughout history, the only way to deal with terrorism, and the parent phenomenon of insurgency, has been to go after the broader target population and eliminate the sources of grievance in the wider society. Doing so eliminates both the motives of the terrorist/insurgent/revolutionary and his or her support in the community. This is the core of both counterinsurgency and counterterrorism strategy. It is the only strategy that has ever been shown to work consistently and over the long term.

Anger and Despair

As best we can tell, the principal factors that move an individual to embrace terrorism, by either creating a new group or joining an established one, are feelings of intense anger, frustration, and desperation. Although terrorists may be psychologically within the spectrum of "normal," killing innocent people you do not know is not "normal" behavior in any society anywhere on Earth. It takes a great deal of emotion to cause people to adopt such a course of action. In a study of the motives of suicide terrorism, the Australian terrorism expert Adam Dolnik explained that "the one feature all terrorists (including suicide terrorists) have in common is that they are incredibly frustrated. Such frustration constitutes an unavoidable prerequisite for an individual's turn to extreme religious belief or active involvement in a struggle for national liberation and independence."[12] Throughout the Muslim Middle East, the underlying and interconnected problems afflicting the economic, social, and political systems, coupled with a strong sense of cultural siege, are producing the requisite levels of anger and despair to condition significant numbers of people ready to join terrorist groups.[13] As Joyce Davis expressed it, "many young men and women, such as Izzidene al-Masri, who blew himself up inside a Jerusalem pizzeria, are easy prey for the world's bin Ladens because the suffering they see around them daily makes them economically, emotionally, and spiritually vulnerable."[14]

TERRORISTS FROM THE ELITES

Since September 11, 2001, there has been a great deal of debate regarding the causes of terrorism, most of it well intentioned and designed to help the United States and its allies better fight groups like al-Qa'ida. Although the vast weight of scholarship accepts that societal factors play an important, but not singular, role in giving rise to the phenomenon of terrorism and encouraging people to join terrorist groups, some observers have argued the opposite. In particular, some have dismissed any connection between economics and terrorism. You often hear this with the glib assertion that since all of the nineteen hijackers who perpetrated the 9/11 attacks were educated and middle class, economics can't have anything to do with it.[15] Though rhetorically appealing, the statement is false both in its specifics (only six of the nineteen were well educated and from the middle class; the others were poor, rural, and not well educated) and in its larger apparent claim.[16] In this regard it is very much like claiming that because Robespierre, Danton, and the rest were from the middle and upper classes, the French Revolution must not have had anything to do with the state of the French economy. It is not just wrong but foolish.

The broader and more common claim that terrorism must be unrelated to economics because so many terrorists are from the middle and upper classes is ahistorical at best.[17] As Tom Farer, the dean of the Graduate School of International Studies at the University of Denver, once put it in a fit of exasperation, "Of course the terrorists are from the middle class—they're *always* from the middle class!" Even a cursory review of history demonstrates that Farer is absolutely correct. The leaders of revolutionary movements and their offshoot terrorist groups are almost invariably scions of the middle class, with exceptions from the upper class being at least as prevalent as those from the lower classes. From the American revolutionaries; to the French revolutionaries; to the Russian terrorists of Narodnaya Volya; to the Bolsheviks; to the Marxist terrorists of the Baader-Meinhof group, the Red Brigades, November 17, and the Japanese Red Army Faction; to the Latin American revolutionaries and terrorists of the 1960s and '70s; to the leaders (both lay and clerical) of the Iranian Revolution; to the leadership of Hizballah and Hamas; to the Islamists and Salafi extremists of today, the leaders of revolutionary and terrorist groups and many of their most trusted lieutenants are invariably from the middle class. And in every one of these cases, economics—or, more properly, a set of grievances derived from interconnected economic, social, and political dysfunctions— played a critical role in setting their movements into motion. Every history of revolution ever written, every exploration, every analysis has concluded that economic conditions played a critical role in creating the environment that gave rise to the revolution or, if it failed, to the insurgency or terrorist campaign that typically followed. They were not always the proximate cause, but they were invariably a crucial underlying cause.

Thus, it is not at all unusual that many of the leaders of a protest movement born ultimately from the anger and despair generated by the economic, social, and political problems of the Muslim Middle East are members of the region's middle (and at times, upper) classes.[18] The principal leaders of al-Qa'ida conform nicely to this pattern: bin Ladin himself is the son of a Saudi billionaire. Ayman az-Zawahiri is a surgeon from a well-known Egyptian family. Ali Mohamed, formerly the group's principal military trainer, is a former Egyptian Army major with a degree in psychology.[19] And the list goes on. Similarly, the rank and file of Hizballah's cadres are largely made up of poor Shi'ah (already one of Lebanon's poorest ethnic groups on average), but its leadership is overwhelmingly from the Shi'i middle class.[20]

In truth, psychologists do not have a good fix on why the middle class invariably seems to spawn the leaders of revolutionary movements and terrorist groups—what the Middle East expert Martin Kramer has called "counter-elites"[21]—although they have suggested multiple possibilities, some, all, or none of which may be correct. They have explained it as an extension of rebellion against bourgeois society—indeed, the ultimate act of rebellion. They have also explained it as the ultimate sense of betrayed expectations. In a pattern that I have already noted is prevalent in the Arab world, the children of the middle class have the greatest sense of entitlement and so are also the angriest and most disappointed when economic and political conditions conspire to prevent them from realizing those aspirations.[22] Still another explanation lies in a typically middle-class sense that it is their duty to look after the lower classes and to champion their rights and needs when they cannot do it themselves, just as the Russian revolutionaries/terrorists were fighting for the good of the peasants and, later, the workers. In analyzing polling data from the Arab world, Mark Tessler and Michael Robbins speculated that what moves many people to terrorism is not necessarily their own circumstances but "an assessment of societal or national well-being" of "economic and political circumstances." They go on to note that a sense of "relative deprivation can prompt rebellious behavior, particularly when such deprivation can be attributed to" actors from beyond their own classes, ethnic groups, or even nationalities.[23]

The unfulfilled expectations of the middle class derived from the region's economic problems, coupled with (and in part caused by) crippling political practices, is almost certainly a powerful element driving many members of the Arab and Iranian middle classes to opposition and, at the extreme, membership in terrorist organizations.[24] For instance, Asef Bayat of Leiden University in Holland reports that "Political Islam in Egypt in [the 1990s] reflected primarily the rebellion of the impoverished middle class who were frustrated by a feeling of moral outrage. Their high expectations, an outcome of their high education and thus social status, were dampened in the job market, which offered few prospects for economic success."[25]

Indeed, many experts have noted a strong connection between educated unemployment, which typically afflicts the middle class (or those aspiring to be middle class), and terrorism in the Muslim Middle East.[26] Among the Palestinians, many suicide bombers recruited by Hamas and Islamic Jihad come from middle-class families and are well educated, "which made them even more bitter about their bleak prospects under Israeli occupation."[27] As one example, *The New York Times* reported on a twenty-year-old Jordanian from Zarqa who went to Iraq in 2007 to conduct a suicide bombing but was caught by U.S. forces. "His family was large and poor, with 17 children. Going to college gave him a glimpse of opportunities, but he failed to win a scholarship to study medicine in England, the sister said. 'Rich people go to his university,' she said. 'He wanted to be somebody and he couldn't.' He then became a devout Muslim, stopped listening to music, became withdrawn," and then decided to become a suicide bomber.[28] This correlation meshes with historical studies, such as that of Goldstone, who found that rebellions and religious movements of the sixteenth and seventeenth centuries in Europe were driven largely by young men from the ruling classes who arrived at adulthood in unusually large numbers at the same time and found that the existing patronage system could not reward them with the state salaries, land, or government positions they felt were appropriate to their class and educational achievement.[29]

Although we may not yet fully understand which, if any, of these explanations is most accurate, the historical evidence supporting the phenomenon itself is overwhelming. When a society's economic, social, and political problems intensify to the point that the country can be said to be in a prerevolutionary state, as so many of the countries of the Muslim Middle East are, intellectuals from the middle class (or occasionally from the upper class, like bin Ladin) invariably take it upon themselves to organize opposition parties, revolutionary movements, and (when the former fail to produce rapid results) insurgencies and terrorist groups. Widespread economic and social problems often delegitimize regimes, especially "in the eyes of those who spend a lot of time thinking about what they see," noted Alan Richards, "such as intellectuals, journalists, and students. Throughout history, most revolutionaries have not come from poor families. Revolutionaries, whether of the Leninist or Islamist variety, can usually 'pronounce their haitches' (are from privileged backgrounds), as George Orwell famously remarked in the 1930s. However, they find the appalling poverty of their societies to be morally outrageous and take action accordingly."[30]

TERRORISTS FROM THE POOR

Although the typical terrorist leader is well educated and a product of the middle class, there are still a great many terrorists from the lower classes, for whom economic and other forms of deprivation are much more direct motives. As discussed above, thirteen of the nineteen hijackers on 9/11 were not well educated and were from the lower classes. They were what Caroline Ziemke has called "muscle hijackers," whose job was to help intimidate and control the passengers. They had few skills and may not have even realized they were on a suicide mission. They were little more than "foot soldiers."[31] A considerable number of terrorist groups employ such foot soldiers, including all of the biggest groups—Hamas, Hizballah, al-Qaʾida, Fatah—and those foot soldiers are usually lower class, with little education, and from either impoverished rural areas or urban slums. As opposed to the well-educated and often highly skilled terrorist leadership cadre who plan and execute operations, these foot soldiers provide little more than bodies, brawn, and trigger fingers.[32]

Terroism experts Ami Pedahzur and Arie Perliger relate the story of one such impoverished terrorist:

> Mohammed Mahmoud Berro was sixteen years old when he was sent by AMAL to detonate a car bomb near the IDF headquarters at the village of Nabatia on 23 February 1985. Berro grew up in the slums of Beirut. In the fifth grade he left school and, in order to help support his family, started to work as a phone installer. However, in 1984, the phone infrastructure in Beirut collapsed and he was left unemployed. At this time, the economic status of the family became more difficult, and after his father had a traffic accident, the family had to borrow money from the AMAL movement in order to meet their financial needs. Soon, the AMAL members demanded that the family repay their debt, and that was when Berro, who knew that the family was unable to do this, volunteered for the suicide mission in order to pay back the AMAL organization.[33]

This is only one anecdote among many, but it illustrates how poor socioeconomic circumstances can prove a source of the kind of desperation that moves men (and women) to terrorism.[34]

In the 1990s, there was a significant shift in the terrorist/insurgency being waged by various Islamist and Salafi extremist groups against Mubarak's regime. As one astute observer remarked midway through the campaign:

> Compared to the 1970s, militants in the 1990s tend to be younger, less well educated, poorer, and more likely to reside in rural areas, shantytowns on urban outskirts, or urban slums. The average age of militants arrested and charged for acts of violence dropped from 27 years in the 1970s, to 21 years by 1990. Of the seven militants executed for attacks on tourists in 1993, three were below the age of 20. Whereas 80 percent of Islamist activists arrested in the 1970s were college students or graduates, by the 1990s they comprised only 20 percent. Those militants who had attended elite faculties, such as

medicine or engineering, dropped from one-half of those arrested to 11 percent in the same time period. In sum, the Islamist movement has become further radicalized and intensified because it increasingly reflects the interests of the lower classes, rather than those of the middle and upper-middle classes. Those youths most negatively affected by Egypt's faltering economy are the ones most likely to be Islamist insurgents.[35]

This trend is documented in Egyptian arrest records, which indicate that those arrested for violent actions against the regime are predominantly from the shantytowns surrounding Egypt's overburdened cities.[36]

In Iraq, many of the foreign terrorists imported by al-Qa'ida are also poorly educated and from the lower classes and are often so poor that they cannot pay their own way to get to Iraq.[37] This trend is even more predominant among Iraqi militants themselves. Both al-Qa'ida in Iraq (the main Sunni militia) and Jaysh al-Mahdi (the main Shi'i militia) are made up overwhelmingly of poor, unemployed young Iraqi men looking to belong to something larger than themselves and looking to lash out at whoever they feel is responsible for their plight. Most of them espouse religious zealotry (although many do not actually practice it), but it is their anger and desperation, derived from their circumstances, that drives them to religion and so to the militant groups, not the other way around.

Indeed, the slums and backwaters of the Arab world are almost uniformly hotbeds of Islamism and provide a seemingly endless supply of new recruits (mostly foot soldiers, but a few leaders) for the Salafi terrorists.[38] Richards notes that "The spread of violent opposition in Upper Egypt is also plausibly related to poverty. The *Sa'id* (Middle and Upper Egypt) is the poorest region in the country. Moreover, there, as elsewhere in the country, poverty has been rising during the past ten years." The Sa'id is also a bastion of Islamism where it is often dangerous for foreigners and regime officials to travel.[39] In December 1992, the Egyptian regime decided that the shantytown of Western Munira in Cairo had become a danger to the regime. The neighborhood was desperately poor, and the government provided it with virtually nothing. As a result, the residents turned to the Ikhwan and other Islamist groups, and many of its residents joined up with the likes of the Gama'a Islamiyya and EIJ. The regime eventually sent 12,000 troops backed by armored vehicles to retake the area, and it took them three weeks of house-to-house fighting to do so. And this was hardly unique as part of the regime's efforts to defeat the terrorists and insurgents.[40] The Shi'ah of Lebanon, one of the country's poorest major denominations, flock to Hizballah's banner not just because they oppose the Israelis and the other Lebanese factions but because Hizballah provides desperately needed social services. In return Hizballah expects, and receives, large numbers of young men from the community, most of them lower class, to serve as Hizballah fighters and terrorists.[41]

Although they constitute a special category, because of their prominence in modern terrorist attacks in the Middle East it is still worth considering that a great number of suicide bombers like Berro have also come from the lower classes.[42] Information on suicide bombers suggests fewer common traits than even the larger profiles of more general terrorists. However, what they do appear to have in common is a perception that they have no future, and poverty and unemployment appear to be frequent elements in this perception.[43] Adam Dolnik observed that suicide terrorists' "source of hopelessness is often socioeconomic in nature: unemployment, poverty, or lack of personal freedoms are all factors that play an important role."[44] For instance, some studies have noted that a fair number of the growing ranks of female suicide bombers are women divorced by their husbands because they were unable to bear children, which in traditional Islamic societies renders them essentially worthless.[45] Socioeconomic circumstances can also create a similar sense of hopelessness, motivating some—in part or in whole—to mount suicide attacks. Hamas leaders recognize that poverty and hopelessness increase support for them by making death and Paradise seem more appealing. "Look around and see how we live here," an elderly resident in Jenin complained in an interview with the terrorism expert Jessica Stern. "Then maybe you will understand why there are always volunteers for martyrdom. Every good Muslim understands that it's better to die fighting than to live without hope."[46] Stephen Dale, a historian of Islam, has documented how three Muslim communities in India, Indonesia, and the Philippines practiced suicide terrorism prior to World War II as a form of anticolonialism. "The activists were often young and almost always poor," in the words of Martha Crenshaw.[47]

That is why so many terrorist groups employ material incentives for new recruits, including suicide bombers.[48] There is no question that the Western media have grossly exaggerated both the munificence of these rewards and their importance to the recruits. The evidence suggests that they are frequently a secondary motivation, behind various psychological motives from commitment to the cause to anger or despair over individual circumstances. However, they do play a role. The proof of the pudding is in the eating: if they were not somehow useful in securing recruits, the groups (which are rarely rich) would not offer them. For instance, as of 2006, Palestinian families were promised anywhere from $12,000 to $20,000 for the death of one of their family members in a suicide attack. Although most families received considerably less in the end, those were the figures advertised, and they clearly were designed to entice men and women looking to help their families financially.[49] The Israeli counterterrorism expert Boaz Ganor states that "The majority of *shahids* [suicide bombers] come from a low-social-status background. The shahid improves his social status after his death, as well as that of his family. The family of the shahid is showered with honor and praise, and receives financial rewards for the attack."[50] Moreover, groups like Hamas and Hizballah have made considerable efforts over the years to see that the families of suicide bombers and other prominent terrorists have been provided with money, foodstuffs, child care, medical care, educational opportunities, jobs, and other material rewards specifically so that others would see that they took care of their own and be willing to join up in expectation that their families would be similarly cared for.[51] As one Hamas activist explained it, "These guys kill Israelis, but they also secure their families from poverty."[52] Overall Hamas is believed to distribute $2 million to $3 million in monthly handouts to the relatives of Palestinian suicide bombers.[53] The Gama'at in Egypt provided members "with low-cost lecture notes, textbooks, minibus transportation for (veiled) women and access to the study groups and tutoring services needed to pass examinations." One radical Islamist group even went so far as to provide its male members with housing, access to work in Saudi Arabia, and even wives.[54] Interestingly, the Saudis have created a program to try to "rehabilitate" captured Salafi terrorists, and they claim that they have enjoyed success by providing the subjects with jobs, cash for their families, and (again) wives.[55]

WHILE RECOGNIZING THE IMPORTANT role that economic problems play in giving rise to Middle Eastern terrorism, it is important not to fall prey to simple economic determinism in which poverty causes people to embrace terrorism. There is lots of poverty in the world, but most of it does not cause terrorism. Other factors must also be at work. Within the Middle East, the underlying causes should not be misconstrued as merely the presence of poverty. First, the problem on the economic side is more often relative deprivation—the sense that people's lives ought to be better than they are, both in an immediate, personal sense and on a grander, societal level. Second, purely economic factors like poverty or unemployment typically produce revolutionary and/or terrorist responses only when they are coupled with oppressive political forces that deny the individual any hope of bettering his (or her) situation but also serve as a tangible focus of anger.[56]

In the case of the Muslim Middle East, its interwoven economic, social, cultural, and political dysfunctions have created a large pool of deeply angry, frustrated, and fearful people. What led them to channel those feelings into terrorism was the fact that a ready model of terrorism was already at hand. Particularly the Palestinians, but also the Algerians (in the 1950s), Afghans, and Lebanese had all adopted terrorism as outgrowths of traditional ethnic-nationalist insurgent campaigns against stronger foes. In every case, these campaigns were viewed in a positive light, as heroic struggles, by the rest of the Muslim Middle East. Thus, when the underlying problems of the region began to produce widespread anger, frustration, resentment, and fear, it was easy for would-be revolutionary leaders to seize upon the terrorist model as a way of harnessing those emotions and for average people to view that model as being a reasonable response—and a potential solution—to their problems. Thus the relatively new phenomenon of Salafi social revolutionary terrorism was largely inspired by the earlier prevalence of ethnic-nationalist terrorism.

Feeding into this pattern has been the apparent success of bin Ladin and al-Qa'ida's campaigns first against the Soviets and then against the Americans (forgetting their failures against the Saudis, Egyptians, and other regional autocrats). Unlike other opposition leaders, bin Ladin seems to many Arabs to have produced tangible results, at least in the sense of actually striking blows at perceived oppressors. Although most Arabs and Muslims don't believe that these blows actually help with their problems, some do, and even those who don't may express sympathy for their motives, if not their methods. All of this can make someone like bin Ladin look attractive, as one of the only "leaders" who is actually taking action to alleviate the suffering of his people. In the words of one thirteen-year-old Moroccan boy, bin Ladin is "very courageous. Nobody did what he did. He challenges the whole world. He even challenges George Bush."[57] In a similar vein, former Deputy Assistant Secretary of the Treasury Matthew Levitt argues that poverty, humiliation, personal suffering, shame, or loss of a loved one can all propel an individual to embrace terrorism, but they typically require an established terrorist organization to do so. Without such a ready-to-hand model, the feelings of anger and frustration those sources create may be channeled into self-destructive behavior—like nihilism, materialism, alcohol and drug abuse, or even suicide—rather than the desire to kill and maim random civilians.[58]

The Friendly Sea

Beyond the direct role that the underlying economic, social, and political problems of the Muslim Middle East play in moving young men and, increasingly, women to join terrorist groups, these same factors play an even more important role in creating a national and regional context in which the terrorists are able not just to survive, but to thrive. Mao Zedong, among the greatest theorists and practitioners of guerrilla warfare, devised a famous analogy comparing the insurgent to the larger population. He said that the insurgent was like a fish and the people were the sea. Just as a fish cannot survive without the sea, so the guerrilla cannot survive without the support of the people. Thus, if the sea (the people) ever turned against the fish (the guerrilla), the fish was lost. More directly, he added that "Because guerrilla warfare basically derives from the masses and is supported by them, it can neither exist nor flourish if it separates itself from their sympathies and co-operation."[59]

Terrorism, of course, is a form of insurgent warfare. Although not all insurgencies employ terrorism, most have historically done so, and every terrorist group is, by definition, employing a form of insurgent warfare.[60] Moreover, as I noted earlier in this chapter, insurgency—and its terrorist component or variant—is a frequent element of the operations of revolutionary groups like the Chinese Communists, the Viet Minh, and various Latin American groups.

Without question, al-Qa'ida and the other Salafi terrorist groups are waging a terrorist insurgency, as a great many other experts have noted.[61] For this reason, maintaining the support of the people is absolutely critical to them.[62] That support comes mostly in the form of passive sympathy for al-Qa'ida's goals, which manifests itself most often in the form of an unwillingness to actively oppose it by aiding the regimes against it.

It is important to understand that the vast majority of Muslims do not like or agree with al-Qa'ida's methods. Most consider attacks on innocent civilians to be abhorrent. Their sympathies lie almost entirely with al-Qa'ida's goals and motives. When you speak to Muslim Middle Easterners about al-Qa'ida, what you typically hear is that they condemn the killing of innocents but then go on to some version of "But what do you expect? We are all desperate for change and the misery that all of us feel has driven some to do awful things."[63] Rami Khouri, the editor of Lebanon's *Daily Star* newspaper and one of the most balanced Arab commentators, implores American audiences to understand that

> most ordinary people in our region have given up hope that change will come from within or be promoted from abroad. Therefore we witness the terrible spectacle of a small number of bombers and terrorists who operate from our region, while

the majority of ordinary people silently watches them in a form of passive acquiescence and a sense of inevitability, feeling that violent rebellion and payback is the predictable consequence of decades of degradation and humiliation in our region. In the same manner, most Black Americans did not support the violence used by a few militants in the 1960s, but they understood why it happened and they watched it, by and large, without actively interceding to stop it.[64]

To some extent, bin Ladin has taken on a Robin Hood quality, as others have noted. As in the case of Robin Hood, people may recognize that his acts are morally wrong, but because they are directed at those whom the people see as their enemies, the source of their unhappiness, the actions are excused. And in some quarters they are positively extolled.

For its part, the al-Qa'ida leadership is well aware of its dependence on this passive support. In July 2005, az-Zawahiri addressed a letter to the then head of al-Qa'ida in Iraq, Abu Musab az-Zarqawi, in which he chastised az-Zarqawi for conducting grisly beheadings and other actions that threatened to alienate his group. He scolded az-Zarqawi that "In the absence of this popular support, the Islamic mujahed movement would be crushed in the shadows, far from the masses who are distracted or fearful, and the struggle between the Jihadist elite and the arrogant authorities would be confined to prison dungeons far from the public and the light of day. This is precisely what the secular, apostate forces that are controlling our countries are striving for. These forces don't desire to wipe out the mujahed Islamic movement, rather they are stealthily striving to separate it from the misguided or frightened Muslim masses."[65]

These sentiments are extremely important for the Salafi terrorist groups. It is just that sort of sympathy upon which they rely. Because the population is broadly sympathetic to their motives and goals, even if not their methods, it allows them to hide among the populace, recruit new members, and plan and conduct new operations. The terrorist, like other guerrillas, has no real ability to fight back against the firepower of the security services. All he can do is stash his weapons, blend into the populace, and hope that his identity is not revealed. Typically, the people generally know (or have strong suspicions) who the insurgents/terrorists in their neighborhood are. The key to victory in any counterinsurgency/counterterror campaign is convincing the people to tell the government forces who the insurgents/terrorists in their midst are. As long as the people see the government as part of the problem, not part of the solution, they have no incentive to give up that information, and that keeps the insurgent/terrorist safe.[66] This is what "passive support" means.

The terrorist or insurgent also relies on the "sea" of the people for recruitment. There is always attrition in any guerrilla war or terrorist campaign. Personnel are killed or captured by the government, they are killed or maimed in operations (especially suicide attacks), they are killed or maimed in accidents, they fight with other members of the group and choose to leave, or they simply tire of the cause or the life of a fugitive. Consequently, new recruits are the lifeblood of any insurgency or terrorist campaign. If the group cannot recruit, it will wither away quickly.[67] The hard core may remain, but it will find itself increasingly isolated and unable to mount operations if it is unable to constantly bring in new recruits, as both foot soldiers and leaders of the organization. As a result, terrorist groups go to enormous lengths to recruit.[68] In an extremely insightful book on suicide attacks, the terrorism expert Mia Bloom has demonstrated that a number of groups have adopted suicide terrorism and conducted specific attacks to better compete for recruits and resources with other, similar terrorist groups.[69]

But recruitment, as the previous section explained, requires a certain level of sympathy from the wider population.[70] There will always be the exceptions who will join no matter what the majority of people may believe. But especially for a vanguard party like al-Qa'ida, that is likely to be inadequate. Al-Qa'ida is not looking for oddballs—rebellious youths or psychotics looking for an excuse to kill—for its ranks, let alone its leadership cadre. Bin Ladin and company are looking for well-educated, intelligent, stable individuals with the skills and demeanor needed to blend into the larger population and carry out quite sophisticated attacks. To find such people, they need to have large numbers of people who want to join, so that they can pick out the best and brightest for membership. If all they could recruit were society's true misfits, that alone would greatly harm their operations. The more the society is broadly sympathetic to a group's motives and goals, the more individuals will be willing to adopt its extreme methods because they share its motives and want to help achieve those goals. There are always numbers of people with the "moral flexibility," to quote an old John Cusack film, to let the ends justify the means, no matter how horrific. But most of these individuals do need to be convinced that the ends are noble and are what their people aspire to. It is why the analogy of bin Ladin as Robin Hood is appropriate; the English all understood that stealing was morally wrong, but because Robin's thefts were aimed at the oppressors of the people (stealing from the rich) and designed to relieve their misery (giving to the poor), they were seen as noble and that made him popular. So, too, bin Ladin's motives and goals are considered noble, and that means that quite a few people are willing to join al-Qa'ida, giving it the pool of recruits it needs to keep waging its terrorist insurgency.[71] Let me reiterate that the vast bulk of Muslims do not seem to approve of his methods, but enough do *because* they see his goals as noble to furnish a sizable pool of recruits for al-Qa'ida and its affiliates.[72]

Finally, the insurgent or terrorist requires a supportive populace so that he can conduct his operations. In many ways this is a corollary of the first point about needing a reasonably sympathetic populace for cover. That was the defensive aspect of a terrorist's reliance on the population, but there is also an offensive aspect. The terrorist needs to be able to gather intelligence on potential targets; raise and transfer funds; purchase weapons and other supplies; manufacture bombs; conduct the attack; and then fade back into the woodwork when it is over. The ability to operate freely in the larger society is the sine qua non of every one of those steps. The terrorists/insurgents typically need information from other members of society. They need to be able to purchase what they need, some of which may be difficult to obtain. Other items may be inherently suspicious and, if information about their purchase were conveyed to the security services, would likely blow the terrorists' cover and/or the entire operation. They often raise money by engaging in various forms of crime, from muggings and break-ins to bank robberies and drug sales. Because their sources of funding are often shady or illegal, they need to help launder their funds.[73] They need safe houses where they can meet, prepare their materials, and then hide afterward without fear that their presence or activities will be reported to the authorities. And they need to be able to move from place to place relatively freely. All of these activities entail actions that will be noticeable to other people. If the general predisposition of society is against the terrorists, there is a fairly high likelihood that someone will not only notice their actions but report them to the security services explicitly so that they can be prevented. On the other hand, if the populace is generally sympathetic to the terrorist or, to be more accurate, generally antagonistic to the regime, there is a much lower likelihood that these actions will be reported to the security services.

Moreover, the more antagonistic the populace is to terrorist operations, the more supportive it typically is of extensive counterterrorist measures. As many Americans are now aware, counterterrorism security measures inflict annoying and costly impositions on an individual's life—from having to take off your shoes at airports to going through metal detectors at museums to more frequent and onerous identity checks. Obviously, there are even greater levels of intrusiveness that compromise basic civil and human rights—wiretaps, government examination of personal information, other forms of surveillance—that can also be extremely helpful in fighting terrorism but intrude much more on the rights and freedoms of the populace. The more the populace is antipathetic to the terrorists, the more willing they will be to tolerate counterterrorism measures and therefore the harder it will be for the terrorists to operate. The more antipathetic the people are to the government itself, the more they will oppose and even evade or subvert its counterterror measures. They may do so because they hope that the terrorists will succeed or merely because they resent the intrusions on their rights and liberties created by the counterterror measures more than they dislike the terrorists.

Some examples might be useful here. Prior to 9/11, the United States had a problem in that most Americans were not even aware that there were terrorists operating in the United States. But since then people have been far more vigilant and, because they oppose the terrorists, are much more willing to report suspicious behavior, making it easier for law enforcement agencies to catch potential terrorists. Moreover, the American people now tolerate considerable intrusions into their lives and infringements on their freedoms in the name of preventing terrorists from operating easily. These are important reasons why there has not been another terrorist attack in the United States since 9/11.

Similarly, Israeli society is hypersensitive to terrorist operations, which has forced Palestinian militant groups to locate all of their bases of operation in the West Bank and Gaza, outside Israeli society. Palestinian terrorists must then try to penetrate into Israel and stay alive and under cover long enough to mount their attack, which is extremely difficult for any period of time because the Israelis are so vigilant. It is why only a small percentage of Palestinian terrorist attacks against Israel actually succeed.

Other examples abound. As I have noted several times, an important element in the demise of the IRA was the Catholics' change in attitudes toward the Provos as their economic and political fortunes improved in the 1990s and 2000s.[74] Indeed, the first two conclusions of a major study by the RAND Corporation on the relationship between terrorism and socioeconomic forces were that "Social and economic development policies can contribute to the expansion of a new middle class in communities that have traditionally lent support to terrorist groups. In many cases, this section of the population has recognized the economic benefits of peace and, as a result, has worked to inhibit local support for terrorist activities" and that "Many terrorist organizations attract new members from communities in which terrorism is generally considered a viable response to perceived grievances. Some terrorist groups also offer recruits financial incentives and additional family support. Social and economic development policies can help to reduce the pools of potential recruits by reducing their perceived grievances and providing the members of these communities with viable alternatives to terrorism."[75]

Another useful illustration of this pattern is Egypt's experience in the 1990s. Egyptians were deeply unhappy because of the same underlying economic, social, and political problems plaguing all of the

Arab states to a greater or lesser degree, and the society had fallen into a prerevolutionary state. As a result, for much of the 1980s and 1990s, there was widespread sympathy for the various Islamist groups trying in various ways to bring about a revolution—whether peacefully like the Ikhwan, via an insurgency (which included terrorism) like the Gama'a Islamiyya, or through a straightforward terror campaign like EIJ. For most of the 1990s, the Mubarak regime could not crush the insurgents and terrorists because the populace was largely supportive of them. However, in the late 1990s, the terrorists went too far: they mounted attacks on Egyptian policemen, who were seen not as members of the government but as average Egyptians trying to do an important job; their attacks killed innocents, particularly children, which outraged the population; and they killed tourists, who are a critical element of Egypt's economy. In fact, the killing of tourists caused a temporary collapse in Egypt's tourism industry, which immediately affected the lives of a great many Egyptians. The result was a sudden, if temporary, volte-face by the populace. They turned on the Gama'a, EIJ, and other Salafi extremist groups, and in about eighteen months the regime was able to smash all of them, forcing most to declare a cease-fire and driving others, like EIJ, out of the country altogether.[76]

Along similar lines, a key element in the success of Saudi efforts to suppress al-Qa'ida in the Arabian Peninsula (AQAP, the branch of the movement working in Saudi Arabia) was an identical change in public perceptions. In 2003 and 2004, AQAP conducted a number of attacks that increasingly alienated the Saudi populace. In May 2003, it launched the famous Riyadh blasts, which killed 30 people in foreign residential compounds. However, in November of that same year it drove a pair of vans loaded with explosives into an Arab residential complex, killing 17 and wounding 120, including large numbers of children. This soured large segments of the Saudi populace, which apparently was willing to tolerate the killing of innocent foreigners but not Saudis and other Arabs. In April 2004, AQAP launched a further attack on a Saudi police headquarters, killing 5 and wounding 148. This too was beyond what the Saudi populace was willing to tolerate, and the Saudi authorities reported increasing cooperation on the part of the populace in rounding up AQAP members. By the summer of 2005, al-Qa'ida in the Arabian Peninsula was effectively nonoperational. Although the ruthless efforts of the Saudi security services were certainly an important element in the campaign, the key difference from other, prior Saudi counterterror campaigns was the support they received from the Saudi people.[77]

Unfortunately, however, in most of the Muslim Middle East, there is extensive support for the goals of the Salafi terrorists. Mark Tessler of the University of Michigan found that polls of Arab and Muslim populations showed a "significant level of approval for events like 9/11, for the principle of 'armed jihad' against the West, and for al Qaeda and Osama bin Laden."[78] As long as the bulk of the people of the region remain desperate and frustrated with their lot, unable to achieve economically, socially, and politically what they believe they are entitled to, and angry at their government for consigning them to this state of affairs through callousness, corruption, and mismanagement, the sentiments will remain. Moreover, in many areas, the failure of the governments to provide basic services allows Islamist groups, some of them attached to terrorist groups, to move in and do for the people instead. The fact that they do so builds tremendous goodwill with the populace and significantly deepens the willingness of the members of the community to overlook, conceal, or even participate in terrorist activities being conducted by the group or its affiliates.[79]

This pervasive passive support has been absolutely critical to the persistence and success of the Salafi terrorist groups, despite the unprecedented level of pressure that has been brought to bear on them.[80] As long as Arab and Muslim populations remain passively supportive of them, it is going to be extremely difficult to ever destroy them fully, and, even if we do, we are likely to find that new groups just like them (and probably worse, if history is any guide) will spring up to take their place. As Joyce Davis has remarked, "Militants find easy recruits in the dust and dilapidation of refugee camps in Jordan, Lebanon, and Gaza and in the rat-infested squalor of Egyptian slums. And many who would never join them, who recoil at the use of Islam to defend such horror, much as Christians recoil at the Ku Klux Klan's claim to be followers of Jesus, say they share the rage that nurtures such evil, that turns young men and women into *shuhada.* Martyrs."[81]

Anti-Americanism

Another way in which the underlying problems of the Muslim Middle East contribute to the terrorist threat we face from the region stems from their role in stimulating anti-Americanism. This too is an important consideration from the perspective of American interests because not all terrorism is a direct threat to the United States and some has little impact on U.S. interests at all. There is an argument to be made, for example, that Baluchi terrorism against the Iranian regime helps legitimize other terrorist actions, including those against the United States. But this is a real stretch. Although we should condemn it for the sake of condemning all acts of terrorism, it is certainly not worth going to war over. Consequently, anything that causes people not just to launch terrorist attacks but to launch them against the United States is something we should seek to address.

Like terrorism itself, anti-Americanism is an extremely complex phenomenon, which seems to be the product of multiple, reinforcing elements. There is no single "cause" of anti-Americanism in the Middle East; therefore it would be inappropriate (and simply wrong) to argue that all anti-Americanism can be traced back to the underlying problems. America is, unfortunately, hated for a great many reasons. Some have to do with policies we pursue that many Muslim Middle Easterners dislike: our support for Israel, our current occupation of Iraq (regardless of what the Iraqi people and their leaders may want),[82] and, especially under the Bush 43 administration, our unwillingness to make a determined effort to broker an Arab-Israeli peace and alleviate the suffering of the Palestinians, to name only the most obvious. Many countries have additional grievances—real and imagined—specific to their own circumstances. The fact that many of these policies are, at least to some extent, imaginary, exaggerated, or misunderstood does not make them any less a source of grievance to those who believe them wholeheartedly.

Another important source of anti-Americanism in the Middle East (and the world) is resentment of America's size and strength. In spite of its troubles in Iraq, America today is still the "hyperpower" with economic and military power unmatched by any other nation on Earth and unlike anything the world has ever seen. As others have observed, our position in the world is analogically closest to that of Rome at the height of its empire—although Rome always had a great rival in the East, the Parthians or the Sassanids, of equal power, whereas the United States has none. With such power invariably come envy and fear, the latter particularly after the reckless aggressiveness of the Bush 43 administration. Indeed, a common but extreme version of this phenomenon is the belief that the United States is seeking to conquer or colonize the rest of the world.[83]

According to the RAND *Chronicle of International Terrorism,* American citizens have been the principal target of terrorist attacks every single year since 1968. Similarly, the U.S. State Department's Special Coordinator for Terrorism reported that during the 1990s, 40 percent of all terrorist attacks around the world were directed against U.S. citizens or property.[84] Since U.S. policy on a wide variety of issues has changed constantly since 1968 and globalization was not much of a problem for the rest of the world before the 1990s, it is hard to blame these patterns on those policies. Instead, it suggests that a good deal of the anger being focused at the United States in the form of terrorist attacks is motivated by America's size and strength, as well as its role as the dominant global power in maintaining the status quo.

Then there is the association between the United States and globalization, modernity, and the homogenization of culture. As I noted in chapter 5, people often react with fear and general antipathy to the invasion of a seemingly alien culture through their television screens, cell phones, computers, iPods, and the like. For better or worse, because the United States is the leading economy of the world, a major source of technological innovation, and the capital of "mass culture," it is typically associated with globalization and modernity. In many ways, the United States was the first to adapt to globalized culture, and, having done so, we then turned around and started to export it to the world, even though many Americans continue to dislike it.[85] Steven Simon, a longtime U.S. government expert on terrorism, quotes a "typical online expression" of Muslim fear and anger at America's decadent cultural imperialism: "This is the America that occupies the world with the culture of sex and deviation. This is the pagan civilization in Christian disguise. . . . This is the American civilization whose object is the body and its means is materialism. The spirit has no place in the system of American values. They are dressed with Christian clothes on hearts that know nothing but stealing, robbing, and occupying the possessions of others. Has America left one place in our lives as Muslims without corrupting it?"[86]

This association of the United States with globalization and modernity is the first of the ways in which the underlying problems of the region—including the widespread perception that their culture is under "attack" by globalization—contributes to the problem of anti-Americanism that has turned the Salafi terrorist groups against us. According to the Bulgarian scholar Atanas Gotchev:

> Globalization . . . fosters political and cultural resistance. The development of global markets for goods, services, and capital compels societies to alter their cultural practices. Globalization brings about cultural Westernization and destroys traditional ways of life. In response, this provokes opposition of broad segments in the affected societies, providing another justification for terrorism. Indeed the infiltration of a supposedly alien and corrupt culture is used by nationalist and radical religious movements as a way of explaining their campaigns. They claim that their violence has the purpose of cleansing their societies and culture from foreign influence. In reality, these are often mere excuses, yet it is also true that the "threat to the local way of life" has become a convenient motivation and justification for terrorist activities.[87]

In support of this, a poll of people in fourteen Muslim countries conducted in 2002 found that "[people who felt that] Islam was under threat were more likely to support terrorism than those who did not have such threat perceptions, all other variables held invariant."[88] A Gallup poll in ten Muslim countries found the same thing: the tiny minority who felt that the 9/11 attacks were "fully justified" were more fearful of American "occupation" or "domination," whereas the majority were more concerned with economic issues.[89]

Of equal or greater importance, however, is the widespread tendency of many people in the Arab world to hate the United States because they believe (rightly and wrongly) that we support the autocratic regimes that they (rightly) hold responsible for their misery. Jordan's former prime minister Taher Masri warns that "those 19 people who were on the planes were not only protesting against the U.S. but against the internal situations in their own countries."[90] Thus the anger and despair they feel because of the actions (and inaction) of their own governments get transferred to the United States in the belief that we are the ultimate power behind the local autocrats. Some go so far as to insist that the United States wants to keep them miserable and essentially orders their regimes to do so. Most simply believe both that the United States is complicit in the policies of the Arab regimes (and therefore equally responsible for the sad state of their economy, educational system, legal system, government, etc.) and that the United States effectively prevents the regimes from being overthrown by revolutionaries—including Salafi terrorists—whom a great many, probably the vast majority, would like to see succeed.[91] In explaining the motives of one Arab suicide bomber, Joyce Davis recounts that he "went every day to pray at mosques where he heard imams lambasting the U.S. and Israel, whom they blamed for the despotism of Middle Eastern governments, for the lack of jobs and for the overall misery so prevalent in the Arab world."[92] Once again, polls of Jordanians and Algerians taken in 2002 lend further support, showing a high correlation between whether people approved of terrorist attacks on the United States and their degree of unhappiness with their own government.[93]

Mark Tessler and Michael Robbins describe a related study of the sources of anti-Americanism that is worth reading in full.

While it is not self-evident that anger at domestic leaders would foster support for international terrorism, a connection is suggested by an insightful study carried out in Morocco during the war to liberate Kuwait following Saddam Hussein's invasion of that country in 1990. As in many other Arab countries, there were popular demonstrations in Morocco against the U.S.-led coalition seeking to expel Iraq's army from

Kuwait. This was puzzling to some observers, since Saddam had invaded a fellow Arab country and was known to be a brutal dictator. Yet it was the United States and its coalition partners, which included the government of Morocco and other Arab countries, who were viewed as the real enemy. Mounia Bennani-Chraibi, a Moroccan sociologist, investigated this apparent puzzle through interviews with young Moroccans and reported that "unshared wealth was the central theme of discourse." More specifically, U.S. and Arab leaders were seen as acting in concert to ensure the survival of a status quo that privileged the few while denying opportunity to the vast majority. Young Moroccans viewed the anti-Saddam coalition as a self-interested partnership in which American and Arab "enemies of the people" worked together to preserve a corrupt political and economic order.[94]

Although al-Qa'ida's assumption that the Arab autocrats are American puppets and would collapse without Washington's support is ridiculous, U.S. support has in some ways helped them retain their grip on power. While the F-16 fighters we sell to Egypt (among other countries) are not ideal for counterinsurgency operations, let alone riot control, the M-1 tanks we also sell it can be useful for these purposes. Moreover, mere possession of such powerful weapons can intimidate the population, making them less willing to openly oppose the regimes. American military personnel and contractors provide extensive training and advice to many of the Arab militaries, including some of their internal security forces. This makes those forces more capable of suppressing domestic unrest. Moreover, the United States provides varying degrees of financial aid to different Arab governments, particularly Egypt, which is the third largest recipient of American aid (after Iraq and Israel), and this money also helps the regimes hold power. On at least one occasion—Lebanon in 1958—the United States sent troops to the Middle East to prevent a friendly Arab government from falling to internal threats when President Camille Chamoun convinced the Eisenhower administration that the domestic opposition to illegally extending his presidency was the work of Nasserists allied with the Soviet Union looking to take over Lebanon. During the Iranian Revolution, the United States encouraged the shah to use whatever means necessary (including a bloody crackdown) to hold power. After the shah fled, the Carter administration sent a U.S. general to Tehran to try to organize a counterrevolution.[95] Although it has never been put to the test, there is reason to believe that many American administrations would react in a similar fashion to similar internal threats in Saudi Arabia, Kuwait, Egypt, Jordan, Qatar, the UAE, and possibly other countries.

As a final point on the question of how the underlying problems of the Arab world contribute to anti-Americanism and in turn to terrorist attacks on Americans, the Middle East experts Barry Rubin and Judith C. Rubin point out a perverse collusion between the Salafi extremists and the regimes they detest. In their words, "While the Islamist revolutionaries were trying to overthrow their Arab nationalist rulers, the latter actually agreed with them on the point of promoting anti-Americanism. The mutual accusations against the United States by Arab nationalist regimes and Islamist oppositions reinforced each other. Rulers even increased the volume of their anti-American rhetoric to co-opt potential supporters of the opposition and to shore up their Islamic, as well as patriotic legitimacy. The result was a spiraling upward of anti-American propaganda."[96]

Alternative Explanations for Terrorist Attacks on the United States

Because anti-Americanism is such a complicated phenomenon and so many different sources seem to feed into it, any number of explanations have been offered for the apparent rise in Middle Eastern terrorist attacks on the United States. For instance, American support for Israel clearly plays some role in inciting various Middle Eastern terrorist groups, including the Salafi extremists, to mount attacks against U.S. targets, but its importance is hotly debated. Some people contend that America's support for Israel is a critical motivation for the Salafi terrorists, arguing (sometimes explicitly, sometimes implicitly) that if there were peace between Israelis and Arabs—or if the United States were to withdraw its support for Israel—these terrorist attacks would greatly abate if not disappear altogether. Others claim that Islam preaches hatred of the West and that this is a principal motivating force for Salafi terror attacks. My own sense of the evidence is that while America's support for Israel almost certainly plays a significant role in Salafi terror attacks against the United States, religion plays only a minor role, and it is religion generally, not anything specific to Islam, that has an impact. Moreover, neither U.S. support for Israel nor the injection of religion into the terrorist mix is as important as the anger felt by so many Muslim Middle Easterners at their economic, social, and political circumstances and the extent to which they blame the U.S. government for these problems.

HATRED OF ISRAEL AS A MOTIVE FOR ANTI-AMERICAN TERRORISM

It is not exactly a revelation to say that there is a great deal of hatred of Israel in the Muslim Middle East (and vice versa). Similarly, there is quite a bit of terrorism directed at the Jewish state, although the vast majority of the terrorist attacks against Israel have been conducted by Palestinian groups and, to a much lesser extent, Lebanon's Hizballah—all of which are predominantly ethnic-nationalist terrorists, not social revolutionaries like al-Qa'ida. There is also no question that a good deal of the anti-Americanism in the region derives from America's strategic relationship with Israel. After the September 11 attacks, one Lebanese expressed the sentiments of a great many Arabs: "People are happy. America has always supported terrorism. They see how the innocent Palestinian children are killed and they back the Zionist army that does it. America has never been on the side of justice."[97] Paul Pillar, long one of the U.S. government's most incisive experts on terrorism and the wider Middle East, adds:

The material and diplomatic support that Washington gives Israel, from arms sales to vetoes at the United Nations Security Council, complements a perception of the United States as leader of the Judeo-Christian West, using Israel as a means for pursuing confrontation with the Muslim world. The details of U.S. policy and the many instances in which U.S. and Israeli policies diverge are noticed by Muslim elites but make little difference to broader Muslim populations, for whom the overall pattern is what matters. It would be very difficult for the United States to stop receiving a generous share of the animosity directed against Israel, until and unless the conflict over Palestine is resolved.[98]

Moreover, bin Ladin, az-Zawahiri, and other al-Qa'ida leaders have routinely trumpeted America's support for Israel as one justification for their attacks. Bin Ladin has been calling for a boycott of American goods by the Islamic world because of U.S. backing of Israel since at least 1989.[99] In virtually every statement or videotape released by the group, there is at least some reference to the U.S.-Israeli relationship, and in some it has been given a fairly prominent role.

However, there is considerable evidence that al-Qa'ida's hatred of Israel, and hatred of the United States for its support of Israel, is a secondary grievance behind U.S. support for the Arab autocracies, as well as its perception that the United States is championing a wider war by the Christian West against Islam. In this cosmic conception, Israel serves as a Jewish cat's-paw of the West, led by the United States. Bin Ladin may or may not have hated Israel his whole life, but he appears to have begun agitating against the United States in 1982 and added American support for Israel to his public calls for action seven years later.[100] His decision to attack the United States was, according to his own history, caused by the American military deployment to Saudi Arabia in 1991 as part of Operations Desert Shield and Desert Storm, when U.S. and other foreign armies deployed to the kingdom to protect the Arab world from Saddam Husayn's armies and then roll them back to free Kuwait from his control.[101]

Even the rhetoric came late. "The furies that moved Osama bin Laden to make war against America did not, in the first instance, include the plight of the Palestinians," as Dana Allin of the International Institute for Strategic Studies and Steve Simon put it.[102] Likewise, Fawaz Gerges, among others, argues that after September 11, when bin Ladin and company suddenly realized that they had awakened a sleeping giant and galvanized the world's only remaining superpower to action, they became desperate to build support for their actions in the Arab and Islamic worlds, "they re-branded Al

Qaeda as a champion of Palestinians and Iraqis, people in whose suffering bin Ladin hadn't previously shown serious interest."[103] Gilles
Kepel echoes this point, observing that Ayman az-Zawahiri wrote
that Palestine provided mostly a rallying cause for Salafi extremists
after the failure of the Oslo Process (in 2000) and that "The downward spiral in Palestine provided the opportunity that the master-
minds of September 11 had been waiting for. They conceived of the
carnage in New York and Washington as an extension of the Palestinian suicide bombings, whose popularity bin Laden sought to
channel for his own purposes."[104]

Of course, actions inevitably speak even louder than words, and
as many of the world's leading experts on terrorism and al-Qa'ida
have observed, despite all of its rhetoric and the many opportunities
to do so, al'Qa'ida has so far not attacked Israel. Bin Ladin and his
compatriots have attacked nearly every Arab government in the region and repeatedly gone after the United States, but never Israel.[105]
As Pillar observes, "The rhetoric of terrorist leaders may be an indicator of what issues they believe resonate with the wider audiences
they are addressing, but it is not necessarily an accurate gauge of
terrorists' motivations, including their own."[106] In other words, al-
Qa'ida's rhetorical attacks on Israel may be more about rallying Muslim support for its actions than about its true priorities.

All of this strongly suggests that no matter how much bin Ladin,
az-Zawahiri, and other Salafi terrorists may hate Israel and hate the
United States for supporting Israel (and they clearly do), this is not
the principal cause of their actions. In particular, there is no reason
to believe that if the state of Israel disappeared tomorrow, it would
diminish their zeal to kill Americans one jot. In this sense, the Salafi
terrorists are very different from the various Palestinian militant
groups like Hamas, PIJ, al-Aqsa Martyrs' Brigade, and others, as well
as from Hizballah. For those groups, Israel is the number one enemy,
and their hatred of the United States is based principally on its support for Israel. However, those groups are not attacking the United
States today and have not attacked Americans in twenty years or
more. Thus, in this area as well, American support for Israel is not
creating a terrorist threat to the United States. Those who are attacking us do not hate us principally for our support of Israel, and

those who do hate us principally for our support of Israel are not attacking us.

But we should not take from this the idea that American support for Israel is unrelated to the terrorist threat we face. It may be less than what is often claimed, and the relationship may be different from what is typically portrayed, but there *is* a relationship. This comes through in the critically important indirect support provided to the Salafi terrorists by the wider population of the Muslim Middle East.

Earlier in this chapter I spent a fair amount of space explaining that the support of the people, even passive support, was vital to terrorist movements and their operations and demonstrated that a great deal of that support was derived from popular unhappiness and anger at their own governments—and that this anger was further projected onto the United States for supporting their governments. Indeed, *that,* not support for Israel, is the principal grievance of the Salafi terrorists against the United States. However, the wider Arab population does hate Israel intensely, perhaps more than average Salafi terrorists do (which would be another way that they are different from other Arabs), and this hatred is another motive for them to provide the passive support that terrorists require to survive and operate. Indeed, it is this very hatred of Israel, and of the United States for supporting Israel, that Kepel, Gerges, and others believe bin Ladin was attempting to tap into when he suddenly began emphasizing al-Qa'ida's opposition to Israel after September 11. Fearing the wrath of the United States, bin Ladin and company needed the support of the wider Islamic population to protect them and so played up the notion that their attacks on America had been motivated by our support for Israel, even though that had previously been a lesser element of al-Qa'ida's grievances.

Of greatest importance, it seems to have worked—at least in a limited way. Some Muslim Middle Easterners did decide that al-Qa'ida's attack had been meant as retaliation against the United States for supporting Israel, and their approval of bin Ladin and his band increased in response, which helped al-Qa'ida withstand the American onslaught when it came. Bergen quotes a former deputy prime minister of Yemen as complaining after the al-Qa'ida attack

on the U.S.S. *Cole* in Aden harbor in 2000 that "There was no justification for the *Cole* bombing. I was shocked and surprised. But the
U.S. bears a great degree of responsibility for the incident for the
way the U.S. deals with issues in the Middle East. It is not just Palestine and its stand on Israel, but the totality of U.S. policies. . . . Since
America is going to continue this policy, it will see a lot of things like
this."[107] In attempting to discern the sources of Arab public support
for Salafi terrorists, Mark Tessler has consistently found in polling
data that Arabs and Muslims are angry at the United States mostly
for its foreign policy decisions—particularly U.S. support for Israel
and, later, the U.S. invasion and occupation of Iraq.[108] Similarly, to
the extent that Western intelligence agencies and terrorist experts
have been able to comprehend how Salafi terrorist groups recruit,
they have often found that hatred of Israel, and U.S. support for Israel, has been one motive (among many).[109]

Nevertheless, this too needs to be kept in perspective. As fierce as
Arab hatred of Israel and Israeli actions may be, and as important as
that hatred may be in making average people tolerate or even admire
Salafi terrorist attacks on the United States for our support (real and
exaggerated) of Israel, the evidence indicates that except for the
Palestinians, this is a secondary motive for most people, behind their
own unhappy existences. For example, in a 2007 Zogby survey of
public opinion in Egypt, Jordan, Lebanon, Morocco, Saudi Arabia,
and the UAE, only 14 percent of respondents said they sympathized
with al-Qa'ida because it stood for "Muslim causes such as the Palestine issue." This was third in a field of five responses, with al-
Qa'ida's willingness to confront the United States first with 33
percent.[110] In other words, to the extent that Arabs sympathize with
al-Qa'ida, it is mostly out of direct anti-Americanism and not because of any perception that it is fighting against Israel on behalf of
the Palestinians. In an important, preliminary study of how Arab behavior may differ from attitudes (i.e., how actions are diverging from
words), Robert Satloff, Eunice Youmans, and Mark Nakhla of the
Washington Institute for Near East Policy compiled a database of
321 acts of public protest in the Arab world against the United States
between 2000 and 2005 and found that 73 percent had been triggered by acts of U.S. policy, whereas only 20 percent had been pro-

voked by acts of Israeli policy.[111] In conclusion, they noted that "a strong likelihood exists that responses to poll questions are skewed by factors ranging from social expectations, to perception of political correctness, to fear of intrusion of intelligence agencies into the polling process, to the ethnic, religious, linguistic, and racial characteristics of both the pollsters and those they poll."[112]

Moreover, it is crucial to keep in mind the link between popular support for Islamist groups and passive support for Salafi jihadists, who are ultimately an outgrowth of the same movement in the Arab world. Most Arabs do *not* support the Islamists because the Islamists hate Israel (although mostly they do); they support the Islamists because the Islamists oppose the autocratic governments and are working to bring about far-reaching (i.e., revolutionary) changes in their societies. The Salafi terrorists are popular/tolerated because they too claim to be trying to bring about exactly the same kind of changes to the status quo, and *that* is the principal source of their support among the population. Anger at the United States for supporting Israel undoubtedly feeds into Arab support for (or merely toleration of) the Salafi terrorists; however, there is little reason to believe that such passive support would evaporate if Israel disappeared but there were no changes in their economic, social, and political conditions. The anger and despair would remain. It would continue to feed the popularity of the Islamist groups and the Salafi terrorists as long as they continued to work for the same kind of revolution in Arab affairs. Indeed, as angry as many Arabs may be about American support for Israel, that is not why they are demanding new governments. The principal rallying cry of the Ikhwan and other Islamist groups is not "Support us, and we will fight Israel and America." It is "Support us, and we will bring you better lives." The people of the Muslim Middle East are angry about a lot of things; Israel is certainly one of them, but it is not their foremost source of anger or the principal reason that they want new governments, and those are the driving forces behind both the Islamist groups and the Salafi terrorists.

ISLAM IS NEITHER THE PROBLEM NOR THE SOLUTION

There is no getting around the fact that in the contemporary world, terrorism from the Middle East has an increasingly "Islamic" flavor

to it. Even formerly secular groups like Fatah—the principal component of the PLO—have adopted religious rhetoric to explain their
actions, naming their military wing the al-Aqsa Martyrs' Brigade.[113]
In Lebanon, the secular Shi'i group AMAL has been all but superseded by the Islamist Hizballah. Although there are important structural reasons why this is the case (described in chapter 7), the fact
that Islamist groups are on the rise across the Arab world and their
Salafi extremist "fellow travelers" have similarly risen to prominence
in the terrorism world creates a superficial impression that everything going on in the Arab and Islamic worlds is somehow about—if
not caused by—Islam. Moreover, since the terrorists now invariably
explain their actions by citing verses from the Qur'an and the Hadiths, and the Islamists have similarly forced all sides to conduct political debates in the context of religious ideas, it is easy for
Americans and other Westerners to make the mistake that somehow
Islam is to blame for all of it.

Islam is not the reason for the rise of Islamist movements, nor is
it the cause of the terrorist threat that the United States faces. As
many scholars of Islam have observed, like all of the great religions of
the world, Islam is so rich and varied in its precepts that individuals
can find bits and pieces they can always twist to justify anything.[114] As
Shakespeare cautioned in *The Merchant of Venice,* "the Devil can cite
scripture for his purpose." It is certainly true that the terrorists invariably justify their actions based on their interpretation of Islam,
but there are two key "buts" to this point: first, a terrorist is hardly
going to say that he killed a group of innocent people because he
hated his job or was denied a license or some other mundane source
of frustration—especially when he can claim instead that he killed
for God—and second, this interpretation is not widely accepted in
the Islamic world. A lot of people have done horrific things based
on their interpretation of Christianity (the Crusades, the Inquisi-
tion, the Thirty Years' War, David Koresh and the Branch Davidians)
or Judaism (Baruch Goldstein, who killed twenty-nine innocent
Arabs at the Tomb of the Patriarchs in 1994; Yigal Amir, who killed
Prime Minister Yitzhak Rabin). That does not mean their actions
were the result of Christianity or Judaism.[115]

A great many Islamic scholars have thoroughly rejected the interpretations used by the Salafi terrorists to justify their actions, and most Muslims do not accept them either. Very few fatwas have been written by Islamic scholars in support of terrorism. Most Muslim scholars regard Salafi extremist ideas as abhorrent and their actions as criminal.[116] "Establishment clerics were virtually unanimous in condemning the [9/11] attacks on religious grounds."[117] Shaykh Yusef al-Qaradawi, one of the most well-known religious scholars in the Arab world; Shaykh Muhammad Sayyid Tantawi, the Grand Imam of al-Azhar; and Grand Ayatollah Muhammad Husayn Fadlallah, the spiritual leader of Hizballah, all condemned both the 9/11 attacks and bin Ladin for perpetrating them.[118] Fadlallah has also famously wrestled with the question of whether Hizballah's own suicide attacks are consistent with Shi'i Islam.[119]

As for the masses of the Islamic world, they tend to like what the Salafi extremists stand *against* far more than they like what the Salafi extremists stand *for*. Some may cheer, openly or secretly, when al-Qa'ida wounds the United States, rails against American imperialism and Western culture, or joins the chorus of voices preaching the destruction of the autocratic Arab regimes (and Israel), but very few want the world that bin Ladin and his followers hope to create. Very, very few Arabs believe that the restoration of the caliphate will solve their problems and should be their principal political goal, as the Salafi extremists claim. In fact, a 2007 survey in Egypt, Jordan, Lebanon, Morocco, Saudi Arabia, and the UAE found that only 7 percent sympathized with al-Qa'ida's goal of creating an Islamic state.[120] Similarly, a 2005 Gallup poll of ten predominantly Muslim countries found that only 7 percent of the respondents felt the September 11 attacks were "fully justified" and had an "unfavorable" or "very unfavorable" opinion of the United States—moreover, this 7 percent was no more or less religious than the other 93 percent.[121] In Iraq, Salafi extremists started a backlash against themselves from Sunni tribesmen in al-Anbar Province when they began imposing their radical version of Shari'a law, including cutting off people's hands for smoking. Moreover, the vast majority of Arabs and Muslims ardently desire the kind of political pluralism (even democracy, discussed in the next chapter) that bin Ladin and his ilk have declared antithetical to Islam—at least their version of it.[122] "What prompts a 20-year-old to blow himself up and kill as many Israelis as he can in the process?" the Jordanian political analyst Labib Kamhawi asks rhetorically. "It definitely takes more than belief in God to turn a boy into a martyr. It takes desperation, anger, loss of hope. It's believing that your life is not worth living anymore."[123]

Even within their own ideology, the Salafi extremists pick and choose what they like, ignoring what they don't like. Thus their interpretations of Islam are largely arbitrary and inconsistent. For instance, the most important Islamic scholar upon which they base their actions is Taqi ad-Din Ahmad ibn Taymiyyah, who wrote at the turn of the fourteenth century. First of all, ibn Taymiyyah is not exactly a mainstream Islamic scholar, and his ideas are largely rejected by most authorities within Islam. However, as the Islamic scholar Abdul Hadi Palazzi notes, the Islamists are willing to base their claim that religion and government are inseparable in Islam on ibn Taymiyyah's ideas but then ignore the fact that he also flatly stated that "there is no Muslim holy place in Jerusalem," which is the cornerstone of their demands for the destruction of Israel.[124]

Nor is it the case, as is often argued, that most of the terrorists we face are products of Islamic schools—madrasas and kuttabs. Every study of the influence of the madrasas on the rise of Salafi terrorism has found little evidence of a direct link. Peter Bergen and Swati Pandey reported that of the seventy-nine worst al-Qa'ida and other Salafi terrorists, only 11 percent had attended madrasas, whereas 54 percent had gone to regular universities. Indeed, they found that of those who had attended college, 48 percent had gone to Western schools.[125] For similar reasons, the terrorism expert Marc Sageman has argued that there is a much stronger correlation between going to school in the West—where Arab and Muslim students often feel alienated or oppressed—than there is with attendance at madrasas.[126]

As with every claim about the sources of Middle Eastern terrorism, we should not throw the baby out with the bathwater. Islam is not the cause, but it is an important complicating factor. However, it is not *Islam* that is the complicating factor, it is *religion*. The fact that Islam is not the cause is important because it means that we do not need to "solve" the "problem" of Islam to diminish or eradicate the threat we face from the Salafi extremist groups—which is good because there would be no easy way for the United States to "solve" any real cause emanating from the religion of Islam if one actually existed.

Nevertheless, the complications are important because they have helped exacerbate the threat we face. Mark Juergensmeyer is probably the leading authority on the relationship between religion and terrorism, and he has concluded that "religious language and ideas play an important role, though not necessarily the initial one. The conditions of conflict that lead to tension are usually economic and social in character. . . . At some point in the conflict, however, usually at a time of frustration and desperation, the political contest becomes religionized. Then what was primarily a secular struggle takes on the aura of sacred conflict. This creates a whole new set of problems."[127] These problems include: providing a justification for violence that supersedes man's law, encouraging egregious acts because they are done in the name of what is good and against those painted as evil, excluding compromise since there can never be compromise with those believed to be evil, providing an easy method of social mobilization through established religious channels, holding out the promise of eternal reward for vicious acts that can inspire people to do things (like suicide bombings) that might make little sense to the individual expected to perform them in a purely secular context.[128] In other words, injecting Islam into the terrorist equation in the Middle East has exacerbated the problems, but Islam itself is not the problem; the problem is that any religion injected into any terrorism problem tends to make the situation worse in the same general set of ways—although the specifics can vary from time to time and place to place.

When presented with the kind of widespread unhappiness typical of prerevolutionary circumstances, people—typically middle-class intellectuals—will go looking for theoretical explanations and will inevitably find them in a variety of sources. For similarly varied reasons, one or more of these rationales will emerge as the dominant explanation. Sometimes it is because the idea is new and therefore avant-garde and widely discussed. Sometimes it is because the idea is old and therefore comfortable and already widely accepted. Sometimes it is because the ideas are simply very seductive. Sometimes it is because they are espoused by one or more highly charismatic or extremely powerful/respected figures.

Religion is a frequent place for such individuals to go looking for such theoretical explanations, because it promises to contain buried truths, unacknowledged explanations, and paths to greater happiness. It is a particularly powerful source because the bulk of the people are predisposed to be receptive to ideas supposedly derived from religion, and because there is often a body of leaders (the clergy) ready at hand and willing to organize on behalf of ideas supposedly derived from religion. It is why religion can be such a powerful and explosive revolutionary force. But the religion itself is not the cause of the unhappiness or of the reaction to it. It is simply being used as a vehicle (sometimes with the best of intentions) by those who would overturn the status quo. Religion, like communism, socialism, liberalism, and other revolutionary ideologies, provides both a justification for demanding change and—what most people have the least idea of—a set of ideas about what should be built instead of the current system to provide the people with the better life they seek.

Draining the Swamp

If we could somehow make the underlying economic, social, and political problems of the Muslim Middle East vanish, imagine the impact it would have on the threat we face from Salafi terrorism. It would eliminate the most powerful forces that have pushed so many of the countries of the region into prerevolutionary states, by eliminating the foremost grievances of the population. There would be little inclination for radical changes in the political and economic structures of the Arab states. There would be little inspiration for revolutionary groups (including terrorist groups like the Salafi extremists of al-Qa'ida and their ilk). There would be much less anger and despair driving people to join these terrorist groups in hope of changing their own situation or that of their community as a whole. Most people would see far more attractive alternative means to address their own individual problems—through economic opportunity, through the courts, through more responsive governments, through civil society organizations that are not operating in tension with a paranoid regime. The populace would likely see terrorists as a threat to themselves and their own increasingly comfortable lives. They would undoubtedly help the security services to round up the die-hard fanatics who might attempt to carry on despite the transformed circumstances.

Such a hard core always exists and rarely perceives when its wider support has evaporated because the majority are satisfied. The Provos lingered on long after most Irish Catholics had lost their enthusiasm for continued bloodshed. Similarly, we should never expect bin Ladin to give up his own personal jihad, both because his thinking appears too warped to acknowledge any victory other than establishing his Islamic utopia and, at a more mundane level, because he appears entirely unwilling to give up the fame and adulation that leading his "jihad" has brought him. But if the people no longer feel the same sense of grievance and therefore no longer support the goals of the terrorists (and instead come to abhor their disruptive and threatening violence), even that hard core will find it ever more difficult to recruit new members or to operate freely in their own societies. This is the way terrorist and insurgent campaigns are invariably defeated.

In the case of the terrorist threat from the Middle East, it would likely do more than just that. If the United States were to play an important role in helping such a societal transformation, it would likely knock down one of the most important sources of the region's endemic anti-Americanism. Gone would be the angry claim by so many Muslim Middle Easterners that the United States is the ultimate source of their misery, either because they think we deliberately want to keep them poor and oppressed or because we back callous autocrats who keep them poor and oppressed. That great grievance would be gone. Of course, other sources of anti-Americanism would remain, so we should not expect this transformation necessarily to result in an end to anti-Americanism entirely. However, it would diminish its intensity and that would be important in itself. In addition, the example of Eastern Europe suggests that when the United States is seen as being one of the principal engines of a positive political and economic transformation, it can create considerable good-will toward our nation—perhaps enough to neutralize some of the anger we may continue to face for those policies that Muslim Middle Easterners will always dislike (especially support for Israel).

Unfortunately, all of this takes time. The British efforts to transform Northern Ireland to eliminate the economic, political, and social grievances that were feeding the Troubles and boosting the IRA took decades to bear fruit. Thus, an effort to undermine the underlying causes of terrorism cannot be the only counterterror campaign we mount. Such an effort would not obviate the need for a traditional, direct counterterror campaign consisting of old-fashioned law enforcement techniques, intelligence operations, diplomatic suasion, and perhaps even the occasional military campaign to kill and capture terrorists, disrupt their operations, and suppress their ability to recruit or operate freely. However, what is equally clear is that such a counterterror campaign cannot be our *only* approach to terrorism. If it is, we will do no more than suppress the threat for some period of time. We will never eradicate it, and so, at some point, when for some reason we are no longer willing or able to make the same kind of full-court press we have since 9/11 or when circumstances change to make it harder for us to do so or our allies more reluctant, the terrorists will be back in full force. Indeed, they will no doubt have learned from prior mistakes and be fired by new anger by their years under suppression. Only by addressing the underlying problems of the Muslim Middle East can we actually eliminate the terrorist threat we currently face.[129]

Perhaps a rabbi should have the last word on this topic. Rabbi Arthur Waskow implored an audience shortly after 9/11 that "Many act as if there is a choice between dealing with the terrorists themselves and dealing with the pools of despair and anger out of which terrorism can [grow] and has grown. . . . It is like dealing with malaria; you attend to the epidemic with medicine, but you also must drain the standing water. . . . If we want to end terrorism in the long term, then we must eliminate the pools of cultural deprivation, poverty and despair."[130]

PART FOUR

THE CORE OF
A GRAND STRATEGY
FOR THE MIDDLE EAST

OF ALL OF THE MANY MISTAKES AND PREVARICATIONS OF the Bush 43 administration in its conduct of the invasion of Iraq, perhaps the most damaging was its claim that Saddam Husayn posed an imminent threat and had to be dealt with immediately.[1] Even if you accepted the (mistaken) judgments of the U.S. intelligence community—and every other intelligence community with the capability to collect information independently against Iraq—that Saddam had reconstituted Iraq's weapons of mass destruction programs, as I did, the threat from Iraq was not imminent. In particular, the intelligence community believed that Saddam was probably at least several years away from having nuclear weapons, not the one year that the Bush administration frequently claimed.[2] This false impression of an imminent threat made the invasion far worse than it needed to be. It was a major factor contributing to the rush to war, a headlong dash that eliminated time for the diplomatic and logistical groundwork that would have been necessary to give the invasion and the subsequent reconstruction of Iraq a realistic chance of success.[3]

The experience with Iraq raises the issue of the relationship between the imminence of a threat and the time required to deal with it. This is an important issue for the grand strategy proposed in this book as well.

The threat of terrorism is already upon us. Since the 1990s, the Salafi terrorists have been attacking not just American interests or Americans abroad but the American homeland itself. In that sense, it is an imminent threat. However, what we have seen since 9/11 is that a determined counterterrorism campaign, coupled with widespread efforts to impove our national defenses against terrorism, can have a dramatic effect. Although they have tried mightily, the terrorists have not been able to conduct another attack on Americans in the United States. That should not make us complacent, because they will keep trying and at some point they may succeed. As I noted earlier, counterterror campaigns merely suppress terrorism; they cannot eradicate it, and so the terrorists will keep coming back at us and at some point will likely find a chink in our armor. Nevertheless, it should reassure us that we do have a good option available that can diminish the immediate threat of terrorism while we adopt other measures that will eliminate it altogether over a longer period of time.

The threat of instability in the Middle East is much harder to pin down in terms of its timing. In some ways, instability is already everywhere in the Middle East, to a greater or lesser extent. However, that instability has not yet risen to the level where it has created a catastrophic problem for American interests, and particularly for America's interest in Middle Eastern oil exports. The threat from instability lies in its *potential* to create such a disaster. Of course, it is very hard to predict revolutions or other forms of internal strife, and they can sneak up on you. Moreover, there is already enough internal unrest in the Middle East that it would not take much to push it past various dangerous thresholds. This should make us wary of assuming that we can know for certain when a truly dangerous threat from the instability of the Middle Eastern states will manifest itself or that we will have much warning when it does.

Weighted against these risks is the simple but inescapable fact that there are no quick fixes to the problem of instability in the Middle East. It would be nice to be able to wave a magic wand and make it all go away, but we simply do not have that power. In the twentieth century, the West, led by the United States, did devise a solution to the problem of regional instability, but it was a solution that has typically taken decades to work. After 1945, Europe was transformed from being the world's worst cauldron of war, ethnic conflict, revolution, civil strife, and terrorism to being the most peaceful, secure, and prosperous region on Earth. That happened only because of the deliberate efforts of the United States and the people of Europe themselves. During the same period, East Asia and Latin America made similar strides along the same path, although they have not come nearly as far as Europe yet.

It is not a coincidence that the only solution known to humanity to cure the problem of instability is the same as the only solution known to cure (as opposed to just suppressing) the problem of terrorism. As explained in part III, terrorism is a common manifestation of instability. When people become so desperate about their political, economic, and social conditions that they want change at any price, terrorism is one of the tools some people typically employ to bring about the revolutionary transformation they seek. Thus, curing terrorism requires curing the same problems that produce instability.[4]

So, for better or worse, the only approach known to mankind to eradicate, and not merely suppress, the kind of problems experienced by the Muslim Middle East is to embrace a long-term process of reform—toward more pluralist forms of government, toward the rule of law, toward a dynamic educational system, toward a market-driven economy, and toward a more "modern" pattern of social interaction.

THUS, WE SIMPLY do not know how much time we have to help the Middle East deal with its underlying problems; but the only way we know how to do so will take time, no matter how dire or distant we believe the threat.

Two additional facts should provide some reassurance. As I noted repeatedly in part III, while the potential consequences of a major internal problem in the Middle East (particularly Saudi Arabia) would be calamitous, the risk is fairly low on any given day or year. If we and the leaders of the region let the current trends continue for decades, the likelihood of such a disaster will rise to dangerous levels, but it seems unlikely, even remote, at this moment and so we should not panic. We may be playing Russian roulette, but the gun has a lot more than six bullet chambers and the cylinder is turning slowly.

Moreover, it has typically been the case that simply starting down the path of transformation can quickly alleviate many of the pressures that produce both instability and terrorism. What triggers revolutions, civil wars, and other internal unrest is psychological factors, particularly feelings of extreme despair. However, as others have observed, humans have a remarkable capacity for hope, and it does not take much to reignite that hope. Simply beginning a process of reform can restore people's hope and relieve the pressure building for violent change.

The one critical point is that that hope cannot be allowed to flag. This is the core of Crane Brinton's scholarship on revolutions: they are most likely to occur when people believe that their situation is improving, only to have their hopes dashed. Like Aesop's tortoise and hare, the pace of the effort is less important than its constancy. We should get started as soon as we can, and to a certain extent we already have. The key now is to keep plodding down the path.

Having explained the need for such a course, it is now appropriate to turn to its nature. This next part lays out broadly what policies the United States should adopt to enable the people of the Muslim Middle East to pursue a course of political, economic, and social reform to address the underlying problems of their societies and addresses the many hurdles that we will have to overcome to do so.

CHAPTER 10

ENABLING REFORM

ARL VON CLAUSEWITZ ONCE FAMOUSLY OBSERVED THAT "everything in war is very simple, but the simplest thing is difficult." The same might be applied to the question of cultivating a process of political, economic, and social reform in the Middle East. It is not hard to spell out, in broad terms, what those reforms should encompass. However, the devil is not just in the details but also in the implementation. Prescribing the needed course of reforms is relatively straightforward.[1] Explaining how to turn theory into practical reality, how to overcome all of the potential problems, how to settle a spate of conundrums, how to encourage the people of the region to follow this course and enable them to do so—not to mention actually executing it over the course of the next several decades—is the hard part. And it is likely to be very hard. But it is also absolutely necessary.

The Reforms

It is worth starting with at least an outline of the needed reforms before wading into the details, as well as the hows, whys, wherefores, and what-ifs. In the political realm, the predominantly Muslim states of the Middle East and North Africa need to move toward a system that guarantees basic individual rights like the right of free speech, free assembly, freedom of religion, and freedom from arbitrary arrest and other abuses by the state, to name only the most basic. They will need to embrace protections for minorities so that the state or the majority cannot oppress unpopular groups and to ensure that every person and every group is ensured full equality. Government will have to be transparent, accountable to the people, and derive its legitimacy by representing the will of the people made manifest in elections (and possibly other methods) by which the people can choose their leaders. There will need to be political and structural checks on the power of the different institutions of governance, and the government must be served by an effective, apolitical, and meritocratic bureaucracy. The wealth of the nation will have to be viewed and treated as the wealth of the people, not of those governing, and that wealth must be employed for the common good. It will undoubtedly be a process of democratization, even if the end result is not quite a liberal democracy in the classic Western sense—although then again it may well be.

These political reforms will have to be built upon a foundation of legal reforms that establish the rule of law. Legal codes must be clear, well articulated, accessible to all, and the product of a meritocratic process of jurisprudence. All citizens must receive the same fair and impartial treatment, and none can be above the law. As part of establishing the rule of law, all of these countries will need to develop an independent judiciary that will be largely (ideally, completely) free of contamination by financial inducement, political pressure, or fear of violence and served by a principled legal process, an effective but respectful law enforcement system, and a humane penal system. They will also require proper anticorruption guidelines, complete with all of the institutions (including an independent press) needed to enforce them.

Educational reforms will be of equal importance. These should focus on transforming the teaching methods of Middle Eastern schools. Middle Eastern schools need to practice modern instructional practices that emphasize active learning and teacher-student and student-student interaction, as well as allowing students to learn through doing and by pushing them to discover answers and solutions themselves. Memorization should be deemphasized (except for disciplines such as language and elementary mathematics, in which it is necessary) in favor of the development of critical thinking. In addition, education should focus not just on the aggressive acquisition of knowledge but on the creation of new knowledge. In this sense, traditional cultural resistance to innovation needs to be superseded by an emphasis on creativity. The educational process should encourage interdisciplinary thinking as well as basic theory development and testing as a means of sorting truth from fiction (and conspiracy theory). Finally, education reform should expunge the racism and xenophobia that have previously littered their textbooks and curricula (and a number of Muslim Middle Eastern countries, including Saudi Arabia, have already begun such a process).[2]

Although the dismal science cannot offer a guaranteed path to prosperity, something like the "Washington Consensus" of reforms is the only path of economic reform that has been proven to work in practice in a variety of countries.[3] This approach builds on a foundation of sound monetary and fiscal policy: balancing government budgets, limiting government spending, keeping inflation low, minimizing balance-of-payment gaps. It stresses the introduction of market forces into the economy by reducing price controls and subsidies, making currencies fully convertible, privatizing industry, deregulating firms and markets, eliminating monopolies, and creating incentives for trade and direct foreign investment. Last, it includes efforts to improve the efficiency of markets and the ease of transactions, as well as improving the efficiency of governmental regulation by modernizing, streamlining, and reforming political and financial bureaucracies (including the banking sector), introducing a progressive taxation system, and eliminating patronage networks that subvert good economic practices and the efficient functioning of markets.[4]

Finally, Muslim Middle Eastern society is going to have to come to grips with modernity, globalization, and the new political, legal, educational, and economic systems that the reforms are meant to create. As with many other societies that have done the same over the years, this will be a process of accepting and adapting to new ways of living and thinking, while preserving and adjusting traditional values, norms, and patterns of behavior. It will mean accommodating the demands of new technology, new economic systems, new methods of communication, and the new possibilities they create, but doing so in ways that the individual, the family, and the community are not cut loose from their history and culture. It is not an easy process, but it is not impossible either. Just as Japanese, Korean, and Chinese cultures all adapted to the demands and the new values of the industrial age and then the information age while maintaining many of the unique aspects of their culture and values, so too must Muslim Middle Eastern society.

Is All of This Really Necessary?

Unfortunately, it is. Change is coming to the Middle East, whether we or the autocratic regimes of the region want it to or not.[5] The underlying economic, political, and social problems are causing deep-seated and widespread unrest across the region. The leaders of nearly all of the Middle Eastern states have acknowledged this by reacting, typically with some combination of greater repression and limited reform. As the democracy expert Marina Ottaway has commented on this phenomenon in the Middle East, "reform from the top usually comes in response to political pressures that make it costly and dangerous for regimes to insist on maintaining the status quo."[6] There is no question that many of the reforming gestures of Middle Eastern autocrats are halfhearted, if not disingenuous, and have left the region still very far from where it needs to be. It is also true that many of the leaders refused to believe that the problems were important until something shocked them. In Saudi Arabia, it was a series of Al Qa'ida bombings in May 2003. In Jordan it was the popular response to the 2000 al-Aqsa intifadah, which surprised King Abdallah II by the depth of anger that it unleashed among his people, an anger that he recognized came from more than just solidarity with their Palestinian brethren across the Jordan River. In other Arab states it was the publication of the first *Arab Human Development Report* in 2002, in which, for the first time, twenty-two prominent Arab authors honestly described the problems of their societies and demanded political, economic, and social reform to remedy them.[7] In other countries, it was still other events, but in every case it was something that stunned the regimes, forcing them to realize that their people were very unhappy and increasingly heeding the siren song of revolutionaries, typically Islamist revolutionaries of one kind or another. As one senior Saudi prince told *The New York Times,* "The fact is, reform is imperative and not a choice, and so is participatory government."[8]

In short, the status quo is eroding and has been for the past three decades. Thus, the question that we, and the regimes of the region, face is whether we want to keep ignoring the problems and allow change to happen spontaneously, and probably explosively, or whether we (and they) want to try to guide it in a direction that would be best for our interests, for the interests of the people of the region, and ultimately (because returning to the past is not an option) the interests of the ruling elites as well.

There is no question that this will be difficult and will entail any number of potential pitfalls, many of which will be addressed in this chapter and the next. However, it is worth contemplating that those who have raised concerns about this course of action have proposed no alternative themselves. So far, no one has been able to offer a different but easier, less risky, more practical program that would have a reasonable chance of success and that could solve the underlying problems of the Muslim Middle East, stave off the violence and instability that already pervade the region and appear likely to worsen over time, and thus secure America's vital interests and create a better world for the people of the region over the long term.

The only alternative that those who dislike this strategy have suggested is to simply keep doing what we have been doing in the assumption that the Arab regimes will be able to keep repressing and manipulating their people in perpetuity. This is not a very good option. It is the approach that gave us revolution in Iran; civil wars in Algeria, Sudan, Syria, Lebanon, Iraq (even before the U.S. invasion), and Yemen; insurgencies in Egypt and Libya; coups in too many countries to list; as well as rebellions, riots, and Salafi terrorist campaigns in nearly every Muslim state in the region. It has also meant severe fluctuations in the price of oil and the threat of economic catastrophe hanging over our heads like a sword of Damocles. It has meant American military forces fighting three wars in the region since 1987, each more costly than the last. And it has meant a savage terrorist campaign turned on us, culminating in the horrors of Sep-

tember 11, 2001. Even if you believe that the status quo can somehow hold for several decades more and are willing to risk the security
of the United States on that bet, it is hard to argue that it has been
good for America so far.

Getting Past the Legacy of the Bush Administration

In some ways, the hardest obstacle to overcome in arguing that the
United States must help foster a process of far-reaching economic,
political, and social reform in the Middle East is that the George W.
Bush administration briefly—but loudly and ineffectively—embraced
this policy.

At least they embraced it rhetorically. And I must admit that
their rhetoric was often magnificent. Bush's 2003 address to the National Endowment for Democracy and his second inaugural address
were beautiful speeches that hit every note that the reformers of the
Middle East had ever wanted to hear from the United States, and hit
them perfectly. His second inaugural proclaimed, "We will encourage
reform in other governments by making clear that success in our relations will require the decent treatment of their own people. America's belief in human dignity will guide our policies, yet rights must
be more than the grudging concessions of dictators; they are secured
by free dissent and the participation of the governed. In the long
run, there is no justice without freedom, and there can be no human
rights without human liberty."[9] Saad Eddin Ibrahim, among the most
courageous of Arab reformists, commented after the 2003 NED
speech that "as a lifelong advocate of democracy in the Arab world, I
could not have written a better speech."[10] The Bush administration
did also establish some new programs meant to advance these causes,
most notably the Middle East Partnership Initiative (MEPI), which
would be the umbrella title for all of its programs meant to push reform in the Middle East, and the multilateral Broader Middle East
and North Africa Initiative (BMENA). Unfortunately, as with so
many things that the Bush administration did, it pursued this policy
badly and abandoned it when it became inconvenient.

We cannot, as a nation, discard this approach just because the
Bush administration championed it rhetorically. Despite the fact

that George W. Bush said it was the best thing for us to do, it actually *is* the best thing for us to do.

It may help to remember that encouraging democracy and other reforms in the region was not their idea nor did it reflect their initial approach to the Middle East. Assisting democratization, fostering economic prosperity through free-market reforms, and helping other nations to adjust to the societal demands of a new age (whatever that age might be) are hallowed traditions of American foreign policy. During the postwar era, they were more often associated with Democratic administrations, particularly those of Truman and Kennedy, who made them the cornerstones of their policies toward Europe and Japan, and the third world, respectively. Even more recently, it was the first President Bush who committed the United States to a major effort to see that democracy and free-market economies replaced communism in the collapsing Soviet bloc. President Clinton went still further, encouraging economic reform around the globe, establishing international groups like the Community of Democracies, and funding aid programs designed to assist any country willing to pursue democratic, free-market reform with know-how, political support, and financial aid. Indeed, even within the Middle East, the Clinton administration was extremely supportive of the nascent reform efforts of King Hassan of Morocco and King Abdallah of Jordan. Few people remember that one of Vice President Al Gore's most difficult assignments was the Gore-Mubarak dialogue, in which he pushed, prodded, wheedled, cajoled, threatened, and did everything else he could to convince President Mubarak to adopt a similar program for Egypt.

The idea of fostering a comprehensive process of reform in the Middle East was not an idea that the Bush 43 administration brought with it to office. It was notably absent from their campaign speeches and initial policy positions. Although there certainly were some among administration officials and their outside supporters who favored the idea of democratic reform in the Middle East prior to the invasion of Iraq, the truth is that few did. Most believed that friendly dictators were preferable to unfriendly democracies. Very few agitated publicly for a policy of democratization in the Middle East. Most of the administration's seniormost foreign policy makers wanted nothing to do with the Middle East at all, let alone adopt a major initiative to try to help the states of the region transform themselves.[11]

Democracy was actually only a minor consideration in the administration's decision to invade Iraq. Indeed, even setting aside the numerous accounts of its deliberations that make this point, the most powerful evidence is its infamous refusal to prepare for postwar reconstruction in a way that might have allowed Iraq to emerge as a democracy. While its members occasionally referred to the examples of Germany and Japan in defense of their bellicose intentions, they did nothing like the massive planning and preparatory work that had made those occupations and transitions to democracy possible—the plans for which were readily available as models had they been serious about building a democracy in Iraq after Saddam's fall. Similarly, they made no effort to learn from the many exercises in nation building/democratization that had been undertaken during the Bush 41 and Clinton administrations, let alone prepare for similar exertions in Iraq. Instead, they insisted that such efforts would be unnecessary and undesirable.

Scholars (mostly on the left) have argued for the United States to embrace a policy of democracy promotion in the Middle East at least since the 1990–1991 Persian Gulf War. For instance, right after the war, Muhammad Muslih and Augustus Richard Norton asserted that Saddam's invasions of Kuwait and Iran had been "the products of flaws inherent in Arab society and politics: the absence of democracy and the alarming, incongruous distribution of wealth and population in the Arab world. These weaknesses constitute the Arab malaise."[12] Norton and Muslih went on to call for Washington to make democracy promotion in the Middle East the centerpiece of its post–Gulf War policy toward the region to head off the prospect of similar conflicts and other forms of instability. Later, the *Arab Human Development Report* would make the need for democratization in the Middle East one of its principal recommendations for dealing with the problems of the region. The seminal 2003 edition stated that "democratic transformation in the Arab world is a fundamental condition for the independence of knowledge, taking into account that such a transformation requires synergy among economic, political, and cultural actors."[13] In this sense as well, this strategy has a long pedigree that dates well back before the Bush 43 administration and has little to do with its philosophy.

In the political arena, the idea is principally an outgrowth of the neoliberal school associated with the Clinton administration, and particularly with names like Madeleine Albright, Richard Holbrooke, and Dennis Ross[14] (and arguably has even deeper roots in the Kennedy administration). The first time I personally advocated this idea came in 2002, when I coauthored an article with Ronald Asmus, my friend and former colleague from the Clinton administration, in which we attempted to rebut the famous neoconservative Robert Kagan's argument that U.S. and European interests were increasingly divergent because the transatlantic alliance had created peace in Europe and therefore no longer faced a common threat.[15] Ron and I argued that although Kagan may have been correct about Europe, the Western Alliance still faced a common threat: no longer the Red Army but terrorism and instability arising from the economic, political, and social problems of the Middle East. We went on to call for a transatlantic partnership to help the Middle East transform itself, just as that same partnership had allowed Europe to do the same during the Cold War.

At the time we wrote it, the right wing of the administration mostly scoffed at the idea. But its centrists were extremely receptive. Ron and I found ourselves in constant conversations with moderate Republicans in the Congress and the administration, many of them quite high-ranking (along with congressional Democrats), who liked our article and determined to make the idea a component of U.S. policy. In fact, it was Richard Haass, then the director of policy planning at the State Department and among the most reasonable and moderate members of the entire first Bush 43 administration, who gave the first speech heralding just such a policy on December 4, 2002. Haass had already been thinking along the same lines (he asked for a copy of our article while it was still in draft), and the ideas in his final speech were very similar to our own.[16] Haass's speech was followed by an address by Secretary of State Colin Powell on December 12, in which that chief moderate of the Bush administration announced the inauguration of MEPI.[17] Both the Powell and

Haass speeches were intelligent, reasonable, modest, and wholly pragmatic. Thus, the idea of helping foster political, economic, and social reform in the Middle East was initially the idea of neoliberals from the Clinton administration who inspired the moderates in the Bush 43 administration. The idea was embraced by its radical Right only later on, particularly after the reconstruction of Iraq began to flounder, when it became clear that there were no weapons of mass destruction anywhere in sight, and to some extent when democracy became their last resort to maintain popular support for our exertions there.

BAD PRACTICES

Unfortunately, the problem is not just that the Bush 43 administration adopted this idea rhetorically and a great many people in the United States and abroad loathe them. It is also that the Bush 43 administration pursued the policy poorly. The administration's actions never lived up to its rhetoric. In the words of the democracy expert Thomas Carothers, "A common theme [today] is that the United States should back away from what is often characterized as a reckless Bush crusade to promote democracy around the world. Although it is certainly true that U.S. foreign policy is due for a serious recalibration, the notion that democracy promotion plays a dominant role in Bush policy is a myth."[18] As a result, we got the worst of both worlds. The administration's rhetoric and limited actions were just enough to get up the hopes of the many reformists and other democracy advocates throughout the Middle East and to anger many of the regimes and their cronies. But because the administration failed so miserably to match its words with deeds, the United States dashed many hopes and paid the consequences for advocating a policy unpopular with many of the regimes while reaping few rewards.[19]

Although the president's lofty speeches might have convinced many that democratization in the Middle East had become America's number one priority, the actual commitment of resources was minimal. The administration established an office in the State Department (initially under the vice president's daughter Elizabeth Cheney as deputy assistant secretary of state) to oversee the Middle East Partnership Initiative. However, the office was not assigned the department's top Middle East officers and had a largely adversarial relationship with the rest of the department's Arabists—which senior administration officials made little effort to ameliorate. The initial funds allocated to MEPI were a bare $29 million, and since then its funding has never risen much beyond the $100 million mark.[20] To some extent, this was understandable because it was hard to know, especially early on, how best to spend that money and who would be willing to accept money from the U.S. government, given the pervasive anti-Americanism in the region. What was far more damning was that the administration made little effort to press Congress to allocate additional funding for bilateral or multilateral aid designed to create incentives for regional governments to move down the path of reform. Along similar lines, the administration was loath to employ its political capital to press regional regimes on issues related to reform and was excessively congratulatory when the regimes took modest, superficial, or ultimately counterproductive steps in the name of reform, all of which convinced both the regimes and the struggling reformists that Washington would be satisfied with cosmetic changes.[21]

In part as a result of this meager commitment of resources, the specific activities of their efforts to promote reform were often mistaken. Rather than funding Middle Eastern nongovernmental organizations (NGOs) that best met the needs of the people of the region, the administration often funded those most palatable to Americans and attempted to force other NGOs to adapt their programs to the American agenda.[22]

Overall, the administration did a poor job seeking out guidance from reformists in the region and too often attempted to impose American ideas on potential allies ill suited to the Middle Eastern context. It concentrated excessively on providing grants to Middle Eastern government agencies, including 70 percent of the program's first $103 million for things such as translating documents, computerizing schools, and running seminars for government officials. All of these programs had utility, but the administration's efforts lacked the core of a real reform program, and by putting so much into government programs it led Middle Eastern reformers to believe that the American effort was little more than an excuse to provide more money to the regimes, rather than a genuine program to stimulate indigenous change.[23] (There were additional funds allocated via USAID and other mechanisms, but the most public part, and what was most closely watched, was the inadequate and often misspent MEPI funds.)

Although the few occasions when the Bush administration put pressure on Arab regimes to adopt political or economic reforms received disproportionate attention, given how modest their impact was, overall, these proved to be exceptions and not the rule.[24] For example, the president, secretary of state, and other high-ranking officials apparently never raised Saudi Arabia's imprisonment of human rights activists for petitioning the regime to adopt a national constitution. Nor, for that matter, did President Bush even mention political reform in his discussions with Egyptian President Husni Mubarak during the latter's visit to the president's ranch in Crawford, Texas, in April 2004, less than three months after the second inaugural address.[25] Even on the rare occasions when the administration pushed for reform, the result was often counterproductive: it demanded that Mubarak allow freer elections for president in 2005 but was quick to accept conditions on those elections that threatened to make future ones *less* free rather than more.[26] When Secretary of State Rice returned to Egypt in 2007, she reportedly did not discuss political reform issues at all.[27] Likewise, the administration's insistence on elections for the Palestinian territories at a point when there were no underpinnings of democracy produced "electocracy" and the triumph of Hamas instead. Far from advancing the cause of political reform in the region, this produced chaos and violence, left the Palestinians (and Israelis, Jordanians, and ourselves) worse off than they had been, and provided more evidence that the regimes and other critics could cite to argue against further reform. The Bush administration was so desirous of securing buy-in for its Foundation for the Future, a multilateral fund intended to aid civil society organizations in the Middle East, that it agreed to give Arab governments a say in selecting its board members, as well as having the foundation register as an NGO in Jordan. The result is that the foundation is "beholden to the very governments it is meant to challenge," in Tamara Wittes's words, which tightly constrains its operations.[28]

It is unclear whether the Bush administration ever had the courage of its convictions, but it was certainly caught in several traps of its own making the moment it set out down the democracy promotion path. In particular, the administration's mishandling of the Palestinian-Israeli conflict, Palestinian internal politics, Lebanon, Afghanistan, and (especially) Iraq left it desperate for the support of Arab governments, which demanded that the administration tone down its support for reform in return.

Iraq created another problem. Washington's claims that what it was doing in Iraq constituted a well-resourced and good-faith effort to build democracy there (which it most certainly was not prior to 2007) and its careless rhetoric suggesting that Iraq might be a model for the rest of the region terrified many people and handed a powerful trump card to the opponents of democratization and free-market transition in the region, both within the regimes and among the Islamist groups.[29] It was too easy for these groups to argue that if reform and liberalization meant what was going on in Iraq, then reform and liberalization were not desirable for their countries.[30] Finally, Bush administration officials seemed to lose faith in their own approach when they saw free elections in the Palestinian territories and Iraq boost many of the worst Islamist militants (Hamas, the Sadrists) into positions of power and score big victories elsewhere. Their fear that Islamists who could not be trusted to conform to democratic practices would take power throughout the region caused the administration to back away quickly from its proud early oratory.[31]

In fairness to the administration, this was the first comprehensive effort on the part of the U.S. government to push a genuine process of reform throughout the Arab world, and any administration—even one more humble, cautious, and competent than this one—would have made many mistakes. As Scott Carpenter, who succeeded Liz Cheney as the deputy assistant secretary of state presiding over the program, once said, "We don't know yet how best to promote democracy in the Arab Middle East. I mean we just don't know. It's the early days. . . . I think there are times when you throw spaghetti against the wall and see if it sticks."[32] Moreover, there is no question that most people in the region (and most in the United States) mis-understood their aims. As Marina Ottaway described the initial un-veiling, "Secretary of State Colin Powell announced a conciliatory Middle East Partnership Initiative (MEPI) that envisaged democra-tization as a slow, gradual process that the United States would en-courage by promoting economic development, education, rights for women, and the funding of civil society organizations."[33] This was a perfectly reasonable approach that should have been acceptable, even desirable, to a great many Muslim Middle Easterners. However, it was immediately so overpromised, oversold, underresourced, and undersupported that it confounded genuine reformers, frightened potential supporters, and paradoxically helped those who were most opposed to it.

Helping the people of the Muslim Middle East devise a program of genuine political, economic, and social reform and then imple-ment it over the decades it will need to succeed will not be easy. However, as a wide range of other experts and commentators is now beginning to reaffirm, there is no reason to see the George W. Bush administration's oratorical acceptance of it as an impediment, nor should we judge its likelihood of success based upon their incompe-tent and halfhearted efforts.[34]

Is Democracy Possible in the Middle East?

Far too often, the debate over whether the United States should be fostering political, economic, and social reform in the Middle East gets hung up on this question. Although aiding political reform—a more accurate way to think of this process than simple democrati-zation—is a key component of the grand strategy the United States must adopt, it is not the only component. Just as it is a mistake to boil down all of the problems of the region to simple economic deficits like poverty, unemployment, and income distribution gaps, it is equally mistaken to assume that political reform is all that is neces-sary to solve the region's problems. Political reform is an important element, but so too is reform of the region's economies, legal sys-tems, and educational systems, as well as helping Muslim Middle

Eastern society adapt to the demands of modernity. We should not reduce this task to just democratization.

Second, though there is no question that political reform in the Muslim Middle East will have to include considerable *democratization,* I hesitate to use the word "democracy" because it often evokes connotations for both Americans and Middle Easterners that are misleading. Scholars have found that there are few differences between Muslim and Western publics in terms of their support for democracy but very big differences in their perceptions of social values like gender roles, abortion, homosexuality, and the like. This further indicates that Middle Eastern discomfort with what often gets lumped in with the term "democracy" comes from the cultural trappings they associate with Western (and principally American) systems, not from democratic principles themselves.[35] Similarly, when Americans think about helping foster democracy in the Middle East—or anywhere for that matter—we tend to imagine a system of government very much like that of the United States. Such a specifically American version of democracy may or may not be right for the Muslim Middle East, although only the people of the region themselves will know that for sure. Arabs often make the same mistake and add to that the assumption that "democracy" also somehow includes American culture, much of which—like hip-hugger blue jeans, sex on television, and antireligious speech and behavior—they find deeply offensive (as do a great many Americans, of course). Fortunately, none of that is what democracy is really about.

Instead, democracy is about basic political freedoms like speech and assembly, representative government, transparency, accountability, rule of law, checks and balances within government, and limits on governmental power, to name only its most basic principles. And fortunately, there are a great many ways that a society can adapt those principles to create a pluralistic political system. There are a great many democracies in the world, and many of them look very different from one another. Democracy in Bangladesh is very different from democracy in Japan, which in turn is almost nothing like democracy in America. These countries are all democracies in that they are all built around the basic principles of democratic governance, but their actual institutions, functions, and methods are very different because each is adapted to the culture, history, values, and traditions of the host nation. With the possible exception of Lebanon before 1975 (and Lebanon is an exceptional Middle Eastern country in many ways), the Arab world has never had a real democracy that could serve as a model to which the rest of the region could aspire. One of the keys to helping the Middle East find its own path of reform will also be that the people of the region, and they alone, will have to decide how best to adapt the basic principles of democracy to their own culture, history, values, and traditions.[36]

With this in mind, there is no reason why democracy should be impossible in the Muslim Middle East if that is the desire of the people. At various times, many theorists have posited one or another factor as being a critical "prerequisite" for democracy—such as a strong civil society, prosperity, or a culture "suited" to democracy.[37] Over the course of time, every one of these notions has been disproven by experience. The Middle East scholar Eva Bellin observes that

> The Middle East and North Africa are in no way unique in their poor endowment with the prerequisites of democracy. Other regions similarly deprived have nonetheless managed to make the transition. Civil society is notoriously weak in sub-Saharan Africa, yet twenty-three out of forty-two countries carried out some measure of democratic transition between 1988 and 1994. The commanding heights of the economy were entirely under state control in eastern Europe prior to the fall of the Berlin wall, yet the vast majority of countries in this region successfully carried through a transition during the 1990s. Poverty and inequality, not to mention geographic remoteness from the democratic epicenter, have characterized India, Mauritius, and Botswana, yet these countries have successfully embraced democracy. And other world cultures, notably Catholicism and Confucianism, have at different times been accused of incompatibility with democracy, yet these cultural endowments have not prevented countries in Latin America, southern Europe, and East Asia from democratizing.[38]

Indeed, at various times in the past, distinguished statesmen and scholars insisted that democracy was inconceivable in Germany and Japan or even the entire Catholic and "Confucian" worlds. The success of democracies in every one of these areas belies every one of these claims.[39] There is no reason to believe that similar claims about the Arab world are anything but equally mistaken.[40]

Despite aspersions to the contrary, the Arab world has already seen one functional, nascent democracy. From 1934 until at least 1975 (and arguably again since 2005), Lebanon has boasted a pluralist system of government—albeit one not without its limits and problems. In particular, the civil war from 1975 to 1989 is often seen as casting doubt on the entire democratic experience in Lebanon. However, current scholarship emphasizes the relative stability of Lebanese democracy. The unhappiness of the Muslim communities prior to the early 1970s has generally been exaggerated, and the system did well in overcoming potential constitutional crises in 1952 and 1958. Indeed, it seems likely that Lebanon would have been able to find political compromises for its problems had it not been for the sudden influx of Palestinian militants fleeing Jordan after Black September in 1970. Unfortunately, as it did in Jordan, the PLO went looking for internal rifts in Lebanon and ripped them wide open in pursuit of its own political agenda. And as was the result in Jordan, this led to civil war—initially between the dominant elite (the Maronites in Lebanon) and the PLO—but the Lebanese government was not strong enough to overcome this as the Jordanian regime was (just barely).[41] The key point here is that the Lebanese demonstrated that they could make a protodemocratic system work, despite the disadvantages of a multicultural, multisectarian society. There was nothing about Arab culture, Islam, or any other facet of Muslim Middle Eastern society that inhibited the function of Lebanese democracy.

Perhaps the most ridiculous aspect of this debate is the claim that Islam is somehow incompatible with democracy. Some Westerners and radical Islamists even insist that passages from the Qur'an and the Hadiths make it somehow impossible for good Muslims to live in a democracy. They argue that because Islamic texts make no particular distinction between politics and religion and make no explicit provision for democracy, this makes it impossible for Muslims to embrace democracy. However, Islam is so rich a religion that it is equally easy for others to demonstrate that there is no incompatibility, and this is where the weight of scholarly opinion in both worlds lies.[42]

Of far greater importance than such abstract theoretical arguments is the fact that there is no validity in practice. The vast majority of the world's 1.2 billion Muslims live in democracies—like Indonesia, India, Malaysia, and Bangladesh. There is nothing about their religion that somehow hobbles their participation in politics in any of these nations. In Indonesia, Malaysia, and Bangladesh, the majority of the population is Muslim, yet none has experienced problems as a result. Even in countries where they are not the majority, as in India and the United States, large Muslim populations have no problem serving as fully functional members of their polities, participating in elections, running for office (and winning), and serving in government. In fact, a recent study found that when you remove a country's wealth from the equation (because wealthier countries tend to be better breeding grounds for democracy), the Muslim "democracy gap" disappears. Of the thirty-eight countries in the world (sixteen Muslim and twenty-two non-Muslim) with a per capita GDP below $1,500 per year, 31 percent of the Muslim states had a competitive electoral process, while 32 percent of the non-Muslim states did.[43] In other words, lack of prosperity, not Islam, tends to explain the lower rates of democracy among some predominantly Muslim countries.

Public opinion polling similarly shows no such incompatibility. A 2005 Gallup poll of people from the ten largest Muslim countries found that large majorities were both very supportive of Islam and very supportive of democracy, and most did not want religious figures drafting or even advising in the drafting of a new constitution.[44] Likewise, the Pew Global Attitudes survey of 2005 found exactly the same thing: Arab Muslims saw Islam's role in politics as positive, and they also favored democracy in their country.[45] Public opinion data for Egypt, Jordan, Morocco, and Algeria show that neither strong Islamic attachment (measured by mosque attendance and personal religiosity) nor adherence to "political Islam" (measured by their sense of the desirability of the role of Islam in politics) discouraged or influenced support for democracy. Instead, there was absolutely no correlation between personal religiosity and support for democracy, and most people were both very pious and very supportive of democracy.[46]

Give the People What They Want

As the last paragraph should have begun to make clear, another mistaken but commonplace conviction in the West is the idea that the people of the Muslim Middle East don't want reform, and particularly don't want democracy. Critics often scoff at the very idea of trying to bring democracy to the Middle East in the mistaken belief that it is antithetical to the wishes of the people themselves.

The truth is the exact opposite. The vast majority of Muslim Middle Easterners both understand democracy and desire it for themselves. In poll after poll in which they have been asked whether they want democracy in their country, Muslim Middle Easterners have resoundingly and consistently answered in the affirmative.[47] As Saudi expert Asad AbuKhalil has put it, "Over the past decade, Arab men and women have clearly voiced their deep desire for democratic changes in their respective countries."[48] As only a few more examples in addition to those polls cited above, in the World Values Survey polls, conducted in 2000–2002, the four Arab countries included in the survey (Algeria, Egypt, Jordan, and Morocco) topped the list of those agreeing with the statement that "democracy is better than any other form of government" and were also the most strongly opposed to authoritarianism.[49] Overall, those who responded that a democratic system was a "very good" or "fairly good" way of governing their country were 99 percent in Egypt, 96 percent in Morocco, 95 percent in Jordan, and 86 percent in Iran.[50] Zogby surveys in 2002 of Kuwait, the UAE, Saudi Arabia, Egypt, and Lebanon showed levels of admiration for specifically American democracy ranging between 50 and 60 percent for each population despite evincing strong anti-Americanism overall. Likewise, a Pew survey in the spring of 2005 in Jordan, Morocco, and Lebanon found that 83 to 90 percent of those surveyed thought that democracy would work well in their country.[51]

As noted earlier, sometimes the word "democracy" itself elicits a lukewarm reaction, but when Muslim Middle Easterners are asked about the component parts of democracy, their responses are often far more favorable—suggesting wholehearted support for the constituent principles of democracy and disapproval of merely some of the unnecessary connotations of the word itself.[52] For instance, the 2005 Gallup poll of ten Muslim countries comprising 80 percent of the global Muslim population reported that "When asked what they admire most about the West, Muslims frequently mention political freedom, liberty, fair judicial systems, and freedom of speech." And in nine of the countries (the question was not asked in Saudi Arabia) over 80 percent of respondents favored the right of free speech— with 99 percent of Lebanese, 94 percent of Egyptians, 92 percent of Iranians, 91 percent of Moroccans, and 84 percent of Jordanians all approving.[53]

In some ways, Iraq immediately after the fall of Saddam's regime was an ideal test because the population had largely been isolated from contact with the outside world by Saddam's totalitarian controls. A poll conducted by the Iraq Center for Research and Strategic Studies in the summer of 2003 found that 56 percent of Iraqis wanted some form of democratic government, with the only other coherent bloc supporting an "Islamic" system, although it was unclear what they meant by that—and most other studies indicated that they did *not* mean an Islamic fundamentalist regime like Iran's.[54] In a Zogby poll conducted with *American Enterprise* magazine in August 2003, respondents were asked which foreign country they should model their new government on. The United States got the most votes (24 percent), while Iran got the fewest (3 percent).[55] A Gallup survey in Baghdad at the same time found that a multiparty parliamentary democracy was both the preferred form of government (39 percent) and the form that was most acceptable to the respondents (53 percent said that such a system would be acceptable to them). By comparison, an Islamic theocracy such as Iran's was preferred by only 10 percent and was acceptable to only 23 percent.[56] The social scientists Mark Tessler, Ronald Inglehart, and Mansoor Moaddel found that in 2004, 91 percent of Iraqis wanted a democratic political system in their country, and by 2006, a remarkable 88.7 percent still wanted a democratic system despite all of the unfulfilled promises and carnage that had transpired since.[57]

Indeed, even when polls found that Iraqis were ambivalent when specifically asked about "democracy" (because of the connotation of Western culture), they invariably found that they were overwhelmingly positive when asked about the building blocks of democratic governance. For example, in October 2003, the U.S. State Department conducted a poll of Iraqis in Baghdad, Basra, Fallujah, Ramadi, Irbil, Sulaymaniyyah, and Najaf. One of its principal conclusions was that

> In all seven cities in the Office of Research poll, large majorities support what are generally considered to be democratic values. Nine in ten think it is very or somewhat important that people vote in free and fair elections (95%), that people abide by the law and criminals are punished (94%), that people can criticize the government (86%), and that major nationality (89%) and religious groups share power (87%). Majorities also value media that are independent of government censorship (78%) and rights for women that are equal to those of men (71%). There is very little, if any, variation among the cities on these components, and there are only minor differences between men and women in their attitudes toward gender equity.[58]

All of the polls that found strong support among Muslim Middle Easterners for the building blocks of democracy also demonstrated a reasonable degree of support for the concept of democratic government, and not just its superficialities. For instance, high levels of support for freedom of religion and speech belie the fears of some that Arabs simply want majority rule when they discuss democracy. Indeed, an important distinction between the majority of public opinion and the more virulent Islamist groups is that although the latter may say they are comfortable with democracy (and many won't even say that), they will not accept freedom of religion or freedom of speech because doing so would allow minority sects to practice a religion other than Islam and be able to speak out in their own defense.

Qualitative research has reached the same conclusions. For instance, Amaney Jamal of Princeton University reports that "In qualitative interviews with Jordanian citizens during the summer of 2005, the vast majority of citizens from all economic and educational backgrounds expressed support for democratic rule based on a worldview of Islamic laws and doctrines. These citizens do not see Islam and democracy as opposed to one another. In fact, in many instances, respondents offered very perceptive analysis on the ways in which Islam could further contribute to the democratization project."[59] Similarly, National Democratic Institute focus groups in Bahrain in July 2002 demonstrated that the greatest complaint of Bahrainis was that the people were unhappy because they believed that the democratic reforms that they had been promised by the king were not being fully implemented. In the words of the final report, "They believe the democratic potential they had embraced is being thwarted by the very measures the government is enacting to structure the reform process."[60]

As another important piece of evidence, the Muslim Middle East has witnessed an increasing number of prodemocracy demonstrations over the past fifteen years.[61] These have been accompanied by a similarly growing number of calls by Middle Eastern leaders like former Jordanian Foreign Minister Marwan Muasher, who wrote in *The New York Times,* "It is becoming clear that the Arab world needs to take the initiative in making its political and economic systems more democratic. The frustrations Arabs feel today—prompted by the slow pace of democratic reform, stagnant economies, and political instability—all threaten the region's future. The moment has come for the Arab world to engage in a homegrown, evolutionary, and orderly process of democratization—one that will respect Arab culture while at the same time giving citizens the power to be part of the process."[62] Likewise, Uraib al-Rantawi of the al-Quds Center for Political Studies has written in Jordan's *Al Dustour* that "The need for political, economic, administrative, and fiscal reform in the Arab world is real, even if it is the Americans that tell us about it."[63]

Too many Americans and Europeans indulge in an outdated, and subtly racist, image of Muslim Middle Easterners as being wholly contented with their "backward" society and political institutions and equally resistant to importation of "Western" ideas of democracy, free markets, and modernity. The reality is entirely different.

Arab media, particularly the out-of-control satellite television networks, routinely discuss the merits of democracy and the problems of their ossified autocratic regimes. They have transformed the way that people (including the regimes themselves) talk about politics, making democratic and Islamic norms the only legitimate forms of political expression. This in turn is beginning to transform people's thinking, as illustrated by the public opinion polling, to reflect the deep embedding of democratic principles as the way that their societies ought to be governed.

To link this discussion back to the earlier point that Islam and democracy are not incompatible—and the related finding of so many pollsters and scholars that most Muslim Middle Easterners hold both a very positive impression of Islam and a very positive impression of democracy—it is useful to understand popular perceptions of Islam in government. As Dalia Mogahed and Geneive Abdo of the Gallup Organization have observed, popular demands for Shari'a in the Muslim world should be understood as a desire for limits on the power of the state. Mogahed and Abdo note that Shari'a establishes a clear compact between the ruler and the ruled, making the ruler responsible for the welfare of the ruled, limiting his power over his subjects, and creating a predictable pattern of governance that is in effect a form of "rule of law."[64] In other words, a key aspect of Muslim desires for incorporation of Shari'a into the governance of their state is to try to constrain the arbitrary exercise of power (and thus the abuse of power) by the ruling autocrats, which is also one of the principal goals of democratic government. Consequently, even the newspapers and magazines of the Arab world, long the mouthpiece for regime boilerplate about the threat from Israel and other conspiracy theories justifying continued emergency rule, now print pieces demanding reform and democratization, even adaptation to globalization and modernity.[65]

One of the many reasons for Middle Eastern anger at the United States is widespread rage that Washington has not done more to promote democracy in the region.[66] "There is a pervasive sense in the Middle East that the United States does not support democracy in the region, but rather supports what is in its strategic interest and calls it democratic," in the words of former Assistant Secretary of

State for the Near East Richard Murphy and the Middle East scholar Greg Gause.[67] Rami Khouri of Lebanon's *Daily Star* is often described as one of the most balanced voices of the Arab world, and in 2003 he warned that "The single most powerful and consistent complaint against the U.S. is that it applies a double standard in its policies to the Arab World. . . . This double standard is seen to apply in many areas, including promoting democracy, fighting terror, and mixing religion and politics, for example."[68] A 2006 Zogby poll of Egypt, Jordan, Lebanon, Morocco, Saudi Arabia, and the UAE found that 65 percent of those surveyed said they didn't think democracy was a real objective of the United States in the Middle East.[69]

Unfortunately, this is not a figment of their imagination. Because of our habitual avoidance of the problems of the Middle East, the desire of consecutive American administrations dating back to the 1940s to minimize America's involvement with the Middle East, and our preference for working with regional autocrats who were willing to guarantee America's interests in stability and oil, the United States has consistently indulged in what has been called "Arab exceptionalism." This is a nasty euphemism for excluding the Arab world from American efforts to promote democracy, which have been commonplace everywhere else in the world (to a greater or lesser degree). Most Arabs and Iranians are deeply unhappy with their lot, they believe that reform—and particularly democratization—are part of the answer to their problems, and it frustrates them greatly that the United States has purposely chosen *not* to try to foster reform and democratization in their part of the world. This anger feeds into conspiracy theories about the United States, because it raises the inevitable question of why America is unwilling to do so. Is it because we are trying to keep them weak so that we (and the Israelis) can dominate them? Is it because we seek to control their oil and we believe that pliant autocrats make for better puppets than unruly democracies? Is it because we hate them because they are Muslims and we seek to destroy Islam? To people desperate for exactly the kind of changes that the United States has seemed to stand for everywhere else in the world, these questions lead easily to equally misguided affirmative answers that play into the ideologies of the hatemongers of the region who seek to harm America and our allies.

The evidence is incontrovertible that the people of the Muslim Middle East are desperate for exactly the kinds of reforms that the United States had mostly eschewed, until the Bush 43 administration came along and adopted them about as badly as could have been imagined. But the evidence still stands. Speaking of her people, but in words that echo the sentiments of the whole region, Mona Makram Ebeid, an Egyptian political activist and former member of Parliament, once proclaimed, "What Americans need to understand is that all that Egyptians want is a job and a voice!"[70] It is time for the United States to help them and their brethren throughout the region gain both.

CHAPTER 11

MEETING THE CHALLENGES OF REFORM

Most middle east experts accept that the United States must try to enable and encourage political, economic, and social reform across the Middle East. However, not all do, and those who don't tend to offer a different set of criticisms from those discussed in the previous chapter. They generally acknowledge the desire for democracy and change throughout the region. They also accept the likelihood that Middle Eastern states could eventually adapt and adopt democratic forms of government, just as so many other nations with equally different cultures have over the course of the past hundred years. And they mostly dismiss the claim that Islam is somehow incompatible with democracy.

Instead, they raise three different sets of issues. The first of these is that promoting reform, including democratization and free-market economics, is very difficult and the United States' track record in this area is uneven at best. Thus, they question whether the United States will be able to foster political, economic, and social reform in the Arab world. In particular, they note that the regimes of the Middle East are pretty much dead set against it and have devised clever and effective methods to stymie the efforts of both internal and external reformers. Second, they argue that even if it were possible for the United States to help the Middle East regimes reform themselves, we probably should not want them to do so, because the likely result of pluralistic political reform would be to put Islamists in power. They note that the liberals of the Arab world are so weak and divided and the Islamists so popular that it is highly unlikely that the

United States would see the reformists we like prevail at the polls.[1] The resulting governments might prove virulently anti-American and take actions that would harm America's interests.[2] Last, they argue that though mature democracies tend to be both pacific and restrained, new democracies tend to be pretty bellicose. Therefore, helping create a lot of new democracies in the Middle East might breed lots of interstate conflicts which would be just as dangerous to American interests as the intrastate conflicts and terrorism we currently face.

These three criticisms encapsulate the most important challenges that a U.S.-led effort to enable reform in the Muslim Middle East will face. They are why such a strategy will be difficult to implement and will require decades to succeed. For that reason, it is crucial to examine each in turn to identify ways to tackle the challenges and overcome them.

Tilting at Windmills?

It is possible to trace a path of success stories through the annals of American democracy promotion, beginning with Germany and Japan, meandering through South Korea, Taiwan, Mexico, and Chile, across the Philippines and on to Eastern Europe. However, there have also been any number of failures or cases where the jury is still decidedly out: Haiti, Bosnia, Russia, much of central Asia, and now Iraq and Afghanistan, to name only a few. Typically, critics of democratization point out that the United States has succeeded mostly in cases where the people wanted democracy and largely built it themselves, with the United States playing only a supporting political and economic role (and military, in the case of our defense of Western Europe and East Asia during the Cold War). In contrast, our failures have often come when the United States made a much greater effort, even to the extent of engaging in processes of nation building, such as in Haiti and potentially Iraq.

In this case, however, that evidence does *not* invalidate a grand strategy of enabling reform in the Muslim Middle East, because such an approach would focus on gradual political, economic, and social change largely by assisting (politically, economically, and perhaps militarily by protecting the Middle East from external military threats) indigenous forces for change. It would *not* entail the same kind of nation-building efforts as in Haiti, Iraq, and Afghanistan. Indeed, one of the many problems with the Bush 43 administration's efforts was that its policies to promote reform became associated with Iraq and Afghanistan, and others assumed that that was what it had in mind for the rest of the region.[3]

Nevertheless, the critics are correct that encouraging, enabling, and assisting reform—especially political reform in the manner of democratization—in the Muslim Middle East is not going to be easy. In the case of the Middle East, the most challenging obstacle is the opposition of the existing regimes themselves. None of them has any interest in acceding to the legitimate desires of their subjects and stepping aside in favor of a new pluralist government. Nor do they seem willing to accede to a gradual transition to more democratic rule, a scenario in which they or their successors might still play an important role, albeit not so all-powerful as at present. All of the rulers appear determined to hold on to absolute power for as long as they possibly can, and then pass it on to their son or some other designated successor. What's more, many of the elites in their countries support their resistance to reform. After all, political and legal reform would likely eliminate the graft and perks on which so many of the current elites thrive. The patronage networks that dominate Middle East economies would be destroyed (purposely) by legal, political, and especially economic reform. Since many of the wealthy in the Muslim Middle East made their fortunes by manipulating these patronage networks, they have every reason to join the autocrats in opposing such reforms.[4]

Moreover, they have devised numerous ways to deflect pressure for reform from both internal and external sources. Although most of the regimes have created parliaments in which they allow some opposition figures to serve, these are invariably powerless "advisory" bodies that lack the right to appoint ministers or allocate funds. Moreover, they typically include members appointed by the regime and/or their power is further weakened by an upper house composed of elites tied to the regime and able to veto any actions taken by the lower house. Nearly all of the regimes allow semicompetitive elections, at least for the parliaments but sometimes for regional and municipal offices and sometimes even for the presidency in the "republics" of the region. But they tightly circumscribe who is able to run for office, often arbitrarily disqualifying or even imprisoning popular opposition figures. They hamstring the fund-raising and organization of opposition parties, employ all of the resources and personnel of the state to back the regime's favored candidates, intimidate voters in regions likely to vote for the opposition, gerrymander voting districts to favor their candidates, and restrict the opposition's access to the media. They have subverted and co-opted the kind of civil society organizations—trade unions, professional associations, women's organizations, even athletic clubs—that could create alternative bases for mobilizing people around common interests in opposition to the government. For instance, they insist on "licensing" such organizations and then simply don't grant licenses to those they don't like. Or they insist on appointing the heads of the organizations or on limiting the size and venues of their meetings. And they routinely ban them from receiving foreign funding (which leaves many dependent on government funding) or engaging in political activities. Even in the economic realm, the Middle Eastern regimes have found ways to turn "gestures" of reform into methods of reinforcing their control. So they will "heed" popular or international calls for privatization by selling off a few state-owned enterprises, but because there is no transparency, these factories are invariably sold to cronies of the regime for undisclosed sums.[5]

The regimes have also figured out how to undermine reform rhetorically, portraying it as a Western effort to subvert or dominate the country, playing into both nationalist and anti-American sentiments (and often anti-Israeli prejudices as well). For instance, after President Bush's 2003 address to the National Endowment for Democracy, Arab regimes claimed that it was somehow illegitimate for the U.S. president to be talking about democracy in the Arab world unless American forces were withdrawn from Iraq and there was peace between Israelis and Palestinians.[6] Many of the more radical Islamists who desire theocracy rather than democracy echo these slanders and diversions. As Barry Rubin has extensively described in his book *The Long War for Freedom,* this is a tremendous problem for liberal Arab reformers.[7] It forces the reformists to engage in all man-ner of convoluted efforts to explain how the reforms they propose would benefit their society, even if it might also be what the United States wants. Moreover, by taking this line of criticism, the regimes (and their Islamist foes) further undermine the liberal reformists by effectively making it impossible for them to accept aid of any kind from the West, and especially the United States, because doing so then becomes evidence of the charge that they are nothing but American agents trying to weaken or even destroy the state.[8]

It should not require a great deal of imagination to understand that it is hard to foster reform in another part of the world when the governments themselves are fighting it tooth and nail. This is espe-cially so when it is their highest priority, and on our list it has typi-cally fallen somewhere below securing aid for Iraq, stabilizing the Israelis and Palestinians, rallying support for harsher sanctions on Iran, securing aid for the Lebanese government, isolating the Syrian government, ensuring that Libya complies with U.N. Security Coun-cil resolutions, convincing OPEC to keep prices relatively low, and a few other odds and ends.

Nevertheless, we should not assume that this is an insurmount-able obstacle either. Middle Eastern kings and dictators are not the first autocrats to oppose liberal political, economic, and social re-forms. The Philippines under Ferdinand Marcos, Chile under Au-gusto Pinochet, Romania under Nicolae Ceauşescu, and South Korea under Chun Doo-Hwan are all examples of iron-fisted dictators forced from office by popular pressure for change. In other cases (such as Spain after Francisco Franco) the death of the autocrat fur-nished the occasion for a transition away from autocracy. In Ar-gentina, military defeat in the Falklands War furnished an occasion to depose the ruling junta and establish democracy. East Asia (Tai-wan, Bangladesh), Latin America (Peru, Mexico), and Africa (Niger, Zambia) furnish other examples of more gradual processes of re-form. All of which is merely to say that reform and political change are not a hopeless goal even in the face of opposition from powerful, entrenched, and unyielding autocracies.

Some have suggested that oil wealth inures Middle Eastern au-tocracies to the same pressure. It is certainly true that oil revenues can help Middle Eastern autocrats buy off some opposition groups and frees them of the need to collect taxes. However, Gwenn Okruhlik's study of the impact of oil on internal stability demonstrates that oil does not prevent the emergence of domestic opposition movements (and can actually foment them), while the examples of the shah of Iran, King Idris of Libya, King Faysal of Iraq, and numerous other rulers of oil-rich Middle Eastern countries overthrown at various times since World War II makes it clear that even those with oil wealth can be toppled.[9] Thus oil wealth can help Middle Eastern regimes cope with some forms of internal pressure but cannot eliminate these pressures altogether and often do no more than take the edge off.

Moreover, the rulers themselves are well aware of this and believe themselves to be vulnerable to popular pressure, which is why they pay such careful attention to public opinion and the emergence of internal opposition groups. It is also why they have tried to make at least superficial gestures toward reform over the past ten years as the demands of their populations have grown louder. The fact that they have not gone farther down the path of reform underlines their opposition to the process, but the fact that they have all started down it—and claim to have gone much farther than they actually have—highlights their fear that if they are not seen as implementing the desire of the people for reform, they risk losing everything.

BRINGING THE REGIMES ON BOARD

There is no magic formula for overcoming the resistance of reluctant regimes to embrace economic and social, let alone political, reform. The United States and its allies will have to be flexible, creative, and adaptive in trying out various tactics and tailoring them to meet the specific circumstances of different countries at different periods of time. However, a number of broader guidelines are already discernible and should be used to tackle this particular set of problems.

The first of these guidelines is that the regimes themselves need to be part of the process. They are simply too strong to try to fight. Despite their paranoia, and to a great extent because of it, few (if any) of the regimes are likely to be overthrown by indigenous forces in the near term. And, as described in chapter 8, it would almost certainly not be in the United States' interests to see them overthrown. Moreover, the fiasco of regime change in Iraq should make Washington very reticent about trying to overthrow another Middle Eastern autocracy from the outside. Consequently, the regimes will remain, and they will remain the most powerful forces in their societies for many years to come. What this means is that rather than see the regimes as our adversary when it comes to fostering reform, we need to find ways to make them our partners and, of greater importance, the partners of those in their own societies hoping to bring about peaceful reform.

The first steps are recognizing that we need to give the regimes incentives to allow reforms, we need to remove their incentives (and excuses) not to reform, and we need to work with them to make them feel comfortable about the reforms. If we start from an adversarial position, as the George W. Bush administration did at times, we are bound to fail. A better model was that of the George H. W. Bush and Clinton administrations, which instead worked to persuade the Arab regimes that change was coming, one way or another, and the choice they faced was either to allow for controlled, gradual transition or face mounting internal unrest and eventual revolts.

Our primary goal must be to convince the regimes themselves that their survival, albeit in modified form, is possible only if they are willing to adapt to the new realities of the world and the region. We should not be averse to the idea that the leadership will retain an important role in governance well into the future. This is both especially true and especially easy with the monarchs of the region, who tend to enjoy greater popular legitimacy and so can imagine ceding some power to democratic institutions while still retaining an important role in governance, one way or another. And this argument has the merit of actually being true. It is also one that people and even government officials throughout the Middle East are coming to recognize themselves.[10]

USING AMERICAN AID AS A STICK AND A CARROT

Such arguments are likely to take us only so far, however. The fact is that these regimes have been suppressing their internal foes for a long time and, like the tsars before them, some are convinced that they can keep doing so forever. Moreover, most tend to think very short term, refusing to recognize longer-term problems, let alone take steps to remedy them. That is why their societies degenerated into prerevolutionary states in the first place. Consequently, the United States is going to need more powerful inducements. The most obvious is American aid. The United States provides significant amounts of economic and military aid to Egypt, Jordan, Lebanon, and Morocco and to a lesser extent Yemen. (The United States is also providing Iraq with massive amounts of assistance, but that falls into a separate category.) Since September 11, 2001, a number of other Middle Eastern states have received substantial increases in American aid to bolster their security establishments to better fight terrorism. This aid has proven to be quite important to the regimes.[11] In addition, American diplomatic support is absolutely critical for these and other Middle Eastern states to receive loans, grants, and membership from international financial and trade organizations. For instance, American approval has been crucial to Saudi Arabia's bid for accession to the World Trade Organization, and the United States has intervened in the past to soften IMF decisions regarding conditions for aid to Egypt.[12]

For the most part, Americans have thought about using this aid principally as a stick with Middle Eastern governments. We have threatened, or talked about threatening, to cut or withhold aid if these governments did not adopt significant reforms. Under the right circumstances, this can be effective. America's unwillingness to fund Latin American dictatorships starting in the 1990s crippled many of those regimes, forcing them to start down the same path of reform we would like to see the Arab states and Iran take.[13] The more the United States can condition its aid and its assistance with international organizations on progress toward reform, the greater the incentive for regional states to take these hard steps. For example, Dennis Ross has proposed holding $200 million of the aid we provide Egypt annually in escrow, to be released only when President Mubarak lifts the highly unpopular state of emergency that he has kept in place since 1981 and that justifies many of the government's most arbitrary actions.[14]

Sticks like withholding aid, however, should be only part of this approach, and probably only a small part. Though significant, cessation of American aid is not likely to break the finances of any of the regional governments. The oil producers don't need direct American funding (although they do benefit from American support with international organizations), and even the non-oil-producing states often receive grants from the wealthy Persian Gulf states that at times match or exceed American funding.[15] All of the Middle Eastern states, and particularly the most important (like Egypt and Saudi Arabia), are fiercely nationalistic and bristle when the United States tries to bend them to its will—especially when the regime's leadership believes that acceding will threaten their grip on power.[16] Thus, it will be critical for the United States to think about its aid to the Arab world in terms of carrots as well. Rather than simply threatening to cut aid if the regimes of the region don't embrace reform, we should be making a much greater effort to entice and reward them for doing so. Such aid should be seen as more than just a bribe; it should be seen as providing necessary economic resources to help the states of the region make these transitions and deal with the inevitable problems and dislocations that large-scale reform would cause. Think about it this way: we will be trying to persuade Middle Eastern governments to fundamentally restructure their societies— rewrite their legal codes, reorganize their judiciaries, revise their curricula, retrain their teachers, privatize their industries, break down monopolies, lift trade barriers, limit state controls, and allow greater political freedoms. All of this is going to cost money—in some cases, a lot of money. And the United States (and its European and East Asian allies, all of which would also benefit from greater stability and prosperity in the Middle East) should be providing the poorer states of the region with generous assistance to make these changes possible without further impoverishing the people or alienating key constituencies.

This is going to require the U.S. government, and particularly the U.S. Congress, to do something it doesn't like to do: give more money to foreign governments. Over the past few decades, the U.S. Congress has made it very difficult to increase aid to foreign governments. The simple fact is that there is not much of a constituency for giving money to foreign governments. It just doesn't win votes the way that giving money to Americans does. The only exceptions are specific communities or lobbies that care deeply about one or more foreign countries and advocate foreign aid for those countries. Unfortunately, such a lobby has not yet coalesced to support increased aid to the Middle East for the purpose of assisting with reform. Arab Americans and Iranian Americans often feel passionately about issues affecting the Middle East, but they have not organized themselves, nor have they been as willing to fund candidates friendly to their perspective, as have Cuban Americans, Jewish Americans, and Indian Americans. Similarly, the Congressional Black Caucus has taken a special interest in issues dear to the hearts of many African Americans, and by banding together, it too has been able to influence American foreign policy on issues like Darfur and Haiti. For the Arab states, the most powerful domestic group that has lobbied on their behalf has been the oil industry. However, traditionally the oil companies have cared only about the oil-producing states, and they tend to be quite comfortable with the current regimes and fearful of political change that could threaten their existing arrangements. (Although some of the oil companies have begun to recognize that their interest in long-term stability in the region and ensuring their profitable positions over the same longer time horizons would be best served by reform programs that would reduce the threat of popular unrest and head off potentially catastrophic upheavals down the road.)

Since it is unlikely that a domestic group will make a compelling case for increasing U.S. foreign aid for the Middle East, the executive branch and the Congress must realize that doing so is absolutely crucial to American interests in the Middle East. Their failure to do so is symptomatic of our wrongheaded policies toward the region over the past sixty years. We have a bad history of trying cheap, quick-fix policies for the region that do not work and only force us to return to the region later to confront bigger problems that cost us far more to address than would prudent early investments. The exception that proves the rule is the Arab-Israeli peace process. This is the lone American policy we have (with the exception of the Bush 43 administration) stuck with for over thirty years and the one policy we were willing to commit significant resources toward on an annual basis in the form of large-scale economic and military aid to Israel, Egypt, and (to a lesser extent) Jordan and Lebanon. Not coincidentally, it is also the only American policy toward the region that has shown real progress over the years. Egypt was weaned away from the USSR, Egypt and Israel made peace, Jordan and Lebanon gave up participating in Arab military coalitions against Israel, and then Jordan and Israel made peace. Obviously, that problem is far from solved, but it is the only piece of the Middle East mess where the situation has gotten better, not worse, since 1973.

This is the point of developing a grand strategy toward the Middle East. It is meant to provide a rational framework for how the United States should identify and pursue its goals in the region by employing all of the necessary political, diplomatic, economic, and military means necessary to do so. We cannot expect to help the Arab states (and perhaps someday Iran) to pursue a course of comprehensive political, economic, and social reforms on the cheap. We essentially tried that approach during the Clinton administration and, in its own dysfunctional way, during the George W. Bush administration, and it failed. We would not provide sufficient incentives for the regimes of the region to embrace reform or to enable them to do so. If we do provide greater funding there is no guarantee that we will succeed over the long term, but if we don't, it is virtually certain that we will fail.[17]

I am always wary of the common comparison between promoting reform in the Middle East and the Marshall Plan because the latter was designed to do something quite different. But where I think the comparison is appropriate is that in the aftermath of World War II, the United States realized that rebuilding Europe was necessary for its own safety and prosperity, and we also recognized that doing so would cost a lot of money but that this expenditure was worthwhile because of the importance of the goal. The Middle East today is, like Europe in the early twentieth century, the source of our greatest immediate and potential security threats. The solution to its problems is going to require a lot of money (albeit for different causes, programs, and costs than the Marshall Plan) committed over time, and we need to recognize that providing at least some of that money for them to do so is in our best interests. Think of the hundreds of billions of dollars that the United States is now sinking into the wars in Iraq and Afghanistan, as well as the wider "War on Terror." Doesn't it make sense to put a fraction of that, perhaps as much as $5 billion to $10 billion per year, into foreign aid programs for the Muslim Middle East to encourage and enable it to carry out the reforms that are vital to ameliorating and eventually eliminating the problems of terrorism and instability that threaten our vital interests in the region—and hopefully head off future wars?

An important complementary idea would be for the United States and its allies in the region and outside it to establish a Middle East development bank that would be capitalized by funds from the United States, Europe, East Asian countries, and the oil-rich Arab states.[18] Ideally, the Arab oil producers would furnish most of the funds so that the regional development bank would have little foreign taint and would instead be seen as a mechanism by which the rich of the Arab world would help the poor of the region. The development bank would be enjoined to seek out projects throughout the Muslim Middle East that could help the people of the region overcome their economic, political, legal, educational, and social conundrums and would be led by a nonpartisan international board to ensure that funds were disbursed based on need, not political connections. This too would be an extremely useful way to help the region move down the path of reform and encourage the regimes to do so by absorbing costs that they might otherwise incur.

POLITICAL AND ECONOMIC REFORM

I noted above that the United States will have to be flexible when it comes to trying to convince the regimes of the region to embrace reform, and finding the right balance between pushing for political and economic reforms may be crucial to our success. Experts debate whether the United States should demand that the Arab states and Iran apply political reforms (i.e., democratization) as fast as they are willing to adopt economic change (like privatization and eliminating subsidies). The debate grows from the simple fact that getting the regimes to adopt economic reforms is likely to be somewhat easier than getting them to pursue political reforms because the former have less impact (but not none) on their own power and might actually make them richer. Everyone agrees that both economic and political reforms are necessary, but some argue that economic reform can be allowed to proceed without political reform for some time or merely to outpace it.[19] Their opponents in this debate argue that the United States cannot afford to allow the Middle Eastern regimes to neglect democratization both because political reform is necessary to bring economic reform to full fruition and because decoupling them could allow the regimes to ignore democratization altogether.[20]

I fall somewhere in the middle but lean in the direction of those who argue that economic and political reform do not need to proceed at the same pace and that it may be necessary to allow economic reform to move faster than political reform. First, because America's efforts need to be geared toward *encouraging* and *helping* the Muslim Middle Eastern states adopt liberal reform programs—rather than trying to force them to do so—and because we do not have a monopoly of knowledge on how best to do so, we should not make perfect the enemy of good enough. We need to acknowledge that we have only a rough idea of how the Middle East can transform itself. Different countries have found very different paths to that goal, and it is typically the case that only the people of the country in question can figure out the specific steps they should take in terms of tailoring reforms to make them work best for their history, culture, and other circumstances. The models of Europe and East Asia furnish some useful analogies, but the fact is that their transformations worked because they were driven largely by indigenous agents of change and tailored to the specific circumstances of their societies. Thus we cannot simply superimpose the European and East Asian experiences on the Middle East. Instead, Middle Easterners are going to have to find their own way, and that means that we are not going to be in a strong position to assert that the path we lay out is the best way, let alone the only way, to reach the desired end state.

This is not an argument for "sequencing," for insisting that some reforms must precede others in the mistaken belief that there is a certain order in which societies evolve.[21] Instead, it is an argument for patience, flexibility, and even opportunism in pushing reform in the Middle East. If there are opportunities to push economic reform because the regimes are better disposed toward economic development, we should take them. We should not insist that all of the different areas of reform—political, economic, social—run perfectly in unison and pass on opportunities to push faster on one track. This is especially so since we should not assume that we know what the right pace of each is for the Muslim Middle East. Moreover, the governments of a number of Middle Eastern countries have taken significant steps toward economic reform in recent years, and although we certainly should try to convince them to take commensurate steps on the political side, we should welcome their economic reforms—and definitely should not tell them not to go any farther down the economic track until they have made more progress on political reform![22]

Second, in the short term, economic reform could be an important means of diminishing the wide popularity of the Islamist groups in the region. A considerable amount of their popularity derives from their willingness and ability to provide basic services like food, jobs, medical care, sanitation, clean water, education, and even housing to those who cannot afford it. Amaney Jamal found that better-educated and wealthier Egyptians and Jordanians were more likely to support democracy and less likely to support Islamism. Poorer and less educated people tended to be more supportive of Islamism and less supportive of democracy. Similarly, she found that people outside Cairo and Amman (where most of the slums are located) were also more supportive of democracy.[23] Thus, the more economic opportunities available and the less poverty, the fewer the numbers of people turning to the Islamist groups. This too would be a useful contribution to the political reform of Middle Eastern societies.

Third, as Fareed Zakaria, Richard Haass, and others have argued, economic growth and modernization are themselves important elements in making democracy possible and typically exert their own pressure for democratic reform.[24] We don't know much about why democracy flowers in some countries at some times but not in others at other times. However, there is a clear correlation between increasing prosperity and successful democratization. This is one of the most consistent findings of scholarly work on democratization over the past forty years: the more prosperous the country, the easier it is for it to transition to democracy.[25]

In what is probably a related phenomenon, economic reform typically creates pressure on regimes to move in the direction of democratization. In the domestic realm, economic restructuring to favor market forces and private industry (rather than the controlled economies and state-owned enterprises that dominate the contemporary Middle East) typically allows more and more members of society to benefit economically. They can create a middle class that does not owe its position or wealth to the regime's beneficence. This, in turn, typically causes those members of society to demand greater rule of law to protect them against arbitrary actions by the state and then a greater say in government for the same reason (and potentially to determine how their money is being spent if the state begins to tax them, which becomes possible when there are people making money from sources other than government largesse).[26] The pressure can also come from international sources, especially international financial and trade organizations, which typically demand greater transparency and accountability when governments petition for aid for economic reforms. The international organizations also require the adoption of various regulations and practices both to improve the efficiency of the relevant institutions and to allow the state's economy to better integrate into the global economy.[27] All of this pushes any regime interested in economic reform to adopt democratic practices as well.

Those who argue that democratic reforms must precede or at least run precisely parallel with economic reforms typically cite examples like China, Chile, and Singapore as examples of autocracies that embraced economic reform without democratization. I would argue that these cases prove the opposite. The embrace of free-market economics in all three of these countries created powerful pressures for democracy. In all three cases, the autocrats resisted and delayed but could not eliminate these pressures. All have been forced to adopt some political reforms in response to them. In Chile, Pinochet's economic liberalization forced him to grant successively greater political rights, to the point where he was denied reelection in 1988 and a democracy was established. Neither China nor Singapore has come as far as Chile, but both are very different polities today than they were twenty years ago. Even in China, which arguably has resisted democratization most, the demands and pressures of its rapid economic modernization are forcing the regime to open up its political space in ways that were unthinkable in the days of Mao and the Cultural Revolution. In fact, in 2006, Chinese Premier Wen Jiabao told a group of American scholars, "We have to move toward democracy. We have many problems, but we know the direction in which we are going."[28]

The United States should not necessarily assume that where China and Singapore are today would be sufficient to address the underlying problems of the Middle East (and thus that all we should be looking to do is to get the Middle Eastern regimes to imitate Singapore and China). However, it is undeniable that economic development is creating pressure for democratization in both of those countries, which in the Middle East could be helpful in cajoling the autocrats there to adopt political reform.

These examples raise another point regarding the relationship between economic and political reform in the Middle East. Afshin Molavi, a keen observer of the Middle Eastern scene, once commented that the road to democracy is a very long one and that although the United States should never give up pushing for that ultimate goal because it is what so many people in the region want, we should also try to help them reach an important intermediate goal, which he described as "decent" government.[29] By this he meant a government that would not dominate (and, in so doing, cripple) the nation's economy, leaving many of its citizens in poverty; a government that would lay out rational laws and regulations and then proceed both to enforce them and to abide by them; a government that would provide a useful education for its citizens to enable them to compete in a globalized economy; and a government that would see its citizens as the ultimate source of its national wealth, rather than a potential competitor for the consumption of that wealth. All of these would be steps in the right direction. All of them would help address the underlying grievances of the people of the region and thus would likely diminish the anger and frustration that is feeding both the terrorism and instability that threaten American interests in the Middle East. Having a "decent" government (what others often call "good governance"), as many argue Singapore has, might not be the ultimate solution to the Middle East's problems or a desirable end state for the people of the region, but it would be quite a bit better than the status quo. Creating the environment for real economic reform would likely compel the Arab regimes and Iran to at least become "decent" governments, which would be a step in the right direction.

In an insightful study of the various patterns of reform and pseudoreform in the Middle East, Marina Ottaway and Michele Dunne of the Carnegie Endowment have demonstrated that this is precisely what King Muhammad VI's reforms in Morocco are probably intended to achieve. While pointing out that these are "not meant to lead to democracy" they also demonstrate that "Changes in Morocco cannot be dismissed as purely cosmetic. The country is without doubt more open, and the government is less repressive, than it was in the past. Nor is there any sign that this process of managed reform has run its course and can go no further."[30] Morocco's drive toward good governance should not be allowed to preclude the development of true democracy, assuming that that is what the people of Morocco want, but neither should it be disdained as irrelevant. Morocco's reforms are positive steps, and we would do well to encourage other Muslim Middle Eastern states to emulate them.

Moreover, we should keep in mind that history does not offer a compelling pattern for the Muslim Middle East to follow. In Western Europe and East Asia, economic reform both laid the foundation and created the desire for democratization.[31] In contrast, in Eastern Europe, democratization had to pave the way for economic reform by unlocking critical political barriers.[32] Thus, we do not know for certain whether economic reform can or should precede political reform or vice versa in the Middle East. So humility alone would suggest that we ought to advocate both simultaneously, and take progress wherever we can get it. If that means greater progress in the economic realm because that is what the regimes are most comfortable with, so be it. Over time, it may become more apparent whether one necessarily must precede the other, and if that is the case, then we ought to be prepared to shift our emphasis to that track. But in the meantime, we should allow pragmatism to guide our actions, and that pragmatism argues for enabling reform wherever it appears possible, whenever it appears possible.

Nevertheless, none of this should be misconstrued as an argument to focus on economic reform at the *expense* of political reform (let alone social, educational, and legal reform). Quite the contrary. Political reform is absolutely crucial, and there are aspects of it, such as pushing for basic political rights, that the United States should never abandon. Moreover, it almost certainly is the case that political and economic reform are reinforcing processes with each dependent on the other for meaningful progress. In particular, in the Middle East it is going to require political changes to dismantle the patronage networks that dominate Arab states and economies.[33] Those political changes need not come together in one fell swoop, but even if they happen piecemeal over time, they still need to happen. Similarly, the states of the region need not necessarily move on all aspects of political reform before they adopt far-reaching economic changes, but some sort of iterative process—with economic liberalization creating the demand for political reform and political reform unlocking the potential for further economic liberalization—will undoubtedly be necessary.[34]

THE VIRTUE OF PATIENCE
The need for flexibility also suggests the need for patience in America's efforts to advance the cause of reform in the Middle East. Because the United States is going to have to overcome the resistance of the regional regimes, we are going to have to be willing to seize opportunities where they are available and calibrate our pressure based on the circumstances of the moment. There will be times when events will create a propitious situation and we will be able to make great strides forward. There will be other times when the opposite will be true and we may have to satisfy ourselves with much smaller gains. On some occasions, the opportunities to advance economic liberalization will be greatest, on others they may be more conducive to political reform, and on still others they may be most conducive to social development. We need to be ready to shift gears as needed to take advantage of whatever the situation has to offer.

One likely scenario is that the states of the region without oil wealth are likely to be far more receptive to American help in advancing the cause of reform than the oil-rich states are. Those without oil wealth are likely to be more desirous of American aid (especially if the United States is willing to provide generous long-term packages) and are those least able to buy off their domestic constituencies, making them generally more fearful of internal unrest. There is no reason that Washington and its allies should not work most energetically with these states. There is no reason that reform needs to advance uniformly all across the region. In fact, if Jordan, Morocco, Yemen, and Egypt make real strides toward economic liberalism, democratization, the rule of law, and advanced educational systems, then, assuming they are seen as prospering (and that is another important role for U.S. economic assistance, to ensure that those who take risks for reform are seen as having benefited from doing so), others in the region will likely follow suit. Even the Gulf states may find it hard not to move down the path of reform, albeit more slowly, if their people believe that such reforms have really helped the other states of the region.

Another important reason to see patience as a virtue is that although reform is coming only slowly and haltingly to the Middle East, it is coming. We just cannot give up on it prematurely or insist that it move faster than is realistically possible. Although the critics are right that the Arab autocracies have devised cunning means of undermining reforms, limiting them, or channeling them into areas that do not have a significant impact on the current state of affairs, one can also see that glass as half (or at least partially) full.[35] Although the reform promotion efforts of the Clinton and Bush administrations did not produce democratic dominos falling across the region, they nevertheless had a meaningful impact. It is true that most of the legislatures in the region are powerless, but there are now legislatures in many countries where before there were none. And those legislatures serve as bully pulpits for opposition figures who can at least call attention to government misdeeds. In some, including Saudi Arabia's, they are now able even to propose laws.[36] Similarly, the regimes have found clever ways to censor the media and the Internet, but the satellite TV channels still broadcast with a great deal of freedom and young people are constantly finding ways around the latest Internet controls. Across the Arab world, editorial pages print columns urging reform and criticizing the status quo—even criticizing the government and, occasionally, specific officials or organizations.[37] In Egypt's heavily manipulated 2005 presidential elections, the Judges' Club, a quasi-official syndicate, nonetheless forced the regime to permit more direct (if inadequate) judicial supervision of the voting.[38] If this small step creates a precedent for eventual judicial review by an independent judiciary, we will look back on it as having been a giant step forward.

Today, democracy is the touchstone of legitimate government throughout the region and the regimes are being forced to justify their actions based on democratic norms. Even if their references are nothing more than a rhetorical facade, their acceptance of it creates a set of expectations that can increasingly bind them over time. The Carnegie Endowment's Nathan Brown and Amr Hamzawy emphatically relate that "In the level of intellectual debate, the battle for democracy has been fought—and won" in the Arab world.[39] As discussed above, virtually all of the regimes have been forced to legalize opposition parties, whereas before there were almost none. These opposition parties are heavily repressed, but they are allowed to run in (heavily manipulated) elections and even win seats—all of which is a major change from twenty years ago. Although much of the privatization that has taken place has favored regime cronies, it has at least set important precedents. The regimes are also being forced by the new democratic zeitgeist to hold more competitive elections. Although all of them find ways to monkey with these elections, they are having to devote lots of effort and resources to do so and then have to be satisfied with garnering 77 percent of the vote rather than the previously typical 99 percent.[40] Again, none is in danger of losing right now, but this opens up the potential that one day they will lose and be replaced, just as Pinochet was. With each election, both locals and outsiders have been able to catch, expose, and even prevent some of these practices, which over time might slowly diminish the regimes' ability to employ them. Moreover, some of the regime's efforts to manipulate elections—like gerrymandering and spreading nasty rumors about the opposition—are unsavory but conform to

democratic principles. The United States has the very same problems. If, over time, the regimes can be reduced to employing only
these methods, we should look on it as considerable progress. In
places like Mexico and Taiwan, autocratic regimes manipulated elections for years, but over time consistent external pressure (particularly from the United States) forced them to curb their abuses to the
point where elections became increasingly fairer and more representative.[41]

The Arab regimes have also adopted a range of economic reforms, despite the importance of their patronage networks and their
control of their national economies. Indeed, they have arguably gone
quite a bit farther on economic reform than on political reform, reinforcing the point that economic reform is a much easier pill for
them to swallow. Since 2004, the Middle Eastern states have seen
much greater flows of trade and foreign investment, with a modest
decline in unemployment. Although high oil prices and a favorable
global economic environment have played the biggest role, economic
reform policies like revised employment laws that give employers
greater flexibility to hire and fire, lower tariffs and price subsidies,
and somewhat greater privatization have also contributed.[42] The
World Bank notes that non-oil-producing states in the Middle East
have generally done better with job creation than have oil-producing
states, which suggests that reform has been a factor.[43] Inevitably, all
this must be taken with a grain of salt. The shifts are still modest and
certainly do not change the overall situation of the national
economies, nor do they touch their deeper structural problems. But
they are additional signs of life—and signs that it is possible to convince the regimes to reform despite their general disinclination to
do so.

In many ways, the modest progress on reform made over the last
ten to twelve years constitutes reasonable first steps as part of a
process that will doubtless take several more decades. The United
States and its allies pushed the regimes to reform (intelligently in
some cases, unintelligently in others). This pressure, coupled with
the demands they faced from their own populations, convinced the
Middle Eastern regimes to make a number of important concessions.

Ultimately, they found ways to stop the reform process and to undercut some of the concessions, but they were not able to roll back the clock to 1970, as they would have liked. The Middle East *is* different today from what it was two or three decades ago, and the differences are important because of the precedents that have been set. In the end, the region took two steps forward and one step back. But that one step of progress that remained is important, and that may be the pattern of reform in the Middle East well into the future. If so, we should accept that this is progress and not simply throw up our hands in despair at its halting pace. Now that the regimes have found a way to block and co-opt the early efforts to pressure them to reform, both we and the Middle Eastern reformists themselves need to find new ways forward. But we should take heart from these early experiences that the combination of internal and external pressure can convince the regimes to make significant concessions, even if it did not cause them to become Middle Eastern Switzerlands overnight.

The Islamist Dilemma

The next great challenge of any strategy designed to foster political reform in the Arab world is how to overcome the dilemma of Islamist popularity. Much as Americans might like Arab secular liberals to succeed to governance in their countries as a result of democratization, the uncomfortable reality is that they don't stand much of a chance against the many Islamist parties—at least not now and probably for some time, if ever. Unfortunately, many of the current crop of secular liberals of the Arab world tend to be isolated elitists with few connections to the mass of the people. They have done a poor job of organizing themselves and a poorer job of recruiting among the population. Few have made anything like the same kind of effort as the Islamists to ingratiate themselves with the mass of the people, let alone to build social service networks to try to help fulfill the populace's basic needs.[44] In their defense, their task is a difficult one because they are so often branded as Western (or even Israeli) agents by their opponents; they lack the vehicle of the mosque and its charitable arms for building support, raising money, and distributing aid; and in some cases they are seen as the vestiges of outdated secular nationalist movements to boot.[45]

In contrast, the Islamist groups tend to be widely popular, as witnessed by their regular electoral triumphs across the Arab world in recent decades. In January 2006 the Islamist group Hamas and its allies won 56 percent of the seats in the Palestinian Parliament. In Iraq's 2005 parliamentary elections the United Iraqi Alliance, a coalition of Shi'i Islamist groups including Da'wa, the Supreme Council for the Islamic Revolution in Iraq (since renamed the Supreme Islamic Iraqi Council), and the Sadrist movement won over 45 percent of the seats, giving it the largest bloc and allowing it to form the new government. In the 2005 Egyptian parliamentary elections, the Muslim Brotherhood won 88 seats, or 20 percent of the total, in a heavily manipulated process. Of greater significance, it ran only 150 candidates, meaning that it won 60 percent of the races it contested. (On the other hand, secular liberals won only 11 seats, or 3 percent of the total.)[46] When King Hussein allowed relatively free elections in Jordan in 1989, Islamists won over 40 percent of the seats, and all oppositionists together held 60 percent. This prompted him and his son, King Abdallah, to circumscribe future elections to ensure that the Islamists would be unable to repeat this performance.[47]

The widespread popularity of the Islamist groups and the likelihood that they would therefore be the greatest beneficiaries of increased democratization create several problems for the United States.[48] Many of these Islamist groups are highly anti-American; thus a true process of democratization that resulted in fair and free elections to legislatures with real power could mean handing control of these countries to groups of people who see the United States as their adversary—an outcome that has not proven beneficial to American interests in places like Sudan and Iran. Moreover, although many Islamist groups now employ the language of democracy, have claimed to be committed to democracy, and are willing to participate in a democratic political process, there is still a lingering fear that any Islamist party that actually gets itself voted into power would then dispense with democratic pretenses and establish a (theocratic) autocracy—as the Nazis did in Germany and the Fascists did in Italy. As former Assistant Secretary of State for the Near East Edward Djerijian once famously noted, "We do not support 'one person, one vote, one time.' "[49] Unfortunately, it is not always clear which Islamist groups have really made a genuine commitment to democracy and which are merely pretending to in hope of achieving the power that would free them of the need to respect democratic traditions.

All of this raises the vexing question of whether the United States should support Islamists in the democratic process. It is an important question because it should influence, if not determine, how hard the United States presses for *rapid* democratic reform. It should also determine whether the United States simply pushes for democratization of any kind as part of an overall strategy of encouraging political reform or if it should go farther and press for certain kinds of democratization and political reforms (such as very explicit separations of church and state) to try to ensure that Islamist parties are unable to dominate the eventual reformed governments. Finally, it affects whether the United States should be providing direct support to Islamist parties or should direct that aid only to secular liberal groups.

In chapter 7, I noted that Islamist parties run the gamut from quite moderate to extremely radical. It seems obvious to suggest that the United States should not be helping radical Islamist groups, which are the most anti-American, the most undemocratic, the most violent, and the most likely to use a democratic process to subvert that very process (assuming that they are willing to participate at all). Consequently, the real question for the United States is whether moderate Islamist domination of the political process would be harmful to our interests or beneficial to the furtherance of reform across the region.

The first hurdle is to define a set of criteria for what it means to be a moderate Islamist party. By "moderate" Islamist groups we should mean those that reject violence; endorse competitive, pluralist political systems; accept the rule of law; accept a secular, public education system; are willing to accept alternative sources of law other than the Shari'a (although the Shari'a can certainly be *a* source of law); and accept religious freedom and gender equality.[50] More-over, in rejecting violence, we should expect these parties not only to eschew employing it themselves but also to condemn its use by others—which is not always the case among even some of the Is-lamist groups on the more moderate end of the spectrum. Some ex-amples of Islamist parties that either have met or appear to be moving toward those criteria include the Moroccan Justice and De-velopment Party, the Egyptian Muslim Brotherhood, the Jordanian Muslim Brotherhood, the Tunisian an-Nahda, the Yemeni Reformist Union, and the Egyptian al-Wasat (Center Party). For instance, Robin Wright of *The Washington Post,* a respected Middle East expert, has pointed out that Shaykh Rachin al-Ghannouchi, the leader of the Tunisian an-Nahda, "advocates an Islamic system that features majority rule, free elections, a free press, protection of minorities, equality of all secular and religious parties, and full women's rights in everything from polling booths, dress codes, and divorce courts to the top job at the presidential palace. Islam's role is to provide the system with moral values."[51]

Similarly, in 2007, Mohammed Mahdi Akef, the Supreme Guide of the Egyptian Muslim Brotherhood, said that "the legitimacy of a ruling in a society of Muslims is based on the satisfaction . . . of the people and on (the rulers') ability to provide people with the space to express opinions and participate in public affairs." He argued that the form was dependent on how the idea of *shura* (consultation) was implemented and that today the shura "converges with the demo-cratic system which puts matters of state in the hands of the major-ity, without prejudice to different minorities' legitimate right to express and defend opinions and positions and to call for supporting these positions."[52] Moreover, the Ikhwan's program for the 2005 parliamentary elections proclaimed its goal of creating, in Egypt, "a democratic, constitutional, parliamentary, republican, system."[53]

Most of these parties have renounced violence, accepted democ-racy and the rule of law and agreed that Shari'a should not be the only source of law. However, they often are not yet willing to accept gender equality, full political rights for non-Muslims, complete reli-gious freedom, or secular public education.[54] The well-known Egyp-tian analyst Abdel Monem Said Aly also warns that what these groups say is often very different from what they advocate, and what they say in English is often very different from what they say in Arabic. For instance, the Egyptian Muslim Brotherhood preaches freedom of religion but still considers conversion away from Islam to be apostasy, deserving of death.[55] On the other hand, Amr Hamzawy notes that most Islamist parties reject out of hand the label "secular" when discussing the importance of neutrality in governance and state policy but mean effectively the same thing when they refer to the need for "civility" instead.[56] In politics, euphemisms should be fine if that is what is necessary to help secure important compromises.

Consequently, although there is evidence that these groups have all fully committed themselves to working within a democratic process, concerns persist about how they would act once in power.[57] Though all of these parties are talking the talk of democracy, since we have not seen any of them in full power with no autocratic checks on them, we just don't know whether they would actually walk the walk. One school of thought contends that the demands of actually governing would moderate the behavior of Islamist parties. Advocates of this perspective argue that while Islamist groups are free to call for pure rule of Shari'a and other abstract notions while they are in opposition, once they were actually responsible for the well-being of the state and its people, the practical realities would force them to give up their more outlandish and (particularly to the United States) harmful theories and govern as responsible leaders. "Islam is the solution," a common slogan of various Islamist groups, makes for a nice rallying cry but rarely turns out to provide an effective blueprint for governing a twenty-first-century nation-state. On the other hand, Europeans (including German conservatives) all believed the same forced moderation would soften the Nazis if they were actually allowed to rule in Germany, and that theory turned out to be badly mistaken. Similarly, the demands of governance only partially moderated the behavior of Islamists in Iran, Sudan, and Afghanistan (the Taliban), although since none of them came to power through a democratic process, these are not really fair tests of this idea.[58]

Based on an analysis of moderate Islamist parties brought into government in Yemen and Jordan, Jillian Schwedler of the University of Maryland argues that although the inclusion of Islamist groups in governance may help moderate their views, this is not sufficient to have faith that they will not subvert a democratic government or otherwise usurp power. Instead she suggests that close examination of internal party debates can demonstrate whether the moderation is genuine or a smoke screen: "If an Islamist party struggles with how—indeed, whether—it can justify particular dimensions of democratic participation in terms of its broader ideological commitments, we can confidently say that it has evolved ideologically when internal policy commitments have shifted toward more inclusivity and tolerance of alternative views."[59] One of the examples she cites is the debate within Jordan's Islamic Action Front (the political wing of the Muslim Brotherhood) over whether participation in democratic processes could be justified on Islamic grounds. After considerable deliberation, they ultimately concluded that it could. This then led to a secondary debate over whether they could cooperate with leftist political parties, which again was decided in the affirmative, as long as the leftists themselves were good Muslims.[60]

There is also some evidence that participation in government helps to discredit Islamist parties, largely because the populace comes to realize that they are no better at fixing the problems plaguing their country than the autocrats acting on their own were. Some scholars have noted that when Islamists are allowed to participate in (politically limited) elections, they typically win 20 to 40 percent of the votes initially but just as consistently lose seats in subsequent elections.[61] However, the evidence for this phenomenon is not compelling. Typically, much (probably most) of the explanation for the poorer performance of Islamist parties in subsequent elections lies in the greater exertion of the regime to tamper with the polling. The regimes are usually surprised by how well the Islamists do the first time they allow partially free elections and so make a much greater effort to manipulate future elections to avoid the same embarrassing result.

For instance, in the 2006 local council elections in Yemen, the Islamist party Islah was trounced by the regime's own political party after much stronger showings in previous elections. The main reason for this was that the regime poured money into the campaign on behalf of its party, gave all state employees a one-month bonus before the election, directed teachers and professors to vote for its candidates, used the intelligence service to spread nasty rumors about Islah, used soldiers in civilian clothes to increase the numbers of people at proregime rallies, deployed military units to areas where there was support for Islah so that the soldiers could vote in those areas, prevented Islah candidates from registering, and doled out gifts (like providing electricity) to key municipalities immediately before the election to sway voters.[62] Nevertheless, it is also true that Islah ran a lousy campaign because its past successes had made it overconfident, its participation in government had tainted it (including with charges of corruption), and many Yemenis did not like the strict Islamic regulations that some Islah members tried to impose on their towns and neighborhoods, including forbidding the work of local artists and musicians and prohibiting music and singing at weddings.[63] A similar pattern held true in Jordan, where King Hussein passed a slew of new regulations after the Muslim Brotherhood's electoral victory in 1989, all limiting political freedoms and disadvantaging the Ikhwan, so that in 1993 it won one-third fewer seats. This prompted the Muslim Brotherhood and ten other opposition parties to boycott the 1997 elections in protest.[64]

THE TURKISH MODEL AND THE ROLE OF AMERICAN MILITARY ASSISTANCE

One predominantly Muslim (albeit not truly Middle Eastern) country that appears to have found an effective solution to the Islamist dilemma, in its own fashion, is Turkey. Since 2003, the Turkish government has been led by the Adalet ve Kalkinma Partisi (AKP, Justice and Development Party), an Islamist faction. The AKP candidate, Abdullah Gül, even won the presidency in 2007. AKP has proven to be capable administrators of the government and responsible custodians of Turkish democracy. Moreover, AKP is actually the second Islamist party to have held the reins of power in Ankara in the past fifteen years.

Although the AKP is probably a truly moderate party with no aspirations to take over the system, it is also true that if it ever tried, it would be prevented from doing so by the Turkish military, which sees itself as the guardians of Mustafa Kemal Atatürk's legacy of sec-ular democracy. The generals have made it painfully clear that if the AKP ever tried to subvert the system, they would step in to stop it from doing so. Over the years the Turkish military has not exactly carried out this role gracefully—it has acted in a heavy-handed fash-ion, overthrown governments that probably were not the threat that they were made out to be, and trampled all over the notion of civil-ian control of the military. Nevertheless, it *has* solved the Islamist dilemma for Turkey.

In the Middle East proper, this was the model that the Algerian military was following when it arbitrarily halted the 1992 parliamen-tary elections (which were going heavily in favor of the Islamist FIS) and imposed a new government. But unlike in Turkey, the result was eight years of bloody civil war. Thus, if Turkey suggests a possible so-lution to the Islamist dilemma, Algeria furnishes an important cau-tionary note to it.

Unlike Turkey, none of the armed forces of the Muslim Middle East can be considered professional and "above" politics. Turkish military interference in politics is hardly a desirable practice of civil-military relations, but it does reflect (paradoxically) both the ideals of professionalism and what may be necessary for the Muslim Mid-dle East. As is the case for any professional military, including the U.S. armed forces, the Turkish military sees itself as the guardian of a *system* of government, not the enforcers of any particular govern-ment. In the Turkish case, the problem is that it is a bit too quick to view certain political parties as threats to that system. At least some of the problems of the Middle East (and particularly the potential for Islamist groups to take power democratically and then overturn the democratic system) could potentially be solved if there were Middle Eastern militaries similarly committed to the preservation of a pluralist system in general, rather than being wedded to a particu-lar party or leader.

The United States already has extensive relationships with most of the militaries of the Muslim Middle East and especially with those of Egypt, Iraq, Jordan, Morocco, and all of the Gulf Cooperation Council (GCC) states. As part of this, the United States provides some training and education to military officers from all of these countries on military professionalism and the role of the armed forces in a democratic society. In addition, the United States furnishes weapons, supplies, advisers, and, in some cases, considerable funding to all of these states. This provides an important point of departure for a much wider program. As part of a grand strategy designed to foster political reform and democratization in the Muslim Middle East, it will be important for the United States to expand its training and educational programs, as well as its advisory missions, with the militaries of the region to make a much greater effort to inculcate professionalism and democratic values in Middle Eastern military personnel.

Of far greater importance, the United States would do well to greatly increase the amount of military assistance it provides to friendly Middle Eastern states. There are actually many reasons to do this, but the one most relevant to dealing with the Islamist dilemma is that the more that Middle Eastern militaries are dependent on the United States for everything from the latest weaponry to high standards of living, the more likely they will be to listen to American advice about professionalism and heed calls from Washington not to intervene in politics. For many decades during the twentieth century, Arab military officers were among the elites of their society, but today many are angry because their armies no longer command the same respect or resources they once did. The precarious state of their national economies has forced the regimes to divert assets away from their militaries. As a result, they no longer boast the modern arsenals, impressive inventories, extensive training time, and other manifestations of martial power they once did. It has also meant that the standards of living for most military officers has declined precipitously. American military assistance could reverse both of those trends, boosting both the pride and material circumstances of the Arab militaries and making them look more and more to the United States as their principal benefactor.[65]

The more the Arab militaries see the United States as their principal benefactor, the more receptive they will be to our training, our philosophy, our advice, and our requests. They are far more likely to accept our assistance in becoming more professional if we are providing them with significant material benefits. If they can reach the point where they truly are apolitical guarantors of a democratic system, rather than the bully boys of the ruler, they can stand as an independent institution outside of politics and give us confidence that whoever wins at the polls will not be able to subvert the system itself.

Whenever the United States thinks about increasing military assistance, let alone providing new weapons, to the Arab states, it makes the Israelis very nervous. They worry that those weapons will eventually be turned on them. However, greater dependence on American military assistance and American weaponry would make Middle Eastern states less willing and less able to attack Israel, not more. Countries like Saudi Arabia and Egypt are now so heavily reliant on American logistical support that they could not mount a serious military effort against any neighbor, including Israel, without our assistance. Perhaps the best example of this is Iran, whose armed forces were virtually crippled when they cut their ties with and evicted their American military advisers after the fall of the shah in 1979. The Iranian military has never regained the strength it once had, and Iran's conventional forces have little capability to project power in the region because they have never recovered from the loss of their American patrons.

In short, greatly increasing military assistance to the Arab states makes good sense. It would give us some reason to hope that the Arab militaries can be professionalized to the point where they could be a help, not a hindrance, to the long process of reform that their countries so desperately require. This would be important to helping solve the Islamist dilemma. It can also be valuable because comprehensive reforms will undoubtedly entail considerable internal dislocation for many of the Middle Eastern states, and a professional military could be a big help in overcoming all such challenges. Finally, American military assistance to the Arab states would generally make them less of a threat to Israel and our other allies, not more.

A FINAL POINT related to this matter concerns the potential for regional monarchs to play a similar role as guarantors of the system. In many of the Arab kingdoms and emirates, the institution of the monarchy, if not always the current king or amir, holds considerable legitimacy among the people, the Army, and other key institutions. In places like Morocco and Jordan, most people feel considerable loyalty to the monarchy and the Army tries to stand outside of politics by declaring its allegiance to the state as embodied by the monarch. Of course, in each of these countries, the monarchs involve themselves heavily in politics, which often can make them quite unpopular. Nevertheless, the general affection and relative legitimacy of the monarchies create the possibility that they, and the army whose loyalty they invariably command, could stand outside of politics, setting the ultimate parameters for political actors and ensuring that no one would attempt to subvert the system. In theory, this would allow the Arab monarchies (along with their militaries) to play the role of the Turkish military in its narrowly positive function of ensuring that no political party, and specifically no Islamist group, is able to subvert or overthrow the democratic system itself. Even in practice, there is reason to be optimistic about this possibility, at least over the long term. The greater legitimacy of the monarchies and their greater confidence in their ability to control their countries have allowed them to embrace reform more willingly and quickly than have the Arab "republics." This is why the regimes in Kuwait, Qatar, Bahrain, Morocco, and Jordan have all been the most receptive to reform.[66]

Inevitably, there will be obstacles on this path. In order for the monarchs to play such a role, they would have to be willing to cede a great deal of the governance and administration of their societies to political leaders from the people. In effect, they would have to give up the day-to-day rule of their country and be willing to move more into the background. Naturally, they are loath to do so because it would mean giving up a great deal of their absolute power and sharing some degree of authority with political leaders not chosen by them. It also frightens many of the elites in these countries, who fear that any diminution in the monarch's control will affect their own power, position, and wealth.

Consequently, if the United States and its allies are to encourage the monarchs of the region to shift to this kind of role, it will have to be a gradual process, full of half steps and partial measures. For instance, we should not expect any of the Middle Eastern monarchs to be willing to become mere figureheads with little more power than the queen of England. None of them is going to go for that. However, it might be possible to convince them eventually to accept a hybrid system, in which the monarch would retain primary responsibility for national security and foreign policy but most responsibility for domestic policy would devolve to a prime minister and a parliament. This would represent a huge political reform, it would give the people the voice in government they sought (in fact, it might satisfy the demands of many), and it would doubtless unlock a variety of economic, legal, educational, and social reforms. At the same time, it would leave a powerful monarch in full command of the Army and thus able to intervene to prevent any political party or group from moving against the system itself. Obviously, there is no perfect corollary for Iran or the Arab republics, but that does not mean that we should not encourage it among the regional monarchies.

A Strategy for Solving the Islamist Dilemma

Ultimately, I do not believe it is wise or possible for the United States to try to exclude all of the various Islamist groups from office or to try to penalize them when they come to power, as they almost certainly will in some fashion in some places. They are simply too popular, and trying to prevent them from coming to power will only confirm the belief of many Middle Easterners that the United States opposes Islam, that we are seeking to control their lives and their political systems, and that we will allow only political parties subservient to our will to rule in the Middle East. Moreover, it is contrary to our own democratic ideals to try to exclude political parties from a democratic process just because we may not agree with their policies. As long as they are willing to conform to the rules of the system and are not a threat to the system, they have to be allowed to participate.[67] We should encourage all of the states of the region to adopt laws prohibiting political parties from attempting to subvert democratic processes but in general will have to leave it to the states themselves—and their professional, independent institutions (like their militaries, someday) to uphold them.

What this discussion suggests is a five-pronged U.S. approach toward the Islamist groups of the region as part of the broader strategy of promoting political, economic, and social reform (including democratization) throughout the region:

1. As noted above, **Washington should encourage economic liberalization to create greater economic opportunity** and thereby diminish popular support for the Islamist groups. Similarly, the more the United States can do to help other groups—including the central government—to provide basic services to the population, the less the people will depend on the Islamist groups for those services.[68]

2. Although the United States should not try to prevent legitimate, popular groups from participating in a democratic political process, neither is it obligated to give its support and funding to groups it doesn't like. Consequently, for those that may desire it, **the United States should provide assistance only to Islamist groups that meet the criteria for moderation** enumerated above (reject violence; accept competitive, pluralist political systems; accept the rule of law; accept a secular, public education system; accept alternative sources of law other than Shari'a; and accept religious freedom and gender equality), but those that do so should be treated no differently from secular, liberal groups. In particular, we should try to employ Schwedler's notion of scrutinizing internal political debates as a further test of the moderation of these groups.

3. **The United States should help build up and professionalize major institutions like the governmental bureaucracy and especially the armed forces** so that they can serve as independent checks on the power of any political party and preserve a future pluralistic system of government against efforts to try to subvert it. Moreover, among the monarchies of the region, we should encourage the rulers to shift their role away from day-to-day domestic political governance, to allow them to better

stand outside politics (along with a more professional military) and play the same role of an external institution able to prevent any subversion of the system by political parties.

4. **The United States should make clear that its friendship, economic relations, and aid are all contingent upon the political parties' abiding by the rules of the system.** We should hold our noses and continue to deal with Middle Eastern countries even if, through a process of democratization, parties we don't particularly like take power—just as we do when parties we don't like assume power in European or East Asian democracies. We should take action only when those in power move to subvert the system. Moreover, we should work to build a multilateral coalition of states willing to do the same and willing to announce their intentions publicly beforehand as a deterrent.

5. Because all of this will take a long time to bear fruit, will be plagued by problems, and will be imperfect even in the end, **the United States should see democratization as a process that should develop gradually.** There are other good reasons for this approach, which I will discuss in the next chapter, but the Islamist dilemma is an important part of it. It will take time for liberal Arab political parties to organize, recruit, and build support that could possibly rival that of the Islamists. With enough time, people may begin to tire of the Islamists and realize that their catchy rhetoric often conceals hollow or misguided political and economic programs (as well as unpleasant social constraints). A more gradual process also allows problems to be caught and rectified before they become disasters. Thus, if only to guard against the inherent difficulties and inevitable mistakes of trying to encourage moderate Islamist groups to participate in a process of democratization, the entire effort would be best undertaken slowly and deliberately. The alternative is the kind of headlong rush to democracy that produced the disastrous Hamas victory in the Palestinian territories.

In his study of the Egyptian Muslim Brotherhood, Abdel Monem Said Aly reaches probably the most important conclusion of all. He argues that what is critical to bringing about the moderation of Islamist groups is the process of reform itself. "In these cases, moderation is induced by the society's experiencing serious political and economic reforms, propelling it toward democracy and a market economy. The latter is crucial not only for development but also for creating strong vested interests against the exercise of violence in an environment ruled by norms of social, political, and economic bargaining."[69] Thus, the process of reform creates a benevolent cycle in which reform moderates the Islamists and the moderation of Islamists helps propel further reform.

The Problem of New Democracies

Some scholars have pointed out that the process of democratization can be messy and war-prone and have extrapolated this to the Middle East, arguing that the United States should not promote democracy in the Middle East because doing so could spark interstate wars that would be just as threatening to American interests there as terrorism or intrastate conflict. These claims rest principally on the work of academics Edward Mansfield and Jack Snyder, who examined historical cases of democratization and compared them to the outbreak of wars.[70] Their bottom line was that

> It is probably true that a world in which more countries were mature, stable democracies would be safer and preferable for the United States. But countries do not become mature democracies overnight. They usually go through a rocky transition, where mass politics mixes with authoritarian elite politics in a volatile way. Statistical evidence covering the past two centuries shows that in this transitional phase of democratization, countries become more aggressive and war-prone, not less, and they do fight wars with democratic states. In fact, formerly authoritarian states where democratic participation is on the rise are more likely to fight wars than are stable

democracies or autocracies. States that make the biggest leap, from total autocracy to extensive mass democracy—like contemporary Russia—are about twice as likely to fight wars in the decade after democratization as are states that remain autocracies.[71]

Mansfield and Snyder cite a number of factors that they believe combine to make countries undergoing a process of democratization more bellicose before they become less so. In particular, they warn that democratic mass politics can lead to demagogic leaders stirring toxic nationalist sentiments as a way of mobilizing public support for themselves, which creates jingoistic pressures on the leadership to undertake wars of aggression or merely act more belligerently with other countries, thus provoking wars. In their words, the "concoction of nationalism and incipient democratization has been an intoxicating brew, leading in case after case to ill-conceived wars of expansion."[72]

It is first worth noting that Mansfield and Snyder's claims are somewhat overstated and a number of their cases are suspect. For instance, they consider countries like Serbia under Slobodan Milošević, Croatia under Franjo Tudjman, Prussia/Germany of the kaisers, and interwar Japan to be "democratizing" states. That is a very dubious description for any of them. Moreover, for their statistical analysis, they looked only at cases prior to 1980. This omits all of the cases of peaceful democratization of the past three decades in Eastern Europe, East Asia, southern Africa, and (as they acknowledge) Latin America.[73]

Nevertheless, it is also probably the case that a weaker version of their conclusions is true: that a transition to democracy can unleash nationalistic sentiments among the population that can lead to aggressive behavior and war. This also seems entirely plausible in the Arab world, where a great many people have been fed a steady diet of anti-Semitism, anti-Americanism, and other forms of xenophobia. Indeed, the Arab autocrats have played upon this fear by warning Washington and other Western governments that their countries' foreign policies would be far more bellicose—especially toward the United States and Israel—if it were conducted according to the desires of their people. This is part of the reason that successive American administrations have shied away from promoting democracy in the Middle East. Washington has often feared that doing so would mean not just the loss of reasonable Arab autocrats who have worked well with the United States because they saw their interests as coinciding with ours but also their replacement by unruly democracies in which the passions, conspiracy theories, and prejudices of the average people could be exploited by demagogues and zealots who would engage in aggressive, reckless, or just anti-American behavior. Unfortunately, it is not a baseless fear.

However, it should be seen as another cautionary note, not a show-stopper. There are at least three reasons to believe that these fears should not preclude the United States adopting a grand strategy that would promote political reform, particularly democratization, in the Middle East. First, as I noted above, change is coming to the Middle East whether we like it or not. The status quo simply is not stable, and even if some, perhaps many, of the region's regimes can stave off change for many years through a combination of limited reforms and repression, not all will. Some will fail disastrously, in revolution and civil strife, and it is unlikely that we will get to choose which ones survive and which collapse. Nor will we have much ability to prevent such collapses from affecting other, neighboring states. Thus, the choice that the United States really faces is not whether to prevent change or not—but whether to try to guide that change or not.

Because the status quo is untenable, the opposite course of action—encouraging the regimes to continue to repress their populations—is not likely to avoid the problem of bellicose emerging democracies. Because most Middle Easterners want democracy, there will probably be some degree of continued democratization in the Middle East whether we like it or not. Even if the United States were to throw its political weight wholeheartedly behind repression, the simple fact is that the regimes tend to be more afraid of their own people than they are of the United States, and so even with our endorsement of repression, they would likely allow some democratization anyway as a way of defusing popular unrest. In so doing, they would be opening up the very same risks of bellicose emerging democracies.

Furthermore, some of the regimes would ultimately fail no matter how much support we gave them, and some of those that did would be replaced by democracies of one kind or another, simply because democracy is so popular across the region. We would also have to expect that since in that scenario the United States would continue to be seen as an arch *opponent* of democracy in the region, this would exacerbate anti-Americanism, making it that much more likely that any acts of aggression undertaken by these fledgling democracies would be designed to hurt American interests. Again, Iranian hatred of the United States at the time of their revolution was derived largely from their belief that Washington was encouraging the shah to repress his people, and that mostly accurate perception has caused us three decades of problems (and counting). In other words, there is no real reason to believe that we can fully avoid the problems of new democracies having a greater propensity for war, and if we were to try to suppress that desire for change, reform, and democracy, we could actually make the problem much worse.

Second, there is reason to believe that if the United States and other countries were to take an active role in the process of democratization (and reform more generally) in the Middle East, this would likely dampen the factors that push new democracies toward war. For instance, one problem that Mansfield and Snyder argue has made democratizing states more belligerent has been the fear of their old elites—landowners, regime cronies, military officers—that they would be the ultimate losers from a process of democratization. Consequently, these people have at times promoted aggressive foreign policies to demonstrate their continuing importance to the state. However, a successful alternative approach has been for outside groups, like the United States and the European Union, to effectively "buy off" these groups either by creating and funding programs that would allow them to learn new skills and otherwise adjust to life in different political systems or by pensioning them off with very generous retirement packages.[74] Thus, there are both know-how and resources that the United States and its allies (and international organizations like the U.N., IMF, World Bank, and others) can employ to ameliorate the dangerous internal factors that propel some new democracies to war.

Last, if there is any problem in the Middle East that the United States is well positioned to handle, it is the problem of interstate war. Especially after the overwhelming displays of American conventional might at the end of the Iran-Iraq War in 1987–1988, the 1990–1991 Persian Gulf War, the 1999 Kosovo war, the 2001 invasion of Afghanistan, and the 2003 invasion of Iraq, there is not a single Muslim Middle Eastern state that is anxious to go to war with the United States, even in spite of the fiasco of reconstruction in Iraq. Thus, if the United States makes it clear that it will intervene against Middle Eastern states launching wars of aggression, this is likely to be an extremely powerful disincentive to aggression by democratizing states.

As military analysts have repeated so often that it has become a cliché, since the 1990s, any Muslim Middle Eastern state looking to employ force against another, or against the United States or Israel, has instead resorted to forms of "asymmetric warfare" like insurgencies and terrorist campaigns. They have done so precisely because they fear American intervention and recognize that defeating the United States (or Israel) in conventional combat is impossible for them. Though insurgencies and terrorist campaigns can be painful and are often the only way that a weak nation or group can fight a stronger one, they are highly inefficient forms of warfare. They typically take many years to produce the kind of results that conventional campaigns can achieve in weeks or even days. It took the IDF two weeks to overrun southern Lebanon in 1982 and Hizballah fifteen years to force it out. Israel conquered Gaza in a few hours in 1967, but it took Palestinian groups forty years to get it out. And Israeli forces still have not left the West Bank, which they conquered in less than three days. Only when the stronger country's interests are very minor—as was the case for the United States in Lebanon and Somalia—can an asymmetric campaign produce results in months rather than years.

Israel's withdrawals from Lebanon and Gaza were certainly victories for Hizballah and the Palestinian militants, but not exactly what a demagogue would be promising the people of a new Middle Eastern democracy to persuade them to launch a war of aggression. Indeed, insurgencies and terrorism are exceptionally poor methods of waging *aggressive* war, which is what Mansfield and Snyder fear from nascent democracies. These kinds of campaigns are most suitable for defensive operations, when a group or a nation is attempting to defend itself against an attacker. It is well nigh impossible to employ such operations to take over the territory of another country. Hizballah and the Palestinians were eventually able to push the Israelis out of land Israel had occupied, but there is no expectation that they are going to be able to destroy the state of Israel itself. The best that countries have been able to do in terms of using insurgency in an offensive fashion is to stoke a dissident group within the target country to start an insurgency against the regime and/or the dominant group, but that too is a very ineffective method of aggression—let alone conquest.

Consequently, if our concern is the kind of wars of aggression that are sometimes caused by emerging democracies, that is exactly the kind of problem that the United States should be able to handle. In fact, one of the most important things that the United States did to help encourage democratization and economic reform in East Asia over the past sixty years was to provide exactly the same kind of military protection that allowed them to concentrate on domestic problems without having to worry about foreign threats. (This also gave Washington the clout to intervene from time to time to protect political activists and other opposition figures.)[75] The conventional militaries of the Arab states and Iran are all extremely weak, and the United States ought to have little difficulty dissuading them from mounting conventional attacks on one another by announcing a doctrine of intervention against conventional aggression in the Middle East. (Such a doctrine would be greatly helped by the kind of regional security structure discussed in chapter 16.) If this were the only problem potentially created by an American grand strategy of promoting and enabling reform in the Muslim Middle East, it would not be much of a problem at all.

The Most Important Question

Dalia Mogahed of the Gallup organization raised a fundamental question to those who argue against America promoting reform, including democratization, in the Middle East. She asked rhetorically, "Who are we to say that Arabs should not or could not have democracy?"[76]

Her question cuts right to the heart of the matter and leads to two important points. First, the people of the region want change. In particular, they want democracy. Even if it were in our interests to do so, as some claim, should the United States actively oppose their aspirations? Should we continue to encourage the despots of the regime to repress their people, as we effectively did for the entire period of the Cold War? Did that policy leave us better off?

I think the answer to that last question is a pretty clear "no." Its consequences plague us to this day. The Iranian Revolution was a catastrophe for the United States, and we continue to suffer from its consequences today (and are likely to suffer even more if the theocratic regime there acquires nuclear weapons). Only slightly less disastrous for American interests were the Iran-Iraq War, the Algerian Civil War, our long war with Saddam Husayn, and our new battle with al-Qa'ida, all of which were the results of that same policy.

Moreover, should we assume that pursuing a Middle East policy of opposing popular desires for reform and democracy will somehow serve us better in the future? Even with our help, the Arab regimes will not succeed in repressing demands for change forever. Inevitably, some will fail. And when they do, we will see further revolutions, civil wars, insurgencies, coups, and terrorist campaigns. And they could be even worse in the future than they have been in the past. As bad as revolution in the shah's Iran was, revolution in Saudi Arabia would be even worse. As bad as civil war in Algeria was, civil war in Egypt or Jordan would be worse. As bad as al-Qa'ida is, another group (or al-Qa'ida itself) armed with weapons of mass destruction would be far worse. In the Middle East, never assume you have seen the worst that things can get. They can always get worse. Trying to oppose popular aspirations for change and reform could easily prove disastrous over the long run, even if it were easy and successful in the near term.

A second implication of Mogahed's question is this: Who are we, the United States of America, one of the oldest democracies on the planet, who are we to *prevent* the Arabs from developing democracies of their own? And who are we *not* to help them on that path?

As I noted when discussing our support for democracies as a reason to support Israel, throughout our history our finest hours and most rewarding actions have come from advancing the cause of democracy both at home and abroad. Never have we felt better about ourselves or been more respected by the rest of the world than when we have promoted the interests of democracy around the globe. Equally consistently, our worst moments have been when we placed narrow, short-term interests ahead of the promotion of democracy and supported repression instead, many of the instances of which backfired badly on us. Indeed, to the extent that the United States is still respected and admired around the world, it is largely as a result of our past efforts to promote democracy. What has been more beneficial to the United States than the democratization of Western and then Eastern Europe? Has anything, even our development of nuclear weapons, made us safer? Many of our closest allies today are those we helped fashion democratic forms of government, like Germany, Japan, and South Korea. Thus, it is not just that we don't have any other practical alternative to promoting reform in the Middle East to stave off future terrorism and instability, it is also that the active fostering of democracy has consistently been the most beneficial thing the United States has done.

In the end, the United States is not omnipotent, and it probably cannot prevent the Arabs from developing democratic forms of government should they choose to do so. As Mogahed's question makes clear, opposing that would be both foolish and wrong. Let me give the last word on this to Harvard's Noah Feldman, who has eloquently written:

> Over the long run, the costs of sticking with the autocrats are great. Continuing this policy will array the United States and the West against the interests of ordinary Muslims, who will be unlikely to forget what they see as a betrayal of the values of freedom and self-government that the U.S. and the West represent to them. It will send the message to Muslims that democracy is less an animating aspiration at the core of American values than a tool to be deployed cynically and selectively. Existing Muslim dreams of democracy will sour. The auto-

cratic governments of the Muslim world, already illegitimate in the eyes of many of their citizens and subjects, will continue to seem like creatures of the U.S. Frustrated dreams of self-determination will continue to attach themselves, however fleetingly, to any Muslim leader who purports to stand up to the U.S., even when he is a notorious butcher like Saddam or a marginal extremist like Osama bin Laden.[77]

CHAPTER 12

PRINCIPLES FOR ENCOURAGING
REFORM IN THE MIDDLE EAST

ALTHOUGH THE PREVIOUS TWO CHAPTERS HAVE DESCRIBED
a number of specific steps the United States and its allies should take
to help foster a comprehensive process of political, economic, and
social reform in the Muslim Middle East, it would be impossible to
list all of them and it is not the purpose of this book to try to do so.
Indeed, the nature of America's role in such a process will inevitably
evolve over time, changing to suit changed circumstances. What is
needed from the United States and the rest of the developed world
today, when the states of the region have only just started down this
path, is very different from what likely will be required in ten or
twenty years, when (hopefully) those states will have overcome the
initial challenges and be facing second- and third-order problems
and priorities.[1]

Instead, what is most useful at this point is to explain the basic
principles that should guide an American effort to encourage and
enable reform in the Muslim Middle East during the coming decades.
Here, the prior discussions of the challenges to reform provide an
excellent starting point. These principles are likely to remain relevant over much, if not all, of the duration of this strategy and should
guide the formulation of specific policies based on the circumstances
of the moment.

1. REFORM MUST PRINCIPALLY BE INDIGENOUS

The United States has considerable influence in the Middle East, despite the pervasive anti-Americanism and the widespread perception (not necessarily incorrect) that Iraq, Afghanistan, and our War on Terror have left us overstretched. The American economy remains a powerhouse with the potential to impoverish or enrich smaller countries around the world, and American military power is both feared and sought after throughout the Middle East. Consequently, the United States can and should try to foster the process of political, economic, and social reform in the Muslim Middle East, and it would be a huge mistake not to do so. Left to their own devices, the regional regimes will invariably opt for the short-term benefits of repression and cosmetic change. It will require both American (and other external) pressure and support to convince the states of the region to pursue the longer-term strategy of reform to deal with the underlying structural problems that plague their societies.

However, even the influence of the United States in the region is ultimately limited—very significantly. Most of what happens in the region happens without any input from the United States, and a lot of what happens in the region happens *despite* the exertions of the United States. Saying that we are still the most influential power in the region is a far cry from saying that we are all-powerful or even that we are as influential as we once were.

We must recognize that the United States, even acting in concert with all of its allies and international organizations, lacks the capacity to impose reform on the entire region (unless we want to repeat our Iraq and Afghan experiences sixteen or seventeen more times by invading and occupying the rest of the countries of the region).

Moreover, only the people of the Middle East themselves can understand how best to adapt the principles of pluralist government, free-market economics, and modern society to their own traditions, cultures, and needs. No matter how conversant Westerners may be with their society, we are never going to understand its nuances as they do. In addition, an externally designed and imposed blueprint would inevitably be rejected by the people of the region out of nationalism alone. Certainly the United States and its allies have much to offer the region: expertise from our own long experiences with such systems, experience helping other countries in other parts of the world undergo the same processes, and resources to make change possible. But the changes themselves must be fashioned by home-grown reformists for them to fit their societies and be accepted by them.[2]

An important corollary to this principle is the importance of listening to the people of the region. Another failing of the Bush 43 administration's approach to democracy promotion in the Middle East has been that, like all of their policies, they had a bad habit of deciding among themselves how to do things and then announcing it to the world in the assumption that the United States knew best what was right for others—hence their determination to make Arab NGOs conform to American guidelines, rather than reshaping them to better suit the peculiarities of Arab NGOs. There has been far too little asking the people of the region themselves what they thought and what they wanted.

To do it right in the future, our most useful allies will be the people of the region themselves who desperately want change. Both at the beginning and throughout this process, we should be talking to as many people in the region as we can to get a sense from them of what they want, and most of our actions should be designed simply to help people who are already trying to do the right thing—by providing them with resources or preventing others (including the regimes) from hindering them. In a similar context, Dennis Ross has wisely counseled that "The point is to use dialogue to generate an activist approach, with specific programmatic suggestions built around a concept. . . . As with any good approach to negotiations, we should engage in active listening—probing, asking questions, demonstrating our interests in learning what can work best—while also putting the responsibility on our local partners in these dialogues to focus on practical suggestions. We should be listening more than preaching, even as we seek to ensure meaningful outcomes."[3]

Of course, there are two important complications in such an approach. The first is that we need to be able to reach out to the would-be reformers of the region in such a way that they are not tainted by their very association with us. Unfortunately, as noted earlier, because of the pervasive anti-Americanism in the Muslim Middle East, those opposed to such a process of reform use any contact with the United States to try to delegitimize the reformists. The more the United States is seen as genuinely trying to support the kind of economic, political, and social changes that so many people in the region want, the more associating with the United States will become acceptable. In addition, as will be outlined in part V, there are a number of specific policies the United States could pursue (especially toward the Israeli-Palestinian conflict) that could help reduce the damage from this association. Nevertheless, the best answer of all to this problem is to ask the reformists themselves. This should be the starting point of the conversations: How can we help you do what you want to do without undermining your ability to do so? Some of the reformists may have specific ideas for how best the United States can help them (for instance, by acting through international institutions or third parties), and we should certainly try those approaches. In other instances, it may be that none of us knows the answer right now, but only by getting the constant input of the people on the ground, in the region, whom we are trying to help are we ever likely to ascertain the right answer.

The second, related conundrum is how to have these conversations without alienating the regimes of the region. To some extent, this too should be a topic of these very conversations with the reformists of the region—how do they believe that we can best develop a relationship with them that the regimes will tolerate? Another part, however, should be having the same conversation with the regimes. We should not be trying to hide our aims from the regimes of the region—quite the opposite if we are going to offer considerable material incentives in the form of increased aid to support their efforts to reform. As part of this, we should make clear that we intend to speak to reformists throughout their societies, including in opposition parties.

This is actually nothing new. It has been a crucial principle of American diplomacy since at least 1979, when American diplomats learned that bowing to the wishes of a Middle Eastern autocrat (the shah) to refrain from contact with opposition elements could be catastrophic in terms of blinding us to internal conditions in the country and preventing us from developing ties to groups that someday might rule the land. Nevertheless, we ought to be willing to have ongoing conversations with the regimes about how we intend to reach out to reformists in their societies, to discern the regimes' red lines, to figure out whether there are ways we could do so that might actually elicit a positive response or even their cooperation, and to make clear that while we do intend to aid the reformists, we would be glad to try to find ways to do so that would not antagonize them, especially if they are already moving in the right direction.

2. REFORM SHOULD BE A GRADUAL PROCESS

Because of the resistance of the regimes and the limited ability of any outside entity, including the United States, to press them for change, reform is likely to be a gradual process.[4] As I have noted several times already, the United States should not only accept that but encourage it.[5]

Many of the people of the region, and even Middle Eastern reformists, argue for a gradual process of reform. The International Crisis Group quoted one Saudi Majlis ash-Shura (Consultative Assembly) member as arguing that "Eventually we need to elect the *Shura* Council and the local councils. But how to run elections without a culture of democracy and institutions of democracy? The local elections are one way the public can learn. These elections will help society elect representatives as citizens and not as members of corporate groups, with experience and practice; it need not be a tribal choice. Elections are the end result, not the beginning."[6] Similarly, a Saudi journalist who once was an Islamic militant explained, "I don't see political participation as the first step. That's why I am not enthusiastic about elections. It would be like putting the carriage in front of the horse. There has to be some kind of political opening up, but our society still thinks along tribal and religious lines. Its political consciousness has not developed to the point where it would elect the most efficient [leaders]."[7]

All over the world, democracy has tended to grow strongest when it has grown slowly. Even American democracy did not spring Athena-like from the minds of Alexander Hamilton and James Madison. Instead it grew out of the long tradition of English democracy and evolved in the thirteen colonies over many decades. There are countries like Japan where democracy was installed quickly with few antecedents, but it still took decades for Japan to become a mature democracy because it lacked those precedents. As is well recognized, a mature democracy (as well as free-market economics and the rule of law) entails the existence of a range of important institutions, norms of behavior, and perspectives, which typically take some time to develop. Rushing too quickly to install some elements of democracy—like elections—typically produces terrible results, such as the "electocracies" installed in Iraq and the Palestinian territories thanks to foolish American demands. It is hard to argue that such a rush to elections produced an outcome that was beneficial for anyone but the warlords, criminals, and extremists of both societies. Similarly, racing to privatize industry before there is an independent entrepreneurial class with the resources to purchase and manage those industries typically results in organized crime bosses and cronies of the regime scooping up all of the leading businesses, creating a kleptocracy or "mob-ocracy," as in contemporary Russia. Indeed, the Cincotta, Engelman, and Anastasion study found that historically the rapid imposition of free-market economics and democratization created greater risks of conflict and instability than more incremental processes did.[8]

Throughout this chapter I have mentioned the need for social reform as part of the comprehensive changes needed to address the problems of Middle Eastern societies but have made few specific recommendations as to how the United States (or other countries) might try to encourage such a process. This is not accidental. Social reform is absolutely vital to the states of the Muslim Middle East, but it is the part of the reform process that is going to be most difficult for outsiders to assist. How a nation adjusts and adapts to the changes of modernity and globalization are both intensely idiosyncratic and extremely sensitive processes. No outsider can know what is best for another society when it comes to the nature of its social structure, and it would be potentially disastrous to attempt this kind of social engineering from afar. The one thing that we can be certain of, however, is that these adjustments will take time because it is the nature of cultures to adapt slowly to new phenomena.

3. WHEN POSSIBLE, TAKE STEPS THAT CAN BENEFIT PEOPLE RIGHT AWAY

Because there is so much anger and frustration in the region, the United States should be looking for ways to defuse the pressure for change whenever possible to try to avert revolutions, civil wars, insurgencies, terrorist campaigns, and coups d'état. The best way to do this is by taking actions that can have an immediate, concrete impact on people's lives, even if it is a limited one. This can change people's psychological state, leading them to feel that perhaps their situation is not hopeless, that someone is listening to them, and that relief may actually be in sight. This perspective is critical to staving off the despair that drives people to join revolutionary movements and terrorist groups.

Although this may seem to contradict the importance of gradualism, it actually complements it perfectly. Because the overall process will take a long time, providing immediate, even if modest or partial, benefits can be invaluable in building the patience that allows the longer term process of reform to succeed. Such limited fixes cannot actually get at the underlying problems that are the ultimate sources of unhappiness in the society, but they create time and space for the processes of real reform to do so.

Some examples of such limited but immediate actions might include the following.

- Shifting over to a free-market economy will involve the elimination of price controls and tariffs, privatization of industry, and competition from foreign labor forces and industries, all of which can devastate the lower and middle classes of the Arab world, who have been sheltered from these forces by governmental protections. Thus, the Arab economist Sufyan Alissa has suggested that the **United States and the other developed nations might set up an aid program to help the Middle**

Eastern countries "build an effective social safety net to help marginalized and underprivileged groups negatively affected by reform programs until more economic opportunities become available."[9]

- Another problem in the Middle East is that small and medium-sized businesses tend to have great difficulty competing with large enterprises, which are owned either by the state or by wealthy patrons who are closely connected to the regime. The United States, working through various international institutions like the World Bank, could establish more small and micro-loan programs, which have proven successful both in the region and elsewhere around the world.

- The United States and other advanced nations might make aid and other forms of assistance dependent on the condition that all of the people working in programs funded by that aid be local nationals. This would help with situations like the one in Jordan, where only about one third of the 46,000 people working in its Qualified Industrial Zones (factories that can export to the United States duty-free) are Jordanian nationals—this despite the fact that unemployment is officially still over 14 percent.[10]

- One of the most important actions that the United States has typically taken all over the world on behalf of these kinds of progressive reforms is to bring pressure on governments that imprison human rights and democracy advocates. Our track record in the Middle East has been uneven at best, with the Bush administration at times complaining loudly and at other times saying nothing at all. Because such imprisonments tend to be blatantly discriminatory, it would be relatively easy for the United States to condemn them—and for the regimes in question to find a face-saving compromise, like commuting their sentences. As in places like the Soviet Union, Eastern Europe, and China, coming to the rescue of these figures would reaffirm the idea of the rule of law, encourage other would-be activists, and suggest to average people that at some point in time they may all be less fearful of arbitrary arrest by the regime.

- One of the problems afflicting many of the Muslim Middle Eastern states is that they lack the institutional capacity to design and implement comprehensive programs of economic, legal, educational, or political reform.[11] Similar inadequacies contributed to the failure of the various reform programs initiated by the shah of Iran in the 1970s. The United States, its Western allies, some NGOs, and international financial institutions could all be tapped to **establish programs to train and advise Middle Eastern bureaucrats to manage comprehensive reform programs more effectively.**

- Washington might create new aid programs to **extend loan guarantees, investment guarantees, tax incentives, and favorable credit directly to Middle Eastern enterprises or foreign firms willing to invest in the Middle East.** These kinds of incentives could help jump-start the private sector.[12]

- Finally, Dennis Ross has proposed a number of other creative programs for U.S., Western, and international aid programs designed to make exactly this sort of immediate impact on people's lives. They include aid programs to establish afterschool programs that teach English and/or computer skills; internship programs for vocational skills, possibly in conjunction with private companies that would commit to hiring the graduates; food distribution centers in destitute areas; and new medical and dental clinics.[13]

If we are willing to make the effort, there are doubtless many other actions we could take that could also have a direct effect on the lives of those people in the Muslim Middle East who are most frustrated with their current circumstances. Taking these actions could quickly restore their sense of hope and patience, creating time and space for more profound reforms to be put in place and gradually transform the system altogether.

4. FOCUS ON BOTTOM-UP, AS WELL AS TOP-DOWN, REFORM

One of the many paradoxes of fostering reform in the Middle East is that democracy, free-market economics, and the rule of law develop best when they grow from the bottom up. When people can experience democratic processes like participating in local councils, voting in local elections, fulfilling civic responsibilities, serving as temporary or local officials, and exercising control over local governance through transparency, accountability, and legal proceedings, they best internalize the practice and theory of pluralist government. Free-market economics is all about limiting the role of the state and allowing market forces to operate "naturally." The principles of the rule of law are best understood at the individual level, when people look for protection from the law against arbitrary acts by government officials. Social change is about helping people to redefine their relationships to others, and those in their immediate communities are always the most important of those relationships. These kinds of changes are very hard to impose upon people from the top, by fiat of the government, but if they grow from the bottom up—by becoming part of the normal activities of the citizenry—the changes they produce in society over time are profound.

However, as an outside power and one that is generally feared, if not despised, by the average Muslim Middle Easterner, the United States has little ability to help bottom-up reform, at least for now. On the other hand, as the principal security guarantor of the region and one of the largest trade partners and aid donors to many regional governments, Washington has a much greater, but hardly complete, ability to affect decisions made by the regimes of the Middle East—meaning that it has a much greater ability to push for reform from the top down, which is a much more difficult way to do things—and especially to do them right.

Consequently, there has been and will likely continue to be an inevitable American tendency to focus its efforts to promote reform on the governments of the region. Although this is not necessarily disastrous and at some level it is necessary to try to bring the regimes on board, it is also not the most effective way to get to the end state we seek. Consequently, the United States should look for every opportunity it can to help the bottom-up processes of reform as well. Again, this is where talking to regional reformists can be helpful in identifying ways to advance the bottom-up processes.

In some instances, American intervention at the top can actually be very helpful to bottom-up processes. My colleague Tamara Wittes at the Saban Center at Brookings cogently argues that one of the most important areas that the United States and other Western states should focus on is demanding that the governments of the region respect basic political rights like freedom of speech, assembly, and religion, as well as basic aspects of the rule of law, like protection from unreasonable search and seizure, freedom from arbitrary arrest and incarceration, and an independent judiciary able to prevent the regime from trespassing on these rights. In her words, "The power of basic political freedoms is that they make other forms of democratic progress possible by creating space for Arab citizens and reform-minded officials to do what they already want to do, giving them greater opportunities to act on their own and to build coalitions on behalf of change. In such an environment, local activists can raise their own demands, and external actors such as the United States can more easily line up behind them. Governments then face a combination of internal and external pressures, both exerted in the same direction. Political freedoms also help prevent autocratic governments from reneging on reforms without facing a backlash."[14] In other words, by insisting that Middle East regimes accept basic political freedoms, the United States can employ a top-down intervention to unlock bottom-up reform—and reform that will be indigenously led.[15]

5. BE FLEXIBLE

An old military adage warns that a plan is nothing but a basis for improvisation. This is certainly true for any grand strategy. Fostering a process of reform in the Arab world over decades is not the kind of operation that can be rigidly mapped out in advance. As the events of the last ten to fifteen years have demonstrated, because the United States and its allies have an imperfect knowledge of the region, we are inevitably going to try things that don't work and we need to recognize and discontinue those efforts, while reinforcing those ideas that do seem to be bearing fruit. As part of the initial push for reform in the Arab world by the Clinton and (with more fanfare and stridency but less skill or modesty) the Bush 43 administrations, the United States and its allies did help persuade many of the Arab regimes to undertake a number of modest but important reforms. However, as described above, the forces of reaction adapted to this pressure and devised countertactics that allowed them to limit the impact of that pressure and, to some extent, roll back some of the gains initially made.

What that should suggest is that the United States and its allies, working hand in glove with the reformists of the region, need to devise new stratagems for advancing a next round of reforms designed to overcome or circumvent the countertactics devised by the opponents of reform to combat our initial pressure. Once we are able to do so, this should move the ball forward again, but we should assume that the opponents of reform will react and will likely devise counters to these measures as well. And so the game will start all over again. The key is to remain patient, persistent, and flexible enough to keep adapting and overcoming the latest lines of defense of those fighting reform. We need to be willing to stick with the overall strategy, even as we constantly revise and refine our tactics to fit the circumstances of the moment.

An important example of the need for flexibility is the battle over civil society. Democracy advocates note that strong civil society organizations were critical in the democratization of places like the Philippines, Eastern Europe, South Africa, Serbia, and Georgia "to carve out independent political space, to learn about democracy, to articulate a democratic alternative to the status quo, to spread the idea within society, and to mobilize millions of their fellow citizens against repressive regimes," in the words of the Middle East democracy expert Amy Hawthorne.[16] Unsurprisingly, and entirely admirably, the United States and other Western powers made a major push to try to generate and nourish civil society organizations in the Arab world as part of the first round of pressure for reform during the 1990s and early 2000s. The result was a massive growth in civil society organizations across the region, with Egypt alone boasting roughly 14,000 of them by 2006.[17]

However, two things happened that subverted civil society in the

Middle East and left it as much a part of the problem as the solution. The first, and most important, was that the regimes purposely proliferated thousands of civil society groups because doing so kept them small, weak, and fighting among themselves for members and resources. The regimes also heavily regulated their activities, circumscribed their fund-raising, and penetrated their membership, which left most of them heavily dependent on the regimes themselves.[18] Second, those that were not subverted by the regime often came under the sway of the Islamist groups—and this was certainly the case of virtually all of the most important and efficacious organizations. As noted previously, the Islamists' bread and butter has been their ties to the communities. Although Islamist control of civil society groups may be fine if the Islamists are genuinely committed to democratic governance, it could be the basis for an authoritarian takeover if they prove otherwise.[19]

Trying to help civil society flourish in the Arab world was a reasonable idea based on the experiences of other nations around the world. Unfortunately, it has had little positive impact in the Middle East. At some point in the future, either Middle Easterners themselves or outsiders may hit on a way of making civil society a greater force for reform in the region, and if so, we should be open to taking up their cause again. But now there appears to be only limited reason to do so, despite the fact that this was a script that worked elsewhere. We are going to hit on things that fail and things that work, and we need to be flexible enough to discontinue our efforts on behalf of the former and increase them on behalf of the latter.

6. Push on All of the Tracks of Reform (Political, Economic, and Social)

The predominantly Muslim states of the Middle East have a broad range of problems. In some ways, that is actually an opportunity. It means that there are always likely to be areas where outsiders can play a positive role in some way or another if we are just opportunistic enough to recognize where they are and put pressure and resources behind them. At times we may be able to push hard and help secure significant results in overhauling aspects of Middle Eastern legal or educational systems, at other times with social issues, at other times with economic, and at other times with political problems. We should never give up on any of them; we should continue to encourage reform across the board because that is what the region needs and what its people want. For the same reason, neither should we ever abdicate advocating reform in any particular area. However, we should recognize that some areas will be easier to help than others because of less resistance from the regimes, fewer structural problems, more obvious solutions or accessible resources. When that is the case, we should not shy away from pushing harder in those areas where more progress is possible. Reform does not need to proceed uniformly from category to category, and in truth we do not know enough about these sorts of transitions to know if there are some reforms that must precede others—history demonstrates few clear patterns, which suggests that every case may simply be unique and the reasons for success or failure too ineffable to use as a guide for our actions.

7. PURSUE THIS POLICY AS A MULTILATERAL APPROACH

Since the Second World War, perhaps America's greatest strength has been its ability to mobilize large international coalitions of the most powerful and prosperous states of the world to confront common threats to the global order. This is no time to abandon that practice. It should be self-evident that helping the Middle East overcome its deep-seated political, economic, and social problems through a process of comprehensive reform is going to be a major undertaking, akin in scale to the rebuilding and restructuring of Europe after World War II. It is just not clear that the United States has the wherewithal to do this by ourselves.

This is especially true given the widespread animus toward the United States throughout the region, which makes it especially compelling that we have other states beside us that may be more acceptable to the local populations. In some cases, it may be necessary to work through the auspices of other countries, or international organizations, to make American encouragement, pressure, and assistance palatable to the states we are seeking to help.[20] One of the better moments of the Bush 43 administration was the establishment of the Foundation for the Future. This derived from an idea first proposed by Senator Richard Lugar to create a fund contributed to by all of the G8 countries to support reform efforts in the Middle East, so that Arab reformists did not need to be seen as accepting money directly from the United States and the pool of available funds might be that much larger.[21]

Moreover, we should recognize that there are many countries and organizations in the world that may have greater abilities when it comes to helping the Middle East deal with key problems than the United States. South Africa can probably provide better advice on how to deal with painful issues of truth and reconciliation related to past human rights abuses. Some of the Eastern European states may know more about how to shift from a command economy to a market economy. Agencies of the United Nations may know more about social and educational reform, and NGOs like Transparency International may be more helpful at inculcating the rule of law. The United States has no monopoly on the kinds of expertise or resources that may be needed in this process, and the most useful thing it can do is to bring as many potentially helpful countries and organizations into it as possible.[22]

Perhaps the most heartening news I can provide on this count is that our European allies have already shown themselves willing, even eager, to participate. With Denmark leading the charge, the European Union countries have often shown greater enthusiasm and tenacity in pressing for reform and trying to construct common approaches to encourage it than has the Bush 43 administration, albeit in a more low-key fashion. From 2000 to 2006, the European Union spent €5.35 billion on its Mediterranean partner countries (MEDA) program for development, which is designed to spur the same kinds of reforms as Washington's (ridiculously less well funded) MEPI.[23] In June 2004, Middle East democratization was the principal issue of the Sea Island Summit of the G8, and this resulted in the declaration of the Broader Middle East and North Africa Initiative (BMENA), which presented a consensus among the leading Western states that political stagnation in the Arab world threatened the peace and stability of the region, which in turn threatened the vital interests of the West. BMENA led to the subsequent inauguration of the Forum for the Future, at which the G8 and all of the Arab governments meet annually to discuss political reform in the Middle East.[24]

Of course, the Europeans have their own reasons for supporting such an effort. As some will readily admit, they hope that by helping to solve the problems of the Middle East, they will turn off the flood of Middle Eastern immigrants inundating their shores. We may not care for their motive, but we should not spurn their assistance. The unhelpful unilateralism of the Bush 43 administration should have made it clear that multilateral efforts are generally preferable to unilateral ones, especially when the scale is grand and the time frame long.

8. TAKE EXTERNAL SECURITY PROBLEMS OFF THE TABLE

For decades, interstate security problems in the Middle East, like the Arab-Israeli conflict, have been an impediment to reform. In some cases, they have led states to maintain a command economy in order to funnel assets toward wasteful defense budgets. In nearly every case, they provide a convenient excuse for rulers to govern by diktat, suppress internal opposition, and justify not taking the hard steps necessary for genuine reform. In this way the regimes use the fear of *external* threats to suppress the *internal* threats that are far more dangerous to their continued rule. Some countries are genuinely scared of threats from other countries and fear that unleashing potentially disruptive internal reforms is unwise when predatory states appear to be waiting to take advantage of any sign of weakness. Whether real or imagined, these external security threats have been a constant stumbling block for homegrown reformists trying to work toward peaceful change in their societies. Moreover, the persistent conflict in the region has helped frighten off investment and trade.

As noted earlier, addressing the external security concerns of the countries of the region is a role well suited to the strengths of the United States. To a certain extent, ever since the end of the Cold War, the United States has more or less acted as the enforcer of the territorial status quo and has implicitly prevented Middle Eastern states from using conventional military force against one another. Not only should the United States and our allies continue to play this role, but it should look for ways to strengthen it, so as to remove external threats as a problem for the states of the region and allow them to focus on their internal problems instead.[25]

One way in which the United States might bolster the interstate security of the region would be to create one or more regional security architectures to formalize defense arrangements, more clearly demonstrate American (and perhaps European or P-5) commitment to collective security in the region, introduce confidence-building and arms control measures, and provide a forum where security problems can be discussed in the hope of heading off conflicts. This could take the shape of one or more regional security alliances in which the United States pledges itself to defend states in the region. Another, preferable approach would be to establish a single, or several smaller, regional cooperative security frameworks similar to the Conference on Security and Co-operation in Europe (CSCE). Depending on the configuration, either all of the states of the region or all of the states of specific subregions (the Persian Gulf, the Levant, North Africa) would participate on an ongoing basis with the United States and other great powers as guarantors of the stability of the region.[26]

A second approach to the same problem would be for the next president to declare a new "doctrine" that the United States will employ all necessary means to prevent armed interstate conflict in the Middle East, preferably through the exercise of collective security measures against aggressors. In truth, this would be nothing more than a codification and slight expansion of a policy that the United States has effectively pursued at least since 1990 and, for key allies like Israel and Saudi Arabia, for decades before. Although it would be preferable to handle such a doctrine multilaterally, Washington could declare and enforce it unilaterally if necessary, unlike an alliance or regional security agreement, which would require the consent and cooperation of numerous regional states.[27]

9. BE TOLERANT OF THE END STATE

In part because this strategy is ambitious, the United States must keep its goals relatively modest. We should not insist that Middle Eastern societies replicate our own, or Switzerland's, or South Korea's, or anyone else's. They may not want to follow such a template. In the end, they may actually come up with an even better model. At the very least, if this process is successful, the people of the Middle East will devise one or more models that are best suited to their needs and their aspirations. That model is unlikely to look like a mirror image of the United States, Switzerland, or South Korea, and we need to be willing to accept that. We need to focus on the underlying principles of political pluralism, market-based economies, and modern society, not the superficialities that are most apparent.

Moreover, we need to keep in mind that American strategic interests do not require that the people of the Arab world and Iran live in a particular way, only that they are no longer as angry and frustrated as they are today. It would certainly enhance America's interests in the region if the Arab states and Iran were to become full-fledged democracies, but our first goal should be the elimination of the threats to our existing interests from the terrorism and instability fomented by that anger and frustration. Therefore, whatever causes that anger and frustration to abate to the point where we no longer face these threats should be good enough for our own needs. That may require a lesser degree of reform than complete transformation. It might require only "decent" government and a prosperous economy, rather than full democracy. But whether it does can be determined only by the people of the region themselves, and right now, they are suggesting that they want farther-reaching change, including democracy. As long as that is the case, the United States and its allies should be willing to help them do so.

10. BE PATIENT

I am very fond of Ralph Waldo Emerson's sage warning that "a foolish consistency is the hobgoblin of little minds," but sometimes consistency is a virtue. This is especially true for great powers and grand strategies, which, by their nature, take time to bear fruit and therefore require a considerable willingness to stick with them to make it work. As I have noted throughout this book, the United States has shown little stomach for long-term strategies toward the Middle East, and that has consistently gotten us into ever-deeper trouble in the region. Our inconsistency has opened us to charges of hypocrisy and unreliability. Making this grand strategy work will be very challenging, and, of course, there are no guarantees that we will obtain the outcome we seek. But neither is it impossible, and so far, no one has been able to devise a better alternative. One thing that does seem certain is that for this approach to have any chance of succeeding, we cannot allow the inevitable problems and setbacks to cause us to abandon our course. In particular, we cannot allow the resistance of the regimes themselves and other reactionary forces in the region to convince us that success is impossible or misguided.

For example, the widespread anti-Americanism in the Middle East is unquestionably a major complicating factor in our efforts to push for reform there. But there is no reason to assume that it trumps all other factors. In the early 1980s, when the United States began its major efforts to promote democracy in Latin America, opinions of the United States were equally antipathetic. However, as Marina Ottaway has observed, "Sustained U.S. support for democratic change in the second half of the 1980s and throughout the 1990s slowly allayed suspicions about U.S. intentions. The same is happening in many African countries, because U.S. support for democratic change has become more consistent during the last decade."[28] Although we should not assume that this course is foreordained to succeed (especially since so much depends on our own execution), neither should we see every obstacle and every setback as proof that our course is failing. If we do, then no grand strategy—whether this one or another—will ever succeed and we will never rid ourselves of the constant threats and crises of the Middle East.

As a final point on the subjects of consistency and tenacity, the United States also needs to consider its own actions, at home and elsewhere around the world, in light of the message that they send to those in the Middle East. In particular, America's overreaction to the threat of terrorism and the willingness of the Bush 43 administration to subvert our own rule of law, as in the cases of wiretaps without judicial oversight and the treatment of prisoners at Guantánamo Bay, adds one more chapter to the double standards we are seen as employing by the people of the region. These trespasses on the principles of democracy allow the regimes to deflect our pressure by noting that we are no better than they are. They feed anti-Americanism, which makes it that much harder for proponents of reform to associate themselves with the United States or with an initiative that the United States favors. It also allows the opponents of reform in the Middle East to claim that democracy and the rule of law will not bring the relief from oppression that the people crave since the government of the oldest democracy itself is abusive to its own people.

A certain amount of hypocrisy in foreign policy is inevitable: a nation always wants others to do things that it would never want to do itself, and that is one of the constant challenges of diplomacy. In the case of bringing reform to the Middle East, however, avoiding such hypocrisy is an important element of the policy. Flagrant abuses of the rule of law and the principles of democracy in the United States buy us little in terms of the overall battle against the threat of terrorism. The one strategy that could actually bring us victory in that fight is to help the people of the Middle East transform their societies to eliminate the underlying causes of terrorism. In *that* struggle, these same abuses hand yet another weapon to those we are fighting against. Enabling reform in the Muslim Middle East is not impossible, but it will be hard and we should not be indulging in gratuitous acts that will make it harder still.

11. Don't Overpromise

The last principle that should guide American efforts to enable and assist reform in the Muslim Middle East is to keep our promises and our rhetoric in check. This is one of the most important lessons of the failures of the Bush 43 administration's efforts. Its lofty rhetoric was inspiring, but because reality could not possibly fulfill the hopes that it inspired in the time frame it seemed to promise, it proved to be a detriment to the entire effort. Because the administration's rhetoric appeared to suggest that it would throw all of the weight of the United States behind this effort, people were disappointed when that was not the case. Because it promised sweeping changes and spoke of Iraq and Afghanistan as being part of that effort, it conjured up the idea of rapid change imposed by pressure or even force. Moreover, it galvanized the regimes to resist however they could, including by being unhelpful to the United States on issues unrelated to reform—like Iraq and Iran.

The United States would be better served by making it clear that it will support this effort while keeping its promises modest and its threats circumspect. The less we promise, the less likely we will disappoint or disillusion people when the changes prove slower and harder than they expected.

Similarly, the more that pressure can be applied on the regimes of the region quietly, the more likely it is that they will respond positively because they will be less afraid of being humiliated. Typically, compromises are easier to work out, concessions are more easily made, and positions are more easily abandoned if they can be handled in private. Given the need to overcome all of the challenges to reform discussed in this and the previous two chapters, keeping expectations low and keeping the public glare away offer the best chance for making meaningful progress and creating a sense of slow but steady progress without the risk of creating the perception of failure when the pace of reform fails to live up to exaggerated rhetoric.

There are certainly occasions when shouting from the rooftops may be necessary, such as the need to embarrass regimes that have arbitrarily jailed political activists and refuse to release them. But even then, the best course is to start out quietly. Oftentimes, charges are more easily dismissed, sentences are more easily commuted, and the convicted are more readily pardoned if the regimes can do so without having to climb down publicly from their position in the midst of a loud confrontation with the United States. When quiet diplomacy does not work, it is always possible to turn up the volume, but it is much harder to turn it down after a loud start. And anytime the United States is widely seen as failing, it will only harm our ability to promote reform more broadly.

The United States should never hide its efforts to promote reform in the Middle East, nor should we allow them to fade into the background, but there is nothing that says that our commitment needs to be measured in decibels. In this sort of struggle, the more our actions surpass our rhetoric, the more likely we are to achieve our true goal.

CHAPTER 13

TRADE-OFFS

YOU MAY HAVE NOTICED THAT ONE THING MISSING FROM the discussion in the last three chapters of what the core of a new American grand strategy toward the Middle East would look like was any mention of the many crises gripping the region today—Iraq, Iran, Lebanon, civil war among the Palestinians, and so on. That is the topic of part V, which explains how to deal with those "subregional" problems in ways that not only will allow us to address the key American interests in each but to do so in ways that are consistent both with the core of the grand strategy and with one another.

However, there is one set of issues related to these specific policies toward specific countries and problems that is also an important piece of understanding the core approach of the grand strategy. This is the question of what trade-offs the United States should be willing to make on the country-specific policies to secure greater cooperation from the regimes of the Muslim Middle East on reform.

As chapter 11 warned, the greatest challenge of a strategy of enabling reform in the Middle East is securing the cooperation of the regimes themselves. Because they would all prefer not to reform themselves and their societies, previous American efforts to encourage reform ran into immediate problems because the regimes demanded that Washington choose whether they should adopt reforms *or* take some other action the United States sought. In the same vein, the regimes have frequently used any other problem or responsibility as an excuse to halt the process of reform. The Bush 43 administration's "Freedom Agenda" crashed on the rocks of these trade-offs: its many disastrous mistakes in the Middle East created a pressing need for help from the regional regimes, who in turn used Washington's desperation as an opportunity to slow-roll, or even ignore, reform programs they had previously accepted. In its later years, the Clinton administration also increasingly faced trade-offs among reform, movement on the Middle East peace process, containing Iran and Iraq, and fighting the Salafi terrorists. The regimes were willing to do some of these things but not all of them simultaneously, so Washington continuously had to decide which it would push and which it would let slide.

Consequently, a grand strategy for the Middle East that argues that enabling reform must be America's overarching objective in the region also needs to address this question of trade-offs. Although it is impossible to specify exactly how to handle each specific conflict of interests, it is both helpful and important to describe how the United States should be thinking about tackling these trade-offs more generally, as a guide to those specific decisions. The place to start thinking about these trade-offs is with the subject of counterterrorism because it is critical both to the core of the grand strategy and to many of the country-specific policies to be discussed in part V.

Counterterrorism and Reform

The core of the grand strategy advanced in this book is meant to erode and eventually eliminate the basis of social revolutionary terrorism, and particularly the lethal phenomenon of Salafi terrorism, in the Middle East. However, it is designed to do so only over the medium to long term. If the United States were to adopt this strategy tomorrow and make an immediate, major push to get it rolling, it would likely have some positive effect on the region and on support for terrorism right away, but not much. It certainly would not cause the people of the region to turn against the terrorists immediately. Moreover, it might have little impact on those already fully inculcated into the terrorist groups themselves since it is a strategy aimed primarily at undermining their ability to recruit new members and secure the active or passive support of the wider populace over time.

What this means is that adopting this grand strategy is not a sub-stitute for the kind of all-out counterterrorism campaign that the United States has been waging since September 11, 2001. That campaign remains vital because it is the best way to eradicate the existing terrorist cadre, prevent or hinder its operations in the short term, and protect the lives of Americans and our friends and allies around the world today. In that sense, a robust counterterrorism campaign is a necessary component of the proposed grand strategy because it is the best way to minimize the current terrorist threat, to make it possible for the longer-term process of encouraging and enabling reform to have its effect. In the short term we need an aggressive counterterrorism campaign to suppress the threat while we push forward with the longer-term strategy to actually eliminate it, and both must be key components of a new American grand strategy.

Because this is a book about grand strategy and because counter-terrorism tactics will have to evolve over time as the terrorist threat evolves, it is not really appropriate to provide a lengthy critique of the current tactics being employed by the United States other than to make a few broad points. The first is that we are clearly doing better than we did before 9/11, as witnessed by the number of plots broken up by American and allied counterterror forces and the absence (so far) of another successful terrorist attack on American soil, and for this the Bush administration deserves real credit. By the same token, it seems equally clear that we do not yet have either our offensive measures (in the form of aggressive counterterror operations abroad) or defensive measures (in terms of homeland security) down pat, and there is still considerable room for improvement. Those seeking useful critiques of how the United States could be pursuing counterterrorism and homeland security more effectively can see the list of recent works in the reference cited at the end of this sentence.[1] But that is largely a question of tactics, not grand strategy.

The second, and potentially more important, point is that our counterterror tactics cannot be allowed to undermine the longer-term struggle to eradicate terrorism by addressing the underlying problems of the Middle East. Unfortunately, the United States has done a good bit of damage along these lines since 9/11. One example of this was our kick-in-the-doors/terrify-the-children/search-the-women raids in Iraq in the first years after the invasion, which drove numerous otherwise ambivalent Iraqis to join Salafi terrorist groups. Another is the draconian new visa regulations that the United States has imposed, which have made it considerably harder for Middle Easterners to go to school in America. Allowing Middle Easterners the opportunity to attend an American school is important to our interests because here they learn exactly the kinds of skills they need to compete in the global economy and because many of them return to their homelands desirous of moving their societies in precisely the directions of modernity and prosperity that we should be encouraging. Unquestionably, as many terrorism experts point out, some of those who go to school in the United States become alienated here and develop a hatred that pushes them to join extremist groups. Others use their time here to learn skills necessary for the development of weapons of mass destruction and other dangerous technologies. However, these are far outnumbered by the ranks of graduates from American schools who return home to the Middle East with new skills and an affection for the United States that makes them the drivers of reform in their societies. As with so many things, we should not be throwing the baby out with the bathwater.

However, the worst mistake in this regard has been the Bush administration's unqualified—financial, military, diplomatic, and even moral—support of a range of regional autocrats to fight terrorism. Although securing the aid of other countries to fight terrorism was clearly necessary, the administration paid too little attention to how it did so, and its own excesses (like the handling of the prisoners at Guantánamo Bay and Abu Ghraib) convinced them that the United States was interested only in the end of fighting terrorism and not the means. Not surprisingly, many used the American imprimatur to crack down on all manner of domestic dissent, suppressing moderate Islamists along with Salafi extremists—and liberal reformists too. It is on this point that counterterrorism and reform come into tension and have in the past created an incentive for the United States to make trade-offs between them, typically favoring counterterrorism at the expense of reform.

A counterterror campaign is designed to suppress the threat of terrorism in the short term. It is probably the only way to do so. A program of political, economic, and social reform is, likewise, the only way to address the underlying grievances that give rise to terrorism and so eradicate it altogether. But reform can have this impact only over the long term. Moreover, counterterror campaigns impose additional hardships on the people (from searches at airports to searches of homes) that can increase their anger and frustration. They also provide excellent camouflage and even justification for wider campaigns of repression, which in the Muslim Middle East have been one of the primary sources of popular grievance. Similarly, political reform will require a loosening of many of the political controls that the governments use to quash terrorist campaigns. Thus, counterterrorism and reform are necessary complements to each other, but each can create problems for the other if handled badly. Moreover, in part because of this tendency, the regimes of the Muslim Middle East have typically portrayed them as a trade-off: they will either pursue terrorists or pursue reform, but not both at the same time. The truth is that it is possible to pursue both reform and counterterrorism simultaneously; the regimes just don't want to—at least not to the extent that we, and their people, want them to.

Understanding the Trade-off Trap

The need to make trade-offs between reform and counterterrorism or other immediate needs, as the Middle Eastern regimes have frequently demanded of us, is a direct outgrowth of our mishandling of reform over the past twenty years. Because the United States has so far always tried to pursue reform on the cheap, it never created positive incentives for regimes to reform. We have tried to get the Arab regimes to embrace reform without being willing to put anything new on the table, and that is what has created the trade-offs.

Given what we have been willing to commit to the Middle East in recent decades, we should not expect to get a whole lot more for our money, our protection, and our political capital. Take Egypt as an example. The United States provides roughly $2 billion to Egypt each year. This aid earns us considerable goodwill in Cairo. The Egyptians are grateful (increasingly grudgingly) both for the aid itself and for the commitment to their security that it represents. In return for both, the Egyptians have been willing to do a lot for the United States in the past. As described in chapter 3, they have sent military forces to the Gulf War and a slew of other American and international stability missions. They have helped move other countries toward peace with Israel. They have allowed American military forces unfettered passage across their territory. They have also been of great help in pursuing al-Qa'ida and other Salafi terrorist groups. However, our aid to Egypt is not quite the munificent bounty it once was because we have not increased the amount in twenty years and so inflation has greatly eroded its buying power.[2] Moreover, its principal purpose was to demonstrate to the Egyptian people the material benefits from making peace with Israel, which it largely did. From Cairo's perspective, we're basically even at this point, with its many actions on our behalf effectively balancing out our aid and support to Egypt.

What the United States provides Saudi Arabia is protection. We protect the kingdom from all external threats and also provide it with some assistance that is helpful to it against some internal threats. That means a great deal to the Saudis, and they too have been generous in repaying us. For many years they actually sold us oil at below market prices and between 1973 and 2005 made sure that the price of oil stayed within reasonable bounds. Even today, the Saudis would argue that the increase in the price of oil is not unreasonable, given historic fluctuations and the rapid increase in global demand. The Saudis have funded numerous American causes over the years and have spent diligently and extravagantly on American goods (including the purchase of billions of dollars of American weapons that the Saudi armed forces are incapable of operating effectively), as a deliberate form of repayment for America's security guarantee. Again, as far as Riyadh is concerned, the books are pretty much balanced between us.

Consequently, we cannot expect our current commitments to the region to buy us additional actions on the part of the Arab regimes. This is especially the case when what we want them to do is something that they are at best ambivalent about, if not flat-out opposed to. Consequently, since the early 1990s, when the Bush 41 administration suggested, the Clinton administration encouraged, and the Bush 43 administration demanded that the Arab regimes adopt policies of reform, their response was to demand that we give up our requests/demands on other issues—in other words, that we make trade-offs among the many things we wanted from them. In truth, this was not an unreasonable request, given what we were asking and what we were willing to put up to get it.

Unfortunately, the Bush 43 administration made this situation worse in two ways. First, it created a series of new crises in the Middle East, which forced a diversion of both our own and Arab resources to deal with them. And second, the administration demanded *rapid* progress on democratization and certain other aspects of reform.

The crises of the region created or exacerbated by the Bush 43 administration in Iraq, Lebanon, and Palestine (as well as the reinvigoration of Iran that these events in turn made possible) created tensions with the goal of reform. They created serious spillover effects that helped destabilize other states of the region. Given the internal problems caused by Iraq, Lebanon, and Palestine, the regimes did not want to stir up more domestic problems by embarking on internal reforms, which, no matter how welcome they were, would almost certainly cause short-term dislocations as the inevitable byproducts of major societal shifts. In addition, the Bush administration recognized that it desperately needed regional assistance to help deal with the crises with Iraq, Lebanon, Palestine, and Iran. Effectively abandoning the Freedom Agenda was the price the Arab regimes then extracted from the Bush administration in return for their help in containing the regional fires the administration had started.

The Bush administration's stridency in demanding major reforms quickly also created unnecessary and unhelpful trade-offs between reform and other, more immediate American objectives. Very simply, the faster the United States wants the Arab states to reform, the more it is going to cost us to get them to do so. To the extent that the regimes are comfortable with any reform, they want it to come slowly. Therefore, getting them to move faster will require either greater pressure or greater incentives to convince them to do it. If we press them on reform, it becomes very difficult to press them on other issues—like the Middle East peace process, Iraq, containing Iran, or anything else—and vice versa. Similarly, unless we are willing to put new chips on the table, the only way to persuade them to do something is to take chips that were being used to get them to do other things in the past. Thus, it is not just that reform adds another thing that we want from them, it is also that wanting reform *fast* costs us a lot more than allowing it to happen more gradually.

What all of this ought to illustrate is that the trade-offs are a trap. It is important to the vital interests of the United States that the autocracies of the Muslim Middle East embark on a process of sustained political, economic, and social reforms to alleviate the chronic instability and the Salafist terrorism plaguing the region. However, it is also important to the vital interests of the United States that these same regimes aggressively fight the Salafi terrorists to suppress the immediate threat to the United States and contribute more toward the stabilization of Iraq, the containment (or possibly accommodation) of Iran, etc. We need all these things. The problem is that the latter problems are more immediate—and often more tangible—than the former, and so, when forced to choose between them, we have typically chosen in favor of the latter. And the regimes know this. They understand that these trade-offs are a trap that consistently force the United States to diminish its pressure for reform in the name of more immediate objectives. That is why they continue to perpetuate the trade-offs and keep forcing us to make this choice. Thus, the more we approach reform as we have over the past decade or more, the harder it will be to advance its cause.

Getting Out of the Trade-offs Trap

The strategy proposed in this book is specifically designed to try to help the United States extract its Middle East policy from the trap of these trade-offs. As with everything about it—and everything about the Middle East—doing so will not be easy, but there is no reason to believe it will be impossible, either. The key is to apply the principles laid out in the previous chapter and to put up the necessary resources to make the strategy work. Specifically, it will consist of four elements: minimizing specifically American demands for reform (as opposed to international or domestic demands); providing significant new positive incentives so that we don't have to give up on one thing to get something else; repairing the colossal screw-ups of the Bush administration so that they are no longer a drain on regional resources and a threat to the internal stability of the other Middle Eastern states; and finding ways to deal with the demands of the regional states on other issues by providing them with benefits within the issue itself rather than having to take them from another issue (like reform). All of this will require sacrifices, of both money and control over certain regional initiatives, but if we are willing to make them, there is real reason to believe that we can get out of this trap.

Minimize Specifically American Demands for Reform

Part of the reason the United States has had to make trade-offs to get Middle Eastern regimes to reform, especially during the Bush 43 administration, is that Washington turned reform into something that we wanted them to do for us. The moment that happened, it became easy for the regional regimes to demand other sacrifices from us in return for their doing so.

A better way to handle reform is the way that Bush 41 and Clinton tried, which was to frame reform as something in the interests of the regimes themselves. This starts with the point I made earlier that change is coming to the region whether any of us likes it or not, and the question for us and for the regimes is whether we all want to be part of a solution, and so guide change in a direction that does not undermine our interests, or bury our heads in the sand and get swept away when change comes anyway.

This is a message that resonates with all but the most obtuse Middle Eastern leaders, and it is why all of them have been willing to enact some reforms. The importance of working with the regimes, rather than seeing them as the enemies of the end state we desire in the region, lies in this truth. This is why our approach to the regimes should start from the idea that we want to help them manage the transition and are amenable to their preserving some degree of their power and status as part of this transition, albeit in modified form. It is also why we should stress that we can't determine either how much power and status they should retain or what the modified form should take, because that is something that only the people of the region themselves can decide.

Counterterrorism itself offers an interesting case for this approach. In the past, and especially since 9/11, the United States has frequently made trade-offs on reform in return for commitments to do more against the Salafi terrorists. During that time, the United States has held its nose and said nothing despite any number of rigged elections, imprisonments of domestic dissidents, muzzlings of the press, and other abuses of the Middle Eastern regimes' own people and political processes. In return, we certainly did get some additional cooperation from these same countries, in the form of greater intelligence and even some active efforts to break up Salafi terrorist operations and capture or kill the group's leadership. However, it is worth noting that major increases in regional counterterror efforts really came only when the countries were themselves attacked by Salafi terrorists. After the Riyadh bombings of 2003, the Saudi security services suddenly launched a full-court press that effectively smashed al-Qa'ida in the Arabian Peninsula. To a lesser extent, Morocco pumped up its efforts against Salafi terrorists after the 2003 bombings in Casablanca. Outside the Middle East, Indonesian counterterror efforts jumped markedly after the 2002 Bali bombings, just as Pakistani efforts did after a pair of assassination attempts against President Pervez Musharraf in 2003. Egypt waged a similarly brutal war against its own Salafi militants during the 1990s.

What is striking about all of these campaigns is that they represented levels of exertion against the terrorists that dwarfed their post-9/11 increases. In other words, what these countries did to help the United States on counterterrorism after 9/11 represented only a fraction of what they were capable of doing—and did when the threat was actually directed at them.[3] This suggests that perhaps we should not have been so willing to make trade-offs with the Arab regimes on reform to secure their assistance on counterterrorism. Had al-Qa'ida not foolishly attacked them directly, our own counterterror campaign might have had far less impact than it did, despite making so many trade-offs. At the very least, it suggests that if we are going to sell out reform, we ought to have demanded a higher price than what we actually got.

A second tactic we should employ as part of this particular course of action is to minimize our own demands and instead highlight those of the people themselves and of international human rights organizations and other NGOs. As I have noted several times, the regimes of the region are all—no matter how heavy the iron fist with which they rule—sensitive to their own public opinion and even to international opinion. Moreover, it is both more legitimate and more appropriate for the people of the region themselves to be given pride of place in demanding change. And despite the efforts of their regimes, they do find ways to give voice to their desires. Our role should be to help echo and amplify their pleas. Likewise, because of the taint of the United States in the Muslim Middle East, it is much better for us to take a backseat to international NGOs, which will be considered more unbiased and more expert on matters of political, economic, and social reforms. The more we simply highlight the demands of the people of the Muslim Middle East and of neutral experts, the more legitimate the calls for reform will be and the less they will become *our* demands that we will have to pay for ourselves—with either increased aid or trade-offs on other issues.

The last piece of this particular approach to the problem of trade-offs relates to the principle of gradualism. If we want the regimes of the region to reform quickly, that becomes an American demand that we have to pay for in some way. This is yet another reason to favor a policy of gradual reform. The more we are willing to accept a process that unfolds somewhat slowly, over a period of decades rather than quickly in a matter of years, the less we will have to pay. It is nice that this is substantively the *right* approach, as well as being the politically expedient course.

Upping Our Ante
The second course of action the United States needs to pursue to get out of the trade-offs trap is to provide the positive incentives for reform described in chapter 11. If you don't want to have to give up something on one policy in order to get something on another, there

are only two alternatives available: either you threaten to use force and so coerce the other state to give you something for free, or you offer it something else it wants, to persuade them to do it. Using force is not a great way to maintain a friendship, and most of the states we would like to see pursue comprehensive reforms (and all of the most important ones) are valued friends. Moreover, if you threaten to use force, you have to be prepared to back it up, and after the experience of Iraq it will be hard to convince the American people to go to war in the Middle East again anytime soon absent a direct act of aggression against us or one of our closest allies. Thus, we are left with increasing the assets available to us, so that we have things to offer states to convince them to enact reforms other than making sacrifices on one or more issues of immediate importance.

This is precisely why I called in chapter 11 for the United States to be willing to commit something on the order of an additional $5 billion to $10 billion per year in aid to create incentive packages for the poorer states of the Middle East. Egypt, Jordan, Morocco, Tunisia, Yemen, Syria, Sudan, and Bahrain all need cash. (So do Lebanon, the Palestinians, and in some ways Iraq, but they fall into a different category.) They also need trade, foreign investment, foreign expertise, and better integration into the global economy. These are all things that the United States can provide in the form of aid, trade credits, investment guarantees, advisers, and help with international financial organizations. The more we are willing to offer large packages of such economic assistance, the more we will create positive incentives for these states to adopt reform programs. There is already some proof that this works: the Clinton and Bush 43 administrations provided entrée into the World Trade Organization and free trade agreements with the United States to a number of the Arab states in return for their agreements to certain reforms—and in fact used the terms of the agreements to ensure that the reforms were enacted. Likewise, it is clear that one reason that Husni Mubarak pays even lip service to reform in Egypt is the annual U.S. aid package he receives. Given that we already get a fair bit from the Egyptians and they feel that we're pretty much even at this point, if we want more from them on reform, we need to be willing to write a bigger check.

Of course, as I also observed in chapter 11, we're not going to write any checks to Saudi Arabia, the UAE, Kuwait, Qatar, Oman, Algeria, and Libya (let alone Iran), so that limits the utility of this approach with them. Nevertheless, there are still some things that we can do for them. In particular, Algeria and Libya still need trade, foreign investment, expertise, and integration into the global economy. The Gulf states present the biggest problem, and I address them separately below.

FIXING THE CRISES

The third track of this approach to escaping the trade-offs trap is the one that is easiest to say but is the hardest of all to accomplish: fix the crises in Iraq, Lebanon, and Palestine that have created so many problems for the region, from increased fears of an Iranian threat to massive refugee flows to enflamed domestic tensions. The less help the United States needs to deal with these problems, the harder it is for the regional regimes to demand that their help come at the expense of their reform programs. The less the states of the region need to fend off the spillover effects of these crises, the harder it will be for them to justify not moving forward on reform and the more willing some of them will be to actually move forward. It is worth keeping in mind that some of the regional rulers—King Muhammad VI of Morocco, King Abdallah II of Jordan, King Abdallah of Saudi Arabia, Amir al-Sabah of Kuwait, Amir al-Thani of Qatar—actually believe it important (even morally right) to help reform their societies, at least to some extent. It is inescapable that these crises are not only dangerous in their own right but also harm U.S. interests by inhibiting such reform throughout the Muslim Middle East. In part for that reason, all are discussed in much greater detail in part V.

MAKING TRADE-OFFS WITHIN ISSUES, NOT ACROSS THEM

The reason that making trade-offs is a trap is that the Arab regimes have forced the United States to make the trade-offs *across* the issues, specifically by giving on reform in order to get something on Iraq, Iran, or some other issue. The last tactic to escape that trap is to find ways and be willing to make trade-offs *within* the issues themselves.

No one likes to make trade-offs. However, in diplomacy, they are necessary. You invariably have to give something in order to get something. Moreover, it is often useful to give up everything on an issue you don't care much about to get everything you want on another that you care about a lot. In the Middle East, there are too many issues we care about. Nevertheless, it is both possible and important to prioritize them. In fact, one of the purposes of any grand strategy is to help prioritize among different interests and problems, and the grand strategy of this book asserts that what ought to come first is encouraging and helping to foster an indigenous process of comprehensive reform among the states of the Muslim Middle East. That does not mean that our interests in Iraq, Iran, the Israeli-Palestinian dispute, and so on, are negligible or that we should not make sacrifices on reform to get other things on these more immediate and narrow problems. Quite the contrary; it simply means that we should do so only when the gains on the specific problem clearly outweigh the harm to the cause of reform or when there is no other way to obtain what we need on those other, more immediate considerations.

However, it is often the case that there *are* other ways to get what we need on those other considerations. In particular, it is often possible to make sacrifices within the parameters of the other policy areas, which can relieve us of the need to make concessions to the Arab regimes on reform in return for their help on those other issues, as they have in the past. I describe a number of such internal trade-offs in the chapters of part V, so a single example will have to suffice here. We need the help of all of Iraq's neighbors in stabilizing that country. In chapter 14, I argue that one way that the United States ought to secure that support is by creating a standing contact group that includes all of the neighboring states and using it to give them a real say in what happens in Iraq. This is something that all of the neighbors want but that we (and the Iraqis) have resisted because it could significantly further complicate the already hellish process of reconstruction in Iraq. Nevertheless, one of the reasons for recommending this is that, as hard as it might be, it is probably the only way to secure the regional support we need for Iraq and better for American strategy toward the entire region over the long term to secure regional support for Iraq by making this concession than to agree to trade-offs on questions of reform.

An important element of this last tactic is to recognize when there are trade-offs to be made within a specific policy area. Counterterrorism offers a good example of our failure to do this. As noted in chapter 9, since 9/11, the United States has provided significant amounts of aid to various Middle Eastern countries to help them wage counterterror campaigns. To a number of these countries, including Yemen, Tunisia, and Jordan, this assistance is quite important, particularly to their security establishments. We provide them with this aid because we want them to go after Salafi terrorist groups on their own territory, so we look at it as something that we do *for ourselves.* That may be true, but this aid is also helpful to them, and, in the Middle Eastern bazaar, that makes it something to be used in bargaining. At the very least, that aid needs to be strictly conditioned to make it clear that it cannot be used for activities related more to repressing their people than to pursuing terrorists. Beyond that, since virtually all of the regimes of the region hate and fear the Salafi terrorists, it is highly unlikely that they would decline our assistance if we insisted that it not be used as cover for more widespread abuses of human and civil rights. Indeed, it should be given with the proviso that since fighting Salafi terrorists is also important to each of these countries *for their own interests,* this aid will continue to flow only if they continue to move ahead with various reform projects.

Making Smart Trade-offs When We Have To

Because of the complexity of the problems of the region, and because of the many missteps of the Bush 43 administration, we probably will not be able to escape the trade-offs trap altogether, at least not for some time. Perhaps when Iraq has been stabilized, the sense of threat from Iran among the Arab states diminished, and processes put into place to ameliorate the situations in Lebanon and the Palestinian territories, we will be able to rid ourselves of the trade-offs completely by using the methods outlined above, but even then it is unlikely. No matter how diligently we apply these tactics or how generous we are willing to be with positive incentives, we can diminish the number and extent of the trade-offs we have to make, but we will probably not be able to avoid them altogether.

That should not be seen as disastrous from the perspective of the grand strategy. It is why I have repeatedly noted that this will not be an easy policy to execute. It is another reason why I have repeatedly stressed the importance of gradualism. The principle of gradualism suggests that when faced with these trade-offs, agreeing to give on a particular issue related to reform in return for getting help from one or more Arab regimes with an immediate problem is a reasonable choice, as long as it does not become an everyday occurrence. Perhaps a good rule of thumb would be to try to make trade-offs in favor of reform at least as often as we make them against it. The process of reform needs to keep moving forward, all across the region at all times, and the United States needs to always be looking for ways to advance it, but, given the messiness of the region, it is not going to be possible to avoid making choices from time to time that will hinder reform.

The key is to make trade-offs against reform only when it is truly necessary to do so. Three rules suggest themselves as a way to ensure that we make trade-offs only when it is necessary:

1. Our default position should be to make trade-offs in favor of reform unless there is a compelling reason to make a trade-off against it. This would put the burden on those advocating the trade-off to prove that it is necessary. It would also be an important reversal of our past practices, which led to making so many trade-offs against reform.

2. The standard for making a "compelling" case should be that the benefit to the other course of action must clearly be shown to outweigh the harm that will be done to the cause of reform.

3. We should make trade-offs against reform only when we cannot find a way out of the conundrum—by attempting to lower our demands on the other issue (or simply deciding that it is not a critical issue), by offering another inducement to try to

get them to take the steps we need on the other issue, and/or by making a trade-off within the other issue.

THE HARDEST CASE: THE GULF OIL MONARCHIES

Let me end by tackling the part of the region that is the most difficult from the perspective of the trade-off trap. It seems likely that in the future we will most often encounter more of these unpleasant trade-off situations with the Gulf monarchies. Because of their oil wealth, they are likely to prove the most impervious to our efforts, even if we employ the various tactics described above with great skill and ample resources. All of them believe that, with the price of oil sky high, they can buy off a great deal of their domestic opposition. Over the long term this is unlikely to succeed, but in the short term they can certainly make a major dent in the popular agitation for reform—and the short term could last for some time. Our ability to provide them with positive incentives is not zero, but it is not nearly as significant as for the poorer states of the region. Some of them do need American assistance in terms of advisory support and further integration into the global economy, and that will help, but only to a limited degree. Repairing the damage to Iraq, Lebanon, and Palestine would definitely help, but accomplishing those herculean labors is going to take some time—if it is possible at all—and will likely require their assistance to do so. There are certainly trade-offs to be made with them within the different policy issues, and these will also help, but we should not assume that they will eliminate the problem completely.

Consequently, the United States is going to have to accept two unpleasant realities when it comes to the Gulf states: we may have to accept that they will move even more slowly down the path of reform than the other states of the region, and we may need to make some trade-offs across issues in order to encourage them to keep moving down the path. In particular, one trade-off we should be willing to make, which I discuss in greater length in chapter 16, is to undertake a greater effort on behalf of peace between the Israelis and Palestinians (as well as between the Israelis and Lebanese/Syrians). This does not mean selling Israel out to the Arabs: not only do we have many reasons of our own not to do that, but the Gulf Arabs do not expect us to. It means making a much greater effort than the seven and a half years of useless wheel spinning during the Bush 43 administration. It means investing the same time, energy, creativity, and political capital into reviving and moving forward a peace process as the Clinton administration did. This is something that the Gulf states want, and, because this would help mollify their own populations, it would make it easier for them to open up their domestic political and economic systems. Fortunately, it is also something that would serve a number of our other interests as well.

As a final point, we should not assume more generally that reform in the Gulf region is a lost cause. The above analysis might lead you to believe that the Gulf states are doing the *least* of all the Muslim Middle Eastern countries to reform their societies, because they have the most resources to use to fend off pressures from their own people and the outside world. In actuality, many of the Gulf states have enacted some of the most important reform efforts so far. Kuwait, Bahrain, and Qatar are among the leaders in democratization in the Arab world, while the UAE is among the leaders in economic reform. These are all relative statements, but their relative progress is important. It speaks to the fact that all of the Gulf leaders are quite enlightened. They understand the underlying anger and frustration of their people, although in each country the anger and frustration stem from different elements of the many factors discussed in part II: poverty and sectarian oppression in Bahrain; political disenfranchisement in Kuwait; unemployment, underemployment, and a sense of cultural siege in Saudi Arabia. Even in Saudi Arabia, where important segments of the Al Sa'ud oppose all manner of reform, other royals, including King Abdallah himself, have pushed for greater accountability in government, giving the people a voice in their governance, fighting corruption, and other progressive steps. None of these rulers seems to be willing to take reform as far as many of their subjects want, but they all recognize the need for reform, and that creates opportunities for the United States where the limitations of our other foreign policy tools may fail us.

The key is to make reform a cooperative venture with the Gulf governments and to listen to the people of the region—both the leaders and the led. Since all of the leaders of the Gulf states have shown some willingness to adopt various reforms, we need to develop an ongoing dialogue with them about how we can work with them to help them continue to move in that direction. We may find that there are things they would like from us that we never would have thought of on our own. Similarly, by talking to members of their societies who want to see greater reform, we may come up with tactics or even strategies to help them do so. The pressure for reform exists in all of the Gulf states, and while the new oil revenues can help dampen it, not only will it not eliminate that desire completely, it could actually intensify it, as was the case in Iran in the late 1970s. The proof of this is the willingness of the leaders to embark on any reforms at all, and because they are both wealthy and monarchies, they have shown a greater willingness to embrace reform than many of their poorer, dictatorial brethren have. Consequently, even in the Gulf, the cause of reform is far from hopeless. We simply need to be patient, opportunistic, and willing to listen to the people of the region themselves.

PART FIVE

—

A REGION OF CRISES

DURING THE COLD WAR, THE UNITED STATES PURSUED A grand strategy of containment designed to prevent the Soviet Union from further expanding its territory or influence and thereby threatening the United States. Bound up with that central goal was a vast range of substrategies about how the United States would seek to achieve it—by building a web of alliances around the USSR; by bolstering the members of those alliances politically, economically, and militarily; by encouraging democracy in Europe and Asia (but just as often tolerating friendly dictatorships in the third world); by deploying American forces on the periphery of the Soviet Union and its satellites; and so on. Moreover, the United States continued to devise other policies directed at specific problems, countries, or even regions, all of which were tailored to fit the needs of containment, even though what they were meant to accomplish may have had little to do with U.S. policy toward the USSR. U.S. policy toward Mexico, for instance, revolved around the familiar issues of immigration, trade, aid, and development, but always conducted with an eye toward ensuring that Mexico never falls prey to a Communist takeover like that in Cuba. Whether the United States overstated the danger of such a takeover is beside the point; what is important is that the United States shaped a policy toward Mexico based largely on bilateral concerns but still influenced by the overarching U.S. grand strategy of containment of the USSR.

What the example of containment illustrates is that the primary goal of a grand strategy is really just its starting point. Grand strategies are too broad to be limited to a single goal and a single set of steps meant to achieve that goal. Because a grand strategy governs so many different aspects of a nation's foreign policy toward a specific region (or its entire foreign policy, in some cases), it must also address a range of other issues that are important to the nation even if they are only tangentially related to the overarching goal of the grand strategy. At the very least, the grand strategy should indicate how best to think about dealing with these other issues in the context of the nation's wider interests.

Another useful example from the Cold War concerns maritime operations. Freedom of navigation on the world's oceans is a time-honored principle of American foreign policy, and Washington has long maintained that nations have the right to claim only twelve miles of territorial waters from their shores, although some insist that certain gulfs, bays, and other semicontained bodies of water are wholly their own. The United States has always felt it important to remind countries that it does not recognize anything beyond the twelve-mile territorial-limit claims and continued to do so during the Cold War. However, in the case of those countries that sided with us against the Soviets, we generally made that point with perfunctory diplomatic notes delivered by low-level officials. In contrast, when it came to countries aligned with Moscow, we were more likely to send carrier battle groups steaming into the disputed waters. Both methods preserved our commitment to freedom of navigation, but the approach was tailored to suit the needs of containment by downplaying our differences with friendly countries and being more provocative with unfriendly ones.

The same arrangement we employed during the Cold War of a core approach coupled with a penumbra of related policies consistent with the core goal but meant to address separate issues will be necessary for a new American grand strategy toward the Middle East. Whereas terrorism may be the most immediate threat to American security interests emanating from the Middle East and instability that can threaten the regimes of the region (and thus, potentially, global oil supplies), the greatest long-term threat we face, these hardly constitute all of the issues confronting American foreign policy in the Middle East. The newspapers are chock-full of stories about problems in the Middle East that have a direct or indirect bearing on U.S. interests there, and many of them are only tangentially related to the problems of terrorism and instability. Civil war in Iraq, Iran's pursuit of a nuclear enrichment capability, civil war among the Palestinians, the endless Israeli-Palestinian dispute, the threat of renewed violence in Lebanon, and whatever mischief the Syrians may be up to, to name only the most obvious, are all pressing concerns for the United States. The central goal of a new American grand strategy should influence, but not necessarily determine, how the United States handles each.

At the same time, it's important that the policies fashioned to deal with each subregional issue pass a "Hippocratic oath test," meaning that they should do no harm to the core goals and methods of the grand strategy. Indeed, it would be better still if they could be designed to *support* the central thrust of the grand strategy. Thus, American policy toward Iraq, Iran, the Arab-Israeli conflict, and everything else should be devised in such a way that it does not hurt U.S. efforts to encourage and enable reform among the predominantly Muslim states of the region, and to help those efforts whenever that is possible.

A last consideration when devising a grand strategy toward the Middle East should be to try to ensure that each of the subregional policies is working in harmony not just with the central goal of the strategy but also with all of the other discrete but related subregional policies. For example, American policy toward the Israeli-Palestinian dispute should be tailored not just to promote reform in the Middle East or, barring that, at least not to hurt that cause; it should also be designed to work in harmony with U.S. policy toward Iraq, Iran, Lebanon, Syria, and other countries, and should at least not undermine those policies either. Our grand strategy should help harmonize America's various policies toward the Middle East so that they work together, not at cross-purposes.

The Historical Record

These points help explain another reason why the George W. Bush administration's policies toward the Middle East have proved so disastrous. First, there has been no overarching goal. The Bush leadership did briefly suggest that democratization (which should have been only one part of a larger agenda of promoting economic, social, and political reform) would be their framing principle for the Middle East, but they never actually followed through on that thought. The closest they came was the "Global War on Terror," which was nonsensical as a grand strategy because terrorism is nothing but a symptom of the region's problems, not the problem itself. Even if we could suppress the use of terrorism by certain Middle East groups, it would not actually end the threat to American interests. As a result, there has been no organizing principle around which to structure American actions in the region.

Moreover, most if not all of the Bush administration's Middle East policies have run at variance with one another, getting in one another's way, undermining one another, and creating a widespread sense of confusion and amateurishness in the minds of governments throughout the region and around the world. The Bush administration compartmentalized virtually every policy, refusing to believe that any of them might have an impact on the others. For instance, as part of its Iraq policy, the administration demanded that Damascus bar Salafi terrorists from using Syrian territory to enter Iraq. Yet it refused to talk to the Syrian regime, let alone offer them anything they wanted (like economic aid and reintegration into the global community) in return for acceding to our demands on Iraq. Instead, Washington insisted that the two were unrelated and would not make any trade-offs. Similarly, for its first six years in office, the Bush administration steadfastly refused to make any effort to restart the peace process between Israelis and Palestinians and seemed oblivious to the fact that its refusal to do so made it hard for Arab states like Saudi Arabia and Egypt to be more supportive of American policies toward Iraq and Iran. Early on, the Saudis practically begged the administration to make a genuine effort to broker peace, in return for which they would support U.S. policy elsewhere, particularly toward Iraq, but this plea was ignored and so the Saudis distanced themselves from the American war effort. The Bush administration similarly refused to understand that their behavior toward Libya after Qadhafi agreed to give up his nuclear program and support for terrorism had important implications for the willingness of other countries to support similar American efforts to sanction Iran for the same things. Nearly every one of their major policies toward various Middle East states and problems have run directly contrary to one or more other major policies.

THE RESULT HAS BEEN a cacophony that limited the progress they made when they had the right policy (their decision to pursue a multilateral, diplomatic, carrots-and-sticks approach to Iran, for example, was limited by their unwillingness to accommodate Russia on issues of concern to Moscow like ballistic missile defenses) and turned bad policies into disasters (for instance, by leaving them with little regional support when, much to their dismay, Hamas won the 2006 Palestinian elections, which Washington had insisted take place).

The Clinton administration, conversely, had a well-integrated and sequenced approach to the problems of the region. As former assistant secretary of state Martin Indyk (full disclosure: I served in the Clinton White House and Ambassador Indyk is my current boss) explained at the start of the administration, the Clinton team's approach to the Middle East involved a major push to secure a comprehensive peace between the Arabs and Israelis, while employing a strategy of "dual containment" against Iran and Iraq to try to prevent them from derailing the peace process, which was considered the most important and most pressing American objective in the region.[1] This strategy did a superb job of harmonizing all aspects of Middle East policy.

In retrospect, the Clinton administration's strategy for the Middle East was ultimately flawed because it was framed by a Cold War paradigm that exaggerated the importance of the Arab-Israeli conflict. During the Cold War, that problem had been the most important in the region because of its potential to trigger a superpower clash. But the demise of the Soviet Union eliminated that risk, elevating the threat to Persian Gulf oil to the preeminent regional problem for international security. The Clinton administration's strategy also failed to include a course of action that could eliminate, not just suppress, the greatest threats to American interests in the region: what were then called the "rogue states" (at the time Iraq, Iran, Syria, Libya, and Sudan), transnational terrorist groups like al-Qa'ida, and the looming problem of Arab instability. Indeed, as the

Clinton administration went on, we found ourselves increasingly distracted from the peace process and forced to concentrate on these other problems—as witnessed by ever-more-frequent crises with Saddam Husayn (including military strikes in 1996 and 1998) and with Iran, as well as the administration's growing preoccupation with Usama bin Ladin after the 1997 East Africa and 2000 U.S.S. *Cole* bombings. Similarly, as the problem of instability in the Arab states became more acute, the administration increasingly tried to push the Arab states on reform, only to find that the demands of our focus on the peace process limited our ability to do so. A comprehensive Arab-Israeli peace would have removed a source of tension and anti-Americanism in the region, which would then have made tackling other problems easier, but by itself it did not constitute a properly focused strategy for dealing with these other, ultimately more threatening problems.

The Clinton administration ultimately failed to secure its principal objective in the region—a comprehensive Arab-Israeli peace—and allowed some problems to get worse by failing to develop a policy that could do more than box them in for a few years. However, by skillfully integrating the many strands of its various Middle East policies, the Clinton team achieved a number of important secondary objectives—like peace between Israel and Jordan—and avoided any catastrophic missteps in a region famous for its literal and figurative minefields. The George W. Bush administration, on the other hand, failed both to devise and implement a coherent strategy able to address the principal threats to American interests in the Middle East *and* to adopt properly integrated policies toward the many crises of the region (several of which were created by their own mistakes). The result of this has been a geostrategic mess that will take years to untangle.

Greater Than the Sum of Its Parts

These examples should make clear that an effective new American grand strategy for the Middle East requires not just a properly pursued central goal but also a properly integrated set of policies toward the many crises, countries, and other issues of the region.

Consequently, the purpose of part V is to address a number of the most important subregional problems and explain, in general terms, how the United States should think about devising policies toward them based on its interests, the requirements of the core of the grand strategy, and the importance of integrating all of them with one another.

Again, because this is a book about grand strategy, and because that grand strategy will have to play out over the course of decades, I am not going to prescribe specific policies regarding what the United States should do about any of these issues *right now*. Because the crises of the Middle East tend to mutate rapidly, most such prescriptions would be irrelevant before this book ever made it into print. Once the United States adopts a coherent grand strategy with a core goal designed to deal with the most important threats it faces from the Middle East and has recognized the importance of integrating the subregional policies so that they are not working at cross-purposes, the specifics of those policies can be defined and redefined based on the changing circumstances of the moment.

CHAPTER 14

THE DILEMMA OF IRAQ

T HE IRAQ WAR OVERSHADOWS EVERY ASPECT OF AMERICAN policy in the Middle East and affects our relationships with countries all over the world. It has strained our resources, further antagonized the Arab street, and alienated many of our staunchest allies. It has unleashed new forces of instability and convinced many Middle Easterners that transformation American-style is neither practical nor desirable. Moreover, its legacy will remain with us for some time to come, no matter what choice we make—stay, leave, or something in between. Any grand strategy toward the region, as well as every policy we pursue toward specific countries and crises within it, will be much harder because of our failures in Iraq, and its future course could make those policies harder still.

On one of my visits to post-Saddam Iraq, a soldier captured the essence of our problem there nicely: "We can't stay, we can't leave, and we can't fail."[1] From the perspective of both the grand strategy proposed in this book and America's wider interests, every course of action toward Iraq has enormous drawbacks—far more liabilities than benefits. That is the legacy of the countless mistakes made by the Bush administration in the months before the invasion and the years after it.[2] All of the good options have long since disappeared, and we are left with only poor choices. We are going to have to choose one of these courses of action, but it is not going to be straightforward or easy, and it is going to be painful to implement whatever we choose.

To Stay or to Leave?

The problems with staying—with maintaining a large military commitment in Iraq to suppress the sectarian violence and try to create the conditions for a stable, sustainable peace—are principally problems of cost. Every month that the United States remains in Iraq costs our country lives, money, and political capital.[3] Even the successes of the surge in troops and the new counterinsurgency strategy adopted when General David Petraeus took over in early 2007 have not eliminated American casualties entirely, nor was it ever expected they would. Moreover, even if the counterinsurgency strategy continues to succeed spectacularly, it will take five, ten, or even fifteen years before American troops will be able to leave Iraqi security entirely in the hands of Iraqi security forces. In those circumstances, the numbers of American casualties might continue to diminish during that time frame, but it is hard to imagine that they will disappear altogether.

From the long perspective of America's wars, several thousand dead is quite modest, but to the families and friends of those killed, each death is a tragedy, and it is fair for all Americans to ask whether those lives were worth the outcome. The war in Iraq has also cost hundreds of billions of dollars, nothing like the cost of the two world wars but again a very meaningful sum when taxpayers want to know what they are getting for their money. Moreover, the Iraq intervention feeds hostility to the United States throughout the Muslim world, if not the entire world. It means that we have to focus a great deal of our diplomacy on Iraqi matters—keeping coalition troops there, convincing other countries to stop making mischief, persuading our allies to give aid, and encouraging still others to assist us in pushing and prodding other countries to be helpful on Iraq. Every one of those favors is a favor we can't call on for another foreign policy priority. Moreover, our freedom of action is badly constrained. I would argue that our commitments in Iraq and Afghanistan need not have prevented the United States from finding ways to participate in the expanded U.N. peacekeeping mission to Lebanon or leading a multinational intervention in Sudan to halt the genocidal killing in Darfur. Nevertheless, the fact is that even a better-intentioned administration, one that genuinely believed in international commitments and humanitarian actions, would have had a hard time providing large numbers of troops for either of those missions because of the wars in Iraq and Afghanistan.

Thus, every month that the United States remains in Iraq is a constant, relentless cost. It may not be a heavy cost when seen in increments, but it adds up over time. And the price seems especially high when Americans don't see any tangible benefits for the lives, money, and political capital being lost, as was especially true in 2003–2006. There are also risks inherent in staying in Iraq—like the potential risk of another war somewhere else—although this risk should not be exaggerated. Iraq and its neighbors in Iran, Kuwait, and Saudi Arabia possess four of the five largest proven reserves of oil in the world. That alone makes the conflict in Iraq more important than almost any other country in which we might imagine a war, except Saudi Arabia itself.[4] Even a war in the Korean Peninsula (which frankly should not require a heavy commitment of American ground troops, given the balance of power between the North and South) would exceed the importance of Iraq to American interests only if there were a high likelihood that the North Koreans were going to nuke Tokyo. Thus the problem with staying in Iraq is primarily a problem of costs.

ON THE OTHER HAND, the problem with leaving Iraq is essentially a problem of risks. Don't get me wrong, there will certainly be costs associated with leaving—the Army may be devastated by defeat and our political standing in the world will be low, as it was after Vietnam. But those costs are not likely to be catastrophic. With time, both the Army and our standing in the world can almost certainly be rebuilt. The highest cost that the United States will have to pay will come in the form of whatever assistance we give to the millions of refugees created by an all-out civil war in Iraq such as would almost certainly follow a near-term American withdrawal. We will (rightly) feel a compelling moral obligation to do something for them—allow some to emigrate to the United States, help others to resettle elsewhere, provide aid for the rest, perhaps even deploy military forces to protect them, wherever they end up. Of course, we absorbed and helped resettle numerous Vietnamese refugees after our withdrawal from Southeast Asia, and we got over whatever guilt we might have felt for the deaths of others in Vietnam, Laos, and Cambodia, so it is reasonable to believe that we could do the same with the Iraqis and not be overly burdened by international opprobrium or our own consciences.

However, even if we are willing to set aside the humanitarian costs, there are very significant strategic risks involved in a decision to withdraw American combat forces from Iraq that can't be ignored. The first of these is the high likelihood that without American forces present Iraq is likely to descend into an all-out civil war far worse than what we have seen so far (think Bosnia, Lebanon, and Congo) and in which hundreds of thousands, possibly millions, more will die.[5] Millions more Iraqis will flee the country, creating humanitarian nightmares for all of its neighbors. It is worth contemplating that the United States has intervened in other countries—Bosnia, Kosovo, Haiti, Somalia—to try to prevent slaughters on a similar scale.

The second risk is the potential for American withdrawal and the ensuing Iraqi civil war that will almost certainly follow to affect the other countries of the region.[6] Iraq is important by itself, but it is not as important to the global economy as Saudi Arabia is. All-out civil war would risk the loss of all of Iraq's roughly 2 million barrels per day (bpd) of oil production. That is not insignificant and would undoubtedly cause oil prices to rise further, possibly by a considerable amount, depending on a variety of other factors. But this pales in comparison with the impact of losing Saudi Arabia's 8 million to 10 million bpd of oil production.

The problem with major civil wars is that there is inevitably "spillover" into neighboring countries. Sometimes that spillover is mild; sometimes it is catastrophic. It is impossible to predict just how bad spillover from Iraq would get, but it has all of the hallmarks of being toward the worse end of the spectrum, not the better—porous, contested borders; ethnic and religious groups that span those borders; ethnic and religious rivalries that are replicated in neighboring states; a history of interstate conflict; and the presence of high-value natural resources. These are exactly the factors that have tended to make spillover bad in other historical cases. There are six common manifestations of spillover—refugees, secessionist movements, radicalized neighboring populations, terrorism, covert (frequently leading to overt) intervention by neighboring states, and economic problems—and Iraq is already manifesting every one of them, again suggesting that spillover from Iraq is likely to be worse, not better. (Although it should be noted that, as of this writing, the early successes of the surge and attendant counterinsurgency strategy have ameliorated all of these problems to a greater or lesser degree.)

At its worst, spillover from an all-out civil war can create two disastrous problems. First, it can trigger civil wars in other neighboring states, just as Rwanda's civil war sparked Congo's civil war; civil war in mandatory Palestine between Jews and Arabs, what has now become the Arab-Israeli conflict, led to civil war in Jordan in 1970–1971 and Lebanon in 1975–1990; and the Lebanese civil war in turn triggered civil war in Syria in 1976–1982. The second potentially catastrophic outcome of spillover is that it can cause civil war to metastasize into regional war, with neighboring states all intervening in the civil war—and even fighting against one another—to secure their interests in the state in civil war. Seven neighboring states invaded Congo to halt refugee flows, prevent unfriendly groups from attacking their own countries from sanctuaries in Congo, and claim Congo's rich natural resources. Israel and Syria both intervened in the Lebanese civil war and came to blows on a number of occasions, most notably in high-intensity combat in 1982. Even on those occasions when the states keep their interventions limited to covert support of proxy forces (which is every country's preference but typically lasts only till one side starts losing, which often causes it to escalate to overt intervention), the results can be disastrous. The Pakistanis successfully waged a proxy war in Afghanistan in the 1980s and '90s, eventually bringing the Taliban to power, but in so doing they bankrupted their own state economically, socially, and politically. Transferred to the Persian Gulf region, similar developments could be disastrous for a range of American interests, especially the potential for sudden major oil disruptions but also including the potential for destabilization to affect the security of various American allies in the region, particularly Jordan, which is both weak and highly vulnerable to problems emanating from Iraq.[7]

Nevertheless, all of the risks of spillover are just that: risks. There is no guarantee that all-out civil war in Iraq would catastrophically destabilize the region. Everything might work out fine. That seems rather optimistic, especially given the extent of Iranian, Turkish, and Saudi intervention in Iraqi affairs already, but it is possible. And even if everything doesn't work out fine, spillover from an Iraqi civil war might be bad but not disastrous. We do not know. The historical record and the existing evidence give reason for concern, but we don't have a crystal ball.

On the other hand, prudent decision makers typically take any risk of catastrophic failure very seriously. As Steve Biddle of the Council on Foreign Relations has said about the risks of spillover from a civil war in Iraq, "there's a roughly thirty-to-forty-per-cent chance that it'll spread. During the Cold War, we spent trillions worrying about infinitesimally small risks. Thirty-to-forty-per-cent chance of a real, honest-to-goodness catastrophe is something that ought to factor into our policymaking now."[8] Indeed, the soundest and most successful policies and military strategies prepare for the worst case because failure to do so often produces it.

This, then, is the choice that faces the American people and the next American president: whether to keep accepting the ongoing costs of staying in Iraq to avoid the risks or pull out to end the costs and run the risk of spillover, which could cause new problems potentially even worse than an Iraqi civil war.

Reconciling the Options with the Grand Strategy

Whichever option toward Iraq the United States chooses, it will have to be crafted in such a way that it minimizes the damage to the broader grand strategy and to America's other interests and policies in the region. The truth is that neither option is "beneficial" to the grand strategy. Both have the potential to hurt it, just in different ways. But since we do not have the option of somehow making the Iraq dilemma go away, it is critical to think through how best to mitigate the potential impact of whatever choice the next president makes regarding Iraq, whether to stay or to go.

If the next president elects to remain committed to Iraq and try to see it through to a stable conclusion, the primary concern, from the perspective of the grand strategy, must be to reduce the political cost of the war (internationally and in the region) and ensure that it does produce "sustainable stability" in Iraq. The former will likely prove as difficult as the latter.

As long as the United States maintains significant forces in Iraq, it is going to contribute to anti-American sentiments both elsewhere in the region and in the wider global community. However, there are a number of things that a new administration can and should be willing to do that would help alleviate that animosity, possibly to a significant extent. Giving the neighboring states a greater stake in Iraq would be a good place to start. One way to do so would be to convene a formal "contact group," like the one we established to help with the conflicts in the Balkans. This should include all of the neighboring states—including Iran and Syria, if they are willing to come—along with the Iraqi government, the U.S. military and civilian authorities, and the U.N. Assistance Mission in Iraq (UNAMI). The group should meet regularly and be briefed by senior Iraqi government officials (as well as American and U.N. personnel when appropriate) on the state of play in Iraq and the policy options they are considering to deal with the situation. The neighbors should be encouraged to give their input and advice in return for providing assistance (certainly diplomatic, political, and economic but possibly even military) either to help with specific projects or, more generally, to bolster stability. The idea would be to try to diminish Arab, Iranian, and Turkish anger at the United States for its early mishandling of Iraq by formally bringing them into the process, taking their advice whenever possible, and giving them a sense that both Iraqis and Americans are trying to accommodate their concerns, while simultaneously soliciting their much-needed assistance to stabilize the country.[9]

A second important method of both increasing the likelihood of success in Iraq and diminishing regional and global anger at the United States for its occupation would be to make a major effort to give the United Nations a much greater role in Iraq. Like the neighboring countries, the United Nations has a great deal to offer a continuing U.S.-led effort to stabilize Iraq. A UNSC-authorized high commissioner or a new and more fully empowered special envoy, could be given primary responsibility for leading the political and economic reconstruction effort. This would make that person, and less the American ambassador, responsible for pushing and prodding the Iraqi leadership toward national accommodation. It would also make it possible to more fully engage a range of U.N. agencies as well as the wide array of international NGOs that have skills in economic, political, social, educational, and legal development that Americans lack. These personnel were critical to previous nation-building efforts in Haiti, East Timor, Bosnia, Cambodia, Somalia, Lebanon, and elsewhere, and their absence from Iraq has been a major source of problems. They have been reticent to go to Iraq, both because of the security situation and because they are loath to become part of the American chain of command, but they would be happy to be part of a U.N.-led structure.[10]

Still another set of things the United States could do to mitigate the impact of a decision to remain engaged in Iraq on the rest of the region (and hence, on the grand strategy) would be to take steps on other issues that would make regional governments and their people happy for unrelated reasons. The most obvious issue on that count is the Israeli-Palestinian confrontation. As the Bush 43 administration finally learned after six years of trying to ignore this problem, it is important for a variety of reasons for the United States to take an active role in trying to broker peace between Israelis and Palestinians (and, ideally, Syrians and Lebanese). One of them is that this is a source of considerable Arab anger at the United States, and mollifying the Arab populations would make it easier for Arab regimes to support other American policies that are also unpopular, such as remaining in Iraq.

As I have already said several times, this is not an argument for selling Israel out. The United States should prod and cajole all of the parties equally but should not try to force any of them to accept a deal they don't like. Instead, what is important is to make the effort constantly—not only in the hope that doing so will allow for progress and the eventual settlement of the dispute on terms acceptable to all sides but also to demonstrate to the Arab publics that the United States understands their anger and is working to solve the problem. Of course, the peace process is only one of a range of things the United States could do. Another would be to increase American economic aid to countries like Jordan, Egypt, and Turkey (which would also be important in the event the United States failed in Iraq or simply decided to withdraw without having established sustainable security). This too would help mitigate anti-Americanism.

However, as helpful as all these steps might be, they pale by comparison with the salutary effect of actually succeeding in Iraq if the United States decides to maintain a major commitment there. In the end, what would be most helpful in advancing a transformative grand strategy for the Middle East would be avoiding the threats to regional security that could emerge from American failure in Iraq and that country's descent into all-out civil war.

As of this writing, in early 2008, the new Iraq strategy devised by General Petraeus and Ambassador Ryan Crocker has begun to demonstrate heartening progress. In the northern half of Iraq, where American forces are present in strength, violence has been dramatically reduced, and growing numbers of Iraqi military units are demonstrating the competence to maintain the peace with reduced levels of American support. These improvements in security have allowed local leaders to strike important political bargains, reinforcing the changes in military tactics and also allowing local economies to begin to revive. These widespread shifts are even beginning to affect the paralyzed national reconciliation effort in Baghdad. Nevertheless, the progress at this point remains fragile and could easily be reversed, especially by a precipitous withdrawal of American forces. Even if U.S. forces remain, however, there will still be very serious challenges that need to be overcome, particularly in southern Iraq, where American efforts have so far had little impact.

The new strategy has demonstrated that it has the potential to succeed in the modest goal of creating a stable Iraq, but it is far from proving that success is ensured.

ON THE OTHER HAND, if the next president chooses to withdraw from Iraq, the United States will have to devote considerable resources to mitigate the risks of spillover from a major civil war in Iraq. Failure to do so would amount to the same kind of reckless disregard for the lessons of history, determination to plan only for the best-case scenario, and unwillingness to guard against the worst-case scenario that characterized the Bush 43 administration's thinking prior to the invasion of Iraq—and that was responsible for so many of the mistakes that created the nightmare we face in Iraq today. We need to plan and prepare for worst-case contingencies, lest our failure to do so make them unavoidable, as was the case in 2003–2006. In addition to our very real humanitarian obligations, we cannot afford to allow tragedy in Iraq to become a catastrophe for the wider Middle East and through it, vital American interests.

It is worth reiterating that the first price of an American withdrawal from Iraq short of establishing sustainable stability there would be the mass slaughter that would likely engulf the country. We should not fool ourselves that we can somehow prevent this if we remove most, let alone all, of our troops. The 130,000 to 160,000 troops deployed there since 2003 have just barely kept a lid on the violence, and still tens of thousands of Iraqis have died each year.[11] By greatly diminishing the numbers of American and Iraqi deaths, the "surge" strategy simply demonstrated the inverse correlation between American troop levels and Iraqi violence. Significant reductions of American troops in the absence of additional progress will almost certainly unleash greater violence and killing. It is one reason why the decision to withdraw should be based on an objective assessment that American forces are unable to prevent a further descent into all-out civil war under any conditions.

Setting aside humanitarian considerations to focus purely on the strategic dimensions of this policy option, containing the spillover from an all-out civil war could prove extremely difficult. We need to be clear-eyed about this risk: depending on how bad the spillover is, we could easily fail to contain it, and unfortunately there is considerable evidence that it is going to be bad, if not very bad. Nevertheless, if we choose to withdraw, we will not have any choice but to make the effort. There are many ways that a containment strategy could be constructed, but it will almost certainly have to include the following five basic elements:[12]

1. **Help build up the neighboring states.** Historically, the more unhappy neighboring populations are, the more likely they are to be inspired to violence by or demand intervention in a neighboring state in civil war. Thus, the more satisfied they are with their own material circumstances, the more likely they will be to resist the emotional assault of a nearby civil war. In addition, civil wars can create numerous problems for neighboring states—caring for refugees, fighting terrorists and other armed groups from the civil war, having foreign trade and investment frightened off by nearby violence—and the richer and stronger the neighboring states are, the less crippling these problems will be. Consequently, the United States and its allies should work to improve the socioeconomic and political resiliency of the neighboring states. Jordan, in particular, needs to weigh heavily in these calculations. Jordan is caught between three civil wars—Iraq, Lebanon, and the Palestinians—and is suffering spillover from all of them. Consequently, the United States should substantially increase its economic aid to Jordan (which also could help make it easier for King Abdallah to keep moving down the path of reform, as suggested in chapter 11).

2. **Prevent or deter outside interference as best we can.** One of the biggest problems with civil wars, especially those in economically and strategically vital countries like Iraq, is the enormous pull they exert on neighboring states, drawing them like a magnet to intervene to protect their interests or exploit the chaos to improve their position. This is invariably a trap: few countries have emerged better off for having intervened in a neighbor's civil war and, frequently, doing so triggers severe

economic, social, and/or political problems in the *intervening* state. Given the importance of so many of Iraq's neighbors to U.S. interests (the great oil producers of Saudi Arabia and Kuwait, our NATO ally Turkey, our Jordanian friends), the United States will have to make every effort to dissuade them from intervening for fear of the repercussions. In addition, Syria and Iran, two states we don't much like, will undoubtedly expand their own ongoing intervention in Iraqi affairs, and the United States will need to persuade them not to do so or, more realistically, to limit that involvement as well. Because of Iraq's wealth and strategic position in the region, both may try to gain dominance of some kind over much of the country. That in itself would be detrimental to U.S. interests, but, perhaps of greater importance, the more they are seen as making gains in Iraq, the harder it will be for Washington to keep Riyadh, Amman, Kuwait, and Ankara from matching Tehran and Damascus's bids or even upping the ante. That is how civil war in Iraq could turn into regional war.

3. **Prepare to assist refugees.** By late 2007, 4 million Iraqis had already fled their homes, according to the U.N. high commissioner for refugees, and 2 million of them had left the country altogether, most for Jordan and Syria. By early 2008, many had begun to return home, again making clear the sensitive relationship between the U.S. presence and the state of Iraq. If a rapid U.S. troop withdrawal prompts Iraq to slide back into a Bosnia- or Congo-like all-out civil war, the number of refugees is likely to increase significantly and the neighboring states are not prepared to take many more. Large numbers of refugees are not only a humanitarian tragedy, they are an economic burden and a strategic threat to the states that receive them. Large refugee populations tend to be breeding grounds for violence and ideal recruiting pools for militias still fighting the civil war—which inevitably prompts their enemies to attack the refugee camps, in turn requiring the host nation to take action either to defend or to expel the refugee population. This is a very volatile situation and is exactly how Palestinian refugees

from their civil war with the Palestinian Jews (who became the Israelis) sparked civil wars in Jordan in 1970 and Lebanon in 1975 (and then brought the Syrians and Israelis into both). Therefore, the United States would have to launch a major initiative with the UNHCR and any willing countries to prepare to absorb, feed, house, protect, and otherwise care for the millions of Iraqi refugees who could be expected to flee an all-out civil war.

4. **Prepare for an oil shock.** Full-scale civil war in Iraq is likely to lead to the loss of much, and quite possibly all, of Iraq's oil production. Iraqi oil facilities are already targeted by a range of militant groups, and the production and export system produces 2 million bpd entirely thanks to enormous exertions on the part of the United States and the Iraqi government (which would likely collapse or become irrelevant in the event of all-out civil strife). Amid the carnage of a Congo-like war, we should not assume that much oil is going to come out of Iraq. Moreover, if spillover from the war is severe, it could threaten the oil production of other regional states, like Kuwait, Iran, and Saudi Arabia, because of both the threat of heightened terror attacks from Iraq and the increased potential for civil strife of one kind or another in those countries. The United States and its allies would do well to build up their strategic petroleum stockpiles, as well as working with groups like OPEC and the International Energy Association to agree on procedures in the event of a major shortfall in oil production.

5. **Bolster counterterrorism measures.** One of the many paradoxes of Iraq is that the horribly mismanaged U.S. invasion and early occupation of Iraq have aided the cause of Salafi terrorists by inspiring hundreds, if not thousands, of them to travel to Iraq to take up arms against the United States; however, if the United States withdraws from Iraq without having established a sustainable stability, it will probably make the terrorism problem worse still. Major civil wars breed new terrorist groups (the IRA, PLO, Hizballah, Tamil Tigers, Hamas, Is-

lamic Jihad, and al-Qa'ida itself were all born of civil wars) and provide sanctuary to existing ones (as al-Qa'ida has found sanctuary and employment in Somalia and now Iraq).

The highly regarded terrorism expert Daniel Byman has astutely observed that there is an inverse relationship between terrorist inspiration and operations in Iraq. If the United States is in Iraq (and especially if we are not making progress toward stabilizing the country), this inspires many Muslims to join groups like al-Qa'ida to fight the United States. However, as long as large American forces are present in Iraq, the al-Qa'ida fighters have their ability to operate constrained, they take constant casualties, and the net result is that they have a hard time mounting operations abroad. This has been especially true because the new counterinsurgency strategy has inflicted severe damage on al-Qa'ida in Iraq and other Salafi terrorist groups. On the other hand, if the United States withdraws from Iraq, this would almost certainly diminish al-Qa'ida's ability to recruit new members (and would probably cause many of the existing members of al-Qa'ida in Iraq to give up their fight and go home). However, it would also give those who remain the ability to resurrect their organizations and provide them with greater freedom to plan, organize, and mount operations against other countries from Iraq.

This was precisely what happened in Afghanistan. During the 1979–1989 war against the Soviets, 25,000 to 30,000 Arabs (and perhaps as many as 70,000 foreign-born Muslims altogether) traveled to Afghanistan to wage jihad against the Russians.[13] During that time, these men were pretty exclusively focused on the Soviets, and even leaders like Usama bin Ladin paid little attention to other enemies, like the Saudis and the Americans. Once the Soviets withdrew, the vast majority of the Arabs and other foreign-born Muslims went home and gave up the fight. However, a hard core remained and became the organization we know as al-Qa'ida, which then turned its attention on other foes. Some continued to wage war in Afghanistan, this time as part of the civil war that followed the Soviet withdrawal, and eventually threw their support behind the Taliban. However, other parts of the organization turned their attention to other targets—initially Arab governments like Egypt and Saudi Arabia but then the United States—and the anarchy of Afghanistan and the friendship of the Taliban gave them much greater ability to mount such attacks.

Unfortunately, we need to be prepared for the same to happen in Iraq. As was true in Afghanistan, many of the foreigners who went to Iraq to wage jihad against the American occupiers would undoubtedly go home and give up the fight if U.S. military forces did, too. Many others would turn their focus more fully on waging the Iraqi civil war against their Shi'i adversaries (and it is worth remembering that probably about 90 percent of al-Qa'ida in Iraq are Sunni Iraqis),[14] but some would doubtless turn their attention on foreign targets—either on local regimes like the Saudis and Jordanians or back onto the United States—and would have much greater freedom to do so without American forces constantly searching for them and trying to capture or kill them. And while the fact that most Iraqis dislike al-Qa'ida suggests that it may not have quite the same support that it did in Afghanistan, where its Taliban allies ran the government, in the context of an all-out civil war against the Shi'ah and the Kurds, a great many Sunnis would likely overlook their dislike of the foreign Salafists and take whatever help they could get, especially from fanatical and often well-trained al-Qa'ida fighters, which would, in turn, give those elements of the group plotting foreign operations considerable operational freedom, as in Afghanistan. Thus, the United States and its allies would have to brace themselves for greater Salafi terrorism from Iraq (and possibly Shi'i terrorism led by Hizballah operating out of Iraq against Sunni countries supporting the Iraqi Sunnis).

A LAST IRONY of Iraq is that whichever course the United States takes in the future—withdrawal or continued engagement—will only increase both the importance of reform in the Arab world and the difficulty of achieving it. A decision to remain in Iraq would place a premium on succeeding, and that in turn would likely require greater assistance from the Arab states. It could also further inflame Arab passions against the United States. Regardless of whether it did any of these things, the Arab regimes would doubtless use both Washington's needs and the growing anger of their populations to deflect pressure for reform. However, reform promises the best way to mitigate the anger of the Arab populations (including the additional fuel on the fire from continued American intervention in Iraq), and therefore reform is the best way to prevent an American decision to remain in Iraq from translating into internal problems elsewhere in the region.

By the same token, an American withdrawal from Iraq short of establishing sustainable stability would increase the need for reform, again because that is the best way to diminish the grievances of the neighboring populations but also because it would strengthen their states, economies, and psyches to deal with the problems likely to spill over out of Iraq. However, in the face of even greater violence from Iraq and the likelihood that Iraqi militant groups will try to use their territories as sanctuaries, recruiting arenas, and staging grounds for operations back into Iraq, the regimes themselves will be much less willing to take even limited risks for reform. Instead, they are likely to clamp down even tighter on any form of domestic dissent, as nearly all of them have in recent years. They will fear, not without some merit, that any social unrest caused by the inevitable dislocations of major internal reforms could be greatly exacerbated by the problems from Iraq infecting their own societies, raising the risk of wider instability. Given that few want to move in this direction to begin with, this is likely only to reinforce their existing inclination to abjure reform altogether.

CHAPTER 15

THE CHALLENGE OF IRAN

IRAN HAS BEEN AMERICA'S MOST PERSISTENT ADVERSARY IN the Middle East since 1979. Although in Iran's fragmented political system views of the United States vary, since the revolution, those who see the United States as an enemy have tended to dominate Tehran's foreign policy, scuttling efforts by those who would like to see a less confrontational relationship. Hard-line elements within the factionalized Iranian regime still cling to Ayatollah Khomeini's ideological dogma that the United States represents the greatest threat to Iran and everything the Islamic Republic hopes to achieve. Nationalists tend to see the United States as a more traditional rival for power in the Persian Gulf region. The most pragmatic members of the regime have repeatedly signaled that they would like to normalize relations with Washington—a view widely shared by the Iranian public—but they have been stymied by the hard-liners whenever they have attempted to effect such a rapprochement. The net effect of these divisions has been to produce an Iranian foreign policy toward the United States that lurches back and forth from schizophrenic indecision to covert warfare, and since the election of the hard-line Mahmoud Ahmedinejad as president in 2005, Iran has inclined more in the latter direction.[1] Given both the regime's current composition and its past history, the United States should assume that this pattern will persist into the future even as we look to take advantage of whatever openings present themselves.

Ahmedinejad's election itself, however, is only part of the reason for Iran's increased assertiveness toward the United States. Another important element has been that the Bush administration's many foreign policy disasters in the Middle East have created both threats and opportunities for Tehran. The civil wars triggered by American mistakes in Iraq and the Palestinian territories, the semianarchy of Afghanistan after the deposition of the Taliban, and the power vacuum created in Lebanon by Syria's withdrawal have all created opportunities for Iran to increase its influence in these states by supporting a variety of militant groups looking for anyone willing to back them. This has fit well with both Iran's short-term interests in maximizing its influence in these key states (especially neighboring Iraq and Afghanistan, where its military, political, and economic interests are huge) and its longer-term interest in seeing the regional status quo replaced by one in which Tehran predominates.

By backing these opponents of peace and stability, Iran has repeatedly put itself at odds with the United States and its allies, which have just as typically backed the opposing groups—those who have (mostly) stood for the status quo and an end to violence. And it is worth noting that in virtually every case, Tehran's hard-liners have seen such conflict with the United States as at least a side benefit of, if not a principal motive for, aiding these groups. Meanwhile, bellicose rhetoric from members of the Bush administration and some of their supporters, the deployment of large numbers of American troops on many of Iran's borders, and the possibility of true chaos in both Iraq and Afghanistan have likewise encouraged Iran's more pragmatic political leaders to support greater intervention in both of those countries to preclude an American military strike and protect Iran's interests in the event that one or both collapses into chaos.

Iran's growing influence and assertiveness are problematic principally because of the threats they create to our allies in the region, not fear of direct Iranian actions against the United States (although in extreme circumstances those cannot be ruled out). Since Khomeini's death, the Iranians have been aggressive, anti-American, and even murderous, but they have generally been prudent and have tried to pursue their anti–status quo agenda without provoking a war with the United States. For instance, they have not directly attacked another country with conventional military forces since the end of the Iran-Iraq War, although in 1998 they threatened to invade Afghanistan. Instead, there is some evidence that the Iranians have continued to try to subvert regional governments they do not like by aiding internal opposition groups.[2] Iran's desire to overturn the regional status quo, its opposition to U.S. influence in the region, and its willingness to back groups that employ violence (including terrorism) to achieve their goals stoke the mayhem in the region. It turns small groups, like PIJ or Hizballah, which might be nothing more than local annoyances without Iranian backing, into serious threats to peace and stability. This, in turn, is unhelpful to American interests because it gives the Arab regimes a pretext for delaying reform and increasing levels of repression, at least in the short term. That greater repression simply makes their populations that much more unhappy, feeding into the overall anger and desperation of the societies, which in turn can lead to further internal unrest. In this way, whether directly or indirectly, Iranian support for these groups tends to make the region more volatile and increases the risks of revolution, civil war, insurgency, and terrorism. Thus, Iran's efforts simultaneously make the underlying problems of the Arab world worse and make it less likely that the regimes will adopt the right solutions.

Unfortunately, there are no easy answers as far as Iran is concerned. In particular, the Iraq problem adds a range of mitigating and complicating factors to the U.S.-Iranian relationship. On the one hand, there is considerable evidence that Iran is providing weaponry, funds, training, and other support (including most of the explosively formed penetrators so lethal to American military personnel) to a wide range of groups, including, but not limited to, all of the major Shi'i militias.[3] This is stoking the fire of civil war in Iraq and contributing to the death of American soldiers and marines. However, it is just as clear that Iranian support to the Iraqi groups could be significantly greater. For example, the Iraqi groups have not received the sophisticated antitank and antiaircraft weapons the Iranians have provided Hizballah, nor are Iranian personnel fully integrated into the command and intelligence hierarchies of any of the Iraqi groups, as they have been at times with Hizballah.[4] In other words, there is a great deal more that the Iranians could do to make the fighting in Iraq—and specifically, attacks on Americans—much worse than it is now. And though the extent of the aid they are providing is unhelpful, to say the least, it is simply not the case that Iran is the primary, or even a major, cause of Iraq's problems. The chaos in Iraq is almost wholly the result of American mistakes and the inevitable Iraqi reactions to those mistakes, and the Iranian involvement is primarily an exacerbating factor.

We don't really know why Iran has chosen to provide extensive but limited assistance, but it seems likely that it is related to a mixture of at least four different factors: (1) Iran's hard-liners doubtless want to hurt the United States as much as possible, and other Iranian leaders may see utility in helping to erode American military power to preclude an invasion of Iran; (2) the Iranians are trying to maximize their influence with different Iraqi groups, particularly among the Shi'ah, in the hope either that they can engineer the accession of a friendly government or that, at the very least, whoever rules in Baghdad will be well disposed toward Tehran and weapons (especially weapons able to deal with the Americans) are what Iraqi militias want most from them; (3) some Iranians, possibly including Supreme Leader 'Ali Khamene'i and other mainstream conservatives, are as fearful (or more) of chaos in Iraq than of American "success," and so they have tried to strike a balance between providing enough military aid to buy influence with the militias but not so much that Iraq slides irretrievably into civil war; and (4) they are almost certainly afraid that providing greater levels of military assistance would risk provoking an American military response. Regardless of Tehran's motives, the fact that its actions are contributing to the problems in Iraq but are not a major cause of those problems (and that the Iranians could make matters much worse if they decided to abandon the relative restraint they have shown so far) adds several more levels of complexity to an already labyrinthine set of problems.

The Iranian Nuclear Program

No one outside the rarefied circles of Tehran's leadership knows why Iran is trying to develop the capability to enrich uranium and separate plutonium, but it seems unlikely that it is simply for energy production and technological development, as the regime claims. You don't need to be able to enrich uranium (let alone separate plutonium) to run either research reactors or power generators. The United Nations and the European Union (backed by the United States) have agreed to sell Iran light-water reactors that would be more than adequate to generate power but hard to use to make nuclear weapons, and Russia has offered to allow Iranian scientists to participate in a program that would allow them to learn how to enrich uranium without actually having the equipment in Iran. Tehran has rejected all of these offers, and its rationale—that accepting them would make Iran dependent on other countries—is not very convincing. Moreover, the Iranians have already endured considerable international opprobrium and economic hardship to continue their program, which does not square well with the notion that this program is somehow designed to benefit Iran economically. From a purely economic perspective, Iran would have been much better off taking the various deals offered to it over the years.

On the other hand, in December 2007, the U.S. intelligence community released a National Intelligence Estimate (NIE) that concluded that Iran had had a program to employ enriched uranium in nuclear weapons but had halted it in 2003. The NIE could not say how far Iran had gotten before shutting the program down and noted that Tehran continued to move as fast as possible in trying to develop the capability to enrich uranium and build ballistic missiles able to carry nuclear warheads. Although widely interpreted as indicating that Iran did not intend to build nuclear weapons, the report itself was much more circumspect. It stressed that the most difficult part of acquiring a nuclear arsenal is getting the enriched uranium, and therefore the suspension of the weaponization program should be seen as evidence of Tehran's desire to avoid international sanctions and not necessarily as proof of peaceful intent.[5]

There are a lot of other things that Iran has done that are not consistent with a peaceful nuclear program. For instance, the Iranians purchased much of the know-how for their enrichment program, including centrifuge designs and some actual centrifuges, from A. Q. Khan, the notorious Pakistani nuclear scientist whose illegal ring was selling weapons technology—if Iran really were only seeking a peaceful program, why get into bed with Khan?[6] When discovered, the Iranians lied repeatedly to the International Atomic Energy Agency (IAEA) about what they had, where they had gotten it, and what they were trying to do. The United Nations also discovered that Iran had produced polonium 210, a short-lived, unstable element whose only real use is as an initiator for nuclear weapons (although the Iranians claimed it was for nuclear batteries to be used in satellites and deep-space exploration, neither of which they have).[7] When the Europeans first sat down with the Iranians to discuss their nuclear program in 2003 (and only because the European Union threatened Iran with economic sanctions), they found that the Iranians had no technical studies to back their claims that it was more cost-effective for them to build and operate nuclear power plants than natural gas plants—which are more cost-effective everywhere else on the planet and would be so especially for Iran, which has the second largest deposits of natural gas in the world. Nor had the Iranians drawn up any plans, let alone tendered any contracts, to build nuclear power plants.[8]

In other words, the evidence is unclear, but there is real reason to fear that the Iranians are at least looking for the *capability* to make nuclear weapons, if not the weapons themselves. Some of the best experts on Iran believe that all Tehran wants is a capacity like that of Japan, which has all the know-how and materials to manufacture nuclear weapons in a matter of weeks or months if Tokyo ever decided to do so. Other experts believe that, especially given how quickly the Iraqi regime fell to an American invasion—which might be Tehran's cardinal fear—the Iranians will feel that a few months is too long and so want an actual nuclear arsenal on hand. It may be that the Iranian regime has not made up its mind yet and, as with so many things, is continuing to debate the issue even as the program continues to move forward.

Whatever the right answer, the United States and its allies would be foolish to assume that the Iranians are not trying to acquire a nuclear weapons capability of some kind, whether it is a stockpile of bombs or simply the ability to build one quickly. Even on the off chance that Tehran really isn't interested in nuclear weapons at all, the mere fact that it has acquired the capability to build them if it so chose would force other states to treat it as if it had the weapons anyway. For many years after its "peaceful" nuclear explosion in 1974, India remained ambiguous about whether it maintained a stockpile of nuclear weapons, but the Chinese, Pakistanis, and other countries had to treat India as if it had them out of simple prudence. The same will be true for Iran, and it is not Iran's use of nuclear weapons that is the real problem for the United States but how both Iran and other countries are likely to behave once it is widely believed that Iran has such a capability.

Tehran's drive to acquire a nuclear capability creates two different threats to the vital interests of the United States. The first, and most direct, is the threat that a nuclear-armed Iran will believe that it is no longer vulnerable to American conventional military retaliation and so could revert to the aggressive, anti-American, anti–status quo foreign policy it pursued in the 1980s and early 1990s.[9] This consisted of energetic efforts to back terrorist groups from Hamas and PIJ to their traditional allies in Hizballah; incitement of such terrorist groups to undermine the U.S.-brokered Middle East peace process; efforts to subvert or overthrow the governments of American allies in the region; and material and moral support to other governments willing to oppose the United States and its allies, like Libya, Sudan, and Syria. Iran abandoned this policy in 1996 because Tehran sensed that it had overstepped, drawing the wrath of Egypt and the Gulf Cooperation Council states, a conviction for murder (assassination) tied to Iranian Supreme Leader 'Ali Khamene'i by a German judge, and the threat of American conventional military retaliation for the bombing of the Khobar Towers housing facility in Saudi Arabia, which left nineteen Americans dead. Some Iranians have suggested that they want nuclear weapons so that they never again have to fear American retaliation.[10] If that is the case, it could mean that once they have a nuclear arsenal, they will resume their efforts to drive the United States out of the region with terrorist attacks, subvert or dominate the Gulf states, attack Israel and the conservative Arab states of the region, and forge a new alliance with other radical anti–status quo nations and terrorist groups. If possession of a nuclear weapon (or merely the perception thereof) emboldened Tehran to ramp up its anti–status quo activities, this would increase the internal threats faced by many of the Arab states and constrain our ability to act in the region and could easily lead to a series of nuclear crises between Iran and the United States (or Iran and Israel), all of which would be very dangerous for American interests in the Middle East.

Nor is the confusion over Tehran's motives terribly reassuring. Even if the Iranians want nuclear weapons (or merely the capability to produce them) only for defensive purposes now, once in possession of them they might come to see them as enabling offensive actions. To some extent, this is what happened with Pakistan. Pakistan originally sought nuclear weapons to deter an Indian attack, but once the Pakistanis acquired them they decided that they were so effective as a deterrent that they could ratchet up their insurgent operations against India in Kashmir—which sparked the Kargil crisis of 2000 and nearly led to an Indo-Pakistani war.

The second dangerous effect of Iranian nuclear development would be to spur further proliferation, both in the region and around the world. Because many countries fear that once Iran acquires nuclear weapons it will pursue an aggressive foreign policy, if and when Tehran crosses the nuclear threshold, other Middle East countries, particularly Saudi Arabia, might decide to follow suit to deter an Iranian attack (covert or overt). Those outside the region considering whether to acquire nuclear weapons could draw the lesson from the Iranian case (and the North Korean and Pakistani cases) that the penalties for developing a nuclear weapon are bearable—and much less than they might have feared.

As a final point on Tehran's nuclear program, and an important note of balance in assessing it as a threat, the fear that Iran might give nuclear weapons to terrorists tends to receive too much attention. Iran has possessed chemical and biological weapons since the end of the Iran-Iraq War, and if it had wanted to, it could have provided them to any of the different Hizballahs it has spawned; to Hamas, PIJ, or any other Palestinian rejectionist groups; or to any of a half-dozen other groups. It has never done so. It has never done so because it has never believed that these groups required such weapons and because it feared that if their use were ever traced back to Tehran, the retaliation it would suffer would outweigh any gains

from the attack itself. In the past, Iran's skilled intelligence operatives have been able to maintain some degree of plausible deniability
for at least some time after many of its terrorist attacks. However, in
the aftermath of a nuclear terrorist attack, the victim—and its allies—
would probably not be too concerned about how good the evidence
linking it to Tehran was. Moreover, so unforgivable a crime would
not have a statute of limitations. Whenever Iran's hand was discovered behind it—and in every case in the past, Iran's hand was eventually proven—Tehran would have hell to pay.

Thus it is hard to imagine why Tehran would want to give nuclear
weapons to a terrorist group except in extreme circumstances, when
the regime itself was threatened by outside attack and this was the
only means at its disposal to stave off the coup de grâce. Iran's support for terrorism has been entirely instrumental—they are not nihilists like the Japanese Aum Shinrikyo, nor do they want to kill huge
numbers of their enemies as al-Qa'ida does. In virtually every scenario imaginable, Iran's need for nuclear deterrence—or even nuclear blackmail, if it were feeling offensively inclined—would be
better served by having a nuclear force deliverable by its own ballistic
missiles, which is precisely the route it seems to be pursuing. From
Tehran's own perspective, giving nuclear weapons even to its most
faithful servants, like Lebanese Hizballah, makes no sense.

Prospects for Regime Change

Everywhere else in the Middle East, the United States should be
pursuing a policy of encouraging reform to *prevent* radical regime
change and diminish the anger of the people at the current regimes.
Iran is arguably the great exception to that rule. American interests
would probably not be hurt by radical regime change in Tehran and
could easily be helped by it, since it is hard to imagine that whatever
regime overthrows the current one would somehow be *more* anti-
American. Throughout the Arab world, the regimes are (mostly)
pro-American and the people are mostly anti-American. In Iran, the
regime officials are largely anti-American, vehemently so in many
cases, whereas the populace is largely pro-American. Consequently,
any popular revolt in Iran would likely bring to power a government

better disposed to the United States than the current one. Thus, there is no particular reason for the United States to be encouraging—let alone helping to enable—reform in Iran.

Instead, at least in theory, the United States should be encouraging the demise of the Iranian regime. In virtually every scenario imaginable, that would benefit the United States both by removing a regime that has often defined its own foreign policy as being in opposition to the United States and often attempted to fan the flames of internal unrest in the Arab states.

The problem is that regime change in Iran is unlikely in the foreseeable future and almost certainly would be hurt by American efforts to encourage it; any such efforts would undoubtedly provoke the Iranian regime to react more aggressively, looking to hurt us in areas we cannot afford, specifically Iraq (and to a lesser extent Afghanistan).[11] The Iranian people do want a different regime, but they have so far proven unable and unwilling to seriously threaten this one despite having had several opportunities to do so. American involvement in internal Iranian affairs has typically been the kiss of death for any group we have tried to support because of deep-seated Iranian anger at American meddling in Tehran's affairs dating back to our role in the overthrow of Iran's popular prime minister Muhammad Mossadiq in 1953. And although the theocratic regime has consistently demonstrated the ability to defeat internal threats easily, it is also hypersensitive to even the rumor of American efforts to trigger an internal revolt and has typically lashed out in response to any perceived threat—for instance, by mounting the attack on the Khobar Towers housing complex, probably in response to the publicly announced American decision to increase the U.S. covert action budget against Iran by $18 million in 1995.[12]

Consequently, the United States would be wise to relegate the pursuit of regime change in Iran to the back burner. This does not mean we should not treat the Iranian regime as we did that of the Soviet Union: hoping that someday it would be replaced, criticizing its abuses while it survived, but dealing with it pragmatically and focusing American policy on changing its behavior, not the regime itself. For instance, it is fine to continue American broadcasting into Iran to try to prevent the Iranian regime from manipulating and censoring information, as is its wont. Moreover, the United States should consistently criticize Iran's human and civil rights violations, as we did those of the USSR, and point out when the regime is deviating from democratic forms of government and the rule of law— especially since the regime claims to subscribe to both. But regime change should not be a principal component of U.S. policy toward Iran, and we should not sacrifice other foreign policy initiatives (on either Iran or some other aspect of Middle East policy) in pursuit of it.

Hold Out an Olive Branch

Since it is unlikely that the regime in Tehran will fall anytime soon or that the United States can take meaningful action to speed its demise, it is important for Washington to watch closely for any signs that the current regime is interested in a rapprochement. The logic of this is simple: Iran is an important spoiler in the region, undermining delicate structures, exacerbating problems, and looking for places to make trouble. If the United States and Iran, the most important status quo power and the most important anti–status quo power in the Middle East, can agree to diminish or end their confrontation, this will be the most effective way to get the Iranians to stop making trouble. The Iranians certainly understand this. In the past when they have attempted to reach out to us, under Presidents Ali Akbar Rafsanjani and Mohammad Khatami, they have indicated a willingness to rein in Iran's more troublesome behavior—like its support to Hizballah, Hamas, PIJ, and other terrorist groups. A reconciliation would inevitably have to include an agreement on Iraq and Afghanistan, as well as some resolution of Iran's nuclear program. Here as well, Iranian pragmatists and reformists have indicated a willingness to "accommodate" the United States on all of these issues, as Khatami's informal emissaries told us during the Clinton administration.[13]

Although such a rapprochement does not seem promising at the moment, it is not unthinkable at some point in the future. Iranians chafe at their isolation from the world and are furious about the state of their economy.[14] Many seem to understand that the various international sanctions against their country (including the unilateral American sanctions) have contributed to their economic problems, and they know full well that only massive trade, aid, and investment from the international community can quickly revive their moribund economy. Indeed, President Ahmedinejad was elected on a platform of economic reform and anticorruption, and his failure to take meaningful action on either score, coupled with his repeatedly provoking the international community (and so adding to Iran's economic woes), has made his administration highly unpopular with key constituencies.

What this means is that Washington needs to consistently make public its desire for détente with Tehran even as it continues to turn up the heat on the Iranians by imposing ever-more-painful multilateral sanctions on their economy. We should remember that détente does not mean that we have to like the regime or approve of its actions (or vice versa, for that matter), as was the case with détente with the Soviets. We should be willing to state unequivocally that American sanctions against Iran will be lifted and U.S. support for UNSC sanctions withdrawn if Iran brings its nuclear program into compliance with the demands of the Security Council, ends its support for terrorist groups, and accepts Arab-Israeli peace accords that are amenable to the parties. We should also offer Iran generous economic incentives for agreeing to do so—not just the willingness to end the UNSC sanctions and World Trade Organization membership that the Bush administration has proposed, but major positive incentives like investment guarantees, trade credits, and aid from international financial organizations.

Convincing the Iranian regime to give up its most radical, anti–status quo policies is going to be very difficult. Iran's hardliners will never agree to it; they would have to be overruled by Iran's supreme leader, 'Ali Khamene'i, who is reportedly deeply suspicious of the United States and very nervous about his right flank, and who prefers to give all factions half a loaf rather than side decisively with one against another. Getting Khamene'i to go against his instincts and his preferred method will require presenting Iran with stark and clear choices: isolation and destitution if it sticks with the hardliners, acceptance and real prosperity if it is willing to change course.

And both because the hard-liners are very powerful and the Iranian people are very proud, only if both the penalties for continued recalcitrance and the benefits of acquiescence are huge are they likely to push Iran's populace and Khamene'i in the right direction.[15] Indeed, although the Bush administration has been quite diligent about threatening very big penalties for noncompliance, it has been frustratingly stingy about promising major rewards if Iran changes course.

Some have argued that the imposition of sanctions on Iran, both unilaterally by the United States and multilaterally by the U.N. Security Council and/or "coalitions of the willing," makes it less likely that Iran would be willing to negotiate an end to its nuclear program, let alone its other anti-American and anti–status quo activities. They may be right, but it is impossible to know. Moreover, there are at least three good reasons to continue to sanction Iran's economy. First, there is evidence that the sanctions have sparked a debate among the Iranian leadership, with more pragmatic figures arguing for concessions in return for a lifting of the sanctions. This is precisely what the sanctions were intended to produce, so this constitutes some evidence that they are having the desired effect. Second, whether they convince the Iranians to negotiate or not, they are critical to making clear to Iranians and other would-be proliferators that defying the international community comes with a heavy price attached, and that is critical to shoring up the crumbling global nonproliferation regime. Third, even if the sanctions do not cause Tehran to change its behavior, they are critical for laying the foundation to contain a nuclear Iran in the future (discussed at greater length below).

Finally, in making clear our desire for better relations with Tehran and the prospect of a deal in which the Iranians give up the dangerous components of their nuclear program, their support for terrorist groups, and their opposition to an Arab-Israeli peace in return for the West lifting all sanctions and instead providing economic benefits, the United States should not be particular about the modalities of the conversation. If the Iranians indicate that they would like to sit down with the United States and negotiate a "grand bargain" that encompassed all of the different aspects of U.S.-Iranian differences, we should be ready to do so. On the other hand, if the Iranians want to discuss things piecemeal, either dividing them up into discrete subjects or taking a step-by-step approach in which we begin with immediate concerns and only then move on to longer-term considerations, that should also be acceptable. If the Iranians want to use the dialogue over Iraq as a starting point to address other issues, we should accept the invitation. If the Iranians want to meet with us directly, that should be fine, but so too should it be if the Iranians prefer to continue to use the European states and others as intermediaries. It is going to be hard enough to get the Iranian regime to take any of these steps, and we should not make things even harder by demanding that things happen in a certain way. When it comes to changing Iran's problematic behavior, the United States should focus on the product and not get worked up about the process.

Beware the Military Option

So far, what I have described above could be considered the proactive elements of a new strategy toward Iran. Since there is little likelihood of changing the regime, the United States should be looking to remove the threat that Iran presents to the Middle East (and America's interests therein) by attempting to reach a set of simple agreements that would result in Tehran's changing its behavior on key issues that threaten American interests. Though this is hardly a lost cause, neither is it a sure thing. Iran has some compelling strategic reasons to acquire a nuclear weapons capability, and its adherence to an anti-American, anti–status quo foreign policy is rooted deeply in both the revolutionary ideology of the current regime (which some Iranian leaders continue to espouse) and more traditional Iranian nationalist aspirations. Moreover, the hard-liners who oppose any accommodation with the United States and our allies in the region (from Saudi Arabia to Egypt to Israel) are a powerful faction who have often been able to quash any move to improve relations with Washington, even if they have not always gotten the kind of ultra-aggressive foreign policy many of them have demanded.

There is, of course, another "offensive" option intended to eliminate the Iranian threat: military operations to obliterate Iran's nuclear program and/or its terrorist support facilities. Certainly American air power can destroy any target in Iran, as long as we are willing to mount a sustained air campaign with thousands of combat sorties over days, if not weeks, to tear up Iran's air defenses, strike all targets, reconnoiter the damage, and then restrike those targets not fully destroyed.

The problem is that this is not a very good option.[16] First, because the Iranians have demonstrated a capacity to hide even large nuclear-related facilities from Western intelligence, we cannot be certain that we know about every facility Iran has. As was the case with Iraq during the 1991 Persian Gulf War, we might not know about entire Iranian nuclear facilities and so might not set the program back much. Along similar lines, given how much the Iranians now know about nuclear enrichment, even if we did raze their entire program to the ground, they could reconstitute it and be back in business quickly. Some experts have estimated that it might take Iran only two to four years to rebuild to prestrike levels unless the United States were willing to keep striking Iranian facilities whenever it started reconstruction. Second, although Iranian public opinion is difficult to predict, it seems most likely that an unprovoked American attack on Iran's nuclear facilities would outrage the vast majority of Iranians (and most of the world) and cause them to rally around the worst elements in the regime, cementing hard-line control of the country and potentially producing an even more paranoid and aggressive Iranian regime that would be far more dangerous to deal with.

Last, we must assume that Iran will retaliate in some way. They could mount terrorist operations against American targets directly, and we should never forget that the Iranians are far more experienced and skillful than al-Qa'ida. More likely is that they would do exactly what some Iranian officials have already threatened to do: go after American targets in Iraq and Afghanistan. Given how delicate the situations in both of those countries are, the last thing we need is for the Iranians to ratchet up attacks on Americans and our allies in either one. We can't afford to lose Iraq or Afghanistan in pursuit of the ephemeral gains of air strikes against Iran. So the military option has little to recommend it, at least at this time, as an "offensive" strategy for dealing with the problem of Iran and its nuclear program.

Fall Back on Containment

Given the potential for a diplomatic approach (either a "grand bargain" or continued reliance on "carrots and sticks") to fail and the poor cost-benefit calculus of military operations against Iran, it would be prudent for the United States to also adopt a "defensive" strategy as a fallback position. That strategy would have to be a form of containment, if only by default. Especially if Iran does cross the nuclear threshold, the United States is not going to have too many good ways to subvert or attack Iran, and if Tehran is not interested in a negotiated deal or a rapprochement of some kind leading to improved relations, containment will be the only option left.

As in the Cold War, the core of a containment strategy toward Iran would be an effort to inhibit Iranian aggression through deterrence. Our history with Iran suggests that this regime can probably be deterred from using its nuclear arsenal. Although willing to tolerate very high costs when core interests are threatened, key members of the regime have also demonstrated that they will concede in the face of very heavy damage and are often unwilling to incur even more modest damage when their core interests are not threatened. Ultimately, Khamene'i is not Khomeini, who believed that he had a God-given mission and was turned from his path only by truly catastrophic levels of damage to Iran, as at the end of the Iran-Iraq War. Although deterring a nuclear-armed Iran does seem possible, it is not guaranteed, and it will not happen by itself. The United States will have to make a considerable investment to make it work, probably similar to our efforts to deal with North Korea for the past fifty years. If we are willing to make that effort, deterrence can become the cornerstone of a new strategy for containment of Iran.

Beyond deterrence, the United States will have to try as best it can to prevent Iran from expanding its influence, making mischief in the region, or otherwise harming American interests by taking action in the following areas.

- **Economic.** If the Iranians are unwilling to meet the Security Council's demands on their nuclear program, especially after Iran acquires an enrichment capability (let alone actual nuclear weapons), it will be critical to maintain the maximum pressure on Iran's economy through sanctions. These sanctions should have three objectives: (1) to prevent Iran from acquiring the economic and conventionanl military strength to be able to make trouble in the region; (2) to keep pressure on Iran's Achilles' heel, its economy, in hope that eventually the regime will come around, just as Libya eventually did; and (3) to make clear to other would-be proliferators that there is a real price to be paid for flouting the will of the international community in hope of dissuading them from following Iran's lead.

- **Military.** In spite of my caution against precipitous use of military options, it will be important, especially if and when Iran acquires a nuclear weapons capability, for the United States to lay out a clear set of "red lines" for Iranian actions that would trigger an American use of force—like attacking any other country in the region, moving uniformed Iranian personnel into Iraq, interfering with the flow of oil from the GCC states, supporting any act of terrorism against the United States, and providing nuclear-related materials to any other country or group. As we learned during the Cold War, clearly communicating to your adversary what actions you consider a threat to your vital interests can be very helpful in avoiding unintended crises and garnering international support in the face of deliberate provocations. In part to enforce these red lines, the United States may need to reconfigure its forces in the Persian Gulf region (which have been focused mostly on containing, then invading, and then rebuilding Iraq) to better deal with Iran. This would also include the need to interdict contraband being shipped to Iran, the ability to deal with renewed Iranian aggression, and the maintenance of forces in place to execute air strikes if the intelligence ever became available to do so and the cost-benefit considerations shifted decisively.

- **Diplomatic.** Closely tied to the military moves, the United States will have to reassure the other states of the region, particularly the GCC states and Iraq (if it is a functional country), that the United States will defend them against an Iranian conventional or nuclear attack, just as we did Europe, Japan, South Korea, and Taiwan during the Cold War. This could include new alliance arrangements or defense pacts with regional states if they feel it necessary. At the same time, the United States would do well to reach out to Iran and attempt to bring it into either bilateral security discussions or a multilateral framework (like the Conference for Security and Cooperation in Europe) that included the GCC and Iraq, in which all sides could discuss security issues, devise confidence-building measures, and perhaps lay the foundation for arms control agreements.

As I noted at the beginning of this section, many of Iran's gains in recent years have had less to do with the Iranians' skill than with our mistakes. Consequently, a critical element of containing Iran in the future will be fixing the messes we have helped make and not making any more. It means stabilizing Iraq, Lebanon, and the Palestinian territories by helping build viable governments able to secure their territories and provide basic services and governance for their entire populations. The more chaotic these places are, the more Iran will be able to exploit that chaos. (This is another aspect of the challenges of withdrawing quickly from Iraq, although over the long term, Iranian involvement in an all-out Iraqi civil war could cripple Iran.) It also means not allowing new failed states, new civil wars, and new insurgencies to arise. Which in turn brings us back to the importance of reform among the Arab states of the Middle East. The best way to keep the Iranians from gaining a foothold in other countries of the region and stoking the fires of unrest is to eliminate the causes of the unrest in the first place. The unhappier the people, the likelier they are to listen to Iran and its agents in the region. The happier they are, the more likely they will be to tell Iran and its allies to get lost. Of course, as in the case of Iraq, the unfortunate paradox is that the fear of Iranian subversion growing all across the Arab world is liable to make the Arab autocrats less willing to embark on new reforms for fear that doing so will cause the kind of dislocation and unrest that Iran would likely try to exploit. This will be yet another challenge for the United States and its allies, and just as in the 1990s we tried to help Israel, Jordan, Syria, and the Palestinians take risks for peace, so in the future must we try to help the Arab regimes take risks for reform.

CHAPTER 16

THE IMPORTANCE OF THE
ARAB-ISRAELI CONFLICT

THERE WAS A TIME WHEN THE ARAB-ISRAELI CONFLICT WAS America's most important problem in the Middle East. During the Cold War, the Arab-Israeli conflict conjured up the specter of World War III at least twice: in 1956, when Nikita Khrushchev threatened to attack Britain and France for their landings at Suez, and in 1973, when the United States alerted its nuclear forces in response to Soviet moves to intervene on behalf of Syria and Egypt. Today, however, there is no risk of escalation to superpower conflict because there is only one superpower left—not to mention the fact that Egypt and Jordan have made peace with Israel—so there is little danger that war between Israel and the Arabs could mushroom into a global conflict. This makes it easy for some to dismiss the Arab-Israeli conflict as irrelevant. But that is a mistake. The Israeli-Palestinian conflict remains an important element in America's overall interests and policies toward the Middle East, just not necessarily in the same way that it once did.

During the 1990s, when I served as a member of the Clinton administration's Middle East team, we had a phrase we used to regularly intone both in public and in private among ourselves: "We can't want a peace agreement more than the parties themselves." Though it was a nice line and seemed like a simple statement of prudence, in retrospect I think it was wrong. Peace between Israelis and Palestinians would benefit them far more than it would us, but our need for it in some ways outweighs their own. For both the Israeli and Palestinian publics, peace with the other side is arguably the most important and volatile issue on their domestic political agenda, and what matters to their publics is the details of the accord—who gets what. To Israelis and Palestinians, the terms of the deal are far more important than the deal itself, which is why so many decades of negotiations have come to naught. For both sides, a peace agreement has both advantages and disadvantages, and the disadvantages (including in domestic considerations) have often ruled out making the kind of concessions that would secure peace. So in the end, both sides have been willing to live without peace if they can't get the terms they want, because the terms matter more to them than peace itself.

For the United States, however, the opposite is true. The terms are not terribly important. We obviously want the existence and security of Israel guaranteed and should also be firmly committed to seeing a viable Palestinian state, but Washington has repeatedly signaled (rightly) that any deal acceptable to the parties themselves would be acceptable to us. The reason for this is that the United States has a lot of interests in the region that would benefit from a resolution of the Israeli-Palestinian conflict, and since the terms of the deal are not an issue for American interests or even American domestic politics, there is no countervailing set of incentives that can overrule our foreign policy interests.

In other words, although peace between Israelis and Palestinians would not benefit us as much as it would them, we have no interests—foreign or domestic—that are served by the prolongation of the conflict. On the other hand, we do have a considerable number of interests that would be improved by its end, and, as long as the terms are acceptable to both parties, there is no particular disadvantage to the United States from any peace deal. No American interests are served by having the conflict drag on, whereas in many cases letting the conflict drag on is a better outcome for Israelis and/or Palestinians than agreeing to a deal unacceptable to their publics. So unlike the parties themselves, we can only gain from an Israeli-Palestinian peace treaty and have nothing to lose from one—or from Israeli-Syrian and Israeli-Lebanese treaties. For this reason, we absolutely *can* and often *do* want peace more than the parties themselves.

Why Peace Matters

Although you could compose a very, very long list of American interests that would benefit from an Israeli-Palestinian peace in some way or another, I am going to stick to the six most important reasons, several of which I have already touched on in previous chapters. The first, preeminent, and most obvious is that peace would greatly benefit Israel and the Palestinians. A real peace would ensure the security and existence of Israel as the only democracy in the Middle East and remove the Jewish people's search for a national homeland as a source of international conflict. It would also allow the Israeli people to devote their considerable talents toward prosperity and away from security. Peace would benefit the Palestinians equally if not more so. Their lives have been nothing but unhappy, thanks not only to their Israeli foes but also to their Arab allies, who have kept them in misery to serve their own ends, and to a rogues' gallery of Palestinian leaders, who have repeatedly put their own interests ahead of those they claimed to serve. As a people who believe that their nation should stand for justice in the world, Americans should see the creation of a viable Palestinian state as a blessing, even if only a moral or psychological one.

Second, peace between Israel and the Arabs would remove a source of tension in the region that can still threaten war (particularly between Israel and Syria). A central component of the grand strategy proposed in this book is for the United States to *dampen* external conflict and other sources of instability in the region to try to make possible a gradual, controlled process of internal reform (which would inevitably be destabilizing at some level) to create more robust, stable nation-states in the future that would be less susceptible to internal convulsion—thereby minimizing the threats of terrorism and catastrophic oil shocks. As our own experience in Iraq and Israel's 2006 experience with Hizballah demonstrated, wars often have very dangerous unforeseen consequences. In a region composed of unhappy populations, unpopular regimes, and a fragile but vital resource base, the United States should be trying to minimize the potential for volatile, unpredictable events. For instance, a new Israeli-Syrian war could lead to the collapse of the Ba'thist regime in Damascus. We may not like the Syrian regime, but there is real reason to fear that its collapse, especially in the context of a war with Israel, could open the way for an even worse successor or a chaotic civil war that would threaten its neighbors with the same problems of spillover that Iraq, Lebanon, and the Palestinian territories are already producing. Again, the risk of a new Arab-Israeli war may seem low, but the whole point of this new grand strategy is to try to minimize the threat of radical regime change and civil conflict in the region, and for the past sixty years external conflict has had a bad habit of causing or contributing to both.[1]

A third benefit of an Arab-Israeli peace to the United States would be to eliminate the ability of Arab leaders to use the Arab-Israeli conflict as an excuse not to engage in the kind of political, economic, and social reforms that their societies so desperately need. Of course, peace alone will not change this overnight: Egypt has been at peace with Israel since 1979, but its government continues to try to make Israel a scapegoat for its own stubborn refusal to reform. Still, that excuse is wearing thin among the Egyptian people, who increasingly recognize that there is little real threat from Israel.

Another American interest in seeing the end of the Israeli-Palestinian conflict is that the prolongation of the conflict regularly creates events that force the United States to choose between supporting our Israeli ally or being popular among the Arab publics. The most obvious example of this is whenever Israel retaliates for an act of violence by an Arab group—and at times overreacts. In most cases, the United States backs Israel in these situations—although less often and less completely than most Arabs and their apologists recognize. Whenever we do so, it feeds the anti-Americanism rampant in the region.[2] I am not suggesting that the United States should do otherwise. In most cases, I believe that support is warranted, although every case is different. The point is simply that peace between Israelis and Palestinians would eliminate most of these problems, meaning that the United States would not be called on to keep making this choice as often as it does.

There is also a relationship between the general phenomenon of terrorism in the Middle East and the perception of progress toward an Israeli-Palestinian peace treaty.³ It is worth pondering the simple fact that, as the noted Middle East expert Shibley Telhami relates, "The number of terrorist incidents in the Middle East declined every year during the second half of the 1990s, reaching its lowest point in the promising years of 1999–2000."⁴ When Middle Eastern publics believe that a peace process is moving ahead and will ultimately deliver justice and security for all sides, there will be fewer angry Arabs willing to join terrorist groups or provide them with the kind of passive support that is vital to terrorist operations. Of course, while terrorism anywhere in the region is ultimately deleterious to American interests (both because it breeds an atmosphere in which terrorism is seen as legitimate, and because even attacks on Arab regimes help destabilize those regimes), the link between American support for Israel and Salafi extremist attacks on the United States is less clear. Hatred of Israel is not the main grievance of the Salafi terrorists, as explained in chapter 9, but it is not irrelevant to their motives and objectives, and it does contribute to the atmosphere that leads some angry young Muslims to join Salafi terrorist groups and others to turn a blind eye to their recruiting and operations. Thus, to the extent that such anger can be mitigated by an Israeli-Palestinian peace treaty, it can only help diminish support for the Salafists, even if this alone does not lead to their ultimate eclipse.

The last reason I will mention that peace between Arabs and Israelis would benefit the United States is that many of our other policies toward the region, those specific to certain countries or issues, would also be helped by a resolution of the Israeli-Palestinian conflict. As noted, the more Arab publics believe that there is a peace process in place and making progress (and therefore that there is reason to believe that the Palestinians will get justice at some point in the near even though indeterminate future), the easier it is for their governments to do things we want them to do—including enacting painful political, economic, and social reforms. For instance, one reason Jordan's King Abdallah suddenly became very reticent about liberalization in 2001, despite his well-known commitment to the process, was that the outbreak of the al-Aqsa intifadah among the Palestinians was enraging his own population (a manifestation of spillover from a civil war) and he did not want to be seen as advocating "American-style" or American-demanded reforms at a time when his own people were angry at Israel and its American patron.[5] Indeed, the more Arab publics believe that the United States is not helping to make it possible for the Palestinians to achieve a viable state through peace negotiations with Israel, the more it plays into the argument of the radical Islamists that a conspiracy of Israel, the United States, and their own American-backed regimes are purposely trying to deny the Palestinians justice.[6]

And so there is indeed a "linkage" between the Israeli-Palestinian conflict and a great many other American policy initiatives in the Middle East (a notion hotly debated in Washington today). Many Americans (and some Israelis) argue that there is no logical reason why this should be the case because U.S. policies toward Iraq, terrorism, democratization, Lebanon, and so on have nothing to do with what is going on between the Israelis and Palestinians. Though that may be true at some level, diplomacy is often about linking logically unrelated things. For instance, China and Russia support Iran in its confrontation with the West over its nuclear program not because they think Iran should have nuclear weapons but because they want Iranian trade. The two issues have nothing to do with each other in a logical sense—in fact, the Russians and Chinese acknowledge that an Iranian nuclear arsenal would be a threat to them. But because they want to trade with Iran and Iran wants their diplomatic help with the West in return for that trade, the Russians and Chinese make it their business to drag their heels in the Security Council and block any sanctions that might be truly painful to Iran. As mentioned before, this is just how diplomacy works: to get something you want, you often have to give on something the other party wants, even if they have nothing to do with each other.

In this sense, "linkage" between the Israeli-Palestinian conflict and other American policies in the Middle East is a manifestation of common diplomatic horse trading: the Arabs want something from us to do something that we want them to do. The fact that these two things have no logical link is irrelevant. It has been another of the consistent failings of the Bush 43 administration that they have so often refused to engage in such deals. They have typically insisted that their policy was right (in all senses of the word) and therefore the other party should assist us because it was manifestly the just, moral, and correct thing to do. They compartmentalized policies, refusing to recognize that to get a country to do something we wanted—no matter how smart or right it was—often required agreeing to do something for them on an issue that was wholly unrelated to what we wanted but was important to the other country. The result was that we often got nothing. Given the importance of the Middle East, the threats to American interests it involves, and the magnitude of what will be required to eventually reduce or eliminate those threats, we cannot afford to make the same mistake. Even though there may be no logical connection between the Israeli-Palestinian conflict and our other policies in the region, if the Arab states need us to do something for them on the former so that they can be more helpful on the latter, we need to take that into account.

Thus, unfortunately, as former Assistant Secretary of State Martin Indyk once put it, "You can argue till you are blue in the face that there should not be any linkage [between the Israeli-Palestinian dispute and other American policies in the region], but the fact is that if the Arabs say that there is linkage, there is linkage." The Arab publics are unhappy about the unresolved Israeli-Palestinian divide, and they get unhappy at their own governments for being close to the United States because we also support the Israelis. This makes Arab governments skittish about supporting American policy initiatives in the region because it underlines those ties and further arouses popular animosity toward them. For the most part, the policies on which they beg off from aiding the United States are issues of secondary or tertiary importance as chapter 2 described, but they can't be entirely dismissed. Thus, we don't have to like it or even believe it makes sense, but linkage is a reality and one we are not likely to be able to change in the near term.

A Modest Agenda

It is not necessary for Washington to conclude a final peace between Israel and the Palestinians (although it is something for which we should all hope) to address most, if not all, of the interests enumerated above. The peace processes of the 1970s and the 1990s showed that simple progress is enough to help advance other American policy objectives in the region. This sets the bar pretty low for the United States.

There is one important caveat to that point. This is that American activity on the Israeli-Palestinian conflict, let alone the wider Arab-Israeli dispute, cannot become mere process for process's sake. As Martin Indyk has cautioned, it must be "process that leads to progress," even if it is gradual. If the people of the region come to see all of the activity as motion but not movement in the right direction, they will quickly sour on the whole process and resort back to the kinds of unilateral actions (and particularly violence) to solve their problems that will aggravate an already difficult and dangerous situation.

Moreover, it is neither necessary nor smart for the United States to demand, let alone force, either of the parties to make major concessions to achieve peace. It is not necessary because the outlines of a viable peace deal have been clear since the late 1990s and have been enshrined in a series of proposals and informal agreements, including the Clinton parameters, the Ayalon-Nusseibah agreement, and the Beilin–Abu Mazen plan. Such a peace agreement will almost certainly involve the Palestinians' receiving virtually all of the pre–1967 West Bank and Gaza (with territory swaps to compensate for small areas heavily populated by Israelis that would become part of Israel proper); capitals for both countries in their respective parts of Jerusalem; only a symbolic right of return for Palestinian refugees to Israel but full right of return to the new Palestinian state coupled with some form of financial compensation; effective demilitarization of the Palestinian state; and each side administering its own holy sites in Jerusalem with sovereignty shared or the issue deferred in some way.[7] Though the details matter a great deal to the parties and it is the details that have precluded an agreement since 2000, the broad outlines are clear to most Israelis, Palestinians, Americans, Arabs, Europeans, and others and so do not require tremendous pressure from the United States. Nor would it be smart for the United States to apply such pressure because any peace deal struck under duress would not last.

THE NEED TO PUSH ON ALL FRONTS AT ALL TIMES

It is crucial that the United States never simply give up on Arab-Israeli peace, because whenever it has done so, notably during the first six years of the Bush 43 administration, the situation got worse, violence increased, and the United States paid the price in a variety of arenas. As long as there is a broad sense in the region that there is progress toward peace, this alone typically ameliorates the problems, dampens violence, and helps the range of other American interests. In a sense, the peace process is like a shark: if it stops moving forward, it dies, and if you try to ignore it, it will bite you hard.

For that reason, one of the most important lessons to take from the experience of the 1990s, when we came closest to securing a comprehensive peace, is that all of the tracks need to be in play at the same time. Historically, the peace process has been broken up into negotiations between Israel and the Palestinians, the Syrians, the Lebanese, the Egyptians, and the Jordanians—with each set of negotiations being referred to as a "track." (Of course, the Egyptian and Jordanian tracks have already produced peace treaties, and the Lebanon track long ago became subsumed under the Syrian track.) At the international level, this means that both the Syrian track and the Palestinian track need to have something happening on them at all times and we cannot simply give up on one to concentrate on the other. If the Syrians think they are being ignored, they can sabotage the Palestinian track by aiding and encouraging Palestinian rejectionists to mount attacks either on Israel or on the Palestinian Authority. If the Palestinians think they are being ignored, they will simply resort to violence themselves. On the other hand, if both are making progress, it tends to spur both of them on because neither side wants to get its peace treaty second, because they assume that whoever is last will have the least leverage with the Israelis. Consequently, like so many things in the Middle East, progress toward Arab-Israeli peace can be either a virtuous cycle, in which progress spurs further progress, or a vicious one, in which problems create other problems.

The importance of pursuing multiple tracks simultaneously is also true within the issue of the Israeli-Palestinian negotiations.

Here the distinction is typically between final status negotiations meant to define the end state between Israel and Palestine and interim negotiations meant to improve conditions between them prior to a final treaty. During the 1990s, it was most often the case that we pursued these tracks *sequentially:* whenever one seemed to get stuck, we would shift and try to get negotiations going on the other. Although this was not a bad approach, what that experience really demonstrated was the importance of always conducting negotiations on both *simultaneously.* In this way, there are always negotiations going on about both sets of issues, obstacles on one can sometimes be overcome by progress on the other, and the leadership on all sides can shift emphasis whenever one seems to be making more progress, but it is not necessary to start again from scratch each time it becomes useful to shift emphasis.

Moreover, simultaneous negotiations hold out the possibility of making compromises on one track in order to secure them on the other. For both Palestinians and Israelis, it is very hard to make compromises on certain issues piecemeal because doing so would make it seem that they are giving up something for nothing. For instance, it is hard for Israeli leaders to agree to borders the Palestinians would accept and that would give the vast majority of the pre–1967 territories to Palestine, except in the context of a final status agreement, when they can show their people that in return for this they secured major concessions from the Palestinians on security and refugees. Likewise, it is very hard for Palestinian leaders to make compromises on the right of return for refugees outside final status negotiations, when they can show their people that in return they secured Israeli concessions on Jerusalem and borders. This argues for the importance of always having final status negotiations going on, even if they are not the primary focus of emphasis. They are just too important to be neglected, and, because they are the only outright solution to the Israeli-Palestinian dispute, they should never be suspended, so that there is always a sense of movement toward that end and reason to hope for a breakthrough. However, it may also sometimes be the case that one side or the other can make a minor concession on some immediate problem in return for the other side making a concession early (i.e., not necessarily making a concession they otherwise would not, just agreeing to sign up for it sooner than they otherwise would be willing to acknowledge) on the final status agreement.

BUILDING A VIABLE PALESTINIAN STATE

Because both progress on and the problems of the Israeli-Palestinian peace process are constantly mutating and evolving, it would not be possible or useful to try to suggest what the United States should be trying to do at the moment I am writing this book. However, there is one other specific point important enough to warrant mention in a book on grand strategy, and that is the need to build a viable Palestinian state.

At least since 2000, Israelis have complained that they do not have a Palestinian partner capable of agreeing to a deal that would be acceptable to them and then enforcing the terms of that deal after it is signed. Unfortunately, they are not wrong about that. The Palestinian Authority, the governmental structure created to administer Gaza and the West Bank and eventually become the government of a new Palestine, is divided, riven by corruption, and incapable of providing basic services to its people. As a government, it has little to recommend it. It is not capable of governing a Palestinian state, seeing that the Palestinian people are properly provided for, or securing its own territory to prevent the use of violence against Palestinians or Israelis. That does make it very difficult for such an entity to negotiate with the Israelis, let alone to make the kind of difficult compromises that will be necessary to secure a meaningful peace. It also makes it unlikely that such an entity could deliver on any promises made to Israel as part of that treaty—or any other deal.

All that said, the blame for this state of affairs lies as much with Israel, the United States, the European Union, the United Nations, and the Arab states as it does with the Palestinians themselves. In 2004, when Yasser Arafat finally died, everyone had a chance to build a Palestinian entity that could do all of the things that it could not while Arafat lived: make peace with Israel, end the violence against Israelis, efficiently administer the West Bank and Gaza, and provide the Palestinian people with the good governance necessary for them to build a prosperous and peaceful new state. Unfortunately, everyone failed to do so. Mahmud Abbas—Abu Mazen, as he is widely known in the Arab world—tried to step forward and do all those things, but no one would help him.[8] The other Palestinian leaders quickly fell to fighting among themselves, dividing up the spoils of Arafat's demise like thieves and petty warlords. The Israelis and the Bush administration demanded that Abu Mazen prove that he deserved their support before they would provide any meaningful assistance. With tragic and foolish myopia, they insisted that Abu Mazen demonstrate that he could control the Palestinians and prevent violence before they would give him any help to do so. But Abu Mazen needed Israeli, American, and other international support to consolidate power, which he needed to be able to control the violence and make peace with Israel. Instead, Israel, the United States, and other key international actors would provide that assistance only if Abu Mazen first shut down the violence and proved he was in a position to make peace with Israel.

The result was predictable (and widely predicted). Abu Mazen was unable to consolidate power, the Palestinian Authority was crippled, the Palestinian leadership was fragmented, the Palestinian people suffered, and when the United States insisted that they hold elections in January 2006—in the face of Palestinian and even Israeli pleas not to do so—the Palestinian people voted for the violent Islamist group Hamas. They did so not because they supported Hamas's policy of violence toward Israel and refusal to negotiate with the Jewish state but because they trusted Hamas to provide them with the good governance, services, and security that the corrupt, feckless, and powerless "government" of Fatah—Arafat and Abu Mazen's party—had so consistently failed to provide.[9] A poll conducted immediately after the election revealed that only 11.8 percent of those who had voted for Hamas had done so because of its political agenda. In fact, the same poll found that 66.3 percent of Palestinians still supported political negotiations with Israel despite the fact that this ran completely contrary to Hamas's political platform.[10] Another poll conducted by the Ramallah-based Near East Consulting Institute found that 84 percent of those surveyed on the

West Bank and Gaza Strip wanted a peace agreement with Israel and 73 percent wanted Hamas to "change its position on the elimination of the state of Israel," according to a report by Al Jazeera.[11]

It may be helpful to see the Bush 43 administration's handling of the Palestinians after Arafat's death as being similar, if not identical, to its handling of Iraq after the fall of Saddam and Lebanon after the Cedar Revolution. In all three cases, the fall of the autocratic ruler created a power vacuum and a failed state. Without Saddam and his chief henchmen, the Iraqi power structure collapsed. Without Arafat, the Palestinian leadership splintered. Without the Syrians, the Lebanese government was incapable of securing or governing its territory effectively. The result in all three places was the rapid and uncontrollable devolution of power to warlords of one kind or another. In Iraq, it was Shi'i militia leaders and Sunni tribal shaykhs (most of whom became leaders in the insurgency) who simply took over the streets. In Lebanon, the traditional confessional warlords—Maronite Christians, Druze, Sunni, and Shi'i Muslims (including Hizballah)—quickly reemerged as arbiters of their communities' fates. Among the Palestinians, it was a variety of Fatah "security" chiefs and Tanzim leaders, who established various fiefdoms, along with Hamas as a semicoherent military-religious entity similar to Hizballah in Lebanon and Jaysh al-Mahdi in Iraq.

In every place, the United States stood by and effectively did nothing while the power structure crumbled, nor did Washington do anything to quickly put into place an alternative power structure capable of securing the country, governing effectively, and providing for the people. Unable to turn to a legitimate government for these basic necessities, the people in all three countries turned instead to the warlords, and a plurality decided that the religio-military militias (Hamas, Hizballah, and JAM) were the least bad of those options. Indeed, it is not accidental that both Hamas and JAM have consciously emulated Hizballah's extensive social networks, economic and medical programs, and provision of other basic services to the community as a way of securing territorial control and the manpower they need both to further enhance their power and to prosecute their political-military agendas.

Recognizing the common pattern of mistakes in all three of these countries also helps illuminate the steps necessary to remedy them. What is desperately needed in all three places is (1) the provision of security across the country so that people do not need protection by or from the militias, organized crime, and other forms of violence that are widespread in all three societies; (2) the creation of new governmental institutions staffed by a professional civil service and able to provide good governance and basic services to the people so that they no longer have to look to the militias to provide them instead; (3) the gradual development of a new political system built from the bottom up by starting with local institutions and building up through municipal and provincial/regional government to a national level government, in which new political leaders can emerge and displace the warlords, zealots, criminals, and ethno-religious chauvinists who currently dominate in all three countries; and (4) a process of political reconciliation or mere accommodation that can heal the rifts that have emerged as a result of the fighting among the warlords in the power vacuum. Although such a process would have to be heavily tailored to the specifics of each country's circumstances, that is effectively what is required for all three. (The progress being made by the new American counterinsurgency strategy in Iraq derives from the fact that it is designed to accomplish items 1 and 3 on the list above, with 2 and 4 remaining major hurdles to be overcome.)

For the Palestinians, this will mean a long and painstaking process. It may require the introduction of an international security force capable of gaining control of the streets of Gaza and the West Bank while a new, national Palestinian police is created—effectively, as the United States finally began to do in Iraq in 2007 and as the newly expanded United Nations Interim Force in Lebanon is trying to do in Lebanon. In both of these cases there was a recognition that only an external force could provide the kind of neutral security necessary to regain control of the situation, enable new, apolitical indigenous security forces to be created, and end the violence among the militias, warlords, and crime lords.[12] If no international force is going to be introduced, outside powers will have to make a major effort to build a new, professional Palestinian police force capable of doing so, which will be very difficult if the police are forced to try to quell the violence and regain control over the territories at the same time that they are being recruited, equipped, vetted, and trained. Either way, such improvements in security are the vital precondition for making progress on any of the other inadequacies of the current Palestinian political and economic infrastructure.[13]

As in Iraq, the international community not only will have to provide all variety of economic assistance to the Palestinians but will also have to undertake a major program to develop the capacity of Palestinian governmental institutions. Both are necessary to allow a new Palestinian government to supplant Hamas (and Fatah and other militias) as the primary benefactor of the Palestinian people. It could mean creating new NGOs (possibly international NGOs) and furnishing them with adequate resources to provide the Palestinian people with basic services and necessities, coupled with microloans and infrastructure development to jump-start the Palestinian economy and so remove Hamas's powerful appeal to average Palestinians, whom Hamas provides with jobs, money, food, medical care, and whatever else they need in return for their support.[14]

Finally, a great deal will rest on Israel's shoulders. First, the Jewish state will need to accept either an international force going into the territories to restore order or else allow considerable international assistance to enable the Palestinians themselves to build a much more capable security force able to achieve the security preconditions for a functional Palestinian government. Especially if it opts for the latter—politically easier but practically much harder—it is going to have to provide considerable assistance to try to dampen incentives for violence by Palestinian groups against Israel and one another. That could involve some very painful moves on Israel's part. For instance, Jerusalem would have to exercise greater restraint in retaliating for Palestinian violence so as not to inflame Palestinian sentiment, which in turn only plays into the hands of the extremists. Likewise, the Israelis might have to release key Palestinian prisoners, particularly Marwan Barghuti, a key Fatah leader who has the stature to reduce the violence but who also has been an important figure in terrorist attacks on Israelis. Israel will also have to be willing to keep releasing Palestinian tax money it collects and might have to do a number of other things to help boost the status of Abu Mazen or another moderate Palestinian leader struggling to build a Palestinian state able to govern its territory and make peace. For instance, the Israelis might have to dismantle some of their five hundred checkpoints on the West Bank, which greatly inconvenience and humiliate Palestinians trying to move around, and/or turn over additional territory on the West Bank to Palestinian control even before the signing of a final status agreement. Another useful action the Israelis could take would be to cut out the unnecessary harassment and inconveniencing of Palestinians at those checkpoints, much of which appears to be driven by sheer spite and enrages Palestinian farmers who have seen their produce spoil while waiting to get through a checkpoint and businessmen who have been unable to fill an order in time for the same reason. Another very useful—but also very painful—action that Israel could take would be to halt all construction of new settlements or expansion of existing settlements in the West Bank. This activity infuriates the Palestinians and strengthens the arguments of the extremists who claim that Israel has no intention of giving back the West Bank.[15]

Nevertheless, today the greatest problem on the Israeli side is that there are pitifully few Israelis who believe they have a real partner for peace among the Palestinians: those Palestinians who are willing to make peace seem too weak to deliver, while those strong enough to deliver seem to have little desire for peace. This is why it is critical for the United States to lead an international effort to build up the capacity of the Palestinian Authority, to empower the moderates who seek peace and simultaneously punish the extremists who oppose it. Only then will the desire for peace reemerge among the majority of Israelis, and when that happens, changes in Israel's own political landscape will inevitably follow. Though Americans should want to do this out of nothing but goodwill toward both Israelis and Palestinians, the truth is that ending the Israeli-Palestinian conflict (and the larger Arab-Israeli conflict) would be a considerable boon to our country's many vital interests in the region.

CHAPTER 17

OTHER SECURITY PROBLEMS

ALTHOUGH THE PROBLEMS OF IRAQ, IRAN, AND THE ARAB-Israeli confrontation loom largest as challenges to American interests and to the implementation of a grand strategy of enabling reform across the Muslim Middle East, they are hardly the only troubles we face. If Iraq, Iran, and the Arab-Israeli dispute are the "big three" of the Middle East, there is a second tier of problems that are only slightly less important but tend to be overshadowed by the first group. In a very real sense, not only the resources but also the attention and patience of American policy makers (and the American public) are finite, and so much is devoted to the highest priority issues that little is left for these second-highest-priority problems. That is unfortunate, not only because they are important—indeed, even tragic—but because several of them have the potential to explode into much bigger problems if they are not cauterized, while others might actually aid both other subregional policies and the core goal of the grand strategy if handled properly.

This chapter briefly examines five of these second-tier problems: Lebanon, Syria, Libya, Sudan, and a new security architecture for the region.

Lebanon

Lebanon is a very small country, but because of its history and its geography it casts an outsized shadow over American interests in the Middle East. Syria continues to see Lebanon as a "wayward province," stripped from it by the French after the First World War. The Ba'th in Damascus covet Lebanon for its prosperous economy, dynamic population, and great port of Beirut and because they wish to control the deep economic and social ties between Lebanese and Syrians. For its part, Israel's interest in Lebanon skyrocketed after PLO fighters found sanctuary in southern Lebanon in the early 1970s and used it to mount terrorist operations against the Jewish state—a problem that has persisted in the decades since, although Hizballah displaced the PLO as Israel's principal antagonist in the 1980s. Lebanon's proximity to Jordan means that developments in Lebanon can also affect the Hashemite kingdom. Of greatest importance, civil strife in Lebanon, such as engulfed the country in 1975–1990 and flared up again during the period after the 2005 Cedar Revolution, has consistently caused spillover into all three of these countries. Israel and Jordan are close American allies, whose security is important to American interests, while Syria is an important American adversary but one that bridges the gap between the Arab-Israeli conflict and the turmoil of the Persian Gulf region.

Since 1943, the Lebanese government has been a confessional democracy, in which power was apportioned among the main religious groups according to the 1932 census, when Christians were a narrow majority. The system was modified slightly by the 1989 Ta'if Accords, which paved the way for the end of its civil war. As a result, the Lebanese president and the chief of staff of the armed forces are always Christians, the prime minister and the minister of the interior are always Sunni Muslims, and the speaker of the Parliament is always a Shi'i Muslim. The seats in the legislature are further apportioned, 50 percent to the Christians and 50 percent to the Muslims. So that no one can reliably challenge this delicate sectarian balance, Lebanon has scrupulously avoided conducting another census since 1932, although the CIA (and most other sources) estimate that the population today is probably 40 percent Christian and 60 percent Muslim.[1]

Lebanon's political system is the first of several reasons for its importance to the United States. As it is the only Arab democracy (or "protodemocracy") and a truly multisectarian state, what happens in Lebanon can influence people's thinking throughout the region.

Moreover, Lebanon's unique cultural heritage—as a descendant of the Crusader states of the Middle Ages—has bound it closely to the West, particularly to France but through the French also to the United States. Washington attempted to come to Lebanon's aid in 1958 and again (unsuccessfully) in 1982–1984. For these reasons as well, Lebanon's fate reflects on the United States in ways that the fates of other Middle Eastern nations do not. If Lebanon is seen as prospering, it conveys a sense that Western notions of governance, economy, and even society can work in the Arab context; it is also seen as a sign of the power and influence of the West in the Middle East. The opposite is also true: if Lebanon is seen as faltering, this casts doubt in many minds upon the feasibility of democracy and free-market economics in the Arab world, as well as on the American commitment to its allies in the Middle East.

The Lebanese Civil War came to an end in 1989–1990 only because all of the other countries with an interest in Lebanon (including Israel and the United States) agreed to allow the Syrians to fill the security vacuum that had existed since 1975. Damascus did so by crushing the forces of the Maronite warlord Michel Aoun, the last Lebanese leader willing to stand against them. Of course, the price for the stability the Syrians brought was their subversion of Lebanon's democratic political system and free-market economy, an onerous state of affairs that was brought to an end only in 2005.

In that year, the Syrians overstepped themselves by (likely) assassinating former Lebanese Prime Minister Rafiq Hariri—a Sunni Muslim and close friend of French President François Mitterrand. Hariri's assassination unleashed the Lebanese people's anger at the Syrians, which spilled out into the streets in the form of the Cedar Revolution. With U.N. Security Council action hanging over its head, the Syrian regime retreated, agreeing to withdraw its troops from Lebanon. Unfortunately, as I noted earlier, the United States, the European Union, and the larger international community then made a terrible mistake. Instead of moving quickly to provide massive aid to the Lebanese government after the Cedar Revolution— perhaps including an international peacekeeping force to give the government time to train an army capable of taking over from the Syrians—the Bush administration and its foreign partners declared victory and went home. In so doing they allowed the same old security vacuum to open up—a vacuum the Lebanese government has been unable to fill completely. Inevitably, Hizballah filled the gap by using its military capability to make itself a political power, one able to block action by the rest of the Lebanese government. The swagger that came with this new political power led it to provoke the Israelis, erupting in the 2006 Summer War between Israel and Hizballah. In truth, both sides lost that fight, albeit in different ways, but the Israelis were more badly humiliated, and so lost more, than Hizballah.

In addition, despite their humiliating withdrawal in 2005, the Syrians did not give up on Lebanon entirely. Damascus backed Hizballah to the hilt, connived with other Lebanese politicians to split the Maronite and Sunni camps, and began a campaign to assassinate prominent Lebanese politicians who opposed Syria's wishes. By 2007, Syria had once again made itself a major player in Lebanese affairs, although it exercised its influence more indirectly than in the past.

A MANY-LAYERED PROBLEM

Broadly speaking, America's concerns in Lebanon can be broken down into three sets of issues: short term, medium term, and long term. The short-term requirement is to prevent Syria from continuing to meddle in Lebanon's affairs, including by murdering opposition politicians. Simply put, Syria's backing of Hizballah and its willingness to kill Lebanese politicians who won't kowtow to Damascus is subverting Lebanon's bid to regain its independence and restore its democratic system. Because the United States should be supporting both self-determination and democracy throughout the Middle East and because of our long-standing commitment to Lebanon, it is simply unacceptable for Washington (and the rest of the international community) to stand idly by while Syria reasserts its stranglehold over Lebanon. The rest of the region is watching to see how willing the West is to support the nascent restoration of democracy in Lebanon, and therefore allowing Lebanon to succumb to Hizballah, Syria, and other antidemocratic forces will have repercussions for political reform elsewhere in the region. However, doing so will require the United States to lead an international coalition to put tangible pressure on Syria to force Damascus to back down on what it considers a critical interest.

Our medium-term goal should be to help build the capacity of the Lebanese government, including its security services, so that it can fill the security vacuum in the country, prevent Hizballah and other groups from employing violence (either internally against other Lebanese or externally against Israel), and provide the people with basic services so that they do not have to rely on Hizballah or other sectarian militias to do so. As in Iraq and the Palestinian territories, the Lebanese state is so weak that the government lacks the ability to provide either basic security (and justice) or basic services to all of its people. Hizballah, and to a lesser extent other militias, exploit this, giving them military, economic, and ultimately political power sufficient to challenge the authority of the government (which it sometimes does in pursuit of the interests of its Iranian and Syrian allies). After the 2006 fighting the Bush administration and the European Union recognized their mistakes, deployed a beefed-up force of UNIFIL peacekeepers (without American troops) and considerably increased their economic and security assistance to the Lebanese government.[2] This aid has already had some impact, allowing Lebanese Army forces to move against a notorious Salafi terrorist group that had set itself up in one of Lebanon's Palestinian camps. However, the government and its security forces are still a long way from being able to take on Hizballah fighters in pitched battle or replace the social services that Hizballah and other groups provide their Lebanese constituents.

Finally, America's long-term consideration in Lebanon must be to help the Lebanese reform the 1943 National Pact and the Ta'if Accords to create a new political system accepted by all of Lebanon's various communities. The current constitution, which favors certain sectarian groups at the expense of others, no longer reflects Lebanese demography, creating considerable unhappiness among underrepresented communities, particularly the Shi'ah, who believe themselves to be a plurality in the country but have the least power in the government. More to the point, Lebanon's confessional system reinforces the divisions throughout the country, making effective compromise difficult and encouraging disputes across the communities.

If Lebanon is to emerge as a stable, prosperous democracy in the future, it will probably be necessary for the Lebanese to overhaul their political system and put into place a new one that is not based on confessionalism. That will probably require decentralizing some power to local authorities to allow all of the country's many communities to manage more of their affairs themselves, without the interference of a central government dominated by another group or constant mediation and compromise among various groups. It will mean a new electoral system and a greatly strengthened judiciary and security services able to assert the rule of law in the face of challenges from various sectarian militias. Not surprisingly, it will require many of the same things that the new American strategy in Iraq is attempting to put in place.

Solving Lebanon's multitiered problems is not going to be easy. The Syrians are not going to unwind their tentacles from around Lebanon without a knock-down, drag-out fight because they regard possession of Lebanon as crucial to their own well-being. Securing the country and building governmental capacity sufficient to meet all of the needs of its citizens for good governance and basic services is going to be very difficult, especially as long as the United States or some other great power is unwilling to furnish large military forces with the capability and the authority to smash Hizballah, drive it from the streets, and help establish the Lebanese government's control over its own territory. Operating within the framework of (even the expanded) UNIFIL and attempting to build government capacity from the outside are both very challenging undertakings. Last, convincing the Lebanese to take the great leap to open up the issue of their political system and the need to abandon confessionalism will be equally difficult. Addressing the first two problems would go a long way toward making many Lebanese feel comfortable taking this last leap, but even then many would fear that raising the idea of a revised political system and abandoning confessionalism will be like opening Pandora's box. Nonetheless, all of this will be necessary if Lebanon is ever to become the stable, prosperous Arab proto-democracy it once was so many decades ago, let alone move beyond it.

And that, in turn, is important for the furtherance of the overall grand strategy. If the United States can help Lebanon meet these challenges, it will send a powerful message to the rest of the region that positive change is possible, that democracy can flourish in the Middle East, and that the United States is ready to help in a sustained, meaningful, and progressive fashion. Naturally, the converse is also true: if the United States does not help and if Lebanon continues to degenerate into renewed civil strife, this will reinforce regional cynicism regarding American motives and fears about the prospects for positive, far-reaching change.

Syria

Syria is also too important and too troublesome to be ignored. In part like Lebanon, the greatest source of Syria's importance is simply its location. For millennia, the land of Lebanon and that of Syria were one state and their societies remain intricately intertwined. The meshing of Syria and Lebanon's economies and communities gives Syria tremendous influence on events in Lebanon. It also means that the Syrians worry that developments in Lebanon will affect their own society, which leads Damascus to interfere constantly in Lebanese affairs, most notably during the Syrian military intervention/occupation from 1976 to 2005. It is widely believed that the Syrian regime (or at least key figures in it) was responsible for the death of former Lebanese Prime Minister Rafiq Hariri in 2005. A U.N. investigation turned up considerable circumstantial evidence backing that supposition, but Syria has staunchly refused to cooperate with the U.N. commission or provide it with access to the Syrian officials suspected of complicity. The Hariri assassination triggered Lebanon's Cedar Revolution, forcing Damascus to withdraw the 25,000 to 30,000 Syrian troops who had garrisoned Lebanon. Although the troops left, it is widely believed that Syrian intelligence remains highly active inside Lebanon, attempting to empower groups like Hizballah that are closely allied with Damascus, while doing everything they can to undermine the March 14th Movement, the democratic opposition led by Hariri's son Saad that seeks to rid Lebanon of Syrian influence. By early 2008, eight prominent March 14th Movement parliamentarians had been assassinated, and their deaths were universally laid at Syria's doorstep.[3]

Syria's location also allows it to provide all manner of support to various Palestinian rejectionist groups operating from the West Bank and Gaza. Syria has threatened its weaker Jordanian neighbor periodically during the postwar era, including assassination attempts on King Abdallah's father, King Hussein, and a brief, dangerous Syrian invasion in 1970 in support of the Palestinian militants fighting King Hussein's government during Black September. Syria borders Turkey as well, and during the 1990s the two almost came to blows because of Syria's provision of support and sanctuary for the anti-Turkish Kurdish terrorist leader Abdullah Öcalan. Of course, Israel still holds the Golan Heights and there are periodic military skirmishes—which entail the constant threat of escalation to a wider conflict—including Israel's September 2007 strike against a purported Syrian nuclear facility at Dayr az-Zawr. Moreover, under Hafiz al-Asad, the Damascus regime carved out a niche for itself as the ultimate Arab nationalists, a claim that still garners some admiration on the Arab street and therefore infuses Syrian actions with a degree of symbolic importance beyond any practical impact. Syria is effectively the only state in the region that remains an ally of Iran, and while the extent of its active collaboration is unclear, there is still considerable tacit support. Finally, since the fall of Saddam, Syria has emerged as a prime conduit for foreign Salafi terrorists seeking to make their way to Iraq. Consequently, Syria is an important player in a great many of the most important issues of the Middle East—Iraq, Iran, and the Arab-Israeli dispute among them.

Strangely, Syria is also important because it is fragile. Syria is a dictatorship, ruled by the Syrian Ba'th Party, which to a considerable extent serves as a facade behind which Syria's Alawi Shi'ah minority (with about 15 percent of the population) controls the country. Not surprisingly, Syria suffers from all of the underlying political, economic, and social problems afflicting the other Arab states, to some extent worse than the others. Syria has a little oil (about 400,000 bpd of production), but it has nothing like the income of the Persian Gulf states or even Algeria or Libya. Unlike Egypt, Jordan, Morocco, and other countries without major oil supplies, it has not been able to count on aid of any kind from the United States or other Western states. Periodically, Saudi Arabia bribes Syria to get Damascus to do things the Saudis want it to (like join the 1991 Persian Gulf War coalition), but Saudi aid has been more sparing recently, initially because of the kingdom's own structural economic problems and later because Riyadh has been increasingly unhappy with the current Syrian leadership. Like Jordan, Syria is bearing the burden of being caught in the cross fire of three civil wars—Lebanon, Iraq, and the Palestinians. As a result, in 2005–2007 this country of 19 million people had to absorb roughly 1 million Iraqi refugees and another 400,000 Lebanese refugees, along with a smaller number of Palestinians. These refugees have exacerbated Syria's own ethnic and religious frictions among the Sunni Arab majority, the Alawi minority that runs the country, and the restless Kurdish population.[4]

Since the death of Hafiz al-Asad, Syrian policy making has been even more opaque, ossified, and inscrutable than in the past. His son Bashar has nominally succeeded to his father's position, but it is not clear to what extent he is actually calling the shots. He came to power promising sweeping reforms along the very lines I have advocated in this book but has done essentially nothing to enact them. Some of his father's cronies remain in important positions of power, and there is considerable speculation regarding the balance of power in Damascus. Some claim that Bashar really is a modern, progressive leader who desperately wants to "do the right thing" by ending Syria's support to terrorist and militant groups, making peace with Israel, improving its relationship with the United States, and reforming his country but is prevented from doing so by the "old guard" of his father's henchmen. Others contend that Bashar is no more enlightened than his father and that he is the one driving the Syrian train, although he conveniently blames his choices on that same "old guard." Whoever is making the decisions in Damascus, they are decidedly unhelpful to American interests and those of most of the states of the region.

Smoking Out the Syrians

America's interests in Syria are easily enumerated. The Syrian regime is itself one of the stagnant autocracies presiding over a corrupt, centralized economy that is failing to provide for its people and so breeding considerable anger and resentment. Despite the oppressive security imposed by the regime, it has periodically had problems with internal unrest, including a civil war led by its own Islamist opposition, the Muslim Brotherhood, in 1976–1982, which was put down only after the slaughter of 20,000 to 40,000 people. The replacement of this regime by one more willing and better able to meet the needs of the Syrian people could only make the Middle East a better, more stable place. Likewise, while we might celebrate the Syrian regime's demise, its collapse into civil war or its replacement by a militant Islamist regime could actually create even worse problems for the region. Syria's ongoing belligerency with Israel and its support for various militant and terrorist groups attacking Israel help legitimize terrorism as a means of political action in the region and create a constant, if mostly low-level, risk of war with Israel. Syria's interference in Lebanon raises both the risk of civil war there and the prospect that Hizballah will become the dominant player in Lebanese politics. At the very least, it appears highly unlikely that Lebanon can be stabilized and removed as a source of spillover and instability in the region as long as Syria is determined to prevent it. Similarly, while it is an exaggeration to claim that Syria's failure to prevent Salafi terrorists from transiting its territory to Iraq is a major cause of the problems in Iraq, it does exacerbate the problems there, and shutting this conduit down would help calm the worst source of mayhem in the region.

How should America approach the problem of Syria? For starters, as long as the Syrian regime continues to kill Lebanese opposition leaders, refuses to cooperate with the U.N. investigative committee, and provides aid to Palestinian militant groups, nonconfrontational options are not going to make much sense. These are very serious offenses and should be met with opprobrium from the international community and sanctions to compel changes in Syria's behavior.

At a broader level, however, the United States must develop an aggressive policy meant to force Damascus to show its true colors. We need to find out who is in charge there and whether they genuinely want a better relationship with Syria's neighbors, the West, and the wider international community. We need to find out if they are interested in the kind of reforms that Bashar al-Asad talks about—the kind of reforms that could alleviate Syria's internal problems. We need to find out whether Syria is willing to play a constructive role in Lebanon, make peace with Israel, shut down the pipeline of Salafi terrorists to Iraq, and more generally cease its efforts to overturn the regional status quo if it is given a real chance to do so.

Doing so will likely require developing a "carrots and sticks" policy similar to the one I have proposed for Iran. The idea would be for the United States to lead an international effort that would very clearly lay out a list of conditions regarding Syrian behavior—on Lebanon in general, toward the U.N. investigative committee, toward Iraq, on weapons of mass destruction, and so on. Those conditions would be tied to a series of sanctions for noncompliance and rewards for compliance, and both the sanctions (the sticks) and the benefits (the carrots) would have to be substantial enough to have a reasonable prospect of swaying the Syrian regime. The sanctions would have to be tough enough that if the Syrians were to thumb their noses at the rest of the world, they would pay a heavy price for doing so. Likewise, the potential rewards would have to be so beneficial that it would be hard for Damascus to turn them down—big enough that the Syrian people would be very unhappy if it did—and so the regime would have to take into account the potential for domestic disturbances if it rejected the deal.

At the very least, such a policy should allow us to "smoke out" the Syrian leadership. If Bashar al-Asad really is a Western liberal trapped in a Middle East autocrat's body and constrained by the rest of his leadership, this would give him powerful ammunition to fight against the old guard. It would allow him to make the case that Syria has to change its ways if it is going to prosper, not suffocate, and if the regime is not willing to do so it will risk widespread internal unrest. Moreover, if the Syrians *are* willing to change their ways, it is in everyone's interest, including our own, Lebanon's, and Israel's, that they be quickly and generously rewarded so that those Syrian leaders who argued in favor of choosing this course of action will be seen as having delivered tangible benefits right away. As others have noted, demonstrating to the Syrian regime and its people that there are worthwhile political and economic benefits from giving up its membership in the region's anti–status quo camp would make it far more difficult for the Iranians to pour fuel on many of the region's fires.

Without a Syrian partner, the Iranians would find supporting Hizballah, Hamas, and Palestinian Islamic Jihad considerably harder.

Even if Syria refuses such an offer, the outcome would still be helpful to the United States. If the list of things Syria is required to do is drawn up by an international coalition, it is likely that the terms will be reasonable to the Syrians. Thus, if Damascus refuses, it will be clear that the Ba'thist leadership simply has no interest in doing the right thing or becoming a responsible member of the international community except on terms that are unacceptable to the international community itself. The sanctions imposed would then become the basis for constructing an international containment of Syria meant to isolate it and prevent it from causing further mischief in the region. If the Syrians declared themselves unwilling to go along with the demands of the international community despite the offer of major benefits, they would effectively be declaring Syria a rogue state determined to overturn the status quo—something few members of the international community would condone. Thus it would make Syria's intentions clear, and that clarity would make it easier either to reward Syria for positive steps or to punish and contain it for negative ones.

Libya

Like Syria, Libya is a troublesome dictatorship with which the United States has more problems than just the need for it to make major reforms to head off the possibility of an Islamist revolution at some point in the future. Like Syria, Libya has been a major state sponsor of terrorism, pursued weapons of mass destruction, opposed American interests throughout the region, and attempted to destabilize friendly governments around the region—including a bizarre attempt to assassinate Saudi Arabia's King Abdallah while he was the crown prince (but already the day-to-day ruler of the kingdom) in 2003. But unlike Syria—or Iran, for that matter—in 2003–2004 Libya essentially surrendered. Muammar Qadhafi agreed to end his support for terrorist groups, give up his WMD programs, and otherwise discontinue his efforts to overturn the regional status quo and expand Libya's power in return for an end to international sanctions and other rewards. This, and this alone, makes Libya important for the prosecution of the overall grand strategy and for the harmonizing of America's other country-specific policies in the Middle East.

In effect, the Libyans took a deal similar to that which the United States has been offering Iran (however ham-fistedly) and that I am suggesting above that the United States ought to offer Syria at some point when it has stopped murdering Lebanese opposition leaders. This makes what happens between Libya and the international community (and particularly the United States) more important than it otherwise would be. The Iranians already recognize that the American carrot-and-stick approach (again, implemented only halfheartedly so far) is meant to prod them into accepting a version of the same deal as the Libyans. In fact, Iranian hard-liners have rejected any compromise with the West, insisting that Iran cannot be treated in the same way as a weak country like Libya. Whether it can or not remains to be seen, although it is certainly the case that it will undoubtedly take both bigger rewards and bigger threats to convince Iran to do so.

However, what is of greatest importance is that whatever conclusions Iranians draw regarding whether Libya benefited or suffered from having taken this deal will undoubtedly influence their own debate, even as they insist that it won't. If the Iranians conclude that Libya ultimately did well by agreeing to give up its WMD, support for terrorism, and other disruptive activities, this will certainly make it easier for Tehran to do the same. By the same token, if Iranian hard-liners are able to argue that the Libyans made a mistake by accepting the deal because they are worse off now than before (and especially if the Libyans believe this), it can only hurt any argument by Iranian pragmatists that a similar settlement would be in Iran's best interests. Should we get to the point where we are willing to lay out the same choices for Syria, the considerations drawn from their perceptions of the Libyan case will doubtless exert the same kind of influence in Damascus as in Tehran.

What this means is that America's handling of Libya has to be seen in the wider context of strengthening our hand with Iran and Syria, the two remaining "rogue" states of the region. The Libyans do not always abide by the terms of the agreement, and they sometimes do things that infuriate the United States. All of this makes American officials reluctant to reward Libya or even fully implement our part of the deal. This is understandable, but it is also probably a mistake. As troublesome as the Libyans are, Washington needs to keep its eyes on the real prizes in the region: Syria and Iran. Whatever our problems with Tripoli, they pale in comparison with the need to get Damascus and Tehran to agree to the same kind of deal that the Libyans did, and the best way to do so is to make sure that the Libyans are seen as having benefited from their decision to end their confrontation with the West.

Sudan

Like Lebanon, Sudan borders on being a failed state. There is at least a partial security vacuum. A civil war continues to rage there, and spillover from it is already affecting many of its neighbors. It should be self-evident that, as with Lebanon, Iraq, and the Palestinians, it is imperative that the security vacuum be filled, the state's capacity built up to the point where the government can provide for the needs of all of its citizens, and the parties to the civil war reconciled in some marginal sense. None of this should sound new, and so it does not bear a great deal of explanation. What makes Sudan *uniquely* important is the genocide currently going on in Darfur.

The United States is a signatory to the 1948 Convention on the Prevention and Punishment of the Crime of Genocide (more commonly known as the "Genocide Convention"). This document makes it incumbent upon all signatories to take "effective" action to prevent acts of genocide and punish those who commit them. The first article of the convention declares very simply, "The Contracting Parties confirm that genocide, whether committed in time of peace or in time of war, is a crime under international law which they undertake to prevent and to punish."[5] There are no loopholes, no extenuating circumstances or exemptions. If a government sees genocide taking place, it is its duty to take action to end it and punish those responsible for it. The Genocide Convention is an essential document of international law and of American foreign policy. It is the foundation upon which a great deal of human rights policy making rests because it asserts that national sovereignty does not super-sede human rights—in some cases, gross violations of human rights nullify the rights of sovereignty—and that all nations have a respon-sibility to take action to prevent the most egregious violations of human rights. In that sense, it asserts both the preeminence of human rights and the requirement for all nations to act to uphold them. If the Genocide Convention is not honored, there is little legal or practical basis to expect other nations to refrain from lesser abuses of human rights, let alone to take action to prevent them by other countries.

Seen in this context, the genocide in Darfur runs counter to core American values, long-standing American foreign policy practices, and global U.S. interests in seeing the advancement of human rights. However, it is also inimical to American interests in the Middle East. Genocide is, of course, the ultimate manifestation of repression. It is also, needless to say, a form of repression so extreme that it typically provokes resistance on the part of those being exterminated, which can quickly escalate into civil war, as it did in Rwanda. The failure of the international community to take action in Darfur contributes to the perception among Middle Eastern autocrats that they will face little but international finger-wagging if they engage in extreme acts of internal repression for their own reasons. Moreover, the corollary is probably even more salient: if the international community roused itself to take action to save the people of Darfur, this could cause Middle Eastern autocrats to think twice before waging similarly re-pressive campaigns against difficult domestic populations. Thus, both in pursuit of broader American values and interests and as part of a new grand strategy for the Middle East, the United States must take concrete actions to end the genocide in Darfur and bring those responsible for it to justice.

New Security Architectures

The twenty-first-century Middle East is decidedly not late-twentieth-century Europe, and for that reason, the analogy of the Cold War tends to obscure more than it reveals. However, there are lessons from the Cold War that can be applied to our efforts to craft a new grand strategy for the Middle East, and in a number of places in this book I have attempted to incorporate those lessons. Another useful lesson from the Cold War is the utility of arms control. Although archconservatives bad-mouthed arms control throughout its history, in the end even they came to appreciate its value. It was Richard Nixon, Ronald Reagan, and George H. W. Bush who negotiated the critical arms control treaties—SALT, the ABM treaty, START, and the Conventional Forces in Europe (CFE) agreements—that helped put an end to the crisis-filled early Cold War, allowed a far more stable late Cold War, and eventually engineered the international environment that made possible the peaceful collapse of the Soviet Union. These treaties were absolutely critical in reducing tensions and uncertainty between the superpowers and so heading off the confrontations, misperceptions, and overreactions that drove the terrifying crises of the early Cold War in Iran, Poland, Berlin, Cuba, and the Middle East. It is no coincidence that the most dangerous superpower confrontations effectively ended with the October War crisis of 1973, just as arms control between East and West began to come into its own. These arms control measures virtually eliminated the threat of inadvertent war and drastically reduced the likelihood of a deliberate attack. For all of those reasons, the United States would do well to contemplate how it might apply the lessons learned about arms control during the Cold War to the contemporary Middle East.

Of course, arms control did not come quickly to Europe, and it is not likely to come quickly to the Middle East. But it will never come at all if we don't start somewhere. The first lesson of the experiences of the Cold War was that the best way to begin down what is inevitably a long path is simply to get all sides talking. Having a forum in which adversaries can express their fears, have them answered by the other side, and simply get to know one another is a very useful start. If nothing else, it can dampen paranoia, so that a suspicious government does not react provocatively to actions by the other side that it simply does not understand. Over time, if the sides are honest with one another, it can create the basis for a minimal degree of trust, which can then pave the way for simple confidence-building measures. If all sides abide by such measures, it can open up the possibility of more meaningful agreements on arms limitations of one kind or another. Beyond that lies the possibility of actual arms *reduction* treaties. Even if discussions do not lead down that path, at least the parties know where they stand.

This history suggests the utility of having a regional security forum. Such a forum should include all of the states of the region, as well as external actors such as the United States that play an important role in regional security issues (as was the case in Europe). Its goal would be to have the participants raise their security concerns, exchange information, and, if there is goodwill, see their words turned into action in the form of tangible improvements in their safety and the aversion of crises or even war. The Conference for Security and Co-operation in Europe or the current incarnation of the Association of Southeast Asian Nations (ASEAN) would both make good models for the Middle East.

START IN THE GULF

In the 1990s, the United States actually tried to set up such a process, at least among the Middle Eastern states involved in the Arab-Israeli confrontation: Israel, Egypt, Jordan, Saudi Arabia, the GCC, and most of the North African states. Notably absent from this gambit were Syria, Iran, Iraq, Libya, and Sudan, the worst troublemakers in the region.[6] The effort (called the Arms Control and Regional Security initiative, or ACRS) was part of the Madrid peace process and after stumbling along for several years died altogether in the latter half of the decade. Its bane was a disagreement between Egypt and Israel over whether ACRS should include discussions of nuclear weapons. The fact that countries with a formal peace treaty were unable to make this process work should make us realistic about what can be accomplished in the region more generally. But it should not discourage us completely.

The ACRS experience suggests that the Arab-Israeli confrontation may not be the best place to start. The Persian Gulf might actually be better suited to such an effort and would likely benefit from it more.[7] Delving a bit deeper into the failure of ACRS is useful to understanding this. Another critical problem with that earlier effort was that the states involved in it did not have enough security issues in common. Most of the Arab participants in the ACRS process, especially the Gulf and North African countries, did not feel particularly threatened by Israel, and the Arab-Israeli conflict was not their major security challenge. For them, the absence of Iraq, Iran, Syria, Libya, and Sudan—their principal threats at the time—made the process irrelevant. In the jargon of political scientists, the states involved in the process did not constitute a discrete "security system" in which all of the members view the other members as their principal security threats and/or partners. The Persian Gulf, on the other hand, *is* a discrete security system. Iraq, Iran, and the GCC states all do see one another as their principal security problems and all will admit as much, at least in private and especially when the United States is included in the mix. Thus, key foes would be part of the forum, not excluded from it, and so all of the members could be confident that their most important security problems would be addressed.

The objective of a Persian Gulf security forum should be to create a standing organization of states willing to meet and discuss security matters in the expectation that regular conversation will help reduce risks and could lead eventually to an arms control process. This is effectively the CSCE model, which gradually changed the atmosphere between NATO and the Warsaw Pact to the point where a process of confidence-building measures and then arms control agreements became possible.

Such an approach has a lot to recommend it. For the GCC states, if a regional security organization succeeded in eventually defanging Iran and locking in limitations on a future Iraqi state, it would address their security problems without having to rely on a heavy, destabilizing American military presence. Moreover, U.S.-GCC military relations might be more agreeable to the Persian Gulf populations if they took place within the rubric of a regionwide forum. For Iraq, a regional security forum would give it a place to complain to its neighbors about unhelpful interference in its affairs and possibly a mechanism to coordinate regional assistance to help the Iraqi government reform itself and secure the country. Iranian officials have already indicated their willingness to participate in such a forum, with Iran's former ambassador to the United Nations advocating it in the pages of *The New York Times.*[8] There is considerable logic to this idea from Tehran's perspective. For twenty years, Iran has demanded that the United States, Iraq, and the GCC take its security concerns seriously, and a regional security forum would give Iran a venue and an opportunity to discuss those concerns for the first time. Inviting Iran to discuss security issues in the Persian Gulf region at the same table with the United States would give Tehran the sense that it was finally getting the respect from Washington that it believes it deserves. More to the point, such a process is the only possible way that Iran could put limits on the regional military forces of its greatest opponent, the United States. If this forum paved the way for real arms control agreements, these would doubtless include limitations on America's regional force deployments (as was the case in Europe). Such limitations by themselves might be worth the price of admission for Iran.

Even if the hard-liners in Tehran opted not to participate, it would not be a disaster since in doing so they would further isolate themselves both internally and internationally. At home, it would be difficult for them to justify any action based on a supposed threat from the United States (or Iraq or the GCC) if they were unwilling to participate in a process in which they would have the opportunity to address these threats by diplomacy and arms control. To foreign audiences, Tehran's refusal to accept this kind of an olive branch from the United States would demonstrate that it was a rogue state uninterested in peaceful means of addressing its security concerns. This, in turn, would make it easier for Washington to muster international support for tighter sanctions and other forms of pressure.

A security framework in the Persian Gulf would still be worth pursuing even if Iran were to cross the nuclear threshold. In fact, under that circumstance it would be even more important to involve Tehran in a Persian Gulf security organization similar to the CSCE. Before Iran acquired nuclear weapons, the purpose of this enterprise would be to try to address Iran's legitimate security concerns through dialogue, confidence-building measures, and (eventually) arms control to eliminate Tehran's strategic impetus for nuclear weapons. Afterward it would be intended to try to work out diplomatic and military "rules of the road" for all of the states of the region to avoid unintended provocations, crises, and the like. Once Iran has nuclear weapons, difficult as it may be, we are going to have to find a way to live with it, deter it, and reassure it enough about our intentions and actions that it does not react aggressively out of fear while also making very clear to Tehran the consequences of going on the offensive itself.

Of course, the Iranians might try to scuttle the entire effort by demanding Israel's inclusion in such a security forum. They would know that it would be hard (but not impossible) for Iraq and the GCC states to ignore such a demand because of the resonance it would have among their populations. Bringing Israel into such a system would mean saddling the Persian Gulf security system with the additional problems and endless disputes of the Arab-Israeli peace process and the Middle East as a whole, which would clearly be impractical. Indeed, all of the parties would inevitably come to the table with their own agendas and might try to subvert or structure the process to address only those issues that interest them. One of the dirty little secrets of the Persian Gulf is that GCC unity is a fiction: the Qataris want American military bases not to shield them from Iran or Iraq but to deter Saudi Arabia. Likewise, Bahrain wants powerful missiles not to make it an effective member of the Peninsula Shield Force but so that it can threaten Qatar if it ever feels the need. A regional security forum coupled with arms control measures could bring out all of these intra-GCC insecurities, further complicating the process.

Nevertheless, the interstate conflicts of the Middle East can help destabilize already fragile governments, they create excuses for Arab autocracies not to reform, they can disrupt oil exports and threaten critical American allies, and they exacerbate a range of other problems, including the dangerous civil wars in Iraq, Lebanon, and Palestine. As part of a new grand strategy meant to stabilize the Middle East over the long term, the United States should employ every tool at its disposal to reduce the risk of interstate war. Helping to create a new security architecture for the region—and ideally a security organization for part or all of it—can only help. It would make the American presence both more palatable and less necessary. It would reduce the risk of war by miscalculation and could lay the foundation for real arms control that would make deliberate war more difficult as well. Even if it failed in those goals, it would clearly identify the troublemakers, making it easier to organize collective action against them—to contain, sanction, or even confront them. It will not be easy to do, we may have to be creative and to "finesse" certain problems early on, but there is no reason not to make the effort and every reason to do so.

PART SIX

—

LOOKING FARTHER

DOWN THE PATH

ACCOMPLISHING THE GOALS OF A GRAND STRATEGY, ANY grand strategy, doesn't happen overnight. That is especially true for the grand strategy toward the Middle East that this book has proposed. Creating an environment in which the United States and its allies can enable and encourage Middle Eastern regimes to engage in an indigenously driven, comprehensive program of political, economic, and social reforms to address the deep-seated problems of the region, let alone seeing those reforms through to completion, is going to take many years. Moreover, as I have noted several times, this is a process that not only will take decades but *should* take decades.

Because this grand strategy will take decades to work, it must also be able to cope with change. The Middle East is not going to remain constant over the next twenty, thirty, or forty years. It never has, and, given the power of the underlying problems of the region, there is every reason to expect it won't suddenly calm down now. Instead, those problems will continue to generate new turmoil until the process of reform can begin to help the states of the region evolve into more functional societies. The many regional challenges discussed in the last four chapters are yet to be resolved. Nor are they likely to be the last that we and the Middle East face between now and that day in the distant future when we are able to look back and realize that this part of the world has become a much better place than it once was, much as we do with Europe today. In the meantime, the region will continue to produce imperceptible shifts, sudden disasters, and even the occasional unexpected opportunity.

Coping with the inevitable surprises will require a dynamic grand strategy, one that can be adjusted to ride whatever the waves of Middle Eastern fortunes have in store. This is one reason why I have refrained from going into greater detail when discussing how our narrower strategies toward particular countries and problems of the current Middle East should be framed. Those problems will change over time—some might even be solved—and will doubtless be replaced by new ones. What is important is to meet each change with a clear understanding of how best to handle it consistent with our grand strategy and the other policies we are pursuing toward the other crises of the region. At bottom, a grand strategy is a set of principles to be applied in devising specific programs of action as they are needed.

TODAY, THERE ARE A NUMBER of potential major changes to the Middle East already discernible on the horizon:

- Despite our best efforts, Iran may acquire a nuclear weapons capability or a nuclear weapon itself. Because Iran has been determined to reorder the status quo in the Middle East since 1979 and has often sought to do so by exacerbating the many problems of the region, such a development could pose a major challenge for the rest of the region and for a grand strategy intended to create the conditions for reform.

- American-led efforts to stabilize Iraq and/or Afghanistan may fail. Both countries have encountered severe difficulties, and, despite some important progress in Iraq, neither appears headed inexorably for success and stability at the time of this writing. If either does implode, it likely will unleash terrible violence internally, which in turn could create tidal waves of spillover beyond its borders.

- A generational change is taking place among the region's leaders. For decades the same leaders ruled the states of the Middle East. They became very experienced at guiding their own countries and in understanding what to expect from one another. Today, that leadership cohort is passing from the scene, with new, younger leaders already enthroned in Morocco, Jordan, Syria, Qatar, Kuwait, and the UAE. Egypt, Saudi Arabia, and perhaps Libya are also likely to experience similar transitions in the next ten years, while the Palestinians and Iraqis have shed their longtime autocratic rulers for highly unstable pseudodemocracies. As a result, the Middle East now has a slew of new rulers and more will follow, none of whom has much experience in either internal governance or external diplomacy. Nor do they know one another or know what to expect from one another the way their fathers did. The result has already been a number of mistakes by novice rulers and a number of miscalculations regarding the likely reactions of other countries. This can only be expected to multiply over the next decade and is likely to add to the overall turmoil and instability in the region.

Each of these changes, if it comes to pass, will require adjustments and even new policies on the part of the United States to cope with their impact. In every case, Washington will have to gauge the potential ramifications of each development, determine which American interests might be affected (threatened), and then fashion a new policy designed to prevent the new development from undermining the overall American goal of promoting a process of gradual internal reform throughout the region. At the same time, we should always be on the lookout for ways in which the new development might help us advance that goal and must be careful to harmonize the response with American policies toward other countries or specific issues.

Another future development of similar or potentially even greater consequence than these others is the likely rise of China to superpower status and its increasing involvement in the Middle East. Since 1989, we have lived in a unipolar world and the United States has effectively been the only external power willing and able to act decisively in the Middle East. Given China's skyrocketing consumption of oil and gas and its parallel economic growth, it seems only a matter of time before we once again have not only a bipolar world but a Middle East dominated by two superpowers. (Others have suggested that India might someday be a third.) Because this development could fundamentally affect everything else the United States is attempting to do in the region, and to illustrate more fully how the United States should approach future changes in the region in the context of a new grand strategy, I think it useful to briefly lay out how the United States should try to apply a new grand strategy to the rise of Chinese interests and influence in the Middle East.

CHAPTER 18

ENTER THE DRAGON

Since the fall of the Soviet Union, the United States has been the only outside country capable of projecting major military forces into the Middle East. The United States also has the largest single economy in the world, making it a highly desirable trade partner and source of economic aid—as well as allowing it to guide its economic activities to fit its political objectives. In part for these reasons, the United States has also exerted enormous diplomatic influence, including through its membership and leadership of critical international organizations like the U.N. Security Council, the World Trade Organization, the World Bank, and the International Monetary Fund. By the same token, because the United States benefits enormously from the international system we built (with help from our European and Asian allies) after the Second World War, it has tended to use that power to maintain the status quo and, by and large, keep the peace throughout the world.

I am not trying to suggest that since 1945 the United States has not used force, attempted to topple governments it did not like, or taken other actions that appeared aggressive to others—only that when we have done so during this period it has most often been to prevent a major, sudden change to the status quo. In Korea, Kosovo, Bosnia, and the Persian Gulf in 1990–1991, the United States fought to defend one group or country against aggression from another. We have participated in a wide range of counterinsurgency campaigns since 1945—Bolivia, Vietnam, and El Salvador come quickly to mind— to prevent the overthrow of a government by internal (and external) opponents. Even when we overthrew (or tried to overthrow) foreign governments, we did so to try to stop a government we expected to challenge the status quo, like those of Allende in Chile, Mossadiq in Iran, Castro in Cuba, and the Sandinistas in Nicaragua. Although the Bush administration clearly exaggerated the threat from Iraq in 2003, there is no question that its motive in invading was to remove Saddam Husayn because of his history of aggressively and violently trying to reorder the Middle East to put himself on top. (The 1989 invasion of Panama is at least one example to the contrary.)

America's general support for the status quo—regardless of whether you believe it to have been intelligent or misguided, well handled or badly botched—has made the United States a good guardian of Persian Gulf oil exports. The United States has consistently intervened in the Gulf to ensure the free flow of the region's oil. We have worked with regional partners to contain those who threatened to curtail it (like Ayatollah Khomeini) or control it for their own purposes (such as Saddam Husayn). The world has not complained that the United States has had the only hand on the Persian Gulf's oil spigot.

However, it is unclear how much longer that status will last. China is finally coming into its own as an economic power. The Chinese economy continues to grow at a blistering pace and, with its 1.3 billion people, threatens to approach or even match the economic power of the United States in the not-too-distant future. Naturally, China's growth has been fueled by massive increases in oil and gas consumption, which have in turn contributed to the steady increase in global oil prices since 2002. China's demand for oil doubled between 1985 and 1995 and then doubled again between 1995 and 2005 when it became the second largest energy consumer in the world (behind only the United States).[1] Moreover, its demand for energy is growing four to five times as fast as that of the rest of the world.[2] Roughly 40 percent of all new world oil demand is attributable to China's growing energy needs.[3] Between 2005 and 2025, China's energy use is expected to grow at a 3.2 percent average annual rate, while that of mature economies is projected at only 1.1 percent annually.[4]

All of this has understandably piqued Beijing's interest in the

Middle East and its bountiful oil and gas reserves.[5] China imports roughly 40 percent of its oil needs, and of this half already comes from the Middle East, including 17 percent (of total oil imports) from Saudi Arabia, 13.6 percent from Iran, and 7 percent from Sudan.[6] Because China's need for oil imports is expected to more than triple by 2025, Beijing has invested $3 billion in developing Sudanese fields and agreed to a $70 billion deal to purchase Iranian oil.[7] Meanwhile, Saudi Arabia has agreed to a $3 billion deal to build a refinery in Fujian Province that will process 8 million tons of Saudi crude per year.[8]

Bad History, Part 1

Of course, the United States has already had considerable experience facing another superpower in the Middle East, and the experience was not happy for anyone. Throughout the Cold War, the Soviet Union attempted to increase its influence in the Middle East, largely to subvert American interests in the region. Though some scholars argue that the USSR's main aim was to find a warm-water port in the Middle East, there is little evidence that this was a driving motive of Soviet foreign policy.[9] To a limited degree, the Soviets feared that the United States might use its alliances with Turkey and the shah of Iran to mount military operations against them, and they knew that we used both countries to conduct intelligence operations against them. Of far greater significance than either of these, however, was that the Soviets understood the importance of Middle Eastern oil to the Western Alliance (Russia, on the other hand, produced enough oil to meet the needs of the Warsaw Pact) and, to a lesser extent, the value of its geographic position to trade, transportation, and communications.

As a result, the Soviets tried early on to gain influence in the region and to use that influence to make trouble for the West by threatening its interests, in particular its interests in Middle Eastern oil exports. The 1955 Czech arms deal allowed Moscow to arm Egypt under Gamal 'Abd al-Nasser, the leader of the pan-Arab movement that threatened to destroy Western dominance of the Middle East. This in turn led Britain and France to instigate the 1956 Suez-

Sinai War, which they hoped to use to overthrow Nasser and reassert their dominance over the region. The Anglo-French intervention prompted Soviet Premier Nikita Khrushchev to threaten war, until the United States defused the situation by demanding that London and Paris back down and so give up their former imperial roles as the arbiters of the Middle East. Thereafter, the Soviets did what they could to make trouble in the Middle East, consistently siding with the most radical forces for change, violence, revolution, and chaos. When Egypt buried the hatchet with Israel in 1978, the Soviets threw their full weight behind Syria and Muammar Qadhafi's Libya, which were left as the most anti–status quo powers in the region. Moreover, after the Iranian Revolution, they tried (unsuccessfully) to establish a closer relationship with Tehran. They backed the PLO and other Palestinian terrorist groups, as well as the pseudo-Marxist regime in South Yemen, the Dhofari rebels, and disruptive Communist movements throughout the Middle East.

The outcome of all of this was to help make the Middle East a very unstable place and a tinderbox of confict. The two superpowers divided the Middle East up into armed camps and did whatever they could to expand their own camp and weaken that of the other side. Any country or group with a grievance knew that it could always turn to one of the superpowers for help if doing so would hurt a client of the other superpower.

Bad History, Part 2

There is another historical pattern that is also worth considering. Over the past two hundred years, there appears to have been a common scheme to the fortunes of dominant, external powers in the Middle East. It was the experience of the British Empire, the first foreign power to dominate the region in the modern era. We are now treading the same ground, and there are already signs that China is about to follow in our footsteps.

This pattern is as follows: what first brings the external great power into the region is trade. For that reason, when it first establishes relationships in the region, it is unconcerned about how the people of the region govern themselves, whom they bow to, whom they fight, or who wins when they fight. This makes the great power the belle of the Middle Eastern ball, courted by every local potentate in the hope that it will help him against his foes, foreign and domestic. Thus, the people of the region try to embroil the external great power, with all its military might, in their own affairs. And since the external great power really doesn't care about who rules in what capital or who owns which province, it seems easy and worthwhile to do so in return for the promise of greater economic benefits. Over time, however, the great power's trade relationships expand to the point where it becomes economically dependent on the Middle East, and particularly on its oil. Once this happens, the great power realizes that it *does* care about who rules where and who conquers whom because these matters can have a profound impact on the great power's own economic stability and fortunes. At that point, the great power begins to use its influence, including its military might, to put into place the local rulers it wants, to aid some military campaigns and thwart others, and ultimately to demand that the locals start running their affairs in ways that are most amenable to the interests of the great power. At that point, the great power becomes the object of hatred across the region, and inevitably the locals go looking for another external great power they can bring in to balance the last, one that doesn't care about their internal politics and military aspirations. And so the pattern repeats itself.

That is precisely what happened to the British (and, to a lesser extent, the Russians). It is also what has happened to the United States, and it is already happening to the Chinese. All across the Middle East, China is the hottest, latest, most popular new external power. From Rabat to Cairo to Baghdad to Dubayy to Tehran, Chinese businessmen and government officials are the new rock stars of the Middle East. The locals roll out their finest red carpets to make the Chinese happy—just as they did for American businessmen and government officials 50 to 60 years ago and British businessmen and government officials 100 to 150 years ago.

The Chinese are popular throughout the Middle East for the same reasons that Americans and Brits were in their time. China is seen as the rising power, the next great source of fabulous riches. China is seen as a source of technology, investment capital, economic aid, trade, and modern weaponry. Best of all, the Chinese have made it crystal clear that they simply do not care how Middle Eastern regimes govern their societies, what they do to their citizens, and whom they choose to imprison or kill.[10] Although China has an important trade relationship with Israel (because the Israelis have sold the Chinese sophisticated weapons technology that they have not been able to develop themselves), the Chinese lack the ties to Israel that both Britain and America developed over time—and because there are virtually no Chinese Jews, many Muslim Middle Easterners assume that China never will develop such ties. Thus many Arabs and Iranians suspect that the Chinese would support them against Israel just as the United States supported Israel against them after 1967. The Chinese are also willing to sell advanced weaponry, and in the past have even sold ballistic missiles and nuclear technology, to anyone who can pay for them, no matter how despotic, corrupt, or aggressive they might be.[11]

China does not yet have the ability to project significant military power into the Middle East, but a great many Middle Easterners assume that that is only a matter of time. They are patiently waiting for that day in expectation that when Beijing is able to do so, they will be able to use China to balance the United States and undermine its efforts to get the regimes of the region to do things they don't want to do—like reform their political, economic, and social systems. The Chinese are building a commercial port at Gwadar, Pakistan, but across the Middle East this is assumed to be a naval base and the first step in an inevitable Chinese military entry into the region. Moreover, even the Chinese themselves are debating whether they should be actively building the capability to project force into the Middle East, even as they expand their capacity to project it throughout East Asia.[12]

A Worse Middle East or a Better One?

This pattern suggests two possible outcomes, one far more desirable than the other. The first outcome—the one that appears to be the direction in which we are headed—is for both of these unfortunate historical patterns to repeat themselves. China's growing reliance on Middle Eastern gas and oil will increasingly bring the Chinese into the Middle East. There, at least some Middle Eastern states unhappy with the United States—because of its support for Israel or some other group (like the Kurds or the southern Sudanese) or, more likely, because of our efforts to convince them to reform their polities and societies—may shift their allegiance to the Chinese because the Chinese will ask nothing from them except trade. Bashar al-Asad of Syria has publicly called on China to step up to this role and fill the shoes of the Soviet Union.[13] Inevitably, this will pit Washington and Beijing against each other just as the United States and USSR squared off in the region during the Cold War. We will compete for client states, we will both attempt to get Middle Eastern states to do what we want, and our client states in the region will themselves clash and expect us to rescue them when they get in trouble. This seems especially likely if the Chinese ultimately decide that the United States is their great rival and, more important still, a competing consumer of finite energy resources, which can only make them struggle more fiercely against us and everyone else to secure as much of the Middle East energy pie as they can.[14] Moreover, as it did with the Soviets, this competition will both encourage the Chinese to develop the capacity to project military power into the region and create new superpower crises once they are able to do so.[15]

However, it is possible to imagine a very different scenario. Bringing this scenario about rests on persuading the Chinese of two things. The first is that there is a crucial difference between China's interest in the Middle East today and Russia's interest in it during the Cold War. Moscow was not interested in the Middle East because the USSR wanted to monopolize its oil but principally just to weaken the Western Alliance. The Soviets saw the Middle East as an Achilles' heel of the West and supported anti–status quo leaders, countries, and movements in the hope of denying the region's vital resources to the United States and its allies. But China's interests in the Middle East are very different. In fact, China has the exact same interest as the United States: to ensure a plentiful flow of oil from the region. This commonality of interests is the first building block for a common Sino-American approach to the Middle East.

The second is to convince the Chinese that they *are* simply following in our (unhappy) footsteps and those of the British in terms of the narrative arc of foreign great powers in the Middle East. Here the trick will be to persuade the Chinese that though they may not care about the internal affairs of the states of the region today, they will in the future—and when they do, they are likely to wish that they had cared about them all along, just as we and the British ended up regretting our initial lack of interest. The Chinese have already taken the first step down that path, showing some concern for Middle East interstate conflict, which they seem to recognize could affect both the quantity and the price of oil coming out of the region. However, what is required is to induce Beijing to understand quickly what it took us fifty to sixty years to learn: that the problems of the region are creating chronic internal instability and that this is ultimately the greatest threat to the oil exports of the region. The British tried, in their own way, to do the same with us, but we chalked it up (not entirely wrongly) to the British addiction to imperialism and chose to ignore it. We have to hope that we can do better with the Chinese.

If we are able to do so, we will succeed in turning a major challenge for our grand strategy into a major asset. If the Chinese insist on seeing the United States as an adversary and are willing to associate with states regardless of their actions—foreign or domestic—this will greatly complicate the ability of the United States to dampen the risk of interstate conflict and to press regional regimes to adopt far-reaching reforms. They will always be able to hide behind the Chinese, getting what they need from Chinese businessmen and using Beijing as a diplomatic and (eventually) military counterweight to the United States. Implementing a grand strategy of enabling reform in the Muslim Middle East will be that much more difficult under these circumstances.

However, if we are able to bring the Chinese around, they would then become our *allies* in the same initiative. Imagine the impact of two superpowers working in tandem to discourage foreign aggression and encourage internal reform. Imagine if regional reformers had an alternative superpower (one without the taints we have acquired) to turn to for aid in all its forms. Imagine if would-be troublemakers met a united front of Washington and Beijing determined to prevent them from causing mischief. Imagine if local regimes found both the champions of East and West determined to move them down the path of reform—and willing to help them do so. Clearly, the latter scenario would be far better than the former.[16]

REASONABLE ODDS

To some extent, China's policy makers and Middle East experts seem to understand all of this. They reportedly find the religion-fueled zealotry of the Middle East perplexing and frightening. A considerable number of Chinese have been killed, wounded, or abducted in the Middle East in recent years.[17] Jon Alterman, a respected expert on Middle East affairs, writes that "The Middle East is a place where China can really get hurt. The region's location and energy resources have made it a focus of global competition for two centuries. Great powers have gotten entangled—from the 'Great Game' in nineteenth century Afghanistan to the 9/11 attacks on New York and Washington—and have rarely emerged unscathed. Indeed, the most common single phrase I heard in Beijing was, 'the Middle East is the graveyard of great powers.' It seemed to be on everyone's lips."[18]

This recognition creates a basis for mutual understanding. If China knows that it needs stability in the Middle East to ensure the free flow of oil but recognizes that the region is fragile and can be a trap for foreign great powers, its policy makers may be receptive to an arrangement that minimizes Sino-American competition in the Middle East, maximizes cooperation, and possibly even establishes a division of labor in which the United States continues to play a leading military and political role, with economic and diplomatic support from Beijing. In a very tentative sense, the precursors of such an arrangement are already evident, with China providing 1,000 soldiers for the Western-led expansion of UNIFIL in Lebanon and Beijing providing some unexpected support, if halfhearted, for U.N. Security Council sanctions on Iran.[19] Many China experts speak of a debate in Beijing over how to handle China's growing interests in the Middle East, with some espousing a hard-line "realist" position, which would increasingly pit China as a rival against the United States, and others arguing for a "liberal" position that would embrace precisely the kind of cooperative relationship with Washington that would be most beneficial from the perspective of a new American grand strategy toward the region.[20]

China's ambivalence about democracy probably won't be a serious stumbling block to Sino-American cooperation in promoting internal reform and helping to make that possible across the Middle East. The Chinese have demonstrated a high degree of cynicism when it comes to systems of government elsewhere, showing few reservations about democratization in South Korea, Taiwan, Malaysia, and Indonesia, let alone farther afield in Europe, Africa, and Latin America. As long as a country is doing whatever China wants and needs, Beijing has shown itself willing to tolerate (and occasionally even support) democratization. Even where China opposes efforts to promote democracy, such as in North Korea and Myanmar, its concern is principally with preserving regimes friendly to it and avoiding chaotic transitions that could affect its interests—and even in those two countries, China has been supporting domestic reform to improve their stability. The kind of gradual, indigenously driven process of political reform (which may or may not produce true democracy, depending on the desires of the people themselves) envisioned in this grand strategy should be acceptable to the Chinese if they come to see it as in their interests because it will ensure long-term stability even if it comes at the expense of short-term dislocations.

A potentially greater obstacle to overcome will be Beijing's tendency to see the world as a zero-sum game among countries and, especially, its perception of global energy resources as finite. A number of experts on China argue that the Chinese leadership has generally viewed any gain by another country, especially a great-power rival such as the USSR or the United States, as being detrimental to their own status.[21] Of greater importance still, many worry that Chinese behavior suggests that Beijing's leaders see the earth's energy resources as finite and are trying to lock up as much of them as they can to fuel their own future growth. At least some Chinese leaders suspect that the global energy crunch has actually been instigated by the West to drive up costs and so prevent China from further growth and modernization.[22] China has been negotiating massive long-term oil and natural gas deals with Middle Eastern states, certainly to ensure that its energy needs are taken care of but possibly also to prevent other states from trying to claim them.[23] Moreover, China has frequently sought to buy development rights to entire oil fields to physically produce the oil itself (through national oil production companies), rather than simply buying the oil via the international petroleum market, as most nations do.[24] Although there are economic rationales for this, many analysts fear that it is intended to allow the Chinese to control the oil from the wellhead to ensure that it flows only to them, especially in time of crisis.[25] Moreover, China has been willing to deal with pariah states like Iran, Zimbabwe, and Sudan because their isolation makes them desirous of making deals with China in the hope that this will encourage Beijing to defend their political interests (as the Chinese did with Saddam Husayn, even while he was under U.N. sanctions).[26] In turn, the Chinese do so because these countries are willing to sign the kind of deals that Beijing wants in order to ensure that it has a big enough slice of the global energy pie.[27] Finally, Beijing's realists fear that the United States might choose to close off Chinese energy supplies from the Middle East, prompting them to push both for the development of military capabilities able to prevent this and more supplies and means of delivery that are less susceptible to such interference.[28] Indeed, a popular online book in China is *The Battle in Protecting Key Oil Routes,* which envisions a climactic sea battle in which the Chinese destroy an American carrier battle group in the Strait of Malacca.[29]

If it is the case that China sees global energy resources as finite—and then for as long as it does so—this will breed rivalry with the United States and other major energy consumers. To some extent, this problematic way of thinking might be assuaged by mere persuasion—explaining that sheer economics make it unlikely that the "last barrel" of oil will ever be pumped (because as demand increases, prices will rise to compensate, eventually making it too expensive to keep using oil and making it comparatively cheaper to switch to other fuels). On the other hand, some of the best China experts believe that fears of Chinese "mercantilist" thinking about energy supplies are greatly exaggerated, if not flat-out wrong, suggesting that this may not be a problem at all.[30] If it is, however, words alone are likely to prove inadequate and the United States and our allies would have to take action.

As if the United States needed any more reasons to shift to alternative sources of energy, this is yet another one. The more the United States and its allies (who tend to be richer than China and so are better able to afford it) are willing to shift to alternative fuels, the more we will reassure the Chinese that we are not competing with them for oil and gas and, of far greater importance, that affordable alternative sources of fuel (nuclear, solar, hydrogen, or whatever) will be available, thereby reducing China's need for Middle Eastern oil and gas in the future. As part of this effort, the United States may want to consider whether to take measures that would make it easier for China to buy or license cutting-edge alternative energy technology from the United States, in the hope that doing so would make it economically more advantageous for China to begin to shift to alternative sources. In the meantime, we should be looking to develop open-ended communications with the Chinese on energy supply issues (perhaps including a standing joint committee from both countries)[31] intended to provide a forum for Beijing and Washington to cooperate on energy issues, rather than competing.

As this last point suggests, persuading China will likely consist of more than just compelling conversation. In particular, a crucial element in making China our partner in this entire enterprise will be giving it a role in the Middle East commensurate with its growing strength and aspirations. This is going to be hard for the United States, because it will mean accepting China as a partner in the geopolitics of the Middle East. Rather than making unilateral decisions after minimal consultation with our regional allies, Washington will have to learn to negotiate common policies with Beijing. It will certainly mean lots of painful coordination with another government, one whose concurrence will often be vital for the sake of the wider partnership if not for cooperation on the specific matter itself. It may mean allowing the Chinese basing rights in the region, both so that they feel comfortable that they can protect their own interests and so that they are able to exercise their influence jointly with us. It will probably mean agreeing to do some things Beijing's way. All of this would be laborious, frustrating, time-consuming, and even enraging for America's leaders and diplomats, but the rewards would be well worth the effort.

The Path before Us

AMERICA'S ROLE IN THE WORLD HAS EXPANDED OVER TIME, along with its strength and prosperity. At first, we were weak and relatively poor and even though foreign trade was of great importance, we had little ability to influence foreign events. About the most we managed was to get some piratical Barbary emirates to stop preying on our merchant ships. Over time, however, our strength grew along with our economic interests. When President James Monroe first announced his famous doctrine in 1823, the United States had virtually no capability to enforce it and depended on the Royal Navy to do so for us. By the end of that century the situation was very different, and under Presidents William McKinley and Theodore Roosevelt we were able to demonstrate that we were plenty strong enough to exclude all other powers from our private demesne in the Western Hemisphere.

Of course, the American economy kept growing and our prosperity brought both greater interdependence with the world and fear that we ourselves would be targeted by a stronger power. Moreover, we came to accept that our wealth and power brought with it new responsibilities to help other nations avoid the worst depredations of conflict and conquest. The result was that when an aggressive Germany attempted to make itself the dominant power, if not the overlord, of Europe, we intervened to stop it. So too with Japan when it tried to make itself master of East Asia. No sooner had we extirpated the threats from Germany and Japan than the Soviet Union emerged to conjure in American minds the same threat of a rapacious great power determined to conquer America's allies and trading partners, make itself the greatest power in the world, and enslave other nations in a brutal totalitarian system. We may never know the extent to which the USSR was as aggressively expansionist as we feared, and it seems likely that we exaggerated that threat during certain periods, but that was how America saw its role in the world.

In the aftermath of the Second World War, as we first began to fear that Soviet Russia would not only fill the shoes of Germany and Japan but surpass the threat either of them posed, the United States did a remarkable thing. Together with our allies in Europe and East Asia, but mostly following our own counsel, the United States built a new international order. It was hardly a perfect international order, but it served American interests brilliantly and helped a great many other nations around the world as well. Because of its success, the Western Alliance and the United States grew stronger and richer while our Communist rivals grew weaker and poorer and finally collapsed altogether in 1989–1991. With that fall, America's international system spread farther around the world, benefiting the United States along with a great many other countries.

In this sense, America's role and our interests in the world have changed dramatically even since the fall of communism. During the twentieth century, America's principal overseas interest and its most important international mission lay in defeating or containing another great power that seemed determined to conquer and enslave our allies, cripple our economy by assimilating our trade partners, and make itself powerful enough to threaten the American homeland directly. Unless and until China rises to fill that role, no such menace to America currently exists. But that should not cause us to assume that our role in the world is over. Quite the contrary; the foundation of our unimaginable strength and prosperity today lies in the international system we built and have helped spread to much of the world. And many other people around the world are much better off for the existence of that order than they otherwise would be, even if they cannot think of the United States without cursing under their breath. That is not to suggest that this system is perfect— perfectly just, perfectly equitable, or even perfectly consistent. It certainly is not. But it does provide greater peace, economic opportunity, and international assistance than any other the world has seen, and enough so that vast numbers of people are living better lives than they otherwise might have under any other likely set of circumstances.

Defending and preserving this international system has become the new paramount interest and the most important mission of the United States in the twenty-first century. Because so many others benefit from that system even as they curse us, we are likely to play it for as long as we are able. Because it is so beneficial to us and to others, we should play it for as long as we can.[1]

It is for this reason that the problems of the Middle East are among the most important of the twenty-first century. Right now, the Middle East is the greatest challenge to that international order. Inadvertently, in devising that international system after World War II, we tied its vital economic underpinnings to oil. Oil is the lifeblood of the international economic order and probably will be for some decades to come, try as we might (and should) to end that dependence. And unfortunately, two thirds of all the world's oil lies under the sands of the Middle East. A major, sudden disruption in the flow of that oil could bring the entire global economy to a halt and thereby bring the entire international order crashing down with it. At a less dramatic but more immediate level, the Muslim Middle East is generating angry revolutionaries and vicious terrorists willing to try to tear down the status quo by violence and to slaughter innocent people in inchoate ventings of their frustration.

In this sense, the problems of the Middle East are also an archetypal example of the kinds of challenges that the United States is likely to face in the twenty-first century. It is a very different kind of challenge from that which the United States faced in the nineteenth or twentieth centuries, and this has led some to misunderstand or underestimate the nature of the challenge. It is not just that we should not walk away from the system we built because it has helped so many others, it is also that we cannot walk away from it lest it collapse and in so doing threaten our own economic development and even physical security. The fall of the American-led international system would be without parallel in modern history because, unlike during the demise of the British and French Empires, there will be no obvious successor—no America—to pick up the pieces and prevent the reemergence of rapacity and fear and the war, anarchy, and poverty they bring with them.

There is no question that the Middle East is a frustrating place for Americans. It often seems to defy logic, as well as what Americans consider practical solutions and obvious compromises. It often does feel as if we are metaphorically lost in the desert sands for which the region is famous. But we simply cannot afford to give up. If we do, it will only come back to make us regret our having done so, just as it has time and again in the past when we tried to ignore or merely patch up Middle Eastern problems and move on. The only path out of the Middle Eastern desert for the United States is the long, hard one of creating the conditions and painstakingly, patiently helping the people of the region transform their society into a different one—one without the anger and frustration, injustice and oppression, ignorance and violence, that have made the contemporary Middle East so desperately unhappy.

This is not impossible. For 1,500 years Europe was the most violent region on Earth. Its wars of conquest, civil wars, religious wars, violent repression, mass murders, ethnic cleansing, plagues, revolutions, and genocides were without parallel anywhere on earth. A great many Americans, right up through the Second World War, were convinced that it would be impossible to change Europe. They insisted that it was bred into European genes, steeped in their culture, embedded in their state system, or all of the above. In the waning days of World War II, Senator Burton Wheeler opposed a lengthy American occupation and reconstruction of Europe by arguing, not inaccurately, that Europe was nothing but a "seething furnace of fratricide, civil war, murder, disease, and starvation."[2] Over fifty years, however, we helped (led is probably more accurate) Europe to become one of the best regions on Earth, where there is widespread prosperity, unparalleled freedoms, and not even the threat of war. During similar spans we have helped East Asia and Latin America follow a similar path, and both of these regions are much the better for it, although neither has achieved Europe's levels of prosperity and security. Even today, there are many in the Middle East who would welcome such help, if only privately.

The great question we face today, in the first decade of the twenty-first century, is whether we are willing to help the Middle East down the path marked out as the only one that can lead them and us out of the desert that has entrapped us all. If we are, we must brace ourselves for the Middle East to remain one of our biggest foreign policy headaches for the first half of this century. If we are not, we had better be ready for the Middle East to remain one of our biggest foreign policy headaches for all of it.

ACKNOWLEDGMENTS

—

THIS WAS A HARD BOOK TO WRITE. IT ENCOMPASSES A VAST range of topics, from economics to politics to military affairs; spans a geographical gamut, from Morocco to Iran; and attempts to suggest courses of action on a daunting list of problems, from the conflict in Iraq today to the rise of China tomorrow. That meant coming to grips with a similarly vast range of material. Consequently, to the extent that there is anything of value in these pages, it is thanks mostly to a range of people who were excessively generous with their time and wisdom.

Because of its broad scope, I asked a number of other regional experts to read and comment on much or all of the manuscript. Peter Bergen and Daniel Byman, two of the leading authorities on terrorism, read the entire volume and also helped me enormously in understanding their maddeningly complex area of expertise. I could not have asked for better guides than the two of them. Dennis Ross has always been one of the models of a policy analyst and policy practitioner to which I have aspired, so I am deeply grateful to him for reading the manuscript, keeping me focused on what really matters in the region, and helping me to understand the subtleties of everything from Arab-Israeli peacemaking to methods by which the United States might approach moderate Islamist groups. No one sees the path ahead more clearly than Dennis, and I am much the wiser for his having helped me discern it. Greg Gause and Steve Spiegel tore an early draft of the book apart and then provided me with more good ideas than I deserved in putting it back together.

They are two of our nation's finest scholars of the Middle East, and their counsel was simply invaluable. Dalia Mogahed guided me through the labyrinth of Middle East public opinion. She also helped me sort through a variety of other topics, from reform and the roots of Muslim rage to the appeal of political Islam. This book would be much the weaker were it not for her profound insights on every one of these topics. Amjad Atallah did the same for me when it came to Salafism and the Arab-Israeli conflict, among other things. Over the years, I have gotten many of my best ideas about solving that conflict and transforming the Arab world from Amjad, and I cannot thank him enough for sharing these thoughts with me. Tamara Wittes, one of the country's leading experts on democratization in the Middle East, not only read the manuscript and smacked me in the head to get me to think straight on several important topics, but also allowed me to read an early version of her own superb new book, *Freedom's Unsteady March.* You will find this work referenced frequently, especially in part IV, because her ideas served as a critical spur to my own thinking. Marin Strmecki also took a big chunk of time out of his busy life to push me on certain points and open my eyes to others. In his understated way, he lent me the wisdom of his own experiences trying to do some of the very things that I advocate, and my arguments are much stronger for it.

In a similar vein, Jeff Bader, one of Washington's sharpest China hands, was kind enough to read through chapter 18 to make sure that I had not said anything egregiously stupid about China's strategy and intentions toward the Middle East. Whatever foolishness remains can only be laid back at my own doorstep.

Whenever I write, I always look for smart people who don't spend their every waking minute thinking about the Middle East to critique the manuscript. This time around I was unusually fortunate in that respect. Three truly exceptional writers and thinkers—Frederick Kagan, Ted Koppel, and Jonathan Rauch—all agreed to wade through my text and help me turn it into something that might be useful and interesting to a broader spectrum of readers. It's hard to know where to begin to thank them or how to stop. Whatever problems remain in this book remain only because I lack the skill and intelligence to fully apply all of the superb suggestions they gave me.

During the course of my career I have had the great good fortune to work for some outstanding bosses. Although I felt that way long before they set pen to paper to help me with this book, Strobe Talbott, Carlos Pascual, and Martin Indyk—my chain of command at the Saban Center and Brookings—surpassed even their prior efforts in helping me through this volume. They gave me the time and the opportunity to write it. They encouraged me at every step, and then all three took more of their own time than they could afford to read and comment on it. Carlos pushed me hard on the question of reform in the Arab world, lending his formidable experience in helping me to avoid many pitfalls. Few people have taught me more about the Arab-Israeli peace process than Martin, and for his help with the book and his many years of friendship, guidance, and teaching I will be forever grateful. And I am even further indebted to Strobe for writing the book's superb Foreword at a time when he had far better things to do.

In some ways, I feel like I have been writing this book for twenty years. Everything I have learned about the Middle East is here in some passage, or even just the turn of a phrase. For that reason, I feel I should thank every person who has ever helped me understand the region—from all of my teachers, to my mentors and colleagues in government, to my compatriots at Brookings and the Council on Foreign Relations, to my students at Georgetown, to everyone I ever met on my many trips to the region. Unfortunately, Random House balked at the idea of a hundred-page Acknowledgments section. However, there are a number of people who deserve to be singled out for my thanks because conversations that I had with them over the past five or six years played a particularly important role in shaping my thinking on specific aspects of this book. For this reason, Raad Alkadiri, Sheri Berman, Dick Clarke, Roger Cressey, Mona Makram Ebeid, Nabil Fahmi, Tom Farer, William Galston, Jane Harman, Saad Eddin Ibrahim, Gal Luft, Rob Malley, Hisham Melham, Afshin Molavi, Marwan Muasher, Tim Naftali, Jim Placke, Bruce Riedel, Gideon Rose, Salim al-Sabah, Karim Sadjadpour,

David Sandalow, Chris and Betsi Shays, Mai Yamani, Judi Yaphe, and Ahmed Younis all have more than my usual share of gratitude. Whether they knew it or not, comments they made to me over the years became epiphanies that grew into the chapters of this book.

The kernel of the book was provided by my friend Ron Asmus. Years ago, soon after we both left the Clinton administration, Ron insisted that we write a piece together on how the United States and Europe should mount a joint effort to help transform the Middle East, just as we had Europe. I was skeptical at first, but Ron persuaded me, and in so doing set me on the path to this book. For that, for his intelligence and energy, and for his friendship over the years, I am deeply grateful. Jim Steinberg, my former boss at Brookings, took it from there, pushing me to expand the work I had done with Ron and integrate it with other writing I had done on Iraq, Iran, Gulf security architectures, and a host of other topics into a cohesive whole. He was right, as he usually is. Will Marshall of the Progressive Policy Institute then allowed me to take a first cut at the problem in an essay that became a chapter in his terrific edited volume, *With All Our Might: A Progressive Strategy for Defeating Jihadism and Defending Liberty*.

It is both customary and appropriate for an author to note that any errors or other failings of the book are his and his alone. Typically, when I write a book, I blame any such problems on Dan Byman. But this time around I feel compelled to observe the custom. Given the number of truly brilliant men and women who helped me with this effort, any praise should be reserved for them and any scorn directed at me alone.

My research assistant, Irena Sargsyan, was a wonder who got me through many of the worst patches, taking it upon herself to master entire fields and then summarizing and categorizing all of the information I needed. Given the immensity of this subject, I could not have gotten my arms around it without her diligence, perspicacity, and Stakhanovite work ethic. Irena and I were greatly assisted by two of Brookings's superb librarians, Laura Mooney and Sarah Chilton, who outdid themselves in turning up obscure books and reference articles that we desperately needed—and usually needed overnight. In addition, Bilal Saab lent his labor and expertise on several subjects near and dear to his heart.

I try not to miss an opportunity to thank Haim Saban, who had the wisdom and the wherewithal to found the Saban Center for Middle East Policy at the Brookings Institution. Likewise, several generous individuals (who have asked to remain anonymous) agreed to fund our Persian Gulf Initiative, under the auspices of which this book was written. Were it not for Haim and the Saban Center, and those who have made our Persian Gulf Initiative possible, this book would have been impossible.

This was the first book I worked on at Random House with a new editor, Timothy Bartlett, and it turned out to be a fruitful partnership. Tim provided much good advice, found lots of places to cut, and always came through in the clutch. Lindsey Schwoeri at Random House was a whirlwind who kept the book moving, kept all the plates in the air, and kept everyone (including me) doing everything they had to do to make sure the book actually saw the light of day. Had it not been for Lindsey's diligence and energy, this book might have fallen through a dozen different cracks. Also at Random House, thanks to my publicist, Dana Maxson; Barbara Bachman, who designed the book; Richard Elman, who oversaw the production process; production editor Steve Messina; copy editor Lynn Anderson; and proofreaders Andrea Gordon and Tita Gillespie.

As every author knows, the writing of any book often weighs heaviest on his or her family, and mine was no exception. I am fortunate that my adorable son, Aidan, was still too young to really understand what his daddy was doing all those days and nights sitting at the computer—even though I clearly was not playing with him. My wonderful wife, Andrea, is a different story. As usual, a great deal fell to her while I was chained to my word processor, and as always, she weathered the storm of my writing with patience and grace. I can only thank her for the love that got us both through one more book.

Finally, it is required of me to note that all statements of fact, opinion, or analysis expressed are those of the author and do not reflect the official positions or views of the CIA or any other U.S. government agency. Nothing in the contents should be construed as asserting or implying U.S. government authentication of information or Agency endorsement of the author's views. This material has been reviewed by the CIA to prevent the disclosure of classified information.

INTRODUCTION: WHY A GRAND STRATEGY FOR THE MIDDLE EAST?

1. Daniel Yergin, *The Prize: The Epic Quest for Oil, Money and Power,* paperback ed. (New York: Touchstone, 1991), p. 460.

2. Stephen Farrell, "The Latest Iraqi Conspiracy Theory: Killer British Badgers," *International Herald Tribune,* July 20, 2007; Michael Slackman, "Evil Deeds in Iran? British Are Suspects No. 1: Even Traffic Jams Are Blamed on Them," *International Herald Tribune,* February 9, 2006.

3. John Ellis, *World War II: A Statistical Survey* (New York: Facts on File, 1993), p. 273.

4. Kenneth M. Pollack, *The Persian Puzzle: The Conflict Between Iran and America* (New York: Random House, 2004), p. 41.

5. Ibid., pp. 44–48.

6. See also Michael T. Klare, "Fueling the Fires: The Oil Factor in Middle Eastern Terrorism," in *The Making of a Terrorist: Recruitment, Training, and Root Causes,* vol. 3: *Root Causes,* ed. James J. F. Forest (Westport, Conn.: Praeger Security International, 2006), pp. 147–148.

7. Yergin, *The Prize,* p. 567.

8. Despite the claims of the "Israel lobby" conspiracy theorists, the archival historical work on this period has consistently found that the U.S. tilt toward Israel in the 1960s and early 1970s was driven principally by Cold War strategic calculations, not American domestic politics. See, e.g., Warren Bass, *Support Any Friend: Kennedy's Middle East and the Making of the U.S.-Israel Alliance* (Oxford, U.K.: Oxford University Press, 2003); Abraham Ben-Tzvi, *Decade of Transition: Eisenhower, Kennedy, and the Origins of the American-Israeli Alliance* (New York: Columbia University Press, 1998); Mordechai Gazit, "The Genesis of the US-Israeli Military-Strategic Relationship and the Dimona Issue," *Journal of Contemporary History* 35, no. 3 (July 2000), pp. 413–422; Charles Lipson, "American Support for Israel: History, Sources, Limits," in *U.S.-Israel Relations at the Crossroads,* ed. Gabriel Sheffer (London, U.K.: Frank Cass, 1997), pp. 129–142; Douglas Little,

"The Making of a Special Relationship: The United States and Israel, 1957–68," *International Journal of Middle East Studies* 25, no. 4 (November 1993), pp. 563–585; Kenneth Organski, *The $36 Billion Bargain: Strategy and Politics in U.S. Assistance to Israel* (New York: Columbia University Press, 1990); Steven L. Spiegel, *The Other Arab-Israel Conflict: Making America's Middle East Policy from Truman to Reagan* (Chicago: University of Chicago Press, 1985).

9. Martin Indyk, "Back to the Bazaar," *Foreign Affairs* 81, no. 1 (January–February 2002), pp. 75–88.

10. Richard A. Clarke, *Against All Enemies: Inside America's War on Terror* (New York: Free Press, 2004), pp. 227–246; Kenneth M. Pollack, *The Threatening Storm: The Case for Invading Iraq* (New York: Random House, 2002), pp. 104–108; Pollack, *The Persian Puzzle,* pp. 343–374.

11. On the administration's thinking and planning for postwar Iraq, see George Packer, *The Assassin's Gate: America in Iraq* (New York: Farrar, Straus and Giroux, 2005). Also see Kenneth M. Pollack, "The Seven Deadly Sins of Failure in Iraq: A Retrospective Analysis of the Reconstruction," *Middle East Review of International Affairs* 10, no. 4 (December 2006), available at http://meria.idc.ac.il/journal/2006/issue4/jv10no4a1.html, downloaded May 19, 2007.

12. Thomas Carothers, "The Democracy Crusade Myth," *The National Interest,* July–August 2007; Tamara Cofman Wittes, *Freedom's Unsteady March: America's Role in Promoting Arab Democracy* (Washington, D.C.: Brookings Institution Press, 2008), pp. 80–110.

PART ONE: AMERICA'S INTERESTS IN THE MIDDLE EAST

1. For a parallel but much briefer account of U.S. interests in the Middle East, see Nora Bensahel and Daniel L. Byman, Introduction, in *The Future Security Environment in the Middle East: Conflict, Stability and Political Change,* ed. Nora Bensahel and Daniel L. Byman (Santa Monica, Calif.: RAND, 2004), pp. 2–7.

CHAPTER 1: OIL

1. Robert L. Hirsch, Roger Bezdek, and Robert Wendling, "Peaking of World Oil Production: Impacts, Mitigation, and Risk Management," February 2005, p. 8, available at www.netl.doe.gov/publications/others/pdf/Oil_Peaking_NETL.pdf, downloaded April 6, 2007. Statistics from Department of Transportation, Bureau of Transportation Statistics, "Ending the Energy Stalemate: A Bipartisan Strategy to Meet America's Energy Challenges," Washington, D.C., December 2006, p. 3.

2. U.S. Department of Energy, Energy Information Administration, "Petroleum Products," available at www.eia.doe.gov/neic/infosheets/petroleumproducts.htm, downloaded April 5, 2007.

3. Central Intelligence Agency, *The World Factbook,* 2006, available at https://www.cia.gov/library/publications/the-world-factbook/index.html.

4. Alan Greenspan, "Monetary Policy and the Economic Outlook," testimony before the Joint Economic Committee, U.S. Congress, April 17, 2002, Federal Reserve Board, available at www.federalreserve.gov/BoardDocs/Testimony/2002/20020417/default.htm, downloaded April 5, 2007.

5. Hillard G. Huntington, "The Economic Consequences of Higher Crude Oil Prices," Final Report, EMF SR 9, prepared for the U.S. Department of Energy, October 3, 2005, p. 24; Keith Sill, "The Macroeconomics of Oil Shocks," *Business Review,* Q1 (2007), pp. 21, 26.

6. Jad Muawad, "Rising Demand for Oil Provokes New Energy Crisis," *The New York Times,* November 9, 2007.

7. There are other reasons beyond simple supply and demand that can cause oil prices to rise or fall, related to factors such as refinery capacity, commercial reserve decisions, and unrelated transportation costs, among others. However, for purposes of this discussion of the importance of Middle East oil production, supply and demand are the dominant factors, especially over the long term.

8. CIA, *The World Factbook,* 2007; Energy Information Administration, "Overview of U.S. Petroleum Trade," *Monthly Energy Review,* March 2007.

9. On this point, see, e.g., U.S. General Accounting Office, "Energy Security: Evaluating U.S. Vulnerability to Oil and Supply Disruptions and Options for Mitigating Their Effects," Washington, D.C., December 1996.

10. GAO, "Energy Security," pp. 32–35.

11. The World Trade Organization, "Trade Policy Review, The United States: October 1996," press release, Pres/TRB/46, October 31, 1996, available at www.wto.org/english/tratop_e/tpr_e/tp46_e.htm, downloaded April 5, 2007; U.S. Department of Commerce, Bureau of Economic Analysis, "U.S. International Trade in Goods and Services, Annual Revision for 2005," June 9, 2006, available at www.bea.gov/bea/newsrel/tradannnewsrelease.htm.

12. Huntington, "The Economic Consequences of Higher Crude Oil Prices," p. 12.

13. Because the United States consumes so much oil, greatly reducing American consumption would mean far less global oil consumption. Environmentally, this would mean a lot less greenhouse gases being released into the atmosphere. In addition, it would make the global oil market much

softer—there would be far more slack in the system, making it less likely that major disruptions could cripple the global economy and likely lowering prices across the board.

14. Elisabeth Bumiller and Adam Nagourney, "Bush, Resetting Agenda, Says U.S. Must Cut Reliance on Oil," *The New York Times,* February 1, 2006.

15. Josef Braml, "Can the United States Shed Its Oil Addiction?" *The Washington Quarterly* 30, no. 4 (Autumn 2007), pp. 117–130; Council on Foreign Relations, "National Security Consequences of U.S. Oil Dependency," Independent Task Force Report no. 58, New York, 2006, esp. p. 14.

16. Matthew Simmons, "Shock to the System: The Impending Global Energy Supply Crisis," *Harvard International Review,* Fall 2006, p. 65.

17. Sill, "The Macroeconomics of Oil Shocks," p. 23.

18. Assuming that the oil-producing states do not turn around and use the petrodollars they are earning from us to buy American goods at an equal rate. James K. Jackson, "U.S. Trade Deficit and the Impact of Rising Oil Prices," Congressional Research Service, CRS Report RS22204, Washington, D.C., June 9, 2006.

19. Michele Cavallo and Tao Wu, "Measuring Oil-Price Shocks Using Market-Based Information," working paper 2006–28, Federal Reserve Bank of San Francisco, September 2006; Hirsch, Bezdek, and Wendling, "Peaking of World Oil Production," pp. 27–31; Lutz Kilian, "A Comparison of the Effects of Exogenous Oil Supply Shocks on Output and Inflation in the G7 Countries," working paper, University of Michigan, July 2006; Lutz Kilian, "Exogenous Oil Supply Shocks: How Big Are They and How Much Do They Matter for the U.S. Economy?," working paper, University of Michigan, October 2006, pp. 2–4, 18–20; Roger Kubarych, "How Oil Shocks Affect Markets," *The International Economy,* Summer 2005, pp. 32–36; Sill, "The Macroeconomics of Oil Shocks," p. 21. Previously, some economists argued that the impact of oil price shocks had been exaggerated and that changes in monetary policy had been responsible for most of the postwar recessions. However, this view has largely been rebutted. See James Hamilton and Ana Maria Herrera, "Oil Shocks and Aggregate Macroeconomic Behavior: The Role of Monetary Policy," *Journal of Money, Credit, and Banking,* 2004, pp. 265–286; Benjamin Hunt, "Oil Price Shocks and the U.S. Stagflation of the 1970s: Some Insights from GEM," *The Energy Journal* 27, no. 4 (2006), pp. 61–80; Donald W. Jones, Paul N. Leiby, and Inja K. Paik, "Oil Price Shocks and the Macroeconomy: What Has Been Learned since 1996," *The Energy Journal* 25, no. 2 (2004), pp. 12–17; Sill, "The Macroeconomics of Oil Shocks," pp. 23–26; Keith Sill and Sylvain Leduc, "A Quantitative Analysis of Oil Price Shocks, Systematic Monetary Policy, and Economic

Downturns," *Journal of Monetary Economics,* 2004, pp. 781–808. As Jones, Leiby, and Paik conclude in their 2004 survey of the field, "the most thorough research to date has found that post-shock recessionary movements of GDP are largely attributable to the oil price shocks, and are not events that alternative monetary policy largely could have avoided" (p. 27). Moreover, former Federal Reserve Board Chairman Alan Greenspan has suggested that the reason that the models being used by those economists to suggest that oil price shocks are not as directly tied to economic performance is that the models themselves simply cannot capture the complexities of these interactions—let alone the potential impact of a very severe oil price shock. See Greenspan, "Monetary Policy and the Economic Outlook." Last, much of the debate regards gradual oil price increases that allow markets to compensate; there is much broader consensus that sudden, rapid increases in oil prices do cause serious macroeconomic problems.

20. Any significant increase in prices could diminish growth and otherwise harm both the U.S. and global economies. The current problems in the U.S. airline industry as a result of the doubling of oil prices since early 2002 are an example of how even a more gradual increase in oil prices can have deleterious effects for the U.S. economy. However, recent research indicates that the impact of a slow increase over several quarters or years is considerably less than a sudden disruption causing a "spike" in oil prices. See, e.g., Huntington, "The Economic Consequences of Higher Crude Oil Prices"; Sill, "The Macroeconomics of Oil Shocks," pp. 21–27.

21. Gal Luft, "America's Oil Dependence and Its Implications for U.S. Middle East Policy," testimony before the Senate Foreign Relations Subcommittee on Near Eastern and South Asian Affairs, October 20, 2005, p. 2, available at http://foreign.senate.gov/testimony/2005/LuftTestimony 051020.pdf; Jad Muawad, "Rising Demand for Oil Provokes New Energy Crisis," *The New York Times,* November 9, 2007.

22. Recent research on oil price shocks has indicated that the impact is more pronounced on unemployment than on inflation, but there is still evidence of considerable impact on inflation. See for instance, Hirsch, Bezdek, and Wendling, "Peaking of World Oil Production," pp. 27–31; Benjamin Hunt, "Oil Price Shocks: Can They Account for the Stagflation in the 1970s?," working paper WP/05/215, International Monetary Fund, November 2005; Jones, Leiby, and Paik, "Oil Price Shocks and the Macroeconomy," pp. 1–28; Kilian, "Exogenous Oil Supply Shocks," pp. 3–4. Note also that as of December 2007, former Federal Reserve Chairman Alan Greenspan was warning that the rapid rise in oil prices in 2006–2007—not quite an oil price shock but still a steep increase—

was already threatening to create stagflation in the United States. Emily Kaiser, "Greenspan Sees Early Signs of U.S. Stagflation," Reuters, December 17, 2007, available at http://www.boston.com/business/articles/2007/12/16/greenspan_sees_early_signs_of_us_stagflation/.

23. George L. Perry, "The War on Terrorism, the World Oil Market, and the U.S. Economy," Brookings Project on Terrorism and American Foreign Policy, Analysis Paper no. 7, Brookings Institution, November 2001, pp. 3–5.

24. The oil companies also maintain reserves of their own. However, these "commercial" reserves are typically not factored into assessments of oil price shocks both because the size of these reserves is typically much smaller than those held by governments and because their size can vary greatly based on specific economic circumstances.

25. Perry, "The War on Terrorism, the World Oil Market, and the U.S. Economy," p. 7.

26. Rachel Bronson, *Thicker Than Oil: America's Uneasy Partnership with Saudi Arabia* (New York: Oxford University Press, 2006), p. 22.

27. Energy Information Administration, "Short-Term Outlook: OPEC Oil Production," March 2007, available at www.eia.doe.gov/emeu/steo/pub/contents.html; Simmons, "Shock to the System," p. 63. Simmons estimates that Saudi Arabia has less than 1 million bpd of spare production capacity.

28. Office of Technology Assessment, *U.S. Oil Import Vulnerability: The Technical Replacement Capability,* OTA-E-503 (Washington, D.C.: GPO, 1991), pp. 12, 39.

29. Ibid., p. 38.

30. Robert F. Wescott, "What Would $120 Oil Mean for the Global Economy?," *Securing America's Future Energy,* Washington, D.C., April 2006, pp. 4–7.

31. Perry, "The War on Terrorism, the World Oil Market, and the U.S. Economy," p. 9.

32. Ibid.

33. Securing America's Future Energy and National Commission on Energy Policy, "Oil Shockwave: Oil Crisis Executive Simulation," June 2005, available at www.secureenergy.org/reports/oil_shock_report_master.pdf, downloaded April 5, 2007. Sperling stated that none of our economic models could accurately predict the consequences of a political crisis that drove oil to $150 per barrel. At the time, oil was selling for $40 to $50 per barrel. What matters in sudden supply disruptions is the relative change in prices, not the absolute change in prices.

34. Author's interview with James Placke, Washington, D.C., March 2002; telephone interview with Phillip Verleger, April 2002; interview with Michael Weinstein, New York, May 2002.

35. Energy Information Administration, *Annual Energy Outlook 2005 with Projections to 2025,* DOE/EIA-0383 (Washington, D.C.: Energy Information Administration, 2005), pp. 166–167. The oil expert Matthew Simmons observes that these projections are based on very optimistic forecasts and real demand could be even higher. See Simmons, "Shock to the System," pp. 63–64.

36. Energy Information Administration, *World Energy Outlook, 2006* (Washington, D.C.: Department of Energy), 2006, p. 155. See also Luft, "America's Oil Dependence and Its Implications for U.S. Middle East Policy."

37. Energy Information Administration, "World Oil Production Capacity by Region and Country, 1990–2003," available at www.eia.doe.gov/oiaf/ieo/pdf/ieooiltab_1.pdf, downloaded April 28, 2007.

38. Special Assistant for Gulf War Illness, Department of Defense, "Environmental Exposure Report: Chronology of Events," available at www.gulflink.osd.mil/owf_ii/owf_ii_s03.htm#III.%20CHRONOLOGY%20OF%20EVENTS, downloaded April 28, 2007.

39. Shaul Bakhash, *The Reign of the Ayatollahs: Iran and the Islamic Revolution,* rev. ed. (New York: Basic Books, 1990), p. 230; CIA, *World Factbook, 1989* (Washington, D.C.: GPO, 1989); Michael M. J. Fischer, *Iran: From Religious Dispute to Revolution* (Madison: University of Wisconsin Press, 1980), p. 224.

40. "Militants Strike Oil Company Properties in Southern Nigeria with Simultaneous Car Bombings," Associated Press, December 18, 2006, available at www.iht.com/articles/ap/2006/12/18/africa/AF_GEN_Nigeria_Oil_Unrest.php.

41. Chip Cummings and Hassan Hafidh, "Iraq's Oil Industry Pumps Away," *The Wall Street Journal,* November 29, 2004; Energy Information Administration, "Iraq Country Analysis Brief: Oil," June 2006, available at www.eia.doe.gov/emeu/cabs/Iraq/Oil.html, downloaded April 28, 2007; Institute for the Analysis of Global Security, "Iraq Pipeline Watch," April 2007, available at www.iags.org/iraqpipelinewatch.htm, downloaded April 28, 2007; Gal Luft, "A Crude Threat," *The Sun* (Baltimore), April 6, 2004.

42. Michael T. Klare, "Fueling the Fires: The Oil Factor in Middle Eastern Terrorism," in *The Making of a Terrorist: Recruitment, Training, and Root Causes,* vol. 2: *Root Causes,* ed. James J. F. Forest (Westport, Conn.: Praeger Security International, 2006), pp. 155–157.

43. Michael Scheuer, Stephen Ulph, and John C. K. Daly, "Saudi Arabian Oil Facilities: The Achilles Heel of the Western Economy," the Jamestown Foundation, May 2006, p. 7, available at Jamestown.org/docs/Jamestown_SaudiOil.pdf.

44. Cited in Alex P. Schmid, "Terrorism and Energy Security: Targeting Oil

and Other Energy Sources and Infrastructure," *MIPT Insight,* Memorial Institute for the Prevention of Terrorism, March 2007, p. 5.

45. Quoted in Ariel Cohen, "The National Security Consequences of Oil Dependency," *Heritage Lectures,* May 14, 2007, p. 3.

46. Jeff Gerth, "Threats and Responses: Desert Targets; Pro-Qaeda Oil Workers a Sabotage Risk for Saudis," *The New York Times,* February 13, 2003; John R. Bradley, "Saudis' Worst Nightmare," *The Straits Times* (Singapore), May 3, 2004.

47. Daniel Benjamin and Steven Simon, *The Next Attack: The Failure of the War on Terror and a Strategy for Getting It Right* (New York: Owl Books, 2005), p. 49; Ariel Cohen, "The National Security Consequences of Oil Dependency," *Heritage Lectures,* May 14, 2007, p. 4.

48. Maggie Michael, "Saudi Militant Plot Mirrored Sept. 11," Associated Press, April 28, 2007, available at www.phillyburbs.com/pb_dyn/news/93_04282007_1337933.html.

49. Daniel Byman, private correspondence with the author, May 2007.

50. OTA, *U.S. Oil Import Vulnerability,* p. 39; Samil Sen and Tuncay Babah, "Security Concerns in the Middle East for Oil Supply: Problems and Solutions," *Energy Policy* 2007, p. 1518; Sill, "The Macroeconomics of Oil Shocks," p. 24.

51. The Saudis also diverged from this approach in the 1980s, fighting for market share by overproducing to try to force other major oil exporters to do the same. In this case, however, the Saudis were still acting as the "enforcer" of the international oil market by moving to punish those who were refusing to play by the rules. Alan Richards and John Waterbury, *A Political Economy of the Middle East,* 2nd ed. (Boulder, Colo.: Westview, 1998), pp. 60–61; Daniel Yergin, *The Prize: The Epic Quest for Oil, Money and Power,* paperback ed. (New York: Touchstone, 1991), pp. 745–768.

52. Bronson, *Thicker than Oil,* p. 250; Richards and Waterbury, *A Political Economy of the Middle East,* pp. 60–61; Yergin, *The Prize,* pp. 638, 670–673, 747.

53. For an account of the shah's efforts to boost oil prices and the role this played in the Iranian Revolution, see Bakhash, *The Reign of the Ayatollahs,* pp. 10–14; Kenneth M. Pollack, *The Persian Puzzle: The Conflict Between Iran and America* (New York: Random House, 2004), pp. 106–140; Barry Rubin, *Paved with Good Intentions: The American Experience and Iran* (New York: Penguin, 1981), pp. 131–180; Yergin, *The Prize,* pp. 522–525, 605–626.

54. Lawrence Freedman and Efraim Karsh, *The Gulf Conflict, 1990–1991* (Princeton, N.J.: Princeton University Press, 1993), pp. 61–63; Phebe Marr, *The Modern History of Iraq,* 2nd ed. (Boulder, Colo.: Westview, 2004), pp. 217–226; Kenneth M. Pollack, *The Threatening Storm: The Case for Invading Iraq* (New York: Random House, 2002), pp. 30–36; Charles Tripp, *A*

History of Iraq (Cambridge, U.K.: Cambridge University Press, 2000), pp. 252–253.

55. Amatzia Baram, *Building Toward Crisis: Saddam Husayn's Strategy for Survival* (Washington, D.C.: Washington Institute for Near East Policy, 1998), pp. 65–74.

56. Ofra Bengio, *Saddam Speaks on the Gulf Crisis* (Tel Aviv: Moshe Dayan Center for Middle Eastern and African Studies, 1992), p. 15.

57. Alix M. Freedman and Steve Stecklow, "How Iraq Reaps Illegal Oil Profits," *The Wall Street Journal,* May 2, 2002.

58. Osama bin Laden, "Declaration of Jihad Against the Americans," *al-Islah,* September 2, 1996.

59. Scheuer, Ulph, and Daly, "Saudi Arabian Oil Facilities," pp. 7–8.

CHAPTER 2: ISRAEL

1. For examples, see Andrew I. Kilgore, "Israel: No Strategic Asset," *Journal of Palestine Studies* 14, no. 2 (Winter 1985), pp. 222–224; Michael Lind, "Israel Is Not America's Greatest Ally," *Newsweek,* April 8, 2002, p. 17; John Mearsheimer and Stephen Walt, "The Israel Lobby and U.S. Foreign Policy," John F. Kennedy School of Government, working paper RWP06–011, March 2006, pp. 2–14.

2. Samuel W. Lewis, "The United States and Israel: Evolution of an Unwritten Alliance," *The Middle East Journal* 53, no. 3 (Summer 1999), p. 365. Also see Clark Clifford with Richard Holbrooke, "Annals of Government: The Truman Years—Part I," *The New Yorker,* March 25, 1991, pp. 59–71; Charles Lipson, "American Support for Israel: History, Sources, Limits," in *U.S.-Israel Relations at the Crossroads,* ed. Gabriel Sheffer (London: Frank Cass, 1997), pp. 129–132.

3. George Shultz, "The United States and Israel: Partners for Peace and Freedom," *Journal of Palestine Studies* 14, no. 4 (Summer 1985), p. 122.

4. Jerome Slater and Terry Nardin, "Interests vs. Principles: Reassessing the US Commitment to Israel," *The Jerusalem Journal of International Relations* 13, no. 3 (1991), p. 87.

5. Clifford with Holbrooke, "Annals of Government: The Truman Years—Part I," pp. 59–71. I would also note that immediately after recognizing the state of Israel, the United States proceeded to wash its hands of it. The Truman administration would do nothing to help the Israelis defend their state against the simultaneous attack by six Arab armies, refusing to sell them weapons and even threatening to prevent individual Americans from making donations to the foundering new nation. The fact that the Israelis ultimately prevailed—handily—does not change the

fact that we did nothing to help preserve the new state and were motivated almost entirely by fear of jeopardizing the revenues of our oil companies doing business in the Arab world.

6. Ibid.

7. Benny Morris, *Righteous Victims: A History of the Zionist-Arab Conflict, 1881–2001* (New York: Alfred A. Knopf, 1999), esp. pp. 48–66, 106–128; Kenneth Stein, *The Land Question in Palestine, 1917–1939* (Chapel Hill: University of North Carolina Press, 1984).

8. Morris, *Righteous Victims,* pp. 67–76, 121–151.

9. On national self-determination as an element of both U.S. foreign policy and policy toward Israel, see Lipson, "American Support for Israel," pp. 131–132.

10. Clifford with Holbrooke, "Annals of Government: The Truman Years—Part I," p. 63.

11. President Woodrow T. Wilson, "Message to Congress," April 4, 1917, available at http://historymatters.gmu.edu/d/4943/, downloaded May 10, 2007.

12. For a superb recent treatment of the post–World War I negotiations that addresses American support for the principles of self-determination and democratic principles throughout, see Margaret MacMillan, *Paris 1919: Six Months That Changed the World* (New York: Random House, 2001).

13. See for instance, Michael Mandelbaum, *Democracy's Good Name: The Rise and Risks of the World's Most Popular Form of Government* (New York: Public Affairs, 2007).

14. Steve Chan, "In Search of Democratic Peace: Problems and Promise," *Mershon International Studies Review,* May 1997, pp. 59–91; Michael W. Doyle, "Kant, Liberal Legacies, and Foreign Affairs," *Philosophy and Public Affairs* 12, nos. 3 and 4 (Summer and Autumn 1983), pp. 205–235, 323–353; James Lee Ray, "Does Democracy Cause Peace?," *Annual Review of Political Science,* 1998, pp. 27–46; James Lee Ray, "A Lakatosian View of the Democratic Peace Research Program," in *Progress in International Relations Theory,* ed. Colin and Miriam Fendius Elman (Cambridge, Mass.: MIT Press, 2003), pp. 205–244; Bruce Russett and Harvey Starr, "From Democratic Peace to Kantian Peace: Democracy and Conflict in the International System," in *Handbook of War Studies,* 2d ed., ed. Manus Midlarsky (Ann Arbor: University of Michigan Press, 2000), pp. 93–128.

15. President William J. Clinton, "The State of the Union," January 25, 1994, available at www.washingtonpost.com/wp-srv/politics/special/states/docs/sou94.htm, downloaded May 10, 2007.

16. For instance, the Or Commission, charged with ascertaining the circumstances of Jewish-Palestinian violence in October 2000, concluded, "Government handling of the Arab sector has been primarily neglectful

and discriminatory. The establishment did not show sufficient sensitivity to the needs of the Arab population, and did not take enough action in order to allocate state resources in an equal manner. The state did not do enough or try hard enough to create equality for its Arab citizens or to uproot discriminatory or unjust phenomenon." See "Official Summation of the Or Commission Report," *Ha'aretz,* September 2, 2003, available at www.haaretz.com/hasen/pages/ShArt.jhtml?itemNo=335594, downloaded May 16, 2007.

17. Freedom House, *Freedom in the World 2007,* available at www.freedomhouse .org/template.cfm?page=15, downloaded May 16, 2007.

18. Also see Lipson, "American Support for Israel," pp. 132–133; Shultz, "The United States and Israel: Partners for Peace and Freedom," p. 123.

19. The six major Arab-Israeli wars are the Israeli War of Independence, the Suez-Sinai War of 1956, the 1967 Six-Day War, the 1967–1970 War of Attrition, the October War of 1973, and the Israeli invasion of Lebanon in 1982.

20. Lewis, "The United States and Israel: Evolution of an Unwritten Alliance," p. 366.

21. According to newly declassified documents, the U.S. intelligence community had concluded by at least 1974 that Israel possessed a nuclear arsenal. On this, see the declassified text of the Special National Intelligence Estimate (SNIE), "Prospects for Further Proliferation of Nuclear Weapons," September 4, 1974, available at www.gwu.edu/ %7Ensarchiv/NSAEBB/NSAEBB181/sa08.pdf, downloaded January 16, 2008. The relevant page is the first page of the SNIE, which was also declassified as page 6 of "Memorandum from Atherton and Kratzer to Mr. Sisco, 'Response to Congressional Questions on Israel's Nuclear Capabilities,'" October 15, 1975, Secret, RG 59, Records of Joseph Sisco, box 40, Israeli Nuclear Capability 1975, available at www.gwu.edu/ ~nsarchiv/NSAEBB/NSAEBB189/IN-30.pdf, downloaded October 21, 2007. The third paragraph of the SNIE begins with the sentence "We believe that Israel already has produced nuclear weapons." This was the estimate's key judgment regarding the Israelis' nuclear arsenal. We do not know whether the U.S. intelligence community reached this conclusion prior to 1974, although scholars contend that Israel had developed nuclear weapons by 1966. For instance, see Avner Cohen, *Israel and the Bomb* (New York: Columbia University Press, 1998), pp. 99–174. In addition, another declassified document ["Parker T. Hart to Secretary Dean Rusk, 'Issues to Be Considered in Connection with Negotiations with Israel for F-4 Phantom Aircraft,'" October 15, 1968, Top Secret/ Nodis Sensitive, SN 67–69, Def 12–5 Isr, available at www.gwu.edu/ ~nsarchiv/NSAEBB/NSAEBB189/IN-02.pdf, downloaded October

21, 2007] states that as early as October 1968, the State Department had concluded that "All evidence suggests that present Israeli policy is to maintain its nuclear option and to proceed with a program to reduce to a minimum the lead time required to exercise that option." In other words, in late 1968—six years before the intelligence community estimate noted above and seven years before the State Department memo arguing that the Nixon administration should continue to assert that the United States had no concrete proof that Israel possessed nuclear weapons—even the State Department believed that Israel at least possessed a program designed to provide a nuclear weapons capability.

22. Warren Bass, *Support Any Friend: Kennedy's Middle East and the Making of the U.S.-Israel Alliance* (Oxford, U.K.: Oxford University Press, 2003); Abraham Ben-Tzvi, *Decade of Transition: Eisenhower, Kennedy, and the Origins of the American-Israeli Alliance* (New York: Columbia University Press, 1998); Mordechai Gazit, "The Genesis of the US-Israeli Military-Strategic Relationship and the Dimona Issue," *Journal of Contemporary History* 35, no. 3 (July 2000), pp. 413–422; Lipson, "American Support for Israel: History, Sources, Limits," pp. 129–142; Douglas Little, "The Making of a Special Relationship: The United States and Israel, 1957–68," *International Journal of Middle East Studies* 25, no. 4 (November 1993), pp. 563–585; Kenneth Organski, *The $36 Billion Bargain: Strategy and Politics in U.S. Assistance to Israel* (New York: Columbia University Press, 1990); Steven L. Spiegel, *The Other Arab-Israel Conflict: Making America's Middle East Policy from Truman to Reagan* (Chicago: University of Chicago Press, 1985).

23. In 2005 and 2006, the United States government declassified a number of important documents detailing the American effort first to convince Israel not to develop nuclear weapons and then to refrain from testing one. Some of the most important of these include (in addition to those mentioned in note 21, above), State Department Briefing Paper for Eshkol-Johnson talks, "Israel: The Nuclear Issue and Sophisticated Weapons," December 31, 1967, Department of State Records, Record Group 59 [RG 59], Subject-Numeric Files, 1967–1969 [SN 67–69], DEF 12, available at www.gwu.edu/~nsarchiv/NSAEBB/NSAEBB189/IN-01.pdf, downloaded October 21, 2007; Henry Owen to the secretary, "Impact on U.S. Policies of an Israeli Nuclear Weapons Capability," February 7, 1969, Secret/Nodis/Noforn☐Source: SN 67-69, DEF 12 Isr, available at www.gwu.edu/~nsarchiv/NSAEBB/NSAEBB189/IN-05.pdf, downloaded October 21, 2007; Richardson to president, "Israel's Nuclear Program," with memorandum of conversation attached, August 1, 1969, Top Secret/Nodis, NPMP, NSCF, box 604, Israel vol. II, available at www.gwu.edu/~nsarchiv/NSAEBB/NSAEBB189/IN-15.pdf, downloaded October 21, 2007; Theodore L. Eliot, State Department execu-

tive secretary, to Henry Kissinger, "Briefing Book—Visit of Mrs. Golda Meir," September 19, 1969, enclosing "Background—Israel's Nuclear Weapon and Missile Programs," Top Secret/Nodis, SN 67–69, Pol 7 Isr, available at www.gwu.edu/~nsarchiv/NSAEBB/NSAEBB189/IN-21.pdf, downloaded October 21, 2007; Kissinger to the president, "Discussions with the Israelis on Nuclear Matters," October 7, 1969, Top Secret/Sensitive/Nodis, NPMP, NSCF, box 605, Israel vol. III, available at www.gwu.edu/~nsarchiv/NSAEBB/NSAEBB189/IN-22.pdf, downloaded on October 21, 2007; "Memorandum from Atherton and Kratzer to Mr. Sisco, 'Response to Congressional Questions on Israel's Nuclear Capabilities.'" Also see Gerald Steinberg, "Israel and the United States: Can the Special Relationship Survive the New Strategic Environment?," *Middle East Review of International Affairs* 2, no. 4 (November 1998), pp. 9–10.

24. Ze'ev Schiff and Ehud Ya'ari, *Israel's Lebanon War* (New York: Simon and Schuster, 1984), pp. 67–70, 205–211.

25. Scott Lasensky, "Friendly Restraint: U.S.-Israel Relations During the Gulf Crisis of 1990–91," *Middle East Review of International Affairs* 3, no. 2 (June 1999); Steinberg, "Israel and the United States: Can the Special Relationship Survive the New Strategic Environment?," p. 5.

26. Lewis, "The United States and Israel: Evolution of an Unwritten Alliance," pp. 374–376; Robert J. Lieber, "U.S.-Israeli Relations Since 1948," *Middle East Review of International Affairs* 2, no. 3 (September 1998), pp. 5–6; Dennis Ross, *The Missing Peace: The Inside Story of the Fight for Middle East Peace* (New York: Farrar, Straus and Giroux, 2004), pp. 6–7.

27. Jonathan Rynhold, "Israeli-American Relations and the Peace Process," *Middle East Review of International Affairs* 4, no. 2 (June 2000), pp. 38–53.

28. Ross, *The Missing Peace*, p. 7. Also see Lieber, "U.S.-Israeli Relations Since 1948," p. 6.

29. Rachel Bronson, *Thicker Than Oil: America's Uneasy Partnership with Saudi Arabia* (New York: Oxford University Press, 2006), pp. 117–118.

30. Steven David, "Bosom of Abraham: America's Enduring Affection for Israel," *Policy Review,* Winter 1991, p. 57. There is one exception that bears mentioning, and that is the Israeli attack on the U.S.S. *Liberty* in June 1967. The *Liberty* was an intelligence collection vessel monitoring the fighting between Israel and the Arabs during the Six-Day War when Israeli warplanes and torpedo boats attacked it, killing 34 Americans and wounding another 173. The Israeli government claimed that the attack was an accident and paid reparations to the United States and the families of the victims. Although I have never been made privy to evidence unavailable to the public, the circumstances of the attack as described by the publicly available sources leave open the possibility that the Israelis

were aware that the *Liberty* was an American ship and that it was targeted deliberately. Many Americans, from then-CIA Director Richard Helms and Secretary of State Dean Rusk to the surviving members of the crew, believe that the attack was intentional. On the *Liberty*, see Chief of Naval Operations, "Record of Proceedings: Court of Inquiry to inquire into the circumstances surrounding the armed attack on USS LIBERTY (AGTR–5) on June 8, 1967," Department of the Navy, available at www.thelibertyincident.com/docs/CourtOfInquiry.pdf, downloaded January 16, 2008; James M. Ennes, Jr., *Assault on the* Liberty: *The True Story of the Israeli Attack on an American Intelligence Ship* (privately published, 1980); Jay A. Cristol, *The Liberty Incident: The 1967 Israeli Attack on the U.S. Navy Spy Ship* (Dulles, Va.: Brassey's, 2002); Michael Oren, "The USS *Liberty*: Case Closed," *Azure,* Spring 2000.

31. David, "Bosom of Abraham," p. 57.

32. Steinberg, "Israel and the United States: Can the Special Relationship Survive the New Strategic Environment?," p. 2.

33. U.S. Department of Commerce, International Trade Administration, "Top 50 Partners in Total U.S. Trade in 2003," available at www.ita.doc.gov/td/industry/otea/usfth/aggregate/H03T09.html, downloaded on May 22, 2007.

34. CIA, *World Factbook,* 2007, available at https://www.cia.gov/library/publications/the-world-factbook/index.html.

35. Ahron Bregman and Jihan El-Tahri, *Israel and the Arabs: An Eyewitness Account of War and Peace in the Middle East* (New York: TV Books, 2000), pp. 38–40; Slater and Nardin, "Interests vs. Principles," p. 97, n. 2.

36. Quoted in Lipson, "American Support for Israel," p. 138.

37. As one example among many, a January 2007 BBC/PIPA poll of twenty-seven nations found that people in Lebanon, Egypt, and the UAR (the only three Arab states surveyed) were all in the top five of nations with the most negative views of Israel. Fully 85 percent of Lebanese, 78 percent of Egyptians, and 73 percent of Emiratis held mainly negative views of Israel, while only 6, 5, and 7 percent, respectively, held mainly positive views of the Jewish state. BBC World Service, "Israel and Iran Share Most Negative Ratings in Global Poll," March 6, 2007, available at http://news.bbc.co.uk/1/shared/bsp/hi/pdfs/06_03_07_perceptions.pdf, downloaded May 16, 2007.

38. The old canard of the "Israel lobby" could be raised here as well—claiming that the reason that we have sanctions on these countries is/was because of AIPAC's lobbying. That is patently untrue in the cases of Sudan and of Iraq under Saddam. The sanctions on Iran and Syria stem from their inclusion in the State Department's "terrorism list." Both states do support terrorist groups, such as Hizballah, although Iran has

not directly attacked Americans since 1996 and Syria has not been tied to a direct attack on Americans since the 1980s. There is no question that AIPAC has agitated for harsh measures against Iran over the years, but Iran's inclusion on the terrorism list had little to do with Israel or AIPAC, and AIPAC's actions to convince the U.S. government to close the loopholes in the Iran sanctions in the 1990s were only part of the motives of the Clinton administration on this issue. See Pollack, *The Persian Puzzle,* pp. 259–289.

39. Lipson, "American Support for Israel," p. 135.
40. Kenneth M. Pollack, *The Persian Puzzle: The Conflict Between Iran and America* (New York: Random House, 2004), especially pp. 93–97, 141–180.
41. See "The Hashemite Kingdom of Jordan: Foreign Affairs, A Commitment to World Peace," available at www.kinghussein.gov.jo/f_affairs 5.html, downloaded May 12, 2007; author's interviews with U.S. Department of Defense personnel, March 1997.
42. Author's interviews with U.S. military officers, February–April 1997, October–December 1997.
43. On the limited military effectiveness and professionalism of many Arab militaries, see Kenneth M. Pollack, *Arabs at War: Military Effectiveness, 1948–1991* (Lincoln: University of Nebraska Press, 2002).
44. Gilles Kepel, *The War for Muslim Minds: Islam and the West* (Cambridge, Mass.: The Belknap Press of Harvard University Press, 2004), pp. 13–14.

CHAPTER 3: AMERICA'S ARAB ALLIES

1. Rachel Bronson, *Thicker Than Oil: America's Uneasy Partnership with Saudi Arabia* (New York: Oxford University Press, 2006).
2. Bronson provides a nice summary of her arguments on pp. 21–27 of *Thicker Than Oil.*
3. Bronson, *Thicker Than Oil,* pp. 129–131.
4. Ibid., pp. 168, 177–185.
5. Ibid., pp. 147–150, 168–177.
6. Alfred B. Prados, "Saudi Arabia: Current Issues and U.S. Relations," Congressional Research Service Brief for Congress IB93113, Washington, D.C., August 4, 2003, p. 11.
7. CIA, *World Factbook,* 2007, available at https://www.cia.gov/library/publications/the-world-factbook/index.html.
8. Kenneth M. Pollack, *Arabs at War: Military Effectiveness, 1948–1991* (Lincoln: University of Nebraska Press, 2002), pp. 131–137; and author's interviews with U.S. and foreign government officials, May 1992–March 1997.
9. Martin S. Indyk, "A Strategy for Resolving the Conflict in Lebanon," *Financial Times,* July 23, 2006.

10. Dennis Ross, *The Missing Peace: The Inside Story of the Fight for Middle East Peace* (New York: Farrar, Straus and Giroux, 2004), pp. 693–694.

11. Author's interviews with U.S. military officers, February–April 1997.

12. United States International Trade Commission: http://dataweb.usitc.gov.

13. Ibid.

14. Gal Luft, "America's Oil Dependence and Its Implications for U.S. Middle East Policy," testimony before the Senate Foreign Relations Subcommittee on Near Eastern and South Asian Affairs, October 20, 2005, available at http://foreign.senate.gov/testimony/2005/LuftTestimony 051020.pdf; Gal Luft and Anne Korin, "Fueled Again? In Search of Energy Security," in *Blindside: How to Anticipate Forcing Events and Wild Cards in Global Politics,* ed. Francis Fukuyama (Washington, D.C.: Brookings, 2007), pp. 71–81; David Sandalow, *Freedom from Oil: How the Next President Can End the United States' Oil Addiction* (New York: McGraw-Hill, 2007).

CHAPTER 4: NONPROLIFERATION AND NONINTERESTS

1. See the sources in chapter 2, notes 21 and 23, above. Also see Warren Bass, *Support Any Friend: Kennedy's Middle East and the Making of the U.S.-Israel Alliance* (Oxford, U.K.: Oxford University Press, 2003), pp. 186–238; Avner Cohen, *Israel and the Bomb* (New York: Columbia University Press, 1998), pp. 99–174; Mordechai Gazit, "The Genesis of the US-Israeli Military-Strategic Relationship and the Dimona Issue," *Journal of Contemporary History* 35, no. 3 (July 2000), pp. 413–422.

2. This was the best strategic rationale for the 2003 invasion of Iraq, although, of course, we later learned that Saddam had shelved his WMD programs and was nowhere near as close to obtaining a nuclear weapon as the Bush administration or most of the world's intelligence services believed at the time. For my own argument on this threat, see Kenneth M. Pollack, *The Threatening Storm: The Case for Invading Iraq* (New York: Random House, 2002), especially pp. 148–153, 168–180, 248–280. For my postwar reassessment, see Kenneth M. Pollack, "Spies, Lies and Weapons: What Went Wrong?," *The Atlantic Monthly,* January–February 2004, pp. 79–92.

3. Mitchell Reiss, *Bridled Ambitions: Why Countries Constrain Their Nuclear Capabilities* (Washington, D.C.: Woodrow Wilson Center Press, 1995); T. V. Paul, *Power Versus Prudence: Why Nations Forgo Nuclear Weapons* (Montreal: McGill–Queen's University Press, 2000); Ariel Levite, "Never Say Never Again: Nuclear Reversal Revisited," *International Security* 2, no. 3 (Winter 2002–03), pp. 59–88; and Kurt M. Campbell, Robert J. Einhorn, and Mitchell B. Reiss, eds., *The Nuclear Tipping Point: Why States Reconsider Their Nuclear Choices* (Washington, D.C.: Brookings Institution Press,

2004); James Walsh, "Bombs Unbuilt: Power, Ideas, and Institutions in International Politics," Ph.D. dissertation, Massachusetts Institute of Technology, Cambridge, Mass., June 2001.

4. I have purposely excluded North Korea from this list. Although the North Koreans did successfully proliferate against the will of the international community, they paid an outrageous price for doing so. In effect, 3 million North Koreans starved to death and many others live in abject poverty because Pyongyang refused to give up its nuclear program. No other nation on Earth would be willing to make such a sacrifice, and so the North Korean case actually reinforces the disincentives for proliferation.

PART TWO: THE PROBLEMS OF THE MODERN MIDDLE EAST

CHAPTER 5: A SEA OF SOCIOECONOMIC PROBLEMS

1. Marcus Noland and Howard Pack, *The Arab Economies in a Changing World* (Washington, D.C.: Peterson Institute for International Economics, 2007), pp. 2, 86–87.

2. Anthony H. Cordesman, "The Middle East: The Broader Forces Shaping Regional Stability," Center for Strategic and International Studies, Washington, D.C., April 28, 2003, p. 4.

3. Noland and Pack, *The Arab Economies in a Changing World*, pp. 86–87.

4. Alan Richards, "Economic Reform in the Middle East: The Challenge to Governance," in *The Future Security Environment in the Middle East: Conflict, Stability and Political Change,* ed. Nora Bensahel and Daniel L. Byman (Santa Monica, Calif.: RAND, 2004), p. 65.

5. Noland and Pack, *The Arab Economies in a Changing World*, p. 1.

6. Cordesman, "The Middle East: The Broader Forces Shaping Regional Stability," p. 15.

7. Richards, "Economic Reform in the Middle East: The Challenge to Governance," p. 61.

8. Noland and Pack, *The Arab Economies in a Changing World*, p. 85.

9. World Bank, *Middle East and North Africa Region Economic Developments and Prospects, 2007: Job Creation in an Era of High Growth* (Washington, D.C.: World Bank, 2007), p. 37.

10. Noland and Pack, *The Arab Economies in a Changing World*, pp. 2–3.

11. International Labour Organization, "Global Employment Trends for Youth," 2006, p. 13, available at www.ilo.org/public/english/employment/strat/download/gety06en.pdf.

12. Daniel Pearl, "Booming Population Forces Saudi Arabia to Address the Resentment of Its Poor," *The Wall Street Journal,* June 26, 2000.

13. Cassandra, "The Impending Crisis in Egypt," *Middle East Journal* 49, no. 1 (Winter 1995), p. 21.

14. Richards, "Economic Reform in the Middle East," pp. 72–73; Alan Richards and John Waterbury, *A Political Economy of the Middle East,* 2nd ed. (Boulder, Colo.: Westview Press, 1998), pp. 257–260. Note that a third edition of Richards and Waterbury was published in 2007. I cite both editions throughout, indicating which by referencing the year of publication.

15. World Bank, *World Development Indicators 2005* (Washington, D.C.: The World Bank, 2005), pp. 166–168; U.S. Census Bureau, International Data Base, available at www.census.gov/ipc/www/idbsum.html, downloaded May 30, 2007.

16. World Bank, *Middle East and North Africa Region Economic Developments and Prospects, 2007,* p. 39.

17. Noland and Pack, *The Arab Economies in a Changing World,* pp. 75–76.

18. Pearl, "Booming Population Forces Saudi Arabia to Address the Resentment of Its Poor"; U.N. Economic and Social Commission for Western Asia, "Youth Unemployment in the ESCWA Region," 2002, available at www.un.org/esa/socdev/poverty/papers/youth_unescwa.pdf, downloaded June 4, 2007, p. 2.

19. Paul Sullivan, "Economic Stress and Instability in the Arab World," *Strategic Insight* 2, no. 5 (May 2003).

20. International Labour Organization, "Global Employment Trends Brief," January 2007, pp. 1, 3.

21. Edmund O'Sullivan, "To Create Jobs in the Middle East You Need to Have Growth: Unemployment Is High and Growing in the Middle East," *Middle East Economic Digest,* October 31, 2003; Robert Looney, "Can Saudi Arabia Reform Its Economy in Time to Head Off Disaster?" *Strategic Insight* 3, no. 1 (January 2004), p. 1; Tarik M. Yousef, "Development, Growth and Policy Reform in the Middle East and North Africa Since 1950," *The Journal of Economic Perspectives* 18, no. 3 (Summer 2004), p. 102.

22. Charles Levinson, "Egyptian President Hosni Mubarak Meets with President Bush Sunday in Crawford, Texas," *The Christian Science Monitor,* April 12, 2004.

23. CIA, *World Factbook,* 2007; Looney, "Can Saudi Arabia Reform Its Economy in Time to Head Off Disaster?," p. 1; "Saudi Arabia's Unemployment Reaches 30 Percent," ArabicNews.Com, March 5, 2003.

24. Nimrod Raphaeli, "Unemployment in the Middle East—Causes and Consequences," MEMRI (Middle East Media Research Institute), February 11, 2006.

25. U.N. Economic and Social Commission for Western Asia, "Youth Unemployment in the ESCWA Region," p. 2.

26. International Labour Organization, "Global Employment Trends for Youth," pp. 3–4, 15.

27. Alan Richards and John Waterbury, *A Political Economy of the Middle East,* 3rd ed. (Boulder, Colo.: Westview Press, 2007), p. 135.

28. Paul Rivlin and Shmuel Even, *Political Stability in Arab States: Economic Causes and Consequences,* Memorandum 74 (Tel Aviv, Israel: Jaffee Center for Strategic Studies, 2004), p. 23.

29. Noland and Pack, *The Arab Economies in a Changing World,* pp. 3, 85, 96.

30. World Bank, *Middle East and North Africa Region Economic Developments and Prospects, 2007: Job Creation in an Era of High Growth,* p. 86.

31. U.N. Economic and Social Commission for Western Asia, "Youth Unemployment in the ESCWA Region," p. 3.

32. Nader Fergany, "Aspects of Labor Migration and Unemployment in the Arab Region," Almishkat Center for Research, Egypt, February 2001, p. 2.

33. Ibid., p. 3.

34. Ibid., p. 5.

35. George T. Abed and Hamid R. Davoodi, "Challenges of Growth and Globalization in the Middle East and North Africa," International Monetary Fund, Washington, D.C., 2003.

36. Noland and Pack, *The Arab Economies in a Changing World,* pp. 100–101.

37. Ibid., p. 101.

38. Ibid., pp. 102–103; Paul Sullivan, "Economic Stress and Instability in the Arab World."

39. Sullivan, "Economic Stress and Instability in the Arab World."

40. Abed and Davoodi, "Challenges of Growth and Globalization in the Middle East and North Africa"; Edward Gardner, "Creating Employment in the Middle East and North Africa," International Monetary Fund, Washington, D.C., 2003, p. 9; Noland and Pack, *The Arab Economies in a Changing World,* pp. 106–107.

41. Noland and Pack, *The Arab Economies in a Changing World,* pp. 105–108.

42. Fergany, "Aspects of Labor Migration and Unemployment in the Arab Region," pp. 2–3.

43. World Bank, *World Development Indicators,* 2007, p. 185. Note that the World Bank figures are for the entire Middle East and North Africa region, which includes Iran, Pakistan, and Afghanistan, which is why this grouping accounts for 7.7 percent of global population, compared to 5 percent for the Arab world alone.

44. *Arab Human Development Report (AHDR)* 2003, p. 137.

45. Ibid., p. 138.

46. The World Bank, *Middle East and North Africa Region Economic Developments and Prospects, 2007: Job Creation in an Era of High Growth,* p. 91.

47. International Labour Organization, "Global Employment Trends Brief," January 2007, p. 4, available at www.ilo.org/public/english/employment/strat/download/getaf07.pdf.

48. Raphaeli, "Unemployment in the Middle East—Causes and Consequences."

49. Delwin A. Roy, "Saudi Arabian Education: Development Policy," *Middle Eastern Studies* 28, no. 3 (July 1992), p. 478.

50. *AHDR* 2003, p. 6; Noland and Pack, *The Arab Economies in a Changing World,* pp. 105–119.

51. Ibid., pp. 111–113.

52. Abed and Davoodi, "Challenges of Growth and Globalization in the Middle East and North Africa."

53. Richards, "Economic Reform in the Middle East," p. 77.

54. Fergany, "Aspects of Labor Migration and Unemployment in the Arab Region," has an excellent and sophisticated discussion of the impact of migrant Arab workers in the Gulf region and their economic impact.

55. Rivlin and Even, *Political Stability in Arab States: Economic Causes and Consequences,* p. 22.

56. The latest oil boom, which began in 2003, has not had the same impact on the non-oil-producing states, largely because the oil exporters are relying more heavily on South and Southeast Asians for labor and are not providing nearly the same levels of aid to their poorer Arab relations. See "Middle East Enjoying Oil Boom—with Restraint: Oil Producers' High Growth Rates Boost Region," World Bank, June 28, 2006, available online at http://web.worldbank.org/WBSITE/EXTERNAL/NEWS/0,,contentMDK:20972276~pagePK:64257043~piPK:437376~theSitePK:4607,00.html, downloaded June 9, 2007.

57. *AHDR* 2003, p. 10. For a more skeptical analysis of the oil curse, see E. Roger Owen, "One Hundred Years of Middle Eastern Oil," Middle East Brief, no. 24, Crown Center for Middle East Studies, Brandeis University, January 2008.

58. Noland and Pack, *The Arab Economies in a Changing World,* p. 14.

59. For a good discussion of the resource curse (of which the oil curse is a subset), see Paul Collier, *The Bottom Billion: Why the Poorest Countries Are Failing and What Can Be Done About It* (London: Oxford University Press, 2007), pp. 39–52.

60. Noland and Pack, *The Arab Economies in a Changing World,* p. 30.

61. World Bank, *Middle East and North Africa Region Economic Developments and Prospects, 2007: Job Creation in an Era of High Growth,* p. 40.

62. Quoted in Noland and Pack, *The Arab Economies in a Changing World,* p. 94.

63. Noland and Pack, *The Arab Economies in a Changing World,* p. 27.

64. For an excellent discussion of this issue, see Richards, "Economic Reform in the Middle East," pp. 68–72.

65. Quoted in Looney, "Can Saudi Arabia Reform Its Economy in Time to Head Off Disaster?," p. 1.

66. Ibid.

67. Marcus Noland and Howard Pack, "Arab Economies at a Tipping Point," *Middle East Policy* 15, no. 1 (Winter 2008), available at http://www.iie .com/publications/papers/noland-pack02081.pdf.

68. Ali M. Ansari, *Modern Iran Since 1921: The Pahlavis and After* (London: Longman, 2003), pp. 192–193; author's interview with Shaul Bakhash, June 21, 2004; Fred Halliday, "Iran: The Economic Contradictions," *MERIP Reports,* no. 69 (July–August 1978), pp. 16–17; Kenneth M. Pollack, *The Persian Puzzle: The Conflict Between Iran and America* (New York: Random House, 2004), pp. 110–114; Barry Rubin, *Paved with Good Intentions: The American Experience and Iran* (New York: Penguin, 1981), p. 143.

69. Ahmed Galal, "The Paradox of Education and Unemployment in Egypt," Egyptian Center for Economic Studies, Cairo, Egypt, March 2002, p. 4; *AHDR* 2003, pp. 3, 71–72.

70. Farrukh Iqbal, *Sustaining Gains in Poverty Reduction and Human Development in the Middle East and North Africa* (Washington, D.C.: World Bank, 2006), p. 45.

71. Milken Institute, "Global Demographics," March 1999, available at www.milkeninstitute.org/pdf/globaldemographics.pdf, downloaded June 4, 2007.

72. *AHDR* 2002, pp. 52–55; Iqbal, *Sustaining Gains in Poverty Reduction and Human Development in the Middle East and North Africa,* pp. 33–46; Noland and Pack, *The Arab Economies in a Changing World,* p. 70.

73. Abed and Davoodi, "Challenges of Growth and Globalization in the Middle East and North Africa."

74. *AHDR* 2002, p. 53.

75. Ibid., p. 54.

76. Iqbal, *Sustaining Gains in Poverty Reduction and Human Development in the Middle East and North Africa,* pp. 44–45.

77. For instance, see Delwin A. Roy, "Saudi Arabian Education: Development Policy," *Middle Eastern Studies* 28, no. 3 (July 1992), pp. 481–483.

78. *AHDR* 2003, p. 55.

79. For the results of these studies, see *AHDR* 2003, pp. 55–56; "Trends in International Mathematics and Science Study, 2003, Chapter 1: International Student Achievement in Math," available at http://isc.bc.edu/ PDF/t03_download/T03_M_Chap1.pdf, downloaded May 28, 2007; and Trends in International Mathematics and Science Study, 2003, chap. 1:

International Student Achievement in Science, available at http://isc.bc .edu/PDF/t03_download/T03_S_Chap1.pdf, downloaded May 28, 2007.

80. For concurring views, see Ahmed Galal, "The Paradox of Education and Unemployment in Egypt," Egyptian Center for Economic Studies, March 2002, pp. 2–4; *AHDR* 2003, especially pp. 51–56; Noland and Pack, *The Arab Economies in a Changing World,* p. 37; Roy, "Saudi Arabian Education," pp. 480, 483–484, 489, 506.

81. *AHDR* 2003, p. 3.

82. Roy, "Saudi Arabian Education," p. 485. This poor quality comes through in a variety of ways. One obvious one is the consistently poor rankings of the various Arab states in the quadrennial International Mathematics and Science Studies described above. Another is that in parallel rankings by *The Times* of London and Shanghai Jiao Tong University of the two hundred best universities in the world and the five hundred best universities in the world, respectively, not a single Arab university made either list—the only region of the world with such a dubious distinction (Noland and Pack, *The Arab Economies in a Changing World,* p. 37). The *Arab Human Development Report* has illustrated the same point by noting that although Arabs constitute 5 percent of global population, on average the Arab states produce only 1.1 percent of the books published in the world each year (*AHDR* 2003, p. 4).

83. *AHDR* 2003, pp. 72–73.

84. Galal, "The Paradox of Education and Unemployment in Egypt," pp. 8–9.

85. Roderic D. Matthews and Matta Akrawi, *Education in Arab Countries of the Near East* (Washington, D.C.: American Council on Education, 1949), pp. 170, 542–543; Joseph Szyliowicz, *Education and Modernization in the Middle East* (Ithaca, N.Y.: Cornell University Press), p. 197.

86. Gerald D. Miller, "Classroom 19: A Study in Behavior in a Classroom of a Moroccan Primary School," in *Psychological Dimensions of Near Eastern Studies,* ed. L. Carl Brown and Norman Itkowitz (Princeton, N.J.: Darwin Press, 1977), p. 152.

87. Szyliowicz, *Education and Modernization in the Middle East,* p. 186. See also Mohamed Rabie, "The Future of Education in the Arab World," *The Arab Future,* ed. Michael Hudson, p. 24; Fahim I. Qubain, *Education and Science in the Arab World* (Baltimore, Md.: Johns Hopkins University Press), p. 8.

88. For instance, my doctoral thesis examined the impact of this educational method—and the cultural patterns of behavior it both reflected and inculcated—on Arab military operations. See Kenneth M. Pollack, "The Influence of Arab Culture on Arab Military Effectiveness," Ph.D. dissertation, Massachusetts Institute of Technology, Cambridge, Mass., 1996.

89. For a lengthy discussion of how culture develops and changes over

time—and making clear that, contrary to many orientalist tracts, culture is not timeless—see Pollack, "The Influence of Arab Culture on Arab Military Effectiveness," pp. 37–44.

90. Halim Barakat, *The Arab World: Society, Culture, and State* (Berkeley: University of California Press, 1993), p. 118.

91. See, e.g., Hamed Ammar, *Growing Up in an Egyptian Village: Silwa, Province of Aswan* (New York: Octagon Books, 1973), p. 127; Halim Barakat, "Socioeconomic, Cultural and Personality Forces Determining Development in Arab Society," in *Arab Society in Transition: A Reader,* ed. Saad Eddin Ibrahim and Nicholas S. Hopkins (Malta: Interprint [Malta] Ltd., 1977), p. 680; Sania Hamady, *The Temperament and Character of the Arabs* (New York: Twayne, 1960), p. 70.

92. *AHDR* 2003, p. 3, also p. 53.

93. Halim Barakat, "Beyond the Always and the Never: A Critique of Social Psychological Interpretations of Arab Society and Culture," in *Theory, Politics and the Arab World: Critical Responses,* ed. Hisham Sharabi (New York: Routledge, 1990), pp. 144, 146. On this point, see also Ammar, *Growing Up in an Egyptian Village,* pp. 50, 52, 127; Barakat, *The Arab World,* p. 23; Barakat, "Socioeconomic, Cultural and Personality Forces Determining Development in Arab Society," p. 680; Morroe Berger, *The Arab World Today* (New York: Anchor, 1962), p. 113; Jacques Berque, *The Arabs* (New York: Praeger, 1965), p. 103; Leonard Binder, "Egypt: The Integrative Revolution," *Political Culture and Political Development,* ed. Lucian W. Pye and Sidney Verba (Princeton, N.J.: Princeton University Press, 1965), p. 409; Raymond Cohen, *Culture and Conflict in Egyptian-Israeli Relations* (Bloomington: Indiana University Press, 1990), p. 27; George H. Gardner, "The Arab Middle East: Some Background Interpretations," *The Journal of Social Issues* 20, no. 3 (1959), pp. 24–25, 39; Hamady, *The Temperament and Character of the Arabs,* p. 32; Ibrahim and Hopkins, *Arab Society in Transition,* pp. 83–84; Ilse Lichtenstadter, "An Arab-Egyptian Family," in *Readings in Arab Middle Eastern Studies and Cultures,* ed. Abdulla M. Lutfiyya and Charles W. Churchill (The Hague: Mouton, 1970), p. 607; Pegrouhi Najarian, "Adjustment in the Family and Patterns of Family Living," *Journal of Social Issues* 15, no. 3 (1959), pp. 35–36; Anthony Pascal, Michael Kennedy, and Steven Rosen, *Men and Arms in the Middle East: The Human Factor in Military Modernization,* RAND R–2460-NA, Santa Monica, Calif., June 1979, p. 27; Hisham Sharabi in collaboration with Mukhtar Ani, "Impact of Class and Culture on Social Behavior: The Feudal-Bourgeois Family in Arab Society," in *Psychological Dimensions of Near Eastern Studies,* ed. L. Carl Brown and Norman Itkowitz (Princeton, N.J.: Darwin Press, 1977), p. 243; Hisham Sharabi, *Neopatriarchy: A Theory of Distorted Change in Arab Society* (Oxford, U.K.: Oxford University Press, 1988), pp. 7–20, 44–47;

C. A. O. van Nieuwenhuijze, *Sociology of the Middle East* (Leiden: E. J. Brill, 1971), pp. 385–386; Unni Wikan, *Life Among the Poor in Cairo,* trans. Ann Henning (London: Tavistock Publications, 1980), p. 65.

94. Ammar, *Growing Up in an Egyptian Village,* p. 231.

95. Cohen, *Culture and Conflict in Egyptian-Israeli Relations,* p. 22.

96. Ibid.

97. Ibid.

98. Barakat, *The Arab World,* p. 106. See also Ammar, *Growing Up in an Egyptian Village,* pp. 48, 132; Barakat, "Between the Always and the Never," p. 146; Barakat, *The Arab World,* pp. 201–205; Berger, *The Arab World Today,* p. 136; Cohen, *Culture and Conflict in Egyptian-Israeli Relations,* p. 22; Hamady, *The Temperament and Character of the Arabs,* pp. 28, 34; Ibrahim and Hopkins, *Arab Society in Transition,* pp. 83–84; Mounah Khouri, "Criticism and the Heritage: Adonis as Advocate of a New Arab Culture," in *Arab Civilization: Challenges and Responses,* ed. George N. Atiyeh and Ibrahim M. Oweiss (Albany, N.Y.: SUNY Press, 1988), p. 188; Abdullah M. Lutfiyya, *Baytin: A Jordanian Village* (The Hague: Mouton, 1966), p. 49; Fatima Mernissi, *Islam and Democracy,* trans. Mary Jo Lakeland (Reading, Mass.: Addison-Wesley, 1992), pp. 104–113; van Nieuwenhuijze, *Sociology of the Middle East,* p. 381; Sharabi, *Neopatriarchy,* p. 47; Afif I. Tannous, "Group Behavior in the Village Community of Lebanon," in *Readings in Arab Middle Eastern Studies and Culture,* ed. Abdulla M. Lutfiyya and Charles W. Churchill (The Hague: Mouton, 1970), p. 100.

99. Ibrahim and Hopkins, *Arab Society in Transition,* p. 83–84.

100. See Barakat, "Beyond the Always and the Never," p. 143.

101. Sharabi with Ani, "Impact of Class and Culture on Social Behavior," p. 250.

102. Sana Al-Khayyat, *Honor and Shame: Women in Modern Iraq* (London: Saqi Books, 1990), p. 53. See also Barakat, *The Arab World,* pp. 105–106; Ibrahim and Hopkins, *Arab Society in Transition,* p. 84.

103. Bassam Tibi, *Islam and the Cultural Accommodation of Social Change,* trans. Clare Krojzl (Boulder, Colo.: Westview Press, 1991), p. 103.

104. Richards and Waterbury, *A Political Economy of the Middle East,* 2007, p. 122. See also Miller, "Classroom 19," p. 144.

105. Miller, "Classroom 19," pp. 142–153; Anthony Pascal, Michael Kennedy, and Steven Rosen, *Men and Arms in the Middle East: The Human Factor in Military Modernization,* RAND R-2460-NA, RAND, Santa Monica, June 1979, p. 25.

106. Pervez Hoodbhoy, *Islam and Science* (London: Zed Books, 1991), 38–39.

107. Dale F. Eickelman, *The Middle East: An Anthropological Approach* (Englewood Cliffs, N.J.: Prentice Hall, 1981), pp. 238–240; Hoodbhoy, *Islam and Science,* pp. 55–65, 123–124.

108. See, e.g., Sharabi, *Neopatriarchy*, p. 85.

109. *AHDR 2003*, p. 54. See also Ammar, *Growing Up in an Egyptian Village*, p. 204, fn. 2.

110. Lisa Anderson, "Arab Democracy: Dismal Prospects," *World Policy Journal* 18, no. 3 (Fall 2001), pp. 53–61; Berger, *The Arab World Today*, p. 119; Hamady, *The Temperament and Character of the Arabs*, p. 211; Hoodbhoy, *Islam and Science*, p. 39; David Lamb, *The Arabs*, paperback edition (New York: Vintage Books, 1988), p. 4; Mernissi, *Islam and Democracy*, p. 78; Pascal et al., *Men and Arms in the Middle East*, pp. 23, 25, 34; Qubain, *Education and Science in the Arab World*, p. 10; Sharabi with Ani, "Impact of Class and Culture on Social Behavior," p. 251; Sharabi, *Neopatriarchy*, pp. 87–96; Szyliowicz, *Education and Modernization in the Middle East*, pp. 183, 195–197, 274, 289, 306; Bassam Tibi, *Islam and the Cultural Accommodation of Social Change*, trans. by Clare Krojzl (Boulder, Colo.: Westview, 1991), pp. 110–112; Milton Viorst, *Sandcastles: The Arabs in Search of the Modern World* (New York: Alfred A. Knopf, 1994), p. 358.

111. Rabie, "The Future of Education in the Arab World," p. 25. Rabie claims this description applies to a universal stage of educational development. However, he makes it clear that he is really describing the Arab educational system, and he makes no effort to demonstrate that this description applies to any other system. Indeed, his work focuses completely on the Arab world, makes no comparison with other societies, and his analysis and conclusions are narrowly focused on the Arab educational experience.

112. Tibi, *Islam and Cultural Accommodation of Social Change*, p. 111.

113. Viorst, *Sandcastles*, p. 358.

114. *AHDR 2003*, p. 71.

115. For a superb discussion of the impact of educated unemployment in the Arab world, see Michael Slackman, "Stifled, Egypt's Young Turn to Islamic Fervor," *New York Times*, February 17, 2008.

116. Noland and Pack, *The Arab Economies in a Changing World*, pp. 200–201; Richards and Waterbury, *A Political Economy of the Middle East*, p. 42.

117. Richards and Waterbury, *A Political Economy of the Middle East*, pp. 100–101; Roy, "Saudi Arabian Education," pp. 477–478.

118. See Galal, "The Paradox of Education and Unemployment in Egypt," pp. 4–6; Richards and Waterbury, *A Political Economy of the Middle East*, 2007, pp. 136–138; World Bank, *Middle East and North Africa Region Economic Developments and Prospects, 2007: Job Creation in an Era of High Growth* (Washington, D.C.: World Bank, 2007), pp. 63–64; U.N. Economic and Social Commission for Western Asia, "Youth Unemployment in the ESCWA Region," pp. 3–4. Also see Slackman, "Stifled, Egypt's Young Turn to Islamic Fervor."

119. Richards and Waterbury, *A Political Economy of the Middle East,* 2007, p. 137.

120. See in particular Mohamed El-Shibny, *The Threat of Globalization to Arab Islamic Culture* (Pittsburgh, Pa.: Dorrance Publishing, 2005); Ira M. Lapidus, "Islamic Revival and Modernity: The Contemporary Movements and the Historical Paradigms," *Journal of the Economic and Social History of the Orient* 40, no. 4 (1997), pp. 444–460. Also see Naji Abi-Hashem, "Peace and War in the Middle East: A Psychopolitical and Sociocultural Perspective," in *Understanding Terrorism: Psychosocial Roots, Consequences, and Intervention,* ed. Fathali M. Moghaddam and Anthony J. Marsella (Washington, D.C.: American Psychological Association, 2004), p. 70; Marwan Adeeb Dwairy, *Cross-Cultural Counselling: The Arab-Palestinian Case* (New York: Hamworth Press, 1998), p. 11.

121. *AHDR* 2003, p. 8.

122. Mark Juergensmeyer, "Terror Mandated by God," *Terrorism and Political Violence* 9, no. 2 (Summer 1997), p. 21.

123. Robert Looney, "The Arab World's Uncomfortable Experience with Globalization," *Middle East Journal* 61, no. 2 (Spring 2007), p. 342. See also John Fox, Nada Mourtada-Sabbah, and Mohammed al-Mutawa, *Globalization and the Gulf* (London: Routledge, 2006).

124. *AHDR* 2003, p. 8.

125. Cordesman, "The Middle East: The Broader Forces Shaping Regional Stability," p. 5.

126. *AHDR* 2003, pp. 3, 59–60.

127. Ibid., p. 4.

128. Ibid., p. 67.

129. Ibid., p. 124.

130. Ibid., p. 75.

131. Ibid.

132. Ibid.

CHAPTER 6: THE CRISIS OF MIDDLE EASTERN POLITICS

1. Also see Alan Richards and John Waterbury, *A Political Economy of the Middle East,* 2nd ed. (Boulder, Colo.: Westview Press, 1998), pp. 275–308.

2. Marcus Noland and Howard Pack, *The Arab Economies in a Changing World* (Washington, D.C.: Peterson Institute for International Economics, 2007), p. 273.

3. See Freedom House, *Freedom in the World, 2007* (Lanham, Md.: Rowman and Littlefield, 2007).

4. Monty G. Marshall and Keith Jaggers, "Polity IV Project," University of Maryland, Center for International Development and Conflict Management, available at www.cidcm.umd.edu/polity/, downloaded June 7, 2007.

5. On Middle East regimes' efforts to suppress political dissent and the impact this has had on their societies, see Kenneth M. Pollack, "The Influence of Arab Culture on Arab Military Effectiveness," Ph.D. dissertation, Massachusetts Institute of Technology, Cambridge, Mass., 1996, pp. 83–116; James T. Quinlivan, "Coup-Proofing: Its Practice and Consequences in the Middle East," *International Security* 24, no. 2 (Fall 1999), pp. 131–165; Richards and Waterbury, *A Political Economy of the Middle East*, 1998, pp. 275–308.

6. On the role and impact of Middle Eastern bureaucracies, see Richards and Waterbury, *A Political Economy of the Middle East*, 1998, pp. 173–212.

7. Richards and Waterbury, *A Political Economy of the Middle East*, 1998, pp. 119, 181–201; Delwin A. Roy, "Saudi Arabian Education: Development Policy," *Middle Eastern Studies* 28, no. 3 (July 1992), pp. 477–478.

8. World Bank, *Middle East and North Africa Region Economic Developments and Prospects, 2007: Job Creation in an Era of High Growth* (Washington, D.C.: World Bank, 2007), p. 76.

9. Paul Rivlin and Shmuel Even, *Political Stability in Arab States: Economic Causes and Consequences*, Memorandum 74 (Tel Aviv, Israel: Jaffee Center for Strategic Studies, 2004), pp. 17–18; Abdel Monem Said Aly, "Understanding the Muslim Brothers in Egypt," Middle East Brief no. 23, The Crown Center for Middle East Studies, Brandeis University, December 2007, p. 6.

10. Rivlin and Even, *Political Stability in Arab States*, p. 18; World Bank, *Jobs, Growth, and Governance in the Middle East and North Africa: Unlocking the Potential for Prosperity* (Washington, D.C.: World Bank, 2003), p. 13.

11. Edward Gardner, "Creating Employment in the Middle East and North Africa," International Monetary Fund, Washington, D.C., 2003, p. 4.

12. Ibid., p. 3; World Bank, *Jobs, Growth, and Governance in the Middle East and North Africa*, p. 13.

13. Noland and Pack, *The Arab Economies in a Changing World*, pp. 71–72; Roy, "Saudi Arabian Education," pp. 477–478.

14. Roy, "Saudi Arabian Education," pp. 477–478; World Bank, *Middle East and North Africa Region Economic Developments and Prospects, 2007*, p. 76.

15. Richards and Waterbury, *A Political Economy of the Middle East*, 1998, p. 119.

16. World Bank, *Middle East and North Africa Region Economic Developments and Prospects, 2007*, p. 76.

17. Richards and Waterbury, *A Political Economy of the Middle East*, 1998, p. 184.

18. Robert Looney, "Can Saudi Arabia Reform Its Economy in Time to Head Off Disaster?," *Strategic Insight* 3, no. 1 (January 2004), p. 2.

19. Richards and Waterbury, *A Political Economy of the Middle East*, 1998, pp. 181–201; Roy, "Saudi Arabian Education," p. 478; U.N. Economic and Social Commission for Western Asia, "Youth Unemployment in the

ESCWA Region," 2002, available at www.un.org/esa/socdev/poverty/papers/youth_unescwa.pdf, downloaded June 4, 2007, p. 2; World Bank, *Middle East and North Africa Region Economic Developments and Prospects, 2007,* pp. 76–78.

20. Nader Fergany, "Aspects of Labor Migration and Unemployment in the Arab Region," Almishkat Center for Research, Egypt, February 2001, p. 1.

21. Noland and Pack, *The Arab Economies in a Changing World,* pp. 200–201; Richards and Waterbury, *A Political Economy of the Middle East,* 1998, pp. 42, 201–204; Rivlin and Even, *Political Stability in Arab States,* pp. 24–25.

22. Noland and Pack, *The Arab Economies in a Changing World,* p. 8.

23. Ibid., p. 215.

24. *Arab Human Development Report (AHDR)* 2003, p. 9.

25. World Bank, *Middle East and North Africa Region Economic Developments and Prospects, 2007,* p. 119.

26. Alan Richards, "Economic Reform in the Middle East: The Challenge to Governance," in *The Future Security Environment in the Middle East: Conflict, Stability and Political Change,* ed. Nora Bensahel and Daniel L. Byman (Santa Monica, Calif.: RAND, 2004), p. 78.

27. *AHDR* 2003, pp. 135–136.

28. Ibid., pp. 3, 61–63, 81–82; Michael Kraig and Kathy Gockel, "Open Media and Transitioning Societies in the Middle East: Implications for US Security Policy," The Stanley Foundation in Association with the Institute for Near East and Gulf Military Analysis, Muscatine, Iowa, 2005–2006, especially p. 6.

29. S. Abdallah Schleifer, "The Impact of Arab Satellite Television on the Prospects for Democracy in the Arab World," Foreign Policy Research Institute, Philadelphia, May 12, 2005. See also Jon B. Alterman, "Arab Media: Tools of the Government; Tools for the People?," United States Institute of Peace, Washington, D.C., August 2005; Jon B. Alterman, "The Information Revolution and the Middle East," in *The Future Security Environment in the Middle East: Conflict, Stability and Political Change,* ed. Nora Bensahel and Daniel L. Byman (Santa Monica, Calif.: RAND, 2004), pp. 227–252; Kraig and Gockel, "Open Media and Transitioning Societies in the Middle East," especially p. 23.

30. *AHDR* 2003, p. 150.

31. Ibid., p. 81.

32. See, e.g., Barry Rubin and Judith Colp Rubin, *Hating America: A History* (Oxford, U.K.: Oxford University Press, 2004), pp. 157–160, 184; Salman Rushdie, "Anti-Americanism Has Taken the World by Storm: The US Has an Ideological Enemy Harder to Defeat Than Militant

Islam," available at www.guardian.co.uk/print/0,3858,4350590–108920 ,00.html, downloaded March 9, 2007.

33. Joyce M. Davis, *Martyrs: Innocence, Vengeance, and Despair in the Middle East* (New York: Palgrave Macmillan, 2004), p. 108.

34. *AHDR* 2003, p. 23.

35. Ibid., pp. 2, 23.

36. Noland and Pack, *The Arab Economies in a Changing World,* p. 276.

37. *AHDR* 2003, p. 152.

38. Ibid., p. 155.

39. *AHDR* 2003, p. 153; Noland and Pack, *The Arab Economies in a Changing World,* pp. 153–155.

40. *AHDR* 2003, p. 152.

41. Richards, "Economic Reform in the Middle East," p. 78.

42. *AHDR* 2003, pp. 152–153.

43. Transparency International, "Corruption Perceptions Index, 2006," available at www.transparency.org/policy_research/surveys_indices/cpi/ 2006, downloaded May 30, 2007.

44. Noland and Pack, *The Arab Economies in a Changing World,* pp. 147–48.

45. Ibid., p. 145.

46. Ibrahim Akoum, "The Governance Cycle and Its Implications for the Middle East," *Economic Reform* 3, no 1 (Spring 2006), p. 32; World Bank, *Jobs, Growth, and Governance in the Middle East and North Africa,* p. 29.

47. Akoum, "The Governance Cycle and Its Implications for the Middle East," p. 32.

48. World Bank, *Middle East and North Africa Region Economic Developments and Prospects, 2007,* p. 110.

49. Noland and Pack, *The Arab Economies in a Changing World,* p. 238.

50. Ibid., p. 238.

51. Robert Looney, "Can Saudi Arabia Reform Its Economy in Time to Head off Disaster?," p. 1.

PART THREE: THE THREATS WE FACE FROM THE MIDDLE EAST

CHAPTER 7: POLITICAL ISLAM

1. For one of the first analyses of how the underlying socioeconomic problems of the Arab states, coupled with the political problems of their regimes, was producing an increase in support for Islamists, particularly among the middle class and the newly educated, see Saad Eddin Ibrahim, "Reform and Frustration in Egypt," *Journal of Democracy* 7, no. 4 (October 1996), pp. 125–135.

2. Fawaz A. Gerges, *Journey of the Jihadist: Inside Muslim Militancy* (Orlando, Fla.: Harcourt, 2006), p. 89.

3. Michael Slackman, "Stifled, Egypt's Young Turn to Islamic Fervor," *The New York Times,* February 17, 2008, p. A1.

4. Asef Bayat, "Revolution Without Movement, Movement Without Revolution: Comparing Islamic Activism in Iran and Egypt," *Comparative Studies in Society and History* 40, no. 1 (January 1998), p. 160; Joyce M. Davis, *Martyrs: Innocence, Vengeance, and Despair in the Middle East* (New York: Palgrave Macmillan, 2004), p. 16.

5. Bayat, "Revolution Without Movement, Movement Without Revolution," pp. 157–158; R. Hrair Dekmejian, "The Anatomy of Islamic Revival: Legitimacy Crisis, Ethnic Conflict and the Search for Islamic Alternatives," *Middle East Journal* 34, no. 1 (Winter 1980), pp. 1–6; John Esposito, "Terrorism and the Rise of Political Islam," in *The Roots of Terrorism,* ed. Louise Richardson (New York: Routledge, 2006), pp. 146–147; Graham E. Fuller, *The Future of Political Islam* (New York: Palgrave Macmillan, 2003), pp. 15–16.

6. Asad AbuKhalil, "A Viable Partnership: Islam, Democracy and the Arab World," *Harvard International Review* 15, no. 2 (Winter 1992–93), p. 23; Esposito, "Terrorism and the Rise of Political Islam," p. 146.

7. A crucial exception—and not the only one—was Hafiz al-Asad of Syria, who was even harsher with the Syrian wing of the Muslim Brotherhood than he was with secular groups because he felt that they were a greater threat.

8. Davis, *Martyrs,* pp. 11–12; Gerges, *Journey of the Jihadist,* p. 9; Esposito, "Terrorism and the Rise of Political Islam," p. 147.

9. Davis, *Martyrs,* p. 165; Gerges, *Journey of the Jihadist,* p. 10.

10. On Muslims' views about the positive role of religion in their lives, see John L. Esposito and Dalia Mogahed, *Who Speaks for Islam?: What a Billion Muslims Really Think* (New York: Gallup Press, 2008), pp. 34–38, 47–48, 85–87.

11. Ted Robert Gurr, "Economic Factors," in *The Roots of Terrorism,* ed. Louise Richardson (New York: Routledge, 2006), pp. 91–92.

12. AbuKhalil, "A Viable Partnership," p. 23; Fuller, *The Future of Political Islam,* pp. 16–27.

13. For an extremely intelligent and compelling argument regarding the growth of poverty across the region despite the claims of the World Bank and other international financial institutions, see Alan Richards, "Economic Reform in the Middle East: The Challenge to Governance," in *The Future Security Environment in the Middle East: Conflict, Stability and Political Change,* ed. Nora Bensahel and Daniel L. Byman (Santa Monica, Calif.: RAND, 2004), pp. 68–72.

14. Sheri Berman, "Islamism, Revolution and Civil Society," *Perspectives on Politics* 1, no. 2 (June 2003), p. 261; Fuller, *The Future of Political Islam*, pp. 27–33; Ira M. Lapidus, "Islamic Revival and Modernity: The Contemporary Movements and the Historical Paradigms," *Journal of the Economic and Social History of the Orient* 40, no. 4 (1997), p. 447.

15. Naji Abi-Hashem, "Peace and War in the Middle East: A Psychopolitical and Sociocultural Perspective," in *Understanding Terrorism: Psychosocial Roots, Consequences, and Intervention*, ed. Fathali M. Moghaddam and Anthony J. Marsella (Washington, D.C.: American Psychological Association, 2004), p. 81; Esposito, "Terrorism and the Rise of Political Islam," p. 147; Fuller, *The Future of Political Islam*, pp. 68–70, 73–80.

16. National Democratic Institute, "Findings of Jordan Focus Groups," 2007; National Democratic Institute, "Findings of Lebanese Focus Groups," 2007; Yasmina Sarhouny, NDI Morocco, "Memo: Focus Group Research Findings on Perception of Political Parties—Morocco," *People's Mirror*, March 17, 2007.

17. For a good introduction to some of the differences among Islamist groups, see "Understanding Islamism," International Crisis Group, *Middle East/North Africa Report*, no. 37, March 2, 2005. Also see Fuller, *The Future of Political Islam*, especially pp. 47–65; Amr Hamzawy, "The Key to Arab Reform: Moderate Islamists," Policy Brief 40, Carnegie Endowment for International Peace, August 2005, pp. 1–5.

18. Fuller, *The Future of Political Islam*, p. 124.

CHAPTER 8: THE THREAT FROM INSTABILITY AND INTERNAL STRIFE

1. See Paul R. Pillar, "Superpower Foreign Policies: A Source of Global Resentment," in *The Making of a Terrorist: Recruitment, Training, and Root Causes*, vol. 3: *Root Causes*, ed. James J. F. Forest (Westport, Conn.: Praeger, 2006), p. 33.

2. Fawaz A. Gerges, *Journey of the Jihadist: Inside Muslim Militancy* (Orlando, Fla.: Harcourt, 2006), p. 5.

3. Alan Richards, "Economic Reform in the Middle East: The Challenge to Governance," in *The Future Security Environment in the Middle East: Conflict, Stability and Political Change*, ed. Nora Bensahel and Daniel L. Byman (Santa Monica, Calif.: RAND, 2004), p. 64.

4. Pillar, "Superpower Foreign Policies," p. 33; Caroline Ziemke, "Perceived Oppression and Relative Deprivation: Social Factors Contributing to Terrorism," in *"In the Same Light as Slavery": Building a Global Antiterrorist Consensus*, ed. Joseph McMillan (Washington, D.C.: National Defense University Press, 2006), pp. 109–110, 117.

5. Peter L. Bergen, *Holy War, Inc.: Inside the Secret World of Osama bin Laden* (New

York: Free Press, 2001), pp. 200–202; Gilles Kepel, *The War for Muslim Minds: Islam and the West,* trans. Pascale Ghazaleh (Cambridge, Mass.: Belknap Press of Harvard University Press, 2004), pp. 72–82; Emmanuel Sivan, "Why Radical Muslims Aren't Taking Over Governments," *Middle East Review of International Affairs* 2, no. 2 (May 1998), p. 3.

6. John R. Bradley, "Iran's Ethnic Tinderbox," *The Washington Quarterly* 30, no. 1 (Winter 2006–2007), pp. 181–190; Cedric Gouverneur, "Iran Loses Its Drug War," *Le Monde Diplomatique,* March 2002, available at http://mondediplo.com/2002/03/13drug.

7. Kenneth M. Pollack, *The Threatening Storm: The Case for Invading Iraq* (New York: Random House, 2002), pp. 20, 50–51.

8. Curtis R. Ryan and Jillian Schwedler, "Return to Democratization or New Hybrid Regime? The 2003 Elections in Jordan," *Middle East Policy* 11, no. 2 (Summer 2004), pp. 138–152.

9. Ihsan A. Hijazi, "Lebanon War Spurs New Emigration," *The New York Times,* April 15, 1990; "Lebanon," GlobalSecurity.Net, available at www.globalsecurity.org/military/world/war/lebanon.htm, downloaded June 11, 2006; Dilip Hiro, *Lebanon: Fire and Embers: A History of the Lebanese Civil War* (New York: St. Martin's, 1992), p. 183.

10. K. T. Abdurrab, "Tackling Labor Unrest in UAE," *Arab News,* June 25, 2006.

11. Nadia Abou el-Magd, "Economic Woes Add to Tension in Egypt," Associated Press, April 20, 2006.

12. Ibid.

13. Jack A. Goldstone, *Revolutions and Rebellions in the Early Modern World* (Berkeley: University of California Press, 1991), pp. 24–62. Also see Paul Rivlin and Shmuel Even, *Political Stability in Arab States: Economic Causes and Consequences,* Memorandum 74 (Tel Aviv, Israel: Jaffee Center for Strategic Studies, 2004), p. 28; Robert S. Snyder, "Hating America: Bin Laden as a Civilizational Revolutionary," *The Review of Politics* 65, no. 4 (Autumn 2003), p. 337.

14. "Economics in Peacemaking: Lessons from Northern Ireland," *The Portland Trust,* May 2007, pp. 7–8. See also the similar conclusions of a RAND study on the relationship of socioeconomic development and violence in Kim Cragin and Peter Chalk, *Terrorism and Development: Using Social and Economic Development to Inhibit a Resurgence of Terrorism* (Santa Monica, Calif.: RAND, 2003), pp. 5–14.

15. Paul Collier and Anke Hoeffler, "Greed and Grievance in Civil War," *Oxford Economic Papers* 56, no. 4 (2004), pp. 563–595.

16. Kepel, *The War for Muslim Minds,* p. 4.

17. Richards, "Economic Reform in the Middle East," p. 57.

18. Gerges, *Journey of the Jihadist,* pp. 193–194; Richards, "Economic Reform in

the Middle East," p. 57; Sivan, "Why Radical Muslims Aren't Taking Over Governments," p. 2.

19. Marcus Noland and John Pack, *The Arab Economies in a Changing World* (Washington, D.C.: Peterson Institute for International Economics, 2007), p. 75.

20. Ibid., p. 85, n. 1.

21. Author's interviews with U.S. and Iraqi military and intelligence officials in Iraq, July 2007.

22. Ted Robert Gurr, "Economic Factors," in Louise Richardson, ed., *The Roots of Terrorism* (New York: Routledge, 2006), p. 90; Noland and Pack, *The Arab Economies in a Changing World,* pp. 75–76; Ziemke, "Perceived Oppression and Relative Deprivation," pp. 110–111.

23. Joyce M. Davis, *Martyrs: Innocence, Vengeance, and Despair in the Middle East* (New York: Palgrave Macmillan, 2004), p. 12.

24. Ibid., p. 90.

25. Crane Brinton, *The Anatomy of Revolution* (New York: Vintage Books, 1965), p. 251; Ziemke, "Perceived Oppression and Relative Deprivation," p. 111. Also see Asef Bayat, "Revolution Without Movement, Movement Without Revolution: Comparing Islamic Activism in Iran and Egypt," *Comparative Studies in Society and History* 40, no. 1 (January 1998), p. 160.

26. Sheri Berman, "Islamism, Revolution and Civil Society," *Perspectives on Politics* 1, no. 2 (June 2003), p. 260; Gurr, "Economic Factors," p. 90; Noland and Pack, *The Arab Economies in a Changing World,* pp. 75–76; Sivan, "Why Radical Muslims Aren't Taking Over Governments," p. 1; Ziemke, "Perceived Oppression and Relative Deprivation," pp. 110–111.

27. Sivan, "Why Radical Muslims Aren't Taking Over Governments," p. 2.

28. Ziemke, "Perceived Oppression and Relative Deprivation," pp. 101–109. Again, the first to expound this theory was Saad Eddin Ibrahim, "Reform and Frustration in Egypt," *Journal of Democracy* 7, no. 4 (October 1996), pp. 125–135.

29. John L. Esposito and Dalia Mogahed, *Who Speaks for Islam?: What a Billion Muslims Really Think* (New York: Gallup Press, 2008), pp. 24–26.

30. Ziemke, "Perceived Oppression and Relative Deprivation," pp. 110–116.

31. Robert P. Cincotta, Robert Engelman, and Daniele Anastasion, *The Security Demographic: Population and Civil Conflict After the Cold War* (Washington, D.C.: Population Action International, 2003), p. 42.

32. Ibid., p. 45.

33. Ibid., p. 44.

34. Ibid.

35. Ibid.

36. Ibid., p. 13.

37. Ibid., p. 48.

38. Noland and Pack, *The Arab Economies in a Changing World,* pp. 86–89.

39. International Labour Organization, "Global Employment Trends for Youth," 2006, p. 47, available at www.ilo.org/public/english/employment/strat/download/getoben.pdf.

40. Anthony H. Cordesman, "The Middle East: The Broader Forces Shaping Regional Stability," Center for Strategic and International Studies, Washington, D.C., April 28, 2003, p. 4.

41. Cincotta, Engelman, and Anastasion, *The Security Demographic,* p. 45; Gary Fuller, "The Demographic Backdrop to Ethnic Conflict: A Geographic Overview," in *The Challenge of Ethnic Conflict to National and International Order in the 1990s: Geographic Perspectives* (Washington, D.C.: Central Intelligence Agency, 1995), pp. 151–154.

42. Richards, "Economic Reform in the Middle East," pp. 71–72.

43. Ervand Abrahamian, *Iran: Between Two Revolutions* (Princeton, N.J.: Princeton University Press, 1982), pp. 447–497; Said Arjomand, *The Turban for the Crown: The Islamic Revolution in Iran* (New York: Oxford University Press, 1988), p. 70; Charles Kurzman, *The Unthinkable Revolution in Iran* (Cambridge, Mass.: Harvard University Press, 2004), p. 81; Kenneth M. Pollack, *The Persian Puzzle: The Conflict Between Iran and America* (New York: Random House, 2004), pp. 106–120; Alan Richards and John Waterbury, *A Political Economy of the Middle East,* 2nd ed. (Boulder, Colo.: Westview Press, 1998), p. 269.

44. Cincotta, Engelman, and Anastasion, *The Security Demographic,* p. 13; also see pp. 51–54.

45. Ibid., p. 43. See also Noland and Pack, *The Arab Economies in a Changing World,* p. 1.

46. For a concurring assessment, see Berman, "Islamism, Revolution and Civil Society," pp. 257–272.

47. Theda Skocpol, *States and Social Revolutions: A Comparative Analysis of France, Russia and China* (New York: Cambridge University Press, 1979); Theda Skocpol, *Social Revolutions in the Modern World* (New York: Cambridge University Press, 1994).

48. Berman, "Islamism, Revolution and Civil Society," pp. 257–272.

49. Ibid., p. 258.

50. Quoted in Abdul Hadi Palazzi, "Orthodox Islamic Perceptions of Jihad and Martyrdom," in *Countering Suicide Terrorism: An International Conference,* International Policy Institute for Counter-Terrorism at the Interdisciplinary Center, Herzliya (Herzliya, Israel: ICT, 2001), p. 65.

51. Bergen, *Holy War, Inc.,* pp. 200–202; Kepel, *The War for Muslim Minds,* pp. 72–82.

52. See, e.g., Ahmad Nizar Hamzeh, *In the Path of Hizbullah* (Syracuse, N.Y.: Syracuse University Press, 2004), p. 6; J. P. Larsson, "The Role of Reli-

gious Ideology in Modern Terrorist Recruitment," in *The Making of a Terrorist: Recruitment, Training, and Root Causes,* vol. 1: *Recruitment,* ed. James J. F. Forest (Westport, Conn.: Praeger, 2006), p. 198; Richards and Waterbury, *A Political Economy of the Middle East,* p. 347.

53. Martha Crenshaw, "Why America? The Globalization of Civil War," *Current History,* December 2001, pp. 425–432; Michael Doran, "Somebody Else's Civil War," *Foreign Affairs* 81, no. 1 (January–February 2002).

54. John Esposito, "Terrorism and the Rise of Political Islam," in Richardson, ed., *The Roots of Terrorism,* p. 149.

55. Muhammad Muslih, quoted in Judy Barsalou, "Islamic Extremists: How Do They Mobilize Support?," United States Institute of Peace, Washington, D.C., USIP Special Report no. 89, July 2002, p. 7.

56. Bergen, *Holy War, Inc.,* p. 200.

57. Jerrold M. Post, Ehud Sprinzak, and Laurita M. Denny, "The Terrorists in Their Own Words: Interviews with 35 Incarcerated Middle Eastern Terrorists," *Terrorism and Political Violence* 15, no. 1 (Spring 2003), p. 172.

58. Bergen, *Holy War, Inc.,* pp. 3, 19, 89; Gerges, *Journey of the Jihadist,* p. 203; Kepel, *The War for Muslim Minds,* pp. 1–2; Snyder, "Hating America," pp. 325–349.

59. Kepel, *The War for Muslim Minds,* pp. 1–2.

60. Snyder, "Hating America," p. 330.

61. Christopher Boucek, "Libya's Return to the Fold?," *Foreign Policy in Focus,* April 2004.

62. Shaul Bakhash, *The Reign of the Ayatollahs: Iran and the Islamic Revolution,* rev. ed. (New York: Basic Books, 1990), p. 63; James A. Bill, *The Eagle and the Lion: The Tragedy of American-Iranian Relations* (New Haven, Conn.: Yale University Press, 1988), p. 273; Daniel L. Byman, *Deadly Connections: States That Sponsor Terrorism* (New York: Cambridge University Press, 2005), pp. 80–84; Elton L. Daniel, *The History of Iran* (Westport, Conn.: Greenwood Press, 2001), pp. 185–186; Hamzeh, *In the Path of Hizbullah,* p. 18; Bruce Hoffman, *Inside Terrorism* (New York: Columbia University Press, 1998), pp. 95–96; Kenneth Katzman, *The Warriors of Islam: Iran's Revolutionary Guard* (Boulder, Colo.: Westview, Conn.: 1993), pp. 7–19, 23–37, 71; Martin Kramer, "The Moral Logic of Hizballah," in *Origins of Terrorism: Psychologies, Ideologies, Theologies, States of Mind,* ed. Walter Reich (Washington, D.C.: Woodrow Wilson Center Press, 1998), pp. 132–135; Robin Wright, *In the Name of God: The Khomeini Decade* (New York: Simon and Schuster, 1989), p. 69.

63. Gerges, *Journey of the Jihadist,* pp. 84–86, 165–166.

64. Michael T. Klare, "Fueling the Fires: The Oil Factor in Middle Eastern Terrorism," in *The Making of a Terrorist: Recruitment, Training, and Root Causes,* vol. 2: *Root Causes,* ed. James J. F. Forest (Westport, Conn.: Praeger,

2006), pp. 151–152; Yaroslav Trofimov, *The Siege of Mecca* (New York: Doubleday, 2007).

65. Richard Crockatt, *America Embattled: September 11, Anti-Americanism, and the Global Order* (London, U.K.: Routledge, 2003), p. 83.

66. The following overview is drawn from Pollack, *The Persian Puzzle*, pp. 101–127.

67. Richards, "Economic Reform in the Middle East," p. 58.

68. Ziemke, "Perceived Oppression and Relative Deprivation," p. 115.

69. Berman, "Islamism, Revolution and Civil Society," p. 259.

70. Zeev Ivianski, "A Chapter in the History of Individual Terror: Andrey Zhelyabov," in *Perspectives on Terrorism*, ed. Lawrence Z. Freedman and Yonah Alexander (Wilmington, Del.: Scholarly Resources, 1983), pp. 87–88, 93–94.

71. David C. Rapoport, "The Four Waves of Modern Terrorism," in *Attacking Terrorism: Elements of a Grand Strategy*, ed. Audrey Kurth Cronin and James M. Ludes (Washington, D.C.: Georgetown University Press, 2004), pp. 50–52.

72. Audrey Kurth Cronin, "Behind the Curve: Globalization and International Terrorism," *International Security* 27, No. 3 (Winter 2002–03), p. 35.

73. Noland and Pack, *The Arab Economies in a Changing World*, p. 82.

74. Martha Crenshaw, " 'Suicide Terrorism' in Comparative Perspective," in *Countering Suicide Terrorism: An International Conference*, International Policy Institute for Counter-Terrorism at the Interdisciplinary Center, Herzliya (Herzliya, Israel: ICT, 2001), p. 26; Rapoport, "The Four Waves of Modern Terrorism," p. 51.

75. Ibid., p. 47.

76. Gwenn Okruhlik, "Rentier Wealth, Unruly Law, and the Rise of Opposition: The Political Economy of Oil States," *Comparative Politics* 31, no. 3 (April 1999), pp. 295–315.

77. Martha Crenshaw, "The Logic of Terrorism: Terrorist Behavior as a Product of Strategic Choice," in *Origins of Terrorism: Psychologies, Ideologies, Theologies, States of Mind*, ed. Walter Reich (Washington, D.C.: Woodrow Wilson Center Press, 1998), p. 10, see also pp. 11–12.

78. Rapoport, "The Four Waves of Modern Terrorism," p. 49.

79. Takeyh, "Islamism in Algeria," pp. 62–69.

80. Ibid., p. 68.

81. Mohammed M. Hafez, *Why Muslims Rebel: Repression and Resistance in the Islamic World* (Boulder, Colo.: Lynne Rienner, 2003), pp. 35–40.

82. Youssef M. Ibrahim, "In Algeria, Clear Plans to Lay Down Islamic Law," *The New York Times,* December 31, 1991.

83. Takeyh, "Islamism in Algeria," pp. 69–70.

84. Bruce Hoffman, *Inside Terrorism* (New York: Columbia University Press, 1998), p. 98.

85. Hafez, *Why Muslims Rebel,* p. 2; Takeyh, "Islamism in Algeria: A Struggle Between Hope and Agony," p. 69.

86. Berman, "Islamism, Revolution and Civil Society," p. 263.

87. Ibid., p. 269, n. 4. Also see Sivan, "Why Radical Muslims Aren't Taking Over Governments."

88. Ira M. Lapidus, "Islamic Revival and Modernity: The Contemporary Movements and the Historical Paradigms," *Journal of the Economic and Social History of the Orient* 40, No. 4 (1997), p. 447.

89. Stephen M. Walt, *Revolution and War* (Ithaca, N.Y.: Cornell University Press, 1996).

90. Daniel L. Byman and Kenneth M. Pollack, *Things Fall Apart: Containing the Spillover from an Iraqi Civil War* (Washington, D.C.: Brookings Press, 2007).

CHAPTER 9: THE THREAT OF TERRORISM

1. According to the December 2007 National Intelligence Estimate, the U.S. intelligence community believes that the most likely time frame for Iran to acquire the capability to enrich enough uranium for one or more nuclear weapons is 2010–2015. National Intelligence Council, "Iran: Nuclear Intentions and Capabilities," December 2007, available at www.dni.gov/press_releases/20071203_release.pdf, downloaded January 18, 2008.

2. Jerrold M. Post, "The Psychological Dynamics of Terrorism," in *The Roots of Terrorism,* ed. Louise Richardson (New York: Routledge, 2006), pp. 19–20.

3. Ibid., p. 17.

4. Ehud Sprinzak, "Rational Fanatics," *Foreign Policy* (September–October 2000), pp. 68–69.

5. See, e.g., Nasra Hassan, "Suicide Terrorism," in *The Roots of Terrorism,* ed. Louise Richardson (New York: Routledge, 2006), pp. 38–39; Charles A. Russell and Bowman H. Miller, "Profile of a Terrorist," in *Perspectives on Terrorism,* ed. Lawrence Z. Freedman and Yonah Alexander (Wilmington, Del.: Scholarly Resources, 1983), pp. 45–57.

6. Post, "The Psychological Dynamics of Terrorism," p. 18.

7. See, e.g., John W. Crayton, "Terrorism and the Psychology of the Self," in *Perspectives on Terrorism,* ed. Lawrence Z. Freedman and Yonah Alexander (Wilmington, Del.: Scholarly Resources, 1983), pp. 33–41; Frederick J. Hacker, "Dialectic Interrelationships of Personal and Political Factors in Terrorism," in Freedman and Alexander, *Perspectives on Terrorism,* pp. 19–31.

8. J. P. Larsson, "The Role of Religious Ideology in Modern Terrorist Recruitment," *The Making of a Terrorist: Recruitment, Training, and Root Causes*, vol. 1: *Recruitment*, ed. James J. F. Forest (Westport, Conn.: Praeger, 2006), p. 200; Caroline Ziemke, "Perceived Oppression and Relative Deprivation: Social Factors Contributing to Terrorism," in *"In the Same Light as Slavery": Building a Global Antiterrorist Consensus*, ed. Joseph McMillan (Washington, D.C.: National Defense University Press, 2006), p. 118.

9. John Horgan, "From Profiles to Pathways: The Road to Recruitment," *Foreign Policy Agenda* 12, no. 5 (May 2007), pp. 24–25; Jerrold Post, "Terrorist Psycho-Logic: Terrorist Behavior as a Product of Psychological Forces," in *Origins of Terrorism: Psychologies, Ideologies, Theologies, States of Mind*, ed. Walter Reich (Washington, D.C.: Woodrow Wilson Center Press, 1998), pp. 25–40.

10. See, e.g., Larsson, "The Role of Religious Ideology in Modern Terrorist Recruitment," p. 201.

11. See, e.g., Fawaz Gerges, *Journey of the Jihadist: Inside Muslim Militancy* (Orlando, Fla.: Harcourt, 2006), p. 131; Scott Gerwehr and Sara Daly, "Al-Qaeda: Terrorist Selection and Recruitment," in *The McGraw-Hill Homeland Security Handbook*, ed. David G. Kamien (New York: McGraw-Hill, 2006), pp. 84–86; Ami Pedahzur and Arie Perliger, "The Making of Suicide Bombers: A Comparative Perspective," in *The Making of a Terrorist: Recruitment, Training, and Root Causes*, vol. 1: *Recruitment*, ed. James J. F. Forest (Westport, Conn.: Praeger, 2006), p. 154; Jerrold M. Post, Ehud Sprinzak, and Laurito M. Denny, "The Terrorists in Their Own Words: Interviews with 35 Incarcerated Middle Eastern Terrorists," *Terrorism and Political Violence* 15, no. 1 (Spring 2003), pp. 174–176; Sprinzak, "Rational Fanatics," pp. 68–72.

12. Adam Dolnik, "Learning to Die: Suicide Terrorism in the Twenty-first Century," in *The Making of a Terrorist: Recruitment, Training, and Root Causes*, vol. 2: *Training*, ed. James J. F. Forest (Westport, Conn.: Praeger, 2006), p. 161.

13. Mia Bloom, *Dying to Kill: The Allure of Suicide Terror* (New York: Columbia University Press, 2005), pp. 35–36; Joyce M. Davis, *Martyrs: Innocence, Vengeance, and Despair in the Middle East* (New York: Palgrave Macmillan, 2004), pp. 14–16, 22–23; Hassan, "Suicide Terrorism," p. 40; Brian M. Jenkins, "Building an Army of Believers: Jihadist Radicalization and Recruitment," testimony presented before the House Homeland Security Committee, Subcommittee on Intelligence, Information Sharing, and Terrorism Risk Assessment, April 5, 2007, p. 4; Marcus Noland and John Pack, *The Arab Economies in a Changing World* (Washington, D.C.: Peterson

Institute for International Economics, 2007), p. 60; Pedahzur and Perliger, "The Making of Suicide Bombers," pp. 155, 163.

14. Davis, *Martyrs*, p. 16.

15. See, e.g., Daniel Pipes, "God and Mammon: Does Poverty Cause Militant Islam?," *The National Interest* (Winter 2001–02), pp. 14–21.

16. There were six leaders among the 9/11 hijackers, and they basically came from educated, middle-class backgrounds. The other thirteen, however, were what Caroline Ziemke calls "muscle hijackers," who may not have even realized they were on a suicide mission. These thirteen all came from "less affluent circumstances, most from the underdeveloped tribal hinterlands of Saudi Arabia. All were young, unemployed, and all but two had no more than high school educations. None came from grinding poverty, but all had seen the economic well-being of their families and tribes decline from the heyday of Saudi economic largesse." Ziemke, "Perceived Oppression and Relative Deprivation," p. 109.

17. Pipes, "God and Mammon," pp. 15–18.

18. Peter L. Bergen, *Holy War, Inc.: Inside the Secret World of Osama bin Laden* (New York: Free Press, 2001), pp. 28–29; Peter L. Bergen and Swati Pandey, "The Madrassa Scapegoat," *Washington Quarterly* 29, no. 2 (Spring 2006), p. 122; Davis, *Martyrs*, p. 10; C. Christine Fair and Bryan Shepherd, "Who Supports Terrorism? Evidence from 14 Muslim Countries," *Studies in Conflict and Terrorism* 29, no. 5 (2006), p. 51; Ted Robert Gurr, "Economic Factors," in *The Roots of Terrorism*, ed. Louise Richardson (New York: Routledge, 2006), pp. 86–88; Noland and Pack, *The Arab Economies in a Changing World*, p. 81.

19. Bergen and Pandey, "The Madrassa Scapegoat," p. 123.

20. Judith Palmer Harik, *Hezbollah: The Changing Face of Terrorism* (London: I. B. Tauris, 2005), pp. 85–87.

21. Cited in Pipes, "God and Mammon," p. 17.

22. For instance, see Audrey Kurth Cronin, "Behind the Curve: Globalization and International Terrorism," *International Security* 27, no. 3 (Winter 2002–03), p. 35; Ted Robert Gurr, "Economic Factors," p. 88.

23. Mark Tessler and Michael D. H. Robbins, "What Leads Some Ordinary Arab Men and Women to Approve of Terrorist Attacks Against the United States?," *Journal of Conflict Resolution* 51, no. 2 (April 2007), p. 310.

24. Ted Robert Gurr, "Economic Factors," p. 88; Jessica Stern has argued that the same phenomenon is responsible for middle-class adherents to similar Islamist and Salafi terrorist groups in Indonesia. Jessica Stern, *Terror in the Name of God: Why Religious Militants Kill* (New York: Harper-Collins, 2003), p. 80.

25. Asef Bayat, "Revolution Without Movement, Movement Without Rev-

olution: Comparing Islamic Activism in Iran and Egypt," *Comparative Studies in Society and History* 40, no. 1 (January 1998), pp. 157–158.

26. Davis, *Martyrs,* p. 133; Gerges, *Journey of the Jihadist,* p. 109; Gurr, "Economic Factors," p. 88; Alan Richards, "Economic Reform in the Middle East: The Challenge to Governance," in *The Future Security Environment in the Middle East: Conflict, Stability and Political Change,* ed. Nora Bensahel and Daniel L. Byman (Santa Monica, Calif.: RAND, 2004), p. 67; Alan Richards and John Waterbury, *A Political Economy of the Middle East,* 2nd ed. (Boulder, Colo.: Westview Press, 1998), pp. 100–101.

27. Davis, *Martyrs,* p. 133. See also Gurr, "Economic Factors," p. 88.

28. Souad Mekhennet and Michael Moss, "In Jihadist Haven, a Goal: To Kill and Die in Iraq," *The New York Times,* May 4, 2007.

29. Robert P. Cincotta, Robert Engelman, and Daniele Anastasion, *The Security Demographic: Population and Civil Conflict After the Cold War* (Washington, D.C.: Population Action International, 2003), pp. 44–45; Jack A. Goldstone, *Revolutions and Rebellions in the Early Modern World* (Berkeley: University of California Press, 1991), pp. 24–62.

30. Richards, "Economic Reform in the Middle East," p. 71.

31. Ziemke, "Perceived Oppression and Relative Deprivation," p. 109.

32. Gurr, "Economic Factors," p. 87; Pedahzur and Perliger, "The Making of Suicide Bombers," p. 153.

33. Pedahzur and Perliger, "The Making of Suicide Bombers," p. 155.

34. Ted Robert Gurr has also observed, in an important study on the relationship between economics and terrorism, "Low levels of development create masses of young people with few alternatives—people with essentially zero opportunity costs—who become natural recruits for rebel and terrorist groups." Gurr, "Economic Factors," p. 87.

35. Cassandra, "The Impending Crisis in Egypt," *Middle East Journal* 49, no. 1 (Winter 1995), p. 21.

36. Richards, "Economic Reform in the Middle East," p. 70.

37. Gerges, *Journey of the Jihadist,* pp. 290–291.

38. Dan Benjamin and Steve Simon note that this problem is not limited to the slums of the Middle East. In discussing the origins of Islamic militants and terrorists now afflicting Europe, they write that "Muslim residents, many of them now citizens, live for the most part in ghetto-like segregation, receive second-rate schooling, and suffer much higher unemployment than the general population. Those who do work are more likely than their non-Muslim counterparts to have low-wage, dead-end jobs." Daniel Benjamin and Steven Simon, *The Next Attack: The Failure of the War on Terror and a Strategy for Getting It Right* (New York: Owl, 2005), p. 82.

39. Richards, "Economic Reform in the Middle East," p. 71. Also see Cassandra, "The Impending Crisis in Egypt," p. 21.

40. Cassandra, "The Impending Crisis in Egypt," p. 21.

41. Harik, *Hezbollah,* pp. 85–87.

42. Davis, *Martyrs,* pp. 10, 129–130.

43. Boaz Ganor, "Suicide Attacks in Israel," in *Countering Suicide Terrorism: An International Conference,* International Policy Institute for Counter-Terrorism at the Interdisciplinary Center, Herzliya (Herzliya, Israel: ICT, 2001), p. 138.

44. Dolnik, "Learning to Die," p. 159.

45. Ibid. Another Palestinian female suicide bomber caught by the Israeli security forces had been abused by her husband and regularly beaten by one of her brothers and sought to escape a painful and miserable life. See Matthew A. Levitt, *Hamas: Politics, Charity, and Terrorism in the Service of Jihad* (New Haven, Conn.: Yale University Press, 2006), p. 113. Similarly, Mia Bloom relates that "In Chechnya, the Black Widows are female suicide bombers who have often lost a loved one. Widowhood may sever the woman from productive society and/or leave her with a sense of hopelessness, especially in traditional societies." Bloom, *Dying to Kill,* p. 87.

46. Stern, *Terror in the Name of God,* pp. 37–38.

47. Martha Crenshaw, " 'Suicide Terrorism' in Comparative Perspective," in *Countering Suicide Terrorism: An International Conference,* International Policy Institute for Counter-Terrorism at the Interdisciplinary Center, Herzliya (Herzliya, Israel: ICT, 2001), p. 28. Also see Stephen F. Dale, "Religious Suicide in Islamic Asia: Anticolonial Terrorism in India, Indonesia, and the Philippines," *Journal of Conflict Resolution* 32, no. 1 (March 1988), pp. 37–59.

48. Sprinzak, "Rational Fanatics," pp. 70–71.

49. Adam Dolnik, "Learning to Die," p. 160.

50. Ganor, "Suicide Attacks in Israel," p. 138.

51. Harik, *Hezbollah,* pp. 82–88; Levitt, *Hamas,* p. 119; Matthew A. Levitt, "Hamas Social Welfare: In the Service of Terror," in *The Making of a Terrorist: Recruitment, Training, and Root Causes,* vol. 1: *Recruitment,* ed. James J. F. Forest (Westport, Conn.: Praeger, 2006), pp. 129–131; Pedahzur and Perliger, "The Making of Suicide Bombers," p. 154; Magnus Ranstorp, "The Hizballah Training Camps of Lebanon," in *The Making of a Terrorist: Recruitment, Training, and Root Causes,* vol. 2: *Training,* ed. James J. F. Forest (Westport, Conn.: Praeger, 2006), p. 249; Stern, *Terror in the Name of God,* pp. 50–51.

52. Stern, *Terror in the Name of God,* p. 49.

53. Lee Hockstader, "Palestinians Find Heroes in Hamas; Popularity Surges for Once-Marginal Sponsor of Suicide Bombings," *The Washington Post,* August 11, 2001.

54. Richards and Waterbury, *A Political Economy of the Middle East,* p. 349.

55. Ian Black, "Saudis Claim 80% Success in Re-educating Al-Qaida Mili-

tants: Programme Finds Jobs and Wives for Former Jihadists, Anti-Extremist Schemes in Schools and Mosques," *The Guardian,* April 2, 2007.

56. For concurring views, see Gurr, "Economic Factors," p. 86; Noland and Pack, *The Arab Economies in a Changing World,* pp. 80–81; Pedahzur and Perliger, "The Making of Suicide Bombers," p. 161.

57. Andrea Elliott, "Where Boys Grow Up to Be Jihadis," *The New York Times Sunday Magazine,* November 25, 2007, p. 73.

58. Levitt, *Hamas,* p. 108.

59. Mao Tse-tung, *On Guerrilla Warfare* (1937).

60. The new U.S. counterinsurgency manual, FM 3–24 *Counterinsurgency,* defines an insurgency as "an organized movement aimed at the overthrow of a constituted government through the use of subversion and armed conflict. Stated another way, an insurgency is an organized, protracted politico-military struggle designed to weaken the control and legitimacy of an established government, occupying power, or other political authority while increasing insurgent control." Thus, every terrorist campaign is a form of insurgent warfare, although not every insurgency is a terrorist campaign. *The U.S. Army and Marine Corps Counterinsurgency Field Manual* (Chicago, Ill.: University of Chicago Press, 2007), p. 2.

61. See, e.g., Daniel L Byman, "Al-Qaeda as an Adversary: Do We Understand Our Enemy?", *World Politics* 56, no. 1 (October 2003), pp. 139–163; Bruce Hoffman, "From the War on Terror to Global Counterinsurgency," *Current History,* December 2006, pp. 423–429; Brian Jenkins, "The New Age of Terrorism," in *The McGraw-Hill Homeland Security Handbook* (New York, N.Y.: McGraw-Hill, 2006), pp. 117–130; Brian M. Jenkins, *Countering Al Qaeda* (Santa Monica, Calif.: RAND, 2002); David Kilcullen, "Countering Global Insurgency: A Strategy for the War on Terrorism," Canberra and Washington, D.C., September–November 2004, available at http://smallwarsjournal.com/documents/kilcullen.pdf; Thomas R. Mockaitis, "Winning Hearts-and-Minds in the 'War on Terrorism,'" in *Grand Strategy in the War Against Terrorism,* ed. Thomas R. Mockaitis and Paul B. Rich (London: Frank Cass, 2003); Angel Rabasa, Peter Chalk, Kim Cragin, Sara A. Daly, Heather S. Gregg, Theodore W. Karasik, Kevin A. O'Brien, and William Rosenau, *Beyond al-Qaeda,* part 1, *The Global Jihadist Movement* (Santa Monica, Calif.: RAND, Project Air Force, 2006); James Risen, "Evolving Nature of Al Qaeda Is Misunderstood, Critic Says," *The New York Times,* November 8, 2004; William Rosenau, *Subversion and Insurgency,* prepared for the Office of the Secretary of Defense (Santa Monica, Calif.: RAND, 2007); John P. Sullivan and Robert J. Bunker, "Multilateral Counterinsurgency Networks," *Low Intensity Conflict and Law Enforcement* 11, no. 2–3 (Winter 2002), pp. 353–368;

Michael Vlahos, *Terror's Mask: Insurgency Within Islam,* Johns Hopkins University, Applied Physics Laboratory, May 2002.

62. On the fact that the groups themselves are well aware of this, see Mark Tessler, "Public Opinion in the Arab and Muslim World: Informing U.S. Public Diplomacy," in *"In the Same Light as Slavery": Building a Global Antiterrorist Consensus,* ed. Joseph McMillan (Washington, D.C.: National Defense University Press, 2006), pp. 21–23.

63. For corroborating discussions, see Davis, *Martyrs,* p. 10; Barry Rubin and Judith Colp Rubin, *Hating America: A History* (Oxford, U.K.: Oxford University Press, 2004), pp. 155–156.

64. Rami Khouri, "Anti-Americanism in the Arab World: Its Roots, Repercussions, and Remedies," February 12, 2003, Lecture at the University of Utah, available at www.hum.utah.edu/mec/Lectures/2003%20lecture%20pages/2003%20lecture%20pdfs/Khouri.pdf, p. 5, downloaded August 3, 2007.

65. Quoted in Michael S. Stohl, "Counterterrorism and Repression," in *The Roots of Terrorism,* ed. Louise Richardson (New York: Routledge, 2006), p. 59.

66. For sources concurring on the critical importance of popular support for terrorist campaigns, see, e.g., Pedahzur and Perliger, "The Making of Suicide Bombers," p. 161.

67. Johanna McGeary, "Hamas: Popular, Extreme, and an Alternative to Arafat," *Time,* December 17, 2001, p. 54; Kim Cragin and Sara A. Daly, *The Dynamic Terrorist Threat: An Assessment of Group Motivations and Capabilities in a Changing World* (Santa Monica, Calif.: RAND, Project Air Force, 2004), p. 35.

68. Donatella Della Porta, "Left-Wing Terrorism in Italy," in *Terrorism in Context,* ed. Martha Crenshaw (State College, Pa.: Pennsylvania State University Press, 1995), pp. 134–137, 157; Cragin and Daly, *The Dynamic Terrorist Threat,* p. 34.

69. Bloom, *Dying to Kill,* especially pp. 1, 19–44.

70. Pedahzur and Perliger, "The Making of Suicide Bombers: A Comparative Perspective," p. 161.

71. Jenkins, "Building an Army of Believers."

72. For one story illustrating the popular admiration of bin Ladin and the "nobility" of his cause, see Elliott, "Where Boys Grow Up to Be Jihadis," pp. 70–81, 96, 98, 100.

73. Amos Harel, " 'The PA Steals from Me, Hamas Takes Care of Me,' " *Ha'aretz,* June 27, 2002; Catherine Hours, "Charity and Bombings: Hamas Gains Ground with Desperate Palestinians," Agence France-Presse, August 15, 2001; Jamie Tarabay, "Islamic Militants Gain Influence Through Philanthropic Work," Associated Press, March 2, 2001.

74. "Economics in Peacemaking: Lessons from Northern Ireland," *The Portland Trust*, May 2007, pp. 7–8; Kim Cragin and Peter Chalk, *Terrorism and Development: Using Social and Economic Development to Inhibit a Resurgence of Terrorism* (Santa Monica, Calif.: RAND, 2003), pp. 5–14.

75. Cragin and Chalk, *Terrorism and Development*, p. x.

76. Bayat, "Revolution Without Movement, Movement Without Revolution," pp. 155–158.

77. Benjamin and Simon, *The Next Attack*, pp. 100–102.

78. Tessler, "Public Opinion in the Arab and Muslim World," p. 21.

79. Christopher Boucek, "Libya's Return to the Fold?" *Foreign Policy in Focus*, April 2004; Harel, " 'The PA Steals from Me, Hamas Takes Care of Me' "; Harik, *Hezbollah*, pp. 81–82; Hours, "Charity and Bombings"; McGeary, "Hamas," p. 54; Tarabay, "Islamic Militants Gain Influence Through Philanthropic Work."

80. Tessler and Robbins, "What Leads Some Ordinary Arab Men and Women to Approve of Terrorist Attacks Against the United States?," pp. 305–306.

81. Davis, *Martyrs*, p. 10.

82. Benjamin and Simon, *The Next Attack*, pp. 31–50; Gerges, *Journey of the Jihadist*, pp. 262–268.

83. Mark Juergensmeyer, *Terror in the Mind of God: The Global Rise of Religious Violence* (Berkeley: University of California Press, 2000), pp. 180–181; Steven N. Simon, "Muslim Perceptions of America: The Sources of Hostility," in *"In the Same Light as Slavery": Building a Global Antiterrorist Consensus*, ed. Joseph McMillan (Washington, D.C.: National Defense University Press, 2006), pp. 39–51.

84. Juergensmeyer, *Terror in the Mind of God*, pp. 178–179.

85. On this see Cronin, "Behind the Curve," pp. 30–58; Michael Mousseau, "Market Civilization and Its Clash with Terror," *International Security* 27, no. 3 (Winter 2002–03), pp. 5–29; Simon, "Muslim Perceptions of America," pp. 39–51; Robert S. Snyder, "Hating America: Bin Laden as a Civilizational Revolutionary," *The Review of Politics* 65, no. 4 (Autumn 2003), pp. 337–342.

86. Simon, "Muslim Perceptions of America," p. 49.

87. Atanas Gotchev, "Terrorism and Globalization," in *The Roots of Terrorism*, ed. Louise Richardson (New York: Routledge, 2006), pp. 106–107.

88. Fair and Shepherd, "Who Supports Terrorism?," p. 52.

89. Dalia Mogahed, "The Battle for Hearts and Minds: Moderate vs. Extremist Views in the Muslim World," Special Report: The Muslim World, Gallup World Poll, Washington, D.C., 2006, p. 2.

90. Davis, *Martyrs*, p. 90.

91. On this general set of beliefs, see Benjamin and Simon, *The Next Attack*,

p. 80; Bergen, *Holy War, Inc.*, pp. 188–189; Daniel L. Byman, *The Five-Front War: The Better Way to Fight Global Jihad* (New York: Wiley, 2007), p. 11; Davis, *Martyrs*, pp. 10–11, 108; Gerges, *Journey of the Jihadist*, p. 167; Kepel, *The War for Muslim Minds*, pp. 63–64; Juergensmeyer, *Terror in the Mind of God*, pp. 180–181; Noland and Pack, *The Arab Economies in a Changing World*, p. 82; Paul R. Pillar, "Superpower Foreign Policies: A Source of Global Resentment," in *The Making of a Terrorist: Recruitment, Training, and Root Causes*, vol. 3: *Root Causes*, ed. James J. F. Forest (Westport, Conn.: Praeger, 2006), pp. 36–37; Rubin and Rubin, *Hating America*, especially pp. 155–157; Simon, "Muslim Perceptions of America," pp. 39–51; Snyder, "Hating America," pp. 337–342.

92. Davis, *Martyrs*, p. 108.

93. Tessler and Robbins, "What Leads Some Ordinary Arab Men and Women to Approve of Terrorist Attacks Against the United States?," p. 305. Also see Benjamin and Simon, *The Next Attack*, pp. 18–19; Bergen, *Holy War, Inc.*, p. 223; Byman, *The Five-Front War*, pp. 11–15; Richard Crockatt, *America Embattled: September 11, Anti-Americanism, and the Global Order* (London: Routledge, 2003), pp. 72–73; Davis, *Martyrs*, pp. 91–92; Gerges, *Journey of the Jihadist*, pp. 4, 114, 160–170, 177; Fawaz Gerges, *The Far Enemy: Why Jihad Went Global* (Cambridge, U.K.: Cambridge University Press, 2005); Juergensmeyer, *Terror in the Mind of God*, pp. 178–180; Kepel, *The War for Muslim Minds*, pp. 1–2, 72–82; Pillar, "Superpower Foreign Policies," p. 42; David C. Rapoport, "Sacred Terror: A Contemporary Example from Islam," in *Origins of Terrorism: Psychologies, Ideologies, Theologies, States of Mind*, ed. Walter Reich (Washington, D.C.: Woodrow Wilson Center Press, 1998), p. 111; Snyder, "Hating America," pp. 327–330.

94. Tessler and Robbins, "What Leads Some Ordinary Arab Men and Women," p. 312.

95. Pollack, *The Persian Puzzle*, pp. 132–133, 147–149.

96. Rubin and Rubin, *Hating America*, p. 158.

97. Ibid., p. 178.

98. Pillar, "Superpower Foreign Policies," p. 39.

99. Bergen, *Holy War, Inc.*, p. 77.

100. Ibid., pp. 64, 77.

101. Crockatt, *America Embattled*, p. 88.

102. Dana H. Allin and Steven Simon, "The Moral Psychology of US Support for Israel," *Survival* 45, no. 3 (Autumn 2003), pp. 133–134.

103. Gerges, *Journey of the Jihadist*, p. 205.

104. Kepel, *The War for Muslim Minds*, p. 2.

105. Bergen, *Holy War, Inc.*, p. 223; Crockatt, *America Embattled*, pp. 73, 88; Gerges, *Journey of the Jihadist*, p. 176.

106. Pillar, "Superpower Foreign Policies," p. 31.

107. Bergen, *Holy War, Inc.*, pp. 188–189.

108. Tessler, "Public Opinion in the Arab and Muslim World," pp. 13–20.

109. Mary R. Habeck, *Knowing the Enemy: Jihadist Ideology and the War on Terror* (New Haven, Conn.: Yale University Press, 2006), pp. 172–173.

110. Shibley Telhami, "2006 Annual Arab Public Opinion Survey," February 8, 2007, unpublished, p. 47.

111. Robert Satloff, Eunice Youmans, and Mark Nakhla, "Assessing What Arabs Do, Not What They Say: A New Approach to Understanding Arab Anti-Americanism," Policy Focus no. 57, Washington Institute for Near East Policy, Washington, D.C., July 2006, p. 3.

112. Ibid., p. 1.

113. John Esposito, "Terrorism and the Rise of Political Islam," in Richardson, ed., *The Roots of Terrorism*, pp. 155–156.

114. Ibid., p. 155; Abdul Hadi Palazzi, "Orthodox Islamic Perceptions of Jihad and Martyrdom," in *Countering Suicide Terrorism: An International Conference*, International Policy Institute for Counter-Terrorism at the Interdisciplinary Center, Herzliya (Herzliya, Israel: ICT, 2001), pp. 64–74.

115. For a concurring view, see Gerges, *Journey of the Jihadist*, pp. 11–14.

116. Davis, *Martyrs*, pp. 8, 99, 112–113; Reven Paz, "The Islamic Legitimacy of Suicide Terrorism," in *Countering Suicide Terrorism: An International Conference*, The International Policy Institute for Counter-Terrorism at the Interdisciplinary Center, Herzliya (Herzliya, Israel: ICT, 2001), p. 89.

117. Benjamin and Simon, *The Next Attack*, p. 66.

118. Davis, *Martyrs*, p. 5; Gerges, *Journey of the Jihadist*, pp. 240–241; Bill Samii, "Terrorism: Islamic Scholars Debate Suicide Bombings and Hostage Taking," Radio Free Europe/Radio Liberty, 2005, p. 1.

119. Martin Kramer, "The Moral Logic of Hizballah," in *Origins of Terrorism: Psychologies, Ideologies, Theologies, States of Mind,* ed. Walter Reich (Washington, D.C.: Woodrow Wilson Center Press, 1998), pp. 142–149; Paz, "The Islamic Legitimacy of Suicide Terrorism," p. 90.

120. Telhami, "2006 Annual Arab Public Opinion Survey," p. 47.

121. Mogahed, "The Battle for Hearts and Minds," p. 1.

122. Gerges, *Journey of the Jihadist*, p. 91; Kepel, *The War for Muslim Minds*, pp. 72–82; Pillar, "Superpower Foreign Policies," p. 42.

123. Davis, *Martyrs*, p. 104.

124. Palazzi, "Orthodox Islamic Perceptions of Jihad and Martyrdom," p. 67.

125. Bergen and Pandey, "The Madrassa Scapegoat," pp. 117–118.

126. Marc Sageman, *Understanding Terrorist Networks* (Philadelphia: University of Pennsylvania Press, 2004).

127. Mark Juergensmeyer, "Religion as a Cause of Terror," in *The Roots of Terrorism*, ed. Louise Richardson (New York: Routledge, 2006), pp. 139–140. Also see Esposito, "Terrorism and the Rise of Political Islam," p. 155.

128. Juergensmeyer, "Religion as a Cause of Terror," p. 142. For a concurring view, see Susanna Pearce, "Religious Sources of Violence," in *The Making of a Terrorist: Recruitment, Training, and Root Causes*, vol. 2: *Root Causes*, ed. James J. F. Forest (Westport: Praeger Security International, 2006).

129. For a similar assessment and prescription, see Byman, *The Five-Front War*, especially pp. 157–172.

130. Quoted in Davis, *Martyrs*, p. 26.

PART FOUR: THE CORE OF A GRAND STRATEGY FOR THE MIDDLE EAST

1. Kenneth M. Pollack, "Spies, Lies, and Weapons: What Went Wrong," *The Atlantic Monthly*, January–February 2004, pp. 78–92.

2. National Intelligence Council, "National Intelligence Estimate: Iraq's Continuing Programs for Weapons of Mass Destruction," October 2002, available at www.gwu.edu/~nsarchiv/NSAEBB/NSAEBB129/nie.pdf, downloaded January 27, 2008; Kenneth M. Pollack, *The Threatening Storm: The Case for Invading Iraq* (New York: Random House, 2002), pp. 173–175.

3. Larry Diamond, *Squandered Victory: The American Occupation and the Bungled Effort to Bring Democracy to Iraq* (New York: Times Books, 2005); James Fallows, "Blind into Baghdad," *The Atlantic Monthly*, January–February 2004, pp. 52–74; Michael Gordon and Bernard Trainor, *Cobra II: The Inside Story of the Invasion and Occupation of Iraq* (New York: Pantheon, 2006); George Packer, *The Assassin's Gate: America in Iraq* (New York: Farrar, Straus and Giroux, 2005); David L. Phillips, *Losing Iraq: Inside the Postwar Reconstruction Fiasco* (Boulder, Colo.: Westview, 2005); Kenneth M. Pollack, "The Seven Deadly Sins of Failure in Iraq: A Retrospective Analysis of the Reconstruction," *Middle East Review of International Affairs* 10, no. 4 (December 2006); Thomas E. Ricks, *Fiasco: The American Military Adventure in Iraq* (New York: Penguin, 2006).

4. For terrorism experts explicitly making the same argument, see Daniel L. Byman, *The Five-Front War: The Better Way to Fight Global Jihad* (New York: Wiley, 2007), pp. 157–172; Cronin, "Behind the Curve," p. 38; Ted Robert Gurr, "Economic Factors," in *The Roots of Terrorism*, ed. Louise Richardson (New York: Routledge, 2006), p. 91; Mary R. Habeck, *Knowing the Enemy: Jihadist Ideology and the War on Terror* (New Haven, Conn.: Yale University Press, 2006), pp. 176–177.

CHAPTER 10: ENABLING REFORM

1. For some good recent works that discuss the need for reform as well as the form it should take, see Nora Bensahel, "Political Reform in the Middle East," in *The Future Security Environment in the Middle East: Conflict, Sta-*

bility and Political Change, ed. Nora Bensahel and Daniel L. Byman (Santa Monica, Calif.: RAND, 2004), p. 19; Daniel L. Byman, *The Five-Front War: The Better Way to Fight Global Jihad* (New York: Wiley, 2007), especially pp. 157–172; Thomas Carothers and Marina Ottaway, eds., *Uncharted Journey: Promoting Democracy in the Middle East* (Washington, D.C.: Carnegie Endowment for International Peace, 2005); Audrey Kurth Cronin, "Behind the Curve: Globalization and International Terrorism," *International Security* 27, no. 3 (Winter 2002–03), pp. 30–58; Larry Diamond, Marc F. Plattner and Daniel Brumberg, eds., *Islam and Democracy in the Middle East* (Baltimore, Md.: Johns Hopkins University Press, 2003); Michael Mousseau, "Market Civilization and Its Clash with Terror," *International Security* 27, no. 3 (Winter 2002–03), pp. 5–29; Marsha Pripstein Posusney and Michele Penner Angrist, eds., *Authoritarianism in the Middle East: Regimes and Resistance* (Boulder, Colo.: Lynne Rienner, 2005); Alan Richards, "Economic Reform in the Middle East: The Challenge to Governance," in Nora Bensahel and Daniel L. Byman, eds., *The Future Security Environment in the Middle East: Conflict, Stability and Political Change* (Santa Monica, Calif.: RAND, 2004); Dennis Ross, "Counterterrorism: A Professional's Strategy," *World Policy Journal* 24, no. 1 (Spring 2007), pp. 19–31; Tamara Cofman Wittes, *Freedom's Unsteady March: America's Role in Promoting Arab Democracy* (Washington, D.C.: Brookings Institution Press, 2008).

2. See, e.g., International Crisis Group, *Can Saudi Arabia Reform Itself?*, ICG Middle East Report no. 28, Cairo and Brussels, July 14, 2004, p. 25.

3. "During the past 20 years, there has been some consensus on what economic policies ought to be adopted to improve economic management and thereby restore growth of incomes and job-creation. This view holds that only a private-sector led, export-oriented economic development strategy has a chance of coping with the development challenges facing the region. . . . No one has formulated a more persuasive policy mix than the Washington Consensus for the Middle Eastern context." Richards, "Economic Reform in the Middle East," p. 59. Eva Bellin notes that early successes in Jordan, Morocco, Tunisia, and Turkey employing this strategy provide some confirmation that it can work in the Middle East. Eva Bellin, "The Political-Economic Conundrum," in *Uncharted Journey: Promoting Democracy in the Middle East,* ed. Thomas Carothers and Marina Ottaway (Washington, D.C.: Carnegie Endowment for International Peace, 2005), pp. 144–145.

4. Bellin, "The Political-Economic Conundrum," pp. 135, 144–145; Thomas Carothers, "Choosing a Strategy," *Uncharted Journey: Promoting Democracy in the Middle East,* ed. Thomas Carothers and Marina Ottaway (Washington, D.C.: Carnegie Endowment for International Peace, 2005), p. 199; Mar-

cus Noland and Howard Pack, *The Arab Economies in a Changing World* (Washington, D.C.: Peterson Institute for International Economics, 2007), p. 274; Richards, "Economic Reform in the Middle East," p. 128.

5. On this point, see also Noah Feldman, *After Jihad: America and the Struggle for Islamic Democracy* (New York: Farrar, Straus and Giroux, 2003), especially pp. 6–16; Wittes, *Freedom's Unsteady March,* pp. 30–55; John P. Entelis, "The Democratic Imperative vs. the Authoritarian Impulse: The Maghrib State Between Transition and Terrorism," *The Middle East Journal* 59, no. 4 (Autumn 2005), pp. 537–538.

6. Marina Ottaway, "The Missing Constituency for Democratic Reform," in *Uncharted Journey: Promoting Democracy in the Middle East,* ed. Thomas Carothers and Marina Ottaway (Washington, D.C.: Carnegie Endowment for International Peace, 2005), p. 155.

7. Amy Hawthorne, "The New Reform Ferment," in *Uncharted Journey: Promoting Democracy in the Middle East,* ed. Thomas Carothers and Marina Ottaway (Washington, D.C.: Carnegie Endowment for International Peace, 2005), pp. 64–65.

8. Patrick E. Tyler, "Saudis Plan to End U.S. Presence," *The New York Times,* February 9, 2003.

9. George W. Bush, "Celebrating Freedom, Honoring Service," Inaugural Address, January 20, 2005, available on the web at www.whitehouse .gov/inaugural/, downloaded January 22, 2008.

10. Saad Eddin Ibrahim, "A Dissident Asks: Can Bush Turn Words Into Action?," *The Washington Post,* November 23, 2003.

11. In Condi Rice's famous 2000 *Foreign Affairs* article laying out the foreign policy approach of the future George W. Bush administration, there was nothing about the importance of reform—let alone democratization—in the Middle East. The entire Middle East was relegated to a few paragraphs on Iraq and Iran at the very end of the article, which spent most of its text on China, Russia, and Europe—which were the real concerns of the Bush 43 administration when it took office. See Condoleezza Rice, "Campaign 2000: Promoting the National Interest," *Foreign Affairs* 79, no. 1 (January–February 2000).

12. Muhammad Muslih and Augustus Richard Norton, "The Need for Arab Democracy," *Foreign Policy* no. 83 (Summer 1991), p. 3. See also Michael C. Hudson, "After the Gulf War: Prospects for Democratization in the Arab World," *Middle East Journal* 45, no. 3 (Summer 1991), pp. 407–426.

13. United Nations Development Programme, Arab Fund for Economic and Social Development, *Arab Human Development Report, 2003* (New York: United Nations Publications, 2003), p. 151. Also see pp. 151–157.

14. For a good summary of neoliberalism (and how it differs from neocon-

servatism), see Dennis Ross, *Statecraft: And How to Restore America's Standing in the World* (New York: Farrar, Straus, and Giroux, 2007), pp. 17–21, 333–341. Also see Ronald D. Asmus and Kenneth M. Pollack, "The Neoliberal Take on the Middle East," *The Washington Post,* July 22, 2003.

15. Ronald D. Asmus and Kenneth M. Pollack, "The New TransAtlantic Project: A Response to Robert Kagan," *Policy Review,* October–November 2002, pp. 3–18.

16. Ambassador Richard N. Haass, "Towards Greater Democracy in the Muslim World," Remarks to the Council on Foreign Relations, Washington, D.C., December 4, 2002, available at www.state.gov/s/p/rem/15686.htm, downloaded November 11, 2006.

17. Secretary Colin L. Powell, "The U.S.-Middle East Partnership Initiative: Building Hope for the Years Ahead," Remarks to the Heritage Foundation, Washington, D.C., December 12, 2002, available at www.state.gov/secretary/former/powell/remarks/2002/15920.htm, downloaded August 16, 2007.

18. Thomas Carothers, "The Democracy Crusade Myth," *The National Interest* (July–August 2007), p. 8.

19. Ibrahim, "A Dissident Asks: Can Bush Turn Words into Action?"

20. Carothers, "The Democracy Crusade Myth," p. 9.

21. Ibid.; Thomas Carothers and Marina Ottaway, "The New Democracy Imperative," in *Uncharted Journey: Promoting Democracy in the Middle East,* ed. Thomas Carothers and Marina Ottaway (Washington, D.C.: Carnegie Endowment for International Peace, 2005), p. 5; Wittes, *Freedom's Unsteady March,* pp. 76–101.

22. Amy Hawthorne, "Is Civil Society the Answer?," in *Uncharted Journey: Promoting Democracy in the Middle East,* ed. Thomas Carothers and Marina Ottaway (Washington, D.C.: Carnegie Endowment for International Peace, 2005), p. 102.

23. Wittes, *Freedom's Unsteady March,* pp. 90, 99–101.

24. Carothers, "The Democracy Crusade Myth," p. 9.

25. Wittes, *Freedom's Unsteady March,* p. 98.

26. Khairi Abaza, *Political Islam and Regime Survival in Egypt,* Policy Focus no. 51, The Washington Institute for Near East Policy, Washington, D.C., January 2006; Tamara Cofman Wittes, "The 2005 Egyptian Elections: How Free? How Important?," Saban Center Middle East Memo no. 8, Saban Center for Middle East Policy at the Brookings Institution, August 24, 2005, available at www.brookings.edu/views/papers/wittes/20050824.htm, downloaded August 16, 2007.

27. John L. Esposito and Dalia Mogahed, *Who Speaks for Islam? What a Billion Muslims Really Think* (New York: Gallup Press, 2008), p. 32.

28. Wittes, *Freedom's Unsteady March,* p. 97.

29. Amy Hawthorne, "The New Reform Ferment," in *Uncharted Journey: Promoting Democracy in the Middle East,* ed. Thomas Carothers and Marina Ottaway (Washington, D.C.: Carnegie Endowment for International Peace, 2005), pp. 62–63.

30. Esposito and Mogahed, *Who Speaks for Islam?,* p. 59.

31. Carothers and Ottaway, "The New Democracy Imperative," p. 5; Wittes, *Freedom's Unsteady March,* pp. 80–110.

32. David Finkel, "U.S. Ideals Meet Reality in Yemen," *The Washington Post,* December 18, 2005.

33. Marina Ottaway, "The Problem of Credibility," in *Uncharted Journey: Promoting Democracy in the Middle East,* ed. Thomas Carothers and Marina Ottaway (Washington, D.C.: Carnegie Endowment for International Peace, 2005), p. 174. Also see Daniel Brumberg, "Liberalization Versus Democracy," in *Uncharted Journey,* ed. Carothers and Ottaway, p. 15.

34. See, e.g., Nathan J. Brown and Amr Hamzawy, "Arab Spring Fever," *The National Interest* (September–October 2007), pp. 33–40; Thomas Carothers, "U.S. Democracy Promotion Efforts During and After Bush," Carnegie Endowment, Washington, D.C., September 2007; Jackson Diehl, "How to Be a Dissident President: A Chance for Bush to Live Up to His Words," *The Washington Post,* June 11, 2007; Michael Mandelbaum, *Democracy's Good Name: The Rise and Risks of the World's Most Popular Form of Government* (New York: PublicAffairs, 2007); James Traub, "Exporting Democracy, but Not Bush's Way," *Los Angeles Times,* June 8, 2007; Fareed Zakaria, "A Quiet Prayer for Democracy," *Newsweek,* May 14, 2007.

35. Esposito and Mogahed, *Who Speaks for Islam?,* p. 47; Ronald Inglehart and Pippa Norris, "The True Clash of Civilizations," *Foreign Policy* (March–April 2003), pp. 63–70.

36. For a similar perspective, see Mary R. Habeck, *Knowing the Enemy: Jihadist Ideology and the War on Terror* (New Haven, Conn.: Yale University Press, 2006), pp. 176–177.

37. For instance, see Valerie Bunce, "The Tasks of Democratic Transition and Transferability," *Orbis* 52, no. 1 (Winter 2008), pp. 29–30; Samuel P. Huntington, "Will Countries Become More Democratic?," *Political Science Quarterly,* Summer 1984; Elie Kedourie, *Democracy and Arab Political Culture* (Washington, D.C.: Washington Institute for Near East Policy, 1992); James Kurth, "Ignoring History: U.S. Democratization in the Muslim World," *Orbis* 49, no. 2 (Spring 2005), pp. 307–310.

38. Eva Bellin, "The Robustness of Authoritarianism in the Middle East: Exceptionalism in Comparative Perspective," *Comparative Politics* 36, no. 2 (2004), p. 141.

39. The seminal works putting the nails in the coffin of the fallacy that "Confucian" culture is incompatible with democracy are Kim Dae Jung,

"Is Culture Destiny? The Myth of Asia's Anti-Democratic Values," *Foreign Affairs* 73, no. 6 (November–December 1994), pp. 189–94; Amartya Sen, *Development as Freedom* (New York: Oxford University Press, 1999).

40. Kurth, "Ignoring History," p. 307; Wittes, *Freedom's Unsteady March*, pp. 50–51.

41. Farid E. Khazen, *The Breakdown of the State in Lebanon, 1967–1976* (London: I. B. Tauris, 2000).

42. Asad AbuKhalil, "A Viable Partnership: Islam, Democracy and the Arab World," *Harvard International Review* 15, no. 2 (Winter 1992–93), p. 65; John L. Esposito and James P. Piscatori, "Democratization and Islam," *Middle East Journal* 45, no. 3 (Summer 1991), pp. 427–440; John L. Esposito, ed., *Political Islam: Revolution, Radicalism, or Reform?* (Boulder, Colo.: Lynne Rienner, 1997); Feldman, *After Jihad;* Graham Fuller, "Islamists and Democracy," in *Uncharted Journey: Promoting Democracy in the Middle East,* ed. Thomas Carothers and Marina Ottaway (Washington, D.C.: Carnegie Endowment for International Peace, 2005), pp. 37–55; Anwar Ibrahim, "Universal Values and Muslim Democracy," *Journal of Democracy* 17, no. 3 (July 2006), pp. 5–12; Benjamin Isakhan, "Engaging 'Primitive Democracy': Mideast Roots of Collective Governance," *Middle East Policy* 14, no. 3 (Fall 2007), pp. 97–117; Amaney A. Jamal, "Reassessing Support for Islam and Democracy in the Arab World? Evidence from Egypt and Jordan," *World Affairs* 169, no. 2 (Fall 2006), pp. 54–56; Farhad Kazemi, "The Inclusion Imperative," *The Middle East Studies Association Bulletin,* December 1996; Bruce B. Lawrence, *Shattering the Myth: Islam Beyond Violence* (Princeton, N.J.: Princeton University Press, 1998); Ahmad S. Moussalli, *The Islamic Quest for Democracy, Pluralism, and Human Rights* (Gainesville, Fla.: University of Florida Press, 2001); Curtis R. Ryan and Jillian Schwedler, "Return to Democratization or New Hybrid Regime? The 2003 Elections in Jordan," *Middle East Policy* 11, no. 2 (Summer 2004), pp. 138–152; David Smock, "Islam and Democracy," Special Report 93, United States Institute of Peace, Washington, D.C., September 2002.

43. Alfred Stepan with Graeme B. Robertson, "An 'Arab' More Than 'Muslim' Electoral Gap," *The Journal of Democracy* 14, no. 3 (July 2003), pp. 35–36.

44. Dalia Mogahed and Geneive Abdo, "Islam and Democracy," Special Report: Muslim World, Gallup World Poll, Washington, D.C., 2006, p. 3; Dalia Mogahed, "Understanding Islamic Democracy," *Europe's World* (Spring 2006), pp. 163–165.

45. Pew Global Attitudes Project, "Support for Terror Wanes Among Muslim Publics: 17-Nation Pew Global Attitudes Survey," Pew Research Center, Washington, D.C., July 14, 2005, p. 22.

46. Mark Tessler, "Do Islamic Orientations Influence Attitudes Toward

Democracy in the Arab World? Evidence from Egypt, Jordan, Morocco, and Algeria," *International Journal of Comparative Sociology* 43, nos. 3–5 (2002), pp. 229–249. For identical conclusions, see Esposito and Mogahed, *Who Speaks for Islam?*, pp. 35, 47–48.

47. See, e.g., Joyce M. Davis, *Martyrs: Innocence, Vengeance, and Despair in the Middle East* (New York: Palgrave Macmillan, 2004), p. 11; Esposito and Mogahed, *Who Speaks for Islam?*, pp. 31–32, 47–48, 57–58; Amaney A. Jamal, "Reassessing Support for Islam and Democracy in the Arab World? Evidence from Egypt and Jordan," *World Affairs* 169, no. 2 (Fall 2006), pp. 51–64; Carothers and Ottaway, "The New Democracy Imperative," p. 8; Abdou Filali-Ansary, "Muslims and Democracy," in *Islam and Democracy in the Middle East,* ed. Larry Diamond, Marc F. Plattner, and Daniel Brumberg (Baltimore, Md.: Johns Hopkins University Press, 2003), pp. 199–201; Hawthorne, "The New Reform Ferment"; Radwan A. Masmoudi, "The Silenced Majority," in *Islam and Democracy in the Middle East,* ed. Larry Diamond, Marc F. Plattner, and Daniel Brumberg (Baltimore, Md.: Johns Hopkins University Press, 2003), pp. 260–262.

48. AbuKhalil, "A Viable Partnership: Islam, Democracy and the Arab World," p. 22.

49. United Nations Development Programme, Arab Fund for Economic and Social Development, *Arab Human Development Report, 2003,* p. 19.

50. Ronald Inglehart, "How Solid Is Mass Support for Democracy: And How Can We Measure It?," *PS: Political Science and Politics* 36, no. 1 (January 2003), p. 52.

51. Pew Global Attitudes Project, "Support for Terror Wanes," p. 2. Also see Mark Tessler, "Public Opinion in the Arab and Muslim World: Informing U.S. Public Diplomacy," in *"In the Same Light as Slavery": Building a Global Antiterrorist Consensus,* ed. Joseph McMillan (Washington, D.C.: National Defense University Press, 2006), pp. 15–16.

52. Filali-Ansary, "Muslims and Democracy," pp. 202–203; Tim Niblock, "Democratisation: A Theoretical and Practical Debate," *The British Journal of Middle Eastern Studies* 25, no. 2 (November 1998), p. 229.

53. Mogahed and Abdo, "Islam and Democracy," p. 2. See also Esposito and Mogahed, *Who Speaks for Islam?*, p. 34.

54. Iraq Center for Research and Strategic Studies, "Results of Public Opinion Poll #3," International Republican Institute, available at www.iri .org/pdfs/iraq_poll_3.pdf.

55. Zogby International Survey of Iraq, August 2003, p. 2, available at www.taemag.com/docLib/20030905_IraqpollFrequencies.pdf. The Zogby survey also points to the problems with using polls in a country with no experience of public opinion and whose citizens lived for thirty-five years in a world of misinformation and rumors. Even more than

elsewhere, in Iraq the results are highly dependent on how the question is asked. Zogby specifically asked a question about democracy but did so in a foolish fashion. The survey asked Iraqis whether "democracy could work in Iraq" or whether it was "a Western way of doing things and it will not work here." At that time, the words "Western way of doing things" were code in Iraq: they referred to the importation of Western cultures, values, and conceivably even religion. Many conservative Iraqis would automatically shy away from anything associated with that term. Indeed, what was surprising was that even with such a poorly phrased question, the results were 40 percent agreeing with the first statement and only 50 percent agreeing with the second.

56. The Gallup poll findings are presented in Appendix Table 2 of Dina Smeltz and Jodi Nachtwey, "Iraqi Public Opinion Analysis," U.S. Department of State, October 21, 2003, p. 13, available at www.cpa-iraq .org/government/political_poll.pdf.

57. Mark Tessler, "The Attitudes of Ordinary Iraqis in 2004 and 2006," *The Journal of the International Institute,* 14, no. 2 (Winter 2007), p. 4.

58. Dina Smeltz and Jodi Nachtwey, "Iraqi Public Opinion Analysis," U.S. Department of State, October 21, 2003, p. 8, available at http:// www.cpa-iraq.org/government/political_poll.pdf, p. 1.

59. Jamal, "Reassessing Support for Islam and Democracy in the Arab World?," pp. 52–54.

60. Thomas O. Melia, "The People of Bahrain Want to Participate in the King's Political Reform Project: A Report on Focus Groups Conducted in the Kingdom of Bahrain," National Democratic Institute, Washington, D.C., August 2002, p. 1.

61. For instance, there were prodemocracy demonstrations in Jordan and Algeria in 1992, which security services crushed violently. AbuKhalil, "A Viable Partnership," p. 22.

62. Marwan Muasher, "A Path to Arab Democracy," *The New York Times,* April 26, 2003.

63. Quoted in Ottaway, "The Problem of Credibility," p. 185.

64. Geneive Abdo and Dalia Mogahed, "What Muslim Women Want," *The Wall Street Journal,* December 13, 2006; author's interview with Dalia Mogahed, August 3, 2007. See also Esposito and Mogahed, *Who Speaks for Islam?,* pp. 35–36.

65. Hawthorne, "The New Reform Ferment," p. 57.

66. Lisa Anderson, "Arab Democracy: Dismal Prospects," *World Policy Journal* 18, no. 3 (Fall 2001), pp. 53–61; Michael Dobbs, "Reform with an Islamic Slant: Saudi Pro-Democracy Movement Poses Dilemma for U.S.," *The Washington Post,* March 9, 2003; John L. Esposito, "Political Islam and U.S. Foreign Policy," *The Harvard International Review,* November 2, 2006, avail-

able at hir.harvard.edu/articles/print.php?article=1453; Esposito and Mo-gahed, *Who Speaks for Islam?*, pp. 32–33, 57; Wittes, *Freedom's Unsteady March,* pp. 16–26; Mohammad Yaghi, "Missing in Action: The Democracy Agenda in the Middle East," *Arab Insight* 1, no. 2 (Fall 2007), pp. 113–124.

67. Richard W. Murphy and F. Gregory Gause III, "Democracy and U.S. Policy in the Middle East," *Middle East Policy* 5, no. 1 (January 1997), p. 59. Also see Feldman, *After Jihad,* pp. 4–5, 9–16.

68. Rami Khouri, "Anti-Americanism in the Arab World: Its Roots, Reper-cussions, and Remedies," February 12, 2003, lecture at the University of Utah, available at www.hum.utah.edu/mec/Lectures/2003%20lecture%20pages/2003%20lecture%20pdfs/Khouri.pdf, p. 4, downloaded August 3, 2007.

69. Shibley Telhami, "2006 Annual Arab Public Opinion Survey," February 8, 2007, p. 15.

70. Mona Makram Ebeid, conversation with the author, Washington, D.C., November 2007.

CHAPTER 11: MEETING THE CHALLENGES OF REFORM

1. On the problems of Arab reformists, see Barry Rubin, *The Long War for Freedom: The Arab Struggle for Democracy in the Middle East* (New York: John Wiley and Sons, 2006).

2. The best and best-known explication of this critique is F. Gregory Gause III, "Beware of What You Wish For: The Future of U.S.-Saudi Relations," *World Policy Journal* 19, no. 1 (Spring 2003), pp. 37–50. Also see F. Gregory Gause III, "Can Democracy Stop Terrorism?," *Foreign Affairs* 84, no. 5 (September–October 2005), pp. 62–76.

3. Whether the Bush administration would have attempted forcible de-mocratization in other Middle Eastern states had the invasions of Iraq and Afghanistan gone better is impossible to know. There were certainly voices within the administration and outside it who were urging them to do so. MEPI itself, which became the centerpiece of the Bush 43 admin-istration's democracy efforts after the United States became bogged down in Iraq, had the right approach—and did not promote forcible de-mocratization—but was implemented poorly and halfheartedly.

4. *Arab Human Development Report (AHDR)* 2003, p. 136; Thomas Carothers, "Choosing a Strategy," in *Uncharted Journey: Promoting Democracy in the Middle East,* ed. Thomas Carothers and Marina Ottaway (Washington, D.C.: Carnegie Endowment for International Peace, 2005), p. 199; Paul Rivlin and Shmuel Even, *Political Stability in Arab States: Economic Causes and Conse-quences,* Memorandum 74 (Tel Aviv: Jaffee Center for Strategic Studies, 2004), p. 23; Tamara Cofman Wittes, *Freedom's Unsteady March: America's*

Role in Promoting Arab Democracy (Washington, D.C.: Brookings Institution Press, 2008), pp. 78–79.

5. On the general phenomenon of regime efforts to subvert reform, see Daniel Brumberg, "The Trap of Liberalized Autocracy," *Journal of Democracy* 13, no. 4 (October 2002), pp. 56–68; Daniel Brumberg, "Liberalization Versus Democracy," in *Uncharted Journey: Promoting Democracy in the Middle East,* ed. Thomas Carothers and Marina Ottaway (Washington, D.C.: Carnegie Endowment for International Peace, 2005), p. 16; Thomas Carothers, "The End of the Transition Paradigm," *Journal of Democracy* 13, no. 2 (January 2002), pp. 5–21; John P. Entelis, "The Democratic Imperative vs. the Authoritarian Impulse: The Maghrib State Between Transition and Terrorism," *The Middle East Journal* 59, no. 4 (Autumn 2005), pp. 550–551; Steven Heydemann, "Upgrading Authoritarianism in the Arab World," Analysis Paper 13, Saban Center for Middle East Policy at the Brookings Institution, Washington, D.C., October 2007; Thomas O. Melia, "The People of Bahrain Want to Participate in the King's Political Reform Project: A Report on Focus Groups Conducted in the Kingdom of Bahrain," National Democratic Institute, Washington, D.C., August 2002, p. 2; Marina Ottaway and Amr Hamzawy, "Fighting on Two Fronts: Secular Parties in the Arab World," Carnegie Paper no. 85, Carnegie Endowment for International Peace, Washington, D.C., May 2007, pp. 3, 7; Marina Ottaway and Michele Dunne, "Incumbent Regimes and the King's Dilemma in the Arab World: Promise and Threat of Managed Reform," Carnegie Paper no. 88, Middle East Program, Carnegie Endowment for International Peace, Washington, D.C., December 2007, especially pp. 5–17; Curtis R. Ryan and Jillian Schwedler, "Return to Democratization or New Hybrid Regime? The 2003 Elections in Jordan," *Middle East Policy* 11, no. 2 (Summer 2004), pp. 138–152; Quintin Wiktorowicz, "Civil Society as Social Control: State Power in Jordan," *Comparative Politics* 33, no. 1 (October 2000), p. 43.

6. Saad Eddin Ibrahim, "A Dissident Asks: Can Bush Turn Words Into Action?," *Washington Post,* November 23, 2003, p. B03.

7. Rubin, *The Long War for Freedom,* especially pp. 38–54, 123–178.

8. Thomas Carothers and Marina Ottaway, "The New Democracy Imperative," in *Uncharted Journey: Promoting Democracy in the Middle East,* ed. Thomas Carothers and Marina Ottaway (Washington, D.C.: Carnegie Endowment for International Peace, 2005), pp. 6–7; Ibrahim, "A Dissident Asks: Can Bush Turn Words into Action?"; Marina Ottaway, "The Problem of Credibility," in *Uncharted Journey: Promoting Democracy in the Middle East,* ed. Thomas Carothers and Marina Ottaway (Washington, D.C.:

Carnegie Endowment for International Peace, 2005), pp. 173–192; Wittes, *Freedom's Unsteady March,* pp. 26–28.

9. Gwenn Okruhlik, "Rentier Wealth, Unruly Law, and the Rise of Opposition: The Political Economy of Oil States," *Comparative Politics* 31, no. 3 (April 1999), pp. 295–315.

10. International Crisis Group, *The Challenge of Political Reform: Jordanian Democratization and Regional Instability,* Middle East Briefing, Amman and Brussels, October 8, 2003, p. 2, available at www.crisisgroup.org/library/documents/middle_east_north_africa/jordan_political_reform08_10_03.pdf, downloaded July 10, 2007; International Crisis Group, *Can Saudi Arabia Reform Itself?,* ICG Middle East Report no. 28, Cairo and Brussels, July 14, 2004, pp. 20–26.

11. Entelis, "The Democratic Imperative vs. the Authoritarian Impulse," pp. 543–545.

12. Rivlin and Even, *Political Stability in Arab States,* p. 25.

13. Eva Bellin, "The Robustness of Authoritarianism in the Middle East: Exceptionalism in Comparative Perspective," *Comparative Politics* 36, no. 2 (2004), pp. 144–145.

14. Dennis Ross, "Counterterrorism: A Professional's Strategy," *World Policy Journal* 24, no. 1 (Spring 2007), p. 27.

15. Bellin, "The Robustness of Authoritarianism in the Middle East," pp. 147–149; F. Gregory Gause III, "The Persistence of Monarchy in the Arabian Peninsula: A Comparative Analysis," in *Middle East Monarchies: The Challenge of Modernity,* ed. Joseph Kostiner (Boulder, Colo.: Lynne Rienner, 2000), pp. 167–185.

16. Wittes, *Freedom's Unsteady March,* pp. 19–21.

17. For a similar argument, see Daniel Benjamin and Steven Simon, *The Next Attack: The Failure of the War on Terror and a Strategy for Getting It Right* (New York: Owl Books, 2005), p. 228.

18. I am indebted to Carlos Pascual for this idea. Carlos Pascual, correspondence with the author, January 2008.

19. See, e.g., Richard N. Haass, *The Opportunity: America's Moment to Alter History's Course* (New York: Public Affairs, 2005), especially p. 72; Fareed Zakaria, *The Future of Freedom: Illiberal Democracy at Home and Abroad* (New York: Norton, 2003), especially pp. 69–73.

20. Wittes, *Freedom's Unsteady March,* pp. 59–66.

21. On sequencing, see Thomas Carothers, "How Democracies Emerge: The 'Sequencing' Fallacy," *Journal of Democracy* 18, no. 1 (January 2007), pp. 13–27.

22. See, e.g., Sufyan Alissa, "The Political Economy of Reform in Egypt: Understanding the Role of Institutions," Carnegie Paper no. 5, Carnegie

Middle East Center, Carnegie Endowment for International Peace, Washington, D.C., October 2007, pp. 1–7; and Ottaway and Dunne, "Incumbent Regimes and the King's Dilemma in the Arab World," especially pp. 1–5.

23. Jamal, "Reassessing Support for Islam and Democracy in the Arab World?," pp. 51–64.

24. Haass, *The Opportunity,* especially p. 119; Zakaria, *The Future of Freedom,* pp. 69–73.

25. Robert J. Barro, "Determinants of Democracy," *The Journal of Political Economy* 107, no. 6 (December 1999), S158–S183. Also see Eva Bellin, "The Political-Economic Conundrum," in *Uncharted Journey: Promoting Democracy in the Middle East,* ed. Thomas Carothers and Marina Ottaway (Washington, D.C.: Carnegie Endowment for International Peace, 2005), p. 143; Carothers, "Choosing a Strategy," p. 199; Larry Diamond, ed., *The Return to Political Culture? Political Culture and Democracy in Developing Countries* (Boulder, Colo.: Lynne Rienner, 1993); Jamal, "Reassessing Support for Islam and Democracy in the Arab World?," pp. 51–64; Seymour Lipset, "The Social Requisites of Democracy Revisited," *American Sociological Review* 59, no. 1, pp. 1–22; Adam Przeworski, Michael Alvarez, Jose Antonio Cheibub, and Fernando Limongi, "What Makes Democracies Endure?," *Journal of Democracy* 7, no. 1 (January 1996), pp. 39–55.

26. Bellin, "The Political-Economic Conundrum," pp. 142–143.

27. Haass, *The Opportunity,* p. 119.

28. John L. Thornton, "Long Time Coming: The Prospects for Demcracy in China," *Foreign Affairs* 87, no. 1 (January–February 2008), pp. 2–22.

29. Afshin Molavi, conversation with the author, Washington, D.C., August 2007.

30. Ottaway and Dunne, "Incumbent Regimes and the King's Dilemma in the Arab World," p. 10.

31. Tom Ginsburg, "Lessons from Democratic Transitions: Case Studies from Asia," *Orbis* 52, no. 1 (Winter 2008), pp. 92–102.

32. Valerie Bunce, "The Tasks of Democratic Transition and Transferability," *Orbis* 52, no. 1 (Winter 2008), pp. 36–38.

33. Bellin, "The Political-Economic Conundrum," p. 141; Carothers, "Choosing a Strategy," p. 199.

34. See, e.g., Sufyan Alissa, "Rethinking Economic Reform in Jordan: Confronting Socioeconomic Realities," Carnegie Paper no. 4, Carnegie Middle East Center, Carnegie Endowment for International Peace, Washington, D.C., July 2007, especially pp. 19–20.

35. See, e.g., International Crisis Group, *Can Saudi Arabia Reform Itself?,* p. 23.

36. *The Europa World Year Book 2005,* 46th ed., vol. 2 (London: Routledge, Taylor and Francis Group, 2005), p. 3732.

37. ICG, *Can Saudi Arabia Reform Itself?*, pp. 21–22.

38. *Freedom in the World,* Egypt: Country Report (Freedom House, 2007), available at www.freedomhouse.org/template.cfm?page=22&country= 7170&year=2007, downloaded July 12, 2007.

39. Nathan J. Brown and Amr Hamzawy, "Arab Spring Fever," *National Interest,* no. 91 (September–October 2007), pp. 33–34.

40. Steven Heydemann often makes the point that in the Middle East, "77 is the new 99."

41. Ottaway, "The Problem of Credibility," p. 197.

42. Alissa, "The Political Economy of Reform in Egypt," pp. 1–11; Heydemann, "Upgrading Authoritarianism in the Arab World," pp. 17–18.

43. The World Bank, *Middle East and North Africa Region Economic Developments and Prospects, 2007: Job Creation in an Era of High Growth* (Washington, D.C.: World Bank, 2007), p. 1.

44. Mohammed Abu Rumman, "Political Stagnation in Jordan: Liberalism Falls Short," *Arab Insight* 2, no. 1 (Winter 2008), pp. 71–79; Ottaway and Hamzawy, "Fighting on Two Fronts," pp. 1–2; Amr Hamzawy, "The Key to Arab Reform: Moderate Islamists," Policy Brief 40, Carnegie Endowment for International Peace, Washington, D.C., August 2005, p. 4; Marina Ottaway, "The Missing Constituency for Democratic Reform," in *Uncharted Journey: Promoting Democracy in the Middle East,* ed. Thomas Carothers and Marina Ottaway (Washington, D.C.: Carnegie Endowment for International Peace, 2005), p. 153; Ross, "Counterterrorism: A Professional's Strategy," pp. 25–26.

45. Rubin, *The Long War for Freedom,* is the best and most comprehensive survey of the many problems facing secular liberal reformists in the Arab world.

46. F. Gregory Gause III, "Beware of What You Wish For," available at www.foreignaffairs.org/20060208faupdate85177/f-gregory-gause-iii/ beware-of-what-you-wish-for.html, downloaded August 24, 2007.

47. Esposito and Mogahed, *Who Speaks for Islam?,* p. 44; Ryan and Schwedler, "Return to Democratization or New Hybrid Regime?," pp. 138–152.

48. Noah Feldman, *After Jihad: America and the Struggle for Islamic Democracy* (New York: Farrar, Straus and Giroux, 2003), pp. 4–8; Dennis Ross, "Counterterrorism: A Professional's Strategy," *World Policy Journal* 24, no. 1 (Spring 2007), pp. 23–24; Emmanuel Sivan, "Illusions of Change," in *Islam and Democracy in the Middle East,* ed. Larry Diamond, Marc F. Plattner, and Daniel Brumberg (Baltimore, Md.: Johns Hopkins University Press, 2003), pp. 22–25.

49. Edward P. Djerijian, "The U.S. and the Middle East in a Changing World," address to Meridian House International, Washington, D.C., June 2, 1992.

50. This is based on the definitions employed by Amr Hamzawy, Abdel Monem Said Aly, and Angel Rabasa. See Hamzawy, "The Key to Arab Reform," p. 2; Abdel Monem Said Aly, "Understanding the Muslim Brothers in Egypt," Middle East Brief no. 23, Crown Center for Middle East Studies, Brandeis University, Boston, December 2007, p. 1; Angela Rabasa, "Moderate and Radical Islam," Testimony Before the House Armed Services Committee, Defense Review, Terrorism and Radical Islam Gap Panel, the RAND Corporation, November 3, 2005, p. 2, available at www.rand.org/pubs/testimonies/2005/RAND_CT251.pdf.

51. Robin Wright, "Two Visions of Reformation," in *Islam and Democracy in the Middle East,* ed. Larry Diamond, Marc F. Plattner, and Daniel Brumberg (Baltimore, Md.: Johns Hopkins University Press, 2003), p. 229. See also Graham Fuller, "Islamists and Democracy," in *Uncharted Journey: Promoting Democracy in the Middle East,* ed. Thomas Carothers and Marina Ottaway (Washington, D.C.: Carnegie Endowment for International Peace, 2005), especially pp. 43–44.

52. Said Aly, "Understanding the Muslim Brothers in Egypt," p. 3.

53. Ibid.

54. Hamzawy, "The Key to Arab Reform," p. 3. Also see Jillian Schwedler, "Democratization, Inclusion and the Moderation of Islamist Parties," *Development* 50, no. 1 (January 2007), p. 58. Schwedler notes that some moderate Islamist parties are often willing to work together with secular and even leftist parties on a range of issues but typically draw the line on topics such as women's rights that they see as touching on their core beliefs.

55. Said Aly, "Understanding the Muslim Brothers in Egypt," pp. 4–6.

56. Hamzawy, "The Key to Arab Reform," p. 2.

57. For an emphatic assertion that the Egyptian Muslim Brotherhood is committed to democracy, see Marc Lynch, "The Brotherhood's Dilemma," Middle East Brief No. 25, Crown Center for Middle East Studies, Brandeis University, January 2008.

58. Fuller, "Islamists and Democracy," pp. 44–45.

59. Schwedler, "Democratization, Inclusion and the Moderation of Islamist Parties," p. 60.

60. Ibid., pp. 59–60.

61. Ibid., p. 57.

62. April Longley, "The High Water Mark of Islamist Politics? The Case of Yemen," *The Middle East Journal* 61, no. 2 (Spring 2007), pp. 240–245.

63. Ibid., pp. 250–259.

64. Ryan and Schwedler, "Return to Democratization or New Hybrid Regime?," pp. 138–152.

65. For a concurring view, see Steven A. Cook, "The Unspoken Power: Civil-

Military Relations and the Prospects for Reform," Analysis Paper no. 7, Brookings Project on the U.S. and the Islamic World, Saban Center for Middle East Policy at the Brookings Institution, Washington, D.C., September 2004, pp. 30–31.

66. Nora Bensahel, "Political Reform in the Middle East," in *The Future Security Environment in the Middle East: Conflict, Stability and Political Change,* ed. Nora Bensahel and Daniel L. Byman (Santa Monica, Calif.: RAND, 2004), pp. 26–27; Brumberg, "Liberalization Versus Democracy," pp. 18–19, 33.

67. For a concurring view, see Mona Yacoubian, *Engaging Islamists and Promoting Democracy: A Preliminary Assessment,* Special Report 190 (Washington, D.C.: United States Institute of Peace, August 2007).

68. Ross, "Counterterrorism: A Professional's Strategy," pp. 26–29.

69. Said Aly, "Understanding the Muslim Brothers in Egypt," p. 7.

70. Edward Mansfield and Jack Snyder, "Democratization and War," *Foreign Affairs* 74, no. 3 (May–June 1995), pp. 79–97; Edward Mansfield and Jack Snyder, *Electing to Fight: Why Emerging Democracies Go to War* (Cambridge, Mass.: Massachusetts Institute of Technology Press, 2005); Edward D. Mansfield and Jack Snyder, "Democratization and the Danger of War," *International Security* 20, no. 1 (Summer 1995), pp. 5–38.

71. Mansfield and Snyder, "Democratization and War," pp. 79–80.

72. Ibid., p. 85.

73. Ibid., p. 95.

74. Mansfield and Snyder recognize this practice themselves. See Mansfield and Snyder, "Democratization and War," pp. 95–97.

75. Ginsburg, "Lessons from Democratic Transitions," p. 102.

76. Author's interview, Washington, D.C., August 3, 2007.

77. Feldman, *After Jihad,* p. 14.

CHAPTER 12: PRINCIPLES FOR ENCOURAGING REFORM IN THE MIDDLE EAST

1. For those interested, there are a number of books that describe in greater detail specific steps that the United States and other countries can take to help promote reform in the Muslim Middle East. For instance, see Nora Bensahel and Daniel L. Byman, eds., *The Future Security Environment in the Middle East: Conflict, Stability and Political Change* (Santa Monica, Calif.: RAND, 2004); Daniel L. Byman, *The Five-Front War: The Better Way to Fight Global Jihad* (New York: John Wiley and Sons, 2007); Thomas Carothers and Marina Ottaway, eds., *Uncharted Journey: Promoting Democracy in the Middle East* (Washington, D.C.: Carnegie Endowment for International Peace, 2005); Larry Diamond, *The Spirit of Democracy: The Struggle to Build Free Societies Throughout the World* (New York: Times Books, 2008); Larry Diamond, Marc F. Plattner, and Daniel Brumberg, eds., *Islam and Democ-*

racy in the Middle East (Baltimore, Md.: Johns Hopkins University Press, 2003); John L. Esposito and John O. Voll, *Islam and Democracy* (New York: Oxford University Press, 1996); Noah Feldman, *After Jihad: America and the Struggle for Islamic Democracy* (New York: Farrar, Straus and Giroux, 2004); Marina Ottaway and Thomas Carothers, "Think Again: Middle East Democracy," *Foreign Policy* (November–December 2004), pp. 18–29; Dennis Ross, "Counterterrorism: A Professional's Strategy," *World Policy Journal* 24, no. 1 (Spring 2007), pp. 27–28; Barry Rubin, *The Long War for Freedom: The Arab Struggle for Democracy in the Middle East* (New York: John Wiley and Sons, 2006); Jillian Schwedler, *Faith in Moderation: Islamist Parties in Yemen and Jordan* (Cambridge, U.K.: Cambridge University Press, 2007); United Nations Development Programme, Arab Fund for Economic and Social Development, *Arab Human Development Report, 2002* (New York: United Nations Publications, 2002) (also see the various editions since 2002, all of which contain numerous constructive suggestions for how to help transform Arab societies); Tamara Cofman Wittes, *Freedom's Unsteady March: America's Role in Promoting Arab Democracy* (Washington, D.C.: Brookings Institution Press, 2008).

2. For similar views, see United Nations Development Programme, Arab Fund for Economic and Social Development, *Arab Human Development Report, 2003,* p. 2; Thomas Carothers and Marina Ottaway, "The New Democracy Imperative," in *Uncharted Journey: Promoting Democracy in the Middle East,* ed. Thomas Carothers and Marina Ottaway (Washington, D.C.: Carnegie Endowment for International Peace, 2005), p. 10; Marwan Muasher, "A Path to Arab Democracy," *The New York Times,* April 26, 2003.

3. Ross, "Counterterrorism: A Professional's Strategy," p. 28.

4. Alan Richards, "Economic Reform in the Middle East: The Challenge to Governance," in Nora Bensahel and Daniel L. Byman, eds., *The Future Security Environment in the Middle East: Conflict, Stability and Political Change* (Santa Monica, Calif.: RAND, 2004), p. 60.

5. For concurring views, see also Muasher, "A Path to Arab Democracy"; Daniel Brumberg, "The Trap of Liberalized Autocracy," in *Islam and Democracy in the Middle East,* ed. Larry Diamond, Marc F. Plattner, and Daniel Brumberg (Baltimore, Md.: Johns Hopkins University Press, 2003), pp. 44–46; Shibley Telhami, *The Stakes: America and the Middle East* (Boulder, Colo.: Westview, 2003), pp. 160–161; Thomas Carothers, "How Democracies Emerge: The 'Sequencing' Fallacy," *Journal of Democracy* 18, no. 1 (January 2007), pp. 23–27.

6. International Crisis Group, *Can Saudi Arabia Reform Itself?,* ICG Middle East Report No. 28, Cairo and Brussels, July 14, 2004, pp. 19–20.

7. Ibid., p. 20.

8. Robert Cincotta, Robert Engelman, and Daniele Anastasion, *The Security*

Demographic: Population and Civil Conflict After the Cold War (Washington, D.C.: Population Action International, 2003), p. 33.

9. Sufyan Alissa, "Rethinking Economic Reform in Jordan: Confronting Socioeconomic Realities," Carnegie Papers no. 4, Carnegie Middle East Center, Carnegie Endowment for International Peace, Washington, D.C., July 2007, pp. 20–21.

10. Ibid., p. 21.

11. Ibid., pp. 17–20.

12. Wittes, *Freedom's Unsteady March,* pp. 131–132.

13. Ross, "Counterterrorism," pp. 27–28.

14. Wittes, *Freedom's Unsteady March,* p. 106.

15. For others supporting this same notion, see Amr Hamzawy, "The Key to Arab Reform: Moderate Islamists," Policy Brief 40, Carnegie Endowment for International Peace, Washington, D.C., August 2005, p. 6; Ross, "Counterterrorism," p. 30.

16. Amy Hawthorne, "Is Civil Society the Answer?," in *Uncharted Journey: Promoting Democracy in the Middle East,* ed. Thomas Carothers and Marina Ottaway (Washington, D.C.: Carnegie Endowment for International Peace, 2005), p. 82.

17. Ibid., p. 90.

18. Sufyan Alissa, "The Political Economy of Reform in Egypt: Understanding the Role of Institutions," Carnegie Paper No. 5, Carnegie Middle East Center, Carnegie Endowment for International Peace, Washington, D.C., October 2007, pp. 15–16; Daniel Brumberg, "Liberalization Versus Democracy," in *Uncharted Journey: Promoting Democracy in the Middle East,* ed. Thomas Carothers and Marina Ottaway (Washington, D.C.: Carnegie Endowment for International Peace, 2005), pp. 21–22; Walid Kazziha, "Political Consciousness and the Crisis of Political Liberalization in the Arab World," *Elections in the Middle East and North Africa,* ed. Sven Behrendt and Christian-Peter Hanelt (Munich, Germany: Bertelsmann Foundation, 1998), p. 6; Wittes, *Freedom's Unsteady March,* pp. 68–69.

19. Sheri Berman, "Islamism, Revolution and Civil Society," *Perspectives on Politics* 1, no. 2 (June 2003), especially pp. 259, 265–266; Ira M. Lapidus, "Islamic Revival and Modernity: The Contemporary Movements and the Historical Paradigms," *Journal of the Economic and Social History of the Orient* 40, no. 4 (1997), p. 447; Sara Roy, "The Transformation of Islamic NGOs in Palestine," *Middle East Report,* no. 214 (Spring 2000), pp. 24–26; Emmanuel Sivan, "Why Radical Muslims Aren't Taking Over Governments," *Middle East Review of International Affairs* 2, no. 2 (May 1998), p. 2.

20. Saad Eddin Ibrahim, "A Dissident Asks: Can Bush Turn Words into Action?," *Washington Post,* November 23, 2003, p. B03; Ross, "Counterterrorism," pp. 28–29.

21. Senator Richard G. Lugar, "A New Partnership for the Greater Middle East: Combating Terrorism, Building Peace," The Saban Center for Middle East Policy at the Brookings Institution, March 29, 2004, available at http://www.brookings.edu/~/media/Files/events/2004/0329 middle%20east/20040329lugar.pdf, downloaded January 22, 2008.

22. In another vein, bilateral agreements struck with the United States by one government might not be honored by a new government replacing it—either in a violent upheaval or by some quasi-democratic process. On the other hand, agreements struck with international organizations from the United Nations to the International Monetary Fund would be much harder for any government to break. Wittes, *Freedom's Unsteady March*, p. 134.

23. "The Euro-Mediterranean Partnership," available on the European Commission Web site at http://ec.europa.eu/external_relations/euromed/meda.htm, downloaded September 4, 2007.

24. Wittes, *Freedom's Unsteady March*, pp. 96–97.

25. Eva Bellin, "The Political-Economic Conundrum," in *Uncharted Journey: Promoting Democracy in the Middle East*, ed. Thomas Carothers and Marina Ottaway (Washington, D.C.: Carnegie Endowment for International Peace, 2005), p. 134.

26. For a more detailed discussion of these approaches as they would relate to the specific subregion of the Persian Gulf (but that could be expanded or replicated for other parts of the region), see Kenneth M. Pollack, "Securing the Gulf," *Foreign Affairs* 82, no. 4 (July–August 2003), pp. 2–26.

27. Announcing such a doctrine would require the United States to back it up, and this could become problematic if American allies (particularly Israel and Turkey) chose to mount conventional military operations in response to unconventional attacks—by Hizballah, Hamas, the PKK, or other militant groups operating from surrounding territory. If Israel or Turkey, or some other American ally, chose to mount a conventional military operation in response to an unconventional attack upon it, the United States would be very unlikely to intervene to prevent the operation—at least not militarily, although we might well weigh in diplomatically to urge restraint and a rapid conclusion. This would be a clear divergence from a stated policy of intervening to prevent cross-border conventional military operations. Nevertheless, this should not necessarily be a show-stopper: it might be seen as hypocritical by the Arab "street" and could reinforce its anti-Americanism but would have little impact on the true targets of the doctrine: rogue regimes contemplating military aggression against neighbors, which would doubtless have to expect an American reaction to any attack they launched. For that reason,

it could still be an important method to remove external security problems as a stumbling block to internal reform.

28. Ottaway, "The Problem of Credibility," p. 188.

CHAPTER 13: TRADE-OFFS

1. On improving American counterterrorism and homeland security oper-
ations, see Graham Allison, *Nuclear Terrorism: The Ultimate Preventable Ca-
tastrophe* (New York: Times Books, 2004); Daniel Benjamin and Steven
Simon, *The Next Attack: The Failure of the War on Terror and a Strategy for Getting
It Right* (New York: Owl Books, 2005); Daniel L. Byman, *The Five-Front
War: The Better Way to Fight Global Jihad* (New York: Wiley, 2007); Daniel
Byman, *Deadly Connections: States That Sponsor Terrorism* (Cambridge, U.K.:
Cambridge University Press, 2005); Richard A. Clarke, *Against All Enemies:
Inside America's War on Terror* (New York: Free Press, 2004); Richard A.
Clarke and Rand Beers, *The Forgotten Homeland* (Washington, D.C.: Cen-
tury Foundation Press, 2006); Audrey Kurth Cronin and James M.
Ludes, eds., *Attacking Terrorism: Elements of a Grand Strategy* (Washington,
D.C.: Georgetown University Press, 2004); Stephen Flynn, *America the
Vulnerable: How Our Government Is Failing to Protect Us from Terrorism* (New
York: HarperCollins, 2004); James J. F. Forest, ed., *Countering Terrorism
and Insurgency in the 21st Century: International Perspectives,* three volumes
(Westport, Conn.: Praeger, 2007); Philip H. Gordon, *Winning the Right
War: The Path to Security for America and the World* (New York: Times Books,
2007).

2. To keep pace with inflation, the $2.1 billion we set as a fixed amount for
annual U.S. aid to Egypt in 1987 should have risen to $3.3 billion in 2008.

3. Interestingly, it is the exceptions that prove this rule. The countries that
"increased" their counterterror cooperation most with the United States
after 9/11 were three states the United States had previously treated as
pariahs: Syria, Sudan, and Pakistan (although Pakistan's cooperation on
terror declined significantly after 2001–2002). These three countries
tried to use cooperation with the United States against Salafi terrorists
as a way of getting into Washington's good graces. Countries that already
had a good relationship with the United States clearly felt less of an incentive to do the same.

PART FIVE: A REGION OF CRISES

1. Martin Indyk, "The Clinton Administration's Approach to the Middle
East," speech given at the Soref Symposium of the Washington Institute

for Near East Policy, May 18, 1993, available at www.washington institute.org/pubs/soref/indyk.htm, downloaded July 24, 2007.

CHAPTER 14: THE DILEMMA OF IRAQ

1. Author's conversations with U.S. military personnel, Ninevah province, Iraq, November 2005.

2. For a recounting of those many mistakes, see Rajiv Chandrasekaran, *Imperial Life in the Emerald City: Inside Iraq's Green Zone* (New York: Alfred A. Knopf, 2006); Larry Diamond, *Squandered Victory: The American Occupation and the Bungled Effort to Bring Democracy to Iraq* (New York: Times Books, 2005); James Fallows, "The Fifty-First State?," *The Atlantic Monthly*, November 2002, pp. 53–64; James Fallows, "Blind into Baghdad," *The Atlantic Monthly*, January–February 2004, pp. 54–76; Noah Feldman, *What We Owe Iraq: War and the Ethics of Nation Building* (Princeton, N.J.: Princeton University Press, 2004); Michael Gordon and Bernard Trainor, *Cobra II: The Inside Story of the Invasion and Occupation of Iraq* (New York: Pantheon, 2006); T. Christian Miller, *Blood Money: Wasted Billions, Lost Lives, and Corporate Greed in Iraq* (Boston: Little, Brown, 2006); George Packer, *The Assassin's Gate: America in Iraq* (New York: Farrar, Straus and Giroux, 2005); David L. Phillips, *Losing Iraq: Inside the Postwar Reconstruction Fiasco* (Boulder, Colo.: Westview, 2005); Kenneth M. Pollack, "The Seven Deadly Sins of Failure in Iraq: A Retrospective Analysis of the Reconstruction," *Middle East Review of International Affairs* 10, no. 4 (December 2006); Thomas E. Ricks, *Fiasco: The American Military Adventure in Iraq* (New York: Penguin, 2006).

3. I do not consider the common complaint that the Iraq intervention is "breaking" the Army a valid reason upon which to base decisions regarding America's involvement in Iraq. Simply put, the Army exists to fight the nation's wars. If the nation concludes that stabilizing Iraq is vital to American interests, then the Army needs to do it, regardless of other considerations—and the soldiers are typically the first ones to make that point. There is no rationale to preserve the current readiness and organizational standards of the Army simply for the sake of doing so. The Army is a tool of the nation's foreign policy; the American people did not pay for it so that it could sit on the mantel and look nice. If there is a task for which the Army is the best tool, then it is there to be employed.

Nor is there another, potentially more important war for which we might want to preserve the current Army. A major war in the oil fields of the Persian Gulf region was one of the two nightmare scenarios that drove American military planning during the 1980s and 1990s (the other was a new Korean war). Indeed, war on the Korean peninsula, although potentially horrific, would threaten American vital interests only if the North were to employ nuclear weapons, and, given the strength of the South Korean ground forces, the United States' commitment to that war should be principally air and naval. In other words, the military demands of a new Korean war should not require a massive commitment of American ground forces, thereby creating an incentive to free up ground forces currently engaged in Iraq. There is no other foreseeable war that rivals the Iraq War in importance *and* that would require a massive commitment of ground troops—unless Saudi Arabia should go up in flames and the U.S. government decide to intervene there to secure Saudi oil production. At the moment, a threat to Saudi Arabia seems distant, and the one foreseeable event that would be most likely to raise its risk would be Iraq's descent into all-out civil war. Consequently, there is no other war that we ought to be "saving" the Army for.

If the Iraq War is truly vital to our nation's interests, the health of the Army is a secondary consideration. Likewise, if we decide that stabilizing Iraq is *not* vital, the organizational well-being of the Army should be pretty low on the list of reasons for getting out. Certainly, it should be far behind the importance of saving American lives (including the lives of our soldiers and marines, which should matter far more than the readiness of the organizations they serve), saving taxpayer dollars, and preserving whatever political capital the nation has left. But the key consideration is whether we consider this war (and the potential ramifications of both success and failure for the region) vital, not whether fighting the war is good or bad for the Army.

4. Proven oil reserves are notoriously hard to measure because governments constantly lie about how much they have. In addition, there is considerable debate as to whether proven oil reserves is a useful measure. Nevertheless, it remains widely employed and, for my purposes, makes the point that Iraq, especially when seen in conjunction with Kuwait, Iran, and Saudi Arabia, is critical to the global economy and therefore to American interests.

5. Daniel L. Byman and Kenneth M. Pollack, "Iraq Runneth Over: What Next?," *The Washington Post,* August 20, 2006.

6. For a longer, more detailed description of the potential impact of an Iraqi civil war on the rest of the region, see Daniel L. Byman and Kenneth M. Pollack, *Things Fall Apart: Containing the Spillover from an Iraqi Civil War* (Washington, D.C.: Brookings Institution, 2007). For a concurring view that civil war can have extremely dangerous consequences on neighboring states, see Paul Collier, *The Bottom Billion: Why the Poorest Countries Are Failing and What Can Be Done About It* (London: Oxford University Press, 2007), pp. 27–32.

7. A great many Israelis share these same concerns. As an example, see Yossi Alpher, "Israel Owes the U.S. a Blunt Word or Two on Iraq," *The Forward,* August 9, 2007.

8. George Packer, "Planning for Defeat," *The New Yorker,* September 17, 2007, pp. 56–65.

9. For a more detailed explanation, see Kenneth M. Pollack and the Iraq Policy Working Group of the Saban Center for Middle East Policy at the Brookings Institution, "A Switch in Time: A New Strategy for America in Iraq," Analysis Paper no. 7, Saban Center for Middle East Policy at the Brookings Institution, Washington, D.C., February 2006, p. 98.

10. For a more detailed explanation, see Pollack et al., "A Switch in Time," pp. 96–98; Carlos Pascual and Kenneth M. Pollack, "The Critical Battles: Political Reconciliation and Reconstruction in Iraq," *The Washington Quarterly* 30, no. 3 (Summer 2007), pp. 7–19; Carlos Pascual and Larry Diamond, "A Diplomatic Offensive for Iraq," Policy Brief no. 162, the Brookings Institution, Washington, D.C., June 2007.

11. As of January 2008, the best estimate, from the World Health Organization, was that more than 150,000 Iraqis had died in the 4½ years since the fall of Saddam's regime. Laura MacInnis, "151,000 Iraqis Killed Since U.S.-Led Invasion: WHO," Reuters, January 9, 2008.

12. For a far more detailed explanation of how to construct a containment strategy to deal with Iraq in a state of all-out civil war, see Byman and Pollack, *Things Fall Apart,* pp. 60–98.

13. Peter L. Bergen, *Holy War, Inc.: The Secret World of Osama bin Laden* (New York: Free Press, 2001), p. 55; Bruce Hoffman, "Al Qaeda, Trends in Terrorism and Future Potentialities: An Assessment," RAND P–8078, May 2003, RAND, Santa Monica, Calif., p. 9.

14. Author's interviews with U.S. military and intelligence personnel, Iraq, July 2007. Also see Karen DeYoung and Walter Pincus, "Al-Qaeda in Iraq May Not Be Threat Here: Intelligence Experts Say Group Is Busy on Its Home Front," *The Washington Post,* March 18, 2007.

CHAPTER 15: THE CHALLENGE OF IRAN

1. For a fuller account, see Kenneth M. Pollack, *The Persian Puzzle: The Conflict Between Iran and America* (New York: Random House, 2004), especially pp. 233–374.

2. "Bahrain Coup Suspects Say They Trained in Iran," *The New York Times,* June 6, 1996; "Bahrain Holds 44 It Says Are Tied to Pro-Iran Plot," *The New York Times,* June 5, 1996; Richard A. Clarke, *Against All Enemies: Inside America's War on Terror* (New York: Free Press, 2004), p. 112; Bruce Maddy-Weitzman, and Joshua Teitelbaum, "Inter-Arab Relations," in

Bruce Maddy-Weitzman, ed., *Middle East Contemporary Survey* XX (Boulder, Colo.: Westview, 1996), p. 89; Shawn L. Twing, "Iran, Bahrain Will Exchange Envoys," *Washington Report on Middle East Affairs,* January–February 1998, p. 38.

3. Based on author's conversations with U.S. military and intelligence personnel in Iraq, July 2007.

4. Ibid.

5. National Intelligence Council, "Iran: Nuclear Intentions and Capabilities," December 2007, available at www.dni.gov/press_releases/2007 1203_release.pdf, downloaded January 26, 2008.

6. George Jahn, "UN Finds Secret Iran Nuclear Documents," Associated Press, February 12, 2004; David E. Sanger and William J. Broad, "Iran Admits That It Has Plans for a Newer Centrifuge," *The New York Times,* February 13, 2004; David E. Sanger, "In Face of Report, Iran Acknowledges Buying Nuclear Components," *The New York Times,* February 23, 2004.

7. International Atomic Energy Agency, "Implementation of the NPT Safeguards Agreement in the Islamic Republic of Iran," Report by the Director General, GOV/2003/40, June 6, 2003; "Iran's Continuing Pursuit of Weapons of Mass Destruction: Testimony by Under Secretary of State for Arms Control and International Security John R. Bolton," House International Relations Committee, Subcommittee on the Middle East and Central Asia, June 24, 2004; Karl Vick, "Another Nuclear Program Found in Iran," *The Washington Post,* February 24, 2004.

8. Author's conversations with European diplomats, Washington, February 2005; Paris, May 2005; Berlin, September 2005.

9. For a concurring assessment, see Michael Eisenstadt, "Living with a Nuclear Iran?," *Survival* 41, no. 3 (Autumn 1999), pp. 124–148.

10. International Crisis Group, "Dealing with Iran's Nuclear Program," October 27, 2003, pp. 11–15, available at www.crisisgroup.org/home/index .cfm?id=2330&I=1; Ray Takeyh, "Iranian Options: Pragmatic Mullas and America's Interests," *The National Interest* (Fall 2003), pp. 49–56; Ray Takeyh, "Iran's Nuclear Calculations," *World Policy Journal,* Summer 2003, pp. 21–26.

11. For a lengthier explanation of the problems with promoting regime change in Iran, see Pollack, *The Persian Puzzle,* pp. 386–389.

12. The best unclassified sources at present are Daniel Byman, *Deadly Connections: States That Sponsor Terrorism* (Cambridge, U.K.: Cambridge University Press, 2005), pp. 79–110, especially p. 85; Richard Clarke, *Against All Enemies: Inside America's War on Terror* (New York: Free Press, 2004), pp. 112–131; Timothy Naftali, *Blind Spot: The Secret History of American Counterterrorism* (New York: Basic Books, 2005), pp. 248–251, 260–261; and the

grand jury indictment against thirteen members of Saudi Hizballah filed
by the U.S. government in Alexandria, Virginia. The indictment in particular provides an excellent overview of the operational elements of the
attack and is available at http://news.findlaw.com/cnn/docs/khobar/
khobarindict61901.pdf, downloaded July 26, 2004. The 9/11 Commission also found that the evidence of Iran behind the Khobar Towers
bombing was "strong." See *Report of the 9/11 Commission: Final Report of the National Commission on Terrorist Attacks upon the United States* (Washington, D.C.:
GPO, 2004), p. 60. Also see Pollack, *The Persian Puzzle,* pp. 282–284. On
the decision to increase the U.S. covert action budget against Iran, see
Tim Weiner, "U.S. Plan to Change Iran Leaders Is an Open Secret Before It Begins," *The New York Times,* January 26, 1996.

13. Pollack, *The Persian Puzzle,* p. 318.

14. "Polling Iranian Public Opinion: An Unprecedented Nationwide Survey
of Iran," Terror Free Tomorrow, July 2007, available at www.terrorfree
tomorrow.org/upimagestft/TFT%20Iran%20Survey%20Report.pdf,
downloaded January 7, 2007.

15. For a fuller explanation of this approach, see Pollack, *The Persian Puzzle,*
pp. 401–412.

16. For a more detailed discussion of U.S. military options against Iran (and
the problems with them), see Pollack, *The Persian Puzzle,* especially pp.
382–386, 391–395.

CHAPTER 16: THE IMPORTANCE OF THE ARAB-ISRAELI CONFLICT

1. As a quick reminder: Arab defeat in 1948 provoked regime changes in
Egypt and Syria; Nasser's political triumph in the 1956 war produced a
change of regime in Iraq and threatened one in Jordan; Arab defeat in
1967 produced a change of regime in Syria and Libya, contributed to another in Iraq, and threatened one in Egypt; and Israel's disasters in
Lebanon caused at least one (arguably more) government to fall in 1983.

2. For instance, see Majed Kyaly, " 'It's Israel, Stupid!' A Source of Anti-
Americanism," *Arab Insight* 1, no. 2 (Fall 2007), pp. 71–82; Stephen W.
Van Evera, "Why U.S. National Security Requires Mideast Peace," MIT
Center for International Studies, Cambridge, Mass., April 2005.

3. Dennis Ross, *Statecraft: And How to Restore America's Standing in the World* (New
York: Farrar, Straus and Giroux, 2007), p. 262.

4. Shibley Telhami, *The Stakes: America and the Middle East, the Consequences of
Power and the Choice for Peace* (Boulder, Colo.: Westview, 2003), p. 21.

5. Amy Hawthorne, "The New Reform Ferment," in *Uncharted Journey: Promoting Democracy in the Middle East,* ed. Thomas Carothers and Marina Ottaway (Washington, D.C.: Carnegie Endowment for International Peace,

2005), p. 65; Curtis R. Ryan and Jillian Schwedler, "Return to Democratization or New Hybrid Regime? The 2003 Elections in Jordan," *Middle East Policy* 11, no. 2 (Summer 2004), pp. 138–152.

6. For a similar view, see Dennis Ross, "Counterterrorism: A Professional's Strategy," *World Policy Journal* 24, no. 1 (Spring 2007), p. 30.

7. Martin Indyk, *Innocents Abroad: Lessons from the 1990s for America's Middle East Diplomacy,* forthcoming, 2009, pp. 560–563; Dennis Ross, *The Missing Peace: The Inside Story of the Fight for Middle East Peace* (New York: Farrar, Straus and Giroux, 2004), pp. 208n, 742–745, 748–758; Ross, *Statecraft,* p. 261.

8. On the lost opportunity in 2004–2005, see Ross, *Statecraft,* pp. 264–268.

9. Ross, *Statecraft,* pp. 267–268.

10. Jerusalem Media and Communication Center (JMCC), "Poll Results on Palestinian Attitudes Towards the Results of the PLC Elections Held on January 25, 2006," poll no. 57, February 2006, p. 1, available at www.jmcc.org/publicpoll/results/2006/no57.pdf.

11. "Palestinians Want Hamas Reform—Poll," al-Jazeera.net, February 2, 2006, available at http://english.aljazeera.net/NR/exeres/92C2A0B5-793F-4409-9CEA-A4F7E4985850.htm, downloaded February 3, 2006.

12. Martin Indyk has already proposed that such a force might be necessary for the Palestinians too. See Martin Indyk, "A Trusteeship for Palestine?," *Foreign Affairs* 82, no. 3 (May–June 2003), pp. 51–66. For a similar approach, see Ross, *Statecraft,* pp. 274–275.

13. Dr. Mohammed Samhouri, "The 'West Bank First' Strategy: A Political-Economy Assessment," working paper 2, Crown Center for Middle East Studies, Brandeis University, October 2007, p. 17.

14. For a concurring view, laid out in greater detail, see Ross, *Statecraft,* pp. 275–278.

15. Shibley Telhami, *The Stakes: America and the Middle East* (Boulder, Colo.: Westview, 2003), p. 107.

CHAPTER 17: OTHER SECURITY PROBLEMS

1. Central Intelligence Agency, *The World Factbook,* January 2008, available at https://www.cia.gov/library/publications/the-world-factbook/index.html.

2. Bassem Mroue, "U.S., Arab Allies Send Aid to Lebanon," Associated Press, May 25, 2007.

3. Scheherezade Faramarzi and Zeina Karam, "Anti-Syrian Lawmaker Killed in Lebanon," Associated Press, September 19, 2007.

4. Yochi Dreazen, "Iraqi Refugees Seek Safe Harbor—in the U.S.," *The Wall Street Journal,* August 9, 2006; Bassem Mroue, "Syria Bars Iraq Refugees, Crisis Worsens," Associated Press, February 12, 2007; Refugees Interna-

tional, "Iraqi Refugees in Syria: Silent Exodus Leaves 500,000 in Need of Protection and Aid," November 15, 2005, available at www.refugees international.org/content/article/detail/7297/?PHPSESSID=5ce))f927 79c166324e1d, downloaded August 9, 2006.

5. The text of the Genocide Convention is available at www.unhchr.ch/ html/menu3/b/p_genoci.htm, downloaded October 5, 2007.

6. The Syrians and Lebanese were invited to participate but refused to do so until their bilateral negotiations with Israel resulted in signed peace treaties.

7. For a fuller discussion, see Kenneth M. Pollack, "Securing the Gulf," *Foreign Affairs* 82, no. 4 (July–August 2003), pp. 2–16. Also see Joseph McMillan, "The United States and a Gulf Security Architecture: Policy Considerations," *Strategic Insights* 3, no. 3 (March 2004); James A. Russell, "Searching for a Post-Saddam Regional Security Architecture," *Middle East Review of International Affairs (MERIA)* 7, no. 1 (March 2003).

8. M. Javad Zarif, "A Neighbor's Vision of a New Iraq," *The New York Times,* May 10, 2003.

PART SIX: LOOKING FARTHER DOWN THE PATH

CHAPTER 18. ENTER THE DRAGON

1. U.S. Energy Information Administration, "Country Analysis Brief: China," U.S. Department of Energy, Washington, D.C., August 2005, p. 1; Xuecheng Liu, "China's Energy Security and Its Grand Strategy," Policy Analysis Brief, Stanley Foundation, Muscatine, Iowa, September 2006, p. 3.

2. Philip Andrews-Speed, "China's Energy Woes: Running on Empty," *Far Eastern Economic Review,* June 2005, p. 1.

3. EIA, "China," p. 2; *Report to Congress of the U.S.-China Economic and Security Review Commission* (Washington, D.C.: U.S. Government Printing Office, November 2005), p. 164.

4. *Report to Congress of the U.S.-China Economic and Security Review Commission,* p. 165.

5. Phar Kim Beng and Vic Y. W. Li, "China's Energy Dependence on the Middle East: Boon or Bane for Asian Security?", *The China and Eurasia Forum Quarterly* 3, no. 3 (November 2005), p. 19; Jin Liangxiang, "Energy First: China and the Middle East," *Middle East Quarterly* 12, no. 2 (Spring 2005), pp. 3–10; Steve A. Yetiv and Chunlong Lu, "China, Global Energy, and the Middle East," *Middle East Journal* 61, no. 2 (Spring 2007), pp. 199–218. On the history of China's relations with the Middle East

during the Cold War, see John Calabrese, *China's Changing Relations with the Middle East* (London: Pinter Publishers, 1991).

6. EIA, "China," p. 5; *Report to Congress of the U.S.-China Economic and Security Review Commission,* p. 168.

7. EIA, "China," pp. 2–3; *Report to Congress of the U.S.-China Economic and Security Review Commission,* pp. 164–170; Liu, "China's Energy Security and Its Grand Strategy," p. 10.

8. Liu, "China's Energy Security and Its Grand Strategy," p. 11.

9. Aleksandr Fursenko and Timothy Naftali, *Khrushchev's Cold War: The Inside Story of an American Adversary* (New York: W.W. Norton, 2006).

10. David M. Lampton, "The Faces of Chinese Power," *Foreign Affairs* 86, no. 1 (January–February 2007), p. 122.

11. *Report to Congress of the U.S.-China Economic and Security Review Commission,* pp. 143–144, 153–157; Richard Russell, "China's WMD Foot in the Greater Middle East's Door," *Middle East Review of International Affairs* 9, no. 3 (September 2005), pp. 108–124; Yetiv and Lu, "China, Global Energy, and the Middle East," pp. 210–213.

12. Erica S. Downs, "The Chinese Energy Security Debate," *The China Quarterly,* March 2004, pp. 21–41.

13. Jin, "Energy First: China and the Middle East," p. 4.

14. Yetiv and Lu, "China, Global Energy, and the Middle East," p. 205.

15. For a sophisticated analysis of the strengths and weaknesses of the Chinese neighbor and its likely improvement in coming years, see Rear Admiral Eric A. McVadon, "China's Maturing Navy," *Naval War College Review* 59, no. 2 (Spring 2006), pp. 90–103.

16. For a broadly similar perspective, see Liu, "China's Energy Security and Its Grand Strategy," pp. 14–15.

17. Jon B. Alterman, "China's Unease," *CSIS Middle East Notes and Comment,* Center for Strategic and International Studies, Washington, D.C., April 2007, p. 2.

18. Ibid.

19. Yetiv and Lu, "China, Global Energy, and the Middle East," pp. 212–215.

20. Beng and Li, "China's Energy Dependence on the Middle East," pp. 19–26.

21. *Report to Congress of the U.S.-China Economic and Security Review Commission,* pp. 147, 170.

22. Wenran Jiang, "Beijing's 'New Thinking' on Energy Security," *China Brief* 6, no 8, April 12, 2006, pp. 1–2.

23. Andrews-Speed, "China's Energy Woes: Running on Empty," p. 3; Peter S. Goodman, "Big Shift in China's Oil Policy: With Iraq Deal Dissolved by War, Beijing Looks Elsewhere," *The Washington Post,* July 13, 2005.

24. Matthew E. Chen, "Chinese National Oil Companies and Human Rights,"

Orbis 51, no. 1 (Winter 2007), pp. 41–54; Amy Myers Jaffe, "Energy Security: Implications for U.S.–China–Middle East Relations," James A. Baker III Institute for Public Policy of Rice University, Houston, July 18, 2005, pp. 3–4.

25. Compare Beng and Li, "China's Energy Dependence on the Middle East," pp. 21–22, and Erica Downs, "China's Quest for Overseas Oil," *Far Eastern Economic Review,* September 2007, pp. 52–56, with *Report to Congress of the U.S.-China Economic and Security Review Commission,* pp. 144, 167–169.

26. Goodman, "Big Shift in China's Oil Policy"; *Report to Congress of the U.S.-China Economic and Security Review Commission,* pp. 146, 164.

27. Antoaneta Bezlova, "Energy: China's Oil Ties to Sudan Force It to Oppose Sanctions," *Global Information Network,* October 19, 2004, p. 1; Goodman, "Big Shift in China's Oil Policy"; Gal Luft, "Oil Puts Iran Out of Reach," *The Baltimore Sun,* August 16, 2005; Xu Yihe, "China to Look Abroad for Natural Gas," *The Wall Street Journal,* June 23, 2004.

28. Beng and Li, "China's Energy Dependence on the Middle East," pp. 23–24; Peter Cornelius and Jonathan Story, "China and Global Energy Markets," *Orbis* 51, no. 1 (Winter 2007), p. 16; Jiang, "Beijing's 'New Thinking' on Energy Security," p. 2.

29. Ibid.

30. Beng and Li, "China's Energy Dependence on the Middle East," pp. 21–22; Downs, "China's Quest for Overseas Oil," pp. 52–56.

31. *Report to Congress of the U.S.-China Economic and Security Review Commission,* p. 175.

CONCLUSION: THE PATH BEFORE US

1. For a similar view by a brilliant political thinker, see Michael Mandlebaum, *The Case for Goliath: How America Acts as the World's Government in the Twenty-first Century* (New York: Public Affairs, 2005). For a more theoretical treatment by a leading scholar of international relations, see Robert Gilpin, *War and Change in World Politics* (Cambridge, U.K.: Cambridge University Press, 1981).

2. Michael Beschloss, *The Conquerors: Roosevelt, Truman and the Destruction of Hitler's Germany, 1941–1945* (New York: Simon and Schuster, 2002), p. 175.

INDEX

—

Page numbers in *italics* refer to tables.

ABOUT THE AUTHOR

KENNETH M. POLLACK is the director of research at the Saban Center for Middle East Policy at the Brookings Institution. From 1995 to 1996 and from 1999 to 2001, he served as director for Persian Gulf affairs at the National Security Council, where he was the principal working-level official responsible for implementation of U.S. policy toward Iraq, Iran, and the states of the Arabian Peninsula. Prior to his time in the Clinton administration, he spent seven years in the CIA as a Persian Gulf military analyst. He is the author of *The Threatening Storm*, *The Persian Puzzle*, *Arabs at War*, and *Things Fall Apart*. He lives in Washington, D.C.